THE BELOVED DISCIPLE

THE BELOVED DISCIPLE

Whose Witness Validates the Gospel of John?

James H. Charlesworth

Trinity Press International
Valley Forge, Pennsylvania

First Edition 1995

Trinity Press International
P.O. Box 851
Valley Forge, PA 19482-0851

Cover design by Jim Gerhard

Library of Congress Cataloging-in-Publication Data

Charlesworth, James H.
    The beloved disciple : whose witness validates the Gospel of John? / James H. Charlesworth
        p.   cm.
    Includes bibliographical reference and index.
    ISBN 1-56338-135-4 (cloth)
    1. Beloved Disciple. 2. Bible. N.T.—Biography. 3. Bible. N.T. John—Criticism, interpretation, etc. I. Title.
BS2452.B36C48 1995
226.5′092—dc20   95-549
                                                          CIP

Printed in the United States of America

95 96 97 98 99 6 5 4 3 2 1

Contents

Preface

In the Gospel of John (GosJn) the author refers five times to "the disciple whom Jesus loved."[1] From the second through the present twentieth century scholars have sought to identify this "disciple," traditionally concluding that he is the author of the GosJn, and indeed none other than John the son of Zebedee. This is rather a remarkable accomplishment since "John" is neither mentioned nor named in the GosJn 1-20, and is perhaps obliquely included in the Appendix, but only in an ambiguous οἱ τοῦ Ζεβεδαίου (21:2). Yet from Irenaeus to the influential commentaries by R. E. Brown and R. Schnackenburg (vol. 1, but not vol. 3) the Beloved Disciple is heralded as John the son of Zebedee.

In the last phase of research on the identification of the Beloved Disciple the arguments in favor of equating the Beloved Disciple with John the son of Zebedee have been exposed as weak and indeed unpersuasive. As Brown and Schnackenburg have stated, P. Parker published the most complete list of objections against the hypothesis that the apostle John was the author of the GosJn.[2] Over sixty years ago Parker[3] argued that the apostle John cannot be the author of the GosJn, according to the picture of John the son of Zebedee found in Paul, the Synoptics, and Acts, because:

---

[1] All translations are my own, and in different discussions I sometimes translate the same passage in different ways in order to bring out a nuance in the Greek that may be lost in a previously acceptable translation. Occasionally I have used other translations: e.g., *TANAKH: A New Translation of the HOLY SCRIPTURES According to the Traditional Hebrew Text*, published by the Jewish Publication Society, and the New Revised Standard Version.

[2] R. E. Brown, *The Gospel According to John*, 2 vols. (Garden City, N.Y.: Doubleday, 1966) 1:xvii; R. Schnackenburg, *The Gospel According to St. John*, 3 vols. (New York: Crossroad, 1968-1982 [1987]) 1:92.

[3] P. Parker, "John the Son of Zebedee and the Fourth Gospel," *Journal of Biblical Literature* 81 (1962) 35-43.

(1) He was a Galilean but the GosJn shows "little interest in Galilee."

(2) He was a fisherman but the GosJn shows virtually no interest in fishing (except in chapter 21, the Appendix).

(3) He had a brother James; yet there is no evidence of this in the GosJn.[4]

(4) According to Mark 3:17 Jesus called the sons of Zebedee "sons of thunder"; yet the GosJn is the most tranquil of the four gospels.

(5) Acts 4:13 calls John "illiterate and ignorant"; although that can have more than one meaning, none would fit the gifted thinker who authored the GosJn (the Greek is "good" as both Dionysius of Alexandria and Deissmann showed).

(6) Acts 4:13 also shows that John was a bold man of action, but the GosJn is a contemplative work.

(7) According to several passages in the Synoptics (esp. Mk 9:38), John was interested in demon exorcism; but the GosJn "never mentions the subject."

(8) Mark 10:35ff. and Mark 13 (and par.) show that John, unlike the author of the GosJn, was interested in apocalypticism.

(9) According to Mark 10:35ff., John and his brother attempted to put themselves above the other disciples; yet the GosJn treats the disciples with "uniform kindness and respect."

(10) John showed a violent disposition towards the Samaritans, according to Luke 9:54, but in the GosJn the Samaritans are treated with respect.

(11) According to Acts (1:13ff., 3:1-7, 8:14-24) Peter and John were missionaries together, and the former was the spokesman; but in the GosJn Peter's companion, the Beloved Disciple, "takes the initiative."

(12) Unlike the Beloved Disciple, the apostle John in the New Testament is portrayed in a "subordinate position" in relation to the other disciples.

(13) The apostle John is "never named in this gospel." The collective "sons of Zebedee" appears only once and that in the Appendix.[5]

---

[4] Parker more than once states that "sons of Zebedee" appears in 21:2 but the Greek has only "those of Zebedee" (which as I state elsewhere can mean the family of Zebedee).

[5] In fact that is misleading, yet it appears virtually everywhere in secondary literature. Only "those of Zebedee" is mentioned (see 21:2).

(14) The author of the GosJn knows the geography only of Samaria and Judea, yet John was from Galilee.

(15) Unlike the Synoptics and Acts in which Peter is the leader of the Twelve and close to John, the GosJn "shows little interest in, or knowledge of, Peter's doings in Galilee."

(16) It is simply impossible that John would have been known to the high priest as is the case of the other disciple in chapter 18.

(17) While Luke 24:12, according to some manuscripts, has only Peter visit the empty tomb, John 20 has Peter and the Beloved Disciple race to the tomb. Moreover, it is not easy to reconcile the prominent and highly spiritual events in which John appears in the Synoptics with the complete absence of such events in the GosJn.

(18) While according to the Synoptics, John witnessed Jesus' agony in Gethsemane, the "Gethsemane agony is not so much as hinted at in the Fourth Gospel."

(19) According to Luke 22:8 John and Peter made the preparations for the Last Supper, but in the GosJn no such preparation is made by any disciple.

(20) According to Mark 5:37-42 and Luke 8:51-55 John observed Jesus raise Jairus's daughter, an event that would have been very appealing to the Evangelist; but it is not mentioned in the GosJn.

(21) Most significantly, according to Parker, John was present at the Transfiguration as reported by each of the Synoptics; but the event is not mentioned in the GosJn. That is virtually impossible if the Evangelist is John, since it depicts what may be called the Johannine concept of Christ's glory.

The cumulative thrust of these observations is devastating to the hypothesis that the Beloved Disciple is both the author of the GosJn and also the apostle John. However, there are many unattractive features of these objections; among them are the tendency to give documents other than the GosJn priority in discerning the meaning of the GosJn, and the propensity to impute historical accuracy to documents that were not primarily intended to present *bruta facta*, and assuredly are not, by genre, histories. Unfortunately, virtually irrelevant details are mixed with highly significant points (for example number 13, and perhaps numbers 1, 10, 14, 15, and conceivably 5 [number 16 may not involve the BD]). The list is not conveniently ordered (numbers 1, 14 and 15 should have been discussed under one heading), and thus the overall force is dissipated. Most importantly, the internal evidence should have been given precedence.

Four prominent hypotheses are now defended by the experts. First, Brown, Schnackenburg, and many others favor the conclusion that the Beloved Disciple is to be identified with *one of the unnamed disciples* mentioned in 21:2. This conclusion is surely on the right track, since the Beloved Disciple is to be identified with one of the disciples noted by the author of 21:2. I have slowly come to the conclusion that the Beloved Disciple is one of the disciples mentioned in this verse, but I am not satisfied with identifying him as an anonymous disciple. If the author of chapter 21 was attempting to clarify without specifying his identity, then he certainly failed by linking the Beloved Disciple with one who was anonymous.

Second, more and more scholars are defending the viability of *Lazarus* as the Beloved Disciple. The specialists who have presented evidence in favor of Lazarus represent a wide range of positions (see chap. 3), from the conservative W. Brownlee to the liberal V. Eller who devoted his monograph, *The Beloved Disciple: His Name, His Story, His Thought*, to defend this hypothesis. It is remarkable that, despite the impressive list of experts who conclude that the Beloved Disciple is surely Lazarus, a scholar of M. Goulder's reputation can offer the opinion, "No one believes that he was Lazarus or John Mark."[6]

Third, some scholars have claimed—too soon—that a consensus exists among scholars.[7] Some report that there is a consensus among the best scholars that all the references to the Beloved Disciple are additions to the GosJn (that is they are redactional). Others even claim that there is a consensus the Beloved Disciple does not represent a real historical figure, arguing instead that "he" is *a narrative fiction or typos.*[8]

Fourth, as the review of scholarly opinions indicates in chapter 3, some Johannine specialists still suggest that the Beloved Disciple is John the son of Zebedee. This possibility is indeed conceivable—at least at the outset—but the best and most influential commentators (notably Brown,

---

[6] M. Goulder, "An Old Friend Incognito," *Scottish Journal of Theology* 45 (1992) 488.

[7] See, for example, H. Thyen's comments that begin the following "Introduction."

[8] The transliterated noun from Greek τύπος does not suggest an archetype as in Plato's *Republic* 379A; it denotes a "pattern" as in Acts 7:44. Hence a literary pattern or model is intended. In searching for the possible identity of the BD we should comprehend that biblical characters are virtually never described as they are today; thus we have no idea what Abashag or Bathsheba really looked like. See A. Berlin, *Poetics and Interpretation of Biblical Narrative* (Sheffield: Almond, 1983) 34 and H. C. Brichto, "Character and Characterization," in *Toward a Grammar of Biblical Poetics: Tales of the Prophets* (New York/Oxford: Oxford Univ. Press, 1994) 6-8.

Schnackenburg, and Haenchen) have abandoned it because of the paucity of internal evidence for it.

After some extended research it became clear to me that the primary texts in the GosJn and the reflections of the modern scholars indicate that any identification of the Beloved Disciple, whether with one of the disciples specified in the GosJn, with one who is anonymous in this gospel, or with some symbolic theme, must fulfill eight requisites. These are as follows:

First is the criterion of *love*. The identification should be able to explain why the author described the Beloved Disciple as "the disciple whom Jesus loved." In this search the net must be cast wide and far, since the concept of "disciple" in the GosJn includes far more men and women than just the Twelve. The latter term in the GosJn is attached to only two disciples: Judas Iscariot and Thomas the Twin (and by implication to Peter, as we shall see). This criterion of "love" is one of the main reasons some specialists are suggesting that the Beloved Disciple is most likely Lazarus, because he is introduced in a word from Mary and Martha to Jesus as "he whom you love" (11:3).

Second is the criterion of *anonymity*. Any proposed identification should be able to explain why the Beloved Disciple is not explicitly given a name in the GosJn. Why does the leading character appear only as "the disciple whom Jesus loved" in the Beloved Disciple's pericopes? The criterion of anonymity does not indicate that the Beloved Disciple is not named in the GosJn (despite the opinion of some specialists); it denotes only that the name of the Beloved Disciple is not explicitly stipulated in the pericopes in which we find the phrase "the disciple whom Jesus loved." Our search, therefore, is to seek to discern if some link may be found between the Beloved Disciple and a disciple presented by name elsewhere in the GosJn. Hence, before beginning our search, it is conceivable that the Beloved Disciple is either a female—Mary, Martha, Mary Magdalene—or a male—John the son of Zebedee, Lazarus, or another. He or she cannot be Nicodemus, Joseph of Arimathea, Pilate, or the anonymous Samaritan woman; these do not fit the author's and editor's criterion for discipleship. The individual must clearly be one who believes in Jesus and who is openly willing to live and die for believing that Jesus is the one who was sent by the Father.

The criterion of anonymity indicates that the name of the Beloved Disciple is not pellucidly evident in the GosJn. But we should not forget that his (or her) name was known to the Johannine Community.[9] Members in this community were traumatized by the death of this disciple to whom

---

[9] At the appropriate place in the following chapters full bibliographical support for this statement will be given.

they had looked for spiritual guidance, teaching, and most importantly, for trustworthy witness to the life, death, and resurrection of Jesus Christ (see chap. 1.2 and the exegesis of 21:20-23; also see criterion 7 below).

This criterion also helps us comprehend why the identity of the Beloved Disciple has been the focal point of intensive scholarly searches for almost two thousand years and has given rise to so many mutually exclusive hypotheses (see chap. 3).

What is the function of anonymity in the GosJn? Why are both Jesus' beloved disciple and mother presented anonymously in the GosJn, and how does anonymity function in this gospel? Brown offers these acute observations:

> At the foot of the cross there are brought together the two great symbolic figures of the Fourth Gospel whose personal names are never used by the evangelist: the mother of Jesus and the Disciple whom Jesus loved. Both were historical personages, but they are not named by John, since their primary (not sole) importance is in their symbolism for discipleship rather than in their historical careers.[10]

While anonymity helps us understand the narrative concept of an implied reader,[11] does it not also serve as a catalyst in understanding our own relationship with a literary figure (who also represents a historical person), enticing us to embody somatically the universal magnetism of symbolism? It seems evident to me that in dramas of mythic proportions like the GosJn, anonymity enables a character to transcend time and place, stimulating the reader to identify with him or her in ways not possible with someone who is limited by a personal name.[12]

At the end of this research I became convinced that anonymity moves to an epithet and finally to a revelation of the identity of the Beloved Disciple. The model disciple is not really anonymous; he is an enigma that is gradually disclosed. The delicate disclosure of the identity of the leading character is concurrent with the basis—the trustworthy wit-

[10] R. Brown, *The Community of the Beloved Disciple* (New York: Paulist Press, 1979) 196.

[11] See the stimulating reflections by W. S. Kurz in his "The Beloved Disciple and Implied Readers," *Biblical Theology Bulletin* 19 (1989) 100-107. Also see D. J. Hawkin, "The Function of the Beloved Disciple Motif in the Johannine Redaction," *Laval Théologique et Philosophique* 33 (1977) 135-50.

[12] As Joseph Campbell saw long ago, great world-shaping myths are often "suffused with the joy of a transcendent anonymity regarding itself in all of the self-centered, battling egos that are born and die in time" (*The Hero with a Thousand Faces* [Bollingen Series 17; Princeton: Princeton Univ. Press, 1949 (2nd ed. 1968)] 46).

ness—for identifying with (even returning to) the One from above. The narrative development of the Beloved Disciple masks a relationship between profundity and anonymity.[13] In subtle ways the master Evangelist lets light sparkle from the actions of the Beloved Disciple so that his real identity is intimated. Ultimately the careful reader learns what was experienced within the Johannine Community: the harmony and oneness of a great literary masterpiece in which kerygma is proved trustworthy because of the witness of one of Jesus' disciples.

Third is the criterion of *closeness or authority*. Any identification of the Beloved Disciple should be able to explain why he or she was allowed the seat of honor during the Last Supper. The Beloved Disciple enters the narrative of the GosJn (which does not imply by any means that he or she is only a narrative fiction) at the scene of the Last Supper. The reader is introduced to this disciple with these words: "One of his disciples, whom Jesus loved, was lying close to the breast of Jesus" (13:23).[14] Noticeably, Peter turns to him to obtain information and insight (13:24). This scene indicates that the author wants to stipulate that the Beloved Disciple is not only the primary source of reliable tradition (he is the true witness), but is also superior to Peter. Any identification of the Beloved Disciple must be able to explain why he or she is the faithful witness, as the author and editor of the GosJn stipulates in 19:35 and 21:24.

An identification of the Beloved Disciple should be able to explain why Mary Magdalene, upon seeing that the stone had been moved away from the tomb of Jesus, ran to Simon Peter and the Beloved Disciple. Why did she seek them to report this news? Why are Peter and the Beloved Disciple apparently in a place together and not with the other disciples? How does the identity of the Beloved Disciple help explain these questions?

Fourth is the criterion of *lateness*. That is, why is the Beloved Disciple not mentioned until chapter 13 in which the Last Supper is described? Why is he not mentioned in the following episodes (many of which occur

---

[13] As F. Nietzsche in a moment of lucidity and perspicacity stated, "Whatever is profound loves masks; what is most profound even hates image and parable. ... Every profound spirit needs a mask" (*Basic Writings of Nietzsche*, W. Kaufmann, trans. and ed. [New York: Modern Library, 1966, 1992] 240–41). Also see the contributions in *Secrecy in Religions*, K. W. Bolle, ed. (Studies in the History of Religions 49; Leiden/New York: Brill, 1987).

[14] As A. Culpepper contends, there is a subtle difference between "one of his disciples, whom Jesus loved" in 13:23 and "the disciple whom Jesus loved" in 19:26, 20:2, and 21:7, 20. The introduction of the BD is couched so that the reader is not supposed to know his (or her at this point) identity. See Culpepper, *Anatomy of the Fourth Gospel: A Study in Literary Design* (Philadelpia: Fortress, 1983) 215.

in Judea and even within Jerusalem): at the wedding feast at Cana, during the discussions in Samaria with the woman, during the episode at the Pool of Bethzatha inside the Sheep Gate of Jerusalem, during the feeding of the five thousand by the Sea of Tiberias, during the Feast of Tabernacles back in Jerusalem when Jesus was in the Temple teaching (7:14), during Jesus' debate with "the Pharisees" (8:13) in the Temple (8:59) over the validity of his testimony, during the central and major scene not far from the Pool of Siloam just south of the walls of Jerusalem when the man "born blind" (9:1) sees first physically and then spiritually, during the winter Feast of Dedication in Solomon's Portico on the eastern side of the Jerusalem Temple (10:22-23), during the raising of Lazarus near Bethany just east of Jerusalem (11:1), during Jesus' escape to Ephraim (11:54) and return to Bethany (just east of Jerusalem) for Passover (12:1) when Mary (either during or after supper) anointed Jesus' feet with "a pound of costly ointment of pure nard" (12:3), and during the triumphal entry into Jerusalem? Some experts in the search for the Beloved Disciple claim that his introduction only late in the gospel indicates he must be a disciple from Judea. Have they adequately accounted for the numerous passages in the GosJn before chapter 13 (noted above) in which the Beloved Disciple is not mentioned?

The fifth criterion is *the cross*. Why has the narrator placed the Beloved Disciple at the cross? Why does he not state that other disciples are present?

Why does Jesus turn to his mother who is depicted at the cross with the Beloved Disciple and state: "Woman, behold, your son!" (19:26)? Then why does the author have Jesus reciprocally turn to the Beloved Disciple and exclaim, "Behold, your mother!" (19:27)? What is the historical meaning or narrative function of "And from that hour the disciple [the Beloved Disciple] took her [Jesus' mother] within his own things [or to his own home]" (19:27)? How does this episode factor in as we search for the identity of "the disciple whom he [Jesus] loved" (19:26)? Any identification should help us answer these questions.

As J. A. Grassi points out in his *The Secret Identity of the Beloved Disciple*,[15] the GosJn portrays an intimacy between Jesus' mother and the Beloved Disciple. Indeed, the Beloved Disciple is almost a twin for Jesus. Is the intimate relationship between Jesus' mother and the Beloved Disciple merely a formal adoption? How can any identification of the Beloved Disciple satisfy all these issues?

What is the meaning of the pericope in which the Evangelist describes the Beloved Disciple seeing water and blood exuding from Jesus'

---

[15] J. A. Grassi, *The Secret Identity of the Beloved Disciple* (New York: Paulist Press, 1992).

side? Why is he described standing by himself, alone with no other disciples narratively in view?

The sixth criterion is *commendation*. Why does the author of chapter
21 feel compelled to endorse the credibility of the Beloved Disciple? Why
did he write, "And we [the members of the Johannine Community] know
that his witness [or testimony] is true" (21:24)? What is the meaning of
the statement that the Beloved Disciple's witness is trustworthy? Does the
need to endorse the Beloved Disciple's testimony eliminate from consideration all well-known and celebrated disciples, including John the son of
Zebedee?

The seventh criterion is *fear and death*. Why did the Johannine
Christians express concern and anguish at the death of the Beloved Disciple? Apparently they had access to an otherwise unknown saying of Jesus
that they took apocalyptically: "The word spread abroad among the brethren that this disciple [the Beloved Disciple] was not to die" (21:23). The
author of chapter 21 instructs the readers of the expanded GosJn that the
meaning of Jesus' words are casuistic not apocalyptic—that is, Jesus did
not intend his words to mean that the Beloved Disciple would remain alive
until he returned at the Parousia: "Jesus did not say to him that he was not
to die" (21:23). He meant, "If it is my will that he remain until I come,
what is that to you?" (21:23).

Hence, any identification of the Beloved Disciple must account for
the threefold fear mirrored in chapter 21: the fear caused by the death of
the Beloved Disciple (which was not a martyrdom as with Peter [21:18-
19]), the fear that Jesus' words were false and that he might not return,
and the fear that the witness of the Beloved Disciple is invalid. These
points seem to make it impossible to conclude that the Beloved Disciple is
merely a narrative fiction.

The eighth criterion is *Peter*. The Beloved Disciple is closely linked
with Peter in the GosJn. But there is much more. At the Last Supper Peter
must turn to the Beloved Disciple not only for insight, but also for access
to Jesus. The Beloved Disciple arrives before Peter at the empty tomb, not
because he is younger (as some commentators speculate); he outruns Peter
because he is "first." The Beloved Disciple and not Peter is celebrated as
"that disciple whom Jesus loved" (21:7). Peter is made to ask Jesus about
the Beloved Disciple, "Lord, what about this [man]?" (21:21) There is
almost a polemical rivalry between them. How is that to be explained?

These eight requisites will guide us as we seek to answer one
focused question: Can we identify the Beloved Disciple?

A convincing case for the identity of the Beloved Disciple should be
persuasive not only to the one making it, but to at least some of the readers of such a claim, especially to those trained to offer a sane and balanced judgment. Each of these criteria is important and should be used in
assessing each argument. Certainly they are not of equal weight, but scho-

lars will not agree which are most important. All may serve as guides for keeping us on the trail of the Beloved Disciple. In a particular passage one will seem more important than another. I have presented them in an order most significant to me and also in line with the development of the GosJn. Perhaps an hypothesis does not necessarily satisfy all of the criteria. However, the hypothesis that I will present does, in my judgment, meet each of these requirements.

It has become clear to me that the search for the Beloved Disciple has been hindered by church dogmatics, systematic theology, a reading of the GosJn in light of the Synoptics, confusing the anonymity of the Beloved Disciple with the anonymity of "the other" disciple in the GosJn, a western resistance to the evidence of Syriac Christianity and the formation of the GosJn in Syria (perhaps southwestern Syria which around 100 C.E. included Galilee), failure to read familiar (even memorized) passages afresh, a pejorative attitude to the Christology of the GosJn (in light of the Gnostics' fondness of it and Käsemann's claim that it is naively docetic),[16] and a resistance to the possibility that the writers who have given us the GosJn are intermittently reliable regarding some aspects of Jesus' life and mission (while it is certain that his sayings are not *ipsissima verba Jesu*).[17]

The identity of the Beloved Disciple cannot be displayed with palpable proof because the author and editor chose to veil him or her from us. Some reviewers may judge this monograph as not only creative, but challenging. It is even conceivable some specialists will contend that the hypothesis presented here is as strong as any put forward previously. I will be

[16] See E. Käsemann, *Jesu Letzer Wille nach Johannes 17* (Tübingen: Mohr [Siebeck], 1980); ET = *The Testament of Jesus*, trans. G. Krodel (Philadelphia: Fortress, 1968). Käsemann's position is often caricatured; he did not say that the GosJn was "docetic." He thought that the GosJn focused on Jesus' glory, and so presented "a naïve docetism." See the critical responses by Germans and Americans: esp. Hengel, "Wird in den Briefen ein 'naiver Doketismus' des Evangeliums kritisert?" in *Die johanneische Frage* (WUNT 67; Tübingen: Mohr [Siebeck], 1993) 210–19; and M. M. Thompson, *The Humanity of Jesus in the Fourth Gospel* (Philadelphia: Fortress, 1988). D. J. Hawkin argues insightfully that the Evangelist attempts to defend his accurate ("orthodox") interpretation of Christ by claiming that the BD stands "both theologically and historically within the Christian fellowship. The Beloved Disciple was the confidant of Jesus, whom the Lord recognized as understanding him well" (150), ("The Function of the Beloved Disciple Motif in the Johannine Redaction," *Laval Théologique et Philosophique* 33 [1977] 135–50).

[17] This world-wide penchant is brilliantly confronted by D. M. Smith in his "Historical Issues and the Problem of John and the Synoptics," in *From Jesus to John: Essays on Jesus and New Testament Christology in Honour of Marinus de Jonge*, ed. by M. C. De Boer (Sheffield: JSOT Press, 1993) 252–67.

delighted, of course. But, the real joy will not be in reading positive responses to the hypothesis. The joy is certainly in the questioning—in the search for the identity of the Beloved Disciple. Scripture is ever fresh for those who attentively read and contemplate. I covet for others, especially the present generation of "seekers," the excitement in acquiring personal knowledge of such passages as the following one:

> These things I have spoken to you, that my joy (ἡ χαρά) may
> be in you, and that your joy (ἡ χαρά) may be full. (15:11)

Finally getting my hands on a personal copy of R. E. Brown's *The Community of the Beloved Disciple*, I resonate with his opening words, especially in an intellectual environment in which far too often Paul is praised and John is damned. These words by Brown represent my own thought: "In this book I hope to impart both a love for John and an enthusiasm for the adventurousness of Johannine thought. It is a thought that marks a high point in early Christology and ecclesiology, and yet offers frightening dangers even to this day."[18]

Indeed, in an academic environment in which far too often the GosJn is disparaged by gifted critics as a product of Gnosticism, as quasi-docetic, and as replete with grotesque anti-Semitic passages, it is essential to see how the light of truth is refracted through it. In this monograph all who may have harbored such pejorative evaluations of the GosJn are urged to consider why, on the one hand, J. Colson stated in his *L'Énigme du disciple que Jésus aimait*, that the Evangelist is "la plus profonde personnalité théologique du Nouveau Testament,"[19] and on the other, why centuries earlier Clement of Alexandria reported that the Evangelist "inspired by the spirit composed a spiritual gospel."[20]

Today many Christians would not be attracted to a lecture on "Who was Jesus' Beloved Disciple?" If they attended, some undoubtedly would relish the expected moment in which they could claim that Jesus loved all his disciples. At the beginning of this century Christians were more familiar with their cherished and formative traditions, and the Bible was much better known. Many about 90 years ago would readily know what was meant by the words "the Beloved Disciple"; they would also tend to assume it was synonymous with John the Evangelist. For example, in the diary of Rev. Dr. Thomas Charlesworth, written on board ship while traveling from the United States to the Holy Land, I find the following entry:

---

[18] R. E. Brown, *The Community*, 5.

[19] J. Colson, *L'Énigme du disciple que Jésus aimait* (Théologie historique 10; Paris: Beauchesne et ses fils, 1968) 25.

[20] Eusebius, *H.E.* 6.14.

Sunday March 31, 1912. Cloudy, dismal day. No sunshine. Cold! Up just a little past seven. Did not feel as well as on Saturday. A little sea sick. Divine service 10:00 a.m. The Rev. Clarence Allen, D.D., preached the sermon. It was an able and a very helpful discourse on John the Beloved Apostle. Text John 21:7. Rested on deck during the afternoon. It was cold, but I felt better there than anywhere else.

Though not feeling well, my grandfather nevertheless heard and found helpful a sermon about the final confession in the GosJn, uttered in a boat on a sea, and by the Beloved Disciple, judged to be John the Evangelist: ὁ κύριός ἐστιν.[21]

In contrast to the tedious tasks of editing the Pseudepigrapha and the Dead Sea Scrolls, the search for the identity of the Beloved Disciple has been a joy. I have observed in a special way what E. F. Scott learned: "the Fourth Gospel, in outward appearance so unstudied and spontaneous, is in reality a work of complex art."[22] As this work goes to press I wish to thank my research assistants, Michael A. Daise and Henry W. Leathem Rietz for their assistance, Loren L. Johns for the final format, President Thomas Gillespie and the PTS Research Council for a major grant, and President Thomas Reuschling of Florida Southern College who made the Bishop's Residence on Lake Hollingsworth available during my fall sabbatical in Lakeland, Florida. Walter Weaver, Moody Smith, and especially Hugh Anderson listened to my exegetical attempts to understand the GosJn and shared with me their insights. I am grateful to each of them for colleagueship and critical understanding.

Finally, let me now explain how this monograph evolved. In the course of an intensive exegetical study of the GosJn,[23] with an eye on the puzzling and as yet unresolved question of the identity of the Beloved Disciple, I was gradually drawn toward a novel hypothesis. So novel and indeed startling was this hypothesis that I wondered whether to pursue it further toward possible publication. I felt compelled to explore, so far as possible, all pertinent suggestions and hypotheses on the identity of this mysterious witness behind the GosJn, from fifty years ago to the present. I

[21] The diary is in my private library. After my father's death I was astonished to discover in his library his father's diary which accompanied him to and from Jerusalem.

[22] E. F. Scott, *The Fourth Gospel: Its Purpose and Theology* (Edinburgh: T. & T. Clark, 1906, 1908 [2nd ed.]) 22.

[23] *Inter alia*, the teaching of M.Div. and Ph.D. courses on the GosJn and related subjects at Duke University and Princeton Theological Seminary. I am grateful for numerous and profitable discussions with such stellar students as Michael Daise, Loren Johns, John Morrison, Henry Rietz, and Brent Strawn, as well as former students (now distinguished professors) like Alan Culpepper and Loren Stuckenbruck.

soon came to realize that I also needed to study comments from the eighteenth, then fifteenth centuries, and finally insights from the period in which Christianity originated. I discovered, quite surprisingly, that my view has never been suggested by a Johannine scholar. Although in my wide and intentionally thorough search I could discover only one or two vague gropings toward the solution that was slowly dawning on me, I decided to push ahead, cognizant that *all* attempted solutions to the identity of the Beloved Disciple, including my own, were at best speculative. The author of chapters 1–20, and the editor of chapter 21, did not identify the witness whose report, oral or written, validates the claims and insights of the GosJn. Is it possible that the author and his editor knew the identity of the Beloved Disciple and left clues, perhaps not so inadvertently as might be imagined, as to his identity? I became convinced that the answer is in the affirmative.

—JHC

Abbreviations

Abbreviations are avoided as much as possible. Those that are used are according to S. Schwertner, *Internationales Abkürzungsverzeichnis für Theologie und Grenzgebiete* (Berlin/New York: Walter de Gruyter, 1992 [2nd edition]). Additional abbreviations are the following:

Abbreviations for "the Beloved Disciple"
BD	"the Beloved Disciple"
DA	"Discipulo Amado" [Spanish] or "discepolo che Gesù amava" [Italian]
DBA	"Le disciple bien-aimé" [French]
GD	"Geliefde Discipel" [Dutch]
LJ or L	"Der Lieblingsjünger" [German]

Abbreviations for Collections and Other Publications
AKGWG	Abhandlungen der Königlichen Gesellschaft der Wissenschaften zu Göttingen
ABD	*Anchor Bible Dictionary*
ABRL	Anchor Bible Reference Library
BIS	Biblical Interpretation Series
BTS	Biblisch-theologische Schwerpunkte
BTSt	Biblisch-theologische Studien
CB	*Cahier biblique*
COL	Christian Origins Library (Crossroad)
CT	*Ciencia Tomista*
CTSAP	College Theology Society Annual Publications
EEC	*Encyclopedia of Early Christianity*
ETR	*Études Théologiques et Religieuses*
EKKNTV	*Evangelisch-Katholischer Kommentar zum Neuen Testament Vorarbeiten*
GLO	Great Lives Observed

IDBS	*Interpreter's Dictionary of the Bible: Supplementary Volume*
IBA	*Irish Biblical Apocrypha*
KUT	Kohlhammer Urban-Taschenbücher
LS	*Life of the Spirit*
NCB	*New College Bulletin*
NEAEHL	*New Encyclopedia of Archaeological Excavations in the Holy Land*
NFTL	New Foundations Theological Library
NJBC	*New Jerome Biblical Commentary*
NRSV	New Revised Standard Version
OTP	*The Old Testament Pseudepigrapha*
PC	Proclamation Commentaries
RSV	Revised Standard Version
SPGS	Scholars Press General Series
SNTSMS	*SNTS* Monograph Series
TANAKH	*TANAKH: A New Translation of the Holy Scriptures.*
Teologia	*Teologia: Rivista della Facoltà Teologica dell'Italia Settentrionale*

Abbreviations for Frequently Cited Books

Ashton, *Understanding*	J. Ashton, *Understanding the Fourth Gospel* (1991)
Beasley-Murray, *John*	G. R. Beasley-Murray, *John* (1987)
Bernard, *St. John*	J. H. Bernard, *Gospel According to St. John*, 2 vols. (1928)
Brown, *Community*	R. E. Brown, *The Community of the Beloved Disciple* (1979)
Brown, *Gospel*	R. E. Brown, *The Gospel According to John*, 2 vols. (1966,1971)
Bultmann, *John*	R. Bultmann, *The Gospel of John* (1971)
Culpepper, *Anatomy*	R. A. Culpepper, *Anatomy of the Fourth Gospel* (1983)
Culpepper, *John*	R. A. Culpepper, *The Apostle in the Fourth Gospel* (1994)
Culpepper, *School*	R. A. Culpepper, *The Johannine School* (1975)
Haenchen, *John 1* or *John 2*	E. Henchen, *John 1* and *John 2* (1984)
Hengel, *Question*	M. Hengel, *The Johannine Question* (1989)
Kragerud, *Lieblingsjünger*	A. Kragerud, *Die Lieblingsjünger im Johannesevangelium* (1959)

Kügler, *Der Jünger*   J. Kügler, *Der Jünger, den Jesus liebte* (1988)

Lorensen, *Lieblingsjünger*   T. Lorenzen, *Der Lieblingsjünger im Johannesevangelium* (1971)

Martyn, *History*   J. L. Martyn, *History and Theology in the Fourth Gospel* (1979)

Painter, *Quest*   J. Painter, *The Quest for the Messiah* (1993 [2nd edition])

Schnackenburg, "Der Jünger"   R. Schnackenburg, "Der Jünger, den Jesus liebte," *EKK* (1970)

Schnackenburg, *St. John*   R. Schnackenburg, *The Gospel According to St. John* (1968–1982 [1987])

Smith, *Composition*   D. M. Smith, *The Composition and Order of the Fourth Gospel* (1965)

Uechtritz, *Studien*   F. Uechtritz, *Studien eines Laien über den Ursprung* (1876)

Other commentaries and monographs are abbreviated less cryptically; e.g. Hengel, *Die johanneische Frage*. A publication is customarily cited first with full bibliography in a footnote.

THE BELOVED DISCIPLE

CHAPTER 1

Introduction

H. Thyen sees a consensus among the best specialists on the GosJn regarding the Beloved Disciple, a figure mentioned, as is well known, only in the Fourth Gospel. This "growing and by no means uncritical consensus," according to Thyen, is that the references to the Beloved Disciple may all be redactional[1] and literary but they "must correspond with a concrete person on the level of the real history of Johannine Christianity."[2]

Are all the references to the Beloved Disciple editorial additions to the GosJn, or are only some of them to be ascribed to the redactor (as Bultmann concluded)?[3] In my judgment, at least chapter 21 is an addition by an editor who cannot be the Evangelist; that observation is based on an assessment of the different meanings sometimes given to terms and the employment of different vocabulary (see chap. 2).

---

[1] J. Kügler concluded that "Die Lieblingsjüngertexte sind nicht nur alle in ihrem Kontext sekundär, sie sind auch *alle* Produkt der *Endredaktion*" (*Der Jünger, den Jesus liebte* [SBB 16; Stuttgart: Katholisches Bibelwerk GmbH, 1988] 434 [italics his]). See also W. Schmithals, *Johannesevangelium und Johannesbriefe: Forschungsgeschichte und Analyse* (BZNW 64; Berlin: De Gruyter, 1992). Also see P. B. Boshoff, "Walter Schmithals en die Johannese Geskrifte," *Hervormde Teologiese Studies* 49 (1993) 728–41, esp. "Die Lieflingsdissipelredaksie," 737–40.

[2] Thyen, "Aus der Literatur zum Johannesevangelium," *Theologische Rundschau* N.F. 42 (1977) 212–70; see p. 223, esp. his words just quoted, "eine konkrete Person auf der Ebene der realen Geschichte des johanneischen Christentums entsprechen muss." Here is one of the places in which Kügler parts company with Thyen; he contends that the BD "war auch kein historischer Jünger Jesu" (*Der Jünger*, 478).

[3] J. K. Thornecroft also argued that the final redactor added "in certain places" the "title." The Beloved Disciple, according to Thornecroft, is "indeed the author of the Gospel" ("The Redactor and the 'Beloved' in John," *The Expository Times* 98 [1986–1987] 135–39).

In seeking to discern the identity of the Beloved Disciple, I gradually became convinced that the references to him were not part of the first edition of the GosJn, and that they were added by the author when he edited his own work, producing a second edition, or by the editor who supplied chapter 21. More rapidly did I become convinced that the founder of the Johannine Community, which incorporated a School, was the Beloved Disciple; hence, he is a real historical person whom many of the Johannine Christians knew and saluted as "the disciple whom Jesus loved."

Perhaps for guidance through the tortuous waters ahead it might be helpful to indicate that at the end of my work—when an introduction is finally redacted—I finally realized that I was in full agreement with the gifted and interconfessional scholars who produced *Mary in the New Testament*.[4] They agreed that

> (1) the Beloved Disciple was a real person thought to accompany Jesus,
> (2) he was fundamentally significant for the Johannine Community,
> (3) he is the ideal disciple,
> (4) he is the special witness who alone guarantees access to the historical Jesus.

They surely would not agree with me, at least not initially, regarding the disciple whom I slowly and surprisingly became convinced should be recognized as the Beloved Disciple.

These conclusions, except for the identity I will eventually propose, are in line with the burgeoning consensus that the Beloved Disciple is a real person of history. The attempts to identify him with a known disciple, however, have unfortunately tended to focus on John the son of Zebedee,[5] and that he was not only the witness behind, but also the author of, the GosJn.

Research over the last two decades has made it obvious that there are insurmountable difficulties in simply identifying the Beloved Disciple with John the son of Zebedee (as we have already seen from the Preface). As D. M. Smith states, "there is no firm basis in the Gospel for the tradi-

---

[4] R. E. Brown, K. P. Donfried, J. A. Fitzmyer, J. Reumann, eds., *Mary in the New Testament* (Philadelphia: Fortress, 1978) 211. Obviously, one of the leading minds in this summary of the BD is Brown, whose own personal conclusion is very similar to that outlined above. See Brown, *Community*, 31.

[5] As can be seen from chapter 3, many scholars during this century have introduced the hypothesis that the BD is Lazarus.

tional identification of this disciple with John, the son of Zebedee."[6]
Brown and Schnackenburg have been forced to forsake their earlier support of this hypothesis in favor of one of the anonymous disciples mentioned in 21:2 (see chap. 3).

Moreover, it is rather obvious that the editor who added chapter 21 incorrectly claimed that the Beloved Disciple is not only the witness that validates the gospel, but also the author of it. It has become much more attractive in the search for the identity of the Beloved Disciple to distinguish between him and the author or editor (see section 1.4 below).

The present monograph seeks to discover if the Beloved Disciple may be identified within the GosJn. The results of my search have proved startling. The hypothesis presented here will prove challenging. After the name is suggested, it will be concluded that the GosJn does indeed claim, with some credibility, to be based on the witness of one of Jesus' disciples—indeed one of the Twelve (see chap. 2.3). It is not merely a literary device. Members in the Johannine Community obviously knew him and were disturbed by an apocalyptic statement of Jesus that seemed to mean that the Beloved Disciple would remain alive, in contrast to Peter who was crucified, until Jesus returned in glory (the Parousia). The Beloved Disciple had in fact died (though no description is provided), so the author of chapter 21 strives to cast the saying so it can continue to be true.

To conclude that the GosJn does stand on the testimony of an eyewitness is not to suggest that it is thereby historically reliable in all details. This monograph is not to be seen as an attempt to support the apostolicity of the GosJn—such a position does not follow from my conclusion that the Beloved Disciple is one of Jesus' disciples. In fact the literal meanings given by extreme fundamentalists to the epithet "the Beloved Disciple" would make the present search impossible, since our methodology assumes the complexity and symbolic subtlety of the author and editor (redactor).

I began this monograph stimulated by my personal reflections during a Ph.D. seminar at Princeton Theological Seminary in which we discussed the Johannine Community (or School), the influence from the Dead Sea Scrolls (and Essenes) upon Johannine thought, the sources behind the GosJn, the redactional shaping of the gospel, and its narrative unity. Oddly, in retrospect, we never discussed the identity or meaning of the Beloved Disciple.

At the beginning of my search for the identity of the Beloved Disciple I was curious about what could be learned about him. It is obviously inconceivable that the Beloved Disciple might have been a woman, per-

---

[6] D. M. Smith, *John* (Philadelphia: Fortress, 1976) 42.

haps Mary Magdalene, because from the cross Jesus told his mother, "Behold your son."

Who was this disciple that was so important to the Johannine Community from which the gospel has come to us? The door has been opened for fresh investigations into his identity, since it is no longer probable either that the GosJn can be attributed to John the son of Zebedee, or that he is the Beloved Disciple. After some research I wondered to what extent a case could be made for one of the disciples named in 21:2 in which the Beloved Disciple is ostensibly mentioned by the final editor of the GosJn, and that if it were not completely convincing, at least it would be heuristically rewarding and stimulating for others to explore one of the central issues in Christian origins. Finally, I became convinced from an exegesis of passages in which the Beloved Disciple was mentioned that an impressive case could be made for one of the men mentioned in the GosJn. This case now (near the end of the research) is far more convincing to me than any that has been attempted in the past for another candidate.

I realize that specialists on the GosJn are trained to debate and differ with all hypotheses. That posture is healthy and desirable; but let us not forget that our central task is to strive to discover the identity of the Beloved Disciple. In so doing we should not forget that his identity was well known not only to the final editor, but also to members of the Johannine Community (as our exegesis of chap. 21 reveals).

Why has the identification proposed herein not been attempted before by experts on the GosJn? The following reflections may provide some answers.

First, experts working on the identity of the Beloved Disciple have come to the GosJn bearing baggage picked up from the Synoptics, as if one is to read Matthew, Mark, and Luke before reading the GosJn. From the Synoptics, scholars have all too often approached the GosJn assuming that we knew the names of the Twelve and of Jesus' mother, that the name of John the son of Zebedee was mentioned in GosJn 1–21, that Jesus left his family in Nazareth and went alone to Capernaum when his teaching was violently rejected in his home city, and that Jesus' brothers rejected him and thought he was demon possessed. Such presuppositions will not blind us from obtaining the meaning of John 2:12, "After this he [Jesus] went down to Capernaum." But they will certainly hinder us from perceiving the information in the completion of the verse: "*with his mother, his brothers*, and his disciples; and there they stayed for a few days." According to the GosJn, therefore, Jesus' mother and brothers—his real blood brothers because they are distinguished from the "disciples"— *followed Jesus* to Capernaum.

It is not easy to work on the GosJn and to forget what has been memorized or learned from previous research. Even experts who insist on listening to the author of the GosJn if we want to hear his own voice, inadvertently slip into thinking that seven disciples are mentioned in 21:2. They derive this total by assuming that οἱ τοῦ Ζεβεδαίου must mean two and no more. In fact, I made that mistake, while thinking that we must concentrate on what is in the GosJn and not assume we know the names of "James and John the sons of Zebedee." I was correct about the names but wrong on the number. The phrase in 21:2, "those [not the sons] of Zebedee," does not necessarily denote sons or males,[7] and it signifies at least two; it does not specify only two.

It is very difficult to hear the notes in the GosJn and be thinking we are tuned only to him when in fact we have memorized the symphonic tones of the earliest Christian authors. J. D. G. Dunn urges us repeatedly to let John be John: "It is important for exegesis to insist that John must first be allowed to be itself before its relation to other expressions of the gospel can be properly and fully explored."[8]

Second, scholars apparently have spent far more hours studying the work of contemporary scholars and less time poring over the primary sources. While it is imperative to know what other specialists have learned, it is far more important to do one's own work first and not be misled by either misinterpretations or the force of peer pressure. The texts are almost always challenging, and an exegete may ponder over many possibilities before advocating one interpretation—sometimes at the expense of not sharing all the options that were conceivable at the first fresh look. Then another commentator will be less likely to spend months reflecting on multifarious possibilities before choosing one. Especially today, with less and less time for pure reflection and research, it is easy to be influenced by another's apparently careful work, when in fact that work may also be derivative.

Third, in reviewing the monographs and articles on the Beloved Disciple I have noticed a western bias and (where it could apply) a certain European and American parochialism. Since we live in the West, it is understandable that at times we are more interested in it than in the East, but such a bias should not hinder us from exploring all avenues as true and honest historians. This trend is especially lamentable when we are searching for someone from the Middle East whose witness is said by the editor of the GosJn to stand behind and verify the message of that gospel. Few Johannine experts have studied in Jerusalem or been significantly involved in archaeological excavations. In the growing awareness of the importance of knowing the topography of the Middle East and the unpar-

---

[7] Note that in Mark 3:21 οἱ παρ' αὐτοῦ denotes "his [Jesus'] family." I am grateful to W. Weaver for discussing this point with me.

[8] J. D. G. Dunn, "Let John be John," in *Das Evangelium und die Evangelien*, ed. P. Stuhlmacher (WUNT 28; Tübingen: Mohr [Siebeck], 1993) 309-39.

alleled importance of what is being discovered by archaeologists at Capernaum, Sepphoris, Gamla, Hammat Tiberias, Scythopolis, Qumran, Masada, Caesarea Maritima, Caesarea Philippi, Petra, and, of course, Jerusalem, such blindness will hinder us from catching sight of the trails of the Beloved Disciple. None of the monographs on the Beloved Disciple utilize and profit from the recent, indeed major, archaeological discoveries and publications by such experts as S. Freyne, H. C. Kee, L. I. Levine, C. Meyers, E. M. Meyers, and J. Strange.[9] The importance of archaeology and topography—and surely ancient Palestinian culture including the sociological study of it—has led B. Pixner to title one of his recent books *The Fifth Gospel*.[10] For Pixner, the Fifth Gospel is topography.[11]

This all too often prevailing western parochialism is unfortunate when it becomes more and more obvious that the GosJn took shape not in Ephesus, but in the Middle East, perhaps in western Syria which in 100 C.E. included Galilee. And, as many experts have rightly concluded, the GosJn surely took shape and was probably composed and edited in that very region (or at least took formative shape in a Semitic culture). The simple syntax, the Semitic morphology and repetitive vocabulary, and the use of chiasm and *double entendre* indicate that the GosJn, and not just its sources, was conceived and nurtured in a Semitic environment.[12]

Fourth, specialists on the gospels often come to the GosJn without focusing first and foremost on it—*and only on it*. If we really want to understand this gospel, we must respect its integrity as a source. It is a source which is independent of others, including all the intracanonical and extracanonical gospels. As the Synoptics must not dictate what may be found in the GosJn, so the other gospels, such as the Gospel of Thomas and the Gospel of Truth, must not be allowed to provide the agenda for studying the GosJn (despite the importance of gnosis, Proto-Gnosticism, and even Gnosticism in search not only for the origins of the GosJn, but also for perceiving its fundamental message). That means that as difficult as it will be, we must remove from our memory banks what we have learned from reading other gospels. Few observations are so impressive as the split-vision of some commentators, with only partial focus on the

---

[9] Some publications of these scholars and the works of the others are conveniently summarized (even highlighted) in L. I. Levine, ed., *The Galilee in Late Antiquity* (New York/Jerusalem: The Jewish Theological Seminary of America, 1992).

[10] B. Pixner, *The Fifth Gospel* (Rosh Pina: Corazin Publishing, 1992). See the review by T. Elgvin in *Mishkan* 17–18 (1992/93) 156–59.

[11] For R. Winterhalter the Fifth Gospel is the Gospel of Thomas. See his *The Fifth Gospel* (San Francisco: Harper & Row, 1988).

[12] See the publications cited by and the position of N. Turner in *A Grammar of New Testament Greek* (Edinburgh: T. & T. Clark, 1976) 4:64–79.

GosJn (evident especially in the commentaries by Loisy and Lindars in which the reader is constantly taken from the GosJn to other gospels). My impression is that often a major insight was almost made, while an intense struggle was developing on the meaning of a passage like 20:8, only to see the attention shift to Luke or another writing. Then, the exegete became blind to what was nearly seen; and sometimes it may well have been the correct identity of the Beloved Disciple.

Fifth, the repetitions in published articles and books are disturbing. They are far too often derivative; that is, the bulk of them contain the reflections of other scholars (sometimes merely regurgitated). I am convinced that we scholars need to be more bold and creative. Fearing adverse criticism, we have not ventured out with suggestions that others have not previously suggested. Of course, in the light of over two hundred years of intensive biblical research—at least since the Enlightenment—there are few suggestions that really can be labeled novel. One of the understandable reasons we are so reticent to be "creative" is that someone will demonstrate that such an ostensibly original idea is found in some unpublished lecture or in a publication in Russian, Polish, or some other language unfamiliar to us who strive to be Johannine scholars.[13] Fortunately, none of us wants to claim that we have read everything in the field—such a position is no longer possible. But, we have been too hesitant to venture out with challenging ideas, or have hidden behind the claim that a novel hypothesis is merely heuristic.

Sixth, the possible identification of the Beloved Disciple may have been missed by experts on the GosJn. Some have been misled by the presupposition that the "other disciple" is *always* to be identified with the anonymous Beloved Disciple.[14] I became convinced that this assumption is invalid (see chap. 6), but it has detoured some experts in the search for the identity of the Beloved Disciple. To avoid this error I have concentrated my exegesis in chapter 2 solely on the passages in which the Beloved Disciple is mentioned, and reserved for chapter 6 an exegesis of passages in which an anonymous disciple appears who may be the Beloved Disciple.

Seventh, after focusing on the Beloved Disciple passages in the GosJn it is necessary to understand it within its milieu. That task is formidable. It demands knowing, not just perusing the Old Testament (the Hebrew Scriptures), the Old Testament Apocrypha and Pseudepigrapha,

---

[13] In fact, at the close of my research I discovered that two experts on the Gospel of Thomas entertained the identification I discovered. But this will be noted at the appropriate places in the following pages.

[14] We must be alert to "the all fallacy." Few statements regarding the NT can be assessed to be "always" true.

the Dead Sea Scrolls, Philo, other documents in the New Testament, the vast array of "gnostic" writings, so-called Patristics, and the New Testament Apocrypha and Pseudepigrapha. The GosJn obviously belongs within the study of gnostic origins, Christian origins, and the origins of Rabbinic (synagogal) Judaism. Hence, R. G. Hall rightly includes the study of the GosJn, the Odes of Solomon, the Shepherd of Hermas, the Prayer of Joseph, and other similar writings in the study of the Beloved in the Ascension of Isaiah.[15]

New Testament scholars also have been confused by an unexamined exegesis of 21:24, and the resulting opinion that the Beloved Disciple is not only the valid witness, but also the author of the GosJn (see section 1.4 below). The present research will proceed without assuming at the outset that the "other disciple" is really the Beloved Disciple and that he is also the author (the so-called Evangelist John). It is prudent to begin and proceed without such possibly misleading assumptions or invalid presuppositions.

The present work is intended for scholars. Greek and other languages are used when necessary for clarification or exegetical precision. Foreign languages are almost always translated into English, but the original (or selections from it), when deemed prudent, is included. All translations are by the author, unless otherwise noted.

1.1 THE PURPOSE OF THE PRESENT MONOGRAPH

The purpose of this monograph is to venture into risky waters in search of some better understanding of *the identity of the Beloved Disciple*. The research has at times been frustrating; the author of the GosJn bewitches and then disappoints me in this search. Often I have experienced D. M. Smith's evaluation that in search for the identity of the Beloved Disciple "John alternately mystifies and tantalizes the reader and defies the historical investigator."[16] To venture into this area is, to use M. Hengel's words about his own exploration, to "find ourselves on the thin ice of hypotheses which are difficult to prove." So with him, all my comments towards a solution are "no more than very hypothetical considerations."[17] But, that is the task of historical research: to explore into unknown areas of history.

---

[15] R. G. Hall, "Isaiah's Ascent to See the Beloved: An Ancient Jewish Source for the *Ascension of Isaiah*?" *JBL* 113 (1994) 463–84. Recognizing the anachronisms in terms such as "Jewish," "Christian," and "gnostic" Hall rightly concludes that "the Vision of Isaiah is sufficiently Jewish to illustrate the history of Judaism, sufficiently Christian to illustrate the history of Christianity, and sufficiently gnostic to illlustrate the history of gnosticism" (484).

[16] Smith, *John*, 42.

[17] Hengel, *The Johannine Question*, trans. J. Bowden (London: SCM; Philadelphia: Trinity Press International, 1989) 124.

The present is a propitious time to once again seek to discern who might be the Beloved Disciple. It is time to assess the research presented in the monographs devoted to this subject published by A. Kragerud in 1959, J. Colson in 1969, R. Schnackenburg in 1970, T. Lorenzen in 1971, R. E. Brown in 1979, V. Eller in 1987, J. Kügler in 1988, K. Quast in 1989, R. S. Kaufman in 1991, W. Eckle in 1991, J. A. Grassi in 1992, A. Culpepper in 1994, and, of course, in the major commentaries on the Gospel of John.[18] One reason it is imperative to rethink our work is that specialists in search of the Beloved Disciple's identity like Schnackenburg and Brown have reversed their opinions. In fact, Schnackenburg warns us that his own contribution of 1970 "should not be the last word."[19]

It is also important to focus again upon the meaning of the pericopes that feature the Beloved Disciple. Were Jülicher, Scholten,[20] Käsemann,

[18] A. Kragerud, *Der Lieblingsjünger im Johannesevangelium: Ein exegetischer Versuch* (Oslo: Osloer Universitätsverlag; Hamburg: Grosshaus Wegner, 1959). J. Colson, *L'énigme du Disciple que Jésus aimait* (Paris: Beauchesne et ses fils, 1969). R. Schnackenburg, "Der Jünger, den Jesus liebte" *Evangelisch-Katholischer Kommentar zum Neuen Testament* (Vorarbeiten, Heft 2; Zürich-Neukirchen: Benziger Verlag Zürich, 1970). T. Lorenzen, *Der Lieblingsjünger im Johannesevangelium: Eine redaktionsgeschichtlicher Studie* (SBS 55; Stuttgart: Katholisches Bibelwerk, 1971). R. E. Brown, *The Community of the Beloved Disciple* (New York: Paulist Press, 1979). V. Eller, *The Beloved Disciple: His Name, His Story, His Thoughts* (Grand Rapids, Michigan: Eerdmans, 1987). J. Kügler, *Der Jünger, den Jesus liebte* (Stuttgart: Katholisches Bibelwerk, 1988). K. Quast, *Peter and the Beloved Disciple: Figures for a Community in Crisis* (JSNT, Supplement Series 32; Sheffield: JSOT Press, 1989). P. S. Kaufman, *The Beloved Disciple: Witness Against Anti-Semitism* (Collegeville, Minn.: The Liturgical Press, 1991). W. Eckle, *Den der Herr liebhatte—Rätsel um den Evangelisten Johannes: Zum historischen Verständnis seiner autobiographischen Andeutungen* (Hamburg: Verlag Dr. Kovač, 1991). J. A. Grassi, *The Secret Identity of the Beloved Disciple* (New York: Paulist Press, 1992). A. Culpepper, *John, the Son of Zebedee: The Life of a Legend* (Columbia, S.C.: Univ. of South Carolina Press, 1994). This book devotes ample space to the identity of the BD, and—though the BD does not appear in the title—is included here to bring the review up to the present.

[19] Schnackenburg, *St. John*, 3:375.

[20] Some authors have claimed that Bacon also thought the BD was pure literary fiction, but he did not hold that view. That erroneous thought might come from a perfunctory reading of p. 320: "The view many times advanced since Scholten that the Beloved disciple is a purely ideal figure is surely more in accord with the nature of his entry on the scene in the three individual contexts." But Bacon definitely argues against that position: "The 'disciple whom Jesus loved' is something more than a purely ideal figure. A very real man has sat for the portrait; although, as already stated, this is not a self-portraiture" (*The Fourth Gospel in Research and Debate* [New Haven: Yale Univ. Press, 1910]

and Kragerud correct to conclude that the Beloved Disciple is not an historical person but an *ideal* disciple—that is, only a narrative creation? Is the Beloved Disciple only a fiction created by the Evangelist? Is Kügler correct in concluding that all the passages that mention the Beloved Disciple are creative editorial additions ("der narrativen Kreativität der Redaktion")?[21] Was the Beloved Disciple only a "fictional historical authority," a fiction of the author ("Verfasserschaftsfiktion")?[22]

1.2 IS THE "BELOVED DISCIPLE" A LITERARY TYPOS?

Obviously, the study of the Beloved Disciple is an exegetical problem. But, does that lead us into narrative theology or historical research? The two are not clearly distinct in the following research, since to examine the function of the Beloved Disciple in the GosJn means to at least enter the mind and community that has given us the GosJn—that is, exegesis demands intense historical research even if it concludes that the author of the GosJn created the Beloved Disciple as fiction, for whatever reason (polemical, political, sociological, to bolster the authority of the special tradition, or to prove the superiority of the Johannine tradition [story and Christology]).

The central question now before us is discerning if the Beloved Disciple is a literary typos. Is he like the fictional characters in *Joseph and Aseneth*, which was composed about the same time as the GosJn but in Egypt?[23] Or, is the Beloved Disciple more like the Righteous Teacher of Qumran?[24] Although he was a powerful symbol for the Qumran Community, 'the צדק,' he was nevertheless a real historical person, who may once have been a high priest officiating in the Jerusalem Temple.[25]

---

325). For a judicious assessment of Bacon's overall views on the GosJn see D. M. Smith, "B. W. Bacon on John and Mark," *Johannine Christianity: Essays on its Setting, Sources and Theology* (Columbia, S.C.: Univ. of South Carolina Press, 1984) 106–44. Also, see the presentation of Bacon's views on the BD in our chapter 3.

[21] Kügler, *Der Jünger*, 420.

[22] Kügler, *Der Jünger*, 488.

[23] See the study on *Joseph and Aseneth* by Chris. Burchard in the *OTP*.

[24] See J. Roloff, "Der johanneische 'Lieblingsjünger' und der Lehrer der Gerechtigket'," *New Testament Studies* 15 (1968–69) 129–51.

[25] Esp. see G. Jeremias, *Der Lehrer der Gerechtigkeit* (SUNT 2; Göttingen: Vandenhoeck und Ruprecht, 1963) and Charlesworth, "An Allegorical and Autobiographical Poem by the *Moreh haṣ-Ṣedeq* (1QH 8:4-11)," *Sha'arei Talmon": Studies in the Bible, Qumran, and the Ancient Near East Presented to Shemaryahu Talmon*, ed. M. Fishbane, E. Tov, with W. W. Fields (Winona Lake, Ind.: Eisenbrauns, 1992) 295–307.

Long ago H. Lietzmann contended that if we look only at the GosJn itself, it comes to light that the Beloved Disciple is not a historical figure. The author of the GosJn intended it to be a pure literary construction, an ideal bearer of the apostolic witness which connected the heart of the reader with the heart of Jesus. Lietzmann concluded that there was no eyewitness to Jesus' life and teaching in the GosJn, and that the author of the GosJn was "the God-inspired interpreter of a supra-historical process."[26] Many scholars have concluded that the Beloved Disciple is indeed only a narrative fiction or a symbol (see chap. 3).

It is clear to me that according to the editor who appended chapter 21, the Beloved Disciple is a real historical person,[27] since the members of the Johannine Community are disturbed by his death.[28] To judge that the portrayal of the Beloved Disciple is highly interpreted, whether or not he is to be identified with the Evangelist, does not mean he cannot be an eyewitness to Jesus. Interpretation and even the symbolical meaning of persons, like Mary and Peter, does not mean that they never were historical figures. This insight is shared by most of the experts today who are working on the GosJn. For example, both the German Hengel and the Australian Painter have pointed out that symbolical meaning does not indicate narrative fiction; they have also correctly warned that reasoning otherwise merely moves us within twentieth century scholarly academies and not back into first century communities.[29]

Not only Schnackenburg and Brown,[30] but many other specialists on the GosJn—who have mastered not only historical exegesis, but also narrative techniques—have concluded that *the Beloved Disciple surely mirrors a real historical disciple.*[31] I use the verb "mirror" because we are not by any means provided with anything like a portrait.

---

[26] H. Lietzmann, *The Beginnings of the Christian Church*, trans. B. L. Woolf (London: Lutterworth Press, 1937 [3rd ed. rev. 1953]) 233. See his *Geschichte der Alten Kirche*, 1:247–48.

[27] So also many scholars; notably Schnackenburg, *St. John*, 3:376.

[28] Bultmann argued that the BD was a fiction created by the Evangelist, and that the redactor misunderstood this point of the narrative of the GosJn and strove to make the BD an eyewitness to Jesus, thereby giving apostolic authority to the gospel. See the pertinent bibliographical data and insightful discussion of Bultmann on this point by Smith, *The Composition and Order of the Fourth Gospel: Bultmann's Literary Theory* (New Haven/London: Yale Univ. Press, 1965) 220–21.

[29] Hengel, *The Johannine Question*, trans. J. Bowden (London: SCM; Philadelphia: Trinity Press International, 1989) 130; J. Painter, *The Quest for the Messiah: The History, Literature and Theology of the Johannine Community* (Nashville: Abingdon, 1993 [2nd ed.]) 91.

[30] See esp. Schnackenburg, *St. John*, 3:374–87, and Brown, *Gospel*, 1:xcv.

[31] See, e.g., J. Blank, "Der Lieblingsjünger (21,20-24): Die zweite Schlussbemerkung (21,25)," *Das Evangelium nach Johannes* (Geistliche Schriftlesung

The author of the GosJn is attentive to details and is concerned with historical accuracy. There is no evidence that he created a character and labeled him "the disciple whom Jesus loved." As Cullmann rightly states, the "evangelist never invents an event or a person for allegorical ends."[32]

At the outset, therefore, it becomes clear that we must work, *inter alia*, with narrative exegesis of the GosJn. But, since the Beloved Disciple is not merely a literary fiction, our questions will lead us into the Johannine Community of the last half of the first century C.E. These initial decisions will be substantiated in the appropriate places, notably in the exegesis of the major pericopes and in the review of scholars' opinions, which will necessarily include reflections on the reasons some scholars have contended that the Beloved Disciple is a fictional creation.

It is important to clarify the road ahead. This monograph is not primarily or only a literary or narrative study of the GosJn. That work is necessary and will continue. But the Beloved Disciple was an actual historical person. At least some members in the Johannine Community were devastated by his death. To miss that point is, as Eckhardt stated, "offensichtlich absurd."[33]

1.3 EIGHT REASONS FOR REOPENING THE SEARCH FOR THE BELOVED DISCIPLE

The major reasons for opening what some scholars may assume is a futile issue are paradigmatic improvements in the study of Christian origins—especially the setting of the Johannine traditions. Since the early seventies at least eight paradigm shifts in methodologies and perceptions warrant a new search for the possible identity of the Beloved Disciple. These shifts tend to disclose that inexact presuppositions and reasonings formerly shaping the arguments by scholars need to be refocused in the search.

First, after more than one hundred years of research, scholars concur that the Gospel of John was not composed by the apostle John, as so many of the early scholars of the Church had contended. This valid insight unfortunately led to the conclusion by many specialists that the GosJn was not historically reliable. Now, thanks to archaeological discoveries in Israel—especially in Jerusalem—and topographical references in the Dead Sea Scrolls, we know that the author of the GosJn was

---

4/3; Düsseldorf: Patmos Verlag Düsseldorf, 1988 [2nd ed.]); Part 3, 208–15; esp. see 212–13.

[32] Cullmann, *The Johannine Circle*, trans. J. Bowdon (London: SCM, 1976) 74.

[33] K. A. Eckhardt, *Der Tod des Johannes als Schlüssel zum Verständnis der Johanneischen Schriftem* (Berlin: Walter de Gruyter & Co., 1961) 14.

familiar with Jerusalem during the time of Jesus. This insight needs to be added to the issue of whether any part of the GosJn might derive, somehow, from an eyewitness to the events of Jesus' life, and that the Beloved Disciple might be such a person.

Second, some influential scholars about one hundred years ago contended that the GosJn probably postdated 150 C.E.[34] Now, however, scholars admit that the author of the GosJn wrote before 100 and depended upon earlier sources. Although the final edition of this gospel probably dates from about 95 C.E., some of its sources surely antedate the burning of Jerusalem in 70. Are any of these sources related in some way to the search for the identity of the Beloved Disciple?

Among the gospels, it is clear that the GosJn took final form latest— near the end of the first century, but is it not conceivable that behind it is an eyewitness to some of Jesus' activities? Or, is the author's claim to base his account on a trustworthy eyewitness merely a narrative device or an aspect of early Christian apologetics? Is it fundamentally the final redactor's attempt to establish the apostolicity of the Johannine tradition?

Third, the GosJn was once thought to be a composition influenced significantly by Greek philosophy. Now, however, scholars affirm that it is a very Jewish composition, perhaps the most Jewish of the gospels in the New Testament.[35] Behind the GosJn lie Jewish sources, such as the Signs Source, which clearly antedate 70 C.E.[36] Scholars now recognize that in light of our increased knowledge of the origin of the GosJn,[37] of Judaism before 135 (when Bar Kokhba was defeated), and of Judea and Galilee prior to 70 (thanks to unexpected and astounding archaeological discoveries)[38] it is misrepresentative to brand the GosJn as theological

[34] Some of this data is documented in chapter 3.

[35] See Charlesworth, "Reinterpreting John: How the Dead Sea Scrolls Have Revolutionized our Understanding of the Gospel of John," *Bible Review* 9 (1993) 18–25, 54.

[36] Among the numerous publications see R. Fortna, *The Gospel of Signs* (SNTSMS 11; Cambridge: Cambridge Univ. Press, 1970) and U. C. von Wahlde, *The Earliest Version of John's Gospel: Recovering the Gospel of Signs* (Wilmington, Del.: Michael Glazier, 1989).

[37] This fact will be obvious as the monograph develops. One of the articles that has been missed unfortunately in recent Johannine studies is D. Flusser's discovery of sources behind the GosJn ("A Jewish-Christian Source for the Gospel of John," *Yahadut u-Meqorot ha-Naẓrut* [Tel Aviv, 1979] 66–72; "What was the Original Meaning of *Ecce Homo*?" in Flusser's *Judaism and the Origins of Christianity* [Jerusalem: Magnes Press, Hebrew Univ., 1988] 593–603).

[38] See, e.g., N. Avigad, *Discovering Jerusalem* (Nashville: Thomas Nelson Publishers, 1980) and esp. the four-volume masterful *The New Encyclopedia of Archaeological Excavations in the Holy Land*, ed. E. Stern, et al. (New York: Simon & Schuster, 1993).

speculation and the Synoptics as history. Thus we come to the following question: How is the search for the possible identity of the Beloved Disciple improved by the significant advances in understanding the "Judaisms" of Jesus' time (prior to 70), and the emergence of Rabbinic Judaism after 70?[39]

It is clear that pseudepigraphy was an essential means for grounding the truths of new insights within Early Judaism. Pseudepigraphical attribution is surely one of the crucibles of Johannine thought. Pseudepigraphical writing is well known, and shaped many early Jewish documents for over three centuries prior to 70 C.E., as is clear from the brilliant writings of more than five books, abbreviated into what we call 1 Enoch. To what extent are we confronted with pseudepigraphical attribution in the GosJn? That is, does the author of 21:24 pseudepigraphically attribute the GosJn to the Beloved Disciple?

Is it possible that anonymity was also a major method that had both literary and historical roots? The anonymity of the Righteous Teacher at Qumran, and in many of the Dead Sea Scrolls, may well be related to the Evangelist's desire to shroud the Beloved Disciple in the mantle of anonymity, as J. Roloff suggested.[40] This anonymity is, of course, at least partly removed by the editor who added chapter 21. The influence from Qumran upon the GosJn is certainly not limited to the shared dualism; and the influence from Qumran is probably to be explained neither by indirect influence, as Brown thinks,[41] nor by the hypothesis that the author of the GosJn was an Essene converted to Christianity, as Ashton suggests.[42] While each of these suggestions is conceivable, it is much more likely that there were converted Essenes living in the Johannine Community (a Qumranic concept [יחד]). It may well have been a school (as Culpepper contends),[43] and have attracted Jewish scholars, including Essenes, the great

---

[39] The early rabbinic literature has often been unduly neglected in light of the excitement caused by research on the Pseudepigrapha and the Dead Sea Scrolls. See the major publications by J. Neusner on early rabbinics and the shaping of Judaism in the Mishnah. Now we have two important translations of the Mishnah into English: H. Danby, *The Mishnah* (Oxford: Oxford Univ. Press, 1933) and J. Neusner, *The Mishnah* (New Haven and London: Yale Univ. Press, 1988).

[40] J. Roloff, "Der johanneische 'Lieblingsjünger' und der Lehrer der Gerechtigkeit," *New Testament Studies* 15 (1968/69) 129-51.

[41] Brown, "The Qumran Scrolls and the Johannine Gospel and Epistles," in *The Scrolls and the New Testament*, ed. K. Stendahl with Charlesworth (COL; New York: Crossroad, 1992) 183-207. Brown's article first appeared in 1955.

[42] J. Ashton, *Understanding the Fourth Gospel* (Oxford: Clarendon, 1991) 237: "The evangelist may well have started life as one of those Essenes who were to be found, according to Josephus, 'in large numbers in every town.'"

[43] Culpepper, *The Johannine School* (Missoula, Mont.: Scholars, 1975).

writers of Early Judaism, as we know from the more than four hundred nonbiblical documents found in the Qumran caves.[44] From such converted Essenes many Qumranic ideas and concepts may have influenced the composition and shape of the GosJn, even if these are only barely discernible.[45] Is it not at least conceivable, as E. Ruckstuhl concludes, that the Beloved Disciple was a Johannine Christian who was formerly an Essene monk who had lived in the Jerusalem Essene Community?[46] Could one of these Qumran influences have been anonymity?

Fourth, a few decades ago most scholars admitted that unfortunately it is now impossible to recover Jesus' authentic words and to reconstruct his life. Now, however, most experts admit that we know far more about Jesus than about most pre-70 Palestinian Jews, and that some of his sayings and actions are reliably reported in the gospels.[47] The new study of Jesus within his time and place is distinguishable as "Jesus Research," because it is not motivated by theological agendas. Jesus Research is demonstrated in numerous books, especially in E. P. Sanders' *Jesus and Judaism*, my own *Jesus Within Judaism*, and J. Meier's monumental two-volume *A Marginal Jew*.[48] How does the impressive shift in the historical

[44] These documents are now ordered, first by number and then by name, in each volume of the Princeton Theological Seminary Dead Sea Scrolls Project. See Charlesworth, et al., *The Rule of the Community and Related Documents* (The Dead Sea Scrolls: Hebrew, Aramaic, and Greek Texts with English Translations; Tübingen: J. C. B. Mohr [Paul Siebeck], Louisville: Westminster John Knox Press, 1994) 1:180–83.

[45] Charlesworth, *John and the Dead Sea Scrolls* (COL; New York: Crossroad, 1991), esp. the 1989 "Foreword." Also, see Schnackenburg's conclusion that the author of the GosJn may have learned from Qumran Essenes "who later entered Christian, Johannine communities" (*St. John*, 1:135).

[46] This suggestion is discussed in the chapters which follow. See Ruckstuhl, "Der Jünger, den Jesus liebte, ein Essene?" in *Jesus im Horizont der Evangelien* (SBA 3; Stuttgart: Katholiches Bibelwerk GmbH, 1988) 393–95. See his clear statement on p. 393: "The disciple, whom Jesus loved, may have been a monk in the Essene Community in Jerusalem."

[47] It is lamentable that specialists, who knew that historical research can at best provide us with a probable reconstruction that needs constantly to be improved, ignored such a primordial perception and attempted to guide generations of students and scholars in the search for Jesus' uninterpreted *bruta facta* and to isolate his own voice (*ipsissima vox Jesu*) and his pure words (*ipsissima verba Jesu*). Now, scholars wisely seek to discern the meaning of Jesus' message (and in the jargon of phenomenologists like M. Merleau-Ponty, his authentic intentionality).

[48] E. P. Sanders, *Jesus and Judaism* (Philadelphia: Fortress Press, 1985); Charlesworth, *Jesus Within Judaism* (ABRL 1; New York: Doubleday, 1988); J. Meier, *A Marginal Jew: Rethinking the Historical Jesus*, 2 vols. (ABRL; New York: Doubleday, 1991, 1994).

study of Jesus help us in the quest for the identity of the Beloved Disciple? What is the meaning of the claim of the redactor of chapter 21 that the Beloved Disciple was an eyewitness to what is recorded in the GosJn (the Beloved Disciple is ὁ μαρτυρῶν περὶ τούτων according to 21:24)?

Fifth, decades ago it was affirmed by most New Testament experts that the author of the GosJn derived his data from the Synoptics (Matthew, Mark, and Luke). Now it is apparent that he did not base his work on them, as D. M. Smith in *John Among the Gospels* lucidly demonstrates.[49] Is it not conceivable, therefore, that since the GosJn is independent of the Synoptics, it might depend on the eyewitness of a disciple? Is he the Beloved Disciple (one of the Twelve), as chapter 21, in fact, claims? Do the author of the GosJn and the Johannine Christians derive their historical insights into Jesus' life and teachings from one of the Twelve who was with Jesus? This question makes allowance both for the shaping of the traditions and their symbolical development and for the grounding of Jesus' life in a pre-70 Palestinian setting, which moves beyond mere verisimilitude to at least occasionally reliable tradition (even history).[50] Among the latter I would include the knowledge of Jerusalem (especially the Pool of Bethzatha); the recognition of the significance of stone vessels and the pre-70 Jewish preoccupation with purity; Jesus' three-year ministry, especially in Judea; and Jesus' frequent visits to Jerusalem, which the Marcan chronology will not allow but seems to presuppose.[51]

Sixth, the study of Christian origins, in which the exploration of a person who may be the Beloved Disciple is alone possible, has been enriched over the last two decades by insights obtained from anthropologists and especially sociologists. It is clear that three major social crises rocked the Johannine Community. First, the Johannine Jews were being expelled from the synagogue, so there was a rift with other Jews. Second, the Johannine Community was divided by a schism, which seems to have been centered on the claim that Jesus did come in the flesh, and which resulted in some leaving the Community (see 1Jn 2:18-25). Third, the death of the Beloved Disciple (the guarantor of the validity of the tradition in the GosJn) was unexpected and traumatic. Obviously some Johannine Christians expected him to remain alive until Jesus came again (21:20-23), but he did not. Would survivors of the Essene sect, who possessed some

---

[49] D. M. Smith, *John Among the Gospels: The Relationship in Twentieth-Century Research* (Minneapolis: Fortress, 1992).

[50] Verisimilitude must not be confused with historicity, but also an historical account that lacks verisimilitude to what could or would have occurred can scarcely be judged "historically" reliable.

[51] See esp. Mk 11:2-11, 14:13-16.

insights into the traumas caused by the death of the Righteous Teacher, and former followers of John the Baptist who joined Jesus' group (1:35-42), who lived through the anguish of his martyrdom, have helped the Johannine sectarians to cope with the death of "the disciple whom Jesus loved" (clearly their honorific title for one of Jesus' Twelve [see chap. 2.3])?

There is a noticeable tension between the Beloved Disciple and Peter. Chapter 21, which is a unity (as Ruckstuhl has shown),[52] first reestablishes Peter who is worthy to feed Jesus' lambs and tend his sheep—which are certainly symbolical and ecclesiastical terms. But, he is then made somewhat lower in prestige than "the disciple whom Jesus loved" (which certainly excludes Peter as the disciple beloved by Jesus and may mirror an anti-Petrine polemic). Obviously, by the end of the first century (the time when chapter 21 was probably added) Peter would represent to many Christians the church in Rome. The GosJn is now rightly (in my opinion) situated in the East, perhaps in western Syria which would include Upper Galilee (a region we now know was distinct from Lower Galilee). Is it conceivable that the GosJn reflects some political or sociological rivalry between West and East in earliest Christianity (see chap. 8)?[53]

Seventh, Bultmann and many other distinguished critics tended to separate the GosJn into strata, redactional layers, and putative sources.[54] These publications led to the assumption that the GosJn was in disarray and perhaps not in its original order (especially with chaps. 5 and 6). Now it seems that the GosJn 1:1–20:30 represents a "second edition" with the expansion of chapters 1, 15–17, and some other verses (especially 4:2).[55] Later another writer added chapter 21 as an appendix, and much later a scribe inserted the pericope concerning the adulteress (7:53–8:11). The unity of the so-called "second edition," however, has been demonstrated by E. Schweitzer and E. Ruckstuhl.[56] Also, the new study of the GosJn

---

[52] E. Ruckstuhl, "Der Jünger, den Jesus liebte," 355–401.

[53] And perhaps, I might add, a tension between northern Palestine, in which there was in many locales (notably Sepphoris) little cultural discontinuity after 70, and southern Palestine, in which there was frequently a sharp discontinuity after 70, with the burning of Jerusalem (especially the Temple) and the direct imposition of Roman rule. The burning of Qumran is a stunning example of this discontinuity (otherwise the Qumranites would have returned and retrieved the Dead Sea Scrolls).

[54] See Bultmann, *The Gospel of John*, trans. G. R. Beasley-Murray (Oxford: Blackwells, 1971) *passim*; Smith, *Composition, passim*.

[55] Additional redactional verses or phrases will be isolated in the detailed exegesis of the BD passages.

[56] E. Schweizer, *Ego Eimi: Die religionsgeschichtliche Herkunft und theologische Bedeutung der johanneischen Bildreden, zugleich ein Beitrag zur Quel-*

stresses the literary unity and the author's use of such paradigms as "above" and "below," the employment of *double entendre* (such as "living water" [for ordinary life and for salvation], "again" [the Greek of which can also denote "above"], "raised up" [which denotes both Jesus' crucifixion and his exaltation]), along with the mastery of rhetoric. These insights into the coherency of the GosJn have helped us understand the beautiful narrative skills of the author of the GosJn.[57]

But as we have already seen (in chap. 1.2), the Beloved Disciple is not to be categorized as another narrative creation. Intensive research demonstrates that the Beloved Disciple is contrasted with Peter, certainly a real historical person who also was accorded powerful symbolical meaning (see GosJn 21 and Mt 16). Hence, there was a trauma within the Johannine Community because a real person died (a symbol does not "die" that way or cause such a crisis). The published researches by Schnackenburg and Brown illustrate quite conclusively that the Beloved Disciple was a real person who was the bearer of tradition—the eyewitness—for the Johannine Community (see chap. 1.2). Also, the rivalry between the Johannine Community (represented in the pericopes in which "the disciple whom Jesus loved" dominates) and the Petrine group would become unintelligible if the Beloved Disciple was only a literary fiction.

Eighth, for centuries Christian dogmatics and even systematic theology bracketed, and sometimes dictated, what a biblical scholar might conclude. Now, however, New Testament experts are free to explore issues and examine questions with as much freedom as any other scholar. To what extent has the search for the identity of the Beloved Disciple been hindered by the claim that Jesus was born of a Virgin and could not have had a biological brother or sister, and certainly not a fraternal twin? To

---

lenfrage des vierten Evangeliums (FRLANT 56; Göttingen: Vandenhoeck & Ruprecht, 1965 [2nd ed.]). See the recent study by E. Ruckstuhl and P. Dschulnigg titled *Stilkritik und Verfasserfrage im Johannesevangelium* (Novum Testamentum et Orbis Antiquus 17; Freiburg: Universitätsverlag; Göttingen: Vandenhoeck & Ruprecht, 1991).

[57] Especially see Culpepper, *The Anatomy of the Fourth Gospel: A Study in Literary Design* (Philadelphia: Fortress, 1983); P. D. Duke, *Irony in the Fourth Gospel* (Atlanta: Scholars Press, 1985); G. M. O'Day, *Revelation in the Fourth Gospel* (Philadelphia: Fortress, 1986). Also see Ashton, "Revelation," *Understanding*, 381–553. Quite distinct from other approaches is that of T. L. Brodie, who sees the contradictions and abrupt shifts (as between chapters 14 and 15) as the author's attempt to warn the reader that he is not writing a biography but a composition focused "on the mind-surpassing realm of the spirit." Thus he stresses the unity of the GosJn. See Brodie, *The Gospel According to John: A Literary and Theological Commentary* (New York/Oxford: Oxford Univ. Press, 1993) 19.

what extent has the Roman Catholic assumption that the Beloved Disciple is John the son of Zebedee stifled creative reflections on focal pericopes?

These are eight major paradigm shifts in New Testament research that directly affect the search for the possible identity of the Beloved Disciple. How is this search improved by the recognition that the GosJn may preserve reliable historical information, that there are sources in it that are as early as those in the Synoptics, and that Judaism of Jesus' time and the time of the Fourth Evangelist was not what scholars once thought? How is our investigation aided by the perception that research on the historical Jesus has been surprisingly rewarding, that John is independent of the other gospels, that one of the social crises confronting the Johannine Community was the death of its "eyewitness," that he was a real person and not narrative fiction, and that Jesus may well have had (and in my judgment certainly did have) real (not just symbolical) brothers and sisters?

The previous pages are categorically introductory; hence the redundancies are intentional to set the stage for a critical and fresh reading of the GosJn. We may now begin an open search for the identity of the Beloved Disciple. Who was he? Why does the author and editor of this literary masterpiece not state clearly who he is? Does the author gradually remove the mask of secrecy which hides the identity of the Beloved Disciple? The following chapters present the inductive search for answers. The exegesis has eventually lead me to conclude that the author not only knew the identity of the Beloved Disciple, but intentionally in extremely subtle ways allowed his perceptive readers to discern that identity. Only one requisite seems necessary: to listen without preconceptions only to the words of the author and editor, in seeking to discern the meaning veiled within the deeply symbolical language.

1.4 THE MEANING OF 21:24

Who is the Beloved Disciple mentioned in the GosJn? Many leading commentators on the GosJn conclude that this disciple, "the one whom Jesus loved" (21:20), is the one referred to by the claims in 21:24, "This is the disciple who has been witnessing to these things, and who has been writing these things; and we know that his witness is true." E. Haenchen contends that "the narrator of chapter 21 had such interest in this disciple (and his destiny)" because he was, according to this chapter,

> the last surviving eyewitness, whose testimony is true, as the "we" which is not more precisely defined knows, has even written this Gospel.... The beloved disciple is not only the witness who has been invoked; he is even the author of the Gospel itself.[58]

---

[58] Haenchen, *John 2*, trans. F. W. Funk with U. Besse (Hermeneia;

Haenchen can appeal to the literal meaning of 21:24, "This is the disciple who has been witnessing to these things, and who has been writing these things; and we know that his witness is true." Is this the meaning of the Greek and is the exegesis correct?

The verse, 21:24, is bewitchingly simple. But, the Greek needs to be studied carefully.

The popular rhetorician, Lucian (c. 125 to c. 180 C.E.), who called himself a Syrian, comically refers to claims such as those found in this verse. In satirical words meant to amuse, Lucian admits his "A True Story" (ΑΛΗΘΩΝ ΔΙΗΓΗΜΑΤΩΝ) is far better than other histories; it has at least one truth: "I shall at least be truthful in saying that I am a liar" (1.4).[59] The following excerpt has numerous important points that should help us comprehend Johannine thought and the meaning of the next to the last verse in the GosJn:

> Be it understood, then, that I am writing about things which I have neither seen nor had to do with nor learned from others—which, in fact, do not exist at all and, in the nature of things, cannot exist. Therefore my readers should on no account believe in them. (1.4)

Apropos for our study of GosJn 21:24, and indeed of the entire gospel and its claims, are these points: Lucian is writing about things he has neither seen nor experienced; the Evangelist is writing about things he (or his witness, the Beloved Disciple) has seen and experienced. Lucian did not learn the things he is about to describe from others; the Evangelist gives evidence of using sources which he may well have received from the Beloved Disciple (if he is not to be identified with this person). Lucian claims that what he is about to chronicle did not and cannot exist; the Evangelist contends that what he has written is factual and truthful, and that he has described the awesome sending of the divine into the human. Lucian warns his readers not to believe his account (μηδαμῶς πιστεύειν αὐτοῖς); the Evangelist concludes his final chapter with the exhortation to believe his writings that Jesus is the Christ and the Son of God (ταῦτα δὲ γέγραπται ἵνα πιστεύ[σ]ητε ... ἵνα πιστεύοντες [20:31]).

These claims, although they postdate the GosJn, help us enter into and comprehend the world confronted by the Evangelist. In his endeavor to deepen (or initiate) the believing of others was he the author and eyewitness or the author who based his work on an eyewitness? Should we categorize the Evangelist with Polybius (c. 208 to c. 126 B.C.E.), the great

---

Philadelphia: Fortress, 1984) 2:228.

[59] Lucian, "A True Story (*Verae Historiae*)," ed. and trans. A. M. Harmon (LCL 14; Cambridge, Mass.: Harvard, 1979) 247–357.

historian and historiographer, who castigated Timaeus for being unacquainted with what he described, and presented (or at least claimed to present) only what he had personally experienced, notably the burning of Carthage in 146 B.C.E.? Certainly the Evangelist would have abhorred Lucia's desire to entertain by telling lies, but he would have agreed with Polybius, and incidentally with Josephus, who apparently had studied Polybius, that in recounting history we must be accurate, base accounts only on truthful eyewitnesses, and avoid numerous false statements (πολλὰ ἱστορεῖ ψευδῆ [12.7.1]).[60]

Hence, to a certain extent it seems that Polybius's historiography would have been attractive to the Evangelist. But was he an eyewitness like Polybius and Josephus, or one who based his writing on an eyewitness? Thus, is 21:24 to be seen as similar to the opening of the *Book of Thomas the Contender*, which claims that Judas Thomas heard what Jesus said but Mathaias wrote it down?

The importance of 21:24 is hence extreme; but it is not necessary to judge it fraudulent if the gospel was not *composed* by an eyewitness like John the Apostle. Much more important is the *witness* of the tradition. Is it from an eyewitness? The great scholar of the École Biblique in Jerusalem, M.-J. Lagrange, couching his words contra the "extrémistees," namely Goguel and Loisy, stated that the GosJn "prétendait être d'un témoin oculaire," and to ignore that claim would leave us with a gospel devoid of authority, and indeed a fake, "une fraude littéraire.[61] That judgment may not be typical of experts on the GosJn today, but it would be phenomenally significant if scientific research could again cast a favorable light on the possibility that the Beloved Disciple was an eyewitness to portions of what was presented in the Fourth Gospel. That is why the search for the authorship of the GosJn, and the identity of the Beloved Disciple,

---

[60] Polybius, *The Histories*, ed. and trans. W. R. Paton (LCL 159; Cambridge, Mass.: Harvard Univ. Press, 1976) 326. In Book XII Polybius articulates the peculiar virtue of historical study: to recover the words actually spoken and to ascertain the cause of the results of actions (12.25b). Polybius's main point is that authors of history must be those experienced in the things to be accounted and described and to have been an eyewitness to at least some of them (12.25g). He stresses the superiority of seeing over hearing, quoting Heracleitus's "The eyes are more accurate witnesses (ἀκριβέστεροι μάρτυρες) than the ears" (12.27). That means that the author must either be an eyewitness or have interrogated ones who were. The Evangelist endeavors through his narrative, and especially in 19:35 and 21:24, to endorse this norm. It then also becomes much more obvious how powerful is Thomas's request in the final scene of the drama.

[61] M.-J. Lagrange, *Évangile selon Saint Jean* (Etudes bibliques; Paris: Librairie Victor Lecoffre, 1925 [2nd ed.]) cxcvi–cxcix.

has been the preoccupation of New Testament experts, and the "Johannine question."

Recently the attention of Johannine experts has been on the sources the author inherited (especially the so-called *semeia* source), on the origins of the gospel, on the "school" or circle from which the gospel arose, on the community that was suffering from a schism and also from being expelled from the synagogue by other Jews, and on the narrative unity of the gospel. Yet the question of authorship never became only a peripheral concern. As Ashton explains, this issue has been central in Johannine research, because "the credibility" of the author and the Beloved Disciple is virtually synonymous with the reliability of the GosJn. If the "witness" is not true, then the credibility of the GosJn "must be severely reduced, if not destroyed completely."[62] Of course, this conclusion would be dismissed by those students of the GosJn who think it is merely a story, a fictional account of Jesus who was worshipped in the late first century.

Schnackenburg has endeavored to prove that 21:24 does not mean that the Beloved Disciple composed the GosJn. It means rather that he is the witness behind it, and that his witness is trustworthy.[63] As Painter points out, however, the *prima facie* meaning of 21:24 is that the Beloved Disciple is both the author of the GosJn and the witness to the tradition.[64] He is correct in that the Greek is no problem; 21:24 states that the disciple (identified from verse 20 as the Beloved Disciple) "also was writing these things" (καὶ ὁ γράψας ταῦτα).

If the author of chapter 21 was closely aligned with the Beloved Disciple, which seems patently obvious, and the Beloved Disciple was the source—the eyewitness—to some of the events in the gospel, then it would be understandable for the author of chapter 21 to attribute the gospel to him. At that time in the history of writing it was inappropriate to claim authorial rights to what really belonged to another. Hence, in terms of pseudepigraphical composition (known not only in the Johannine School with the Epistles and Revelation, but also in the Pauline School and obviously outside Christianity in Judaism and the literature of the Hellenistic and Roman Age) it is requisite to think about the meaning of "writing" in antiquity.[65] Hence, I agree with F. C. Baur in the sense that the GosJn has a "pseudepigraphischen Charakter."[66]

---

[62] Ashton, *Understanding*, 15.

[63] Schnackenburg, *St. John*, 3:379.

[64] Painter, *Quest*, 87–95.

[65] See Charlesworth, "Pseudepigraphy," in *Encyclopedia of Early Christianity*, ed. E. Ferguson, et al. (New York and London: Garland Publishing, Inc., 1990) 765–68.

[66] F. C. Baur, *Kritische Untersuchungen über die kanonischen Evangellen, ihr Verhältniss zu einander, ihren Charakter und Ursprung* (Tübingen: Mohr, 1847) 377–79.

We must not assume that a monovalent meaning was intended by the author; and we should think about the intention of the verse. The thrust of 21:24 is decidedly on the *trustworthiness of the witness* of the Beloved Disciple.

Beasley-Murray makes another interesting suggestion. He states that when it is written "that the beloved disciple 'wrote' these things, it must mean he wrote down his *witness*. According to this interpretation, the GosJn is based on "the written testimony of the beloved disciple."[67] Much earlier in a note published in *The Expository Times*, D. G. Rogers wrote the following: "We know that the Beloved Disciple wrote some kind of diary or memoir which the final editor of the fourth gospel used as his principal source (Jn 21^{24})."[68] L. Johnson replied to this claim with the sane comment, "But we really know nothing of the kind."[69] Beasley-Murray's comment is more nuanced than are Rogers' words. His position is not impossible; but it is equally possible, perhaps probable, that the GosJn was written by someone who based it on the witness of the Beloved Disciple. There is no reason to conclude that the Beloved Disciple wrote portions of the GosJn (or for that matter anything incorporated into it).

D. M. Smith pointed out to me, *viva voce*, an analogy in the GosJn to 21:24. According to 19:1 Pilate "scourged" Jesus. That would be rather remarkable. The meaning of ἐμαστίγωσεν is surely that Pilate ordered Jesus to be scourged by someone else. Likewise, according to 19:19 Pilate wrote (ἔγραψεν) a title for the top of Jesus' cross; but surely he caused this title to be written. The literal meaning of the Greek is that Pilate did these deeds; but like καὶ ὁ γράψας ταῦτα (21:24) we are confronted with a causative meaning of these two verbs.[70] Pilate caused Jesus to be scourged and the title to be written; likewise, I am convinced, the Beloved Disciple caused the GosJn to be written.

Barrett correctly advises that ὁ γράψας ταῦτα in 21:24 does not mean that the Beloved Disciple is the author of the GosJn. He suggests

[67] G. R. Beasley-Murray, *John* (Dallas: Word Publishing, 1989) 5.

[68] D. G. Rogers, "Who was the Beloved Disciple?" *The Expository Times* 77 (1965-1966) 214. It is rather interesting to observe what can be claimed as knowledge.

[69] L. Johnson, "The Beloved Disciple—A Reply," *The Expository Times* 77 (1965-1966) 380.

[70] The causative (and permissive) verbal form is pervasive in Semitics. See Charlesworth, "The *Beth Essentiae* and the Permissive Meaning of the Hiphil (Aphel)," in *Of Scribes and Scrolls: Studies on the Hebrew Bible, Intertestamental Judaism, and Christian Origins*, ed. H. W. Attridge, J. J. Collins, and T. H. Tobin (College Theology Society Resources in Religion 5; New York/London: Univ. Press of America, 1990) 67-78.

that this expression could be translated "who caused to be written." His paraphrase of this section is attractive: "We, who are actually publishing the gospel, recognize that the authority and responsibility for it are both to be found in the beloved disciple, who gave us the necessary information, and thus virtually wrote the gospel."[71]

In early Christianity there was not a clear distinction made between words attributed to someone and the words uttered by that person. For us to claim that the GosJn contains the Evangelist's editing of Jesus' words or even hermeneutical expansions of what he intended to say could mean in the early centuries of Christianity that the author of the GosJn preserved what Jesus actually said. That point would be tantamount to saying that Jesus may as well have written these words down himself. Proof of this insight is Aphrahat's quotations from the GosJn. He wrote neither that the Evangelist recorded Jesus' sayings nor that he preserved Jesus' words. Rather this fourth-century Persian sage wrote "as He, our Lord, wrote ..." (Syriac = *'yk dktb hw mrn*). He continued: "Jesus who is called your teacher wrote to you" (Syriac = *yšw^c dmtqr' mlpnkwn ktb lkwn* ...).[72] That this relationship between Jesus and the text of the New Testament dates much earlier, even to the time of the GosJn, is demonstrated by a passage in the Didache: "as the Lord commanded in his gospel" (ὡς ἐκέλευσεν ὁ κύριος ἐν τῷ εὐαγγελίῳ αὐτοῦ [*Did* 8.2]). For many readers of the Didache this comment meant that Jesus wrote the gospel.

In modern narrative methodology we might say that the Beloved Disciple is not the author, but the implied author of the GosJn. That is to say, the author of chapter 21 intends to ascribe authorship of the GosJn, all twenty-one chapters, to none other than the Beloved Disciple. L. Doohan presents this perspective in well-couched sentences:

> The Beloved Disciple, the real founder of the Johannine community, is contrasted with Peter and the mainline churches. He represented the source of the community's theology. The Fourth Gospel's editor used the Beloved Disciple as the implied author, whose position of special stature close to Jesus became adequate defense of the community's peculiar understanding of the Gospel.[73]

---

[71] C. K. Barrett, *The Gospel According to St. John* (Philadelphia: Westminster, 1978 [2nd ed.]) 119.

[72] See the text and discussion by Tj. Baarda in *The Gospel Quotations of Aphrahat the Persian Sage* (Amsterdam: Krips Repro B.V. Meppel, 1975) 1:324–25.

[73] L. Doohan, *John: Gospel for a New Age* (Santa Fe, N.M.: Bear & Co., 1988) 39.

Hence, we are to comprehend the composition of the GosJn from multiple sources, the oral witness of the Beloved Disciple, the literary work of the Evangelist, and the editing by at least one hand (the one who added the Appendix which is chapter 21). The recognition that the Beloved Disciple is the implied author is in harmony with what R. A. Culpepper calls "a consensus among Johannine scholars." I agree with him that this consensus exists regarding the search for the Beloved Disciple. It can be represented, in his judicious words, as follows: "it is that there was a real person, who may have been an eyewitness to events in Jesus' ministry, and who was later the authoritative source of tradition for the Johannine community."[74]

Finally, it would be appropriate only if someone besides the Beloved Disciple referred to him with the honorific words "the disciple whom Jesus loved." Hence, we shall distinguish three people: the author of the GosJn (= the Evangelist), the editor who added chapter 21, and the eyewitness, the Beloved Disciple, whose account lies behind chapters 1–20.[75] Thus the literary parallel to 21:24 is the opening of the *Book of Thomas the Contender*: "The secret words which the Savior ($\sigma\omega\tau\acute{\eta}\rho$) spoke to Judas Thomas, the ones which I wrote down, even I, Mathaias."[76] The Evangelist is the author of what the Beloved Disciple had personally witnessed.

The significance of this distinction needs to be accentuated. We shall not be seeking to discern who wrote the GosJn; we shall seek to discern *who may in fact be the witness behind the writing*. Our focal question becomes: Can we identify the Beloved Disciple, the witness behind the composition of the GosJn?

What is the meaning of "and we know that his witness is true" (21:24)? Scholars have defended four interpretations of this clause, which in the order of lesser to probable validity are as follows:

(1) The "Presbyters of Ephesus" added it;
(2) The author of the GosJn used "we" to include readers who concur;

---

[74] Culpepper, *Anatomy*, 47. I wish to acknowledge indebtedness to Culpepper in helping to develop my understanding of narrative analysis.

[75] Brown stressed long ago that since 21:24 refers to the BD in the third person we must think about an author of the GosJn and a "disciple-editor" as the final writer. When he made that point, Brown still thought that the basic tradition stemmed from John the son of Zebedee. See Brown, "The Problem of Historicity in John," in *New Testament Essays* (Garden City, N.Y.: Doubleday, 1968) 187–217; esp. 200.

[76] For the Coptic and ET see J. D. Turner, *The Book of Thomas the Contender* (SBL Dissertation Series 23; Missoula, Mont.: Scholars Press, 1975) 8–9.

(3) The "we" is an editorial "I" by the author of the GosJn;

(4) The redactor revealed that the GosJn was based on this eyewitness.

The first interpretation was defended by Westcott, Calmes, Lagrange, and Streeter; it was the exegesis defended when most commentators concurred that the Beloved Disciple was the apostle John.[77] The second interpretation was the view of medieval commentators, namely Euthymius Zigabenus, Albertus Magnus, and Thomas Aquinas.[78] It is no longer defensible because of the evidence that another writer added chapter 21. The third interpretation was defended by Chapman, who claimed that the Evangelist wrote chapter 21 "before publication."[79] This possibility is unlikely, since (*inter alia*) it is contrasted grammatically with the two singular participles which precede it: ὁ μαρτυρῶν and ὁ γράψας. Moreover, these participles are introduced by "This is the disciple ...."[80]

The fourth interpretation is most likely. All manuscripts of the GosJn contain the final chapter and the final two verses;[81] hence they belong to the author of chapter 21. The redactor who added it spoke for those who in the Johannine Community believed in Jesus as the Christ the Son of God because of the truthful testimony of the eyewitness of the GosJn, the Beloved Disciple. Let us now turn to an exegesis of the passages in the GosJn in which this epithet appears. Do the author of chapters 1–20 (in the first and second edition of the GosJn) and the editor who added chapter 21 provide any clues for the identity of the Beloved Disciple?

[77] See the bibliographical data and discussion in J. Chapman, "We Know That His Testimony is True," *Journal of Theological Studies* 31 (1930) 379–87. Chapman was convinced that the BD is the apostle John; see p. 380 and his article in *JTS* 29 (1928) 16–23.

[78] For additional names see Chapman, *JTS* 31 (1930) 382.

[79] Ibid., 383–87.

[80] It is true that both Nicodemus and Mary Magdalene use οἴδαμεν. However, in the first (3:2) it signifies the group Nicodemus represents (he comes to Jesus ἐκ τῶν φαρισαίων) and in the second (20:2) it is probably a remnant of the *early tradition* which described Mary Magdalene and *other women* going to the tomb early on the first day of the week (cf. Mk 16:1).

[81] The last verse is omitted in ℵ*.

CHAPTER 2

An Exegesis of Passages in the Gospel of John that Mention the Beloved Disciple

The person we are seeking to identify is called "the disciple whom Jesus loved" (τὸν μαθητὴν ὃν ἠγάπα ὁ Ἰησοῦς 21:20). Should we use that expression or employ the idiomatic construct "the Beloved Disciple"?[1] In his first volume of *The Gospel According to St. John*, which appeared in 1965, Schnackenburg suggested we avoid "the expression 'beloved disciple.'"[2] He preferred the literal translation, "the disciple whom Jesus loved." However, in his third volume, which was published in 1975 (after his monograph on the subject), he wisely changed his mind.[3] I shall thus follow the well-established custom of representing the noun and its relative clause with the epithet "the Beloved Disciple."[4]

We must keep in mind, however, that "the Beloved Disciple" is a modern construct and an epithet. The research that follows has convinced me that the "disciple whom Jesus loved" was an honorific designation

---

[1] I intend to be focused. The BD must not be confused with the many individuals in Christian origins who have received the title "beloved." Indeed, Jesus is often called the Beloved in the Odes of Solomon and in the eastern gnostic texts. See especially Ode 38 and the "Crucifixion Hymn" in H.-J. Klimkeit, *Gnosis on the Silk Road: Gnostic Texts from Central Asia* (New York/San Francisco: Harper) 71–72.

[2] Schnackenburg, *St. John*, 1:97.

[3] Schnackenburg, *St. John*, 3:375.

[4] In notes and parenthetical comments "the Beloved Disciple" will be abbreviated as BD. In non-English speaking academic circles the jargon is the following: "Discipulo Amado" (DA) [Spanish], "discepolo che Gesù amava" (DA) [Italian], "Le disciple bien-aimé" (DBA) [French], "Geliefde Discipel" (GD) [Dutch], "Der Lieblingsjünger" (LJ) [German].

given to the disciple who was the witness to Jesus' life for the members of the Johannine Community; it was probably given to him by a person (or persons) in the Johannine School.[5] I have also learned that it is conceivable that the person who created this clause is the Evangelist; but it does not seem to be invented as a literary device by an editor (*pace* Kügler).

We must also remember that the Beloved Disciple appears anonymously (at least initially). Nowhere does an author or editor of the GosJn clearly and unambiguously identify the disciple with a named disciple in the GosJn; but it does not follow that his name never appears in the GosJn. That assumption is virtually inconceivable in light of the growing world-wide recognition that members of the Johannine Community knew him personally and saluted him as their revered teacher and founder of the Johannine School.[6]

Our task is to study all of the GosJn, and not focus only on the passages in which the Beloved Disciple is mentioned (see also chaps. 2.3, 4, 5, 6, and 8, which are also primarily exegetical). No solution can be presented as if it is the definitive solution. Only after much reflection on the GosJn have I concluded from focusing exegetically on it that a very attractive identity is implicitly given to the Beloved Disciple. This identity surprisingly has not yet been seen by Johannine exegetes. Perhaps the present work will spur much debate and renewed interest in the search for the meaning, function, and especially the identity of the Beloved Disciple. There can be no doubt that the Beloved Disciple serves above all to ground and authenticate Johannine theology and Christology. He is the trustworthy witness to the veracity of the gospel about the One who has come from above.[7]

2.1 TEXTS

Let us now begin our exegetical examination of the GosJn, seeking to discern—if possible—who may be the Beloved Disciple. Our work commences without any presuppositions, even though in the preceding pages

---

[5] I use "Johannine Christians" to denote the members (mostly Jews) in the Johannine Community in which there was a school for study and reflection on the origins and in-depth meaning of the Christian faith. Scholars in this School produced numerous literary works, including the first and second editions of the GosJn (which included a "hymn" or "psalm" of the Community—the Logos Hymn), the Appendix (chapter 21), and the Johannine letters (1, 2, and 3Jn). Perhaps the Revelation of John and the Odes of Solomon also come from the Johannine School.

[6] This point will be demonstrated in the following chapters.

[7] As Schmithals stated, "Er ist Joh 21,24 zufolge als Augenzeuge der Verfasser des Evangeliums." *Johannesevangelium und Johannesbriefe*, 220.

and paragraphs, we have already shared some insights obtained from the following work. That organization is necessary in order to clear the way for a fresh look into this question and the issues involved with it.

The disciple whom Jesus loved appears in the GosJn in the following six passages:

13:23-26 (BD was at the Last Supper and close to Jesus)
εἷς ἐκ τῶν μαθητῶν αὐτοῦ ... ὃν ἠγάπα ὁ Ἰησοῦς (13:23)[8]

19:25-27 [35] (BD was at the cross and Jesus entrusts him to his Mother)
Ἰησοῦς ... καὶ τὸν μαθητὴν ... ὃν ἠγάπα (19:26)

20:2-10 (BD runs with Peter to the open tomb; he believes)
τὸν ἄλλον μαθητὴν ὃν ἐφίλει ὁ Ἰησοῦς (20:2)

21:7 (BD is the only one who recognizes Jesus)
ὁ μαθητὴς ἐκεῖνος ὃν ἠγάπα ὁ Ἰησοῦς (21:7)

21:20-23 (BD has died)
τὸν μαθητὴν ὃν ἠγάπα ὁ Ἰησοῦς (21:20)

21:24 (BD is the eyewitness source of the GosJn)

It is odd that only in 20:2 is the verb φιλέω employed with respect to the Beloved Disciple.

Most scholars conclude that no distinction should be made between φιλέω and ἀγαπάω; and it is correct to observe that both verbs are used to express the Father's love for the Son in the GosJn (e.g., 3:35 for ἀγαπάω, 5:20 for φιλέω).[9] It is interesting to wonder, however, why in the

---

[8] The term for Jesus' intimate followers in the GosJn is "disciple" (μαθητής), which appears 78 times. The noun "apostle" is not present in the GosJn. The term "Twelve" is used only in 6:67, 70, 71 and is applied to define Thomas in 20:24. G. Klein offered the novel hypothesis that Luke created the concept of an apostolate of Twelve—and so, for our research, the virtual insignificance of the Twelve in the GosJn is thus not a problem, since we would not have to contemplate what redactional moves the author of the GosJn was making (*Die Zwölf Apostel, Ursprung und Gehalt einer Idee* [FRLANT 59; Göttingen: Vandenhoeck und Ruprecht, 1961]). W. Schmithals demonstrates that Klein's hypothesis is unacceptable, because (*inter alia*) Justin knows the concept but does not know Luke-Acts (*The Office of Apostle in the Early Church*, trans. J. E. Steely [Nashville/New York: Abingdon, 1969] 265–67. Schmithals claims that the GosJn and the Johannine epistles "do not know the disciples as apostles" (239).

[9] J. N. Sanders suggested that there is a discernible difference in the use of the Greek verb. Of 20:2 he wrote, "I do not want to strain language, but it may be that the writer felt that the sense (though not the grammar) included Peter in the clause, and that while ἐφίλει could describe the attitude of Jesus to him, ἠγάπα was not appropriate." See his "'Those Whom Jesus Loved' (John XI.5)," *New Testament Studies* 1 (1954–55) 29–41; esp. 33.

first and second editions of the GosJn the Beloved Disciple is presented in three consecutive passages with the sequence ἀγαπάω, ἀγαπάω, and then φιλέω (13:23, 19:26, 20:2) and that Peter in the Appendix is presented thrice with the same sequence of verbs (21:15, 21:16, 21:17). Perhaps this intimates something symbolically significant about the relation between the Beloved Disciple and Peter.[10] At this point it suffices to observe that the Beloved Disciple is really an epithet; it signifies "le disciple bien-aimé," the ideal disciple in whom "convergent toutes les démarches de disciples-croyants."[11]

At the outset, it is necessary to consider the origin of the Beloved Disciple passages. Are they from some pre-Johannine oral or written source; part of the first edition; added in the second edition when, *inter alia*, the Prologue and probably chapters 15–17 were incorporated into the gospel; or part of the editorial rewriting when chapter 21 was added by the original author or by an editor? Or, are some of the Beloved Disciple passages part of an edition (the second most likely) and others added by a subsequent editor who may have added chapter 21? Furthermore, are the Beloved Disciple passages derived from the life of Jesus, from the needs of the Johannine Community, or are they purely a literary creation by the author to symbolize a real historical person (see chap. 1.2)?

It is not easy to find methodology and criteria by which to make such judgments; nevertheless, we need to be cognizant of these options because they do affect our exegesis, since it must be informed of related meanings in other passages from the same source, author, or editor. Thyen is convinced that all the Beloved Disciple passages are secondary additions ("*literarisch* sekundär sind"), but he also holds that chapter 21 is not an appendix by an editor, but may well be an epilogue by the author of the GosJn.[12] The conclusion that the Beloved Disciple passages, or at least some of them, may be redactional additions to an earlier form of the GosJn is not new and was argued long ago by W. Bousset in 1896,[13] J. Weiss in 1912 and 1917,[14] and W. Soltau in 1916.[15]

---

[10] I intend to explore this possibility in a subsequent publication.

[11] See M. Morgen, "Devenir disciple selon Jean," *Cahier biblique* 26 (1987) 71–73.

[12] Thyen, "Entwicklungen innerhalb der johanneischen Theologie und Kirche im Spiegel von Joh. 21 und der Lieblingsjüngertexte des Evangeliums," in *L'Évangile de Jean*, 259–99; cf. 267 (italics his).

[13] W. Bousset, *Die Offenbarung Johannis* (Göttingen, 1896 [1st edition]); also see Bousset, "Johannesevangelium," *RGG* (1912) 3:608–36. Bousset was also one of the first to perceive that the GosJn comes to us from a Johannine School.

[14] J. Weiss, *RGG* (1912) 3:2199–2201; *Das Urchristentum*, 611–24.

[15] W. Soltau, *Das vierte Evangelium in seiner Entstehungsgeschichte dargelegt* (Heidelberg: Carl Winters Universitätsbuchhandlung, 1916). He introduced

There can be no doubt that chapter 21 is early. It is even conceivable that it may preserve the earliest tradition of Jesus' resurrection appearances.[16] As K. Aland pointed out, the final chapter cannot be a second-century expansion of the GosJn.[17] Now we possess second-century papyri containing at least portions of the GosJn, and there is no textual evidence that chapter 21 was ever missing. It is relatively certain that by about 140 C.E. the GosJn was circulating widely.[18]

I am impressed by the linguistic links between 1–20 and 21, and yet am cognizant of the different meanings and phrases found only in chapter 21; hence, I conclude with Ruckstuhl that chapter 21 was written after 1–20 by another member of the Johannine Community.[19]

It is unlikely that any disciple would create the elevated designation "the disciple whom Jesus loved" and attribute it to himself, so it must have been given to a disciple by others (most likely by his own students if the BD is a real historical person, as we concluded in chap. 1.2). If some of the phrases and words used to describe the Beloved Disciple are reminiscent of the work of the redactor who added chapter 21 (if it is composed by another author), it does not follow that these are added in total by him (or her).[20] We know from the study of the redactional quality of some of the Pseudepigrapha and from the insights obtained from the *redaktionsgeschichtliche* examination of the Synoptics that the perception that some words are added does not imply, let alone denote, that a whole sentence, or an entire section, has been inserted in an earlier document.[21] The result

---

this theory earlier in articles.

[16] This was the considered argument of Bultmann in *John*, 705. Recently D. M. Smith suggested "that the narrative of Jn 21.1-14 may well be the earliest account of Jesus' appearance to his disciples that we possess" ("Historical Issues and the Problem of John and the Synoptics," in *From Jesus to John: Essays on Jesus and New Testament Christology in Honour of Marinus de Jonge*, ed. M. C. De Boer [Journal for the Study of the New Testament Supplement Series 84; Sheffield: JSOT Press, 1993] 252–67; see esp. 266.

[17] K. Aland, "Petrus in Rom," *Historische Zeitschrift* 183 (1957) 497–516.

[18] Brown, *Gospel* 1:lxxxiii, rightly points out that "it is quite clear that John circulated in many copies in Egypt in the period 140–200."

[19] Ruckstuhl: "Wenn man will, kann man auch annehmen, dass nicht er (der Verfasser), sondern ein anderes Mitglied des joh Zeugenkreises Joh 21 schrieb" (367). See Ruckstuhl, "Der Jünger, den Jesus liebte," *Jesus im Horizont der Evangelien*, 355–401.

[20] See the similar judgment by Ruckstuhl, *Jesus im Horizont der Evangelien*, 368.

[21] See my discussion of Mark 12:1-9 and the Gospel of Thomas 65 in *Jesus Within Judaism*, 131–64.

of the exegesis that now follows has slowly convinced me that some of the Beloved Disciple passages are indeed additions to a "primitive" gospel, but these were most likely editorial additions by the author of the GosJn, who had composed the putative primitive work from sources (written and oral).

GosJn 21:1-7

Where do we begin? Which of these six episodes (or pericopes) should be studied first? As Schnackenburg stated in 1965, the "strongest statement" with regard to the Beloved Disciple appears in 21:24, so perhaps we should begin there.[22] After publishing his monograph on the subject in 1970, he again, in 1975, advocated starting "from the closing editorial chapter, because the disciple is characterized there most clearly from a historical viewpoint."[23]

This method—that is, to begin at the end—may seem odd, but it is wise not only to start with the clearest data, but also to take seriously the advice of the editor who lived in the Johannine Community and sought in chapter 21, as we shall see, to remove some of the ambiguity concerning the Beloved Disciple. This starting point is also warranted by the valid assumption (which will also be demonstrated) that not only the editor, but also other members of the Johannine Community probably knew his identity (again the analogy with Qumran seems significant, since the Qumranites, at least during the early period of their history, clearly knew the Righteous Teacher personally even though none of the over four hundred sectarian Dead Sea Scrolls contain his name).[24]

To begin with chapter 21 is also prudent since in this work the Beloved Disciple obviously refers to a historical disciple, as we have seen (chap. 1). It is impressive to note the full conclusion of Bultmann, the dean of Johannine studies in the twentieth century. His position is almost always misrepresented; scholars simply report that he concluded that the Beloved Disciple was not an historical person, only a literary symbolism. But that is inaccurate. Bultmann judged the Beloved Disciple to be symbolical in chapters 1-20; but he argued that in chapter 21 (which was added by an editor) "the beloved disciple is ... a definite historical person."[25]

---

[22] Schnackenburg, *St. John*, 1:97.

[23] Schnackenburg, *St. John*, 3:375-76.

[24] See the seminal and authoritative studies by J. Collins, P. Davies, G. Jeremias, J. Murphy-O'Connor, H. Stegemann, S. Talmon, and G. Vermes. For bibliographical data and a summary of Qumran history, see Charlesworth, "The Origin and Subsequent History of the Authors of the Dead Sea Scrolls: Four Transitional Phases Among the Qumran Essenes," *Revue de Qumran* 38 (1980) 213-33.

[25] Bultmann, *John*, 701.

If we are to catch a glimpse of this historical person, we should start with the strongest clue which could reveal him. Hence, we shall begin with the Appendix of the GosJn: chapter 21, which as both B. H. Streeter and H. P. V. Nunn correctly claimed was written by a literary genius who at least shared the mind of the author of chapters 1–20.[26]

Chapter 21 begins with Jesus and some disciples beside "the Sea of Tiberias." Despite commentators' reports and captions in modern Bibles, there is no way to know how many disciples are with him. The reference is to "those of Zebedee" (οἱ τοῦ Ζεβεδαίου)[27] and that simply denotes an ambiguous number of at least two.[28] It is a post-resurrection narrative which may have originally been a pre-Johannine miracle story.[29] According-ing to 21:2, with Jesus are the following disciples:

Simon Peter,

Thomas called the Twin (Didymus),

Nathaniel of Cana in Galilee,

those of Zebedee (if we want to focus on understanding the GosJn we should not depend upon the Synoptics; we do not know their names nor how many are indicated),[30]

and others from his disciples, (specifically) two.

"Simon Peter" said *to them* (λέγει αὐτοῖς Σίμων Πέτρος·) that he was going fishing. After stating that they were going with him, they climbed into the boat with Simon Peter (καὶ ἐνέβησαν εἰς τὸ πλοῖον). The author portrays these disciples in the boat out on the Sea of Tiberias. From the

[26] Nunn castigated Streeter, but this is one of the few areas where he could "agree heartily with" him. See Streeter, *The Four Gospels: A Study of Origins* (London: Macmillan, 1951 [1924]) 471. Nunn, *The Son of Zebedee and the Fourth Gospel* (London: SPCK, 1932 [1927]) 101.

[27] Some early and important manuscripts, notably ℵ D pc C θ and 700, clarify the Greek by adding υιοι, "sons."

[28] We must again emphasize that if we want to understand the GosJn we should examine it and not turn to other texts (like Mark) for answers. The Greek text, despite the impression found in almost all publications, does not contain the noun "sons."

[29] See R. Pesch, *Der reiche Fischfang. Lk 5, 1-11/Jo 21,1-14* (KBANT; Düsseldorf: Patmos, 1969) and R. T. Fortna, *The Gospel of Signs* (SNTSMS 11; Cambridge: Cambridge Univ. Press, 1970).

[30] Almost all scholars assume that 21:2 refers to "the sons of Zebedee." Some authors even state that it refers to "due figli di Zebedeo." See, e.g., P. Iafolla, "Giovanni, figlio di Zebedeo 'il discepolo che amava' e il IVe vangelo," *Bibbia e Oriente* 148 (1986) 95–110.

beach Jesus (a stranger to them at this point) instructs the men how to fish. None of the disciples know who has called to them with the advice (21:4), but for some reason—perhaps a night's failure (21:3)—they do what the stranger suggests. The subsequent catch of fish is impressive, and the number 153 may be symbolical.[31]

The author reveals to the reader that the stranger is Jesus: "Jesus stood on the beach ... Jesus said to them ..." (21:4-5). The narrator thus invites the reader to imagine the confusion of the disciples. The stage is set for their recognition of the one standing on the beach.

From the boat the Beloved Disciple—and he alone—recognizes the man is Jesus. He turns to Peter ($\tau\hat{\varphi}$ $\Pi\acute{\epsilon}\tau\rho\varphi$) and declares, "It is the Lord" ($\acute{o}$ $\kappa\acute{\upsilon}\rho\iota\acute{o}\varsigma$ $\acute{\epsilon}\sigma\tau\iota\nu$). Why does the Beloved Disciple address the confession to Peter?[32] Why does the author attribute to the Beloved Disciple this recognition; why did he, and no other disciple, know the unrecognizable man was Jesus? In *The Good Wine* B. Barnhart correctly states that the Beloved Disciple, especially in contrast to Peter, "is presented as the one who is gifted with quickness of insight, with depth of understanding, and with fidelity to his Master."[33]

---

[31] The distinguished Semitists J. A. Emerton and P. Ackroyd suggest that the number 153 is a gematria for En-gedi and En-eglaim which bring to memory (at least for the original readers of the GosJn) Ezekiel's vision of waters pouring out of the Temple (Eze 47:1-10). See Emerton, "The Hundred and Fifty-three Fishes in John XXI.11," *Journal of Theological Studies* NS 9 (1958) 86–89; and Ackroyd, *JTS* NS 10 (1959) 94; Emerton, *JTS* NS 11 (1960) 335–56. Schnackenburg rejects the proposal (*St. John*, 3:357), but it is supported by B. Grisby in "Gematria and John 21:11—Another Look at Ezekiel 47:10," *Expository Times* 95 (1983-1984) 177-78. This suggestion and link with early rabbinic traditions (t.Sukk 3:9) that has Ezekiel's water flow into the Sea of Tiberias (and that the Sea of Galilee receives this name only in the GosJn) is intriguing and needs further information and discussion. Hoskyns also attempted to explain the number, concluding that 153 reflects the Greek notion that there are 153 kinds of fish (according to Oppianus Cilix *apud* Jerome in *CommEzek* 47.9-12), and that the perfect catch of fish of every kind fulfills both Eze 47:10 and Mt 13:47-48. See Hoskyns, *The Fourth Gospel*, ed. F. N. Davey (London: Faber & Faber, 1947 [2nd ed.]) 552-56. For more on Johannine numerology see M. J. J. Menken, *Numerical Literary Techniques in John: The Fourth Evangelist's Use of Numbers of Words and Syllables* (SuppNovTest 55; Leiden: Brill, 1985).

[32] Many other questions arise that are not focused on the BD. Among these are the odd actions by Peter. Why does the author state that he was naked? In *L'Évangile de Jean* (264-65) Thyen insightfully points out that the author of chapter 21 weaves into his narrative motifs from the Paradise myth. Like Adam, Peter is aware of his nakedness when he perceives it is the Lord. He then puts on his clothes and dives into the sea (perhaps to signify ritual cleansing).

[33] *The Good Wine* (New York: Paulist, 1992) 379.

If the editor who added chapter 21 is correct, then one of these disciples (21:2) is surely the Beloved Disciple.[34] Which one is he? The Beloved Disciple cannot be Simon Peter, because he talks to Peter (21:7). He is probably not one of the sons of Zebedee, since only John would be likely and long and weighty tomes have been devoted—in vain—to establish this identity.[35] We are left now with only four candidates: one of the two anonymous disciples, Nathanael, or Thomas.

As mentioned above, both Schnackenburg and Brown changed their minds, independently, about the identity of the Beloved Disciple (also see chap. 3). Although they once thought he was John the son of Zebedee, they now conclude that he is one of the unnamed disciples of 21:2.

In my judgment, two telling arguments undermine this attempt at identification. First, the author of chapter 21 attempts to identify the Beloved Disciple. As Bultmann stated, "The author's interest in the figure of the Beloved Disciple, and therefore in the episode he has just related, emerges clearly in the conclusion, for the beloved disciple is now expressly stated to be the one whose authority stands behind the gospel (v. 24)."[36]

In favor of the author's interest in removing some of the ambiguity surrounding the Beloved Disciple is a striking shift from his preference for simple construction,[37] for an unusual redundancy apparently mars his customary straight-forward Greek. An odd but seemingly intentional repetition appears at the outset of the chapter in 21:1. Twice the author who edited the GosJn by adding chapter 21 employs the same verb in precisely the same form "he showed" ($\dot{\epsilon}\phi\alpha\nu\dot{\epsilon}\rho\omega\sigma\epsilon\nu$). What is the author intending by this redundancy? On the one hand, the verb can be seen to form an *inclusio* in what is now labeled verse 1.[38] The emphasis then would be upon "to the disciples by the Sea of Tiberias" which appears between the two verbs. The NRSV translators present the following rendering:

> After these things Jesus showed himself again to the disciples by the Sea of Tiberias; and he showed himself in this way.

[34] This is the position of most commentators and exegetes. See, however, the comments by F. Neirynck who judges that the role of the BD in chapter 21 "can begin and end in v. 7a" (331). See Neirynck, "John 21," *New Testament Studies* 36 (1990) 321–36.

[35] See the Preface and chapter 3.

[36] Bultmann, *John*, 717. (The alternation between "Beloved Disciple" and "beloved disciple" is from this volume.)

[37] See Bultmann's study of the language and style of chapter 21; *John*, 700.

[38] Obviously there were no verses or chapters when he wrote, and the writing was probably *scripta continua* and uncial.

After the semicolon the translators supplied the word *himself*, which is not in the text. Moreover, the Greek connective is not "and"; it is a mild adversative "but" (δὲ). The Greek, in fact, has neither "and" nor "himself." The Greek may mean "After these things Jesus showed himself again to the disciples by the Sea of Tiberias; but it (or he) showed thus."

What is the meaning of the second "it (or he) showed thus"? Should we make the natural, and perhaps obvious, move and supply "himself"? Such assumed resumptive pronouns are evident elsewhere in the GosJn (cf. 1:18 in which we need to supply in English the accusative "him" which, however, is indicated by the power of the accusative "God" which begins the verse). Since the author was certainly a gifted linguist and lived in a community (a School) in which *double entendre* was obviously admired (as we know from studying not only the GosJn, but also the Dead Sea Scrolls and the Odes of Solomon), then he may have intended more than one meaning by "it (or he) showed thus." *Double entendre* appears in chapter 21; as Bultmann pointed out, the verb translated "he followed" (ἀκολούθει) in chapter 21 is employed by the author "in a double sense."[39]

It is conceivable, therefore, that the verb "it (or he) showed" may be a *double entente*. The first meaning would be to pick up the denotation of the first occurrence; that is, Jesus showed himself; the second may well be the showing (the partial disclosure) of the Beloved Disciple.

Further evidence indicates that chapter 21 was composed not only to commend Peter and then make him subservient to the Beloved Disciple, but also to clarify to a certain extent the identity of the Beloved Disciple—perhaps to some members of the Johannine Community who had not known him personally. Does not the narrative thrust suggest that the name of the Beloved Disciple is provided when the names of the disciples are specified (21:2)?

The second telling argument that tends to undermine the conclusion that the Beloved Disciple is one of the anonymous disciples mentioned in 21:2 is the result. Is it helpful, as an exegete, to conclude that the Beloved Disciple is to be identified with one of the unnamed disciples of 21:2? To what extent is it fruitful to conclude that the anonymous Beloved Disciple is to be identified with an anonymous disciple in 21:2? Have we as exegetes removed the ambiguity that has shrouded the identity of the Beloved Disciple? What clarity has been gained by concluding that the anonymous Beloved Disciple is "anonymous"? If the author of chapter 21 wanted to remove some of the ambiguity surrounding the Beloved Disciple—as many leading commentators have stressed (and correctly in my judgment)—we certainly have not attended to his intentionality by being satisfied with

[39] Bultmann, *John*, 714.

anonymity.[40] Have we not already seen that the author wanted us to recognize the Beloved Disciple as one of the disciples *named* in 21:2?

If the answer to this question is "yes," then we are left with only Nathanael and Thomas. Let us see if either of these is conceivable; and if so, to what extent possible and even probable. According to my present knowledge, no scholar working on the GosJn has suggested that the Beloved Disciple is Thomas and the arguments put forward for Nathanael are weak (see chap. 3).[41]

Could the Beloved Disciple be Nathanael? Except for 21:2 the name "Nathanael" appears only in chapter 1. He plays a distinct role in the beginning of the GosJn. He is mentioned in 1:45, 46, 48, and 49. The pericope of 1:43-51 presents Nathanael in a fashion similar to other people in the gospel. He is the first person in the narrative who moves from incredulity to clear confession. He rebuffs Philip's affirmation concerning Jesus with the well-known retort, "Can anything good come out of Nazareth" (1:46)? This colorful question sets the scene for a stunning confession. Before presenting it, the narrator has Jesus bless Nathanael, "Behold, an Israelite indeed, in whom there is no guile!" (1:47).

Nathanael then introduces a series of confessions in the GosJn with the strong affirmation, "Rabbi, you are the Son of God! You are the King of Israel!" (1:49). His confession is powerful and succinct.

We now know not only that "King of Israel" is a pre-Christian Jewish term, but also that "Son of God" was employed by Jewish scholars before the first century C.E. From the Dead Sea Scrolls we learn about the apocalyptic belief in the coming of one who will rule in peace with everlasting prosperity and "be called Son of God and Son of the Most High": ברה די אל יתאמר ובר עליון.[42]

---

[40] See Brown, *Gospel*, 2:1070-71. Redaction and tradition are obviously mixed in chapter 21, as elsewhere, and Schnackenburg is probably correct in judging "that the editors themselves brought in the scene with the disciple whom Jesus loved" (*St. John*, 3:355). Godet, who followed the variant text and saw "sons of Zebedee" in 21:2, pointed out that they are thus listed uncharacteristically last, and published this judgment: "The only reason which explains this circumstance is that the author of this narrative, in its oral or written form, was himself one of the two sons of Zebedee" (*Commentary on John's Gospel*, trans. T. Dwight [Grand Rapids: Kregel, 1985 (1886) 999]).

[41] I learned from a conversation with John Meier that Hans-Martin Schenke (a distinguished gnostic expert living in Berlin), working on texts in the Nag Hammadi codices, had published the suggestion that the Beloved Disciple might in fact be Thomas the Twin. See Schenke, "The Function and Background of the Beloved Disciple in the Gospel of John," in *Nag Hammadi, Gnosticism, and Early Christianity*, ed. C. W. Hedrick and R. Hodgson, Jr. (Peabody, Mass.: Hendrickson, 1986) 111-25. In contrast to Schenke, I do not think that the Beloved Disciple is only, or primarily, a literary typos.

[42] For text, translation, commentary, and bibliography see J. A. Fitzmyer,

Nathanael is certainly a significant disciple in the GosJn. But his presentation is confusing and raises many questions. For example, why is he only in chapter 21 identified as from Cana in Galilee? Why do he and Thomas present a confessional *inclusio* in the GosJn? As Schnackenburg noted, the author of chapter 21 mentioned Nathanael and Thomas, because he wanted to "remind the reader" of the confessions which opened (1:49) and closed (20:28) the gospel. [43]

Among the disciples, Nathanael opens the confessions, following Andrew's then Philip's declarations about Jesus: "you are the Son of God! You are the King of Israel" (1:49). Thomas completes them: "My Lord and my God" (20:28). As impressive as the presentation of Nathanael is in the GosJn, he is not a very viable candidate for the Beloved Disciple. While F. S. Gutjahr, H. Spaeth, and M. A. N. Rovers have concluded that the Beloved Disciple is Nathanael (see chap. 3), Nepper-Christensen, in contemplating the possibility that Nathanael could be the Beloved Disciple, rightly judges him to be too peripheral in the narrative of the GosJn to be the Beloved Disciple. [44]

What about Thomas? Is it possible to construct a case for Thomas, the Twin, as the Beloved Disciple? He certainly looms large in the Johannine account of Jesus' life; thus, an identification is surely conceivable.

In 21:7 the Beloved Disciple alone is reported to recognize the stranger as Jesus. Since the reader already knows this identification, the spotlight is thrown squarely upon the disciples in the boat on the Sea of Tiberias. Who will recognize that the stranger is Jesus? The answer is provided as attention is drawn to Peter and the Beloved Disciple. The latter's declaration resounds: "It is the Lord."

To what previous words is this declaration linked? When does the confessional use of *Kurios*, "Lord"—which is rightly translated "Sir" in 20:15—appear previously and indeed significantly, just before this verse (21:7)? The answer is revealing in our search for the identity of the Beloved Disciple, for the word *Kurios* is found just prior to this verse in the stunning climax to the original, "first edition," of the GosJn. It is in the confession attributed to the disciple called "Thomas the Twin," who looks at the resurrected Jesus and proclaims "My Lord, and my God!" (20:28). [45] That confession appears only eleven verses before the Beloved

---

"4Q246: The 'Son of God' Document from Qumran," *Biblica* 74 (1993) 153-74.

[43] Schnackenburg, *St. John*, 3:352.

[44] P. Nepper-Christensen, "Hvem var den discipel, som Jesus elskede?" *Dansk Teologisk Tidsskrift* 53 (1990) 81–105; see esp. 83.

[45] It is interesting to note that the confession contains "and" when one familiar with the author's use of asyndeton might have expected "My Lord—my God!"

Disciple's "It is the Lord!" Both affirmations might well have appeared on the same sheet of papyrus, or at least on a facing sheet (or on the back of the same sheet). The proximity is impressive. Moreover, the declaration of 21:7 is the highlight of the pericope in 21:1-14, since each of the disciples eventually "knew it was the Lord" (21:12).

Yet, not one of the disciples makes a declaration (or confession) similar to that of the Beloved Disciple. He alone has thus been so singularly centered in the spotlight. Similarly, "Thomas, one of the Twelve, called the Twin" (20:24) is the one placed on center stage in the final scene of the original ending of the GosJn. Thomas is the central character of the passage 20:24-28. Surely, an exegete should ponder the possibility that the author of chapter 21 may be intending to reveal that the Beloved Disciple is none other than Thomas.

Both the author of 1-20 and the editor of the gospel as well as the one who added chapter 21 concluded their treatment of Thomas or the Beloved Disciple with a similar affirmation. The last words of Thomas and the last words of the Beloved Disciple link them at least narratively; they may well forge a tie between them as to identity.

GosJn 21:20-23

Chapter 21 in verses 15-19 is an interlude focused on Peter. In it Jesus questions Peter, using the paradigm of love—which has a double meaning[46] since the one to whom the focus will shift is "the disciple whom Jesus loved."[47] The disciple intended is surely not Peter. Thus it is significant that Jesus finally commissions him. Verses 18 and 19 indicate that Peter will face martyrdom and conclude with Jesus' invitation to him, "Follow me."

The light on center stage now shifts from Peter to the Beloved Disciple. These are the final scenes in the Appendix of the GosJn.

Questions abound: Why is the Beloved Disciple reintroduced with such a full description? Why is the description placed in verse 20 and not earlier, when the Beloved Disciple is introduced in verse 7? Why is the author taken back to the scene at the Last Supper and not to the cross or the race with Peter to the tomb—episodes in which the reader had most recently encountered the Beloved Disciple?

---

[46] Paronomasia, especially in the form of double meaning and polyvalence, is abundant in the GosJn (and a literary feature it shares especially with the Dead Sea Scrolls and the Odes of Solomon).

[47] For discussions of *double entendre* in the GosJn see O. Cullmann, "Der johanneische Gebrauch doppeldeutiger Ausdrücke als Schlüssel zum Verständnis des vierten Evangeliums," *Theologische Literaturzeitung* 4 (1948) 360-72; and Hengel, *Die johanneische Frage*, 266.

Is the description out of place? Was Bultmann correct in judging that the characterization of the Beloved Disciple in 21:20 may be "a secondary interpolation" not only because it is out of place (in comparison with 21:7), but also because the verb "following" (ἀκολουθοῦντα) is "meaningless"?[48] As Bultmann saw, the contrast is between the Beloved Disciple and Peter; the former will "remain" but the latter only "follows." This insight helps indicate that 21:20 has probably not been marred by "a secondary interpolation." The reason the description is full at this point may be to serve as a transition in the narrative. The focus shifts from Peter to the Beloved Disciple. And, more importantly, the author now wishes *to maintain* the Beloved Disciple's superiority over Peter. He was not satisfied merely to raise him to the "same rank as Peter," or primarily to "transfer" authority to the Beloved Disciple, as Bultmann thought.[49] Peter is singled out for recognition and commissioning and there is no pejorative chastising of Peter as may be the case in some passages in Mark;[50] hence, Peter and the Beloved Disciple are not portrayed in the GosJn as adversaries, although they do mirror some rivalry (see chap. 8). The editor who added chapter 21 intends to elevate Peter, but also to continue the portrayal of the Beloved Disciple as exalted above him.

Additional answers lie both in the fact that the Beloved Disciple is reintroduced from the scene in which he is introduced in the GosJn, and in the emphasis that "the disciple whom Jesus loved" lay close to Jesus' chest at that most important event, Jesus' last supper with his disciples. Thus Peter again comes off a distant second; he was not elevated to the "seat" of honor at that pivotal time in Jesus' life. There is surely a rivalry experienced by Christians who celebrate Peter and those who stress the superiority of the Beloved Disciple (as we shall see in chap. 8). Probably it is more global in scope than the social problems reflected in 1 Corinthians 1:12, which signals that the Corinthian church is divided by those who follow Peter (= Cephas) or Apollos or another (1Co 1:10-17).

Why does the author describe the Beloved Disciple as following Peter and Jesus? Is the RSV (2nd ed.) translation correct: "Peter turned and saw following them the disciple whom Jesus loved" (21:20)? The use of the highly symbolical verb "following" (ἀκολουθοῦντα) is odd; but should the translator add "them" which is not in the Greek? Hengel attempts to solve the problem: "the strange participle *akolouthounta* is meant to indicate that this disciple who is following behind Peter will also follow Peter in his death and that both together are following Jesus."[51]

[48] Bultmann, *John*, 714.

[49] Bultmann, *John*, 706.

[50] According to Mark 8:33, Jesus said to Peter, "Get behind me Satan!" Also see Peter's lame advice according to Mark 9:5-6.

[51] Hengel, *Question*, 76.

Why does the author of chapter 21 portray Peter turning and asking Jesus, "Lord, what about this one?" (21:21)? Perhaps the flow of the narrative is from one who apparently only tags along behind Peter and Jesus, but who is in reality the disciple whom Jesus loved most, who lay close to Jesus' chest during the Last Supper, and who has been and will again be presented as superior to Peter. Thus, the scene is set for the author to address and correct a major crisis within the Johannine Community (and perhaps also within early Christianity [see chap. 8]).

The Johannine Christians preserved an otherwise unknown apocalyptic saying of Jesus (which is reminiscent of Mark 9:1 and parallels). According to it the Beloved Disciple would not die until Jesus came again (the Parousia): "The word was transmitted among the brethren [this meaning of ἀδελφός appears only here in the GosJn] that this disciple [the Beloved Disciple] would not die" (21:23).[52] The author attempts to clarify that Jesus did not say that the Beloved Disciple would not die. What had been said had to do with Jesus' will, which was not fully known by the group; hence, a misperceived apocalyptic prediction is disclosed to be a casuistic subjunctive: "If (ἐάν) it is my will that he [the Beloved Disciple] remain [a key term in Johannine theology] until I come, what is that to you?" (21:23) With these teachings the author not only explains a saying of Jesus, he also points out that Christians do not know everything. Thyen introduces an interesting exegesis: to the Johannine Christians "remain" has a meaning other than "remain alive"; it signifies to them that his witness will remain until the end of time.[53]

This emphasis is directed to at least three crises being experienced in the author's community, i.e., the Johannine Community (see chap. 1.3). First, the Beloved Disciple has died (ὅτι ὁ μαθητὴς ἐκεῖνος οὐκ ἀποθνήσκει [21:23]). Eckhardt devoted a full monograph to this section of the GosJn, and advanced our understanding of the implications of the death of the Beloved Disciple. He concluded that 21:23 demonstrates that the Beloved Disciple is no literary construction (this disciple existed), that the Johannine Community believed that the Parousia would occur during his lifetime, and that the final sentences in the GosJn were written after his death.[54] Eckhardt's insights are exegetically sound.

---

[52] In 2:12, for example, Jesus moves to Capernaum with his mother, his *brothers* (οἱ ἀδελφοί), and his disciples.

[53] Thyen in *L'Évangile de Jean*, 273: "Eines ist Petrus ... Ein anderes aber ist der Lieblingsjünger, der in seinem Zeugnis präsent bleibt bis ans Ende." M. de Jonge also rightly defends this exegesis in "The Beloved Disciple and the Date of the Gospel of John," *Text and Interpretation*, ed. E. Best and R. McL. Wilson (Cambridge: Cambridge Univ. Press, 1979) 99–14: "The 'remaining' of the disciple is explained as his continuing witness in the gospel which he has written" (101).

[54] Eckhardt continued to claim that the Beloved Disciple is none other than

The members of the Johannine Community perhaps feared that the living link with Jesus had been severed. They may have been convinced that he would not die. He has died unexpectedly—and not like Peter with a martyrdom that would have reinstated him as authoritative.[55] The modern Greek scholar of the New Testament, S. Agourides, is convinced that the purpose of chapter 21 was to compare the deaths of Peter and the Beloved Disciple, whom he is convinced is John the son of Zebedee. Agourides shows that although the Beloved Disciple was not martyred, as was Peter, he was nevertheless—in the minds of the Johannine Christians—more authoritative and reliable than Peter.[56]

Martyrdom was beginning to be celebrated about the time that chapter 21 was composed. In Revelation 20:4 we learn that only the martyrs, those who have been beheaded (τῶν πεπελεκισμένων), will reign with Christ for a thousand years. And Ignatius of Antioch, who was contemporaneous with the author of chapter 21 and perhaps from the same geographical region, openly sought martyrdom. But the Beloved Disciple simply died; and thus the faith of some Johannine Christians was shattered (for a further discussion of martyrdom and the BD, see chaps. 4, 5, and 8).

Second, the Beloved Disciple's authority—witness—is now being undermined. The Christians who trusted his witness are questioning their support of him. Perhaps they are mistaken. They may even have been pondering whether his identity as the Beloved Disciple was false. This crisis would be severe if, as L. Schenke claims,[57] the Beloved Disciple's superiority rested not on any office but on his charisma (which as Weber showed is powerful only so long as those who have deemed one to be charismatic continue to support that one with power).

Third, Jesus has not returned in glory as the Johannine Christians had hoped, indeed expected. To forestall massive disenchantment and

---

Lazarus (Der Tod des Johannes: Als Schlüssel zum Verständnis der Johanneischen Schriftum [Berlin: Walter de Gruyter & Co., 1961]; see esp. "Jener Jünger stirbt nicht," 11-28; for the discussion mentioned above see 15-16).

[55] The author of chapter 21 apparently knew the tradition which placed Peter's martyrdom in Rome. In the fourth century Eusebius recorded a tradition that clearly antedates him: Πέτρος ... ὃς καὶ ἐπὶ τέλει ἐν Ῥώμῃ γενόμενος, ἀνεσκολοπίσθη κατὰ κεφαλῆς, οὕτως αὐτὸς ἀξιώσας παθεῖν. H.E. 3.1.2.

[56] S. Agourides, "The Purpose of John 21," in Studies in the History and Text of the New Testament in Honor of Kenneth Willis Clark, ed. B. L. Daniels and M. J. Suggs (Studies and Documents 29; Salt Lake City: Univ. of Utah Press, 1967) 127-32.

[57] L. Schenke, Das Johannesevangelium (Kohlhammer Urban-Taschenbücher 446; Stuttgart: Verlag W. Kohlhammer, 1992) 113.

defection from the Community it was necessary to shore up the Johannine tradition.

These observations lead cumulatively to the conclusion that the Beloved Disciple was a real historical person, and that the members of the Johannine Community who learned from him and conversed with him knew him personally. They knew his name. As de Jonge states, "The 'disciple whom Jesus loved' remains anonymous though his identity is known to the ἀδελφοί in vs. 23 and to the 'we' group who wrote vs. 24."[58]

GosJn 21:24

Hence, we are led to ponder the meaning of 21:24: "This is the disciple who is bearing witness to these things." This collective support indicates that the Beloved Disciple is the source of the Johannine tradition.

The Greek is instructive: the genitive "his" (αὐτοῦ) precedes "witness" (ἡ μαρτυρία) and thus puts an emphasis upon the pronoun, which denotes the Beloved Disciple. Is the genitive one of possession or source? It is conceivable that the author would have wanted us to understand that the Beloved Disciple not only possessed the tradition, but was also the source of the tradition and the means by which it was transmitted, through oral channels and finally in writing, to the reader.

The full meaning of "we know that his witness is true" (καὶ οἴδαμεν ὅτι ἀληθὴς αὐτοῦ ἡ μαρτυρία ἐστίν) can be seen in the forensic meaning of the noun "witness" (μαρτυρία) in the GosJn.[59] It appears no less than fourteen times. It never appears in Mark, only once in Luke, and only three times in Matthew.

The verse also discloses that the author and editor of the GosJn were concerned about "truth" probably because of polemical charges thrown at them by others, including the Jews who controlled the synagogue. These writers wanted to make certain to the readers of the GosJn that the Beloved Disciple's witness was absolutely trustworthy and *true* (see also

---

[58] M. de Jonge, *Jesus: Stranger from Heaven and Son of God*, ed. and trans. J. E. Steely (SBLSBS 11; Missoula, Mont.: Scholars Press, 1977) 211. Also see de Jonge, "The Beloved Disciple and the Date of the Gospel of John," 101–02.

[59] See J. Beutler, *Martyria: Traditionsgeschichtliche Untersuchungen zum Zeugnisthema bei Johannes* (Frankfurter Theologische Studien 10; Frankfurt: Josef Knecht, 1972). Also see the insightful review by P. Borgen in *Biblica* 55 (1974) 580–83; he points out that the author of the GosJn "presupposes Jewish debate on the forensic rule against self-witness and the problem that arises when it is applied to God." Borgen rightly points out that Jesus, according to the GosJn, can "witness to himself because of his divine origin." Borgen notes that this idea was articulated previously by Philo, who stated that only God can witness to himself.

19:35 in which the BD's witness is "true"). As Barrett points out, on the one hand scholars now strongly reiterate the Jewish background and foreground of the GosJn; and on the other, the gospel cannot be simply defined "as a missionary tract for the Jews."[60]

The author of chapter 21 continues, "and who has written these things ..." (21:24). Those words have misled scholars who were seeking to identify the Beloved Disciple. He was the witness behind the GosJn; and most likely he was not the author (as we saw in chap. 1). Earlier we pointed out the importance of pseudepigraphical attribution in antiquity, especially in Early Judaism and in Early Christianity (a phenomenon well known in the Johannine Community with the composition of 2 and 3 John and Revelation). The Beloved Disciple could well have used a scribe (an amanuensis) who copied what he dictated; but it is much more likely that his student wrote the GosJn. In either case one of his followers is the one who copied the tradition by writing it and lauding "the real author"—that is, the source of the tradition about Jesus—with an honorific title most inappropriate for a disciple to attach to himself. It seems rather obvious, as so many commentators have stressed for over a century, that only a follower of the Beloved Disciple would have chiseled into the tradition the formula, "the disciple whom Jesus loved."[61] The phrase should in no way lead to the erroneous opinion that Jesus loved only this disciple (which is not possible in light of the GosJn, especially 13:34, "as I have loved you").

It is important to point out, especially, that the meaning of 21:24 is probably that the Beloved Disciple commissioned or empowered the writing of the GosJn; he did not write it himself. He is the witness; another is the author. The analogy is within the GosJn. As we have seen in chapter 1, Pilate neither scourged Jesus (19:1) nor wrote the titulus (19:19); he ordered these actions from his own authority. Hence, along with Schnackenburg,[62] and other eminent specialists on the GosJn like Brown,[63] I think it is imperative—in the search for the Beloved Disciple—to distinguish between the Beloved Disciple and the author of the GosJn. The former is the reliable witness to the tradition; the latter is the author of chapters 1–20 and the putative editor of chapter 21.

The "these things" ($\tau\alpha\hat{v}\tau\alpha$) of 21:24 probably refers to the full GosJn, as most scholars have judged,[64] and not to just the words of chap-

---

[60] Barrett, *The Gospel of John and Judaism*, trans. D. M. Smith (Philadelphia: Fortress, 1975) 7, 75.

[61] See the discussions in chapters 1, 3, and 6.

[62] Schnackenburg, *St. John*, 3:373.

[63] Brown attributes only the first stage in the transmission of the GosJn to the BD. He is not the author (*Gospel*, 1:xxxiv–xxxix; 2:1123, 1127).

[64] See, e.g., I. de la Potterie, "Le témoin qui demeure: le disciple que Jésus aimait," *Biblica* 67 (1986) 348.

ter 21. I have become persuaded that the Beloved Disciple is most likely the one who witnesses to Jesus from the time he was in the wilderness leading a baptist movement until the time of his resurrection (see chaps. 4, 5, and 6).

The thrust of the final word about the Beloved Disciple is the answer to any who would challenge his authority: "and we know that his witness is true" (21:24).[65] Such words are exceptional; there must have been an extreme need to support the trustworthiness of the Johannine tradition. Perhaps the word that the tradition is reliable was dispatched not only to the Johannine Christians, but also to fellow Jews who controlled the synagogue. The witness of the Beloved Disciple obviously caused rebuke and scorn from other Jews, those who rejected Jesus, his tradition, and his authority—and surely the high Christology of the GosJn.

Finally, it is imperative to comprehend the function of the Beloved Disciple. He functions above all as the trustworthy witness to Jesus and his message. No similar role is given to one of Jesus' disciples in the other three intracanonical gospels (but see the claims in the Gospel of Thomas).

The meaning of 21:25 has often been taken literally (following Cyril of Alexandria). Another much more likely meaning began with Origen and has been stressed recently by I. de la Potterie. Since the GosJn is a profoundly spiritual writing, the most likely meaning of this verse is a metaphorical one. That is, humanity cannot comprehend the grandeur of "l'intelligence spirituelle du Christ."[66] The Beloved Disciple is thus the witness to the awesomeness of Christ's revelation.

From chapter 21 we may learn about five crises probably shaking the Johannine Community: (1) The Beloved Disciple has unexpectedly died. (2) Although his death is not described, the author cannot state that he was a martyr; but his rival, Peter, has conceivably been martyred according to 21:18-19. (3) Jesus' words, especially those with apocalyptic meaning, are being questioned. (4) Jesus has not returned as he promised; yet it has been about seventy years since his crucifixion and resurrection. Both of these are reported by the Beloved Disciple (but some are now apparently questioning his authority). (5) The validity of the whole Johannine group is being questioned not only by those outside it, such as the synagogal Jews, but also by some formerly ardent defenders of the faith.

Had the Beloved Disciple claimed, like Paul in 1 Thessalonians 4, that he would remain, and be alive, when Jesus returned? Were those now in authority red-faced with the task of defending someone who was wrong

---

[65] Thyen is convinced that the person who wrote 21:24 also composed 1:14 (*L'Évangile de Jean*, 273).

[66] See I. de la Potterie, *Biblica* 67 (1986) 343-59.

on one major point that was believed by many in the Johannine Community? Were they now confronted with a revered and celebrated *logion* that promised the Beloved Disciple would not die?

What have we learned about the identity of the Beloved Disciple? We have seen that the author of chapter 21 probably presents him in the list of disciples mentioned in 21:2. Unfortunately, he has lifted only part of the veil that conceals the identity of the Beloved Disciple and, even more disconcertingly, he states that two disciples remain anonymous. These facts indicate that *the Beloved Disciple is a disciple*.

At the outset of our search, we saw that John the son of Zebedee is virtually inconceivable as the Beloved Disciple. Although he may be noted only as one of οἱ τοῦ Ζεβεδαίου, he is certainly not named in the GosJn. There are virtually insurmountable objections now—thanks to scholars' indefatigable research—that make the apostle John a very unlikely candidate for the Beloved Disciple (see Parker's list in our Preface). The one name that alone looms large as the Beloved Disciple seems to be Thomas, the Twin—the one to whom the Evangelist gives the spotlight in the final and concluding scene in the GosJn.

GosJn 13:23-26

Upon leaving chapter 21 we turn now to chapters 1–20 which were composed, according to many scholars, by *another member* of the Johannine Community.[67] If chapter 21 was composed by someone other than the Evangelist (as seems likely), then he may well have been the Evangelist's disciple. A consensus on this point is reported in *Peter in the New Testament*:

> What scholars do not agree upon is whether the redactor was a disciple of the Evangelist, favorable to his thought, who added stray Johannine material to the Gospel lest it be lost, or whether he was one who disagreed with basic thrusts of the Evangelist's thought and sought to correct him by additions.[68]

[67] See the comments with which this chapter opened. What we learn from chapter 21 has direct bearing on what we might learn from chapters 1–20. Thyen is even convinced that the author of 21 is the "editor unseres Johannesevangeliums" (*L'Évangile de Jean*, 288).

[68] R. E. Brown, K. P. Donfried, and J. Reumann, eds., *Peter in the New Testament: A Collaborative Assessment by Protestant and Roman Catholic Scholars* (Minneapolis: Augsburg; New York: Paulist, 1973) 139. Note also the comment: "The very fact that, in order to interpret chapter 21, we have constantly needed to refer back to the earlier chapters suggests that the thought pattern is not so markedly different" (146).

The two options are not mutually exclusive. The author of chapter 21 may well have been a disciple of the Evangelist and one who was favorable to his ideas, but he may also have belonged to another generation who either intentionally or inadvertently corrected some ideas in 1–20. That possibility seems attractive to me; nevertheless, let us proceed with the recognition that he was not the author of chapters 1–20, but a disciple of that author.

With these additional preliminary comments, we shall follow the same order as with chapter 21; that is, we shall proceed seriatim through the Book of Glory, from chapter 13, in which the Beloved Disciple is described in the position of honor and authority at the Last Supper, to chapter 20, in which the Beloved Disciple runs with Peter to the tomb.

A danger may now inadvertently appear in our methodology. We should not assume that what we learned from the author of chapter 21 is synonymous with the meaning of the author (or final editor) of chapters 1–20. To conclude from chapter 21 that the Beloved Disciple is to be identified with one of Jesus' disciples should not color the open search for the meaning of the Beloved Disciple passages in chapters 13, 19, and 20. Bultmann may be correct, as mentioned earlier, that the Beloved Disciple is a historical person only in chapter 21, and that in chapters 1–20 he has only a symbolical meaning. Initially, this possibility should be admitted as conceivable.

If chapter 21 suggests that the Beloved Disciple is possibly Thomas, the same conclusion may not derive from a careful exegesis of the "second edition" of the GosJn, namely chapters 1–20 inclusive (but without 7:53–8:11). The burden of proof may be on an exegete who assumes, without a careful study of each passage, that the author of chapter 21 wishes to present a novel hypothesis which is at odds with the gospel of his community and to which he is adding an appendix. Many scholars have shown the literary links between chapter 21 and 1–20 (notably Ruckstuhl and de Solages), so we should avoid the thought that chapters 1–20 are distinctly different from chapter 21.[69]

There is no evidence to warrant the conclusion that the author of chapter 21, living probably in the Johannine School,[70] wanted to suggest

---

[69] Thyen rightly points to the many links between 1–20 and 21, and concludes that the BD passages are from the author of the GosJn (which to him may also include the writing of the "epilogue" of chapter 21). See Thyen, "Johannes 13 und die 'Kirchliche Redaktion' des vierten Evangeliums," in *Tradition und Glaube: Das frühe Christentum in seiner Umwelt; Festgabe für Karl Georg Kuhn zum 65. Geburtstag*, ed. G. Jeremias, H.-W. Kuhn, and H. Stegemann (Göttingen: Vandenhoeck & Ruprecht, 1971) 343–56.

[70] P. S. Minear doubts that chapter 21 was written by a "redactor." He points to the numerous studies by Ruckstuhl, Schweizer, and others which disclose far more and extensive homogeneous vocabulary between 21 and 1–20. He

that the Beloved Disciple might refer to someone different than the one indicated by chapters 1–20.[71] As Brown contends, "the thesis that the Beloved Disciple stands behind the Gospel as its authority is not peculiar to the redactor but was shared by the Evangelist as well."[72] With many Johannine experts I have come to recognize that the author of chapter 21 is different than the author of chapters 1–20; but I am convinced that he was also a member of the Johannine Community, and that he may well have been a student of the author of chapters 1–20.[73]

Hence, we should not forget completely the progress we have already made, working on the Beloved Disciple's identity. Such results must not be read into the exegesis of passages most likely written by another member of the Community; but, at the same time, they may help us understand the meaning of a passage presently placed under a microscope for exegesis.

The clause ὃν ἠγάπα ὁ Ἰησοῦς at the end of 13:23 looks linguistically otiose. It is superfluous grammatically and can easily be removed without affecting the sense of the passage; hence: "One of his disciples was reclining on the chest of Jesus, so Simon Peter beckoned to him." In fact, one could argue that the reason for Peter's question is clarified by the removal of those words; he addresses the one between him and Jesus. Thus, it is conceivable, even perhaps probable, as Bultmann concluded,[74]

---

suggests that a redactor may never have existed. Cf. "The Original Functions of John 21," *Journal of Biblical Literature* 102 (1983) 85–98. See esp. 98: "I find cogent if not overwhelming evidence to support the theses that in the original design of the gospel the last two verses of chapter 20 served only as the conclusion of that chapter and that the last chapter served as the conclusion of the entire document." Hanhart quotes these words approvingly; in *Vervulling en Voleinding*, 244.

[71] Again it is important to note that Thyen is not convinced that chapter 21 is an appendix by a writer different from the one who wrote 1–20. He points out that an epilogue is not an appendix by another author. Cf. "Die Entwicklungen innerhalb der johanneischen Theologie und Kirche im Spiegel von Joh 21 und den Lieblingsjüngertexte des Evangeliums," in *L'Évangile de Jean: Sources, rédaction, théologie*, ed. M. de Jonge (Louvain, 1977) 259–99.

[72] Brown, *Gospel*, 2:1127.

[73] I agree with Ruckstuhl, who contends that the one who composed chapter 21 was an author other than the one who wrote chapters 1–20, and that he was "ein anderes Mitglied des joh Zeugenkreises" (*Jesus im Horizont der Evangelien*, 367).

[74] Bultmann concluded that the Evangelist is the one who is "responsible for describing the disciple who 'reclined on Jesus' bosom'—whose closer identity is left unspecified in the source—as the one ὃν ἠγάπα ὁ Ἰησοῦς v. 23" (*John*, 480).

that the clause which identifies this disciple as the Beloved Disciple has been added by the Evangelist to the source he received.[75] The concept of the Beloved Disciple may well be redactional, but it reflects the mind of the Evangelist. He and not another editor introduced it into the tradition.

How does the author of chapter 13 frame the introduction of "the disciple whom Jesus loved," which is presented in the pericope 13:21-30?[76] It is impressive. Before it, in 13:1-20, he describes Jesus' washing of the disciple's feet, thereby demonstrating how completely *he loves them* (εἰς τέλος ἠγάπησεν αὐτούς. [13:1]).[77] He describes how Jesus instructs his disciples that they "should do as I have done to you" (13:15).

Immediately after the footwashing, in 13:31-35, the author presents a commandment he claims was created by Jesus.[78] The commandment is to "love (ἀγαπᾶτε) one another; even as I have loved (ἠγάπησα) you,

---

[75] Lorenzen is convinced that the Evangelist used an oral tradition in 13:21b, 22, 26b, 27, and 30a; but that he added verses 23 through 26a (*Der Lieblingsjünger*, 15). This position is conceivable, and it would attribute to the Evangelist himself—perhaps in his second edition—the entire reference to one of the disciples resting on Jesus' breast. As is clear by now, I agree with Ashton, Brown, Lindars, Martyn, and many others (against Schnackenburg and Becker who tend to attribute redactions to another editor) that the Evangelist composed a first edition and then a second edition. For a helpful discussion, see Ashton, "The First Edition," in *Understanding*, 198-204.

[76] Thyen is convinced that the BD passages in chapter 13 are secondary redactions (*L'Évangile de Jean*, 276). Ruckstuhl, rightly in my opinion, rejects this idea in favor of the probability that it is early and traditional (*Jesus im Horizont der Evangelien*, 369).

[77] For examinations of the footwashing pericope see especially the following: G. Richter, *Die Fusswaschung im Johannesevangelium* (Regensburg: Pustet, 1967); W. Lohse, *Die Fusswaschung (Joh 13.1-20): Eine Geschichte ihrer Deutung* (Dissertation, Friedrich-Alexander-Universität zu Erlangen-Nürnberg, 1967); and J. C. Thomas, *Footwashing in John 13 and the Johannine Community* (JSNT SS 61; Sheffield: JSOT Press, 1991).

[78] Of course, Jesus' "new commandment" is found only in the GosJn and the Johannine epistles, but elsewhere in the New Testament Jesus' unusual stress on love is also highlighted. See, for example, Matthew's record that Jesus taught love of enemies (ἀγαπᾶτε τοὺς ἐχθροὺς [Mt 5:44]). That paraenesis is exceptional within Judaism. The erudite Jewish expert on the New Testament, C. G. Montefiore reported, "Jewish critics usually take the line that in the command, 'Love your enemies,' there is indeed an original feature." See the excerpt and the discussion by H. Anderson, in *Jesus* (GLO; Englewood Cliffs, N.J.: Prentice-Hall, Inc., 1967) 156. As J. Piper showed, Jesus' new commandment helped shape early Christian exhortation (*"Love Your Enemies": Jesus' Love Command in the Synoptic Gospels and in the Early Christian Paraenesis* [Grand Rapids: Baker, 1980, 1991]).

that you also love (ἀγαπᾶτε) one another" (13:34).[79] The significance of this narrative framework becomes more obvious when we recall that the Beloved Disciple is a modern construct; the author refers to him as the disciple "whom Jesus loved" (ὃν ἠγάπα ὁ Ἰησοῦς [13:23]). Note the framing of the commencement of interest in the Beloved Disciple:

13:1-20	Jesus' absolute love for his disciples
13:21-30	Introduction of the disciple whom Jesus loved
13:31-35	Jesus' new commandment to love as he loved them

The scene and the drama is the same: Jesus' Last Supper with those close to him during Passover week in Jerusalem.

The *inclusio* needs to be clarified. In 13:1 the scene opens with the author's declaration of Jesus' perfect and continuing love (εἰς τέλος) for "his own" (ἀγαπήσας τοὺς ἰδίους). In 13:35 it concludes with the distinguishing characteristic of Jesus' sect: "if you have love for one other" (ἐὰν ἀγάπην ἔχητε ἐν ἀλλήλοις).

The narrative genius of the Evangelist is stunningly apparent. He introduces on center stage "the disciple whom Jesus loved" immediately after describing Jesus' embodiment of love in the washing of his disciples' feet—an arresting portrayal of Jesus as one who cannot be categorized as "Rabbi"—and immediately before Jesus' new commandment to "love one another." How is this love defined? It is in Jesus' selfless "love," specifically in his servile service of others.[80]

Within the narrative another crucial event is developing. Judas Iscariot, Simon's son, is revealed to the reader to be the "Betrayer" (but the

---

[79] Many scholars conclude that 13:34-35 is a redactional addition to the GosJn. The link with 15:1-17, clearly in my judgment a redaction to the "first" edition, suggests this probability. See F. Segovia, *Love Relationships in the Johannine Tradition* (SBLDS 58; Chico: Scholars, 1982) 121–25; Segovia, "The Structure, *Tendenz*, and *Sitz im Leben* of Joh 13:31–14:31," *Journal of Biblical Literature* 104 (1985) 471–93; J. Becker, "Die Abschiedsreden Jesu im Johannesevangelium," *ZNW* 61 (1970) 215–46; esp. 220; U. von Wahlde, *The Johannine Commandments: 1 John and the Struggle for the Johannine Tradition* (Theological Inquiries; New York/Mahwah, N.J., 1990) 84.

[80] As is too well known to warrant discussion here, soon the concept of love for another in the Johannine Community is reduced to love of a fellow member of the Community. This meaning is obvious in the Johannine epistles. It is also evident to me that this move to an insular reduction of love is probably caused by the polemical ambience of the GosJn and the influx of Essenes into the Community (which has become more like the יחד). For a discussion of how in the Johannine Community "the radical inclusiveness of 'neighbor' found in Jesus has vanished," see W. Schrage, *The Ethics of the New Testament* (Philadelphia: Fortress, 1988) 316–19.

disciples do not understand). Judas will be the catalyst for the final drama that will conclude Jesus' life on earth. What does he do? What does he intend? Is he the beloved accomplice or the despicable betrayer? Or, are both the beloved and betrayer introduced in the same dramatic moment to signify that each person has some portions of each? I intend to suggest this latter possibility (see chap. 4).

Specifically, what is the meaning of $\pi\alpha\rho\alpha\delta\acute{\iota}\delta\omega\mu\iota$ in 6:64,71; 12:4; 13:2, 11, 21, and in chapters 18 and 19? This verb is a *terminus technicus* for the handing on of tradition, as we know especially from Paul (1Co 11:23). The Johannine Christians would have known the early rabbinic formula "to transmit" (מסר) and "to receive" (קבל) as in *Sayings of the Fathers* 1.1: משה קבל תורה מסיני, ומסרה ליהושע.[81] The author of the GosJn is using the traditional verb for "to hand over" which has already obtained the extended philological meaning of "to betray" (Mk 14:21, Mt 26:24, Lk 22:22).[82]

There should be no doubt about the meaning of this pericope. Judas is not the Beloved Disciple, although he is beloved of Jesus. As Judas is departing the room in which the Last Supper is in progress, Jesus instructs his disciples to "love one another" (13:35). That will include Judas. In a similar vein after Judas's apparently treacherous deed,[83] Jesus informs his disciples that if they forgive *any* ($\tau\iota\nu\omega\nu$)—which would include Judas— they will be forgiven (20:23). The author of the GosJn, in contrast to Matthew and Luke, neither presents Judas pejoratively nor informs his readers of his fate.[84]

The focused intention of the passage 13:21-30 thus becomes clear: It is not to reveal the identity of the Beloved Disciple, but to review that one of the disciples will betray Jesus (13:18-20 and 21-30). Who will ask Jesus the identity of this disciple—the betrayer? The attention is drawn to the Beloved Disciple, who is described as "reclining on the chest of Jesus" (13:23 and 25).[85] The verb "lying" ($\dot{\alpha}\nu\alpha\kappa\epsilon\acute{\iota}\mu\epsilon\nu\sigma\varsigma$) does not in itself denote a privileged place; but this favored position is obvious through the mention of "the chest of Jesus."[86] Thus, as Origen perspicaciously perceived

---

[81] For the Hebrew text that is pointed see S. R. Hirsch, *Chapters of the Fathers* (Jerusalem: Feldheim Publishers, 1989 [new corrected edition]) 4.

[82] See F. Büchsel, *TDNT* 2.169-72.

[83] It is difficult to discern Judas's intentionality. It is clear, nevertheless, that according to the GosJn Jesus does not condemn him and that there seems to be some complicity between them.

[84] I am persuaded that an editor may have added 12:6. It is virtually the only verse in which Judas is castigated. See the discussion of GosJn 18 in chap. 6.

[85] See the discussion in chapter 4.

[86] In Mark 14:18 the same verb is used to designate the Twelve present at the Last Supper.

long ago,[87] like the Logos who is "the one who exists in the bosom of the Father" (ὁ ὢν εἰς τὸν κόλπον τοῦ πατρὸς [1:18]) so the Beloved Disciple is *introduced* as reclining "on the bosom[88] of Jesus" (ἐν τῷ κόλπῳ τοῦ Ἰησοῦ [13:23]).[89]

Thus, like Jesus, the Beloved Disciple will function as the Paraclete. He will provide most especially the trustworthy witness to him (see especially 15:26, 19:35, 21:24; cf. 3Jn 12); but he will also dwell with the Johannine Christians (14:17), teach them all things (14:26), and help them remember Jesus' teachings (14:26).

None other than Simon Peter asks him to query Jesus "of whom he speaks" (13:24). The author may have implied that the Beloved Disciple obliges Peter, and presumably the other disciples. He asks Jesus, "Lord, who is [the one who will betray you]?" (13:25). Jesus' reply is somewhat ambiguous, but the reader will certainly understand that it is Judas Iscariot (who may well be in central focus in 13:21-30).

It is singularly important to observe that the Beloved Disciple's question discloses that he does not know who will betray Jesus—or that Jesus is predicting his own death. The Beloved Disciple is included within the sweeping authorial comment that the disciples did not know the meaning of Jesus' words to Judas, the son of Simon Iscariot:

> No one at the table knew why he said this to him. Some thought that, because Judas had the money box, Jesus was telling him, "Buy what we need for the feast"; or, that he should give something to the poor. (13:28-29)

This passage has numerous features of the Evangelist's writing and style. The use of irony is rather obvious. The use of misunderstanding in the GosJn is also a well-known Johannine feature. What is not so obvious—

---

[87] Origen, *InJn* 32.20.264 (see *GCS* 4:461).

[88] For the sake of illustrating the link between 1:18 and 13:23 I have used the word "bosom" here. See the further discussion in chapter 4.

[89] See the insightful comments by Thyen in *L'Évangile de Jean*, 292; by Ruckstuhl in *Jesus im Horizont der Evangelien*, 369-71; by W. Eltester in *Der Logos und sein Prophet: Fragen zur heutigen Erklärung des johanneischen Prologs* [Haenchen Festschrift] (BZNW 30; Berlin: Walter de Gruyter, 1964); by I de la Potterie in "Le témoin qui demeure: Le disciple que Jésus aimait," *Biblica* 67 (1986) 343-59; and by G. Segalla in "'Il discepolo che Gesù amava,' e la tradizione giovannea," *Teologia: Rivista Della Facoltà Teologica dell'Italia Settentrionale* 14 (1989) 217-43; see esp. 238-39. Of course, the better reading of μονογενὴς θεός in 1:18 needs to be incorporated into the discussion. (Thyen used the inferior reading.)

and indeed rather surprising—is the inclusion of the Beloved Disciple among those who are presented in the narrative as lacking understanding.

Having completed an exegesis of the first reference to the Beloved Disciple in the GosJn, we can confront two major questions which are interrelated: (1) Why does the author introduce the Beloved Disciple here and not earlier (or to be inclusive, later); and (2) does his appearance only at the Last Supper, the cross, and the empty tomb not indicate that the Beloved Disciple must be a Judean disciple, perhaps Lazarus?

First Question: Why did the author introduce the Beloved Disciple in chapter 13 with the passage in which the Last Supper is described? Of course, we can never be certain why the author, or narrator, chose to introduce the Beloved Disciple at this point in the gospel. He may have not intended a vast amount of symbolism by the setting in which the Beloved Disciple is introduced.

It may be, perhaps, that since many of the *dramatae personae* are introduced for the first time in chapter 11, during the Lazarus episode—namely Mary, Martha, Lazarus, Thomas, and Caiaphas—that the Beloved Disciple is simply another one who is introduced at this point in the narrative. It also may be because the author of the GosJn (unlike the author of Mark, Matthew, Luke, and Acts) has not given us a full list of the Twelve, let alone the names of all Jesus' disciples, almost all of whom are anonymous (a point that may include the man born blind, according to chapter 9). The use of anonymity in the GosJn is rather stunning. As was mentioned in the Preface, Jesus' mother is also left anonymous in this gospel.

Finally, we should not forget the way the narrator has framed the presentation of the Beloved Disciple, and the fact that with chapter 13 the second half of the gospel begins. Surely, it is not insignificant that the opening scene in the Book of Glory is the author's choice for the time to introduce the Beloved Disciple.[90]

Second Question: Is it not apparent that the Beloved Disciple must be a Judean disciple? This conclusion is affirmed by many specialists and assumed to be true by others. For example, in *The Beloved Disciple* Eller argues that "the only conceivable reason for his not giving us Beloved Disciple scenes out of the Galilean phase of Jesus' ministry is that the Beloved Disciple was not there" (48). This opinion is certainly possible and is shared by many exegetes, but is it convincing? And is there perhaps another "conceivable reason" why the Beloved Disciple appears only in Judean scenes,[91] except for chapter 21 which is centered in Lower Galilee, and the Sea of Tiberias (21:1)?

---

[90] It would be jejune to refer to chapters, since these are much later than the time of the Evangelist.

[91] In the following discussion I point out that prior to chapter 13 there are

The argument is certainly not so convincing as it once was formerly, because we now know that Lower Galilee, in which Jesus centered his Galilean ministry (according to both the GosJn and the Synoptics) was culturally linked with Judea and Jerusalem.[92] Archaeological research and astounding discoveries in Lower Galilee make this insight now certain. While Upper Galilee is culturally tied to Tyre and Sidon, Lower Galilee is clearly commercially and ideologically linked with Judea. The latter point is now a fact; it is obvious when we observe the elaborate means for purification developed in Jerusalem and reflected textually in the GosJn (especially GosJn 2) and in the cultural remains now appearing in Sepphoris, Tiberias, Capernaum, Gamla, and elsewhere.

We know, moreover, that the depiction of Galilee as verdant and pastoral in contrast to a cosmopolitan Jerusalem derived more from Romanticism—even Liberal theology—than from historical insights (and the archaeological exploration of Galilee had not yet begun). During Jesus' ministry Sepphoris, Tiberias, Capernaum, and Gamla were "cities" and not villages.[93] It is simply not possible to portray in stark contrasting ways Jesus' Galilean disciples from his Judean disciples. Between the time of Herod and the destruction of 70 C.E., Judea and Lower Galilee were not separated into hermetically sealed distant regions.

Also, chapter 13 does not begin Jesus' Judean ministry according to John. In chapter 2 he is in the Jerusalem Temple, and in chapter 11 he is in Judea to call Lazarus back from the dead. The author of the GosJn makes it clear that Jesus has been to Jerusalem numerous times, and that the end of his ministry depicts him spending months in Judea (not a week as in the Synoptics). The Beloved Disciple does not appear in these Judean episodes, so it is not evident that he must be a Judean disciple.

We should also remember that in the first century many people living in ancient Palestine moved about, sometimes frequently. Pilate lived not only in Caesarea Maritima, but also, especially during the times of pilgrimage, in Jerusalem. Herod and his descendants had "palaces" virtually throughout the land, in Galilee (especially in Caesarea Philippi) and in Judea (especially in Jerusalem, the Herodium, and Masada).[94] Jesus' family moved from Nazareth to Capernaum (or that seems to be implied in the GosJn), and after the Easter event they moved to Jerusalem (if we

---

Judean scenes in which the person known as the BD is present (although not with the epithet "BD").

[92] See, e.g., the chapters in *The Galilee in Late Antiquity*, ed. L. I. Levine (New York/Jerusalem: The Jewish Theological Seminary of America, 1992).

[93] See the discussions in Levine, ed., *Galilee in Late Antiquity*.

[94] For a discussion of these sites and photographs, see *The New Encyclopedia of Archaeological Excavations in the Holy Land*.

can trust the accounts of some second and third-century scholars).[95] Hence, the fact that the Beloved Disciple shows up as an epithet for the first time in a Judean setting in the GosJn does not preclude the possibility that he is a Galilean.

We must comprehend that chapter 13 is situated in Jerusalem during the Passover Feast; and at that time most of the people in the Holy City were not from Judea. Finally, chapter 21 would make *prima facie* sense if the Beloved Disciple went back fishing on the Sea of Tiberias because he, like all the others named in chapter 21, was a Galilean.

GosJn 19:25-27, 35

In chapter 19 the Beloved Disciple is described as present at the crucifixion of Jesus.[96] According to 19:17 Jesus bore his own cross to a place called "in Hebrew Golgotha." It was near Jerusalem (19:20). There he was killed by Roman soldiers. Two men were crucified with Jesus, one on his left and the other on his right. Pilate wrote (*sic* [ἔγραψεν]) a title (in Hebrew, Latin, and Greek) which read, "Jesus of Nazareth, the King of the Jews" (19:19).[97] While he was on the cross, four soldiers stood by and divided his garments, except for his tunic (τὸν χιτῶνα). For it they cast lots (which is surely an incident created out of Psalm 22:19).

Verses 25-27 describe Jesus' followers who witnessed the crucifixion. The narrator names as present only his mother (always anonymous in the GosJn), his mother's sister, Mary the wife of Clopas, and Mary Magdalene. The Beloved Disciple is also singled out to be present, but described in a way that might suggest he was not standing close to the four (or three) women. Jesus tells his mother to behold him as "your son." He then tells the Beloved Disciple, "Behold, your mother." From that hour the Beloved Disciple took Jesus' mother "into his own things" (εἰς τὰ ἴδια).[98]

The passage raises many questions. Why was Jesus crucified at Golgotha? Is it to be identified with the rock now highlighted inside the Church of the Holy Sepulcher?[99] What is the name of Jesus' mother?[100]

---

[95] See the relevant texts and discussions in R. Bauckham, *Jude and the Relatives of Jesus in the Early Church* (Edinburgh: T & T Clark, 1990).

[96] Thyen is convinced that 19:25-27 is "sekundär" and was added by the author of chapter 21 (*L'Évangile de Jean*, 281–82). Ruckstuhl is convinced that "ganz oder teilweise" of 19:25-27 was composed by the author of chapter 21, but "nicht ohne einen Ansatz in der joh Überlieferung" (*Jesus im Horizont der Evangelien*, 371).

[97] It is obvious that Pilate *caused* the title to be written. This use of Greek philology is important for understanding 21:24 (see chapter 1).

[98] For the meaning of this idiom see the discussions which follow.

[99] See my affirmative answer in *Jesus Within Judaism*, 123-27.

[100] Thyen rightly points out that we must avoid "Harmonisierungsinteresse"

Who is her sister? Is she to be identified with "Mary the wife of Clopas"? Is this Clopas to be identified with Cleopas in Luke 24:18? Does the Evangelist expect his readers to know who these people are, and if so then how, and does that mean he was not writing for future generations? What is the relationship among these women, and especially between Mary Magdalene and Jesus' mother?

Why is the Beloved Disciple the only male mentioned as present? Where is Peter? Where are Joseph of Arimathea and Nicodemus, who will soon appear to help bury Jesus, apparently in haste (19:38-42)?[101] Where is the Beloved Disciple placed; what is meant by "standing near"? Is he standing in a place by himself? Is he "standing near" the women, or the cross? If so, where are they? Is he standing near Jesus' mother, as the text may indicate (19:26)? And if so, what distance is denoted by this frustratingly ambiguous expression? Why are the women and the Beloved Disciple described as "standing" (is the reader to imagine that they stand the entire time that Jesus was on the cross)? Did they talk to each other or to Jesus during the hours he was on the cross? Why does the author show no interest in such details? And why is the Evangelist so gifted symbolically, theologically, and dramatically, but so inept occasionally at telling a good story?[102]

---

(278) and then subsequently refers repeatedly to Jesus' mother as "Mary" (285). She, like the BD, is not given a name in the GosJn.

[101] O. Holtzmann offered the opinion that "the distinguished member of the Synedrium, who had in the first instance afforded the body a resting-place in his rock-sepulchre, was not disposed to permit a crucified man to lie permanently beside the dead of his own family. As soon as the Sabbath was at an end, he must have been careful to have the body quietly buried in some other place. Such seems to be the best explanation of this secret transaction." He also claimed (in a footnote to this statement) that the GosJn 20:1-10 was "perhaps based on a good tradition." Holtzmann stressed that the possession of Jesus' corpse would not be proof against his resurrection, as we know from Paul's reflections (1Co 15:50, 2Co 5:1-4). See Holtzmann, *The Life of Jesus*, trans. J. T. Bealby and M. A. Canney (London: Adam and Charles Black, 1904) 499. Strauss severely criticized Schleiermacher for holding somewhat similar views, namely that Joseph of Arimathea only temporarily placed Jesus' corpse in the tomb, and sent servants to transfer it to his own sepulchre; and that Mary Magdalene met these two persons and confused them with "angel-men." Strauss rightly saw the shadows cast by Bahrdt and Venturini, who had earlier claimed that Essenes placed Jesus in a secret cave and then resuscitated him (*The Christ of Faith and the Jesus of History: A Critique of Schleiermacher's Life of Jesus*, trans. and ed. L. E. Keck [Philadelphia: Fortress, 1977 (from the work of 1865)] 136-37).

[102] Jews are gifted authors in telling a story with interest and appropriate detail, as we know from reading the marvelous stories in the Hebrew Bible (= OT), especially the stories of Joseph, Moses, and David, and in the Apocrypha,

What is the meaning of Jesus' words? Why does he call his mother, "woman" (γύναι), and what is the relation of this passage to the same word found in 2:4?[103] What is the meaning of Jesus' words to his mother and to the Beloved Disciple? What is the denotation of "son" in this context? Is the filial relation only symbolical, or is the Beloved Disciple disguised because he is Jesus' blood brother?

Did any of Jesus' brothers become his disciples during his lifetime? Is that reconstruction suggested by 20:17 and 2:12 (according to this verse Jesus' brothers, distinct from his disciples, follow him—along with his mother—to Capernaum)? What is the meaning of the phrase εἰς τὰ ἴδια in 19:27, which is almost always translated (perhaps too idiomatically) "to his own home"? Should this prepositional phrase be translated that way? Why does it appear in 1:11 and 16:32?[104] It literally means "to (or into) the (or his) own things"; but what do these words denote and connote?[105] I. de la Potterie examined the use of ἴδιος in the GosJn and observed that it never denotes material things, as in Luke 18:28; rather it signifies "réalités spirituelles."[106] V. H. Stanton, formerly Regius Professor of

---

notably in Susanna, and in the Pseudepigrapha, most dramatically in *Joseph and Aseneth*. By contrast, our author, obviously a Jew, frequently leaves the reader frustrated, wondering (for example) how the water was turned to wine, and how Mary Magdalene returns to the tomb.

[103] E. J. Kilmartin sees the parallelism between the portrayal of Jesus' mother in chapters 2 and 19, and concludes that symbolically she represents "the spouse" of Christ: "One could argue that Mary is considered to be the spouse of Christ in the sense that the Church is named spouse in *Ap.* 22, 17" (224). While that exegesis is barely conceivable, the following leaves the realm of exegesis: "Hence *Jn* 19, 25-27 depicts the mystery of the marriage of Jesus and Mary, the betrothal of which took place at Cana" (226) "'The Mother of Jesus Was There' (The Significance of Mary in Jn 2,3-5 and Jn 19, 25-27)," *Sciences Ecclésiastiques* 15 [1963] 213-26).

[104] Since these two verses are most likely redactional additions to a "first" edition of the GosJn, the supposition becomes attractive that this verse, and perhaps this pericope concerning the BD, was also added by the same hand, and perhaps at the same time. Since it seems clear that chapters 15–17 were added by the Evangelist himself, it would follow that at least some of the BD passages were added when the writer expanded the GosJn to serve the needs of the Johannine Community. Perhaps he edited his work in such a way that we can refer to a "second" edition.

[105] See the careful discussion by F. Neirynck (and the publications by I. de la Potterie and Schnackenburg he cites) in "ΕΙΣ ΤΑ ΙΔΙΑ: Jn 19,27 (et 16,31)," *Ephemerides Theologicae Lovanienses* 55 (1979) 357-65.

[106] I. de la Potterie, "La parole de Jésus 'Voici ta Mère' et l'accueil du disciple (Jn 19,27b)," *Marianum* 36 (1974) 1-39; see esp. 26.

Divinity in the University of Cambridge, suggested insightfully that if we must retain "home" in a rendering of this verse, the result would be "'from that time the mother of Jesus made her home with that disciple'— that is to say, wherever for the time being his home might be."[107]

If the phrase denotes "to his own home," where is that home?[108] Is it in Jerusalem, somewhere else in Judea, or in Galilee? If it is Galilee, then "from that hour" is merely figurative, since the Beloved Disciple cannot make such a journey and be present for Mary Magdalene to find him on the morning of the first day of the week. Not only the Sabbath limitations for a journey, but also the distance make it inconceivable that the Beloved Disciple could take Jesus' mother from Jerusalem late "Friday" evening to Galilee and be back before sunrise "Sunday" morning. Brown is surely right to point out the symbolic meaning of "his own," and to explain it as embodying the special discipleship enjoyed by the Beloved Disciple.[109]

What is the relationship among these three: Jesus, his mother, and the Beloved Disciple? What does the narrator intend to communicate by placing the Beloved Disciple at the cross? Finally, we exegetes are left contemplating how and in what ways a methodology can be developed that will enable us to discern how much of this section is reliable history and how much of it is creative narrative (including the need for teaching in the Johannine Community and for apologetics in a social world that is often threateningly polemical). As J. H. Neyrey clarifies, Johannine thought took shape in a crucible of social stress and even revolt.[110]

Let us now turn to the interpretation of 19:25-27. The author of this section may be making several points. First, he knows that thousands witnessed Jesus' crucifixion in such a public arena, because it was probably outside the walls of Jerusalem and near a road leading to a city gate;[111] but he wants reliable witnesses representing Jesus' Palestinian Movement to be present at the cross.[112] They can verify against later charges what

[107] Stanton, *The Gospels as Historical Documents*, 3 vols. (Cambridge: Cambridge Univ. Press, 1903-1920) 3:144.

[108] Thyen rightly points out that too many exegetes with their "Blindheit für den symbolischen Sinn der Szene" mistakenly attempt to locate the BD's "house" (*L'Évangile de Jean*, 284).

[109] R. Brown, *The Death of the Messiah* (ABRL; New York: Doubleday, 1994) 2:1024.

[110] J. H. Neyrey, S.J. *An Ideology of Revolt: John's Christology in Social-Science Perspective* (Philadelphia: Fortress, 1988).

[111] The gate is not the present Jaffa Gate; it was east of it and the major western gate in the wall that before circa 41 C.E. was the western barrier of the city.

[112] The technical term, Palestinian Jesus Movement, denotes the followers of Jesus in Palestine before 70 C.E.; they were almost all Jews and constituted a

actually happened. Yet, I am convinced that their presence was not primarily motivated by narrative concerns or apologetic motives. The Evangelist shows that while Jesus suffered alone, he was not abandoned in his last hours, and—most importantly—that the reliable witness behind the GosJn himself verified Jesus' physical death.

Second, the presence of perhaps four women is impressive.[113] What was the relationship of these women to Jesus? Especially, what was the relationship between Jesus and Mary Magdalene, causing her to be by his side at the end and to visit his grave alone in the dark, when the Sabbath had passed and it was permitted to make such a journey? What was her relationship with the Beloved Disciple? It must have been special, developing from the time together at the cross, and her desire to go and inform him that the grave was empty.

The Beloved Disciple is the only male from among Jesus' numerous male disciples depicted as present at the crucifixion. That is rather remarkable. Were the other males afraid (perhaps of the ruling authorities [cf. 20:19])? If so, was the narrator attempting to tell us something about the Beloved Disciple? Was he not afraid also, or were there reasons why he did not have to fear? That is, was he respected by the Jewish establishment (which may well be the case for Lazarus and for John Mark, but not for Thomas)? Does such an observation suggest that the Beloved Disciple was a "priest," perhaps an Essene as E. Ruchstuhl has consistently argued?[114] Is his devoted presence at the cross (at least narratively if not historically) one of the main reasons he received the epithet "the disciple whom he [Jesus] loved" (see 19:26, καὶ τὸν μαθητὴν παρεστῶτα ὃν ἠγάπα)?

Third, it is obvious why Mary Magdalene ran to Peter and the Beloved Disciple; she needed to inform them that the tomb was empty. Was she primarily interested in sharing the information regarding Jesus' tomb with the only male who had been with her at the cross? Did she need at this time a male, because of the sociological barriers and power struc-

---

group within Early Judaism. I introduced this term years ago to replace such terms as "Urchristentum," "Early Christianity," and "the Early Church," because they are anachronistic and separate the history of Jesus' group from Judaism.

[113] The text is ambiguous. The Evangelist may be referring to two, three, or four women. Brown rightly sees problems with any solution except concluding that four women are intended. That is the solution of Tatian and the Peshitta. Cf. Brown, *The Death of the Messiah*, 2:1014–15.

[114] Among his many publications, see especially Ruckstuhl, *Jesus im Horizont der Evangelien*; see 393–95: "Der Jünger, den Jesus liebte, ein Essene?"

tures of the patriarchal, and dominant priestly, society of first-century Jerusalem? The exegete is enticed to ponder on the relationship between Mary Magdalene and the Beloved Disciple.

Fourth, the exegete wonders why Jesus united his mother with the Beloved Disciple. Did the author want to portray Jesus caring for his mother now that he would no longer be present to help her? Surely, in a deeply symbolical book like the GosJn, the meaning is deeper than this common idea.

It is clear that chapters 2 and 19 are parallel. In 2:1-12 and in 19:25-27 "mother" appears four times and "woman" only once.[115] This is hardly mere coincidence in a literary masterpiece so well composed as the GosJn. More importantly, as Grassi has demonstrated, chapters 2 and 19 are united by a possible chiasm in the seven signs:

(1) Jesus, his mother, and the wedding at Cana (2:1-12)
(2) restoration of dying son (4:46-54)
(3) Sabbath healing at Bethesda (5:1-16)
(4) multiplication of loaves (6:1-71)
(5) Sabbath healing of blind man (9:1-41)
(6) restoration of dead Lazarus (11:1-14)
(7) Jesus, his mother, the BD, the blood and water (19:25-37)[116]

The importance of Jesus' mother in the GosJn is highlighted by this chiasm. The Johannine Christians, some of whom knew the identity of the Beloved Disciple, would have grasped more readily than modern exegetes the importance of the drama in which Jesus entrusts his mother to the model disciple, the one authentic witness to him.[117]

Roman Catholic exegetes have defended at least four meanings of Jesus' words to his mother and the Beloved Disciple according to 19:25-27: the *literal (or moral) sense* (Jesus' act of filial piety toward his mother [espoused by Chrysostom, Theodore of Mopsuestia, Euthymius, Cyril of

---

[115] I am indebted to Grassi for this observation ("The Role of Jesus' Mother in John's Gospel: A Reappraisal," *Catholic Biblical Quarterly* 48 [1986] 71).

[116] See Grassi (Ibid., 68–69) who is dependent on the chiastic studies of M. Girard.

[117] Grassi unfortunately exaggerates the importance of Jesus' mother in the sense that he claims (incorrectly) that "the beloved disciple and Jesus' mother are associated in witnessing the meaning of the key event in Jesus' life, sign seven, which culminates in the unusual prodigy of the issue of watery blood from Jesus' side" (Ibid., 73). According to the GosJn only the BD clearly sees this flow of water and blood; it is possible that the drama has depicted his mother (who was described standing separate from the BD) as moving away from the scene as Jesus enters death pangs.

Alexandria, and Augustine]),[118] the *full sense* (the spiritual meaning is affirmed but it was probably not intended by the Evangelist),[119] the *sensus plenior* (the deep and spiritual meaning intended by God was only partially perceived by the Evangelist),[120] and the *typical sense* (the maternal spirituality of Mary).[121] Ceroke is convinced that the literal sense of GosJn 19:25-27 "certainly invokes the spiritual maternity of Mary over mankind."[122] I. de la Potterie affirms that Jesus' mother has "une valeur représentative," since Jesus calls her γύναι and not "Mother"; thus she receives salvific functions, and represents "la nouvelle Sion, le peuple de Dieu messianique et eschatologique."[123] Regarding the Beloved Disciple, he understands Jesus' words to have profound symbolic meaning: "le Disciple accueillit la mère de Jésus et l'Eglise comme sa Mère; c'est l'heure de la naissance de l'Eglise."[124] For our purposes it is imperative to note that these exegetes customarily assume that the Beloved Disciple is the apostle John, and are seeking to discern the symbolic meaning of Jesus' mother.[125]

Is the Beloved Disciple Jesus' real brother, the one so close to him? Was Jesus hoping to heal any possible rift his life and message had caused within his family?[126]

[118] See J. Leal, "Sentido literal mariológico de Jo. 19, 26-27," *Estudios Bíblicos* 11 (1952) 303-19. Here I am grateful to the article by C. P. Ceroke, "Mary's Maternal Role in John 19, 25-27," *Marian Studies* 11 (1960) 123-51; and to the presentation by I. de la Poterrie, *Marianum* 36 (1974) 3-19.

[119] M. de Tuya, "Valor mariológico del texto evangélico: 'Mulier, ecce filius tuus' (Jn. 19,25-27)," *Ciencia Tomista* 82 (1955) 189-223.

[120] See I. Zudaire, "Mujer, he ahí a tu hijo: Jn. 19,26," *CB* 11 (1954) 365-74.

[121] See J. M. Bover, "'Mujer, he ahí tu hijo,' maternidad espiritual de María para con todos los fieles, según S. Juan 19, 26-27," *EE* 1 (1922) 5-18.

[122] Ceroke, *Marian Studies* 11 (1960) 151.

[123] I. de la Potterie, *Marianum* 36 (1974) 38.

[124] Ibid., 39.

[125] Ceroke, *Marian Studies* 11 (1960) 128: "There does not seem to be any reason to doubt that this unnamed person is John the apostle and the author of the fourth gospel." R. Potter, "The Disciple whom Jesus Loved," *Life of the Spirit* 16 (1962) 293-97; 296: "The disciple loved by our Lord, the mysterious follower without a name, and the author of the gospel are all one St John, as Catholic tradition has held from the earliest times." F. S. Voigt, "O Discípulo Amado Recebe a Mãe de Jesus 'Eis Ta Idia': Velada Apología de João em Jo 19,27?" *Revista Eclesiástica Brasileira* 35 (1975) 771-823; 819: "O mesmo se poderia dizer do fato de esta perícope se referir a João como o discipulo *que Jesus amava* ...."

[126] I doubt that this is the answer. The GosJn does not contain the friction so typical of the Marcan account of Jesus and his family.

The passage 19:35 is linked with 25-27. In this verse the Beloved Disciple is meant because he is the only male disciple of Jesus described as being present at the crucifixion to make the observation.[127] The verse, 19:35, is not easy to comprehend, "And he who saw [it] has borne witness—and the witness from him is true; and that one knows that he speaks truthfully, so that you may believe."

What is its meaning? What perspective is the author attempting to emphasize?

First, he wants to make pellucidly clear that the witness of the Beloved Disciple is true. The words of 19:35 are editorial; that is, they come from the author who is editing pre-Johannine traditions (the words are not later redaction).[128] Thus the words "he who has seen it has borne witness" refer to the Beloved Disciple; but the third person discourse, "he ... has borne witness," indicates the theological position of the author of the GosJn. The statement "his witness is true" certainly indicates the author's judgment, although I am convinced it also represents the position of the Johannine Community. Perhaps "and he knows that he tells the truth" is a redundant way to state that the witness of the Beloved Disciple is trustworthy, so that those who are in the Community may continue to believe (taking the present form of the verb "to believe" in 19:35). The redundancy reveals that the author of 19:35, like the editor of 21:24, felt compelled to defend the trustworthiness of the witness of the Beloved Disciple. Research scholars have disclosed a sociological milieu in which the claims of the GosJn were being challenged both by those within the Johannine Community (and we also need to keep in mind the "gospels" that may have been available at that time, not only orally, but also in written form), and those without it.[129]

[127] As de Jonge saw, "the eye-witness referred to in 19:35 can be no other than 'the beloved disciple' mentioned in 19:25-27 and at the end of chapter 21" (*Jesus: Stranger from Heaven and Son of God*, 210). This position is affirmed by many commentators; see esp. Brown, *The Death of the Messiah*, 2:1019-20, who argues persuasively that 19:35 is not a creation by the Evangelist but is pre-Johannine.

[128] Even so, one should acknowledge that by removing 19:35 the narrative flows more smoothly from 19:34 to 19:36.

[129] In addition to the many discussions cited of this well-accepted position, see J. D. G. Dunn's insight that "*by the time the Fourth Gospel was written, there was a form of official Judaism which no longer regarded it as acceptable for Jews to confess Jesus as Messiah, and which could enforce its ruling on the subject among the local synagogues*" (*The Partings of the Ways Between Christianity and Judaism and their Significance for the Character of Christianity* [London: SCM; Philadelphia: Trinity Press International, 1991] 222 [italics his]).

The validity of the Beloved Disciple's word has been challenged. Thus, the author of 1–20 and the editor of 21 both stress that the reader can "trust" the witness of the Beloved Disciple. The verses 19:35 and 21:24 seem to indicate that some unspecified persons have been questioning the validity of the Beloved Disciple's witness. The questioning came from within and without the Community. From chapter 21 we learn that the witness of the Beloved Disciple was being questioned because he had died, which was apparently against Jesus' prophecy. The source seems to be within the Johannine Community.

Obviously there is abundant evidence within the GosJn, as most Johannine experts have demonstrated, that those outside the Johannine Community—especially the synagogal Jews—did not trust the witness of the GosJn. They disparaged the foundation, and the source, for the believing Johannine Community, and expelled Johannine Christians from the synagogue.

Second, the author of 19:35 intends to show that, like Thomas who witnesses that Jesus' resurrection is physical, the Beloved Disciple testifies that Jesus' death was certainly not illusory (which surely was one of the charges addressed to the Jews in the early Palestinian Jesus Movement who were proclaiming that Jesus had been raised by God).[130] The point is driven home by the account, peculiar to the GosJn, that a soldier thrust a spear into his side (19:34), even though he was "already dead" (ἤδη αὐτὸν τεθνηκότα, [19:33]). Out of Jesus' side came blood and water (αἷμα καὶ ὕδωρ.), not the ichor or juice that flows in the veins of Greek gods (ἰχώρ).[131] As D. E. H. Whiteley points out, "The effusion of blood showed that Jesus was human."[132] The multivalent anti-docetic overtones of the passage would be an attractive message for the schismatics who denied that Jesus had come in the flesh (but unlike chapters 1 and 15–17 there is no reason to conclude this section is redactional). As de Jonge stated, 19:4-35 "certainly has an anti-docetic thrust (cf. also 1 John 5:6-8)."[133]

---

[130] From the time of the Enlightenment until the present, that is from Venturini to Thiering, there has been an attempt to use logic and reason to explain how it was possible that Jesus was crucified yet seen alive again three days later. The most viable rationalistic answer has been that he only appeared to have died on the cross, that the drink given to him caused him "to swoon," and that some Jews (usually Essenes) revived him with special medicines in the coolness of a cave.

[131] See *Iliad* 5.340; LSJM, 846.

[132] Whiteley, "Was John Written by a Sadducee?" *Aufstieg und Niedergang der Römischen Welt* II.25.3 (Berlin: Walter de Gruyter, 1985) 2481–2505. See esp. "The B.D. Died While Finishing John: He Was a Sadducee," 2492–2502; cf. esp. 2499.

[133] M. de Jonge, *Jesus: Stranger from Heaven and Son of God*, 210.

Both the synagogal Jews and the docetic Christians may well have been targeted by such descriptions and statements in the GosJn. As P. Borgen points out, "John tries to show that the docetic spiritualists in the Church are like Jewish externalists, because both reject the Incarnate One as the only mediator between God and man."[134]

Third, like Thomas who insures that there is a continuity between the resurrected Lord and the crucified Jesus, the Beloved Disciple grounds the sacraments of Baptism and the Eucharist in the reality of Jesus' life and crucifixion. That is symbolized in what the Beloved Disciple has witnessed: from Jesus' side "immediately poured out blood and water ($\alpha\tilde{\iota}\mu\alpha$ $\kappa\alpha\grave{\iota}$ $\ddot{\upsilon}\delta\omega\rho$)" (19:34). It is evident, as Schnackenburg, Brown, and von Wahlde have seen,[135] that the pouring out of water from Jesus' side fulfills the promise of 4:10-15 and 7:39—Jesus' baptizing with the Holy Spirit occurs at the end of his ministry, on the cross (which is not a defeat) and when he breathes on his disciples (20:22).

The culminating thrust of 19:35 is to give prominence to the Beloved Disciple.[136] The account of the death of Jesus depends upon his witness. The author testifies that the Beloved Disciple's witness is true and accurate (perhaps in contrast to other accounts, some of which we have—possibly in Mark, as well as in Matthew and Luke—and others of which are lost).

Readers of the GosJn who were not intent on discerning the narrator's art nor his intention, that is those who were guilty of eisegesis, could well have conjured up the idea that the witness in 19:35 was none other than Judas Iscariot and that therefore this gospel is the Gospel of Judas ($\varepsilon\mathring{\upsilon}\alpha\gamma\gamma\acute{\varepsilon}\lambda\iota o\nu$ 'Ιούδα) mentioned by Irenaeus and Epiphanius.[137] One move in that direction would be to take literally the meaning of the scriptural

---

[134] P. Borgen, *Bread from Heaven: An Exegetical Study of the Concept of Manna in the Gospel of John* (NTSup 10; Leiden: Brill, 1965) 184.

[135] Schnackenburg, *St. John*, 1:305; Brown, *Gospel*, 2:946-51; and U. von Wahlde, *The Johannine Commandments*, 132.

[136] As M. J. J. Menken demonstrates, the Evangelist does not use the LXX ("because the piercing is absent from it") of Zech 12:10 but a pre-Johannine *testimonium*. It concerned the Parousia of Christ; thus it becomes evident that the Evangelist indicated that the BD "was the first of" the believers who will see "in the crucified Jesus the risen Lord, and in the risen Lord the crucified Jesus" (511). I am impressed with these insights and the way they link the BD with Thomas. See Menken, "The Textual Form and the Meaning of the Quotation from Zechariah 12:10 in John 19:37," *Catholic Biblical Quarterly* 55 (1993) 494-511.

[137] Irenaeus, *Adv.Haer.* 1.31.1. See *New Testament Apocrypha*, ed. W. Schneemelcher and trans. R. McL. Wilson (Cambridge: James Clarke & Co.; Louisville: Westminster/John Knox, 1991 rev. ed.) 1:386.

quotation: "They shall look on him whom they have pierced," which is from Zechariah 12:10. Obviously, this verse can be interpreted to suit Judas Iscariot better than the Beloved Disciple.

The second move would be to portray Judas as the one who worked with Jesus to fulfill the predetermined economy of salvation. That would make Judas a partner not in the crime of crucifixion but in the exaltation of Jesus on the cross, which is a well-known Johannine *Tendenz*. Note how this seems to be what Irenaeus indicated:

> And furthermore—they say—Judas the betrayer was thoroughly acquainted with these things; and he alone was acquainted with the truth as no others were, and (so) accomplished the mystery of the betrayal. By him all things, both earthly and heavenly, were thrown into dissolution.
>
> And they bring forth a fabricated work to this effect, which they entitle *The Gospel of Judas*.[138]

This reasoning, however, does not present us with a possible exegesis of the GosJn; rather, it presents us with perhaps the stimulus for a gnostic, Cainite composition of about 140 to 170 C.E.

The verse, 19:35, refers not to Judas, but to the Beloved Disciple. He is the only male the narrator places at the crucifixion. And the Evangelist puts stress on his testimony being true, which applies only to the Beloved Disciple, as we know from chapter 21 (21:24). The redundancy that his witness is true fits only the witness who has supplied the eyewitness information for the GosJn and whose witness is trustworthy according to both the Evangelist and the Johannine Community (19:35, 21:24). Finally, the plural form "they have pierced" makes it unlikely that Judas is meant by 19:37.

How does chapter 19 help us understand the identity of the Beloved Disciple? Let us imaginatively move back and forth within the narrative of the GosJn up to chapter 19. The Beloved Disciple, who had been beside—indeed touching—Jesus during their last meal together, stood beneath the cross; he looked up at the corpse of Jesus and saw the lance pierce Jesus' side. He must have suffered greatly. Did the narrator expect the sympathetic reader to recoil at the horrific event? Perhaps so, since not only is Jesus depicted as dead, but his corpse is mutilated. Does the author invite the reader to stand empathetically beside the Beloved Disciple? Does he subtly move the reader to feel the horror of the traumatic moment?

---

[138] Irenaeus, *Adv.Haer.* 1.31.1. See B. Layton, *The Gnostic Scriptures* (Garden City, N.Y.: Doubleday, 1987) 181.

The narrator has woven the full fabric of his story with exquisite skill. Did he intend the perspicacious reader to remember that this moment had been foreshadowed? *If the Beloved Disciple is Thomas, then his willingness to die with Jesus* (ἄγωμεν καὶ ἡμεῖς ἵνα ἀποθάνωμεν μετ' αὐτοῦ)—*uttered in 11:16—was experienced empathetically beneath Jesus' cross.*

In the darkness of that hour, there was no hope and surely no anticipation of what would transpire on the first day of the next week. Narrative exegesis helps us understand that if the Beloved Disciple is Thomas, the pathos of much of the story is now, finally, adequately perceived and felt. Moreover, the developing harmony of the whole gospel comes alive for the first time.

GosJn 20:1-10[139]

This section of the GosJn portrays Mary Magdalene going to the tomb, seeing the stone removed, running to "Simon Peter and the other disciple, the one whom Jesus loved," and delivering her report: "They have taken the Lord out of the tomb, and we (who?)[140] do not know where they have laid him."[141] Peter and the "other disciple," that is the Beloved Disciple, run to the tomb, with the latter outrunning the former. Upon arriving at the tomb the Beloved Disciple stoops, looks into the tomb, and sees only "the linen cloths." Then Peter arrives, enters the tomb, and sees the linen cloths and the face-cloth (or head napkin) that had been on the corpse. Subsequently, the Beloved Disciple enters the tomb; "and he saw

---

[139] P. S. Minear warns that in 20:1-18 the exegete confronts "many anomalies. Baffling questions proliferate and confident answers are hard to come by" ("'We don't know where ...' John 20:2," *Interpretation* 30 (1976) 125-39; see esp. 125.

[140] Here it is obvious that the author of chapter 20 knows the sources, or at least traditions, according to which many women came to the tomb. His slip into the first person plural, "we," shows he is working from earlier traditions, and probably not that we have a Galilean use of the plural for the first person singular. These traditions are also reflected in the passages in which women are described as present at the empty tomb (see Mk 16:1, Mt 28:1, Lk 24:10). P. Benoit showed that the literary genesis of 20:1-10 is complex, and pointed out the striking resemblances to the Synoptic tradition and the obviously independent Johannine traditions ("Marie-Madeleine et les disciples au tombeau selon Joh 20:1-18," in *Judentum, Urchristentum, Kirche: Festschrift für Joachim Jeremias,* ed. W. Eltester [BZNW 26; Berlin: Verlag Alfred Töpelmann, 1960] 141-52).

[141] I am convinced that the author of the GosJn is here working over—that is editing—earlier traditions (oral or written). Thyen defends the other possibility, that is, that 20:1-10 has been edited by the author of chapter 21 "den ich den Evangelisten nenne" (*L'Évangile de Jean,* 288).

and he believed" (20:8). Nothing is said about Peter's reaction,[142] but the conclusion is clear: both disciples did not know the Scripture (not plural) that Jesus must rise from the dead, so they went home.[143]

The locations of the *dramatis personae* are vague.[144] Dipping back into chapter 19 we wonder where Joseph of Arimathea and Nicodemus come from, and why they not were not mentioned at or near the cross. Where did Nicodemus find nearly one hundred pounds of spices, and is this not hyperbolic? Where were Peter and the Beloved Disciple and how did Mary know where they were? Where is Mary as they run to the tomb? Then they return πρὸς αὐτοὺς but can we be sure this prepositional phrase means "to their own homes"? Mary is said to be left weeping by the tomb; but how did she get there? In contrast to the pericope of the high priest's courtyard, the end of chapter 19 and all of chapter 20 read like a series of separate cameo sketches: 19:31-37 (the BD witnessing Jesus' physical death), 19:38-42 (Joseph of Arimathea and Nicodemus), 20:1-10 (Mary, Peter, and the BD), 20:11-18 (Mary), 20:19-23 (some disciples), 20:24-29 (Thomas).

Numerous questions spring forth from a fresh reading of this passage: How much of this report is theological expansion and how much is authentically remembered history (perhaps we should not talk about *bruta facta*)? Why does Mary Magdalene go to the tomb? Has the author risked his credibility with some of his readers by reporting that she made such a journey alone when it was still dark?[145] Why does she not look into the tomb, but only run away when she sees the stone has been moved? What is the meaning of her running, and the running of the two disciples? Why is the Beloved Disciple linked here with the expression "the other disciple"? To whom do "we" and "they" refer in Mary Magdalene's report, "We do not know where they have laid him"? Are these impersonal plurals remnants of an Aramaic source? Why does she go only to Peter and the Beloved Disciple? Where did she find them, and how did she know where they were staying? Why are they together, and not with other disci-

---

[142] Numerous scholars conclude that Peter believed that Jesus was raised from the dead. Among those are Bultmann, *John*, 684; Lorenzen, *Lieblingsjünger*, 34; Kragerud, *Lieblingsjünger*, 30. I agree with Brown that Peter sees, but does not come to faith (*Gospel*, 2:1004–1005).

[143] The Greek is literally "to themselves"; but as Bruce states, the idiom is "practically synonymous with *eis ta idia* (19:27, etc.)" (*The Gospel of John*, 387).

[144] In this paragraph I am especially indebted to Hugh Anderson for suggestions and discussions.

[145] Obviously, the use of "dark" is a Johannine theme to depict the absence of Jesus, the light of the world. The light-darkness dualistic paradigm clearly shapes the theology of the GosJn.

ples? Why do they run to the tomb? What is the meaning of the Beloved Disciple arriving before Peter at the tomb? Does that comment indicate he was younger, as many commentators have suggested,[146] or does it reflect some other meaning, perhaps his superiority over Peter? Why does the Beloved Disciple not enter the tomb? Is his hesitancy perhaps caused by a fear of becoming impure?[147]

How is our search for the identity of the Beloved Disciple improved by recent archaeological, sociological, and textual studies? We know from archaeological work (and indeed the study of the Temple Scroll), from sociological study,[148] and especially from a more sensitive reading of the GosJn (e.g., GosJn 2)[149] and related texts that the fear of impurity and "death" was surely an ever growing social concern within Early Judaism,[150] especially in the first century until the destruction of the Temple in 70.[151] The fear of going near—let alone into—a tomb, which may be

---

[146] For example, Bruce was of the opinion that the BD beat Peter to the tomb "probably because he was younger and fleeter of foot; it is hazardous to seek some allegorical significance in John's statement" (*The Gospel of John*, 385).

[147] P. Billerbeck suggested that it was not out of fear of Levitical impurity that he drew back, but because of shyness. In light of our increased knowledge of the fear of impurity in Judaism, especially just before 70 C.E. in ancient Palestine (especially Jerusalem), it is much more likely to specialists today that a pious man would fear the dangers of impurity before a tomb. See Billerbeck [that is, so-called Strack-Billerbeck], *Kommentar zum Neuen Testament aus Talmud und Midrash*, ed. H. L. Strack and P. Billerbeck (Munich: C. H. Beck, 1924 [8th unalt. ed. of 1983]) 2:584.

[148] See esp. M. Douglas, *Purity and Danger: An Analysis of the Concepts of Pollution and Taboo* (London: Ark, 1984); R. Huntington and P. Metcalf, *Celebrations of Death: The Anthropology of Mortuary Ritual* (Cambridge/New York: Cambridge Univ. Press, 1979).

[149] The six "stone" jars were for the Jewish rites of purification (2:6). Archaeologists have found such stone jars not only in Jerusalem, but also in the Galilee; and these stone vessels postdate Herod's building plans of circa 20 B.C.E. and antedate the destruction of 70 C.E. The full archaeological reports have not yet been published.

[150] See P. Sacchi, "Il sacro e il profano, l'impuro e il puro," in *Storia del Secondo Tempio: Israele tra VI secolo a.C. e I secolo d.C.* (Turin: Società Editrice Internazionale, 1994) 415–53.

[151] R. K. Fenn, a sociologist, points to the social problems caused by the increase in taxation by the Romans and the concomitant increase in taxes and heightened rules for purification by the Pharisees and the sacerdotal aristocracy based in Jerusalem ("Sociology and Social History: A Preface to a Sociology of the New Testament," *Journal for the Study of the Pseudepigrapha* 1 [1987] 95–114; see esp. 109–11).

behind the Beloved Disciple's reticence to enter Jesus' tomb, is clarified by the problems encountered when the building of Tiberias (a city mentioned only in the GosJn in the New Testament [6:1, 23; 21:1]) commenced in 18 or 20 C.E.[152] In the place marked out for Tiberias, tombs and graves were found; and sepulchers had to be removed to prepare for building projects. Even then many Jews refused to enter the city because of the fear of becoming contaminated.[153] As Josephus reported about Tiberias, contamination from graves made one ritually "unclean" for seven days (*Ant* 18.2).[154] Is the narrator of the GosJn assuming that his readers would know that a fear of impurity was one reason the Beloved Disciple hesitated before entering Jesus' tomb? In pondering such issues it is well to consider that Jesus' tomb may have been like the tomb of Herod's family on the west of the Hinnom Valley or like the graves of the kings and queens of Adiabene; that is, it was probably underground, and thus there would have been many other corpses in adjacent niches and rooms.

When the author has Peter see the linen clothes and the face-cloth neatly rolled up, does he intend to confront the claim that the corpse had been stolen? Why is the Beloved Disciple not depicted entering the tomb first? What was Peter's reaction upon seeing that the tomb was empty? Why did the author leave Peter's reaction, or belief, out of the account? Does the narrator mean that "one disciple becomes a believer, the other doesn't," as Haenchen contended?[155] The commentators' views on such issues is markedly diverse.

This pericope elicits a torrent of questions. Paramount among them is the following: What did the Beloved Disciple "believe"? Other questions follow: What Scripture is being referred to in 20:9, and how is it related to the claim in 2:22?

Does 20:10 mean that Peter and the Beloved Disciple went home? Do they return to Galilee (as McCasland claimed),[156] or back to where they were staying during the Passover Festival in or near Jerusalem (as

---

[152] See "Tiberias," in *The New Encyclopedia of Archaeological Excavations in the Holy Land* 4 (1993) 1464-73 [sections written by Y. Hirschfeld, G. Foerster, and F. Vitto].

[153] Soon after the completion of the GosJn, in the middle of the second century C.E., Rabbi Simeon Bar Yohai purified Tiberias from the desecration and impurity—indeed danger—caused by the graves (*GenRab* 79h; *j.Shab* 9.1-38d).

[154] See J. F. Strange, "Tiberias," *The Anchor Bible Dictionary* (1992) 6.547-49.

[155] Haenchen, *John 2*, 208.

[156] McCasland, *The Resurrection of Jesus: A New Study of the Belief That Jesus Rose from the Dead, of Its Function as Early Christian Cult Story, and of the Origin of the Gospel Literature* (New York: T. Nelson and Sons, 1932) 49.

Brown claims)?[157] Michaels also contends that the disciples "went back to their respective lodgings in Jerusalem (cf. 16:32; 19:27)."[158] Do they both exit now from the story, and are both absent when Jesus appears to some disciples, according to 20:19-23? Neither is mentioned again in the GosJn (that is, in chapters 1–20). Does the author of the GosJn thereby leave the reader with the impression that neither the Beloved Disciple nor Peter were present when Jesus appeared to some disciples, unnumbered and unnamed, on the evening of that day, the first day of the week? The pericope of 20:19-23 becomes more important for understanding the flow of the Johannine narrative, since not only the Beloved Disciple but Peter, according to 20:1-10, expresses no belief in Jesus' resurrection.[159] Surely, the possible exegesis that neither the Beloved Disciple nor Peter may appear again in the narrative is one of the main reasons it was necessary to add the Appendix, chapter 21.

Why is there a rough transition from 20:10 to 20:11, since as Haenchen stated, 20:11 "does not go well with what precedes"?[160] How are traditions, sources, and redactions in this section to be perceived and explained (I see no reason to assume interpolations)?[161]

This is clearly one of the most misunderstood chapters in the GosJn. Critics have not sufficiently considered the possibility that the Beloved Disciple may be Thomas because the former "sees and believes" that Jesus has been resurrected; hence, he could not be Thomas who subsequently questions the disciples' claim that they have seen the resurrected Jesus.

Bultmann was a remarkably independent thinker; yet he concluded that "the empty grave does clearly count as proof for the resurrection,"

---

[157] Brown argues that "home" in 20:10 does not denote "Galilee, but wherever they had been in Jerusalem when Magdalene called them" (*Gospel*, 2:988). Brown also points to Lk 24:24, which according to him portrays Peter going "home, wondering at what had happened." I am not persuaded that Lk 24:24 indicates this exegesis.

[158] Michaels, *John* (Peabody, Mass.: Hendrickson, 1984, 1989 [repr. 1993]) 338.

[159] B. Weiss, who assumed the BD was John, concluded that both of them, according to 20:1-10, believed in Jesus' resurrection: "at the empty tomb they attained to belief in Jesus' resurrection" (*The Life of Christ*, trans. M. G. Hope [Edinburgh: T. & T. Clark, 1884] 3:394 [also see fn. 1]).

[160] Haenchen, *John 2*, 208.

[161] Bultmann saw 20:9 as "a gloss of the ecclesiastical redaction" (*John*, 685). Schnackenburg (*St. John*, 2:312–13) also supposes that 20:9 comes from "a source akin to the synoptics," and that the Evangelist received it "without wholly getting rid of the contradiction in his presentation which arises because of it." According to him, only Peter and Mary were originally portrayed as those who "did not attain faith in Jesus' resurrection."

and that the Beloved Disciple believes that Jesus has been raised.[162] The Beloved Disciple does see the empty tomb, the grave-clothes, and finally the face-cloth;[163] but was he the first one, according to the GosJn, to believe that Jesus rose from the dead?

Such an exegesis represents a consensus today; note these comments by the leading commentators on the GosJn:

> Peter and the disciple believed then in the resurrection of their master, when they saw the empty tomb. If they had known the sense of the scriptures, they would not have needed to see the sepulchre to know that Christ had already risen. (Loisy, 1903)[164]

> The other disciple ... believes, not what Magdalene had told him (*pace* Augustine) since he has come to the tomb to verify her report; he believes in the resurrection. (Lagrange, 1927)[165]

> The Beloved Disciple then entered, saw, and believed. From *vv.* 25, 27, 29 it is clear that *believed* means belief in the Resurrection of the Lord. (Hoskyns, 1947)[166]

> What did he believe? That Jesus was actually risen from the dead, and was the real Messiah, the Lord of Glory, the Son of God in the most exalted sense. This is nothing less than living faith in the act of embracing the truth of the resurrection. (Hendriksen, 1954, 1959)[167]

---

[162] Bultmann, *John*, 684. This is a rather startling conclusion for the following reasons: First, the empty tomb, according to Paul and other New Testament authors, is no proof in the resurrection. Second, the very next verse clarifies that he and Peter did not "yet" know that Jesus must rise from the dead. Third, the following verses (11-14) show that the section concerns the confusion regarding the location of Jesus' corpse, and contains no belief that Jesus rose from the dead.

[163] See especially the following: B. Osborne, "A Folded Napkin in an Empty Tomb: John 11.44 and 20.7 Again," *Heythrop Journal* 14 (1973) 437–40; S. M. Schneiders, "The Face Veil: A Johannine Sign (John 20:1-10)," *Biblical Theology Bulletin* 13 (1983) 94–97.

[164] Loisy, *Le Quatrième Évangile* (Paris: Nourry, 1921 [2nd ed.] 902).

[165] The translation is intentionally idiomatic. See M.-J. Lagrange, *Évangile selon Saint Jean* (Paris: Librairie Victor Lecoffre, 1927) 508: "L'autre disciple ... crut ... à la résurection."

[166] E. C. Hoskyns, *The Fourth Gospel*, ed. F. N. Davey (London: Faber and Faber, 1947 [2nd ed.] 540 [italics his]).

[167] Hendriksen, *A Commentary on the Gospel of John*, 2 vols. (London: Banner of Truth Trust, 1954, 1959) 2:451.

[The] Beloved Disciple ... is the first to believe in the risen Jesus. (Brown, 1966)[168]

John does not say what the Beloved Disciple believed. He means that he drew the only possible conclusion from the facts, and the reader is expected to be able to do the same. The Disciple has reached Resurrection faith without an appearance of Jesus. (Lindars, 1972)[169]

[The Beloved Disciple] understood the situation, so to say at a glance, and immediately came to believe .... To what kind of belief? According to the context, undoubtedly, to the full faith in the resurrection of Jesus; any kind of diminution, with a view to v. 9, is ruled out. (Schnackenburg, 1975, 1982)[170]

[The Beloved Disciple] understood that Jesus had risen bodily from the dead (20:8) and he was the first to recognize the risen Lord on the border of the lake of Tiberias (21:7). (de Jonge, 1977)[171]

The beloved disciple, who was the first to reach the tomb, followed Peter into it, and, when he saw, believed that Jesus had risen from the dead. (Barrett, 1978)[172]

[The Beloved Disciple] saw what Peter had seen, but with the eye of faith he saw more. Like a flash it came home to him what had happened: the Lord had risen from the dead and left the tomb. (Bruce, 1983)[173]

Now for the first time the 'other disciple' also enters the tomb and sees what Peter had seen. In his case, however, what he sees causes him to believe in the resurrection. ... That he does not say anything about Peter having this faith makes it clear that the other disciple alone returned home from the empty tomb as a believer. (Haenchen, 1984)[174]

---

[168] Brown, *Gospel*, 2:987.

[169] Lindars, *The Gospel of John* (Sheffield: JSOT Press, 1990) 602. I wish Lindars had informed us of how he discerned what the author "means" and how he is so certain that "the reader is expected to be able to do the same."

[170] Schnackenburg, *St. John*, 2:312. Schnackenburg thinks the verb denotes the ingressive aorist, which is surely possible. If that is correct, then it means he began to believe (but in what?).

[171] M. de Jonge, *Jesus: Stranger from Heaven and Son of God*, 213.

[172] Barrett, *The Gospel According to St. John*, 561.

[173] Bruce, *The Gospel of John*, 385.

[174] Haenchen, *John 2*, 208.

But what exactly did the beloved disciple believe? ... He believed Jesus had returned to the Father, just as he said he would (cf. 14:29: 'I have told you now before it happens, so that when it does happen, you will believe'). The basis of his belief was the simple fact that Jesus' body had disappeared. (Michaels, 1984, 1989)[175]

The Beloved Disciple is the first to the grave and above all the first believer in the resurrection of Jesus (cf. 21:7). (Becker, 1984)[176]

The beloved disciple then enters, sees the same thing Peter had seen, and believes that his master has risen from the tomb (although he did not yet fully understand what had taken place, John adds). (Kysar, 1984)[177]

Above all it is clear that 'the other disciple' (the BD) enters the tomb, 'he sees' what is visible in the empty tomb, 'and believes'. It requires fundamentally no encounter with the resurrected one; the 'other disciple' is with perceptive view the contrast to 'Doubting Thomas' and to him (the BD) belongs the praise: 'Blessed are those who do not see and believe.' (Blank, 1988)[178]

[The Beloved Disciple, in contrast to Peter, is] the first to come to resurrection belief. (Porsch, 1989)[179]

The Beloved Disciple is introduced as an example of faith which immediately perceives the truth of the resurrection events (also 21:7). He serves as a sharp contrast to the doubts expressed by Thomas (20:24-29). (Perkins, 1990)[180]

John (if he is the Beloved Disciple) 'believes.' *What* does he believe? Without any doubt, that Jesus is resurrected. (Voigt, 1991)[181]

The beloved disciple sees the empty tomb and believes. He comes to faith without seeing Jesus himself. He, thereby, becomes not only a

---

[175] J. R. Michaels, *John*, 337.

[176] Becker, *Das Evangelium nach Johannes*, 2:614.

[177] Kysar, *John's Story of Jesus* (Philadelphia: Fortress Press, 1984) 86.

[178] Blank, *Das Evangelium nach Johannes*, 3:163.

[179] Porsch, *Johannes-Evangelium* (Stuttgart: Verlag Katholisches Bibelwerk, 1989 [2nd ed.]) 211.

[180] P. Perkins, "The Gospel According to John," in *The New Jerome Biblical Commentary*, ed. R. E. Brown, J. A. Fitzmyer, and R. E. Murphy (Englewood Cliffs, N.J.: Prentice Hall, 1990) 983.

[181] G. Voigt, *Licht, Liebe, Leben: Das Evangelium nach Johannes* (Göttingen: Vandenhoeck & Ruprecht, 1991) 278. The italics and parenthetical words are his.

witness to the authenticity of the tradition of the empty tomb (21:24), but also a prototype of faith for those of subsequent generations who will believe without themselves seeing the risen Jesus (20:29b). (Talbert, 1992)[182]

The experience of the beloved disciple—*"he saw and believed"*—has an importance in the fourth gospel far beyond what would be inferred from these few words.... The implication of these words ... is that *he is the first of the disciples to experience the resurrection of Jesus*: he is the *firstborn*, as Thomas will be the last. (Barnhart, 1993)[183]

[The beloved Disciple is said] to believe. (Crossan, 1994)[184]

This consensus among the commentators and leading New Testament experts is impressive (as is the intermittent comment that the BD is contrasted with Thomas).[185] The conclusion is even fortified by publications of four independent thinkers, Colson, Moloney, Byrne, and Schneiders.[186] Colson, in his careful research into the identity of the Beloved Disciple, postulates that "'Il vit et il crut.' Il crut à la Résurrection de Jésus."[187] Moloney attempts to depict the journey of the Beloved Disciple to resurrection faith.[188]

Schneiders claims that the neat arrangement of the face veil is a "sign" for the Beloved Disciple; it indicates that like Moses (Ex 34) Jesus put aside the flesh and ascended to the Father.[189] Byrne rejects this explanation, because it cannot be reconciled with Jesus' subsequent statement to Mary Magdalene that he has not yet ascended to the Father; yet Byrne is

---

[182] C. H. Talbert, *Reading John: A Literary and Theological Commentary on the Fourth Gospel and the Johannine Epistles* (New York: Crossroad, 1992) 250.

[183] B. Barnhart, *The Good Wine*, 220. Much more insightful (in my view) is his comment about Thomas: "Such is the deep personal root of his relation to Jesus that he cannot accept the witness of the others, however unanimous and emphatic" (255).

[184] J. D. Crossan, *Jesus: A Revolutionary Biography* (San Francisco: Harper, 1994) 187.

[185] Also affirming that the BD was the first to believe in Jesus' resurrection is J. Goettmann, *Saint Jean: Évangile de la nouvelle genèse* (Paris: Cerf-Pneumathèque, 1982) 260–61.

[186] Roloff also concludes that the BD is the first to believe in Jesus' resurrection, and refers to his "Osterglaubens," *NTS* 15 (1968/69) 137.

[187] Colson, *L'Énigme du disciple que Jésus aimait*, 99.

[188] Moloney, *Australasian Catholic Record* 59 (1982) 417–32.

[189] S. M. Schneiders, "The Face Veil: A Johannine Sign (John 20.1-10)," *Biblical Theology Bulletin* 13 (1983) 94–97.

convinced that the Beloved Disciple believed in Jesus' resurrection because of what he saw in the tomb.[190]

Scholars' attempts to explain how the Beloved Disciple obtained resurrection faith leave me with an appreciation of the Evangelist's succinct "he saw and believed." Perhaps he did not intend his readers to complete his report with affirmations of resurrection faith. Yet, there is an amazing consensus that 20:8 denotes resurrection faith. I wonder if there is such a world-wide consensus on the meaning of another verse in the GosJn.

Dare one go against the formidable force of such an armada of experts? But are they correct in interpreting 20:8? Have they perhaps been too influenced by a previous commentator's conclusion? Have they, each one, published a fresh, penetrating, and independent examination of 20:1-10? Have they dealt sufficiently with the contextual force of 20:9? The *prima facie* meaning of this verse is that the Beloved Disciple and Peter did not believe in Jesus' resurrection at that point in the narrative, because they were ignorant of the scriptural proof of Jesus' resurrection. Thus 20:9 cannot be ignored, removed, or attributed to a foolish redactor. If one intends to observe the contextual force of this verse, then one cannot exegetically conclude that resurrection faith was advocated by the Beloved Disciple who merely did not know the appropriate scriptural proof text.

In his *Understanding the Fourth Gospel*, Ashton leaves no doubt that he thinks the Beloved Disciple went home, believing that Jesus had been raised from the dead. His words, however, show a keen attachment to the text and a gift for theological insight:

> He [the author of 21] is able to record the response the beloved disciple makes, not to the voice of an intermediary, but to a vision of emptiness. The head-band and the grave-clothes are themselves signs of absence, mute witnesses to the truth of one half of the angelic witness: he is not here. The other half has to be supplied by the disciples themselves. Peter, it seems, failed to make the necessary leap of faith (that is supplied in the Appendix, 21:7); the other disciple 'saw and believed.'[191]

Let us attempt to understand the commentators' exegetical method. How do they come to the conclusion that 20:8 portrays the Beloved Disciple "believing" in Jesus' resurrection?

---

[190] Byrne, *Journal for the Study of the New Testament* 23 (1985) 84, 88–89. See esp. 89: "But greater love had quickened in him (the Beloved Disciple) a keener sensitivity to signals of Jesus' risen life."

[191] Ashton, *Understanding*, 506.

The best place to begin is to focus on the Evangelist's intentionality. What is the intention of the author? He introduces the Beloved Disciple at the Last Supper, places him at the crucifixion, describes how he outruns Peter to the tomb, but allows him only to stoop and to look, allowing Peter to rush in ahead of him. Finally he has the Beloved Disciple enter himself, to see the graveclothes and face-cloth, and states cryptically that he "sees and believes." The very next verse, however, states rather clearly that the Beloved Disciple and at least one other person do not understand yet that a certain passage in Scripture (never identified by the author) proves that Jesus must rise from the dead. With this ignorance the Beloved Disciple is said to "go home."

Is that not an odd way for our author to orchestrate the exit from center stage by the major actor? Is the interpretation of 20:8 by the leading commentators adequately sensitive to the dramatic skill and linguistic ability of the author of the GosJn? Is he not too gifted with rich symbolism to have the Beloved Disciple slip away into the shadows of ambiguous verses?

Within this context we are urged by the commentators to understand that the Beloved Disciple "believed" that Jesus had arisen. If so, then why has the author followed his confession with an editorial comment regarding ignorance of some ambiguous passage in Scripture? Does not the Beloved Disciple "go home" without making any confession? Does he not now merely as it were slip away somewhere? What is then the meaning of the author's editorial comment that he "believed," but did not understand the Scripture regarding Jesus' resurrection?

Even removing verse 20:9 as a later addition (as Bultmann advised) does not eliminate the problems with the narrative. The Beloved Disciple believes and "goes home." If he believed Jesus rose from the dead, why is the reader not told that clearly? If he did so, why would he merely disappear from the story? Would that not be absurd, according to the narrative? Why would he not share his newly acquired faith, which is unprecedented in the story up to this point according to the commentators, with others? Why does he keep his insight from Peter, and especially from Mary Magdalene, who had informed him about the tomb being empty and is now left standing devastated and crying?

Do not these questions expose some exegetical problems? Are these not indicative of serious objections to the reigning consensus? The commentators do not defend or demonstrate how, and with what philological insights, they have obtained the conclusion that "believe" must denote resurrection belief in this context. Categorically they do not seem to be carefully articulated exegetical insights; they appear to be subjective pronouncements. In my opinion the exegesis proposed by the commentators raises more problems than it solves.

Let us focus again upon the primary question: What did the Beloved Disciple "believe"? That is the crucial question today for an exegete of the opening verses of chapter 20. E. Bammel astutely points out that in 20:6-8 the author uses "to see" in a double sense: first for seeing (θεωρεῖν) without believing, which applies to Peter, and second for seeing (ὁρᾶν) and believing, which qualifies the Beloved Disciple.[192] Both of them saw the same things—that is the empty tomb and graveclothes—but only the Beloved Disciple is the one of whom the author adds the categorizing words καὶ ἐπίστευσεν. Now, the question is more carefully focused. What does the Beloved Disciple believe?

Reading 20:1-10, cognizant of all the questions these verses raise, leads me to ponder what Peter thought. Some experts, for example Bultmann, are convinced that Peter is the first to believe: "Clearly, it is presupposed that Peter before him (the BD) was likewise brought to faith through the sight of the empty grave."[193] Other specialists, for example Haenchen, are convinced that Peter exits without any belief: "That he does not say anything about Peter having this faith makes it clear that the other disciple alone returned home from the empty tomb as a believer."[194]

Neither of these interpretations, however, is sufficiently supported by exegesis and a study of the narrative of the GosJn. According to 20:1-10, Peter makes no confession, does not understand Scripture, and goes "home." According to narrative exegesis, it would be rather odd if the author only here elevates Peter over the Beloved Disciple and portrays him as the first to believe.

We are not told what Peter thought or believed as he went ostensibly homeward. The author of the GosJn is interested in clarifying that the Beloved Disciple "saw and believed."

It is attractive, in terms of the full narrative of the GosJn, to assume that the Beloved Disciple may have gone home, continuing to believe that Jesus is the Son who was sent by the Father. Or, perhaps now he believed that Mary was correct in reporting that the tomb was empty.[195] Hugh Anderson correctly contemplates that the author of this section perhaps intended to say that not from reading Scripture, but only from personal

---

[192] E. Bammel, *Judaica: Kleine Schriften I* (WUNT 37; Tübingen: Mohr [Siebeck], 1986) 169.

[193] Bultmann, *John*, 684. I am impressed that often the adverb "clearly" reveals that the exegete is forcing an interpretation.

[194] Haenchen, *John 2*, 208. The appearance of "clear" is indicative of forced exegesis.

[195] J. F. O'Grady contends that the BD is a real historical person who received the "office of witness" and the "epitome of believer." The "empty tomb is sufficient" for him to believe in Jesus' resurrection ("in the Risen Lord"). Cf. "The Role of the Beloved Disciple," *Biblical Theology Bulletin* 9 (1979) 58-65.

experience ("he saw," in this case not the risen one, but an empty tomb) did belief arise (cf. Luke's Emmaus Story).[196]

The Beloved Disciple saw even more: the graveclothes neatly organized in some unclear way which prove not only that the corpse was not stolen,[197] but also, in Ashton's words, that Jesus "is not here." That is obviously the meaning when one looks at the immediate context. According to the author of the GosJn—who wrote a gospel not a treatise—saving faith can only be based on the one *kairos* of Jesus, the Christ the Son of God, and that perception is present in the whole message of the gospel as the movement from beginning to end of "the One Sent" back to "the One Who Sends."[198] No one should equate believing that Jesus is on his way to the Father with believing in a physically resurrected body.

Perhaps the Beloved Disciple believed Jesus' words that he is going to his Father (πορεύομαι πρὸς τὸν πατέρα [14:28]), and his claim that he is going away so that he may come again (ὑπάγω καὶ ἔρχομαι πρὸς ὑμᾶς [14:28]). Jesus, according to the GosJn, must go away in order to return to the disciples. Jesus is said to have informed his disciples of these teachings so that they "may believe" when they take place.

In 14:29 and 20:8 we confront the intransitive use of the verb "to believe." The Beloved Disciple may well have believed that Jesus had gone to his Father. Anderson rightly points out that an exegesis of 20:8 must not forget that in the GosJn "the way of Jesus is from the first the way to the Father, a way that has to be traveled through suffering and death towards 'that day' when he will have reached his heavenly glory by the Father's side."[199] Equally important is a recognition of how Jesus' crucifixion is portrayed in the GosJn. The soteriological significance of Jesus' death is noticeably absent, especially in light of Paul's emphasis. M. de Jonge insightfully states that "Jesus' death on the cross is, in the Fourth Gospel, primarily a stage in his return to the Father, characterized as δοξασθῆναι and ὑψωθῆναι."[200] That is, the Evangelist does not call his

---

[196] Anderson, personal letter of 10 October 1994.

[197] Grayston expresses this fact in an attractive manner: "So it was not tomb robbery, but some neat and orderly proceeding (note the contrast with the haste and agitation of the disciples)" (*The Gospel of John* [Philadelphia: Trinity Press International, 1990] 166).

[198] See Anderson's comments in "John's Easter Witness," in *Jesus and Christian Origins: A Commentary on Modern Viewpoints* (New York: Oxford Univ. Press, 1964) 233–37, see esp. 234.

[199] Anderson, "The Easter Witness of the Evangelists," in *The New Testament in Historical and Contemporary Perspective: Essays in Memory of G. H. C. Macgregor*, ed. H. Anderson and W. Barclay (Oxford: Blackwell, 1965) 35–55; cf. 52.

[200] M. de Jonge, *Jesus: Stranger from Heaven and Son of God*, 210.

readers to believe, first and foremost, that Jesus has been resurrected. The Beloved Disciple can "believe" without having to believe that Jesus has been resurrected; his faith would be complete if he continued to believe in Jesus as the One who was going back to his Father above.

There is no reason to contend that 20:8 must mean that the Beloved Disciple believed in Jesus' resurrection; it may signify in ways uncomprehended by the Beloved Disciple that Jesus has done exactly what he had claimed. Hence, the meaning of "believing" in 20:8 may be linked with 14:29 (ἵνα ὅταν γένηται πιστεύσητε). It has happened; the Beloved Disciple believes (ἐπίστευσεν).

The aorist in 20:8 may be either inceptive (before the empty tomb the BD only began to believe that Jesus had been raised [but the faith will need further demonstration in the GosJn]), or perfective (he believed fully [either what Mary had reported to him or that Jesus was truly the One from above who had returned to his Father]).

Why have commentators defended, *en masse*,[201] the exegesis that 20:8 must be interpreted to mean the Beloved Disciple believed that Jesus was resurrected?[202] Two reasons seem paramount, but they are seldom mentioned and certainly are not developed in the commentaries.

First, according to the commentators the Beloved Disciple must be portrayed as believing in Jesus' resurrection because he is now exiting from the story. It would be unthinkable that the author of this masterpiece would allow him, the model for discipleship, to leave the narrative without clear evidence that he believed in the resurrection.

They presuppose that the Beloved Disciple will not appear again in the narrative of 1–20, and that he is not to be equated with a named disciple who, subsequent to 20:10, will do or say something. Such presuppositions, in my opinion, need to be carefully reexamined. Contrary to the conclusions of these experts, it is far from clear that this disciple does not return. What if he were to be identified with a major character who has a powerful confession to make? If that were so—especially if he were Thomas—then their presuppositions are no longer valid.

Second, the commentators assume that the Beloved Disciple must be one who believes in Jesus' resurrection because he "saw and believed" (καὶ εἶδεν καὶ ἐπίστευσεν), and they correctly point out these two verbs have been developed and imbued with deep symbolic meaning by the

---

[201] Even the contributors to *Peter in the New Testament*, ed. R. E. Brown, K. P. Donfried, and J. Reumann, have no trouble concluding that "the first one to have come to resurrection faith was the Beloved Disciple" (138).

[202] R. Russell assumes that the Evangelist and BD is the apostle John and thus the GosJn contains his own experience of the "newness" of that "Day" ("The Beloved Disciple and the Resurrection," *Scripture* 8 [1956] 57–62).

author of the GosJn. The verse 20:8 must—they tend to assume—be read in light of 20:27-29 in which we are confronted with the last, indeed stirring, words from the risen Lord to Thomas: "Blessed are those who have not seen and yet believe" (οἱ μὴ ἰδόντες καὶ πιστεύσαντες). Hence, Brown—who has written one of the most careful, detailed, and perceptive commentaries on the GosJn—concludes that the Beloved Disciple could not have been put in central focus of the narrative only to confirm that the corpse was no longer in the tomb. He argues that

> the Evangelist certainly did not introduce the Beloved Disciple into the scene only to have him reach such a trite conclusion. Rather he is the first to believe in the risen Jesus (compare the combination of seeing and believing in vs. 29).[203]

While it is helpful to point to the linguistic relation between 20:8 and 20:29, only the latter verse and context obviously articulate a belief in Jesus' resurrection.

How can an empty tomb, even with Jesus' burial face-cloth rolled up in a place separate from the linen cloths,[204] be proof of Jesus' resurrection? Would a Jew at that time and place have jumped from seeing the linen cloths and face-cloth to believing that Jesus had been raised? Would such a person have *assumed* that one who had been resurrected would spend time and focus his interest on rolling up neatly the face-cloth (as seems to be implied in some commentaries)? Or, is the description of the face-cloth indicative of the way Jesus' face had been wrapped, which would indicate, as many Roman Catholics contend, that "Jesus' body had become a spiritual body and passed through the linen and the napkin without moving them from their position."[205]

Have commentators read 20:8 in its context or have they read it in terms of a much later verse, 20:29? Does such an exegesis not miss the narrative flow and the development of thought from the Beloved Disciple at the empty tomb to Thomas's triumphal confession? Does chapter 20 not show an attractive movement from belief that the corpse has been removed to the confrontation with a living being who reaches from

---

[203] Brown, *Gospel*, 2:987.

[204] Scholars frequently refer to the face-cloth as *neatly rolled up in a place by itself*. That interpretation goes beyond what is in the text. It does not state that the face-cloth had been neatly wrapped by someone (human or angelic). All that is said is that the face-cloth was "rolled up in a place by itself." It is possible that it remained where it had been—that is, where Jesus' face had lain in the grave.

[205] F. Salvoni, "The So-Called Jesus Resurrection Proof (John 20:7)," *Restoration Quarterly* 22 (1979) 72-76; the quotation is from 76.

another dimension, calls out a personal name: "Mariam" (20:16), and later invites Thomas to touch and see? Has the author of the GosJn not attempted to demonstrate that belief in Jesus' resurrection is always a relationship with a living Lord who knows us by name and invites us to obtain eternal life in and with him? If so, then the content of the Beloved Disciple's belief in 20:8 needs to be reexamined.

The author of the GosJn has not written his masterpiece so that the reader is called by him to come and to believe that Jesus has been raised by God. The gospel does not exhort the reader to believe in Jesus' resurrection. Yet, such a presumption seems to be in the back of the minds of some exegetes who want to interpret 20:8 to mean that the Beloved Disciple could not be beloved unless he believed in Jesus' resurrection.

The gospel clearly concludes that it was written so that those who read it may continue to believe "that Jesus is *the Christ, the Son of God*, and that believing you may have life in his name" (20:31). Hence, Marsh rightly suggests that according to 20:1-10 the Beloved Disciple does not come to resurrection faith; he comes rather to believe that Jesus is indeed the Christ the Son of God. Note his words:

> The beloved disciple, perhaps encouraged by Peter's example, joined Peter inside the tomb. He saw the same arrangement of the contents, but reacted quite differently: he saw *and believed*. There can be no doubt that what John means his readers to understand is that this was the point at which the beloved disciple really came to believe in Jesus as the Christ, the son of God. What John is trying to leave clear is that the beloved disciple did not jump to the conclusion that some astoundingly unique miracle had been performed; that did not constitute 'belief'. He had come to believe that the one who could thus be free from death must be what he had been claiming to be, the very Son of God.[206]

The author of the GosJn repeatedly shows the reader how others believed that Jesus was sent from the Father. And the author of the GosJn invites and exhorts his reader *to believe* that Jesus is the one who has been sent into the world (this would bring out the dimension of completion of an action specified by the verb [effective or perfective aorist]). Does 20:8 mean that the Beloved Disciple believed that Mary was correct that Jesus' corpse had been removed, and continuing in his belief that Jesus was the one sent by the Father who sends, then go home? That is conceivable, and points up the need to study the immediate context of 20:8.

---

[206] Marsh, *The Gospel of St. John* (The Pelican Gospel Commentaries; Hammondsworth, Middlesex: Penguin Books, 1968) 631.

P. Perkins sees this problem. She asserts that 20:8 means belief in Jesus' resurrection, and advises, "The faith ascribed to the Beloved Disciple in v 8 has no relationship to the action. Verse 9 asserts that 'they did not understand.'"[207] She also wisely states that 20:9 makes "it clear that the empty tomb was not proof to the disciples that Jesus had been raised."[208] Though she thinks that the Beloved Disciple is the first to believe in Jesus' resurrection, she rightly recognizes that the context of 20:9 undermines the customary interpretation of 20:8.

Her comments should be arresting, and cause more caution in the exegesis of 20:8. We should hesitate to conclude that we know the content of the intransitive verb and that the Beloved Disciple believed in Jesus' resurrection. Minear correctly stressed that there are many anomalies and "baffling questions in 20:1-18."[209] The *context* of 20:8 undermines the regnant exegesis, which requires at this point in the narrative that the Beloved Disciple believe in Jesus' resurrection.

Why is there a clash between "*he* saw and believed" and "*they* did not yet know the Scripture, that he (Jesus) must rise from the dead"? Numerous commentators attempt to solve this problem by appealing to varied traditions unsuccessfully combined by the author of the GosJn. This research is on the right track in terms of seeking to discern sources used by the Evangelist, but it certainly undermines attention to and sensitivity for the flow of the story given to us by the author. Bultmann saw the problem and so removed the verse, but it is now impossible simply to remove verses as early scholars habitually did[210] in order to reconstruct a putative pure text.[211] The passage 20:1-10 cannot be cut and pasted. The words of 20:9 cannot be simply marked out, as did the scribe who in the Middle Ages copied the *Cairo Damascus Document*—he frequently took his pen and drew a horizontal line through words he had incorrectly written. The words of 20:9 must remain before us to examine; they cannot be ignored. As Schnackenburg saw, "The supposition of an editorial gloss represents no solution."[212] This verse must be understood, and that means interpreted and allowed to affect our exegesis of 20:8.

---

[207] Perkins in *The New Jerome Biblical Commentary*, 982.

[208] Perkins, *The Gospel According to St. John* (Chicago: Franciscan Herald Press, 1978) 233.

[209] P. Minear, "'We don't know where ...' John 20:2," *Interpretation* 30 (1976) 125–39; see 125.

[210] This method was characteristic of some of the best work during the first half of this century. I think in particular of Bultmann's commentary on the GosJn and R. H. Charles' two volume commentary on the Revelation of John.

[211] As textual critics, moreover, we are no longer endeavoring to discover the pure original text, of which C. von Tischendorf dreamed. We seek to reconstruct the less corrupt text.

[212] Schnackenburg, *St. John*, 3:313.

Some commentators make the exegetical move of removing the Beloved Disciple from the inclusive plural in 20:9 in order to preserve the interpretation that depicts the Beloved Disciple believing in Jesus' resurrection. But surely the Beloved Disciple is included in that plural verb: "*they* did not yet know the Scripture." Schnackenburg correctly observed that the plural verb is difficult to understand in light of the exegesis that 20:8 means the Beloved Disciple believed in Jesus' resurrection; but he does not seem to show requisite sensitivity to the Johannine narrative when he proceeds to argue that originally, in a putative but lost source, "the concern was with Peter and Mary who, through the inspection of the tomb, did not attain faith in Jesus' resurrection." He can thus conclude "then v. 9 fits excellently in that connection."[213] Has he not succumbed to the temptation to interpret a text that is lost, and missed the meaning of the narrative given to us?

A few commentators even tend to contradict themselves in attempting to isolate 20:8 from 20:9 and to interpret each as if it is hermetically sealed from the other. Hence, Lindars concluded that 20:8 means that the Beloved Disciple "has reached Resurrection faith without an appearance of Jesus." Then he interpreted 20:9 to mean something appreciably different: "It is important at this point to see what John is doing. That Jesus should rise from the dead has not so far even been thought of. The tomb has been found empty. Mary Magdalene drew the wrong conclusion, that the body had been stolen."[214]

I can agree with Lindars in only two of his points. First, we must attempt to see what the narrator "is doing." According to 20:9 Mary Magdalene, Peter, and the Beloved Disciple did not consider, or think, that the empty tomb meant Jesus had been resurrected.[215] Second and most importantly, 20:9 occurs in the Johannine narrative when resurrection faith "has not so far even been thought of."

Some theologically insightful commentators have interpreted 20:9 to denote the truth that Christian "believing" is a life-long adventure. Hence, Marsh wrote that this verse should be interpreted as follows: "the process of understanding all that Jesus Christ was and did sets the Christian out upon an unending adventure in coming to know more and more of the fullness of God's purpose as revealed in scripture."[216] This insight is axiomatic, but it is not anchored in the intention of 20:9. Even though Marsh

---

[213] Schnackenburg, *St. John*, 3:313.

[214] Lindars, *The Gospel of John*, 602.

[215] I am aware that Lindars may have been striving to understand 20:9 so that the author of the GosJn was awkwardly expressing the truth that inspired reading of Scripture has not yet developed in the Palestinian Jesus Movement.

[216] Marsh, *The Gospel of St. John*, 635.

correctly understood 20:8, has he allowed the brilliance of a theological profundity to blind him to the problems encountered in relating two *contiguous* verses, 20:8 and 20:9?

Two scholars have focused attention on the meaning of the face-cloth for comprehending the belief of the Beloved Disciple. B. Osborne asks what the presence of a face-cloth "would have conveyed in first-century Judaism." He draws attention to Isaiah 25:7-8 and with the use of an Aramaic Targum (namely Jonathan) concludes that first-century Jews conceptually linked face-cloth (or veil) with the abolition of death. Thus, by studying the use of face-cloth in the GosJn, Osborne surmises that Lazarus comes out of the grave with the face-cloth because he will die again. In contrast, Jesus is said to leave his face-cloth behind to signify that he "has conquered death definitively himself and will never die again, thereby through his Resurrection ushering in the age to come."[217] Osborne, convinced that the Beloved Disciple is the apostle John, thus concludes that he "believes that Christ has risen from the dead because the folded napkin tells him that the prophecy of Isaiah has been fulfilled: God has swallowed up death for ever."[218]

This is a clever and erudite study.[219] However, it is unconvincing. The latter Targums, including Targum Jonathan, should not be mined for ideas to understand first-century Jewish thought.[220] They all too often reflect the social and ideological world of much later centuries. Also, the text of the GosJn does not make a clear link between Jesus' face-cloth and the belief of the Beloved Disciple. S. M. Schneiders, who apparently did not know of Osborne's article, came to a different meaning of the face-cloth for the Beloved Disciple's belief.[221] For her it is a "sign" through

---

[217] Osborne, *Heythrop Journal* 14 (1973) 440.

[218] Ibid.

[219] See also W. E. Reiser, "The Case of the Tidy Tomb: The Place of the Napkins of John 11:44 and 20:7," *Heythrop Journal* 14 (1973) 47-57. Reiser, who influenced Osborne, rightly pointed out that the Evangelist most likely intended the reader to perceive Jesus' resurrection in terms of Lazarus's rising out of the grave. I am convinced the Evangelist is indicating the difference between the resuscitation of Lazarus and the resurrection of Jesus.

[220] For a succinct and carefully controlled exegesis of early Jewish resurrection thought, see H. Lichtenberger, "Resurrection in the Intertestamental Literature and Rabbinic Theology," *Concilium* 5 (1993) 23-31.

[221] She does in more than one place tend to include in her conclusion the Beloved Disciple's belief in Jesus' resurrection; but it seems her stress is on the paschal mystery and not the resurrection, which is only implicit in the account of the BD as "the first stage in the revelation of the meaning of Easter as it is perceived by the fourth Evangelist" (Schneiders, *Biblical Theology Bulletin* 13 [1983] 97).

which "the properly disposed person can encounter the glory of God revealed in Jesus."[222] Rightly arguing that the GosJn must be interpreted in terms of its own pericopes, and not in light of the Synoptics, she concludes that in contrast to the Synoptics, the Beloved Disciple came to belief "on the basis of what he saw in the tomb." What did he believe? Seeing the "Johannine tomb account" as an "integral part of the fourth Evangelist's theological interpretation of the resurrection" and using "Peter's experience as a foil," the Evangelist, according to Schneiders, indicates that the Beloved Disciple's belief is "the perfect response and precisely that which is evoked by the 'signs' throughout the fourth gospel."[223] The Beloved Disciple believes in the paschal mystery, "the glorification of Jesus ... the return of Jesus to his own."[224] Hence, the face-cloth is not intended to indicate that the Beloved Disciple believed in Jesus' resurrection.[225] Consequently, an examination of the meaning of the face-cloth does not elicit resurrection faith.

Let us leave the apparent confusion among the commentators and return to the text, which alone is our source for understanding. The words "they did not know the Scripture, that he must ($\delta\varepsilon\hat{\imath}$)[226] rise from the dead" (20:9) mean not only that the scriptural basis for understanding resurrection faith had not yet been developed, but they also that they—Peter *and* the Beloved Disciple—did not yet believe in Jesus' resurrection. The author of chapters 1–20 never portrays Peter believing in Jesus' resurrection; hence, it becomes obvious why an editor felt compelled to add the Appendix.[227]

The former Professor of Biblical Theology at Yale Divinity School, Paul S. Minear, rightly emphasizes that the prevalent exegesis of 20:8 is unacceptable: "the context wholly fails to support that answer."[228] He correctly perceived that

> verse 9 makes no sense at all if at this time the beloved disciple saw and believed in the Resurrection: "for as yet they did not know the scripture, that he must rise from the dead." This is clearly said *after*

---

[222] Ibid., 94.

[223] Ibid., 96.

[224] Ibid., 96–97.

[225] Schneiders' presentation tends to mix resurrection belief into the Evangelist's portrayal of the BD's belief in Jesus' glory.

[226] Note the apocalyptic tone of this verse. Scripture is deterministic for the future.

[227] And it is certainly understandable why some scholars, e.g., Minear and Thyen (as noted earlier), have concluded that chapter 21 is not an appendix but the conclusion of the GosJn.

[228] Minear, *Interpretation* 30 (1976) 127.

the notice of the disciple's "belief." As in the case of Mary, the story discloses a misunderstanding by the disciples. John wanted his readers to learn that *even* the two leading disciples had been baffled by the empty grave and that this ignorance was the result of their ignorance of scripture.[229]

Minear continues to accentuate the point that the Beloved Disciple does not at that point in the narrative believe that Jesus has been resurrected. He states, "In a similar way, verse 10 excludes the possibility that this text refers to faith in the resurrection: 'then the disciples went back to their homes.'"[230]

Now, another problem emerges in the customary exegesis proposed by the commentators and Johannine experts. Can the author of the GosJn compose a drama in which the leading character exits in such a way? Surely in his concluding chapter, which is devoted to explaining that Jesus arose from the dead, he will intend to clarify that the Beloved Disciple professes personal belief in Jesus' resurrection.

But, when does the Beloved Disciple believe that Jesus has been raised? In my judgment, this essential and final development occurs in the final verses of the final chapter (in the original gospel). The Beloved Disciple—once anonymous—is probably disclosed to be Thomas. He presents the final and most beautiful confession in the gospel. He confesses "my Lord and my God." He is thus revealed before the Revealer; he is the "twin," Thomas.

Let us observe that if the Beloved Disciple really believed in Jesus' resurrection upon seeing the empty tomb and garments inside, then he was surely filled with joy. What a change would have occurred: he had witnessed Jesus die, observed a soldier pierce his side, and now he was confronted with the most sensationally glorious news that Jesus was spectacularly alive again. How could one think that he would thus simply return "home"? He could not have merely left Mary Magdalene standing outside the tomb, despondent and therefore weeping. He would have shared his joy with her.

She had run to him to report that the corpse had been moved. There is no reason to contend she thought the body had been stolen. The description of the grave garments, especially the face-cloth, makes that point clear, as do the words of 20:15, "Sir, if you have carried him away, tell me where you have placed him, and I will take him away." These words hark back to 19:41-42, according to which Jesus' corpse seems to have been hastily, and therefore possibly temporarily buried.

[229] Ibid., 127.
[230] Ibid.

Can the anonymous one be saluted as the *Beloved* Disciple when he does not show love for Mary Magdalene?[231] There is no evidence that he shares his ostensible "resurrection" faith with her. The narrator does not even hint that the Beloved Disciple shared his joy with her.

How can one assume a gifted author like the Fourth Evangelist would compose a passage which would tend, upon reflection, to contrast the ideal disciple with Mary Magdalene and even with his Lord? Jesus does show love for Mary in 20:16 when he calls to her. Unlike the Beloved Disciple, according to the commentators' exegesis, he does not leave her crying. He calls to her by name: "Mariam." The loving bond between them is surely represented in the affectionate reply of Mary: "Rabboni." This address is Semitic, and within the Semitic environment in which we now know the GosJn was formed and written, it not only denoted "teacher," but also connoted a fondness for the one who has revealed spiritual knowledge to her.

The contrast between Jesus' personal call to Mary Magdalene and the Beloved Disciple's lack of compassion for her is strikingly unattractive if one reads the narrative according to the commentators. They have him slip away in the shadows to some unknown place. This interpretation would generate an impression in the attentive reader that the "ideal disciple" was not a true disciple of Jesus, and certainly not a model for discipleship (as is surely demanded by the portrait of the BD in the GosJn).

If the author of the GosJn intended the scenario placarded by our long list of affirmations that 20:8 denotes resurrection faith, then the Beloved Disciple is portrayed in a way that does not enable him to follow Jesus' commandment and the concomitant demonstration that he is Jesus' disciple: "A new commandment I give to you, that you love one another; even as I have loved you, that you also love one another. By this all will know that you are my disciples, if you have love for one another" (13:34-35). If he knew Jesus was alive and did not share that insight with Mary Magdalene, who is grieving, then he did not show the love for her requisite of a disciple. That certainly cannot be the intention of the author and editor of the GosJn who endeavored to portray the Beloved Disciple as the ideal disciple and authentic witness to Jesus.

W. Schrage stipulates correctly that in the GosJn "Jesus' commandments are inseparable from his person," and that the love displayed by Jesus, especially in the humble washing of his disciples' feet, is paradig-

---

[231] Mary Magdalene appears in some later gnostic texts as if she is the Beloved Disciple. According to the *Gospel of Peter* 55b Jesus often kissed her on the mouth because he loved her more than the other disciples. According to the *Second Apocalypse of James* (Nag Hammadi, Codex V, 270) Jesus kissed her on the lips, embraced her, and hailed her as "My Beloved!"

matic. That means all the disciples are thus "bound by Jesus' example of love."[232] Any exegesis that portrays the model of discipleship—"the disciple whom Jesus loved"—as unloving is certainly unthinkable.[233] That means the Beloved Disciple cannot be "beloved" and at the same time believe in Jesus' resurrection and leave Mary weeping. The author of the GosJn apparently did not intend to suggest that the Beloved Disciple saw the empty tomb and graveclothes and went home happy and pleased that all was well, that indeed Jesus had arisen.

As scholars who come to familiar texts seeking to interpret them afresh, we should be resistant to any exegesis that presupposes that the context has no meaning. Is it not true that context is determinative in discerning the precise meaning of a word and a statement? Is the exegesis of 20:8 by the commentators not simply an example of ignoring context? Is their exegesis not clearly derived from preconceptions about the Beloved Disciple? To what extent is their interpretation of 20:8, "he saw and believed," an example of what J. Barr calls "*our* control" of texts in which we "allow our own preconceived ideas to dictate what we got out of the Scriptures"?[234] Have preconceived understandings of the Beloved Disciple detoured a fresh reading of chapter 20?

Is it not apparent that 20:1-15, *inter alia*, concerns the location of Jesus' corpse? It begins with Mary Magdalene going to the tomb and returning—running—to Peter and the Beloved Disciple with the report, "They have taken the Lord out of the tomb, and we do not know where they have laid him" (20:2).[235] This section continues with her asking someone whom she thinks is the gardener, "Sir [not Lord],[236] if you have

[232] W. Schrage, *The Ethics of the New Testament*, trans. D. E. Green (Philadelphia: Fortress, 1988) 307.

[233] One of the reasons commentators seem to defend the interpretation that has the BD almost slinking away and not sharing his newfound belief in Jesus' resurrection is the preoccupation with sources. Our eyes should be alert to possible *aporiai* and sources; but our vision should primarily be upon the text as we have received it.

[234] J. Barr, *The Semantics of Biblical Language* (London: SCM; Philadelphia: Trinity Press International, 1961, 1983, 1991) 5.

[235] The use of the plural "we" indicates that the author of this section is working with earlier traditions, according to which more than one person went to the tomb with Mary Magdalene (cf. Mk 16). Yet, what is impressive is the independent tradition in the Johannine narrative of the passion. As C. H. Dodd judged, the Johannine tradition here and its "apparent contacts with Jewish tradition, and the appreciation it shows of the situation before the great rebellion of A.D. 66, make it probable that this tradition was formulated, substantially, before that date, and in Palestine" (*Historical Tradition in the Fourth Gospel* [Cambridge: Cambridge Univ. Press, 1963] 150).

[236] This cannot be an example of the Evangelist's fondness for *double entendre*; but it may be an example of his use of irony.

carried him away, tell me where you have laid him, and I will take him away" (20:15). These are consistent thoughts.[237]

They are meaningful not only in light of the tomb being open and without a corpse inside, but also of the hasty burial: "In the place where he was crucified there was a garden, and in the garden a new tomb in which no one had ever been laid. There, because of the Jewish day of Preparation, as the tomb was close at hand, they laid Jesus" (19:41-42). Is not the impression given that the burial was not only rushed, but also, perhaps, provisional? In light of the common practice of "secondary burials" before 70 C.E. in and around Jerusalem, verified time and again by the recovery of "disarticulated bones" in ossuaries, it is not unthinkable that a corpse may be recovered (even though almost always this practice occurred much later when the flesh had decomposed). Mary Magdalene certainly thinks that the corpse has been moved to some other place; she even offers to "take it [or him] away." Nicodemus brought what appears to be an excessive amount of spices to enwrap Jesus' corpse. Perhaps these excess spices betray his intent to bury Jesus' body temporarily.[238]

Have we adequately understood the full dimensions of "believing" in the GosJn? Certainly the author wants the reader to continue (or begin)[239] believing that Jesus is God's Son, the one sent from above, and from the Father who sends, so that through believing the person may have "eternal life." Also, it is clear that in the GosJn "to believe" is almost always Christological, as it appears in numerous chapters with the meaning of believing "in me" (which means Jesus), or believing that Jesus had been sent from God.[240]

While Bultmann was correct to point out that "to believe" in the GosJn is "used in the general Christian sense for acceptance of the message about Jesus,"[241] not all uses of "to believe" in the GosJn are Christo-

---

[237] W. A. Meeks demonstrates that the question "where is Jesus?" is a very important and indeed ironical theme in the GosJn (*The Prophet-King: Moses Traditions and the Johannine Christology* [Leiden: Brill, 1967] 38).

[238] What happened to these spices? The narrator does not inform us.

[239] The Greek manuscripts report confusion between the aorist subjunctive and the present subjunctive in 19:35 and 20:31 (between πιστεύσητε and πιστεύητε).

[240] In the GosJn "to believe" is often used with the dative. As Bultmann stated, "Specifically Johannine is the fact that πιστεύειν is often used with the dat." Hence, the author of the GosJn attempts to rectify a possible problem in the kerygma: "He wants to make it plain that it is the One proclaimed who Himself meets and speaks with us in the kerygma. What the kerygma proclaims as an event, God's act, has itself the character of word." Thus the author of the GosJn "can call Jesus Himself the Logos (1:1)" ("πιστεύω κτλ.," *TDNT* 6.222).

[241] Ibid.

logical. In 5:46 πιστεύω is employed to express the thought that Judeans do not "believe" Moses. Furthermore, chapter 4 centers upon the belief of a Roman officer near Capernaum whose son was ill. He "believed" (ἐπίστευσεν) the word Jesus spoke to him that his son would live (according to 4:50); but upon knowing the hour of the healing it is said that he advances to a Christological belief: "he himself believed (καὶ ἐπίστευσεν αὐτός) and all his household" (4:53). Hence, the first use of πιστεύω was not Christological; it denoted only a belief in Jesus' power to heal. That observation makes it possible that the Beloved Disciple "believed" Mary's report or that the corpse was not in the tomb.

In chapter 11 we find the absolute use of πιστεύω as in 20:8. Jesus says, according to the GosJn, that he is pleased he was not present when Lazarus was ill, so that his disciples (11:12) might believe (ἵνα πιστεύσητε; 11:15). What does Jesus hope his disciples will believe?[242] The context suggests only that they will believe him that Lazarus is dead; they had thought, erroneously, that he was only asleep (11:13). The disciples are not intended here to have a belief that is Christological; there is no intention here to believe *in* Jesus.[243]

In 11:26 Jesus asks Lazarus's sister, Martha, "Do you believe this?" (πιστεύεις τοῦτο;). What is the noun or phrase to which "this" refers? It is to Jesus' words.[244] Likewise, according to 11:40, Jesus said to Martha, "Did I not tell you that if you would believe you would see the glory of God?" What is she to believe? Again πιστεύω is without an object. In light of 11:4, to which this verse refers, Martha is to believe not *in* Jesus, but that in raising Lazarus Jesus will be glorified: "so that the Son of God may be glorified by means of it" (δι' αὐτῆς; 11:4).

As is well known, πιστεύω is used throughout the GosJn with εἰς and with the dative. As Brown states, "*Pisteuein* with the dative is used for believing both in someone (Moses, Jesus, the Father) and in something (the word, Scripture) .... Of course, many times *pisteuein* is used absolutely without any object, and this construction has various shades of meaning."[245] Precisely; the verb itself is no proof of a Christological confession, let alone a confession in Jesus' resurrection (as so many scholars have tended to assume when interpreting 20:8). As Bultmann pointed out,

[242] Brown states that the verb here is "an attempt to represent the aspect of a single act in the aorist" (*Gospel*, 1:424).

[243] Schnackenburg, *St. John*, 2:327, argues that Jesus is striving (according to these verses) to strengthen the disciples' faith, because of the shaking events of the passion to come. I am convinced that this exegesis does not do justice to the immediate context of 11:15.

[244] Of course, in his words Jesus includes belief in himself.

[245] Brown, *Gospel*, 1:513.

πιστεύειν in the GosJn is customarily used in the "sense for acceptance of the message about Jesus."[246] This verb does not by definition, or context, denote or connote resurrection faith. Far from it, to believe in the GosJn, in the religious sense, is to trust "the word which is proclaimed by Jesus, and which proclaims Him."[247]

For the author of the GosJn, πιστεύω is not static. "To believe" is a verb and indicates that believing dynamically develops and grows, as is shown in so many passages (e.g., 4:46-54 and 9:1-41). It is not mere coincidence that the GosJn does not contain the noun πίστις, although it appears 142 times in the Pauline School (which includes Paul's own letters and those composed later under his name). The use of the noun πίστις might indicate that "belief" is a once and for all act. The Evangelist rather stresses the verb πιστεύω, which indicates that "believing" is a process.

In fact, the GosJn contains the verb πιστεύω 98 times, which is far more than in any other gospel (Mt = 11; Mk = 14; Lk = 9). The verb is employed more in the GosJn than in the letters written by and even attributed to Paul (54 times).[248] Hence, for the author of the GosJn "to believe" is a personal, continuous, dynamic commitment to the one believed to be sent into the world by Him Who Sends. In a certain sense, to believe is a process that is conceptually a miracle; it certainly is not a worldly act. To believe is an act of radical desecularization.[249]

The Evangelist presented πιστεύω in six morphological patterns.[250] First, he employed "to believe in" (πιστεύειν εἰς) with the accusative 36 times. Second, he wrote "to believe" (πιστεύειν) with the dative 18 times. Third, he chose the expression "to believe that" (πιστεύειν ὅτι) 13 times. Fourth, he penned "to believe" with a neuter accusative one time. Fifth, he used the verb in a nonsoteriological sense twice. Sixth, and most importantly for our exegesis of 20:8, he utilized "to believe" without an object 30 times.

The use of πιστεύω in 20:8 falls under the final category. In this passage the author did not choose to use his most repetitive expression, "to believe in." He could have written that the Beloved Disciple "believed in Jesus' resurrection." He chose not to do so.

---

[246] Bultmann, *TDNT* 6.222.

[247] Ibid., 223.

[248] The statistics are from R. Morgenthaler, *Statistik des neutestamentlichen Wortschatzes* (Stuttgart, Zürich: Gotthelf-Verlag, 1958, 1973) 132.

[249] As Bultmann argued, "The desecularization achieved in faith is not an act which man may freely accomplish for himself, as though the Word of Jesus were simply the occasion for it" (*TDNT* 6.224).

[250] I wish to acknowledge dependence on Schnackenburg, "The Notion of Faith in the Fourth Gospel," *St. John*, 1:558-75.

Why? It is because the Evangelist chose to write a gospel. Paul stressed that "faith" is essentially believing in the salvific nature of Christ's death and resurrection. The author of the GosJn rather emphasized that "believing" is grounded in the σάρξ and πνεῦμα of Jesus' earthly life. To believe is conceived as encountering Jesus—the Christ, the Son of God—as the One from Above who came to humans in the fleshly world in which they breathe, which is poetically presented in the incarnational Christology of the Prologue (1:1-18).

The uses of πιστεύω in 5:46, 4:40-53, 11:12-15, 11:26, 40 and the pervasive use of the verb "to believe" also indicate that this verb in the GosJn does not necessarily demand a Christological confession. Hence, the use of πιστεύω in 20:8 does not indicate that the Beloved Disciple upon seeing the empty tomb and graveclothes must have obtained a resurrection faith. It is conceivable that the author of the GosJn in the opening verses of chapter 20 intended the reader to perceive that the Beloved Disciple believed Mary Magdalene's report, perhaps whatever Peter may have said to him, and especially what he saw.

After Peter arrived and entered the tomb, the Beloved Disciple also entered the tomb. Then he saw the linen clothes and the face-cloth which were signs that Jesus' corpse was not there. He could have continued in his faith in Jesus as God's Son; but if the next verse helps us understand 20:8, then the Beloved Disciple could not have yet (οὐδέπω) understood the Scripture that Jesus must rise from the dead.[251]

It is interesting to ponder why no manuscript contains the plural "the Scriptures" in 20:9. There is a variant in 20:9 on "the Scripture." One manuscript omits this word, thus presenting the following: "for as yet they did not know that he must rise from the dead." Only one Vulgate manuscript has omitted this word; hence, the reading cannot be original and must postdate 384.[252] It is either a copyist's error or an intentional correction by some scribe who may have been struggling to comprehend the meaning of 20:9 in light of 20:8, which was assumed to denote resurrection belief (probably because of dogma and theological treatises by the time of the Vulgate version).

We can only speculate what passage in "Scripture" was intended; but we do know that 20:9 means: *"for as yet they did not know the Scrip-*

---

[251] Interesting, but unpersuasive, is the attempt to claim that the reference to Scripture in 20:9 "would implicitly confirm" the BD's resurrection faith. See Brown, et al., "Simon Peter and the Beloved Disciple (John 13-20)," *Peter in the New Testament*, 137.

[252] Jerome completed the Vulgate version of the Gospels in 384. For a succinct and authoritative study, see A. Vööbus, *Early Versions of the New Testament* (Papers of the Estonian Theological Society in Exile 6; Stockholm: 1954) 56-57. No publisher is given for this book.

ture *that he must rise from the dead.*" This reading makes it pellucidly clear that 20:8 cannot contain full resurrection belief. The Greek ἐπίστευσεν cannot be a perfective aorist denoting resurrection belief that is fully developed. Perhaps the intended meaning is an inceptive aorist, which would mean "he began to believe." Let us focus on the meanings of the aorist.

The verb in 20:8, an aorist ἐπίστευσεν, represents a punctiliar action.[253] It is not likely that the aorist here signifies an action that is presented as a whole without respect to its duration (constative aorist).[254] Grammatically, philologically, and syntactically ἐπίστευσεν in 20:8 can be an aorist either in which the end of an action is stressed (a perfective aorist) or in which the beginning of an action is emphasized (an ingressive aorist). Thus the author may be indicating that the Beloved Disciple believed either *what he saw*, Mary Magdalene's report, or *what he had been taught by Jesus*, and believed it at that time fully and completely (perfective aorist). This is entirely possible; but it is more likely in light of the developing drama of chapter 20 and the context, which *commences the resurrection stories*, that the author is implying that the Beloved Disciple, as he went into the empty tomb and saw the clothes and face-cloth, *began to develop a belief* that culminated in a full awareness that Jesus had been raised (inceptive aorist).

The last possibility certainly demands more narrative action for the Beloved Disciple. He cannot merely exit with Peter somewhere (πρὸς αὐτοὺς [20:10]). Note the well-attested variant πρὸς ἑαυτοὺς which would denote: "Then the disciples departed again to themselves." Neither reading allows for any communication with others, including Mary. We are left with the editorial comment that they left without understanding (20:9).

The importance of 20:9 for understanding 20:8, and the foundational need to observe the context of a possibly difficult passage, may not be reflected in modern commentaries on the GosJn, but it surely is evident in an ancient Greek version of the gospel. As Bultmann pointed out, Codex Bezae (D) inserts οὐκ before ἐπίστευσεν, which shifts 20:8 so that it means: "The other disciple, who reached the tomb first (the BD), also went in, and he saw and did not (*sic*) believe."[255] Bultmann judged that by

---

[253] Some exegetes fail to perceive that the Greek verbal system does not divide easily into past, present, and future tenses. It rather presents the kind of action (*Aktionsarten*).

[254] See Blass-Debrunner-Funk, Par. 332.

[255] In Codex Bezae the ουκ επιστευσεν is not added by a later hand. It is on the line with all the other words which are arranged on Folio 175 in one neat column. See *Codex Bezae Cantabrigiensis: Qvattvor Evangelia et Actvs Apostolorvm Complectens Graece et Latine* (Cambridge: C. J. Clay et Filios, 1899) which is available in ALTA microfilm; see ALTA Film 1987–B002.

this means "the gloss v. 9, which is difficult to understand, is manifestly made comprehensible; nevertheless the insertion is unreasonable, for the story would lose its point if it dealt in a skeptical fashion with the rivalry of the two disciples."[256]

It is clear that the reading in Codex Bezae is secondary. The Uncials Vaticanus and Sinaiticus are clear at this place in the text (each has an ε as augment and no evidence of a negative particle).[257] The Bezae οὐκ is a variant; it cannot be what the author of the GosJn intended. Codex Bezae of the fifth or sixth century C.E., as is well known, represents a challenging (even) aberrant text of the Greek New Testament. It does present alterations which improve the narrative (as in 20:8) and which sometimes support theological interpretations.[258] But, the variant does make it clear that some early Christians, and Greek scholars, thought 20:8 meant that *the Beloved Disciple did not at that point believe in Jesus' resurrection.* That interpretation seems demanded by the literal meaning of 20:9, as Bultmann and other distinguished commentators note.

They are also correct in judging that the story would lose its point if the Beloved Disciple would be portrayed as not believing, and then exit from the gospel. But, perhaps at this point he believed Mary's report, that Jesus was not in the tomb, or more likely, he began to receive the first inklings that Jesus had arisen. He then must return later in the narrative.[259] Such an interpretation of 20:8 explains away the problem Brown

---

[256] Bultmann, *John*, 684.

[257] The possibility must be dismissed that there is evidence that the Urschrift had ἀπιστέω, "to refuse to believe." There is no scribal correction in Codices Vaticanus or Sinaiticus and no trace of another reading. See the facsimiles: C. V. S. Barnabitae and I. C. M. Basiliani, eds., *Bibliorum Sacrorum: Graecus Codex Vaticanus* (Detroit: Brown & Thomas, 1982 [from the original book of 1868]) 146 (the first column, second line); and H. and K. Lake, eds., *Codex Sinaiticus: Petropolitanus—The New Testament* (Oxford: Clarendon Press, 1911; repr. Brown & Thomas of Detroit in 1982) on the page marked by John 20:1 (column one, 13 lines up from the bottom). The verb ἀπιστέω appears in the secondary ending of Mark at 16:11 and in Luke 24:11; and in each case describes how the disciples did not believe that Jesus had been resurrected. I am grateful to D. M. Smith for discussions on this dimension of the gospels.

[258] See E. J. Epp, *The Theological Tendency of Codex Bezae Cantabrigiensis in Acts* (SNTSMS 3; Cambridge: Cambridge Univ. Press, 1966) and C. K. Barrett, "Is There a Theological Tendency in Codex Bezae?" in *Text and Interpretation*, 15-27. Barrett judges that the tendency of D is "to exaggerate existing tendencies" (26). Unfortunately, D's variant in 20:8 was not included in the discussion.

[259] We are seeing more clearly not only the narrative flow of chapter 20, but also the need for an appendix (or epilogue).

recognizes: that the "belief of the Beloved Disciple has no effect on Magdalene nor on the disciples in general (19)."[260]

Has no scholar seen or perceived that the Beloved Disciple could have believed in something other than Jesus' resurrection? Yes. The Bishop of Hippo, St. Augustine (354–430), who immensely influenced Christian thought and shaped medieval theology, saw the obvious meaning of 20:8, by pointing out the contextual control over the meaning. In his homilies on the GosJn, in Tractate 120, he reflected on the meaning of this verse. He wrote,

> "And he saw, and believed." Here some, by not giving due attention *(Hic nonnulli parum attendentes)*, suppose that John believed that Jesus had risen again; but there is no indication of this from the words that follow *(sed quod sequitur, hoc non indicat)*. For what does he mean by immediately adding, "For as yet they knew not the scripture, that He must rise again from the dead"? He could not then have believed that He had risen again *(Non ergo eum credidit resurrexisse)*, when he did not know that it behooved Him to rise again. What then did he see? What was it that he believed? What but this, that he saw the sepulchre empty, and believed what the woman had said, that He had been taken away from the tomb? "For as yet they knew not the scripture, that He must rise again from the dead."[261]

Why would the author of the GosJn want to report that the Beloved Disciple believed Mary Magdalene's report? Is it not obvious that it was necessary to prove forensically her claim regarding the tomb of a Jew who had been crucified and not accepted by the Temple establishment? Her claim would not only be rejected, but it would cause derision, since she was a woman who may not have owned a sterling reputation. Who could better supply this credibility, prove the validity of Mary Magdalene's witness, than the one who is the witness to the traditions in the gospel—and whose witness is substantiated in the GosJn? The need for shoring up Mary Magdalene's report seems rather obvious; thus, both Peter and the Beloved Disciple are presented as the two male witnesses needed to establish the fact that the tomb was empty. The author of the GosJn knew

---

[260] Brown, *Gospel*, 2:995. He also lists what he rightly perceives as "an extraordinary number of inconsistencies" in the GosJn 20:1-18, "that betray the hand of an editor who has achieved organization by combining disparate material." There can be no doubt that the author of the GosJn inherited and edited sources, more than one, and that they have left their mark on chapter 20.

[261] Augustine, "Homilies on the Gospel of John," in *A Select Library of the Nicene and Post-Nicene Fathers of the Christian Church*, ed. P. Schaff (Edinburgh: T & T Clark, [repr. 1986]) 7:436. The Latin is from J.-P. Migne, *Sancti Aurelii Augustini* (Paris, 1841) 3:1955.

Jewish law and even stated the requisite statute: "In your Torah it is writ-ten that the witness of two men is true" (8:17). Few scholars have seen the importance of presenting two males as witnesses to what Mary reported; but Marsh wisely stated that the author of the GosJn "now tells how Peter and the beloved disciple come and witness the fact of the empty tomb. He is concerned to have witness and testimony that could be regarded as adequate in the courts of men—two adult male witnesses."[262]

St. Augustine's exegesis, that the Beloved Disciple believed Mary's report, has been examined by I. A. Ramsey, who rejects it. He observes that in 20:1-10 three different verbs for "to see" are used by the author (βλέπω, θεωρέω, ὁράω). According to him, each is a progression in per-ception. In 20:5 the Beloved Disciple arrives at the tomb and stooping down only "saw" the linen clothes; the verb for "saw" is βλέπω, which according to Ramsey means merely "what happens when I turn my head in a particular direction in good light and keep my eyes open."[263] In 20:6 Peter arrived, entered the tomb and "saw" not only the linen clothes, but also the face-cloth; the verb this time is θεωρέω, which according to Ram-sey denotes seeing to behold, look at, and notice.[264] Then the Beloved Disciple entered the tomb, "saw and believed." A third verb is used; it is εἶδεν (second aorist of ὁράω). According to Ramsey, this is confirmation that the Beloved Disciple alone obtained spiritual insight: "Here is a "see-ing" which tells of a discernment, a seeing which is a response to a dis-closure: something breaks in on us and around the appearances."[265] For Ramsey, then 20:1-10, through three different verbs for "to see," denotes "the glancing eye; the eye for detail; and the eye of faith."[266]

In his book, *Two Disciples at the Tomb*, R. Mahoney judges that Ramsey has judiciously understood the intention of the author of chapter 20 and the development of the narrative. Mahoney states that here is a "build-up to the leap of faith in verse 8."[267]

How insightful are Ramsey's comments? First, it is probable that Augustine knew that three different verbs were employed by the author of the GosJn; but he did not think that different meanings were thereby intended. Indeed, the meanings of these verbs are not as neatly distin-guished as Ramsey contends. They are different verbs and may be trans-

---

[262] Marsh, *The Gospel of St. John*, 631.

[263] I. A. Ramsey, *Christian Discourse: Some Logical Explorations* (London: Oxford Univ. Press, 1965) 2.

[264] Ibid., 3.

[265] Ibid.

[266] Ibid., 4-5.

[267] R. Mahoney, *Two Disciples at the Tomb: The Background Message of John 20.1-10* (Theologie und Wirklichkeit 6; Bern: Herbert Lang; Frankfurt: Peter Lang, 1974) 262.

lated with different English words, as did James Moffatt.[268] The verb βλέπω can mean not only "to see," or "to look at," but it also connotes spiritual sight. In fact, our author uses this verb to denote the spiritual seeing desired by Jesus. According to 9:39 Jesus has come into the world so that those who do not see may see (βλέπω). The verb θεωρέω means not only seeing some details; it also means "to look at," "to observe," and "to perceive." Focusing myopically on this one verb, one could continue Ramsey's argument to "prove" that Peter "perceived" the truth. Finally, the verb ὁράω in the GosJn can mean not only "perceive," but also "see." In fact, according to our author this same verb is used to contrast "seeing" with "believing": "Blessed are those who do not see (ἰδόντες which is the second aorist participle from ὁράω) and yet believe" (20:29). The case for the Beloved Disciple's believing in Jesus' resurrection according to 20:1-10 cannot be built on a philological study of the three verbs used by the author of the GosJn. It seems that Ramsey is not primarily interested in Greek philology, let alone in the Jewishness of the GosJn and the narrative thrust and contextual meaning of 20:8. He is interested in and focused upon how this section of the GosJn helps him understand and explain "Christian discourse."[269]

Even if Ramsey's argument regarding the meaning of the three Greek verbs could be substantiated, we would have to admit that we have not yet struggled with the meaning of the context of these verbs within 20:1-10, especially 20:8. The very next verse contains the information that the Beloved Disciple did not understand the Scripture that Jesus must rise from the dead (20:9). That verse alone, especially following directly on the statement that the Beloved Disciple "saw and believed," certainly means that the Beloved Disciple has not yet fully and unequivocally believed in the resurrection.

Scholars, other than St. Augustine, have also advocated that 20:8 does not mean that the Beloved Disciple believed that Jesus had been raised from the dead. Martin Luther (1483–1546) added a note to the verb "believed" (gleubets) in his translation of 20:8. In the margin he clarified what the Beloved Disciple believed. What did he believe? He believed what Mary Magdalene had said to him: "They have taken the Lord out of the tomb, and we do not know where they have laid him" (20:2).[270]

---

[268] James Moffatt used "seeth" in 20:1, "*looking in,* saw," in italics in 20:5, "seeth" in 20:6, and "saw" in 20:8. J. Moffatt, *The New Testament: A New Translation* (New York: Harper & Brothers Publishers, 1935 [new ed., rev.]) 284.

[269] Ramsey, *Christian Discourse*, 5.

[270] See the recent edition: M. Luther, *Biblia/das ist/die gantze Heilige Schrifft Deutsch*, 2 vols. (Frankfurt: Röderberg-Verlag, 1983) vol. 2, ad loc. cit. (In the left margin Luther wrote: "Das er were weg genomen wie Magdalena zu im gesagt hatte.")

Later in the same sixteenth century, John Calvin (1509–1564) discussed the meaning of 20:8 in his commentary on the GosJn, which was completed in 1552, and published in January 1553.[271] He rejected Luther's exegesis (which he did not mention by name) as "poor exposition." Displaying his advanced exegetical skills, but causing some problems with his own interpretation of 20:9, Calvin pointed out that the verb "to believe"—"when used simply and without any addition"—nowhere in the GosJn bears Luther's meaning.[272] As we have seen earlier, in the GosJn the verb "to believe" without an object can, and does, have a non-Christological meaning suggested by Luther. Calvin was clearer on what the Beloved Disciple (to him John) did not believe than in what he did believe (according to 20:8).

Calvin was well aware of the importance of context and the meaning of 20:9. According to him, "*Peter and John* [= the BD] return home, while they are still in doubt and perplexity."[273] These comments may well represent the intention of the author of the GosJn; but I doubt that he would have agreed with Calvin's choice of words when he contended that Peter and the Beloved Disciple had not yet been "awakened from their carnal stupidity."[274] It is also highly dubious that the narrator of the GosJn would agree with Calvin that Mary Magdalene remained at the tomb, after Peter and the Beloved Disciple went home, because of "only a mixture of superstition and carnal feeling."[275]

Most importantly, Calvin saw that 20:8 cannot denote resurrection faith without some fundamental qualifications. He must have contended that the aorist ἐπίστευσεν is an inceptive aorist; it denotes only the point at which resurrection belief may first be observed. Calvin recognized the importance of 20:9 in interpreting 20:8 and cautioned that the Beloved Disciple is "still far from the pure and clear knowledge of faith."[276] Calvin's insights, exegetically and philologically sound, should have protected exegetes from the wholesale affirmation, during this century, that the Beloved Disciple believed in Jesus' resurrection when he saw the graveclothes in the tomb. He grasped that the Beloved Disciple and Peter went home without obtaining full resurrection faith. He warned:

---

[271] Calvin, *The Gospel According to St. John*, trans. T. H. L. Parker, ed. D. W. Torrance and T. F. Torrance (Grand Rapids: Eerdmans, 1988) part 1, v.

[272] Calvin, *Commentary on the Gospel According to John*, trans. W. Pringle (Grand Rapids: Baker, 1989 [1848]) 2:251–52.

[273] Ibid., 2:252.

[274] Ibid., 2:254.

[275] Calvin, *The Gospel According to St. John*, part 2, 196.

[276] Ibid., part 2, 194.

> It is possible that their minds were still doubtful and uncertain when they returned home. For, although John [= the BD] says that they believed, it was not a steady faith, but only some confused sense of the miracle, and was like a trance until they received more confirmation.[277]

Thus, according to this interpretation, which is sound, narrative criticism would expect for the Beloved Disciple to return once again in the drama to illustrate pellucidly full resurrection faith. As the model for Johannine believing and discipleship, he cannot leave the drama representing only "some confused sense of the miracle" or exiting somewhat lost in a "trance." He should be the paradigm for full-blown commitment, and that would demand, in terms of drama, that he return again in the narrative. Perhaps Calvin's own native genius peers through, despite the centuries of denigrating Thomas which influenced Calvin,[278] when he admits—subsequent to these words—that "substantial faith could not be conceived by sight alone."[279]

In the eighteenth century John Wesley (1703-1791) commented on the meaning of 20:8. His exegesis points back to Luther's insight and indicates the meaning evident in the contextual setting of what the Beloved Disciple saw and believed. According to Wesley, the Beloved Disciple saw that "the body was not there." He believed that "they had taken it away, as Mary said." He adds that both Peter and the Beloved Disciple "had no thought of His rising again." They both went home, not "seeing what they could do further."[280] From these giants in church history—Augustine, Luther, Calvin, and Wesley—we jump to the modern historical critical period.

In 1882 Westcott, a brilliant Greek scholar, pointed to the different verbs for "to see," and explained that the Beloved Disciple's "simple sight" ($\beta\lambda\acute{\epsilon}\pi\epsilon\iota$) is contrasted with Peter's "intent regard ($\theta\epsilon\omega\rho\epsilon\hat{\iota}$)." He then focused upon the meaning of 20:8. It is clear that the Beloved Disciple saw, specifically what Peter had seen in the empty tomb: "the clear signs of the removal of the body of the Lord."[281] That statement leaves

---

[277] Ibid., part 2, 195.

[278] Calvin's words about Thomas are stunning: "Here is related Thomas' unbelief .... He was not merely slow and reluctant to believe. He was downright obstinate.... Thomas' stupidity was astonishing and monstrous.... He was not only obstinate, but also proud and insulting towards Christ." Calvin leaves the text when he advises that Thomas "boldly and fearlessly stretches out his hand as if unconscious of any wrongdoing" (Ibid., part 2, 209).

[279] Ibid., part 2, 195.

[280] J. Wesley, *Explanatory Notes Upon the New Testament* (London: Epworth Press, repr. 1952) 385.

[281] Westcott, *The Gospel According to St. John*, 290.

many options open. Westcott warned that the "exact interpretation" of 20:9 is "difficult." Here is his exegesis:

> It is not likely that it [the verb "believed"] means simply "believed that the body had been removed as Mary Magdalene reported." Such a conclusion was rather a matter of natural and immediate inference from what he saw. The use of the word absolutely rather points to the calm patient acceptance of a mystery as yet in part inexplicable with full confidence in the divine love. The threefold sign of the stone removed, the empty sepulchre, the grave-clothes leisurely arranged, indicated something still to be more fully shewn, and the apostle waited in trustful expectation for the interpretation.[282]

Westcott wisely perceived that 20:8-10 indicated that "something" was "still to be more fully shewn." Was that something the disclosure of the full resurrection belief of the Beloved Disciple?

In 1903 E. von Dobschütz, the distinguished professor of theology at the University of Jena, stated clearly that the empty tomb was not proof of Jesus' resurrection. His attention was primarily drawn to 1 Corinthians 15—which all specialists admit indicates that the empty tomb was not a proof of Jesus' resurrection; it was confirmed, according to the earliest teaching, preaching, and prophecy only by direct encounters with Jesus himself as risen Lord.[283]

E. von Dobschütz also discussed the GosJn. According to him, 20:8 denotes to the "mystical and anonymous" Beloved Disciple something "completely other than an Easter belief."[284] For proof he points to the contextual control of the next verse. It is, indeed, an editorial explanation of 20:8.

In 1934 G. W. Broomfield concluded that according to 20:8 the Beloved Disciple did not believe in Jesus' resurrection; he believed the report by Mary Magdalene. Broomfield rightly saw that this exegesis "removes all difficulties with regard to the story, and it has the great advantage of being the most obvious and natural interpretation of the text as it stands."[285]

---

[282] Ibid.

[283] A recent discussion of these points, along with the claim that early Christian prophecy was grounded on the kerygmatic explanation of Christ's victory over death through the crucifixion, is found in T. W. Gillespie, *The First Theologians: A Study in Early Christian Prophecy* (Grand Rapids: Eerdmans, 1994) see esp. 199–235.

[284] E. von Dobschütz, *Ostern und Pfingsten: Eine Studie zu I Korinther 15* (Leipzig: Hinrichs'sche Buchhandlung, 1903) 16.

[285] G. W. Broomfield, *John, Peter, and the Fourth Gospel* (London: S.P.C.K./New York: Macmillan, 1934) 49.

In 1956 W. Nauck asked, "What meaning does the empty grave have for belief in the resurrection according to the Evangelists' reports?"[286] After examining each intracanonical gospel, he sees that the reports about the empty grave are devoid of Christological confessions, and are theologically unreflective. They are totally uninfluenced by the Christology of the earliest Christians. He points out that despite its apologetic and polemical character, the GosJn does not present the empty grave and its graveclothes to demonstrate that Jesus has risen from the dead. The motive is simply to demonstrate the impossibility of believing that his corpse had been stolen. Nauck clarifies that the verb πιστεύω means not only "to believe," but also "to be convinced of." That is certainly a possible meaning of πιστεύω. Hence, according to Nauck, the Beloved Disciple was "convinced of" something (he does not specify what). The Fourth Evangelist thus does not understand the open grave to represent proof to awaken faith in Jesus' resurrection. The context, 20:9, surely indicates this interpretation.[287] Thus, I am in full agreement with J. A. T. Robinson when he stated, "No one expected to find a grave empty ... nor if they had would they have associated this with 'the resurrection.'"[288]

In 1968, without apparent knowledge of the position of Augustine, Luther, or Nauck, J. Kremer discussed the meaning of 20:8. In his book on the Easter faith of the four Evangelists, he asks if it is really possible to conclude that this verse means the Beloved Disciple believed in Jesus' resurrection. He stressed that this interpretation can never be demonstrated with any degree of certainty because of the clarifying force of 20:9. He concludes that the Beloved Disciple probably "believed" Mary Magdalene's report and confirmed it. That is a very important point, since the author of chapter 21 goes to such lengths to undergird the faithfulness of the Beloved Disciple's witness. Kremer also indicates, with philological insight, that ἐπίστευσεν can mean not only "he believed," but also "he certified." Hence, the Beloved Disciple serves in the narrative of the GosJn to certify the facts about the empty tomb.[289] This exegesis makes

---

[286] W. Nauck, "Die Bedeutung des leeren Grabes für den Glauben an den Auferstandenen," *Zeitschrift für die neutestamentliche Wissenschaft* 47 (1956) 243-67; esp. 249.

[287] See Nauck, *ZNW* 47 (1956) 254.

[288] J. A. T. Robinson in *Christ, Faith and History*, ed. S. W. Sykes and J. P. Clayton (New York/London: Cambridge Univ. Press, 1972) 49.

[289] J. Kremer, *Die Osterbotschaft der vier Evangelien: Versuch einer Auslegung der Berichte über das leere Grab und die Erscheinungen des Auferstandenen* (Stuttgart: Verlag Katholisches Bibelwerk, 1968, 1969 [3rd ed.]) 91: "Es ist gut möglich, dass Johannes hier das griechische Wort 'er glaubte' (ἐπίστευσεν) in dem Sinne von 'er vergewisserte sich' (von dem Tatbestand des leeren Grabes) verwendet."

eminent sense, since—as we have already seen—the forensic proof of Jesus' tomb being empty demands the independent report of *two men* (δύο ἀνθρώπων [8:17]),[290] Peter and the Beloved Disciple. The author of the GosJn knew well how to appeal rhetorically to Jewish norms of forensic argument (see 8:17-18).

In 1971 L. Morris, the Principal of Ridley College in Melbourne struggled to understand 20:1-10, and in particular 20:8. He rightly pointed out that the verbs "saw and believed" do not have an object. The object of the first verb seems to be "the grave clothes," because they are "at the moment the centre of attention." He continues his exegesis by rightly perceiving the context. What did the Beloved Disciple believe? Morris wrote, "That Jesus rose is the natural answer, but immediately John goes on to tell us that they did not yet know the scripture that Jesus must rise." It is not clear, however, that the "natural answer" is a belief in Jesus' resurrection. Fortunately, Morris continues in the attempt to understand the full context of 20:8. The meaning of 20:9 is important; the context may mean that the Beloved Disciple "believed that a resurrection had taken place, even despite his ignorance at this time of the significance of the scripture bearing on this point." Morris concludes his discussion by admitting that the Beloved Disciple may not have believed at this point in Jesus' resurrection (despite the meaning of the verb "to believe" in later sections of the chapter, in 20:25, 27, 29). The Beloved Disciple may have attained "some sort of faith." Or, he may have simply believed Mary Magdalene's report.[291]

In 1985 Whiteley, a Greek scholar in Oxford, perceptively argued that "believed" in 20:8 is an inceptive or ingressive aorist and that it "must be given its full force."[292] It denotes that at this point the Beloved Disciple began to believe. He begins to believe in Jesus' resurrection and "to believe in him as Lord."[293] For those who share my thesis that the Beloved Disciple is Thomas, Whiteley's philological insight helps galvanize the link between the Beloved Disciple and Thomas: the one whom the narrator portrays as believing fully in Jesus' lordship is Thomas, who subsequent to 20:8 looks at the resurrected Jesus, who is the crucified one, and confesses, "My Lord ...."

In 1987 L. W. Countryman presented a challenging exegesis of 20:8. He argued that Mary Magdalene assumed that "the body had been

---

[290] J. Gaffney rightly points out that we must attend not to forensic procedure, but to forensic rhetoric ("Believing and Knowing in the Fourth Gospel," *Theological Studies* 26 [1965] 215–41; see esp. 235–36).

[291] L. Morris, *The Gospel According to John* (Grand Rapids: Eerdmans, 1971) 833–34.

[292] Whiteley, *ANRW* II.25.3, 2499–50.

[293] Ibid., 2500.

stolen." He continued: "The beloved disciple fears that graverobbers have ransacked the tomb and that there is still a corpse inside that might pollute him if he should touch it."[294] While the fears of the Beloved Disciple probably have nothing to do with grave robbers, they may well be related to the exaggerated and elevated fears about pollution that were regnant in pre-70 Jerusalem (as indicated earlier).

Countryman's comment that the two disciples, Peter and the Beloved Disciple, found in the tomb "only an absence" is well couched. He then attends to what the Beloved Disciple believed:

> That is what the beloved disciple came to believe at this moment—a real absence of the polluting corpse, no more. It all means nothing to them because they "did not know" the writings that prophesied the resurrection. Peter and the beloved disciple are as much in the dark as the Magadalene.[295]

Countryman seems far better interpreting 20:8 in light of 20:9 than he is in discerning the various possible beliefs that the Beloved Disciple may have held according to the author of the GosJn. His comments are insightful and help point out the weaknesses in the claim that the Beloved Disciple must believe in Jesus' resurrection as he stands before the empty tomb.

Also in 1987, J. Zumstein pointed to the "difficile remarque du v. 9," and argued that the verse signified "l' extraordinaire foi" of the Beloved Disciple. In the previous paragraph he had stressed that when the author of the GosJn (who is not the BD) stated of the Beloved Disciple that "il vit et il crut" he meant that he was "par excellence le témoin compréhensif du destin du Christ, celui qui en donne, avant tout autre, la juste interprétation."[296] Thus the content of "he believed" need not be focused upon nor even inclusive of a resurrection belief. Zumstein emphasizes the superior cognitive powers of the Beloved Disciple ("sa supériorité dans l'ordre de la connaissance").[297]

In 1988 R. T. Fortna, well known in Johannine studies because of his pioneering work on the Gospel of Signs, published *The Fourth Gospel and its Predecessor*.[298] He argued that 20:1-22 contains a source inherited by the author of the GosJn. That is clear to most Johannine experts; what

---

[294] L. W. Countryman, *The Mystical Way in the Fourth Gospel* (Philadelphia: Fortress, 1987) 123.

[295] Ibid.

[296] Zumstein, "Le disciple bien-aimé," *Cahier biblique* 26 (1987) 53.

[297] Ibid.

[298] R. T. Fortna, *The Fourth Gospel and its Predecessor* (Philadelphia: Fortress, 1988).

is debated is whether the source can be isolated and recovered behind the text.[299]

For our purposes it is singularly important to note that Fortna sees behind 20:1-10 *a source* that concerns only Mary and Peter. Fortna's source has, "And he (Peter) went into the tomb and he saw the burying cloths lying. [And he wondered.] For as yet they (Mary and Peter) did not know the scripture." This is eminently sensible; it clarifies many problems. In particular it removes the tension between verses 8 and 9, and (unlike the present text of the GosJn) links verse 10 with 11. I think there are reasons to conclude that the Evangelist added the references to the Beloved Disciple.

Fortna, influenced by C. F. Evans's publication on resurrection in the New Testament,[300] states that the resurrection stories in the GosJn have no real place in the GosJn. That is certainly correct if we turn our reflections from Johannine narrative to Johannine theology. The author of the GosJn presents Jesus' crucifixion as his exaltation, since according to 12:32 Jesus will draw all to him when he is "lifted up ($\dot{v}\psi\omega\theta\tilde{\omega}$) from the earth." The Evangelist interprets this exaltation to refer to Jesus' crucifixion (12:33). Fortna rightly states that in 20:8 there "is no thought of the resurrection," even though the Christian reader (who must obviously know all about this belief) is informed concerning it.[301] Peter and the others "neither knew nor understand this *yet* ...."[302]

According to Fortna, the Evangelist added, among other words, "and to the other disciple whom Jesus loved" in 20:2, as well as "And then the other disciple, who had come first to the tomb, also went in and saw and believed" in 20:8. For Fortna the "napkin ... had been rolled up in a place by itself" is also added by the Evangelist, who uses it as a *sign* that the Beloved Disciple's faith was "exemplary since it was not prepared for even by scriptural prophecy."[303] Fortna does not delimit the Beloved Disciple's faith to Jesus' resurrection.

These erudite comments on the meaning of 20:8 are atypical. Commentators today, as became clear at the beginning of our study of 20:8, unanimously conclude otherwise. They contend that the Beloved Disciple "believed" that Jesus had been raised. We need again to attend to the sem-

---

[299] Fortna admits his "reconstruction contains some guesswork" (Ibid., 188).

[300] C. F. Evans, *Resurrection and the New Testament* (Studies in Biblical Theology Second Series 12; London: SCM, 1970) 116.

[301] The verse 20:9 indicates that subsequently "they"—Peter and the Beloved Disciple—knew the Scripture that Jesus must rise from the dead.

[302] Fortna, *The Fourth Gospel and its Prececessor*, 188 (italics his).

[303] Ibid., 191.

antic domain represented by the combining of "seeing" and "believing" in the GosJn, indeed the joining of them as in 20:8, καὶ εἶδεν καὶ ἐπίστευσεν. Both O. Cullmann and F. Hahn, outstanding New Testament scholars, have focused on the meaning of "seeing and believing" within the GosJn. They both point out that it embodies a characteristic Johannine theme. But the theme is not Jesus' resurrection. It is an affirmation of Jesus' Lordship (Herrlichkeit) within earthly history (irdischen Geschichte) which is introduced in the Prologue (1:14).[304]

The exegesis of 20:8 paraded in the major commentaries—we have seen—is not persuasive, and at times it is forced and insensitive to the intent of the Evangelist. The consensus has seriously hindered scholars in the search for the identity of the Beloved Disciple.

Has no recent commentator on the GosJn defended the exegesis of 20:8 that indicates the Beloved Disciple at that point in the narrative does not yet believe in Jesus' resurrection? Fortunately, one recent commentator, indeed one of the most gifted exegetes and a specialist who had an exceptional grasp not only of the New Testament and Jewish literature, but also of Gnosticism,[305] argued for the exegesis that I am laboring to establish in the field, focusing anew on 20:8. The author was G. W. MacRae. In his *Invitation to John* MacRae wrote the following:

> The real issue is what the beloved disciple "saw and believed." It is not actually said that Peter did not believe, and we need not pursue an unexpressed contrast. But what did the beloved disciple believe? Verse 9 says that "they had not yet understood the teaching of scripture, that he must rise from the dead" (the JB translation is too interpretative here).[306]

---

[304] O. Cullmann, "Εἶδεν καὶ ἐπίστευσεν: La vie de Jésus, object de la 'vue' et de la 'foi', d'après le quatrième Évangil," in *Aux sources de la tradition chrétienne: Mélanges offerts à M. Maurice Goguel à l'occasion de son soixante-dixième anniversaire* (Bibliothèque Théologique; Paris: Delachaux & Niestlé, 1950) 52–61; and F. Hahn, "Sehen und Glauben im Johannesevangelium," in *Neues Testament und Geschichte [Oscar Cullmann zum 70. Geburtstag]*, ed. H. Baltensweiler and B. Reicke (Zürich: Theologischer Verlag/Tübingen: Mohr [Siebeck], 1972) 125–41.

[305] It was because of his international reputation in New Testament research, in the Pseudepigrapha, in Gnosticism—indeed his overall competence—that I asked George MacRae to write a statement regarding the importance of the Pseudepigrapha to help introduce the *OTP*. I admired this person, and lament that he is no longer present to discuss such challenging issues as the identity of the BD.

[306] G. W. MacRae, *Invitation to John: A Commentary on the Gospel of John with Complete Text from the Jerusalem Bible* (Garden City, N.Y.: Image Books, 1978) 219.

MacRae thus pointed out the difficulty of claiming that the Beloved Disciple understood that Jesus had risen. In my opinion MacRae is correct. The text is not simple; it is profoundly symbolical. The context of 20:8 needs to be highlighted again: 20:9 states that he (and Peter) did not understand the Scripture that Jesus must rise from the dead, and the narrative continues with Mary Magdalene standing alone weeping. The following verses contextualize 20:8 and cumulatively indicate that the Beloved Disciple has not yet believed in Jesus' resurrection.

Verse 20:9 is indicative of the fact that up until the study of Israel's Scripture, the necessity of Jesus' resurrection was not perceived by the Beloved Disciple and other followers of Jesus. It is imperative to recall D. Juel's valid insight that the "beginnings of Christian reflection can be traced to interpretations of Israel's Scriptures, and the major focus of that scriptural interpretation was Jesus, the crucified and risen Messiah."[307] It was not a grave with burial clothes inside that elicited resurrection faith; but a tomb devoid of Jesus' body may constitute the first beginnings towards believing in Jesus' resurrection. Yet focusing too much on resurrection faith misses the *Tendenz* of Johannine theology. Since this point was made by MacRae, let us return to his exposition.

What does the Beloved Disciple believe according to MacRae? He continued,

> In light of other statements in the Gospel (see, e.g., the comment on 16:30), we may suppose he believed that Jesus had indeed returned to the Father, as he had promised. This is what constitutes true christological faith in the Fourth Gospel. Thus the resurrection as such is not (yet) the object of faith.[308]

MacRae accurately perceived that "believing" in the GosJn is not a static given, and that the content of "believing" is not primarily focused in Jesus' resurrection. That is why the noun πίστις is never used by the author or editor. Commentators have not adequately grasped the import of what has been developing in the field of New Testament studies. Exegetes must attend to the narrative mode in the GosJn. G. R. O'Day rightly points to the dynamic of revelation in the GosJn, notably in the scenes we have been studying. This dynamic, she writes, "cannot be conveyed by the categories of event or content, kerygma or dogma. Revelation is not static in the Fourth Gospel and therefore cannot be understood independently of the Fourth Gospel narrative. Without full attention to the revela-

---

[307] D. Juel, *Messianic Exegesis: Christological Interpretation of the Old Testament in Early Christianity* (Philadelphia: Fortress, 1988) 1.

[308] MacRae, *Invitation to John*, 219.

tory dynamic of the Fourth Gospel text, we are not in the world of the Fourth Evangelist."[309]

Thus let us turn to the passage mentioned by MacRae, namely 16:30. In 16:31 Jesus asks his disciples, "Do you now believe?" How is that "believing" defined? That would be significant in our exegesis of 20:8. His disciples had declared, "we believe that you come from God" (16:30). That is the very verse to which MacRae alluded. There is in this concept of "believing" no resurrection faith, even if the author of the GosJn obviously believes that Jesus is resurrected. Hence, the Beloved Disciple could have believed according to 20:8 that Jesus came from God (that would be the perfective meaning of the aorist). Perhaps the Evangelist has more than one meaning in his use of ἐπίστευσεν in 20:8; he may well have also employed the verb as an ingressive aorist, as I indicated earlier, to indicate that the Beloved Disciple now at this point began to consider that his full faith would also include the affirmation that Jesus had arisen.

Perhaps some critics will complain that MacRae has left the Beloved Disciple faced with Jesus' tomb, which is empty except for the grave-clothes and face-cloth, and not believing in Jesus' resurrection at this point in the narrative. They will point to his words, "we may suppose he believed that Jesus had indeed returned to the Father, as he had promised." How can MacRae claim that, critics will ask, and still hold that the Beloved Disciple did not believe in Jesus' resurrection? The answer is surely in the perception that the empty tomb means merely that Jesus' body is not there. It does not indicate where it may be. A disciple may well have believed that Jesus had returned to the Father without believing in a physical resurrection. Perhaps this possibility led the author of the GosJn to continue with his narrative, which contains the only intracanonical account that Jesus' crucifixion wounds could still be seen by those who saw the risen Jesus. The link between the Beloved Disciple and Thomas becomes even more obvious with this observation.

There is an additional unattractiveness to the consensus among commentators regarding 20:8. The regnant exegesis of this passage leaves the narrative of the GosJn with a confused ending. A reader in the first century (and, of course, of subsequent centuries also) could well have received the impression that the Beloved Disciple exits the scene, confused and devoid of the appropriate knowledge of God's providence clarified in Scripture, and goes home never again to return in the story.

As Neirynck astutely points out, "the Beloved Disciple did not communicate his belief to Peter."[310] The reader would be puzzled with numer-

---

[309] O'Day, *Revelation in the Fourth Gospel* (Philadelphia: Fortress Press, 1986) 45.

[310] Neirynck, *New Testament Studies* 36 (1990) 330.

ous questions: Why does he go home? What did he think and believe? If the Beloved Disciple is none other than Thomas, then the narrative—from beginning to end—has an impressive development and a resounding final scene. Narrative exegesis may well indicate the link forged between the Beloved Disciple and Thomas.

Another point needs to be made regarding the exegesis of 20:1-10 as we seek to understand the actions and thoughts of the Beloved Disciple. As many experts point out, 20:1-10 was written "to establish the fact that, though it was empty, the body of Jesus could not have been stolen, because the grave-clothes were still there (against the suggestion, therefore of Mt. 28.13)."[311] Since the face-cloth was "rolled up in a place by itself" (20:7), there is narrative proof that one cannot appeal to any disruption caused by either thieves or disciples.[312]

The possibility needs to be confronted that some readers of the GosJn may have thought that robbers stole the body. The motive for such a robbery certainly could have been stealing grave treasures, such as the approximately "100 pounds" of spices in which Jesus had been wrapped (19:39). The weight, nearly 100 Roman pounds, is equal to a little more than 65 pounds; and that is an excessive amount of very valuable commodities.[313] Ancient tomb robbers eagerly sought spices, as we know from the opening of Tutankhamun's tomb in which much of the gold and precious jewels were still present, but the spices had been stolen.[314] Two

---

[311] Lindars, *The Gospel of John*, 597.

[312] As G. Lüdemann perceives, "In v. 7 the rolled-up cloths are evidence of the impossibility of a tomb-robbing, since this would have been done in great haste, and it was difficult to fold up the linen clothes carefully. So this must be something other than a body snatching" (*The Resurrection of Jesus: History, Experience, Theology* [London: SCM, 1994] 153).

[313] On the one hand, the mention of an excessive amount of spices may be due to the Evangelist's penchant for extravagant numbers (cf. the excessive amount of wine [chap. 2] and the large number of fish caught [153 in chap. 21]). On the other hand, it may be due to the Evangelist's attempt to celebrate Jesus as a great teacher. At the death of Herod the Great 500 slaves ported spices for his funeral (*Ant* 17.199), and at the death of Rabbi Gamaliel the Elder (within two decades of Jesus' crucifixion) a proselyte named Onkelos is reputed to have offered up 80 pounds of spices (Billerbeck, 2:584). See the informative discussion by Beasley-Murray, *John*, 358–59. Also, see Dodd, *Historical Tradition in the Fourth Gospel* (Cambridge: Cambridge Univ. Press, 1965) 139; Brown, *Gospel*, 2:940–41. It is unlikely, as M.-J. Lagrange suggested, that the text contains "une erreur de copiste" (*Évangile selon Saint Jean* [Paris: Gabalda, 1936] 503).

[314] I am grateful to many Egyptians for discussions on this point, and for showing me the gold and then the tomb of Tutankhamun. Howard Carter reported that the ancient plundering of Tutankhamun's tomb "was done within a very few years of the king's burial" (1:188). The thieves "were either trapped

reasons for this choice is the portability of spices and the ease with which it can be sold.

Does that mean that robbers had stolen Jesus' corpse? The narrator's description of the graveclothes and face-cloth dispel that interpretation. Talbert rightly comments,

> If anyone had removed the body of Jesus, would he have stripped it first? Would he have left the cloths lying in an orderly fashion on the floor? Would he have taken the time to roll up the napkin and put it in a place by itself? Would he have left the costly cloths (so John Chrysostom, *Sermon on John* 85:4)? Jesus' body is absent from the tomb, but not because it has been stolen.[315]

Let us look again more closely at 20:7. The description of what was inside the tomb is often misunderstood. Are the "cloths lying in an orderly fashion on the floor?" Is the "face-cloth" rolled up in a place by itself? What did the Beloved Disciple see? What happened to the roughly 100 pounds of spices ("a mixture of myrrh and aloes")?

In the tomb, which was probably cut into the rock, were the cloths with which Jesus' corpse had been bound (19:40). Also, the Beloved Disciple saw the σουδάριον,[316] which probably denotes a face-cloth placed over Jesus' head above the skull wrapped in clothes.[317] It was not neatly folded. The Greek is ἐντετυλιγμένον, a perfect-passive verbal tense that denotes that the face-cloth was "rolled up," or "wrapped around." It does not have to mean someone rolled it up after Jesus' resurrection; it can denote that it remained the way it had been: rolled around, or still wrapped as it was when the corpse was there. Yet, as Brown points out,

---

within the tomb, or overtaken in their flight" (1:194). Tutankhamun's tomb was robbed twice during pharaonic times. The object of the "second robbery" was "the costly oils and unguents contained in the alabaster jars" (3:105). Carter offers the opinion that the "second robbery was evidently by another class of thiefs [*sic*], who sought only the costly oils and unguents contained in the numerous stone vessels" (3:103). Howard Carter, *The Tomb of Tut.Ankh.Amen*, 3 vols. (New York: Doran Company, 1923; London: Cassell and Co., Inc., 1933).

[315] Talbert, *Reading John*, 250.

[316] This Latin loan word (*sudarium*) denotes a towel or handkerchief for wiping away sweat (*sudo*, "to sweat").

[317] This face-cloth is not to be confused with the apocryphal story of Veronica (= Bernice). This legend took final shape around the fourteenth century. According to it Jesus wiped his face on her head cloth and left an imprint of his face. The legend evolved out of many traditions, including the Acts of Pilate, esp. chapter 7.

the attempts to claim that the graveclothes and face-cloth still portrayed the outline of the corpse, which was no longer there, would mean that Peter would also have believed, and the Evangelist has not even subtly at this point in his narrative intimated that Jesus, as resurrected Lord, can pass through objects.[318] These graveclothes signaled to the Beloved Disciple not that Jesus had been physically raised by God; they denoted—perhaps initially—that he had gone to his Father, as he said, or that Mary Magdalene's report was correct and the tomb no longer contained Jesus' corpse. The apologetic tone of 20:1-10 seems apparent, if not absolutely clear. The author of the GosJn leaves no doubt that the members of the Johannine Community knew that the body could not have been stolen.

The regnant consensus that the Beloved Disciple believed in Jesus' resurrection and left the stage for good in 20:10 depicts an awkward way for this leading character, the model of ideal discipleship, to exit this dramatic literary work. Minear pointed out this fact:

> Simon Peter and the beloved disciple ... had left the stage in 20:10, following an episode that can at best be termed indecisive. At that point the Evangelist had underscored two things about them: their ignorance of the scriptural predictions of the resurrection and their return to their own homes. Those two points disprove the usual inference that at that moment they believed that Jesus had been raised from the dead.[319]

Minear was convinced that what the Beloved Disciple "believed" according to 20:8 was what Mary had informed him.[320] This suggestion—as I have already indicated—makes admirable sense. It is in line with what I have been attempting to show: Given the forensic character of the GosJn and the recognition that two male witnesses are needed, it was incumbent on the Evangelist to state that Peter and the Beloved Disciple substantiated her report: the tomb was empty.

Numerous commentators assume, without exegetical support, that the author of the GosJn presents the Beloved Disciple as an antithesis to Thomas in chapter 20. These scholars contrast the Beloved Disciple with Thomas, contending that the former believed without seeing, but the latter needed tactile and visual proof. Crossan, for example, claims that "the story in John 20 exalts the Beloved Disciple over Thomas." He continues, "The Beloved Disciple *saw* only empty cloths and empty grave but

[318] Brown, *Gospel*, 2:1008.

[319] Minear, "The Original Functions of John 21," *Journal of Biblical Literature* 102 (1983) 85–98; esp. 91.

[320] Minear, "We Don't Know Where ... John 20:2," *Interpretation* 30 (1976) 129–39.

believed; Thomas needed to *see* and even wanted to touch the risen Jesus himself."[321]

One of the few scholars at least to consider the possibility that Thomas may be the Beloved Disciple, but only later to dismiss it, was Kraeling. In arguing that the Beloved Disciple is one of the disciples mentioned in 21:2, he writes that the choice cannot be "Thomas ... in the light of the contrast established between him and the beloved disciple."[322] We are not informed by Kraeling what the "contrast" is between Thomas and the Beloved Disciple.

A pattern, however, in the Johannine narrative may link favorably the Beloved Disciple and Thomas. Here is the schema:

Empty Tomb	*Resurrection Appearances*
Mary Magdalene's report	Mary Magdalene's report
Peter "saw"	The disciples "saw"
BD's need for verification of both	Thomas's need for verification of both
BD's seeing and believing	Thomas's seeing and believing

The transition from the empty tomb to the disciples' resurrection experiences are Mary Magdalene's words, "I have *seen* the Lord" (20:18). The transition from the disciples' experience to Thomas's confrontation with Jesus are the words, "We have *seen* the Lord" (20:25). Thomas must not be disparaged because he demanded "to *see.*" He and the Beloved Disciple, as well as Mary Magdalene and the unnamed disciples, see and so believe. The conceptual world of the Evangelist becomes clearer, perhaps, when we recall the Christian *Sententiae* of Sextus (c. 200 C.E.), especially 415b:

> The soul of a sage hears God.
> The soul of a sage is joined by God to God.
> The soul of a sage always sees God.

The final line, σοφοῦ ψυχὴ ἀεὶ θεὸν ὁρᾷ,[323] applies characteristically to both the Beloved Disciple and Thomas. The GosJn claims to be built on

---

[321] Crossan, *Jesus: A Revolutionary Biography*, 189 (italics his).

[322] Kraeling, *The Disciples* (Chicago: Rand McNally, 1966) 136.

[323] For the Greek and ET of Sextus I am indebted to W. T. Wilson, *The Mysteries of Righteousness: The Literary Composition and Genre of the Sentences of Pseudo-Phocylides* (TSAJ 40; Tübingen: Mohr [Siebeck], 1994) 30. Wilson used the Greek text published by H. Chadwick, ed., *The Sentences of Sextus* (TextsS 5; Cambridge: Cambridge Univ. Press, 1959) 58.

the trustworthy words of an eyewitness; such a trustful eyewitness must be able to claim to have *seen* the important aspects of Jesus' life just recorded. Both the Beloved Disciple and Thomas believe *only after seeing*, as is obvious by comparing 20:8 and 20:29.

This vital point is often missed by exegetes who have failed to ask how and in what ways the author of the GosJn links seeing and believing. Cullmann demonstrated that the GosJn opens and closes with an emphasis on the necessity of seeing for believing. In 1:14 we are told "we have seen his glory." Finally, the GosJn culminates "dans le récit de l'apôtre Thomas." Thomas's confession on seeing Jesus and Jesus' blessing on those who have not seen yet believe are "le couronnement de son ouvrage, à la fin même de l'évangile, parce qu'elle s'applique aux leceurs de tout le livre."[324] Jesus' words have been unfortunately misunderstood to denote that seeing, as Thomas demanded, is not important. In many publications Jesus' blessing is portrayed inaccurately as a malediction on Thomas. Such is certainly impossible in light of the narrative development from Andrew's declaration in 1:41 to Thomas's confession in 20:28 (and the BD in 21:7).

In a subsequent discussion we shall endeavor to show that Thomas is included in the blessing. Now it is wise to point out that the blessing is really a beatitude. The beatitude in 20:29 ($\mu\alpha\kappa\acute{\alpha}\rho\iota o\iota\ o\acute{\iota}$ ...) is unlike the second-person beatitudes of Luke 6:20-26 ("Blessed are you ..."); they are like the Beatitudes in Matthew 5:3-12, Sirach 14:20-27,[325] and the recently published Qumran Beatitudes (4Q525), in that the blessing is upon "those." GosJn 20:29, "Blessed are those who not seeing also continue believing," is similar to the Qumran beatitude formula: "Blessed are those who ...."[326]

It is essential to grasp the connection between Thomas's request to see with his own eyes and the claims that the GosJn is founded on an eyewitness. Note Cullmann's insight that the author of the GosJn "ne veut nullement dire par là que le témoignage oculaire soit sans importance. Au contraire, il est nécessaire que du vivant de Jésus, il y e ait eu qui aient vu ...."[327] Moreover, the author of the GosJn (and of 1 John)[328] empha-

---

[324] Cullmann, "Εἶδεν καὶ ἐπίστευσεν: La vie de Jésus, objet de la 'vue' et de la 'foi', d'après le quatrième Evangile," in *Aux sources de la tradition chrétienne*, 52-61.

[325] The link is closer with Matthew and Qumran; Sirach uses a third person singular: "Blessed [better: Happy] is he ...."

[326] See E. Puech, "4Q525 et les péricopes des Béatitudes en Ben Shira et Matthieu," *Revue biblique* 138 (1991) 80-106, and the judicious commentary on 4Q525 and Matthew by B. T. Viviano, "Beatitudes Found Among Dead Sea Scrolls," *Biblical Archaeology Review* 18 (1992) 53-66.

[327] Cullmann, in *Aux sources*, 54.

[328] 1John 1:1 founds Christian faith on that "which we have heard, which

sizes that Christian belief is founded on what eyewitnesses have really seen with their own eyes. Thus, Thomas—alone with Jesus—anchors the fact that believing has been founded on trustworthy, and not wishful, seeing. This point resounds with profundity when the exegete perceives that Thomas is indeed the Beloved Disciple, the trustworthy eyewitness that substantiates the claims in the GosJn.

These arguments are bolstered by the recognition that the Evangelist does not inform the reader what the Beloved Disciple saw and what he believed. In a profound sense it is misleading to attempt to perceive what he saw and believed. The drama is not experienced if we miss the fact that what we have in 20:8 is a rhetoric of suspense[329] or ambiguity (*amphibolia*).[330] As Cicero pointed out, the gifted linguist must delight and stir his audience (*De oratore* 69).[331] At this point the reader wonders: What did he see? What did he believe? The reader will read further to see how this drama will end. In reading on he will see what Johannine Christians knew: the identity of the Beloved Disciple.[332]

Summary

The exegesis of 20:8 has taken an extraordinary amount of space, because in my opinion the leading commentators for centuries, and especially in the last half century, have misinterpreted it. Most importantly, without a proper perception of its meaning we will miss the narrative and

---

we have seen with our eyes, which we have looked upon and touched with our hands." The exegesis of the GosJn which disparages Thomas for wanting to touch Jesus fails to see the importance of this concept in the Ancient Near East and within the Johannine Community.

[329] Here I am grateful for discussions with Hugh Anderson. See G. Kennedy, *The Art of Persuasion* (Princeton: Princeton Univ. Press, 1963) [The τάξις must be interesting (11)]; Kennedy, *The Art of Rhetoric in the Roman World: 300 B.C.-A.D. 300* (Princeton: Princeton Univ. Press, 1972); Kennedy, *Greek Rhetoric under Christian Emperors* (Princeton: Princeton Univ. Press, 1983); and esp. Kennedy, *New Testament Interpretation Through Rhetorical Criticism* (Chapel Hill/London: Univ. of North Carolina Press, 1984).

[330] See Kennedy, *Greek Rhetoric*, 83, for a chart that represents the rhetorical teachings of Hermogenes, who probably represents the general rhetoric of the first century C.E.

[331] See Kennedy, *The Art of Rhetoric*, 255.

[332] Kennedy rightly stressed the Evangelist's skills with rhetoric. The author's art is "especially" apparent in "the striking story of Thomas (20:24-29) and the fine concluding chapter on the encounter of Peter and the beloved disciple with the Lord" (*New Testament Interpretation Through Rhetorical Criticism*, 101).

sociological functions of chapter 20, and the subtle ways in which the Evangelist removes the mask hiding the identity of the Beloved Disciple.

We now see that experts could not have perceived that Thomas is probably the Beloved Disciple because of their erroneous interpretation of 20:8. Four points made in the study of this verse need to be summarized:

First, the variant in Codex Bezae is informative. It may indicate that some early Greek Christian scholars took 20:8 to mean that the Beloved Disciple did not then believe in Jesus' resurrection.[333]

Second, an examination of "to believe" in the GosJn indicates that this verb has multivalent meanings. It often means believing in Jesus as the one sent by the Father, and does not usually denote believing in Jesus' resurrection. We must observe that the verb is intransitive; the reader is informed only that "he believed." We are not informed "in" what or given an object of belief. The rhetoric of suspense moves the reader to ponder what has happened.

Third, the immediate context must not be ignored, explained away, or dismissed as an interpolation. All such suggestions seem to be self-serving hermeneutical moves that violate the exegetical norm that context is the key to interpretation. Clearly 20:9 means that Mary, Peter, and *also the Beloved Disciple* did not believe in Jesus' resurrection when faced with an empty tomb or with what might have been left inside.[334] The thrust of the GosJn is clear: belief in Jesus' resurrection is unexpected and even resisted. And this insight harmonizes beautifully with the reconstruction of the social setting of the GosJn: it is in a polemical relationship with followers of John the Baptist (who was not raised), Docetists (who caused a schism in the Johannine Community and needed to be told that Jesus *physically died and was physically raised*), and especially fellow Jews (who controlled the nearby synagogue and who, we can readily imagine, would decry any claim that Jesus had been resurrected because of the witness of a woman or contention that he was the only way to the Father).

A fragment from Hippolytus (c. 170–c. 236) is significant as we summarize our exegesis of the passages in which we find a clear reference to "the disciple whom Jesus loved." In a letter to a certain unnamed queen, Hippolytus writes that Jesus

> having risen, and being desirous to show that the same (body) had been raised which had also died, when his disciples were in doubt,

---

[333] One should also admit the possibility that Bezae's text is simply the result of an error by a copying scribe.

[334] Lüdemann speculates that a possible solution is that *edeisan* be understood as a "pluperfect: up until then—namely until what is depicted in v.8—they had not yet understood the scriptures" (*Resurrection*, 153).

called Thomas to him, and said, "Reach here; handle me, and see; for a spirit does not have bone and flesh, as you see that I have."[335]

The purpose of the Johannine narrative is correctly perceived by Hippolytus. Moreover, Thomas is given elevated prominence. Far from being a "Doubter" he is portrayed in this fragment as the disciple whom Jesus chose to serve others as the witness to his physical death.

The fragment might even give the impression that only Thomas did not doubt; the other disciples "were in doubt." Be this as it may, it is clear that Thomas is not contrasted unfavorably with the other disciples. He is the one to whom Jesus chose to reveal the truth about his resurrection. Thus he is the trustworthy witness to Jesus' resurrection, and it is this witness which is the mark of the ideal disciple whose witness validates the GosJn.

Fourth, experts are correct that the narrative of the GosJn indicates that the Beloved Disciple must not be allowed to exit the story without clearly professing belief in Jesus' resurrection, even if that content of believing is not central to the gospel. Their objection is partly removed by the completion of the GosJn with chapter 21. In it—and only in it—not only does Peter experience the risen Jesus and reinstatement by Jesus' empowering commands, but also in it the Beloved Disciple is given the confessional recognition of the man on the shore: "It is the Lord."[336]

When one realizes that the Beloved Disciple is indeed Thomas, then it is evident that 20:8 should be interpreted to mean that the Beloved Disciple, like Thomas, is not easily persuaded that Jesus has been raised. He does so later in the chapter, as Thomas—his real name—confronts the living Lord.[337] Also, in character with his actions in chapter 21, the Beloved Disciple does not immediately believe the stranger is Jesus. In fact, the one who composed the account states that "the disciples did not know that it was Jesus" (οὐ μέντοι ᾔδεισαν οἱ μαθηταὶ ὅτι Ἰησοῦς ἐστιν); hence, the Beloved Disciple is also included in this sweeping comment regarding the lack of knowledge. The Beloved Disciple obtains this knowledge only

---

[335] Hippolytus, apud Theodoret, Second Dialogue ἀσύγχυτος [*Works* 4.88]. See the translation and notes in ANF 5:240.

[336] Experts, like Minear and Thyen, who contend that chapter 21 is not an appendix by an editor, but the epilogue composed by the Evangelist to complete his own work, will appreciate the narrative necessity of 21 for Peter and the Beloved Disciple. In my assessment, chapter 21 completes what is missing for those who wish to elevate Peter and to clarify that the BD did expressly believe that Jesus had been raised. That was not necessary for those in the Johannine School who understood that the BD was Thomas, the one who presents the climactic and perspicacious expression of resurrection faith.

[337] It is conceivable that Thomas is also a nickname.

later (we are not informed how), out on the Sea of Tiberias and in a boat; then he declares and confesses ὁ κύριός ἐστιν.

Both the author and editor portray the Beloved Disciple as trustworthy, because he does not readily, and unreflectively, jump to conclusions. The link between the Beloved Disciple and Thomas looms as a very attractive, and highly probable hypothesis, at least to my comprehension of the GosJn and its setting. Is the Beloved Disciple Thomas; and is that hypothetical identity not only conceivable, but also probable, and even relatively certain?

In the following pages we shall explore additional evidence for this hypothetical identity for the Beloved Disciple. We shall also grow to perceive that the Beloved Disciple passages in the GosJn may well have been added by the author in a "second edition." They do, as Thyen stated, tend to control the Johannine tradition and protect it from outside and inside problems and polemics ("als Instrument für innerjohanneisches Krisenmanagement").[338]

2.2 RESULTS OF THE EXEGESIS: A SYNTHESIS

A disciple who is distinguished as "the disciple whom Jesus loved" appears for the first time in chapter 13. He is introduced at the Last Supper in a position of prominence. It is clear that he is one of Jesus' disciples, but he cannot be Peter.

He is superior to Peter, who must ask him to obtain insight from Jesus concerning the meaning of some of his words (13:23-26, 20:2). The author clarifies that the tradition of the GosJn is based on the witness of the Beloved Disciple, and that this male disciple, not Peter nor any other person, is the "disciple whom Jesus loved." If he is one of the Twelve (which explicitly includes only Thomas and Judas Iscariot), he is above Peter in prominence, insight, and witness. His superiority to Peter is further affirmed, *inter alia*, by his reaching the tomb first, and his paramount stature according to 21:20-24.

The Beloved Disciple is the only male disciple specifically mentioned as present at the crucifixion. His eyewitness account of Jesus' death verifies that Jesus was already dead when a soldier pierced his side (19:26-27). According to the Johannine narrative, Jesus' last pronouncement was to unite the Beloved Disciple to his mother as a "son."

Before that time the Beloved Disciple was obviously close to Jesus and may have also been close to his mother. The reader obtains the impression that he could have been a special friend also of Mary Magdalene (2:1-10); but this may well be too speculative. She and he were pres-

---

[338] Thyen, *Theologische Rundschau* N.F. 42 (1977) 251.

ent at the crucifixion. Because he was the only male disciple specifically mentioned with her at the cross, one could imagine that she runs to tell him, and incidentally Peter, that Jesus' corpse has been removed from the grave. The text, that is 20:2, however, states that she goes to Peter and to the Beloved Disciple. Peter is mentioned first. She certainly goes to both. At this point in the narrative the author does not elevate Peter over the Beloved Disciple; such prominence is only implied in the report that he beats Peter to the tomb.

The reader now wonders why Peter and the Beloved Disciple were together. Were they staying together in the same house and the other disciples living elsewhere? If they were living in the same house, then what is the intention of the conclusion of the account of their visit to the empty tomb? What is the meaning of the narrative that seems to imply that each goes to his respective home ($\pi\rho\grave{o}\varsigma$ $\alpha\grave{v}\tauo\grave{v}\varsigma$)?

The Beloved Disciple cannot be Lazarus, although the latter is introduced into the narrative as one Jesus "loved," for he is never identified as a disciple of Jesus. This is impressive when it is obvious that Joseph of Arimathea is clearly identified as "a disciple of Jesus" (19:38). Furthermore, the Beloved Disciple is a model of discipleship, for action and belief; yet the Evangelist never reports an action by Lazarus, or a saying of his—it is not even clear that he believes in Jesus, and he certainly does not witness to him.

The reader is left in suspense regarding the identity of the Beloved Disciple. His name is never clarified. The reader does not know if he is from Galilee or Judea. No passage describes how and when he—as "the disciple whom Jesus loved"—became a disciple of Jesus. We shall explore that issue in chapter 6.

Perhaps all the passages that mention the Beloved Disciple are after the raising of Lazarus because the second portion of the GosJn begins with chapter 13. That is, the GosJn is divided into two parts: the Book of Signs (1:19–12:50) and the Book of Glory (13:1–20:31). That means that the Beloved Disciple is the hero of the Book of Glory, since he appears for the first time in 13:23. There can be no doubt that he alone is the paramount witness to Jesus' glory. He saw the horrible death and the vacant grave; but he continued to believe in Jesus as the only One sent from the Father. Perhaps he also began at that time to begin to believe that Jesus had arisen.

According to the editor who expanded the GosJn, and added especially chapter 21, the Beloved Disciple is either Thomas called the Twin, Nathaniel of Cana, one of those of Zebedee, or one of the two anonymous disciples (21:2). We have observed that the only likely choice is the second name given: Didymus Thomas. It is obvious that the identity of the Beloved Disciple was known to the Johannine Community, because chapter 21 mirrors frustration, and perhaps even apostasy in the Community because of his death, and perhaps loss of faith in his witness. Some members of the Johannine Community misunderstood one of Jesus' sayings. They held that he was not to die until Jesus returned; yet he had passed away. There can be no doubt that the Beloved Disciple is the source of the Jesus tradition upon which the GosJn is founded. The author, editor, and others (note the "we" of 21:24) stress that his witness is reliable and true (19:35, 21:24). This indicates that his credibility was challenged not only by those outside the Community (especially the synagogal Jews), but also by those within the Community (cf. 21:22-23).

It is probable that the Beloved Disciple is Thomas. As the Beloved Disciple he sees the empty tomb, and along with Peter provides the requisite verification for the account of a woman, Mary Magdalene. He continues believing in Jesus and may begin to inculcate some resurrection belief. He goes home continuing to believe in Jesus as God's Son, not concerned about the empty tomb. Later Jesus appears to some disciples, but he—as Thomas—is not present, because he has gone home. He provides the model for discipleship: the empty tomb and its contents are not a threat to Johannine believing; they are also no proof of Jesus' resurrection. As Thomas he is critical of others who believe in ascents into heaven, visions and dreams, claims of angels, and even the reports of trustworthy friends, like Mary Magdalene and the other disciples. He is inquisitive; he is not a doubter. As Thomas, he asks Jesus concerning the way, framing Jesus' famous revelation "I am the way, the truth, and the life." As the Beloved Disciple, he seeks to know personally—by seeking and experiencing it himself—what Mary Magdalene had reported regarding the tomb. Later, as Thomas, he will not simply believe the reports of other disciples who enthusiastically claim that Jesus has been physically raised from the dead. The Beloved Disciple, Thomas, is the disciple who verifies accounts and proves that they are trustworthy so that others may believe in Jesus.

Eight days after Jesus appeared to the disciples for the first time, the Beloved Disciple, as Thomas, is with the disciples. Jesus appears to them a second time. He shows his marks of crucifixion and invites Thomas to touch him and to even place his hand in his side, thus allowing the request of Thomas. Earlier, as the Beloved Disciple, Thomas verified Jesus' physical death; now as Thomas he provides the final proof that Jesus physically rose from the dead.

Later, while fishing on the Lake of Tiberias, he sees Jesus' fourth resurrection appearance to his followers. Of the disciples in the boat, he is the only one who recognizes a stranger on the shore as Jesus. Peter responds by jumping into the sea and swimming to him. The GosJn concludes originally by quoting Thomas's words as a model of the supreme confession of a Johannine Christian. The Appendix concludes by blessing and affirming the trustworthiness of the Beloved Disciple's eyewitness report regarding Jesus, the Christ, the Son of God.

Thus, the thrust of chapter 20 is a reflection of the social crises confronting the Johannine Christians. Their adversaries, who were powerful enough to bar them from frequenting the synagogue for services, had polemically castigated them. They were more than ostracized; some were even killed for their faith (16:1-4). One can imagine their enemies pillorying them: you believed that a crucified Jew is the Son of God and resurrected from the dead. Your faith is without trustworthy foundation; it simply derives from an irreputable woman's report that in the darkness she saw that Jesus' tomb was empty, and that she had talked with angels. She even subsequently reported that a gardener was actually in the dim light perceived to be Jesus. If that is not absurd enough, you believe because of the report by frightened men who claimed to see a resurrected person. Such nonsense!

The author consummately forensically defends his fellow Christians in the Johannine Community. They did not believe because of an empty tomb. They did not believe angels ostensibly sitting in a tomb. They believed not primarily because of a woman's report. They believed because the disciples had seen Jesus alive again; and most importantly, they believed because one among them, Thomas the Beloved Disciple, did not believe unsubstantiated reports. He demanded empirical proof. Only after checking them out and proving that they were worthy of trusting did he confess.

Through Thomas's hard-won and examined knowledge and belief, the Evangelist presented the gospel as based on the trustworthy report of a reliable eyewitness, the Beloved Disciple. His report is trustworthy because he was critically inquisitive. He espoused no wishful belief. Such is the appropriate paradigm for model discipleship in the Johannine School.

2.3 WAS THE BELOVED DISCIPLE ONE OF THE TWELVE?

Was the Beloved Disciple one of the Twelve? New Testament scholars have been sharply divided as they attempted to answer this question. Those who are convinced he is John the son of Zebedee assume or try to demonstrate that the Beloved Disciple is one of the Twelve.[339] Those who contend he must be Lazarus presuppose or try to prove that he was not one of the Twelve. Clever exegetes can manipulate the evidence in the attempt to prove either option, but the methodology of the exegete must be inductive in seeking to discern answers the text itself may provide.

In attempting to ascertain the identity of the Beloved Disciple and to learn if the author of the GosJn assumed he was a member of the Twelve,

---

[339] See for example D. Muñoz León, "¿Es el apóstol Juan el discípulo amado?" *Estudios Biblicos* 45 (1987) 403–92.

I have appreciated scholars' insights regarding the dramatic nature of the Johannine narrative.[340] S. S. Smalley, for example, rightly perceives that the GosJn "is presented not simply as a story with dramatic elements, but as a highly-wrought and sustained drama, by means of which the Evangelist helps his audience to perceive the real significance of his message, and to respond to it."[341]

Not only is the GosJn high drama, but it is also a highly symbolical narrative. The whole helps to explain the parts. That is to say, the identity of the Beloved Disciple is not disclosed in one verse, pericope, or chapter; it becomes evident only when the whole work of art is appreciated and absorbed from numerous perspectives. While the early members of the Johannine Community obviously knew the identity of the Beloved Disciple, the author of the GosJn instructs his readers in subtle ways—perhaps inadvertently—regarding his identity.

In striving to discern whether the Beloved Disciple is one of the Twelve, numerous observations have either not been made or have been lost in other discussions. Let us begin with the following focused question: Where is the Twelve mentioned in the GosJn? This group plays a dominant role in the Synoptics,[342] but is mentioned only four times in the GosJn, and in only two chapters: 20 (20:24) and especially 6 (6:67, 70, 71). These statistics can be deceiving; looking only at them and knowing where the Beloved Disciple is mentioned would lead to the conclusion that he was not one of the Twelve. That conclusion would be premature, and could reflect the predilection to deny that he belonged to this group.

We learn little about the Twelve from chapter 6; but we are informed that Jesus speaks privately to the Twelve, that they do not leave Jesus as do many of his disciples, and that Peter (by implication), and Judas Iscariot are members of the Twelve. From chapter 20 we are told that Thomas, called the Twin, was a member of the Twelve. While the author wants the reader to know that Thomas was not present when Jesus appeared to some disciples, he has not introduced him cavalierly. There is an *inclusio* between the entrance of Thomas on stage and the culmination of the gospel. Note the formula:

11:16   Θωμᾶς ὁ λεγόμενος Δίδυμος
20:24   Θωμᾶς δὲ εἷς ἐκ τῶν δώδεκα, ὁ λεγόμενος Δίδυμος

---

[340] See the pioneering and still heuristically stimulating volume by R. H. Strachan titled *The Fourth Evangelist: Dramatist or Historian?* (London: Hodder and Stoughton, 1925).

[341] S. S. Smalley, *Thunder and Love: John's Revelation and John's Community* (Milton Keynes: Nelson Word Ltd., 1994) 66.

[342] According to Morgenthaler: 13 times in Matthew; 15 in Mark; 12 in Luke.

Perhaps one of the reasons the author must clarify that Thomas is one of the Twelve is because his readers were not aware of which disciples belonged to the Twelve and of the status of Thomas in that elite group.[343] Only at the end of the gospel is the reader informed that Thomas is one of the Twelve. There does, however, seem to be a subtle animosity against the Twelve (as we shall see). Yet, the Evangelist does not polemicize against it; he places Peter, Thomas, and Judas within it. Perhaps it is best to acknowledge that the Twelve is part of the tradition the Evangelist inherited, but its function and prestige are certainly not lauded in the GosJn.

There is another clue that the author either intentionally sequestered for the careful reader or inadvertently left in his narrative, as he apparently intended to diminish the importance of the Twelve.[344] The clue should not be missed in chapter 6.[345] The Twelve are distinguished from other disciples. They are the ones Jesus chose: οὐκ ἐγὼ ὑμᾶς τοὺς δώδεκα ἐξελεξάμην; "Did I not choose you, the Twelve?" The verb ἐκλέγομαι ("to choose," "to pick out") always appears in the GosJn in the aorist. Four of the five times it is the same form "I have chosen." It always denotes Jesus' action of selecting the Twelve from other disciples.

This verb and the noun "Twelve" appear for the first time in the GosJn in 6:70; and they are introduced with the formula just given. This verse denotes that the Twelve are those Jesus has chosen. That is significant; it may imply that the author of the GosJn indicates that only the Twelve were chosen by Jesus. He does not say that Jesus chose, for example, Mary Magdalene, Lazarus, or anyone who was not one of the Twelve.

It is certainly obvious that the Beloved Disciple is present at the Last Supper. He is depicted in the singular place of honor, resting on Jesus' chest (see also chap. 4, below). Does that not suggest he was one of the Twelve? Certainly not in itself alone; supporting evidence is necessary. Note the following recognitions.

[343] Here is another indication that the GosJn 1–20 should not be read as if it presupposes the Synoptics.

[344] Certainly, chapters 6 and 20 show the varied sources the author has inherited.

[345] If chapter 6 is redactional—that is, added as part of the second edition of the GosJn—then the editor of 1–20, the Evangelist in a second edition, has clarified that the "chosen" mentioned in chapter 13 are the Twelve. This suggestion is in line with the numerous observations made in this monograph that the author in the second edition has helped to lift the veil of secrecy from the face of the BD. The editor who added chapter 21 has removed the mask even more; but the original intention not to declare too obviously who the BD is continues in force.

Observe how the Twelve is subtly introduced in the beginning of the Last Supper scene. Jesus blesses his "disciples." The author of the GosJn knows that Judas is one of the Twelve, and that Jesus has chosen him as one of the Twelve (6:70-71); but he must not be included in the blessing (13:17). He thus has Jesus qualify the blessing (13:18), by employing the *terminus technicus* ἐξελεξάμην: "I am not speaking of all of you; I know whom I have chosen" (13:18).[346] One may deduce from these observations that Jesus washes the feet of the Twelve, and only those disciples. That is, when the author has Jesus say "I have chosen you" (ἐξελεξάμην) he means that Jesus has spoken only to those whom he has chosen, specifically the Twelve.

If this interpretation is sound, then the Beloved Disciple is clearly one of the Twelve. He is introduced in the next pericope. He is not only on center stage, but the spotlight falls upon him. He is the disciple "lying on the chest of Jesus" (13:23).

Further indication that the Beloved Disciple is one of the Twelve comes from the information preserved in the chapters added in the second edition of the GosJn, specifically chapters 15-17. In chapters 15-17 the ones addressed by Jesus are not specified; he speaks only to a group of disciples. No names are given and the Beloved Disciple is also surprisingly not mentioned. As is well known, the scene does not change. Disturbing the flow of the narrative, the Evangelist has Jesus launch into long speeches as the Last Supper apparently continues. During these revelatory discourses, Jesus refers to those present. He says to them, "You did not choose (ἐξελέξασθε) me, but I chose (ἐξελεξάμην) you" (15:16). A few lines later Jesus reiterates his thought, "I chose (ἐξελεξάμην) you out of the world" (15:19). He appears to be speaking only to the Twelve, since 6:70 and 13:18 indicate that the Twelve are the disciples whom Jesus has chosen.

The implications of 17:14-19 are that Jesus is addressing the Twelve. They are "men" and one of them is the Betrayer (17:12). A key phrase that helps identify the disciples is found in 16:4. In that verse Jesus apparently refers to those who have been with him "from the beginning" (ἐξ ἀρχῆς). This meaning becomes certain from 15:27, "you have been with me from the beginning (ἀπ᾽ ἀρχῆς)." This qualification would exclude Joseph of Arimathea, Nicodemus, Lazarus, and Mary Magdalene; it would apply aptly only to the Twelve. And most importantly, as we will discover in chapter 6, it applies most aptly to the Beloved Disciple.

It seems to follow that Jesus and the Twelve—and most likely only they, according to the drama of the narrative—were at the Last Supper.

---

[346] The narrator is restricted by history. He cannot dismiss Judas Iscariot from the Twelve nor present a drama in which he does not betray Jesus.

Thus the Beloved Disciple is not only one of the Twelve; but because of his honorific position, he is probably portrayed as their leader. As we have seen only three men are disclosed to be in that elite group, namely Peter, Judas Iscariot, and Thomas. Thus it seems to follow that the Beloved Disciple is either Peter, Judas Iscariot, or Thomas.

The leadership role of Thomas was made clear in chapter 11, when he exhorted his fellow disciples to follow Jesus even if it meant death (11:16).[347] His leadership role is also dramatically presented in chapters 13 and 14, in which the drama unfolds with questions which remind one of early rabbinic writings. The main characters in this scene are presented in the following order: Peter, Thomas, Philip, and Judas not Iscariot. The latter two may be members of the Twelve, but they are not dominant. The leaders are clearly Peter and Thomas, just as Peter and the Beloved Disciple are the main actors in chapters 13, 20:1-10, and 21.

In evaluating this data we need to remember that the author of the GosJn reduces the significance of the Twelve and expands the group represented by "disciples." Hence we need to wonder, as we continue our search for the identity of the Beloved Disciple, why the author stressed the importance of the Beloved Disciple and yet seems to disclose that he was one of the Twelve.

The same tension is found in the passage in which Thomas is finally revealed to be one of the Twelve. While the author attempts to reduce the importance of the Twelve, probably because of politics from western Christian groups, he also intends to present the Beloved Disciple and Thomas as members of this recognizably elite group. The narrative tension between the Twelve and the Beloved Disciple is paralleled by the friction between Peter and the Beloved Disciple. The GosJn seems not only to embody brilliant Christological reflections, but also to refract the flickering flames of political tension between a Petrine group and a Beloved Disciple group (we shall explore these social and political issues in chap. 8).

I can agree with Cullmann that the Beloved Disciple was "the representative of a particular group." But I must disagree with him and side with numerous Johannine experts in concluding that, while it is conceivable that the author of the GosJn may have reduced the significance of the Twelve, perhaps because some other Christians were exaggerating its importance and Peter as its head, there is no reason to conclude that the Beloved Disciple was "not one of the Twelve."[348]

Later we shall see that the Beloved Disciple is most likely the anonymous disciple of GosJn 1 (see chap. 6). We have been detecting and

---

[347] It is not insignificant that Thomas, if he is the BD, is the only disciple who followed this exhortation. Only the BD was at the cross.

[348] Cullmann, *The Johannine Circle*, 76.

amassing evidence that Thomas is the Beloved Disciple, and the author states explicitly that he was one of the Twelve. Thus it would seem to follow from those explorations that the Beloved Disciple was a member of the Twelve.

J. J. Gunther, in an article on "The Relation of the Beloved Disciple to the Twelve,"[349] concluded that the Beloved Disciple was a member of the Twelve. In Gunther's judgment the Beloved Disciple was added to the Twelve "in the final months" of Jesus' ministry. For him then to be called "the disciple whom Jesus loved" would suggest he was Jesus' brother: "Who but a brother could receive the special attention of Jesus without violating the other disciples' sense of propriety and equity?"[350] These are challenging thoughts; they may be on the right track since the author of the GosJn states that Jesus' brothers followed him to Capernaum (2:12; see 20:17 in which τοὺς ἀδελφούς certainly denotes Jesus' brothers, and contrast 7:5). Gunther speculates that the brother is Judas.[351] There may be some link then between the GosJn and the early Syriac tradition, preserved in many apocryphal documents and also in the Old Syriac Gospels, that Thomas is actually Judas Thomas, Jesus' brother (the Didymus).

The Johannine Community experienced a polemical ambience, especially with other Christian groups, notably those who elevated the Beloved Disciple's opponent, namely Peter. Chapters 1 through 20 indicate that the leader of the Twelve is not Peter; he is the Beloved Disciple (GosJn 13) or Thomas who leads and exhorts his fellow disciples (11:16). If the GosJn portrays the Beloved Disciple as the trustworthy witness to Jesus' traditions and the one who struggles successfully for supremacy over Peter, then he cannot be inferior to Peter who is a member of the Twelve. It has become virtually certain, according to the Johannine narrative, that the Beloved Disciple was one of the Twelve.

---

[349] J. J. Gunther, "The Relation of the Beloved Disciple to the Twelve," *Theologische Zeitschrift* 37 (1981) 129–48.

[350] Ibid., 148.

[351] Ibid., 144. Also see Gunter's "The Family of Jesus," *Evangelical Quarterly* 46 (1974) 33–35.

CHAPTER 3

The Beloved Disciple:
Scholars' Suggestions

According to 21:24 the Beloved Disciple is the witness who validates the gospel.[1] He is the unnamed disciple mentioned in the GosJn by the phrase "the disciple whom Jesus loved" ($\varepsilon\hat{\iota}\varsigma$ $\dot{\varepsilon}\kappa$ $\tau\hat{\omega}\nu$ $\mu\alpha\theta\eta\tau\hat{\omega}\nu$ ... $\ddot{o}\nu$ $\dot{\eta}\gamma\dot{\alpha}\pi\alpha$ $\dot{o}$ $'I\eta\sigma o\hat{\upsilon}\varsigma$).[2]

3.1 SCHOLARS' SUGGESTIONS OF THE IDENTITY OF THE BD

In this review of scholarly opinions of the historical background of the Beloved Disciple (das historischen Hintergrunds der Lieblingsjünger) I shall endeavor to be focused and succinct. Usually I begin, when appropriate, with a brief biographical sketch of the person being identified as the Beloved Disciple. Then scholars' opinions are presented chronologically. Finally, I often make some personal observations. This research ends with a question: "Who is the Beloved Disciple?" The present chapter of the book was written after the chapter on the exegesis of Beloved Disciple passages, but—of course—both chapters were intermittently edited during the same months.

In his 1992 publication, *The Secret Identity of the Beloved Disciple*, J. A. Grassi reviews five candidates for the Beloved Disciple:[3] John the son of Zebedee, Lazarus, John Mark, John the Presbyter, and a literary typos (that is, not a real person of history but a representative symbolic

---

[1] See esp. my chapter 1.4; also see Lindars, *The Gospel of John*, 31; Hengel, *Question*, 125, 129.

[2] See, e.g., 13:23. (The noun "apostle" does not appear in GosJn.)

[3] Earlier, in 1988, J. Kügler reviewed eight options: the apostle John, the elder John, John Mark, Matthias, the Rich Young Ruler, Judas Iscariot, Lazarus, and a literary fiction (*Der Jünger, den Jesus liebte*, 439–48).

figure).[4] In the same year Schmithals reported that scholars had suggested ten hypotheses for the identity of the Beloved Disciple: the apostle John, John the Elder, John Mark, Lazarus, the Rich Young Ruler, a beloved brother of Jesus, the unknown disciple of Mark 14:51-52, Andrew, Nathanael, and a literary fiction.[5] In 1994, in *John, the Son of Zebedee: The Life of a Legend*, A. Culpepper examined eleven scholarly hypotheses presented to identify or explain this epithet: the apostle John, Lazarus, John Mark, Matthias, the Rich Young Ruler, Paul, Benjamin, Gentile Christianity, An Itinerant and Prophetic Community, and the Elder who wrote 2 and 3 John.[6] Our review has turned up even more candidates, and most have been defended with erudition and insight by scholars famous in the field of Christian origins.[7]

There is a myth among scholars that until the last few decades Johannine specialists defended, almost *en masse*,[8] the conclusion that the author of the GosJn was John the son of Zebedee, and that he is the Beloved Disciple.[9] This review shows, on the one hand, that for over two hundred years experts on the GosJn have argued that the author of the

---

[4] J. A. Grassi, *The Secret Identity of the Beloved Disciple* (New York: Paulist Press, 1992) 5-18.

[5] W. Schmithals, "Die Lieblingsjünger-Redaktion," *Johannesevangelium und Johannesbriefe* (BZNW 64; Berlin/New York: Walter de Gruyter, 1992) 220-59.

[6] A. Culpepper, *John, the Son of Zebedee: The Life of a Legend* (Columbia, S.C.: Univ. of South Carolina Press, 1994).

[7] One of the best reviews of nineteenth-century scholarly opinions is by F. L. Godet in *Commentary on John's Gospel*, trans. T. Dwight (Grand Rapids: Kregel Publications, 1978, 1985 [1886]) 8-28.

[8] In 1966, for example, N. E. Johnson contended that for "years the traditional view was unchallenged" ("The Beloved Disciple and the Fourth Gospel," *Church Quarterly Review* 167 [1966] 278-91; cf. 278). Johnson defended the traditional view that the BD was the apostle John. I agree with Johnson that in the BD passages "it is interesting to note the great amount of detail, which must have come only from an eyewitness account or source" (280).

[9] In 1882, for example, S. Davidson of the University of Halle argued that the GosJn could not have been written by John the Apostle. He demonstrated that Justin Martyr did not know or use the GosJn, although his teaching on the Logos should have made him turn to it; hence, he concluded that the GosJn could not have been written by Justin's time. Davidson showed also that the GosJn was not accepted as the work of the apostle John until after 170, with the work of Irenaeus, Clement, and Tertullian (*An Introduction to the Study of the New Testament* [London: Longmans, Green, and Co., 1882 (2nd ed.)] 2:275-437). It will be important to remember his valid insights, but to distinguish between the late reception of the GosJn and its early composition.

GosJn cannot be John the Apostle,[10] and on the other hand, that many brilliant insights and heuristic perspectives have not been picked up by the leading commentators of this century.

Impossible to Decide (Jackson, Dodd, Colson, MacRae, Martyn)

In 1918 H. L. Jackson of Christ's College, Cambridge, distinguished himself from others who had been writing in the field. He knew most of the hypotheses that had been suggested by that time: the attempts to identify the Beloved Disciple with, for example, Judas Iscariot, Paul, Nathanael, Lazarus, John the son of Zebedee, and the suggestions that he is only symbolical. He found the hypothesis for the Rich Young Ruler a "tempting" conjecture, but he concluded with a *non liquet*: "the veil which hides the identity of 'the disciple whom Jesus loved' refuses to be drawn."[11]

In his influential commentary on the GosJn, which appeared in 1960, C. H. Dodd showed little interest in the identity of the Beloved Disciple. He was not in favor of a symbolic meaning, and felt that the individual was "enigmatic."[12]

In a penetratingly thoughtful monograph on the Beloved Disciple, titled *L'Énigme du disciple que Jésus aimait*, J. Colson strove to show that the author of the GosJn and the Beloved Disciple cannot be John the son of Zebedee. Colson was convinced that the former disciple of John the Baptist mentioned in 1:43-44 was not the Beloved Disciple but Philip, and that the anonymous disciple of 18:15-16 surely cannot be John the son of Zebedee. Colson gave considerable credence to the early martyrdom of John the son of Zebedee, who was not necessarily martyred at the same time as his brother. It is not clear what Colson concluded regarding the identity of the Beloved Disciple; he was more content to prove that the Beloved Disciple cannot be the apostle John.[13]

---

[10] Bruno Bauer, for example, concluded that the GosJn results from the creative work of a gifted reflective poet. See his first murmurings on this issue in *Kritik der evangelischen Geschichte des Johannes* (Bremen: Carl Schünemann, 1840; repr. Zürich/New York: Hildesheim, 1990) 59–60. Bauer, as is well known, is one of the first critics to claim that Jesus never existed.

[11] H. L. Jackson, *The Problem of the Fourth Gospel* (Cambridge: Cambridge Univ. Press, 1918) 168.

[12] C. H. Dodd, *The Interpretation of the Fourth Gospel* (Cambridge: Cambridge Univ. Press, 1960) 428, n. 2. Dodd judiciously evaluated the relationships among the GosJn and 1Jn and concluded that the "simplest hypothesis, however, seems to be that the author of the Epistle was a disciple of the Evangelist and a student of his work" (*The Johannine Epistles* [New York/London: Harper & Brothers, 1946] lvi).

[13] Colson, *L'Énigme du disciple que Jésus aimait*; for the discussions of the points made above see respectively pp. 15, 96–97, 65–84, and 73.

In 1978 G. W. MacRae did not feel compelled to seek a resolution between an ideal figure or a real person of history. He judged that perhaps "it is not essential to choose between these options."[14]

In 1979 J. L. Martyn published the second edition of his influential *History & Theology in the Fourth Gospel*. He rightly saw the need to clarify the historical origins of the GosJn, but also acknowledged that the "origin of the Fourth Gospel is enveloped by mists of unusual density." He set out to "achieve a single clearing among them." His task was focused; he endeavored to dispel only part of the mist, and warned that too often "interpreters have mistaken the achievement of a small clearing for a complete removal of the mists."[15] He certainly achieved much more than his modest expression of purpose allowed; he has helped show how Jewish is the matrix of the GosJn and that fear of being cast out of the synagogue was one of the concerns of the Johannine Christians. What did he think, however, about the identity of the Beloved Disciple? Regarding this issue he offered a sweeping judgment: "the 'Johannine Problem,' far from being settled, has grown during the last quarter-century, both in extent and in depth. Relatively few firm conclusions are shared by scholars who have troubled themselves to work with the document itself."[16]

A discussion of the Beloved Disciple and of the passages in which he appears are conspicuously absent in Martyn's book; hence, I called him and discussed the issue with him. He stated that he had given up on trying to understand the identity of the Beloved Disciple.[17] In his reconstruction of the origins of the GosJn and the tense synagogal drama, the Beloved Disciple plays no part.[18]

Ananda (Edmunds, Bruns)

In the sixties I argued that the caravan routes which brought spices, silk, and incense from the East to the West through ancient Palestine also brought cultural and religious ideas. Interest in the caravan and trade routes has been stimulated by the search for the origins of the cosmological ideas found in the erudite Jewish writings in the Old Testament Pseudepigrapha (notably the Books of Enoch) and by the evidence that many of the monumental buildings in Petra, the great caravan city in Jordan, date from the time of Hillel and Jesus. Hence, we can understand that the

---

[14] MacRae, *Invitation to John*, 173.

[15] J. L. Martyn, *History & Theology in the Fourth Gospel* (Nashville: Abingdon, 1979 [rev. and enl. ed.]) 11.

[16] Martyn, *History*, 17.

[17] The telephone conversation occurred in June 1994.

[18] Here is a major contrast between the reconstructions by Martyn and Culpepper.

dualism developed in the Rule of the Community was most likely influenced by Zurvanism (a form of Zoroastrianism).[19]

As Boyce shows, Theopompus referred to Zurvanism about 330 B.C.E. Additional evidence that Zurvanism has influenced Qumran thought is the observation that according to 1QM there will be three wars won by the Sons of Light and three by the Sons of Darkness, until finally the forces of Light will win the battle with God's intervention. This sounds very much like the Zurvanite concept of one god dominating another in war alternately for three thousand years until, after another three thousand years, one will smash the domain of the other. Zurvan is called the God of gods and the King of the gods in the recently published eastern gnostics texts.[20]

Scholars have also speculated that the East—especially Buddhism—has influenced the West before the rise of Christianity in the second half of the first century C.E. In 1969 J. E. Ménard claimed that the earliest forms of Gnosticism appeared in Alexandria, in which he traced influences from Buddhism as early as the time of the Ptolemies.[21] In 1973 M. Philonenko speculated that some of the ideas and phrases in the Epistle of James come from Essene circles in which Buddhism had helped shape Jewish thought.[22] It is no surprise, therefore, that some scholars trained in Buddhism have sought to help our search for the identity of the Beloved Disciple by turning to the East.

In 1911 A. J. Edmunds expressed his opinion that the Beloved Disciple may reflect some of the ideas associated with Ananda, Gautama's special disciple.[23] In 1973 J. E. Bruns, after authoring two books on possible influences from Buddhism on the GosJn,[24] published an article

[19] See Charlesworth, *John and the Dead Sea Scrolls*, esp. the Foreword of 1989. Also see M. Boyce, ed. and trans., "A Zoroastrian Heresy: Zurvanism," *Zoroastrianism* (Textual Sources for the Study of Religion; Chicago: Chicago Univ. Press, 1984) 96–99.

[20] See H.-J. Klimkeit, *Gnosis on the Silk Road: Gnostic Texts from Central Asia* (San Francisco: Harper, 1993) 340 and 351.

[21] J. E. Ménard, "Le origines de la Gnose," *Revue des Sciences Religieuses* 43 (1969) 24–38.

[22] M. Philonenko, "Un Écho de la prédication d'Asoka dans l'épître de Jacques," *Ex Orbe Religionum Studia Geo Widengren Oblata* (Leiden: Brill, 1972) 1:254–65.

[23] A. J. Edmunds, *Buddhist Texts Quoted as Scripture by the Gospel of John: A Discovery in the Lower Criticism* (Philadelphia: Maurice Brix and A. J. Edmunds, 1906) 22.

[24] J. E. Bruns, *The Art and Thought of John* (New York: Herder and Herder, 1969); Bruns, *The Christian Buddhism of St. John: New Insights into the Fourth Gospel* (New York: Paulist, 1971).

devoted to proving that "the only real parallel to the beloved disciple in religious literature" is in Buddhist scriptures that focus on Ananda.[25] Bruns pointed out that, like the Beloved Disciple, Ananda remembered the words of his master (Buddha), repeated them openly to the assemblies, was very near to his lord (Gautama) in "acts of love," and remained by his master's side until the very end. Bruns is convinced that "some of the mystery surrounding" the GosJn and its community "may perhaps be sought in its (hypothetical) contact" with Buddhism.

I would be more willing to accept the hypothesis that the Beloved Disciple did not develop within Early Judaism and earliest Christianity but from contacts with Mahayana Buddhism, even with Gautama's Ananda, if the latter would have been labeled the disciple (or student) whom Gautama loved, and if there were other *Stichworten* that would link the GosJn and Buddhism. In fact, Ananda is portrayed in ways inappropriate for a model disciple like the Beloved Disciple. While he is depicted as "the body attendant" of Buddha, he complains to him.[26] Ananda is portrayed in error and he misunderstands; he claims prematurely that Gautauma has passed into Nirvana.

To be complete, I must at least note that in Hinduism there is a far more stunning parallel to the Beloved Disciple than Ananda. He is Arjuna, whom R. C. Zaehner identified as "Krishna's bosom friend."[27] Thoughts about the possible background of the GosJn in 1:18 and 13:23 are thus appropriate when we hear the Johannine-like aspect of Krishna, "the incarnate God and inseparable friend of Arjuna,"[28] who imparts salvific knowledge to his favorite disciple.[29] Arjuna can appeal to his divine teacher, "Krishna, I beg you, tell me frankly and clearly what I ought to do. I am your disciple. I put myself into your hands. Show me the way."[30] Reminiscent of "the disciple whom Jesus loved" is the emphasis

[25] J. E. Bruns, "Ananda: The Fourth Evangelist's Model for 'the Disciple Whom Jesus Loved'?" *Studies in Religion/Sciences Religieuses* 3 (1973) 236–43.

[26] Note the following: "the body attendant of The Blessed One, Ananda, complained to The Blessed One" (trans. from H. C. Warren, *Buddhism in Translations* [Harvard Oriental Series 3; Cambridge, Mass.: Harvard Univ. Press, 1896] 95–110, and cited by Campbell, *The Hero*, 362).

[27] R. C. Zaehner, *Hinduism* (London/New York: Oxford Univ. Press, 1962) 124.

[28] Ibid., 123.

[29] Is there any link between the conversation between Krishna and Arjuna at the place of pilgrimage and the Johannine introduction of the Beloved Disciple who is resting on the bosom of Jesus at the time of the great Jewish pilgrimage?

[30] *The Song of God: Bhagavad-Gita*, trans. S. Prabhavananda and C. Isherwood (New York: Mentor, 1954, 1960) 35.

that Krishna, the beginning and the end,[31] loved Arjuna "as dearly as himself."[32] Also in line with the Johannine portrayal of the Beloved Disciple is Krishna's explanation that he has revealed truths to Arjuna "because I love you."[33] Similar to the Johannine Jesus, Krishna urges his disciples to be "united always in heart and consciousness with me";[34] and he, like John's Jesus, can offer the promise of unending life: "The man that loves me. He shall not perish."[35] Like the Jesus of the GosJn, Krishna can bewail that "the world fails to recognize me as I really am."[36] To what extent has Hinduism helped shape the GosJn or some of the traditions in it? Have the scholars in the Johannine School met and been somewhat influenced by Hindus, perhaps through international caravan trade?[37]

Has the portrayal of Arjuna helped provide a model for the Beloved Disciple? Since an ivory statue of Lakshmi, the Indian goddess of Prosperity, has been found at Pompeii,[38] and since a first-century sea-captain describes the trade from Rome to India,[39] then it is not so unthinkable that some influences from India might have been felt in and around the cosmopolitan Johannine Christians. Research devoted to a better understanding of trade between Rome and India has concluded that "the peak period" for this trade was the first century C.E., and that "the most dynamic trade network was the one which connected the Mediterranean and India via the Red Sea during the first century A.D., when Rome had come to dominate both the Mediterranean and the Red Sea."[40] Of course, the Johannine Christians may have been influenced by Hindus who moved westward via the land-based caravan routes, along especially the silk road from China

[31] Krishna informs Arjuna, "I am the beginning, the life-span, and the end of all" (*Bhagavad-Gita*, section X [p. 88]).

[32] Zaehner, *Hinduism*, 85.

[33] *Bhagavad-Gita*, section XI [p. 96].

[34] *Bhagavad-Gita*, section XVIII [p. 128].

[35] *Bhagavad-Gita*, section IX [p. 85].

[36] *Bhagavad-Gita*, section VII [p. 71].

[37] To what extent is it insightful to think about Muhammed who had been a caravan driver?

[38] A. Maiuri, "Statuetta eburnea di arte indiana a Pompei," *Le Arti* 1.2 (1939) 111–15. V. Begley drew my attention to a study I have not yet located: E. C. L. During Caspers, "The Indian Ivory Figurine from Pompeii—A Reconsideration of Its Functional Use," in *South Asian Archaeology*, ed. H. Härtel (Berlin, 1981) 341–54.

[39] See the focused discussion by M. P. Charlesworth in *The Roman Empire* (London: Oxford Univ. Press, 1951) 130–31.

[40] V. Begley, "Introduction," in *Rome and India: The Ancient Sea Trade*, ed. V. Begley and R. D. De Puma (Madison: Univ. of Wisconsin Press, 1991) 3–7.

that accepted the flow of commodities from India, and the trade route from India itself that poured through Persepolis, Susa, and perhaps Petra, then northward to Jerusalem or Tyre (a caravan route which had been stimulated by Alexander's conquests around 331 B.C.E.).

It is obvious—but virtually unperceived by most scholars—that Indian philosophy, especially Hinduism, helped shape some aspects of early Jewish theology. For example, in his creative rehearsal of Eleazar's speech before the fall of Masada, Josephus discloses that he and other Jews knew about Hinduism and admired some aspects of it. Eleazar is reputed to have pointed admirably to "those Indians" who willingly choose death by setting themselves afire (*War* 7.8).

Do these diverse observations about the evidence of Hinduism in ancient Palestine and Italy prove that Arjuna is a prototype of the Johannine Beloved Disciple? The evidence is at best suggestive.[41] While such investigations are certainly warranted and needed, I must confess that there are better parallels to the Johannine Beloved Disciple within the world of Early Judaism, in the Wisdom traditions, the Old Testament Apocrypha and Pseudepigrapha (especially in the testamentary literature),[42] in the Dead Sea Scrolls, in Philo, and especially in Rabbinics (see chap. 4).[43] Moreover, the commonality of humanity would suggest that great teachers like Jesus and Gautama would attract beloved disciples who would serve as guarantors to their truths.

An Ideal, Fictitious, or Symbolical Figure (Scholten, Jülicher, Loisy, Schillito, Goguel, Lindars, Kügler)

Beginning in 1864 J. H. Scholten, Hoogleeraar te Leiden, argued that the Fourth Evangelist was not a Jew, and was not John the son of

---

[41] Would not Nagarjuna be a better candidate for the BD if we should look to Buddhism? He lived about the time of Jesus, according to Sen-Jui's preface to the *Tattvasiddhisastra*, and as Bruns states, "the balance of the evidence is tipped rather heavily in favor of a date not later than the first century A.D." See Bruns, *The Christian Buddhism of St. John*, 13. Nagarjuna is like Enoch and Thomas (according to the GThom) in that he receives the secret teachings of Buddha.

[42] Grassi correctly draws attention to Joseph typology. According to the author of Genesis 33, Joseph was singled out by Moses as "Blessed by the Lord," and "prince among his brothers" (Gen 33:13, 16), (Grassi, *The Secret Identity of the Beloved Disciple*, 47–50). Far more than Genesis, the T12P is important for studying this parallel to the BD.

[43] In particular the elevation of Torah study, the joy and faithfulness of disciples and fellow students, the place of the Rabbi, and the yearning for a better understanding of the will of the God of Israel all show how deeply rooted the GosJn is within Judaism. See in particular Aboth and 1QS 6.

Zebedee. He concluded that the Beloved Disciple was an ideal person, who was not an historical person.[44] Scholten's work is erudite and his insights are well informed. He was ahead of his time in arguing that the Beloved Disciple is an ideal figure. Unfortunately no one who has worked on the BD seems to know and benefit from his pioneering insights.

A. Jülicher claimed that whoever thinks that the apostle John wrote the GosJn "might just as well accept the Second Epistle of Peter as the work of Simon Peter." He was convinced that the author of the GosJn cannot have been an eyewitness to Jesus' life, since he was dependent on the Synoptics. Since such events as the Johannine miracles—"the changing of the water into wine, the healing of the sick man at the Pool of Bethesda"—are simply "artistic intensification of well-known Synoptic stories," the GosJn is of no value in reconstructing Jesus' life and teaching. Jülicher judges the author of the GosJn to be anonymous and to have been "high-handed" in the way in which he composes Jesus' words and arranges Jesus' actions. Yet, the GosJn is distinct from the apocryphal "fantasy-gospels" (*Phantasieevangelien*). The author is thoroughly apologetic, and cannot be dated before the second century. As did Justin, he championed Christianity against Judaism, using the form of a gospel. The author of the GosJn was a "little-known and perhaps comparatively young Christian theologian" who attributed his work pseudepigraphically to Jesus' disciple John. This son of Zebedee "evidently prided himself" upon not only "having once belonged to the circle of the Twelve, but [on] the fact that as *disciple* he had seen and still was bound to his Master by special and indissoluble ties of love." He had passed away, and to him the anonymous admirer applied the title the "Beloved Disciple."[45]

In the 1903 edition of his *Le quatrième Évangile*, A. Loisy saw that the editor of chapter 21 thought the Beloved Disciple was a person of history and the author of the GosJn. But in Loisy's judgment, he was mistaken and was indeed attempting to establish the authority of the GosJn. The gospel itself, chapters 1–20, are highly symbolical, and thus the

---

[44] J. H. Scholten, *Het Evangelie naar Johannes: Kritisch Historisch Onderzoek* (Leiden: P. Engels, 1864); see 274–85, 335–36 [German: *Das Evangelium nach Johannes: Kritisch-historische Untersuchung*, trans. H. Lang (Berlin: G. Reimer, 1867) see 258–68, 315–16; also see 367–82]; Scholten: The disciple "dien Jezus liefhad" was "geen bekend historisch persoon" (*De Apostel Johannes in Klein-Azië: Historisch-critisch Onderzoek* [Leiden: S.C. van Doesburgh, 1871] 90).

[45] Jülicher, *An Introduction to the New Testament*, trans. J. P. Ward (London: Smith, Elder & Co., 1904) 410–29. See also, Jülicher, *Einleitung in das Neue Testament*, rev. by E. Fascher (Grundriss der Theologischen Wissenschaften 3.1; Tübingen: Mohr [Siebeck], 1931) 400–23. (This edition is substantially altered.)

Beloved Disciple is "a purely typical person."[46] It is not a he, but a fictional character. It represents the type of the perfect gnostic.[47] As Jesus' mother is a symbol of messianic Judaism, so the Beloved Disciple represents spiritual Christianity. The only difference is that Mary alone is linked with a historical person. The nonhistorical nature of the Beloved Disciple is obvious in 19:25-27, according to which this perfect Christian attests to spiritual truths.[48]

Loisy, who represents one aspect of the early phase of Roman Catholic critical biblical scholarship,[49] argued that the author of the GosJn used the Beloved Disciple to guarantee the gospel. This author is a convert from Judaism, probably Alexandrian Judaism. He also certainly knew Philo's writings, was a profound and enthusiastic mystic, and was a theologian without any interest in history.[50] He was literarily dependent on the Synoptics, but he allegorizes the ancient and sacred history. The special traditions in the GosJn thus do not go back to an eyewitness called the Beloved Disciple; they are "symbolic, and represent not the memories" of an eyewitness but are "the personal conceptions of the author" of the GosJn.[51]

Many of Loisy's conclusions are reminiscent of those obtained by Scott and Bultmann. Hence, he not only probably influenced them, but also he is to be considered, at least in some ways, typical of the scholars who contend that the Beloved Disciple is a symbol of the church. Again, it is imperative to stress that scholars' conclusions can be arranged only in categories that have flexible borders.

At the height of the First World War, E. Schillito painted the picture of the Beloved Disciple as the one who is intimately close to the Mas-

---

[46] A. Loisy, *Le quatrième Évangile* (Paris: Alphonse Picard et Fils, 1903) 123–39.

[47] W. Bauer was of the opinion that the intimate connection between the Beloved Disciple and Jesus means that he is one of three disciples: Peter (who is not conceivable because of the narrative), James (who is impossible because of his early martyrdom), and John; and so it "bleibe nur der Zebedäide Johannes übrig ...." Bauer was impressed with Loisy's argument and concluded concerning his position: "Das ist zweifellos zum guten Teil richtig" (*Das Johannes-Evangelium* [Tübingen: J. C. B. Mohr, 1933] 173–74).

[48] The dependence of Bultmann on Loisy seems obvious, but is seldom pointed out.

[49] Unfortunately Loisy was excommunicated in 1908 and the encyclical *Pascendi* denounced him as *vitandus* (he was to be avoided).

[50] Loisy, *Le quatrième Évangile*, 129: "C'est un théologien aussi étranger que possible à toute préoccupation historique."

[51] These quotations are from a question Loisy asked about the spuriousness of the unique traditions in the GosJn. He answered it affirmatively (*The Gospel and the Church*, trans. C. Home [Philadelphia: Fortress, 1976 (1903)] 30).

ter during the Last Supper when the Betrayer is introduced, who is close to the cross of Christ, who is bonded forever with Mary, Jesus' mother, and who "saw and believed" without needing communion with the Risen Lord. This anonymous disciple is everyone; "he can be the one whom Jesus loved—the passing embodying of the undying disciple-heart—the contemporary response to the Eternal Invitation."[52] While this article is certainly not an example of historical research, it does evidence how meaning pours from Scripture amidst a world choked by gas, trenches, and barbed wire fences.

In 1923 M. Goguel, at that time Professeur à la Faculté libre de Théologie protestante de Paris, examined in detail, and with unprecedented (indeed unusual) thoroughness and openness, the identity of the Beloved Disciple.[53] He was impressed with the symbolic nature of the figure, but his own thoughts cannot be neatly categorized. He saw no reason to suspect the historicity of the anonymous disciple in 1:35-42 and 18:15-27. The anonymity of 20:2-10 impressed him, and he was convinced the account was fabricated to shift the first belief in Jesus' resurrection from Mary Magdalene to a disciple. He judged that 13:21-30 was an ingenious combination of primitive traditions taken from the Synoptics and artificial embellishment. For Goguel the episode at the cross, 19:26-27, was simply doctrinal and nonhistorical. The thrust of the lance, 19:34-35, was composed to combat Docetism,[54] and it has no historical character. The redactor of the GosJn may have attached certain aspects of Paul's personality to the ideal depiction of the Beloved Disciple (see the following discussion of the hypothesis that Paul or a Paulinist is the BD). This does not mean that the Beloved Disciple may not represent also a real person.

Goguel pointed out that only two persons, according to the intracanonical gospels, are reported to have been loved by Jesus: the Rich Young Ruler and Lazarus. He disagreed with Swete regarding the former and with Völter regarding the suggestion that the Beloved Disciple is John Mark. He judged Erbes' reconstruction of the origin of the GosJn to be a flight of fancy from "le terrain de l'histoire pour celui du roman."[55] In summation, none of the suggestions for the Beloved Disciple can be maintained.

---

[52] E. Schillito, "The Beloved Disciple," *The Expository Times* 29 (1917–1918) 473–74.

[53] M. Goguel, "Le témoignage de l'évangile sur son auteur le disciple bien-aimé," in *Introduction au Nouveau Testament: Tome II Le Quatrième Évangile* (Paris: Éditions Ernest Leroux, 1924) 315–54.

[54] Goguel, *Le Quatrième Évangile*, 336–37: "One may well completely explain this pericope by the attempt to establish against the docetics the unquestioned reality of Jesus' death" [free translation].

[55] Goguel, *Le Quatrième Évangile*, 348.

Goguel claimed that chapter 21, which represents the editor's view (which may not be assumed to be identical with that of the author of the GosJn), suggests that the Beloved Disciple may have once been a historical person, but he is now an ideal figure. There is certainly a polemic between the Beloved Disciple and Peter and the form of Christianity he represents, which is obviously Rome.

In 1972 B. Lindars argued that "there is no warrant to see a reference to the Beloved Disciple in 1.35." He also resisted the claim that he appears in chapter 18 and that he is the one who witnessed the piercing of Jesus' side (19:35). Lindars was convinced that "the only authentic references to him are 13.23; 19.26; 20.2; and the Appendix."[56] He argued against the hypotheses of John the Apostle, Lazarus, John Mark, and Paul. He stressed that "the anonymity of the Beloved Disciple must be taken seriously." In the seventies Lindars thus concluded that the Beloved Disciple may well be an ideal figure, a symbol.[57] But in 1990 this ambiguity was removed:

> To me the Beloved Disciple is a creation of the evangelist in order to serve a specific function. He is one of the Twelve, who at crucial moments gives expression to the evangelist's own views. He represents true discipleship, understanding the necessity of the death of Jesus when all others fail. He is thus a foil to Peter ....[58]

In 1988 in a monograph of over five hundred pages on the Beloved Disciple, J. Kügler examined the passages in which this epithet appears. Kügler found that a historical-critical examination of the GosJn shows that there is no validity to the old tradition which concluded that the Beloved Disciple is the apostle John. The redactor has created a fictional character, a Beloved Disciple, whose witness substantiates the claims in the GosJn and thus serves to legitimate and stabilize the Johannine Community. The figure and function of the Beloved Disciple, therefore, is "Verfasserschaftsfiktion."[59] Neirynck offers the opinion, that we "may welcome Kügler's study as an attempt at understanding the Beloved Disciple in the Gospel of John without identifying him with a concrete historical figure."[60]

---

[56] B. Lindars, *Gospel of John* (London: Marshall, Morgan & Scott; Grand Rapids: Eerdmans, 1972, 1987) 32.

[57] Lindars, *The Gospel of John*, 33-34.

[58] Lindars, *John* (New Testament Guides; Sheffield: JSOT Press, 1990) 22.

[59] J. Kügler, *Der Jünger, den Jesus liebte: Literarische, theologische und historische Untersuchungen zu einer Schlüsselgestalt johanneischer Theologie und Geschichte* (Stuttgarter Biblische Beiträge 16. Stuttgart: Verlag Katholisches Bibelwerk, 1988) see esp. 429-38 and the summary on 488.

[60] Neirynck, *New Testament Studies* 36 (1990) 335.

A Symbol of the Apostolic Prophet (Kragerud)

In 1959 A. Kragerud published an extensive monograph on the Beloved Disciple. He concluded that this epithet does not refer to an historical person. It is a symbol which signifies the "apostolischen Wander-prophetismus."[61]

The criticisms of Kragerud's hypothesis have sometimes been severe. Schnackenburg rightly states that a collective meaning of the singular in 21:24, as Kragerud attempts to do, is unlikely, and that it is "scarcely possible" that the collective meaning of the alleged symbol of the Beloved Disciple was misunderstood by the editor.[62] Dauer in *Die Passionsgeschichte im Johannesevangelium* judges that Kragerud's exegesis is unacceptable. He stresses that the Beloved Disciple is certainly not a purely symbolic figure, and that in summation "Krageruds Hypothese hat das Problem des 'Lieblingsjünger' nicht wirklich gelöst."[63]

In *New Testament Prophecy*, D. Hill judges that Kragerud's hypothesis "suffers from major weaknesses." Here are his points: (1) While the Beloved Disciple has symbolic meaning, so do Mary and Peter, but "he is a real person whose actions are significant on the Gospel scene: his possible symbolic value must remain secondary to his real historical identity." (2) It is doubtful that the Beloved Disciple represents "the charismatic spirit active in prophecy: it is much more likely that he symbolizes the disciple or believer *par excellence*, the example to be followed by the reader of John's book." (3) The attempt to make the GosJn a manifesto for charismatic freedom and prophetism against ecclesiastical order "cannot be judged successful."[64]

A Symbol of the Church (Scott, Bultmann, Pamment)

In 1906 E. F. Scott claimed that the Beloved Disciple "represents the Church in its essential idea. All the rest is temporary and external, and the one thing necessary is the inward fellowship, by faith and love, with Jesus Christ."[65] Scott was convinced that the Beloved Disciple, as well as

---

[61] A. Kragerud, *Der Lieblingsjünger im Johannesevangelium: Ein Exegetischer Versuch* (Oslo: Osloer Universitätsverlag, 1959).

[62] Schnackenburg, "Der Jünger," 98.

[63] Dauer, *Die Passionsgeschichte im Johannesevangelium* (Munich: Kösel-Verlag, 1972) 330-31.

[64] D. Hill, *New Testament Prophecy* (New Foundations Theological Library; Atlanta: John Knox Press, 1979) 147-48. It is at least noteworthy that the BD and Kragerud's ideas are not discussed in the distinguished book by D. E. Aune titled *Prophecy in Early Christianity and the Ancient Mediterranean World* (Grand Rapids: Eerdmans, 1983).

[65] E. F. Scott, *The Fourth Gospel: Its Purpose and Theology* (Edinburgh: T. and T. Clark, 1906, 1908 [2nd ed.]) 144.

Nicodemus, Thomas, and Philip, "are not so much individuals as religious types."[66]

In the forties Bultmann developed the symbolic interpretation,[67] which as we have observed was earlier articulated by Loisy.[68] According to 19:35, which is a redactional gloss, and 21, which is a redactional appendix, the Beloved Disciple represents "a particular historical figure, clearly an authoritative one for the circle which edits the Gospel and one whose authority is placed side by side with that of Peter." According to Bultmann, the redactor's portrait is incredible: "it cannot be maintained that the beloved disciple ... is a particular historical figure." This is impossible because "there would be no accounting for the fact that the Evangelist does not speak of him by name, as he does the other disciples, but refers to him in that mysterious way."[69] Thus the Beloved Disciple is "an ideal figure." He is a symbol of "Gentile Christendom" (as Peter represents "Jewish Christendom").[70]

In 1983 M. Pamment argued that the Beloved Disciple was a Gentile, primarily because the GosJn in chapter 21 is concerned with the Gentile mission. The Beloved Disciple is neither one of the Twelve nor the author of the GosJn. He rather "represents gentile Christianity. It is with gentile Christianity that the mother of Jesus finds her home."[71] There are no notes, nor expressions of indebtedness, but it is apparent that Pamment is influenced by Bultmann. She does not clarify that the Beloved Disciple

---

[66] Scott, *The Fourth Gospel*, 57.

[67] It is well to remember, as E. Baasland has stipulated, that Bultmann perceived the GosJn as "das mythische Evangelium" (see Baasland, *Theologie und Methode: Eine historiographische Analyse der Frühschriften Rudolf Bultmanns* [Zürich: Brockhaus, 1992] esp. 308).

[68] Bultmann, *Das Evangelium des Johannes* (Kritisch-exegetischer Kommentar über das Neue Testament; Göttingen: Vandenhoeck & Ruprecht, 1941). Note 369: "Der Lieblingsjünger ist vielmehr eine Idealgestalt.... Der Lieblingsjünger repräsentiert also das Heidenchristentum."

[69] Bultmann is not convincing at this point. The names of the sons of Zebedee are not given in the GosJn, and we do not know the name of Jesus' mother. The anonymity of the GosJn functions narratively to heighten the symbolism and to extend and undergird the timelessness of the gospel. It entices the reader to struggle with symbolism and indeed with mysticism. See the discussion of "anonymity" in my Preface.

[70] Bultmann, *John*, 483-85. Bultmann thinks Bacon's view that the BD is Paul "is the best as regards subject matter." But, he continues to show that this hypothesis is impossible (*John*, 484, n. 5).

[71] M. Pamment, "The Fourth Gospel's Beloved Disciple," *The Expository Times* 94 (1983) 363-67.

is only a symbol, yet a few of her comments seem to suggest that interpretation.

A Real Human Whose Identity is Lost (Baur, Garvie, Lofthouse, Roloff, Lorenzen, Dauer, Culpepper, Cullmann, D. M. Smith, Thyen, de Jonge, Moloney, du Rand, Becker, Beasley-Murray, Porsch, Byrne, Zumstein, Ruckstuhl, Bonsack, Quast, Collins, Ernst, Grassi, Whiteley [S. Brown])[72]

Chapter 21 makes it abundantly clear (at least to the vast majority of Johannine experts) that the Beloved Disciple was a real human. The members of the Johannine Community not only knew his identity but held him to be an eyewitness to Jesus' life and teaching. Most importantly, they were disturbed that he had died. As Blank states, during the time from Jesus death until the writing of chapter 21 "the Beloved Disciple has actually died."[73] Chapter 21 cannot be jettisoned from the GosJn by the claim that it is a mere addendum. It is now an integral part of the GosJn and was most likely produced within the Johannine Community (as we saw in chap. 2). Thus, the author of chapter 21 cannot be misinformed. He also cannot be deceptive, since his whole program is to win the readers' confidence in the trustworthiness of the hero of the GosJn.

Despite the unique vocabulary of chapter 21, judiciously pointed out by Bultmann,[74] it is also linguistically linked with chapters 1–20. Like chapters 1–20, chapter 21 has a distinct style that distinguishes it not only from other books in the New Testament, but also from other contemporary writings.[75] Bultmann concluded that the editor who supplied chapter 21 was also the person who has given us the present order of the GosJn.[76] He also held that the Beloved Disciple was a fictional creation of the author of the GosJn.

This conclusion has been widely and wisely criticized. Note, for example, the words of Brown in *The Community of the Beloved Disciple*:

> The thesis that he [the BD] is purely fictional or only an ideal figure is quite implausible. It would mean that the author of John 21:20-23 was deceived or deceptive, for he reports distress in the community

[72] The arguments of scholars who defend this hypothesis are similar in many ways with those presented by experts who conclude that the BD is one of the anonymous disciples mentioned in GosJn 21:2. The two categories, however, are not identical.

[73] Blank, *Das Evangelium nach Johannes*, Part 3, 212.

[74] Bultmann, *John*, 700–701.

[75] See E. Ruckstuhl and P. Dschulnigg, *Stilkritik und Verfasserfrage im Johannesevangelium*, esp. 34–35, 236.

[76] Bultmann, *John*, 700–706. Also see, D. M. Smith, *Composition*, xiii–xiv.

over the Beloved Disciple's death. The Disciple was idealized, of course; but in my judgment the fact that he was a historical person and a companion of Jesus becomes all the more obvious in the new approaches to Johannine ecclesiology. ... The "one-upmanship" of the Beloved Disciple in relation to Simon Peter in the Fourth Gospel illustrates this [claim to possess the authoritative witness to Jesus].[77] But such a depiction would have been counterproductive if the Beloved Disciple were a purely imaginative symbol or if he had never been with Jesus, for the community's self-defense would surely have crumbled under such circumstances.[78]

Peter is not only a symbolical figure in the GosJn, but also certainly a real person of history, as we know from tradition within and without the New Testament. Hence, it would seem to be demanded that since he is contrasted with the Beloved Disciple, the latter cannot be merely categorized as a mere literary typos or narrative fiction (see chap. 1.2).

It seems relatively certain that the Beloved Disciple represents a real historical person. No symbol dies and causes consternation in a social group, like the Johannine Community. Culpepper is obviously correct; there is a growing consensus that the Beloved Disciple "is a real historical person."[79] There is no doubt that the Beloved Disciple obtained ideal and symbolical meaning, but that does not in any way undermine the fact that he was a real person of history. As B. Byrne states in the recently published and authoritative *Anchor Bible Dictionary*,[80] a "lack of any corresponding historical identity would severely undermine his leading role as witness and guarantor of the gospel." Hence, contemporary scholars conclude that the Beloved Disciple is "a genuine historical personage who is presented in the fourth gospel in a symbolical and idealized way."[81]

Many Johannine experts conclude that the Beloved Disciple is a real human, but stress that his identity is lost in the shadows of time (see chap. 1.2). Long ago, in fact in 1847, at the beginnings of the historical and critical examination of the New Testament, F. C. Baur pointed out that the GosJn cannot have been written by the apostle John, and that the Beloved Disciple (whom he called "der Lieblingsjünger Jesu" or "Busenjünger") is an unknown gifted author who, like Paul a century earlier, felt

---

[77] This clarifying parenthetical phrase has been added by me. It represents what was omitted from Brown's discussion.

[78] Brown, *The Community of the Beloved Disciple*, 31–32.

[79] Culpepper, *Anatomy*, 121.

[80] Bryne, B. "The Beloved Disciple," *Anchor Bible Dictionary* (1992) 1.658–61.

[81] Byrne, *Anchor Bible Dictionary* (1992) 1.658.

the soul of an apostle.[82] He began by asking how it is conceivable that an apostle, let alone John the son of Zebedee, could have composed a gospel like the GosJn in which is found "einer mystisch-spekulativen Anschauungsweise" (327–28). He pointed out that there is no Beloved Disciple in the Synoptics (328). Quite understandable in Baur's time—before the discovery of the Dead Sea Scrolls in the winter of 1947 and the recognition that Rabbinics before 70 C.E. was not the same as after 200—is his contention that the author of the GosJn is far removed from all forms of Judaism.[83] His slavish dependence on Josephus, who reported that Caiaphas was high priest from 25 to 36 C.E. (*Ant* 18.2.2), is noticeable as he judges the author of the GosJn to be out of touch with Jewish customs when he writes that Caiaphas ἀρχιερεὺς ὢν τοῦ ἐνιαυτοῦ ἐκείνου (GosJn 11:51 cf. 18:13).[84] In summation, Baur's position on the identity of the Beloved Disciple is as follows:

> Woher wissen wir denn, dass der Verfasser selbst seinem Evangelium die Ausschrit κατὰ 'Ιωάννην gab? Das Evangelium selbst enthält ja keine Andeutung über den Verfasser, erst der unächte Anhang schreibt die Abfassung der Schrift dem Jünger zu, welchem Jesus liebte, und selbst der Name dieses Lieblingsjüngers ist im Evangelium nirgends ausdrücklich genannt.[85]

He continues by pointing out that the identification of the GosJn with the apostle John is found "nur in der kirchlichen Tradition" (365) and in literature that dates from the end of the second century (371). For Baur the author of the GosJn comes from a time far removed from the apostolic period.[86] Baur had a very high esteem for the brilliant theology preserved in the GosJn and was struggling against the powerful consensus that the GosJn was composed by the apostle John; note his words that the "Ansicht von dem Charakter des Evangeliums kann ja auf keine Weise nur an dem Namen des Verfassers hängen" (388).

---

[82] It is not easy to follow Baur, who is fond of long run-on sentences and statements that ultimately end with question marks. See F. C. Baur, "Der Verfasser des Evangeliums," in *Kritische Untersuchungen über die kanonischen Evangelien, ihr Verhältnis zu einander, ihren Charakter und Ursprung* (Tübingen: Ludw. Fr. Fues., 1847) 327–89; see esp. 328, 365, 378, and 383.

[83] His language is interestingly distinct from the jargon of today; note his words: "Wie frei sich der Verfasser des Evangeliums von allen Banden des Judenthums gemacht hat" (Baur, *Kritische Untersuchungen*, 330).

[84] It is salubrious to note that even the great Baur can fail twice to put the circumflex accent over the last syllable.

[85] Baur, *Kritische Untersuchungen*, 365.

[86] "Dass ausserhalb des ursprünglichen Apostelkreises noch ein anderer Apostel erstanden ist" (Ibid., 386).

Any self-serving contemporary celebration for recognizing finally the subjective in all writing that professes to be historical will be embarrassed by the skills apparent in Baur's following insight:

> Was, wie bei der Geschichte, so auch bei den evangelischen Geschichte, ganz besonders aber bei einem Evangelium, wie das johanneische ist, nie vergessen werden darf, dass wir die Geschichte nirgends in ihrer reinen Objektivität vor us haben, sondern nur in Berichten und Darstellungen, in welchen wir erst kritisch ausscheiden müssen, was an ihnen nur subjektiv ist, um der historischen Wahrheit mehr oder minder nahe zu kommen, bleibt immer der Hauptgesichtspunkt, aus welchem das johanneische Evangelium zu betrachten ist; es kann in dem einen Falle wie in dem andern nur als eine durch die Subjektivität ihres Verfassers hindurchgegangene und durch sie vermittelte Darstellung genommen werden.[87]

It is important to observe that Baur concluded that the Beloved Disciple was a real person but that he wrote the GosJn in the second half of the second century, perhaps around 170, because he shares the Zeitgeist of the Montanists.[88]

Other scholars concluded that the identity of the Beloved Disciple is unknown, but they perceived that the person to whom this epithet was attached lived sometime in the first century C.E. This position is defended by A. E. Garvie in *The Beloved Disciple*.[89] In 1936, in his *The Disciple Whom Jesus Loved*, W. F. Lofthouse argued that the evidence indicates that the author of the GosJn is not John the son of Zebedee, but he is an eyewitness. He claimed that "we must distinguish between the beloved disciple and the son of Zebedee." He cautiously advises that the Beloved Disciple may not even be "identical with one of the unnamed disciples of i. 37, of xviii. 15, and of xx. 2." It is far from certain that the Beloved Disciple was one of the Twelve. The arguments that have been presented to identify the Beloved Disciple have been built "from wood, hay, stubble, rather than from granite or even brick."[90] The Beloved Disciple was a real person, although anonymous, but that does not leave us emptyhanded: "We may now claim the right to regard the Fourth Gospel as evidence, not simply for what an old man, who had once been in touch with the companions of Jesus, had come to think about Him; but for what Jesus actually said and was."[91]

---

[87] Ibid., 388–89.

[88] Ibid., 373–75.

[89] Garvie, *The Beloved Disciple: Studies of the Fourth Gospel* (London: Hodder and Stoughton, [1922]).

[90] W. F. Lofthouse, *The Disciple Whom Jesus Loved* (London: Epworth, 1936) 35–36.

[91] Ibid., 43.

With the first discovery of the Dead Sea Scrolls in 1947 and their initial publication in the fifties, scholars should be expected to contemplate a relationship, perhaps only literary, between the anonymity of the Qumranic Righteous Teacher and the Johannine Beloved Disciple. In fact this was the purpose of an article in 1968/69 by J. Roloff.[92] Despite some comments that he concluded the Beloved Disciple was only a fictitious figure, his arguments are quite the contrary. His insights can be presented under six points: (1) Historical-critical research indicates that the Beloved Disciple passages are not built upon older traditions; they are throughout "literary compositions."[93] (2) The Beloved Disciple is one who knows and understands Jesus in a special way; he is the confidant who is known and loved by Jesus. (3) He is not only the guarantor of the actuality (Faktizität) of Jesus' death, he is also its interpreter. (4) These observations may lead to the impression that the Beloved Disciple is only a literary fiction, but in no way is he simply the product of literary fiction. (5) Not only chapter 21, but also chapters 1–20 are to be understood together in presenting the reader with an individual historical person. (6) Like the Qumranic Righteous Teacher, the Johannine Beloved Disciple was understood allegorically and symbolically; but he was also a real historical person.[94]

In 1971 T. Lorenzen published his *Der Lieblingsjünger im Johannesevangelium*. He was particularly alert to the social and theological crises that forged the present shape of the GosJn. He rightly stressed that the search for the identity of the Beloved Disciple is enriched by the ideas and social world represented by the Dead Sea Scrolls. In particular, like the Beloved Disciple, the Righteous Teacher of Qumran is a real historical person, an anonymous figure, and the source of truth and scriptural exegesis for a focused Jewish community. The Beloved Disciple was of interest to the Johannine Community as a person and as bearer of the message. Note these insights:

> *Sachlich* dürfte der Lieblingsjünger die Funktion haben, zu bezeugen, dass Jesus von Nazareth wirklich verraten, verhört und gekreuzigt worden ist, und dass sich in diesem Tod das jetzt erfahrene eschatolo-

[92] J. Roloff, "Der johanneische 'Lieblingsjünger' und der Lehrer der Gerechtigkeit,'" *New Testament Studies* 15 (1968–69) 129–51.

[93] Ibid., 133.

[94] This is unassailable, as Schnackenburg states (*St. John*, 3:377). For a study of an allegorical self-portrait of the Righteous Teacher, see Charlesworth, "An Allegorical and Autobiographical Poem by the Moreh haṣ-Ṣedeq (1QH 8:4-11)," in *"Shaʿarei Talmon": Studies in the Bible, Qumran, and the Ancient Near East Presented to Shemaryahu Talmon*, ed. M. Fishbane and E. Tov, with W. W. Fields (Winona Lake, Ind.: Eisenbrauns, 1992) 295–307.

> gische Heil gründet.... Theologisch heisst das, dass der Evangelist
> mit der Person des Lieblingsjüngers sein anti-doketisches Interesse
> zur Sprache bringt.[95]

He concludes that while the Beloved Disciple is surely "keine literarische
Fiktion" his identity cannot be discerned.[96] He is the ideal disciple who
"als Mittler zwischen dem erhöten Herrn and seiner Gemeinde stand und
daher theologisch das Kriterium für rechte Theologie und Gemeindefröm-
migkeit ist."[97]

In 1972 A. Dauer published his *Die Passionsgeschichte im Johannesevangelium*. Although he was not focused on identifying the Beloved
Disciple, he did reveal his own understandings of the issue. He is convinced that the Beloved Disciple does not have only a purely symbolic
meaning.[98] As Jesus is the only exegete and revealer of the Father, so the
Beloved Disciple in a special way is Jesus' exegete, "in besonderer Weise
der 'Exeget Jesu.'"[99] Most importantly, the Beloved Disciple is the true
witness who guarantees the tradition and truth preserved in the GosJn.[100]
In chapter 19 this epithet is employed to ground the unity of the church in
Jesus' commission to his mother and to the Beloved Disciple.[101] As in the
Dead Sea Scrolls the Righteous Teacher remains anonymous, so in the
GosJn the name of the Beloved Disciple is never clarified.

In 1975 R. A. Culpepper argued that the GosJn has come to us from
a school, which is similar to other schools in the Hellenistic and Roman
Period. Convinced that "the Johannine community was a school,"[102] Culpepper argues, persuasively, that "Jesus viewed teaching as an integral
part of his ministry and called together and taught a group of disciples."[103]

---

[95] Lorenzen, *Der Lieblingsjünger im Johannesevangelium* (Stuttgart: Verlag
Katholisches Bibelwerk, 1971) 106.

[96] Ibid., 107.

[97] Ibid., 109.

[98] Dauer: "Auch die Annahme, die Gestalt des L habe rein symbolische
Bedeutung, ist nicht wahrscheinlich" (*Die Passionsgeschichte im Johannesevangelium*, 330 [L = Lieblingsjünger]. His words were directed against Kragerud's
hypothesis.

[99] Dauer, *Die Passionsgeschichte im Johannesevangelium*, 331.

[100] Dauer: "Nun verstehen wir auch, warum der 4. Evangelist den 'Jünger,
den Jesus liebte', immer wieder so betont herausstellt, seine Nähe zu Jesus und
seine intime Kenntnis Jesu unterstreicht; denn das wahrhafte Zeugnis dieses
Jüngers ist die Garantie für das zuverlässige Zeugnis seines Evangeliums" (Ibid.,
333).

[101] Ibid., 333.

[102] Culpepper, *The Johannine School* (Missoula, Mont.: Scholars Press,
1975) 290.

[103] Ibid., 226.

The Johannine School is based on Jesus' teachings and a devotion to his life and ministry, but the honor of founding the School should probably be given to the Beloved Disciple: "The actual founder of the Johannine community is more likely to be found in the figure of the Beloved Disciple."[104] Thus, while Martyn has little use for the Beloved Disciple in reconstructing the origins of the Johannine Community, Culpepper depends on him and sees him as the founder of the Johannine School.

In 1975, in his *Der johanneische Kreis*, O. Cullmann argued that the Beloved Disciple was not merely an ideal figure for numerous reasons, notably the crisis caused by his death (chap. 21). He was rightly convinced that the Beloved Disciple's identity cannot be solved by resorting to the Synoptic tradition. He also pointed out that in the Fourth Gospel the Twelve—as a group—plays no significant role. From this valid insight he (erroneously) contended that the Beloved Disciple does not belong to the group called the "Twelve." Instead, as Peter is the representative of the Twelve, so the Beloved Disciple is the leader of another group of disciples. After dismissing the attempts to identify him with John the son of Zebedee, John Mark, and Lazarus, he concludes that we must be satisfied with the understanding that the Beloved Disciple's name cannot be known.[105] He concluded, "We must therefore be content with *remaining in ignorance about the name of this beloved disciple.*"[106]

In contrast to many scholars who present complex hypotheses and never summarize their own position, Cullmann conveniently brought his ideas into final focus: The Beloved Disciple is from Judaea. He is a former disciple of John the Baptist: "He began to follow Jesus in Judaea when *Jesus himself was in close proximity to the Baptist.*"[107] He was acquainted with the high priest, and much later "collected a whole group of followers about himself."[108] Cullmann was convinced that the Beloved Disciple was indeed the author of the GosJn, but that he was an eyewitness of only "a limited number of the events which he records."[109]

---

[104] Ibid., 265.

[105] O. Cullmann, "Der Verfasser des Johannesevangeliums im Rahmen des johanneischen Kreises," in *Der johanneische Kreis* (Tübingen: Mohr [Siebeck], 1975) 67–88; ET: *The Johannine Circle*, trans. J. Bowden (London: SCM, 1976) 63–85. Note his comment on 84: "Ich neme sogar an, dass der Verfasser des Johannes-Evangeliums nur für eine beschränkte Zahl der berichteten Ereignisse als Augenzeuge in Betracht kommt. Für die anderen hat er Traditionen benützt." This quotation is highlighted at the beginning of W. Eckle's *Den der Herr liebhatte: Rätsel um den Evangelisten Johannes* (Hamburg: Verlag Dr. Kovač, 1991).

[106] Cullmann, *The Johannine Circle*, 78 (italics his).

[107] Ibid., 78 (italics his).

[108] Ibid., 78; *Der johanneische Kreis*, 82.

[109] Cullmann, *The Johannine Circle*, 80; *Der johanneische Kreis*, 84.

In the supplementary volume to *The Interpreter's Dictionary of the Bible*, D. M. Smith suggested that the verses in which the Beloved Disciple appears are "almost certainly secondary in their present context," and may belong to some editor. He is critical of the attempts to link the Beloved Disciple with John the son of Zebedee, because that tradition cannot be traced into the period prior to 135 C.E. Smith is convinced that the Beloved Disciple represents not a symbol, but a real historical person. Note these focused and insightful comments:

> Probably he was a historical figure, even though the gospel accounts of him may be largely legendary. Certainly 19:35 and 21:24 presume his actual existence. If his historicity is denied, such passages must be construed as the product either of ignorance or of intentional fabrication, and neither of these alternatives is satisfactory.[110]

Elsewhere Smith reports that there is today a consensus that the Beloved Disciple was an historical figure,[111] and that "however much he may have been idealized, is tied to the recognition that he is somehow important for Johannine origins and self definition."[112]

In 1977 H. Thyen expressed his opinion that chapter 21 may not be a "sekundärer Nachtrag" by an author different from the one who wrote 1–20, but an "Epilog" by the redactor of chapters 1–20. He is convinced that "alle Lieblingsjüngertexte in ihrem jeweiligen Kontext *literarisch* sekundär sind."[113] He opined that the "einzigartiges Pseudonym 'der Jünger, den Jesus liebte'" represents a real historical person whose death caused a trauma in the Johannine Community.[114] The name of that person is unknown: "Der unter dem Pseudonym, 'dem Jünger, den Jesus liebte', verborgene Anonymous ist ein wohl hochbetagter und allseits verehrter Mann im johanneischen Christentum gewesen."[115] While his identity is not known to us, he was well known to the members of the Johannine

---

[110] D. M. Smith, "Beloved Disciple," *IDBS* (1976) 95.

[111] See Smith, "The Fourth Gospel: A Report on Recent Research," in *Aufstieg und Niedergang der Römischen Welt* II.25.3 (1985) 2389–2480; esp. 2439: The GosJn "was written by an anonymous figure in the community who preserved the traditions of his group centered in a distant figure of the past known in the gospel as the BD."

[112] Smith, in *The New Testament and its Modern Interpreters*, ed. E. J. Epp and G. W. MacRae (SBL The Bible and its Interpreters; Philadelphia: Fortress; Atlanta: Scholars Press, 1989) 285.

[113] Thyen in *L'Évangile de Jean*, 267.

[114] Ibid., 272, 293–94. He is rightly convinced that the "hochbetagten und verehrten Lehrers die Gemeinde" has actually died ("tatsächlich gestorben").

[115] Ibid., 269.

Community.[116] He concludes with posing the hypothesis that he may be linked or identified with the Presbyter who wrote 1 John and 2 John.[117] In any case he rightly points out, in my opinion, that the Beloved Disciple passages serve the needs of the Johannine Community and often have clear anti-docetic functions.

In 1979 M. de Jonge, an expert distinguished for his research on the *Testaments of the Twelve Patriarchs* as well as on the GosJn, focused on the function of the Beloved Disciple and sought to discern if all references to him were editorial additions to a core document. In the process de Jonge offered the opinion that the identity of the Beloved Disciple was well known to the members of the Johannine Community, but his identity is unknown to us: "He remains anonymous for us, but was not so for the original readers who knew him and revered him as an 'apostolic' eye-witness."[118] In 1980 and 1982 F. Moloney expressed a similar opinion.[119] In 1991 Jan A du Rand also concluded that the identity of the Beloved Disciple "remains unknown to us."[120]

In 1984 J. Becker argued that the Beloved Disciple cannot be a literary fiction because he is contrasted with Peter. Becker evaluated the attempts to identify the Beloved Disciple, and was forced to conclude that the "personal identity of the Beloved Disciple has sunk into the shadow of history."[121] In 1989 G. R. Beasley-Murray questioned the identity of the Beloved Disciple. He suggested that the Beloved Disciple's "written testimony" is the main source for the author of the GosJn. He discussed his possible identity, but finally concluded, "We cannot pretend to be able to solve this issue."[122]

F. Porsch wrote his *Johannes-Evangelium* in the same year as Beasley-Murray's abridged commentary. Porsch reports that after two thousand years research specialists have been forced to give up trying to prove that the Beloved Disciple is John the son of Zebedee. He rightly

---

[116] Ibid., 294: "Sondern ein Anonymus dessen Inkognito nur dem eigenen Kreis durchschaubar ist."

[117] Ibid., 296–99.

[118] M. de Jonge, "The Beloved Disciple and the Date of the Gospel of John," in *Text and Interpretation*, 105; see also 109.

[119] F. Moloney, "From Cana to Cana (John 2:1–4:54) and the Fourth Evangelist's Concept of Correct (and Incorrect) Faith," in *Studia Biblica 1978: II. Papers on the Gospels*, ed. E. A. Livingstone (JSNT Supplement Series 2; Sheffield: JSOT Press, 1980) 185–213; Moloney, "John 20: A Journey Completed," *Australasian Catholic Record* 59 (1982) 417–32; see esp. 426.

[120] Jan A. du Rand, *Johannine Perspectives* ([Johannesburg]: Orion, 1991) 87.

[121] Becker, *Das Evangelium nach Johannes*, 2:438.

[122] Beasley-Murray, *John*, 7.

states that scholars are seeking to discern the identity of the Beloved Disciple. Porsch considers it improbable that the Beloved Disciple denotes only a symbol. He is a historical disciple, but "for us he must always remain as a nameless unknown (namenlose Unbekannte)."[123]

In 1985 in the *Journal for the Study of the New Testament* B. Byrne, in his attempt to sidestep the "actual identity" of the Beloved Disciple, may give the impression that he considers him to be a literary symbol that, on the one hand helps later generations to avoid the impression that they should envy the first disciples, and on the other hand helps such later readers of the GosJn to know "how the historical Jesus of Nazareth remains for all generations of mankind the abiding and saving revelation of God."[124] However, in 1992 in *The Anchor Bible Dictionary*, Byrne espoused the same opinion as articulated by Porsch. He added (under the influence of Culpepper) that the Beloved Disciple was "the head of the Johannine school in its formative period," but "was not widely known or recognized outside his own moment."[125] Nevertheless, he is the guarantor of the truthfulness of the Jesus tradition in the GosJn.

In 1987 J. Zumstein contended that the Beloved Disciple is "un personnage mystérieux et captial" who is "un personnage historique" and not "une création littéraire à valuer symbolique." He points out that the Beloved Disciple, like Peter and Judas, is described as present at the Last Supper. Most importantly, the intention of the author of the GosJn to ground the claims of the gospel on a trustworthy witness faces grave problems if the Beloved Disciple was merely his own literary and symbolical creation. Zumstein astutely stresses what has been clear to me: the Beloved Disciple was "une figure centrale et reconnue du milieu johannique."[126] He also rightly perceives that one "des traits classiqes du personnage" is the dramatic opposition with Peter. The person remains anonymous. His main function in the GosJn is to witness to the truth of the Johannine gospel and to guarantee and legitimate its claims.[127] He is certainly not the author of the GosJn, but he is at the "origines de la tradition johannique." He is thus the unnamed founder of the Johannine movement and "le fondateur d'une école."[128]

---

[123] F. Porsch, "Der Jünger, den Jesus liebte," in *Johannes-Evangelium* (Stuttgarter Kleiner Kommentar; Neues Testament 4. Stuttgart: Verlag Katholisches Bibelwerk, 1989 [2nd ed.]) 145–47.

[124] B. Byrne, "The Faith of the Beloved Disciple and the Community in John 20," *Journal for the Study of the New Testament* 23 (1985) 83–97, esp. 94.

[125] B. Byrne, "Beloved Disciple," *Anchor Bible Dictionary* (1992) 1.658–61; esp. 660–61.

[126] J. Zumstein, "Le disciple bien-aimé," *Cahier biblique* 26 (1987) 47–58; see 48.

[127] Ibid., 55.

[128] Ibid., 57.

In 1988 E. Ruckstuhl in "Der Jünger, den Jesus liebte," presented some more of his careful reflections on the GosJn. He concluded that one can scarcely doubt that a real historical person is meant by 13:23 and 19:20; the Beloved Disciple is depicted along with Judas, Peter, and other of Jesus' disciples at the Last Supper and was thus a real historical individual.[129] The Beloved Disciple stands by Jesus at the cross as an "einziger Jünger und treuer Freund."[130] The author of the GosJn employs the Beloved Disciple as a many faceted anti-docetic character.[131]

While the name of the Beloved Disciple may not be discernible from the GosJn, he was certainly known by many Johannine Christians: "Als solcher war die Ausage für die Johanneschristen eindeutig, weil zur Zeit, als Joh 21 geschrieben wurde, fast alle von ihnen den Träger des Names persönlich noch gekannt hatten, wie 21,23 überdeutlich macht." Even more interesting is Ruckstuhl's suggestion that in light of the tension between Peter and the Beloved Disciple in the GosJn, it is conceivable that the "petrinische Gemeinden" in the vicinity of the Johannine Community also knew this disciple and his honorific title (the BD), perhaps even if only by word of mouth.[132] He disagrees with Thyen on a number of points, especially on the attribution of all the Beloved Disciple passages to a secondary literary level. He surmises that the Beloved Disciple may have been a converted Essene who formerly lived in the Essene quarter in Jerusalem.[133] Such a possibility is no longer too speculative in light of the growing textual and archaeological evidence of an Essene quarter in Jerusalem, precisely where Jesus and his disciples' may well have celebrated the Last Supper.[134] Indeed Ruckstuhl's insightful perception is fascinating in light of Ashton's argument that the author of the GosJn was a converted Essene, and my own contention that the author of the Odes of Solomon lived in the Johannine Community and was a former Essene.[135]

In 1988 B. Bonsack argued that the Beloved Disciple is a composite figure. He is not one historical person. He represents all who have func-

---

[129] Ruckstuhl, *Jesus im Horizont der Evangelien*, 359.

[130] Ibid., 361.

[131] Ibid.

[132] Ibid., 363.

[133] Ibid., 393–95.

[134] See the numerous chapters in Charlesworth, ed., *Jesus and the Dead Sea Scrolls*.

[135] See Ashton, *Understanding*, 237: "The evangelist may well have started life as one of those Essenes who were to be found, according to Josephus, 'in large numbers in every town': ἐν ἑκάστῃ [πόλει] μετοικοῦσιν πολλοί (BJ ii. 124)." Also see the discussions in Charlesworth, ed., *John and the Dead Sea Scrolls*.

tioned as witnesses and leaders in the Johannine Community.[136]

In 1989 K. Quast focused on the rivalry between the Beloved Disciple and Peter. In his *Peter and the Beloved Disciple: Figures for a Community in Crisis* he concluded that the Beloved Disciple was certainly a real historical person. He left the identity unresolved.[137]

In 1990 R. F. Collins contended that the Beloved Disciple was "a real individual," like John the Baptist and Peter. All the Beloved Disciple passages are compositions by the Evangelist or a final redactor. Collins is convinced that it is "best to leave to him the anonymity which was certainly intended by the author of the final gospel."[138] He is the quintessential believer, disciple, beloved, and witness.

In 1991 J. Ernst wrote his *Johannes: Ein theologisches Portrait*, and one might obtain from the title the impression that he held that the Beloved Disciple was John the son of Zebedee. That is not the case, although he takes at face value the meaning of 21:24-25 that the Beloved Disciple is the author of the GosJn. He concludes with the speculation that the Beloved Disciple may perhaps be the Elder John. But he admits that the only certain identification is that the Beloved Disciple belongs to the Johannine School, that he has died, and that he now has this honorific title.[139]

In 1992 J. A. Grassi published his *The Secret Identity of the Beloved Disciple*. He is convinced that the Beloved Disciple "certainly" cannot be the apostle John and that he was not even a member of the Twelve. Grassi concluded that the name of the Beloved Disciple is "secret," but he was a real historical person. He stresses the ties between the Beloved Disciple and John the Baptist under whom he had been a close disciple and "protégé." This anonymous disciple, who was from Judea, may have been from a priestly family. "Jesus adopted the youngster as his own son in a strong affectionate relationship."[140] Grassi sees the possibility of the Joseph tradition in the accounts of the Beloved Disciple. Like Joseph (Gen 37:3) he may have been Jesus' youngest. The tension between the Beloved

---

[136] B. Bonsack, "Der Presbyteros des dritten Briefs und der geliebte Jünger des Evangeliums nach Johannes," *Zeitschrift für die neutestamentliche Wissenschaft* 79 (1988) 45-62.

[137] K. Quast, *Peter and the Beloved Disciple: Figures for a Community in Crisis* (Journal for the Study of the New Testament, Supplement Series 32; Sheffield: JSOT Press, 1989) 16-21.

[138] R. F. Collins, *These Things Have Been Written: Studies on the Fourth Gospel* (Louvain Theological & Pastoral Monographs 2; Louvain: Peeters, 1990) 43.

[139] J. Ernst, "Der Lieblingsjünger," *Johannes: Ein theologisches Portrait* (Düsseldorf: Patmos Verlag Düsselverlag, 1991) 17-26.

[140] Grassi, *The Secret Identity of the Beloved Disciple*, 115.

Disciple and Peter in the GosJn is traced back into the time of the historical Jesus: "Jesus' affectionate relationship to the beloved disciple ... was a
source of friction as well as embarrassment to the chosen twelve who saw
John (sic) as a threat to their own special position."[141] I wonder to what
extent these tensions originate only in the milieu of the Johannine Community.

Also to be categorized here are those scholars who have studied the
use of the plural personal pronoun in the GosJn and have pointed out that
it demonstrates the importance of the witness behind the gospel. A. Harnack and E. C. Hoskyns argued that this "we" not only has the power to
extend to a group larger than the original disciples, but also to contract to
a singular person.[142] Hoskyns stressed that "we do not have the capacity"
to name the man represented by the ego and the one who wrote the
GosJn.[143]

Also under this category of those who see the Beloved Disciple as a
real person of history whose name, or identity, cannot be recovered
should be placed the idiosyncratic, yet intriguingly insightful hypothesis of
D. E. H. Whiteley.[144] This gifted and influential Oxford scholar argues
that it is highly improbable that the Evangelist is John the son of Zebedee
(2486-87, 2493). He is, though, the Beloved Disciple, and was once a
Sadducee, even a member of the Sanhedrin. His knowledge of Hebrew
and mastery of midrashic technique reveals that he "was an outstanding
Rabbinic scholar."[145] The Beloved Disciple "died in the course of finishing his work, and left it virtually as we now have it."[146] One of his main
sources was his own vivid memory of events from Jesus' life that he had
witnessed.

Whiteley is influenced by the Synoptic account that depicts high
priests at the scene of the crucifixion (οἱ ἀρχιερεῖς in Mk 15:31 and Mt
27:41; cf. Lk 23:35, οἱ ἄρχοντες). He connects this tradition, which he
assumes is reliable historically, with Polycrates' claim that the Evangelist

---

[141] Ibid.

[142] A. Harnack, Das "Wir" in den Johanneischen Schriften (Situngsberichte
der Preussichen Akademie der Wissenschaten; Philosophisch-historische Klasse;
Berlin, 1923) 95-113. (I am indebted to Hoskyns for this citation.) See Hoskyns,
The Fourth Gospel, ed. F. N. Davey (London: Faber and Faber, 1947) 86-88.

[143] Hoskyns, The Fourth Gospel, 87.

[144] D. E. H. Whiteley, "Was John Written by a Sadducee?" Aufstieg und
Niedergang der Römischen Welt II.25.3 (Berlin: Walter de Gruyter, 1985) 2481-
2505. See esp. "The B.D. Died While Finishing John: He Was a Sadducee,"
2492-2502.

[145] Ibid., 2487.

[146] Ibid., 2488.

wore the πέταλον (which does indicate a priest),[147] and with the exegesis that places the Beloved Disciple at the foot of the cross observing the thrust of the soldier's lance (19:35). Thus the Beloved Disciple is an unknown Sadducee who is an eyewitness to aspects of Jesus' life and crucifixion; and he is the anonymous man who wrote the so-called Gospel According to John. He "ceased" being a Sadducee and became a Christian, "sharing the Pharisaic belief in the resurrection," when he "saw and believed" (20:8). This verb "believed" is an inceptive, or ingressive aorist, which denotes that the Beloved Disciple began to believe that Jesus is "Lord."[148]

Also under this category may be placed the hypothesis of S. Brown. Impressed by the anonymity of the Beloved Disciple, he contends that the "Beloved Disciple's anonymity has led me to suggest that he may not even have been a contemporary of Jesus." He is persuaded by H. Koester's observation that anonymity was a "characteristic of the second generation of the Christian church"; and this prompts him to suggest that "the Beloved Disciple is a second generation Christian leader, who has been written into the story of Jesus."[149]

Matthias (Titus)

Biographical Sketch: Matthias is mentioned only briefly in Acts 1:23 and 1:26. He is the one chosen by lot to replace Judas Iscariot among the Twelve. He fits the criterion for election: a man who beginning from the time Jesus was baptized by John the Baptist until the time of the election had "accompanied" the disciples. He also fulfills the requirement of being a witness to Jesus' resurrection (Acts 1:22).

In 1950 E. L. Titus, who taught at the University of Southern California, claimed that the Beloved Disciple is to be identified as Matthias. While some scholars may think such a suggestion is ludicrous, the argument is made with insight; it does have an attractive cogency that is often missing in articles that defend another historical person.

---

[147] Polycrates' letter of circa 191 C.E. is preserved by Eusebius in *HE* 5.24. Note Whiteley's contention that "on one occasion the B.D., a young member of a high-priestly family, did duty for Caiaphas" (*ANRW* II.25.3, 2497).

[148] If Whiteley is correct on the meaning of the aorist in 20:8, which is likely, and the BD begins to believe that Jesus is "Lord," then the link between the BD and Thomas is forged. My thesis is that it is Thomas as the BD to whom the narrator gives the climactic confession: "My Lord ...."

[149] S. Brown, "The Beloved Disciple: A Jungian View," in *The Conversation Continues: Studies in Paul and John in Honor of J. Louis Martyn*, ed. R. T. Fortna and B. R. Gaventa (Nashville: Abingdon, 1990) 336–77; esp. 371. Also, see S. Brown, *The Origins of Christianity: A Historical Introduction to the New Testament* (Oxford: Oxford Univ. Press, 1984) 137–38.

Titus's argument may be summarized under twelve points: (1) Matthias fulfills both the criterion of "witness" according to Acts, and the major characteristic of the Beloved Disciple according to the GosJn. (2) The Acts criterion of witnessing Jesus' resurrection is a key feature of the Beloved Disciple. (3) Since the Beloved Disciple is perhaps alluded to in the GosJn in 1:35-40, he would thus, like Matthias, have participated in Jesus' group from the time of his baptism, since he would then have formerly been a follower of John the Baptist and a "witness" to Jesus' baptism. (4) As Matthias replaces Judas, so the Beloved Disciple is introduced for the first time "in the section dealing with Judas' departure from the group." (5) As Matthias was chosen by divine lot, so the disciple who was a "witness to Jesus' most inmost intention" (13:21-26) was none other than the "one who was predestined ultimately to succeed Judas himself." (6) The objections that Matthias does not fit the description of the Beloved Disciple in 18:15-16 and 19:35 are irrelevant; it is "not clear that it is the Beloved Disciple who is referred to in these sections." Furthermore, these passages may not be genuine to the GosJn. (7) Matthias and the Beloved Disciple are representatives of Christians. (8) Matthias is integrally connected with Mary, the mother of Jesus and Jesus' brothers (Acts 1:14) which fits the scene of Jesus' mother and the Beloved Disciple at the cross (19:25-27). (9) Matthias and the Beloved Disciple are admirable symbols of the church. (10) Both Matthias and the Beloved Disciple are cast in obscurity, and hence both help the New Testament authors portray Christianity as "a universal religion bound in no way by time or place." (11) Anonymity strengthened the symbol of the Beloved Disciple; and the best the author of the GosJn could do, in face of the influence from the Synoptics, was to cast Matthias in an anonymous role in the narrative. (12) The author of the GosJn knew Acts and used it as a source. Finally, Titus does not deal with the Appendix of the GosJn, because he is convinced it is the work of an editor who intended to "identify the Beloved Disciple with John the son of Zebedee."[150]

In 1953, along with E. C. Colwell of Emory University, Titus wrote *The Gospel of The Spirit: A Study of the Fourth Gospel*. Twice the Beloved Disciple is mentioned, and neither time is there any suggestion of his actual identity (or what the epithet might mean).[151]

In Titus' subsequent *The Message of the Fourth Gospel*, the references to the Beloved Disciple are of a decidedly different kind from the claims in his article.[152] He considers favorably the possibility that the

[150] E. L. Titus, "The Identity of the Beloved Disciple," *Journal of Biblical Literature* 69 (1950) 323–28.

[151] E. C. Colwell, E. L. Titus, *The Gospel of the Spirit: A Study in the Fourth Gospel* (New York: Harper & Brothers, 1953) 83, 181.

[152] E. L. Titus, *The Message of the Fourth Gospel* (New York/Nashville: Abingdon, 1957).

Beloved Disciple may be a symbol of the church.[153] The identification of the other disciple of 18:15-16 with the Beloved Disciple "is entirely gratuitous."[154] The Beloved Disciple is intentionally anonymous so it can represent the church, perhaps Gentile Christianity.[155] While his identity has been suggested—"Paul, the rich young ruler, Lazarus, Matthias"—it is more "plausible" that he is a "representative type"; he stands for "the ideal disciple."[156] He does not cite his article in which he argued for Matthias; and that name appears only here in his discussion of the Beloved Disciple.

Titus has significantly distanced himself from wild speculation. He stated that the author of the Appendix (chapter 21) wrote as a representative of the Johannine Community. He claimed that the Beloved Disciple was both witness and author of the GosJn.[157] The following is well couched:

> The less personality attaching to a name the more flexibility it could have as a symbol. Seen in this light, the role of the beloved disciple becomes understandable. He is the true disciple, whose faith, unlike Peter's, is unwavering. He is in the bosom of Jesus as Jesus is in the bosom of the Father. He is the one who alone can be entrusted with the care of Jesus' mother. His faith brings him first to the empty tomb.[158]

The hypothesis that Matthias can be the Beloved Disciple fails to convince, since it does not meet the major criterion. The identity of the Beloved Disciple must be found within the GosJn. Matthias does not appear in the GosJn; therefore he cannot be the Beloved Disciple.[159]

---

[153] Ibid., 187. Titus obviously came under the influence of Bultmann's interpretation; see esp. 221 and n. 85. I am also convinced he changed his mind on the identity of the BD.

[154] Ibid., 215.

[155] Ibid., 221 (text and footnote 85).

[156] Ibid., 218.

[157] Ibid., 253.

[158] Ibid., 220. Titus continues to claim that the BD cannot be a member of the Twelve. Obviously, my own research and conclusion forced me to end the quotation as it does above, otherwise I could not introduce the citation as "well couched."

[159] As I indicated earlier, Titus probably abandoned his suggestion that the BD is Matthias. In 1968 he authored an article that showed keen insights into the meaning of the GosJn, pointing out that the BD was contrasted with both Peter and Judas. He wrote, "The identity of the 'beloved disciple' is not indicated" ("The Fourth Gospel and the Historical Jesus," in *Jesus and the Historian: Written in Honor of Ernest Cadman Colwell*, ed. F. T. Trotter [Philadelphia: Westminster, 1968] 98–113; esp. 109).

Apollos (Tobler, Dechent, Pétrement)

In 1860 J. T. Tobler, a Pfarrer in Zürich, argued that the Beloved Disciple is to be identified with Apollos. Tobler wisely saw that "alle dog-matischen und traditionellen Gesichtspunkte" must not influence critical research, but he, as others of his time, was too optimistic about the limits of so-called "wissenschaftlichen Untersuchung." His method was to gather passages which he was convinced were historically true and to combine them with the model disciple. While the "innere Charakter des 4. Evan-geliums" is that of a Jew, the composition is by an unknown person who was a Greek, or non-Jew, living outside ancient Palestine. Alexandrian influence seems clear from the use of Logos. Some Philonic influence should be recognized, since Philo was the first to combine cosmological reflections on Logos with Plato's philosophy. He contended that Apollos was the first philosopher to combine Philonic ideas with a portrayal of the historical Jesus; hence, as Apollos wrote *Hebrews*, so he composed the GosJn near the end of the first century C.E. (which was not in line with *consensus communis* in the late 19th century).[160] The GosJn was written "gegen die Juden für Hellenen."[161] Apollos obtained Jesus traditions from the apostle John.

That Apollos was the author of the GosJn was upheld by H. Dechent,[162] and most impressively by S. Pétrement in 1984.[163] Pétre-ment's claim is as follows: "it can be affirmed that *we know of no other person of the time who as much as Apollos unites the qualities and condi-tions necessary to allow one to attribute the Johannine writings to him.*"[164] He defends this conclusion by organizing his thoughts into twelve obser-vations regarding Apollos and the author of the GosJn (who to him is the BD):[165] (1) Both show a "grandeur or force of spirit." (2) Both are elo-

---

[160] J. T. Tobler, "Ueber den Ursprung des vierten Evangeliums," *Zeitschrift für Wissenschaftliche Theologie* 3 (1860) 169–203. Under his name is the following notice: "Verf. der *Evangelienfrage im Allgemeinen und der Johan-nisfrage insbesondere*. Zürich, 1858." I have not read this book.

[161] Tobler, *Zeitschrift für Wissenschaftliche Theologie* 3 (1860) 174.

[162] H. Dechent, "Wer hat das vierte Evangelium verfasst?" *Theologische Studien und Kritiken* (1911) 446–61. I am grateful to Pétrement for this citation.

[163] S. Pétrement, "Apollos and the Fourth Gospel," *A Separate God: The Christian Origins of Gnosticism* (San Francisco: Harper, 1990 [French original 1984]) 276–97.

[164] Ibid., 276–97; esp. 288 (italics his).

[165] These are numbered by him; habitually I have organized presentations into clear observations.

quent. (3) Both were Jews. (4) Apollos was from Alexandria; the Evangelist was theologically influenced, especially in his concept of the Logos, by Philo of Alexandria. (5) Both were judged in antiquity to be linked with John the Baptist, and both may have once belonged to a group associated with John the Baptist. (6) Paul thought Apollos was "imperious and violent (2Co 11:20)," and this description fits the author of the GosJn. (7) If Apollos presented a life of Jesus as found in the GosJn, then "one could understand very well why in Paul's eyes he preached another Jesus, another Gospel." (8) Most of Luke's portrait of Apollos "agrees perfectly with the author of the Fourth Gospel." (9) The theological links between Paul and the GosJn can be explained by recognizing that Apollos was "instructed in part by Paul's disciples." (10) The striking similarities between the Gospel of Luke and the GosJn are explained by recognizing that both authors belonged to the circle of Paul's disciples. (11) Gnosticizing tendencies erupted in Corinth after Apollos's visit, and the GosJn is characterized by a "tendency toward Gnosticism." (12) If Apollos wrote the epistles of John, then the reference to a certain Gaius (3Jn 5-7) makes sense, since both he and a Gaius were in Corinth (Ro 16:23, 1Co 1:14).

This hypothesis is creative and thoughtful, but it fails to persuade for numerous reasons, among them the following: It is now clear that the "Anti-Judaisms" in the GosJn reflect not the time of Apollos, but the later period; after circa 80 C.E. sociological conditions permit the probability of a Jewish community estranged from the "synagogue." The discovery of the Dead Sea Scrolls proves that the GosJn is fundamentally Jewish in terms of ancient Palestine and not Alexandrian Judaism. Philonic ideas do help us understand the Logos concept, but that does not move us out of ancient Palestine. We know so little about Apollos—who never appears anywhere in Johannine literature (within or without the "canon")—that we are left explaining one unknown through another. Apollos is mentioned only somewhat obliquely in Acts 18:24, 19:1, 1 Corinthians 1:12, and four times in 1 Corinthians 3–4.

Nevertheless, fruitful for further exploration, in my judgment, are the insights into the parallels between Philo and the GosJn (which are deepened by the magisterial research by Borgen today),[166] the insight into the preponderance of ἐκεῖνος in the GosJn,[167] which Tobler thought indicates Apollos' "Bekanntschaft" with the apostle John, and the list of Latin loan words in the GosJn:

---

[166] See especially P. Borgen's *Logos was the True Light and Other Essays on the Gospel of John* (Publications Edited by the Department of Religious Studies in the Univ. of Trondheim 9; Trondheim, 1983).

[167] According to Morgenthaler: 54/23/33/70.

titulus	τίτλος	19:19, 20
sudarium	σουδάριον	11:44, 20:7
mansiones	μοναί	14:2, 23
litra	λίτρα	12:3, 19:39
cadus	μετρητής	2:6
stadium	στάδιον	6:19, 11:18

Paul or a Paulinist (Bacon, Hanhart, Goulder)

Biographical Sketch: The apostle Paul is so well known that a biographical sketch can be abbreviated, bringing out what I am persuaded are the main aspects of his life obtainable through historical research.[168] He was born a Roman citizen in Tarsus, and may have studied in Jerusalem under the famous Gamaliel (if Acts can be trusted). He first persecuted the followers of Jesus, but after an experience during which he claimed to have been blinded by an appearance of the risen Jesus, Paul believed Jesus to be his Lord, Savior, and the Son of God. Subsequently he became one of the most prominent Christian missionaries. He wrote some of the most brilliant epistles in antiquity, and his own authentic writings are probably 1 Thessalonians, Romans, Galatians, 1 and 2 Corinthians, Philippians, and Philemon.

In 1907, in the *Expositor*, B. W. Bacon discussed the identity of the Beloved Disciple. His position has been inaccurately portrayed by scholars working on the identity of the Beloved Disciple. Some think that Bacon concluded the Beloved Disciple was a "purely ideal figure"; others report he opted for Paul. His opinion appeared in many publications; I shall focus on his 1907 article and his books on the GosJn of 1910 and 1933.

In the *Expositor* Bacon argued that the Beloved Disciple is a "type of true discipleship." The editor of the Appendix, chapter 21, clearly understood the Beloved Disciple to be John the son of Zebedee; but that does not indicate this identification is reliable. John 19:35 is "redactional" and indefinite as regards the Beloved Disciple. He is convinced that chapter 13 and the Last Supper is not history, but "doctrinal interpretation" in line with the teaching of Paul in 1 Corinthians 10 and 11. The third appearance of the Beloved Disciple in chapter 20 is also only a type of faith, and "no disciple of flesh and blood." In these three contexts the Beloved Disciple is phantasmal; he results from "the symbolic adaptations of synoptic scenes in which he figures."[169] His appearance in the GosJn is

---

[168] I am convinced that his own letters are the primary sources for Paul's life, but I am not convinced that the historian can completely ignore Acts (despite the penchant of so many Pauline experts).

[169] B. W. Bacon, "The Disciple Whom Jesus Loved," *The Expositor* 4 (1907) 324–39; see 336.

the result of the editor's interpolations. The Beloved Disciple is more than an ideal figure; he is an idealized person.

Bacon is not easy to comprehend. When he states that "a very real man has sat for the portrait," does he mean that the idealization evolves from a real person of history? His words are ambiguous; but he is intent on showing the link between the GosJn and Paul, to whom the figure of the Beloved Disciple makes "a primary reference." The secret of the GosJn is framed by the great utterances of Paul. "The disciple whom Jesus loved" is to be seen in light of Paul's statement that the Son of God "loved me" (Gal 2:20). He concludes, "In this sense Paul, and whosoever has had Paul's experience ... is the disciple whom Jesus loved."[170] The qualification is fundamental; but its real meaning is left imprecise.

In 1910, in his *The Fourth Gospel in Research and Debate*, Bacon continued to explain his understanding of the Beloved Disciple. He struggled with the traditional interpretation that the Beloved Disciple should be identified as John the son of Zebedee. It is clear that he was forced to reject it.

The work and discussion by the Buckingham Professor of New Testament Criticism and Exegesis at Yale University was scientific and subtle. He did see striking affinities between the GosJn and Paul's letters. He argued that the language of the GosJn is beautifully framed by Paul's brilliant utterances. He judges, "If the Fourth Gospel be 'the heart of Christ,' the heart of the Fourth Gospel is Paul's confession of his faith in Galatians 2:20."[171] He actually cites Galatians 2:19-20; that passage is as follows: "I have been crucified with Christ; and it is no longer I who live, but it is Christ who lives in me. And the life I now live in the flesh I live by faith in the Son of God, who loved me and gave himself for me" (NRSV). Bacon continues (italics mine): "In this sense Paul, *and whosoever has had Paul's experience*—whosoever has thus seen the Lord, whether in the body or out of the body, whosoever has come to 'know him and the power of his resurrection'—is the 'disciple whom Jesus loved'."[172] Thus, much of his discussion in this book is from his article; but he now adds the necessary clarifications.

The italicized words indicate that Bacon really thought the Beloved Disciple was one who had been deeply influenced by Paul. For Bacon he remains anonymous, "the figure itself will gain no appreciable degree of

---

[170] Ibid., 339.

[171] Bacon, *The Fourth Gospel in Research and Debate: A Series of Essays on Problems Concerning the Origin and Value of the Anonymous Writings Attributed to the Apostle John* (New York: Moffat, Yard and Company, 1910) 326.

[172] Ibid.

historicity."[173] He was, in summation, "a Greek-speaking, Pauline Christian of 100 A.D."[174] who has been idealized.

In 1933 in his *The Gospel of the Hellenists* Bacon continued to stress that the GosJn does not come from the hand of the son of Zebedee, but is closely aligned with the teachings of Paul. If Bacon seems confusing it may be because of what he sees developing in Jerusalem in the latter half of the first century C.E. John the son of Zebedee was martyred in 63 and another John, John Mark, left Jerusalem in 46; these two were "inextricably confused and interchanged." The confused portrait of the Beloved Disciple is just what the "Christian visitor from Ephesus to Jerusalem would be shown as relics and traditions of his patron Apostle, 'the disciple whom Jesus loved.'"[175] Bacon uses the image of a photograph that has "a double exposure." The stronger image is that of "another John" who "eventually became a partner of Paul in his world-wide apostolate to the Gentiles." The fainter image reflects John the son of Zebedee. It is not representative to conclude that Bacon thought the Beloved Disciple was Paul; he is a Paulinist.

In 1984 K. Hanhart argued that the Beloved Disciple represented "een historisch persoon" and that he seems to be the apostle Paul.[176] The Evangelist was apparently thinking about Paul when he created the Beloved Disciple.[177] For Hanhart "Paulus past op die raadselachtige scènes als een sleutel in een slot."[178] During the *SNTS* Congress in Edinburgh in August 1994 Hanhart reiterated his position to me *viva voce*. He is convinced that the Beloved Disciple is not "een symbolische figuur," but a real historical person who has died.

In my judgment Hanhart concludes that the Beloved Disciple represents Paul because of the following reasons: (1) The Beloved Disciple appears only three times in the GosJn: at the Last Supper, at the cross, and in confrontation with the risen Lord (in the Appendix). He is not present at the empty tomb; that is another figure, the "another disciple"

---

[173] Ibid., 331.

[174] Ibid.

[175] Bacon, *Gospel of the Hellenists* (New York: H. Holt and Company, 1933) 427.

[176] K. Hanhart, "Johannes," in *Vervulling en Voleinding: De toekomstverwachting in het Nieuwe Testament*, ed. H. Baarlink, et al. (Kampen: Uitgeversmaatschappij J. H. Kok, 1984) 221–72. See esp. "De Geliefde Discipel," 239–47.

[177] Hanhart claimed that *"De schrijver moet gedoeld hebben op de apostel Paulus"* (*Vervulling en Voleinding*, 241 [italics his]). Also see 242: "Dit gedeelte is dus duidelijk een creatie van Johannes."

[178] Ibid., 247.

(20:2).[179] Hence, each of these events in the life of Jesus corresponds with a Pauline emphasis. (2) The Beloved Disciple's confession that Jesus is *kurios* found in 21:7 reminds Hanhart of Paul's confessional theology. (3) The ταῦτα of 21:24 points to Paul's own writings, which were considered important to read in the early church and were studied in the Johannine Community.[180] (4) The claim that the Beloved Disciple would not die until Jesus returned is consonant with Paul's belief that he would still be alive when Jesus returned in glory (see 1Th 4 and 1Co 15). (5) In chapter 19 at the foot of the cross we have symbolically Jesus' mother, who represents Zion, and the Beloved Disciple, who symbolizes Paul and his mission to the Gentiles.[181] (6) The Beloved Disciple in chapter 13 is Paul, who replaces Judas, who exits as the twelfth disciple.[182] (7) Paul is admirably suited as "the disciple whom Jesus loved" because he not only stressed that Christ, the Son of God "loved me and gave himself for me" (Gal 2:20), but also composed the sterling description of love in 1 Corinthians 13.[183] (8) The two great figures in the early church were Peter and Paul, so Peter's rival in the GosJn, the Beloved Disciple, may well represent Paul.[184] In summation, Hanhart is convinced that "Paulus is dus een veel logischer kandidaat voor de GD, dan b.v. Johannes, die volgens de klassieke exegese deze rol moet vervullen."[185]

In 1992 M. Goulder began his investigation of the identity of the Beloved Disciple with the claim that he "cannot be John bar-Zebedee," because there would "be no reason to suppress the name of so high an authority" in earliest Christianity.[186] He raised into new focus the question why "Jesus' favourite and the Gospel community's hero" would be "sup-

[179] Ibid., 247. The above is from my conversations with Hanhart; in 1984 he stated that the BD appears four times in the GosJn, including 20:3-10 (see 240). Orally he stressed that since in chapter 20 another verb is used to describe this disciple, he is most likely not to be identified as the BD.

[180] Ibid., 244-47. He claims that Paul's letters were studied in the Johannine Community; see Hanhart in *Studies in John*, 46.

[181] Ibid., 243. He cites Eph 2:11-22 as an example of "Paulinische theologie." Under the influence of Bultmann, Hanhart earlier argued that the BD represents the Gentiles to whom Israel, represented by Jesus' mother, is given as a son. See Hanhart, "The Structure of John I 35-IV 54," in *Studies in John Presented to Professor Dr. J. N. Sevenster on the Occasion of his Seventieth Birthday* (NTS 24; Leiden: Brill, 1970) 22-46; see esp. 29-30.

[182] Hanhart in *Vervulling en Voleinding*, 242-43.

[183] Ibid., 244.

[184] Ibid., 242.

[185] Ibid., 243.

[186] M. Goulder, "An Old Friend Incognito," *Scottish Journal of Theology* 45 (1992) 487-513.

pressed." He continues by stressing that the Beloved Disciple cannot be "an anonymous Jerusalem disciple," a "totally fictitious 'symbolic' figure," Lazarus, or John Mark. He concentrates on trying to ascertain the provenience and social world of the GosJn. He argues that the Beloved Disciple cannot be Paul; "but could John have *thought* he was?"[187] His answer is affirmative. He hypothesizes the following scenario:

> John was writing round the turn of the century, and had not known Paul personally. He did know at least some of the Pauline letters which we have; and he inferred from them, reasonably but erroneously, that Paul had been one of the Twelve Apostles. He also inferred from them that Paul had been present at the Last Supper, the Passion and the Resurrection. He found reason for thinking that Paul had been loved by Jesus; but his reconstruction was met with so much incredulity that he felt obliged to keep his hero incognito.[188]

Goulder is attracted to the "*explanatory power*"[189] of his hypothesis. The important witness in the GosJn helps "an Asian Pauline church embattled against a Jewish Christian mission which boasts its descent from Peter, and is currently led by Jesus' family. So he needs to promote the position of Paul over against Peter."[190] He is convinced that this explanation "fits well with the picture we form from elsewhere of John as a beleaguered defender of Pauline doctrine, and a redoubtable master of creative exegesis."[191]

Bultmann offered the opinion that as to "subject matter" the view introduced by Bacon that Paul represents the Beloved Disciple "is the best."[192] He, however, was ruminating about and advocating his own position that the Beloved Disciple represents "Gentile Christendom." Despite implications that Bultmann's comments shore up the hypothesis that the Beloved Disciple represents Paul, we need to continue to read Bultmann.[193] He went on to point out that this position is "of course impos-

---

[187] Ibid., 495; (italics his).

[188] Ibid., 495–96; (italics his).

[189] Goulder's italics.

[190] Ibid., 511.

[191] Ibid., 513.

[192] Bultmann, *John*, 484. *Das Evangelium des Johannes* (1941) 370: "Unter den Begriff des heidenchristentums fällt also auch das paulinische Christentum; und wenn schon auf eine historische Gestalt geraten werden sollte, die dem Evangelisten dieses freie Christentum repräsentiert, so ist Bacons Ansicht: Paulus sie gemeint, sachlich die beste."

[193] As J. E. Kay states, there are vast theological differences between Paul and the Fourth Evangelist. The former grounds eschatological salvation primarily on the cross and resurrection, the latter stresses that it is perceived "throughout the mission of the *Logos*, the incarnate Son of God." Hence, the wit-

sible, because the Johannine theology and terminology, while being theologically akin to the Pauline, bears no historical relation to it, and John develops his argument against Judaism in a completely different way from Paul."[194]

Benjamin (Minear)

P. S. Minear made an interesting case for the possibility that the author of the GosJn had the Benjamin traditions in mind when he introduced the Beloved Disciple into the gospel record. In 1977 Minear opined that every search for the identity of the Beloved Disciple "ends in impasse."[195] He offered two insights: recognizing that we have failed "to grasp the intention of the Evangelist," and that "his immediate audience understood his references to the beloved disciple better than we do," we "should lay aside our preoccupations and become more alert to what was important to them." Secondly, it is surely significant that "in every context where the disciple (the BD) remains unnamed, other disciples are carefully identified by name."[196] Thus, the Evangelist considered descriptive epithets, like mother and beloved disciple, "to be more significant than a name would have been." Pointing out that the evocative epithets would have been more appealing than mere names, Minear proceeds to "recover some of the nuances in that dialogue."

The Evangelist "defended his faith in Jesus as that prophet like Moses," and directed his apology to four segments of his society: his own church, secret synagogal believers, unbelievers in the synagogue, and Jamnia (Yavneh) loyalists. Minear endeavors to demonstrate that the Mosaic typology in the GosJn is to be supplemented by Benjamin traditions. It is at this point that we see his contribution to understanding the imagery, if not the identity of the Beloved Disciple.

Deuteronomy, in 18:15-22 and 34:1-12, contains traditions about the coming of "a prophet like Moses." In Deuteronomy and in the GosJn, the prophets Moses and Jesus are both mediators of a covenant, and their deaths in a Passion Story are described as necessary for God's economy. Deuteronomy 33 and GosJn 17 are farewell addresses with the latter pro-

---

ness of the GosJn cannot be Paul or a Paulinist. See Kay, *Christus Praesens: A Reconsideration of Rudolf Bultmann's Christology* (Grand Rapids: Eerdmans, 1994) 63. Moreover, the Pauline futuristic eschatology cannot be simply equated with the Johannine realizing eschatology. This fact was pointed out long ago by T. W. Manson, *On Paul and John* (SBT 38; London: SCM, 1963) see esp. 114.

[194] Bultmann, *John*, 484.

[195] P. S. Minear, "The Beloved Disciple in the Gospel of John: Some Clues and Conjectures," *Novum Testamentum* 19 (1977) 105-23, cf. 105.

[196] Ibid., 105.

viding "an appropriate climax to the earlier dialogue."[197] Minear now asks how Deuteronomy 33 helps the exegete of the GosJn to comprehend the Evangelist's interest in the Beloved Disciple.

The answer is supplied in Deuteronomy 33:12 in which Moses blesses Benjamin. He is "the beloved of the Lord" (ידיד יהוה). Indeed, the portrayal of Benjamin as the best-loved son of Jacob (Israel) was alive in the Evangelist's time as Jubilees 42:11 clarifies. Benjamin was the best loved brother of Joseph, whom—in contrast to the other sons of Jacob—he did not betray. The conceptual links with the Beloved Disciple are obvious and would be readily recognizable to the social group behind the GosJn. R. C. Fuller offered the opinion that the Beloved Disciple was "the youngest of the apostles" and received this epithet because of "his being the Benjamin of Christ's immediate followers and not because of any special merits he might possess."[198]

Secondly, Benjamin is promised continuing protection "all the day long." The link with the belief that the Beloved Disciple would not die should not be missed.

Thirdly, God will dwell between Benjamin's shoulders. This tradition probably helped shape the description of the Beloved Disciple who rested close to Jesus, on his shoulders (or breast; 13:23, 25; 21:20). For Minear, the Evangelist "found in Deuteronomy the assurance that because Benjamin was beloved by the Lord, the Lord assured him of two basic things: long-term security and intimate knowledge of the Lord's will and way."[199] Minear thus concludes that the Evangelist has portrayed the Beloved Disciple in part "to conform to the picture of Benjamin" in Deuteronomy 33:12. He is convinced that this clue will help in the search for the identity of the Beloved Disciple (see further in chap. 4).

Minear has contributed significantly to the study of the Beloved Disciple. In light of the social environment of the GosJn, specifically its Jewish context (both background in traditions and perspectives, and foreground in social crises), there can be no doubt that Jewish traditions, including those associated with Benjamin, helped shape the portrayal and reception of the Beloved Disciple. Despite Grassi's rejection of Minear's

---

[197] Ibid., 109.

[198] R. E. Fuller, "The Authorship of the Fourth Gospel," *Scripture* 5 (1952/1953) 8–11; see esp. 9. Fuller was writing for Roman Catholics, and he was defending tradition that the apostle John wrote the GosJn and is the BD. Another *defensor fidei* is B. de Solages who with considerable integrity and skill came to the conclusion that the apostle John is the BD ("Jean, fils de Zébédée et l'énigme du 'disciple que Jésus aimait,'" *Bulletin de litterature ecclesiastique* 73 [1972] 41–50).

[199] Minear, *Novum Testamentum* 19 (1977) 113.

insight,[200] I agree with Culpepper, who points to the fact that "all three features of the blessing on Benjamin are evoked by the sparse references to the Beloved Disciple in a context in which Deuteronomy and the Mosaic traditions serve as the background for the Gospel story, [and that] these correspondences can hardly be accidental."[201]

The Rich Young Ruler (King, Swete, Erbes, Lewis, Macgregor)

As far as I know, the first scholar to suggest that the Beloved Disciple is the Rich Young Ruler of Mark 10 was E. G. King of Sidney Sussex College, Cambridge in 1909. Professing the truth that those "who love the light eventually come to the Light," he contended that the Rich Young Ruler eventually "became a disciple, that he wrote the Fourth Gospel, and that, when he calls himself 'the disciple that Jesus loved,' he alludes to that look of love which appealed to his better self and drew him 'at the eleventh hour' into the Master's vineyard."[202]

In 1916 H. B. Swete, who is famous for his edition of the Septuagint (*The Old Testament in Greek*), intimated that the Beloved Disciple is the Rich Young Ruler mentioned in Mark 10:17-31.[203] He did not indicate any foreshadowing of this hypothesis in his commentary on Mark, which was published in 1905, or in his book on the GosJn, which appeared in 1913.[204]

Swete begins by suggesting that the Beloved Disciple may be one of the anonymous disciples of 20:2, which is now a rather popular move (as we know by following the searches of both Brown and Schnackenburg). Swete, however, intended to identify the disciple who is anonymous. Here are his arguments: (1) The Beloved Disciple was present at the Last Supper. He is in a prominent place which leaves out the sons of Zebedee to whom no author would accord such a high honor after they "roused the indignation of the Ten by their request that they might sit on the Lord's right and left." (2) The Beloved Disciple, the ἄλλος μαθητής of 13:15ff., must have been an influential person within the Jerusalem aristocracy.

---

[200] Grassi, *The Secret Identity of the Beloved Disciple*, 49–50, 129.

[201] Culpepper, *John*, 81.

[202] E. G. King, "The Disciple that Jesus Loved—A Suggestion," *The Interpreter* 5 (1909) 167–74.

[203] H. B. Swete, "The Disciple Whom Jesus Loved," *Journal of Theological Studies* 17 (1916) 371–74.

[204] H. B. Swete, *The Gospel According to St Mark* (London: Macmillan and Co., 1905). Some comment would have been expected regarding the BD on p. 225, when he discussed Mark 10:21. In *The Last Discourse and Prayer of Our Lord: A Study of St. John XIV–XVII.* (London: Macmillan and Co., 1913), one would have expected some comment on the BD on pp. viii–x, 13, 38–39, and 93–95.

(3) The Beloved Disciple takes Jesus' mother εἰς τὰ ἴδια which means he must have been rich, perhaps extremely rich, owning a *home* "in Jerusalem or in the neighbourhood." (4) The Beloved Disciple is the one ὁ γράψας ταῦτα. These observations lead to the conclusion that "the Beloved Disciple was not a Galilean, but a well-to-do inhabitant of Jerusalem or its environs, who belonged to a class socially superior to that from which the Galilean disciples of Christ were drawn."[205] He was also "not one of the Twelve."

Who was he? He was most likely either Lazarus or the Rich Young Ruler, since these are the only two men whom the gospels report that Jesus loved. Lazarus is unlikely because "if the Beloved Disciple had been the subject of our Lord's greatest miracle, the fact would not have been passed by without notice either in the Fourth Gospel or in early Christian tradition." Also, it is not "easy to conceive" how Lazarus of Bethany can become "the θεολόγος, the leader of Greek Christianity who survived under the name of John to the end of the first century."[206]

That leaves us with only the Rich Young Ruler, and recall Jesus ἠγάπησεν αὐτόν (Mk 10:21). He was "rich, even very rich," and he was a ruler, and thus "probably a member of the Sanhedrin." As a young man he ran to meet Jesus as he was coming up to Jerusalem. He asked Jesus the key question. Swete continues,

> The Lord's answer disappointed him, at least for the moment; he went away with clouded brow, a sadder man. But who shall say that Christ's love did not avail to bring him back? or that on his return he may not have attached himself to Jesus with a fervour and whole-heartedness which justified the Lord's immediate recognition of his worth?[207]

Thus Swete made an impressive case for the Beloved Disciple as the Rich Young Ruler. His hypothesis did not go unnoticed.

In the same year as Swete published his article (1916) C. Erbes issued his thoughts on the identity of the Beloved Disciple.[208] Without dependence on Swete's arguments or even knowledge of them, Erbes claimed that the Beloved Disciple cannot be one of the sons of Zebedee; he is rather to be identified with the Rich Young Ruler, who is to be identified with John Mark. The Zebedee John is not to be confused with the

---

[205] Swete, *The Journal of Theological Studies* 17 (1916) 373.

[206] Ibid., 374.

[207] Swete, *The Journal of Theological Studies* 17 (1916) 374.

[208] C. Erbes, "Der Jünger, welchen Jesus lieb hatte," *Zeitschrift für Kirchengeschichte* 36 (1916) 283–318.

Jerusalem John (Acts 12:12).[209] He must have been rich because the followers of Jesus congregated there, and Peter went directly there after being released from prison (Acts 12:6-17).[210]

In 1922 F. W. Lewis argued that the author of the GosJn "is the work of Lazarus issued (and perhaps edited) by the Apostle John—or that other John, beloved of critics!" The Beloved Disciple, Lewis continued, was not one of the Twelve, because he was one for whom Jesus had "special affection." His concluding words are important, "The story begins, I think in Mk 10[21]—Jesus loved him at sight—the young ruler was Lazarus."[211] Hence, Lewis thinks the Beloved Disciple is the Rich Young Ruler who did eventually follow Jesus and is known to us today by the name "Lazarus."

In his 1929 *The Gospel of John*, G. H. C. Macgregor of Glasgow presupposed "quite clearly" that the author of the GosJn not only knew the Gospel of Mark, but also expected his readers to know this earlier gospel, and hence he can "omit explanations which would otherwise be necessary (e.g., 3:24)."[212] Macgregor also argued that the author of John was literarily dependent on the Gospel According to Luke.[213] His search for the identity of the Beloved Disciple makes admirable sense only within these presuppositions.[214]

Macgregor begins by pointing out why the Beloved Disciple can be neither John the son of Zebedee nor an ideal figure. The former is

[209] Ibid., 287.

[210] Ibid., 295-318.

[211] F. W. Lewis "The Disciple Whom Jesus Loved," *The Expository Times* 33 (1921-1922) 42.

[212] G. H. C. Macgregor, *The Gospel of John* (Garden City, N.Y.: Doubleday, 1929) x.

[213] Macgregor, *The Gospel of John*, xi. "Literary dependence on Luke seems suggested by a comparison of Jn. 18:10 with Lk. 22:50, Jn. 19:41 with Lk. 23:53."

[214] Of course, as stated elsewhere in this monograph, today it is now being perceived by many experts on the GosJn that there is not one place in the GosJn where it is obvious that the author of the gospel was dependent on any one of the Synoptics. We are now thinking more in terms of the force of living oral traditions (recall Papias' penchant for the living word years after the composition of the GosJn), and we are more aware today of the other written traditions that were available by about 100 C.E., when the GosJn probably took the shape as we know it today. We are much more aware of the early traditions that appear in other (so-called extracanonical) gospels. See Smith, *John Among the Gospels*; also see Smith, "The Problem of John and the Synoptics in Light of the Relation Between Apocryphal and Canonical Gospels," in *John and the Synoptics*, ed. A. Denaux (Bibliotheca Ephemeridum Theologicarum Lovaniensium 101; Leuven: Univ. Press, 1992) 147-62.

unlikely because of the "thundering" character of John. The latter is unthinkable because no reader could guess what ideal the author "means to portray." Three individuals have given us the GosJn in its present form: the witness (that is the BD), the author (the Evangelist), and the redactor. The former was "a young Jerusalemite of good family, possibly with priestly connexions, not one of the Twelve, but a 'super-numerary,' whom Jesus admitted to peculiar intimacy during the closing period of his ministry."[215] He was introduced for the first time in chapter 13 (not as many have suggested in 1:35), and may have been "an unconfessed disciple, whenever our Lord was in Jerusalem."[216]

Macgregor is willing to venture into the "perilous realm of conjecture." He suggests that Swete's suggestion is perhaps "the most plausible."[217] That is "the Beloved Disciple" is to be identified "with the 'Rich Young Ruler.'"[218] These are the steps in his reflection: Both the Beloved Disciple and the Rich Young Ruler are introduced towards the close of Jesus' public ministry. The Rich Young Ruler asks Jesus the question so central to the GosJn: "O Good teacher, what should I do in order to inherit eternal life?" (Mk 10:17) Jesus is said to have loved the young man (Mk 10:21). Admitting his final comments may be "nothing more than 'pious speculation,'" Macgregor adds that the Rich Young Ruler "may have repented of his 'great refusal' and thrown in his lot with Jesus."[219]

What should be said about the suggestion that the Beloved Disciple is to be identified as the Rich Young Ruler? Jesus is said to have loved the young man ($\dot{\eta}\gamma\dot{\alpha}\pi\eta\sigma\epsilon\nu$ $\alpha\dot{\nu}\tau\dot{o}\nu$ [Mk 10:21]). He also is one who claims publicly to have obeyed the Torah from his youth (10:20). If the author of the GosJn knew Mark, and assumed his readers were very familiar with it, then this is not an impossible suggestion, at least at the outset. However, the man does not follow Jesus; he goes away sorrowful (10:22). He exits the scene of the gospels, and we never hear from him again. Moreover, he cannot be a viable candidate for the Beloved Disciple because it is highly unlikely that the author of the GosJn could have presupposed that his readers knew the account in Mark 10, and he never alludes to or mentions the Synoptic account of this possible episode in Jesus' life.[220] The hypothesis

---

[215] Macgregor, *The Gospel of John*, xlvi.

[216] Ibid.

[217] Ibid.

[218] Ibid.

[219] Ibid.

[220] Obviously there are some leading scholars who are persuaded that the GosJn has used one or more of the Synoptics as sources. See the numerous publications by F. Neirynck, especially "John and the Synoptics," in *L'Evangile de Jean*, 73–106, and "John and the Synoptics: The Empty Tomb Stories," *New Testament Studies* 30 (1984) 161–87. Also see T. L. Brodie, *The Quest for the*

is not even mentioned today in commentaries, monographs on the Beloved Disciple, or examinations of the identity of the Beloved Disciple.

Judas Iscariot (Noack, Griffin)

We now turn to the individuals mentioned in the GosJn. The Beloved Disciple must be a μαθητής[221] and a male, because of Jesus' words to his mother from the cross, "Behold your son" (ἴδε ὁ υἱός σου [19:26]).

Recent reviews of Johannine research give the reader the impression that there has been a consensus among scholars regarding the identity of the Beloved Disciple. Many Johannine experts today assume that we scholars concurred until recently that the Beloved Disciple was John the son of Zebedee. The benchmark is alleged to be the defection of Brown and Schnackenburg from the John-hypothesis to the suggestion that the Beloved Disciple is one of the anonymous disciples mentioned in 21:2. Virtually no critical review of research mentions the arguments published to substantiate the hypothesis that the Beloved Disciple may be Judas Iscariot, which probably meant "man from Cariot."[222]

In 1876 L. Noack argued that the Beloved Disciple is to be identified with Judas Iscariot, and indeed the author of the GosJn. Beneath layers of redaction in the GosJn (which includes all Jewish doctrine and miracle) is hidden the primitive gospel which was composed in 60 C.E. Jesus knew that he must die so that others might live, so he chose Passover in Jerusalem as the time for his death. He needed a helper, a beloved disciple, from among his chosen seven to assist him. Only Judas understood Jesus, so he was chosen "to deliver up" Jesus. Thus Judas, the Beloved Disciple, helped Jesus so that he would not be arrested as a troublemaker and disturber of the crowds, but rather be taken to die on the day of Passover. He claimed that the Greek παραδίδωμι in the GosJn 13:11, 21 means "to deliver up"; it never means "betray," which would be προδίδωμι (see my discussion in the exegesis of this passage). During the Last Supper Jesus made a symbolical gesture and only "the Bosom-disciple understood the sign." The Beloved Disciple was Judas, who is also known as Judas "Thaddäus oder Lebbäus."[223]

Origin of John's Gospel: A Source-Oriented Approach (Oxford/New York: Oxford Univ. Press, 1993). Brodie is convinced that the author of the GosJn "reshaped the synoptic narratives in order to give a clearer portrait of the working of the Spirit" (155).

[221] The one whom Jesus loved is always called μαθητής (13:23, 19:26, 20:2, 21:7, 21:20, 21:23).

[222] Jer 48:24, Am 2:2; cf. Jos 15:25. See also the variants to "Judas Iscariot" in the GosJn, viz. 6:71 in which ℵ* θ f¹³ sy^hmg have απο Καρυωτου.

[223] L. Noack, *Die Geschichte Jesu auf Grund freier geschichtlicher Untersuchungen über das Evangelium und die Evangelien*, 4 vols. (Mannheim: J.

Noack's study goes unperceived and without critique in the monographs on the Beloved Disciple and in the works on Judas Iscariot by D. Haugg,[224] R. B. Halas,[225] G. Buchheit,[226] K. Lüthi,[227] H. B. Dickey,[228] H. L. Goldschmidt and M. Limbeck,[229] and W. Vogler.[230] If Noack's three-volume work on Jesus went unnoticed by scholars working on the Beloved Disciple or Judas Iscariot, his publications were also not mentioned in the classic works on nineteenth-century biblical research on Jesus by H. Weinel and A. G. Widgery and by K. Barth.[231] And while M. Kähler in his epoch-making *The So-called Historical Jesus and the Historic Biblical Christ* referred to Noack only in passing,[232] the great A. Schweitzer devoted considerable space to him and his arguments.

Schweitzer rightly (even prophetically) stated that Noack's work "passed unnoticed." The great physician of Lamboreen judged him to be a free thinker, an ingenious scholar with considerable acumen, but one whose insights were vitiated by "too much of the poet in him."[233] Valu-

---

Schneider, 1876 [2nd ed.]) 232–36. S. Tarachov (M.D.) approaches the BD from psychological and psychoanalytical perspectives. He concludes that Judas, before "the betrayal," was the most beloved disciple of Jesus ("Judas the Beloved Executioner," *Psychoanalytical Quarterly* 29 [1960] 528–54, esp. 531–34). Tarachov attempts "to delineate the libidinal aspects of the Judas-Christ relationship as well as to provide clinically related phenomena" (551).

[224] D. Haugg, *Judas Iskarioth in den neutestamentlichen Berichten* (Freiburg im Breisgau: Herder & Co., 1930).

[225] B. Halas, *Judas Iscariot* (Washington: Catholic Univ. of America Press, 1946).

[226] G. Buchheit, *Judas Iskarioth* (Gütersloh: Rufer-Verlag, 1954). Buchheit lists Noack's book under "Allgemeine Literatur" on p. 279, but I find no discussion of his position.

[227] K. Lüthi, *Judas Iskarioth* (Zürich: Zwingli-Verlag, 1955).

[228] H. B. Dickey, *Judas Iscariot* (New York: Exposition Press, 1970).

[229] H. L. Goldschmidt and M. Limbeck, *Heilvoller Verrat? Judas im Neun Testament*, with a Foreword by A. Vögtle (Stuttgart: Verlag Katholisches Bibelwerk, 1976).

[230] W. Vogler, *Judas Iskarioth* (Berlin: Evangelische Verlagsanstalt, 1983).

[231] H. Weinel and A. G. Widgery, *Jesus in the Twentieth Century and After* (Edinburgh: T. & T. Clark, 1914) and K. Barth, *From Rousseau to Ritschl*, trans. B. Cozens and rev. H. H. Hartwell (London: SCM, 1959).

[232] M. Kähler, *The So-called Historical Jesus and the Historic Biblical Christ*, trans. C. E. Braaten (Philadelphia: Fortress, 1964 [1896]) 62.

[233] A. Schweitzer, *The Quest of the Historical Jesus*, 2nd ed., trans. W. Montgomery (London: A. & C. Black, 1931 [1910]) 173. An example of Noack's poetic distortion: "It is in the Galilaean district which forms the scene of the Song of Solomon that the reader of this book must be prepared to find the Golgotha of the cross" (see Schweitzer, 175).

able insights were the following thoughts by Noack:[234] The author of the GosJn introduced the Logos Christology and so would not have undermined its possibility of being heard by inventing a topographical and chronological perspective which is so different from the Synoptics as to question his position; hence, his account of Jesus' life cannot be easily dismissed as mere redaction. The GosJn is heavily redacted by more than one author, and there is a primitive core which antedates the destruction of 70 C.E.[235]

In 1892 C. S. Griffin published a "pamphlet" titled *Judas Iscariot: The Author of the Fourth Gospel*.[236] He was convinced that Judas wrote the GosJn and was the Beloved Disciple: "I believe Judas Iscariot was the author of the book of St. John, the fourth gospel; also the author of the three epistles ascribed to John." Griffin agreed with what he considered a unanimous consensus, "the 'beloved disciple' is the author of the book."[237] Here is a summary of Griffin's arguments:

(1) The "suspicion" is raised that Judas Iscariot is the author of the GosJn because "the author purposly (*sic*) hides his identity on several occasions" (preface and p. 1).

(2) Combining an exegesis of 1:35-42 and 6:71 ("Judas the son of Simon Iscariot") Griffin concludes that Judas was the "son of Simon Peter, and the nephew of Andrew" (pp. 1-2).

(3) Judas's death, especially in Acts, "has every appearance of a false tradition" (p. 2); hence, Judas can be said to write the GosJn "when he was an old man" (p. 4).

(4) At the Sea of Tiberius (20:1-2) Jesus separates Judas from the others; the book ends with the scene in which Peter asks Jesus, "Lord and what shall this man do?"

(5) The Beloved Disciple wrote the GosJn and is Judas, "probably the youngest of the twelve because his father was also a disciple with them" (p. 2).

---

[234] These are obviously shaped by my own reading of Schweitzer.

[235] Absurdities also abound in Noack's book and are pointed out in Schweitzer's report. Noack claimed erroneously that the primitive gospel contained no Jewish doctrine and no miracles (an amazing statement in light of the present consensus on Jewish elements in the GosJn and the probable isolation of the Signs Source), and that the Johannine Jesus focused his ministry in Galilee. Noack's reconstructions were based on Eusebius' *Onomasticon* mixed with references by Crusaders and others; thus these were evaluated correctly by Schweitzer as the result of "a recklessness which is nothing short of criminal" (175).

[236] C. S. Griffin, *Judas Iscariot: The Author of the Fourth Gospel, Which is Ascribed to St. John* (Boston: The Scott-Parkin Printing Company, 1892).

[237] Griffin, *Judas*, 2.

(6) Jesus trusted Judas and chose him to carry the purse—in part because he was young—so the older disciples could attend to more religious duties.

(7) Judas may have employed a scribe, as the use of "we" indicates.

(8) Judas "was not a traitor"; he "only did as Jesus told him privately to do" (p. 3).

(9) Jesus "consigned his mother to the life-long care of Judas, who alone of all the disciples could live in safety among the Jews, because he was no longer considered one of the hated Christians" (pp. 3, 8).

(10) The rumor that the Beloved Disciple would not die (21:23) fits only Judas "because he was not around to carrect (*sic*) it" (p. 3).

(11) The author of the GosJn "was a very ignorant man" because he thought the world could "not contain the books that would give an account of all that Jesus did" (pp. 3–4).

(12) The aside that Judas was a thief (12:6) "was certainly a hard thing for one to say about himself," but Judas was no doubt selfish and looked back as an old man on his youthful mistakes, and "he loved to write about himself as 'the disciple whom Jesus loved'" (p. 4).

(13) According to Acts, Peter speaks about Judas "as a guide prophesied" (4; cf. Acts 1:16: Ἰούδα τοῦ γενομένου ὁδηγοῦ).

(14) Acts 1:18 and 19 "are historical" (p. 5).

(15) GosJn 13:1–17:26 belongs "to another book"; he is convinced this conclusion follows from the valid observation that Judas would not have been present.[238]

(16) Jesus answers the Beloved Disciple by giving him the sop; "only Judas understood Jesus" (p. 6).

(17) The words "some of them thought" in 13:29 make sense only if Judas had written them.

(18) The "other disciple" of chapter 18 must have been Judas, since only he would have been known to the high priest (7–8). Griffin concludes as follows:

> Seeing that the "beloved disciple" twice declared that he wrote the book, and many times purposly [*sic*] covers his own name, and leaves out everything that was specially important to John, and also did things that Judas alone could have done—does not this all point to one conclusion, namely, that Judas Iscariot wrote the book ascribed to John?[239]

Obviously, these eighteen points are of differing value. They should not all be dismissed as insignificant. It is conceivable that Jesus' disciple,

---

[238] GosJn 14:31–17:26 probably does belong to a later edition of the GosJn.
[239] Griffin, *Judas*, 10.

Judas, may have written the GosJn. What is conceivable is, however, far removed from what is probable.

In 1992—one century after Griffin's work appeared—H. Maccoby examined the myth of Judas and the rise of Anti-Semitism. He reported that "modern scholars" do not think that the Beloved Disciple is John the son of Zebedee; they "regard the Gospel as being of unknown authorship."[240] Maccoby, the librarian at Leo Baeck College in London, is impressed with the "air of personal authenticity" and the complicity between Jesus and Judas according to the GosJn. Regarding the search for the Beloved Disciple, observe these words by Maccoby:

> After all, Judas himself was a "beloved disciple" ("mine own familiar friend," in the words of the Psalm Jesus quotes in this Gospel). The more beloved Judas was, the greater horror in his betrayal. There is thus, as in a dream, a coalescence between Judas and the beloved disciple.[241]

Most New Testament experts will not take seriously a suggestion that Judas could be identified in any way with the Beloved Disciple. The resistance will be immediate, unsympathetic, and the credentials of one supporting such an hypothesis will be severely questioned. Such is the power of the Judas myth, and perhaps of the academy.[242] Yet, as historians on the trail of the Beloved Disciple, we must admit that there are some observations that warrant contemplating that Judas Iscariot is conceivably the Beloved Disciple. Why should this hypothesis be branded absurd, unthinkable, idiotic, inconceivable? Out of conceivability might come some light for our journey. The clues will be hidden, of course, behind the heavily edited Johannine narrative.[243]

According to the GosJn—upon which our eyes should alone be focused if we want to see the trail of the Beloved Disciple in this highly

[240] H. Maccoby, *Judas Iscariot and the Myth of Jewish Evil* (New York: The Free Press; Oxford: Maxwell Macmillan International, 1992) 72.

[241] Ibid., 74. See also Maccoby, "Judas Iscariot," *The Sacred Executioner* (London: Thames and Hudson, 1982) 121-33.

[242] K. Lüthi emphasized the pejorative portrayal of Judas in the GosJn; he is the antithesis of Jesus. He is the Devil ("Das Problem des Judas Iskariot—neu untersucht," *EvTh* 16 [1956] 98-114).

[243] Thinking about "John's literary skill," F. Kermode points out that if the BD is Judas Iscariot we are confronted with "an excellent midrash." Narrative exegesis would then reveal that Jesus "indeed hands the bread to the man who asked the question" (*The Genesis of Secrecy: On the Interpretation of Narrative* [Cambridge, Mass.; London: Harvard Univ. Press, 1979] 92). See also Maccoby, *The Sacred Execution*, 127.

symbolical work—Judas was chosen by Jesus ("Did I not choose you, the Twelve, and from you one is a devil?" [6:70]). He was even elevated to a high position; he was the treasurer of Jesus' group. Surely the author of the GosJn, especially with his stress on Jesus' foreknowledge, would not want to suggest that Jesus erred in choosing Judas and making him a leader in the group.[244] Only he and Thomas are signaled out clearly as members of the Twelve.

He is present at the Last Supper, and the first disciple mentioned in that account. The reader is given the impression that his feet are washed by Jesus (13:5); and that would mean that he was forgiven by Jesus. He has a prominent role. He must be seated very close to Jesus, in a seat of honor, so that Jesus can reach out and give him the honorifically dipped unleavened bread ($\tau\grave{o}$ $\psi\omega\mu\acute{\iota}o\nu$ [13:26]).[245] The account is written so that one may obtain the impression that Judas is lying precisely where the author has placed the Beloved Disciple at the table. Jesus converses in confidence with him, giving the impression that he not only knows what Judas is about to do, but also does not resist it (13:27). Peter must ask the Beloved Disciple what is the meaning of Jesus' words. Is not the Beloved Disciple closer to Jesus than Peter? Is Judas also that close? All the other disciples, including the Beloved Disciple, are devoid of understanding what Jesus and Judas are intending: "No one ($o\grave{v}\delta\varepsilon\grave{\iota}\varsigma$) at the table knew why he said this to him [Judas]" (13:28). Among the disciples Judas alone knows what is about to happen. Here the author of the GosJn demonstrates his skill with the narrative technique of irony through misunderstanding.[246] The authorial stress upon Jesus' foreknowledge was made evident earlier in the narrative (6:70).

There must have been some confusion in the Johannine Community regarding Judas, since the author of the GosJn must at least once refer to another "Judas" who was "not Iscariot" (14:22). The author of the GosJn portrays Judas and Jesus on a cosmic scale; Satan is said to be involved,

---

[244] R. Brownrigg writes, "The very fact that he was his rabbi's choice to be treasurer of the band of disciples shows that he could be trusted with an important office" (*The Twelve Apostles* [New York: Macmillan, 1974] 204).

[245] I agree with Brownrigg that according to the GosJn the Beloved Disciple and Judas sat in the two seats of honor, one to the right and the other to the left of Jesus (*The Twelve Apostles*, 207). J. S. Billings also concluded that Judas reclined immediately to Jesus' left, and illustrated how during the Last Supper "Judas is paid special honour by our Lord." This scene contrasts with the unfair treatment of Judas elsewhere in the GosJn ("Judas Iscariot in the Fourth Gospel," *The Expository Times* 51 [1939/40] 156–57).

[246] H.-J. Klauck rightly sees the element of "Jüngermissverständnis." Klauck, *Judas—Ein Jünger des Herrn* (Quaestiones Disputatae 111; Freiburg: Herder, 1987) 86.

yet he is somewhat demythologized in the sense that he is now inside Judas. The author specifically states that Satan entered into Judas immediately after he ate what Jesus gave him (13:27). The drama is heightened in terms of the pervasive light-darkness paradigmatic dualism. As a son of darkness Judas leaves Jesus and his group and ventures out into the night (13:30).

He returns again at night, with lanterns and torches, accompanied by some Roman soldiers and a selection of the Temple guard. Judas knows Jesus' secret place (18:2). Is it not conceivable that "the other disciple" (18:15), who was known to and by the high priest, who entered the high priest's courtyard with the soldiers and ordered the door opened for Peter, was none other than Judas Iscariot?[247] Would any of Jesus' disciples, other than Judas, have been allowed at that moment and with soldiers into the high priest's *aulē*?

What happened to Judas after Jesus' arrest? Was he banned, condemned, and cast out as unforgivable by his former close friends? Or does the statement that Jesus lost not one of his close followers (18:9, 6:39), which includes Judas Iscariot, denote that Judas was forgiven of his actions that night?[248] Are his actions those of a betrayer? If so, what did he betray? Was Judas not included in the commission by the risen Jesus to the disciples? In the GosJn Jesus commissions his disciples, "Receive the Holy Spirit. If you forgive the sins of any, they are forgiven. If you retain

---

[247] Bernard mentioned that Abbott adopted the view that the "other disciple" of 18:15 was "Judas Iscariot, whose face would have been familiar to the portress, because of his previous visit or visits to the high priest in pursuance of his scheme of betrayal." Bernard, however, is critical: "But that Judas should *wish* to introduce Peter, or that Peter would have tolerated any advances from him or accepted his good offices, is difficult to believe" (*St. John*, 2:593). Whether Abbott or Bernard is closer to the historical truth will depend upon the truthfulness of our sources, and we scholars have been stressing that the gospels are heavily redacted (and not just those outside the so-called canon).

[248] How are we to relate 18:9 ("Of those whom you gave to me I lost not one from them") and 6:39 ("this is the will of him who sent me, that I should lose none whom he has given me,") with 17:12 ("I have guarded them, and none of them is lost [ἀπώλετο] but the son of perdition [ὁ υἱὸς τῆς ἀπωλείας], that the scripture might be fulfilled." The latter is probably a later addition to the GosJn, as experts have shown. The addition of chapters 15–17, in my judgment, reflects a later stage in the evolution of the GosJn, when Judas was considered lost, and when the study of Scripture had helped the members of the Johannine School understand episodes in Jesus' life. The sentence in 12:6 also defames Judas, disrupts the flow from verses five to seven, and is clearly editorial; it probably belongs to the stage when chapter 17 was added to the GosJn. It is intriguing to ponder how Judas was perceived during the early decades of the Johannine Community.

the sins of any, they are retained" (20:22-23). Although Jesus seems to reprimand Peter, according to chapter 21,[249] he never condemns Judas. On the contrary, Jesus speaks with him in the most cordial terms.[250] He urged his followers to love as he had loved them. And he issued his new commandment immediately after Judas exited from the room of the Last Supper (13:34). Would this love now include Judas once again? According to the Evangelist, Jesus loved his "own," his close disciples like Judas, "until the end" ($\varepsilon i \varsigma$ $\tau \acute{\varepsilon} \lambda o \varsigma$ [13:1]). As the one who demanded Jesus' full love, Judas could be considered as the disciple Jesus loved in a special way.[251] Is it possible that the Evangelist is ruminating on the Betrayer and the Beloved in each of us?[252]

How strong is the hypothesis that Judas Iscariot may be the Beloved Disciple? It at least fits four of the necessary criteria: the Beloved Disciple must be a historical person, a male, a disciple, and he must appear in a significant capacity in the GosJn.

Is there any possibility that the lost Gospel of Judas, mentioned by Irenaeus, Epiphanius, and Theodoret, is in any way derivative from or related to the GosJn?[253] This is unlikely if it was the gospel in which Judas is portrayed as the only disciple who knows the relation of the world above with the world below, the possessor of celestial gnosis, and the honoree of the sect of the Cainites.[254] The improbable could become impossible if the Gospel of Judas explains how Judas accomplished "the

[249] Of course in the Synoptics Peter is reprimanded by Jesus.

[250] This is discussed insightfully by H. Stein-Schneider in "A la recherche du Judas historique," *Études Théologiques et Religieuses* 60 (1985) 403-24.

[251] Maccoby defends a challenging and controversial thesis, which does have at least some grounding in the GosJn. He is convinced that Judas Iscariot is indeed Jude, the apostle and brother of Jesus, and perhaps the author of the Epistle of Jude. Judas the Betrayer is a creation of Christian myth making: the Pauline Gentile Church "turned Jesus into a deity, and gave Judas the role of archetypal traitor." Originally Judas had only one personality (*Judas Iscariot*, 152-54; cf. 152).

[252] Including the Synoptics one can ask what is the meaning of the two Jews hanging on a tree near Jerusalem. W. Jens poetically incorporates Judas within the necessary dimensions of the Christian drama of salvation with the words, "Dank sei dem Judas!" (*Der Fall Judas* [Stuttgart: Kreuz Verlag, 1975] 9). Seeing Judas as one of Jesus' favorites helps us understand the theological profundity that we betray only those whom we love, and that the gospel is about the forgiveness of God. For further reflections on these points, see R. S. Anderson, *The Gospel According to Judas* (Colorado Springs: Helmers & Howard, 1991).

[253] Charlesworth, with Mueller, *The New Testament Apocrypha*, 10, 15 (which contains a bibliography).

[254] See J.-P. Migne, *Dictionnaire des Apocryphes* (Encyclopédie Théologique 24; Paris: J.-P. Migne, 1858) vol. 2, cols. 449-50.

mystery of the betrayal" (*proditionis mysterium*, μυστήριον προδοσίας) and threw "all things into dissolution," as Irenaeus reported (*adv.Haer.* 1.31.1). In addition Iraenaeus would never confuse the GosJn with the Gospel of Judas, which is far too late to be equated with the GosJn, since it apparently must postdate 130.[255]

Then again we must not be too categorical. The apocryphal gospel is lost, and we simply do not know what was in it; moreover, Judas was not always the hero of the gnostics, as we know from Ptolemy's view of Gnosticism. According to him some gnostics thought Judas was an apostate.[256]

As in early Christianity there were many men named "John," so there were numerous significant men known as Judas: the patriarch Judah, Judas Barsabbas, Judas who was Jesus' brother, the two men named Judas who were the first and third bishops of Jerusalem, Judas who was James' son, Jude (or Judas) who was James' brother,[257] Judas Iscariot, and finally Judas Thomas the Twin. Does this extensive list not raise the question of the place of Judas in early Christianity? If he was so evil, then why did fathers give their sons that name? There is virtually no doubt that Thomas was known by that nickname, Didymus, and not by what is apparently his actual name, Judas, because of the abundance of men named Judas. The popularity of the name "Judas" in early Christianity is surely not because of the prestige of Judas Maccabaeus, Judas of Damascus, and Judas of Gamla.

The place of Judas in the life of Jesus is something quite other than the portrayal of him in the final edition of the GosJn or in other early Christian literature. The more we study Judas Iscariot, the more we become impressed by the aggregation of pejoratives concerning him than we are with *bruta facta* from his life.

What about the hypothesis that Judas Iscariot is the Beloved Disciple? Jackson pointed out that this hypothesis "breaks down" because Judas is distinguished from the Beloved Disciple in chapter 13.[258] To a certain extent this advice is sound, but on closer examination one wonders why the author has written this section so that the Beloved Disciple (13:23) and Judas (13:36) are presented in such an ambiguous way. Readers can derive the opinion that they are really lying on the same couch because they are one and the same person. Why are distinctions blurred narratively?

---

[255] See H.-C. Puech's comments, revised by B. Blatz in *New Testament Apocrypha*, 2:386–87.

[256] See Layton, *The Gnostic Scriptures*, 287.

[257] The Evangelist refers to a Judas who is not Iscariot; he is most likely one of the men given in the list above.

[258] Jackson, *The Problem of the Fourth Gospel*, 165.

Indeed, it is odd that in the crucial scene in the drama (chapter 13) Judas is not presented in disparaging ways as he is elsewhere (as in 6:71 and 12:6). An exegete is forced to admit that the Beloved Disciple and Judas Iscariot are not portrayed in clearly distinct ways when Jesus is described foretelling his betrayer (13:21-30). The distinction between so-called Betrayer and Beloved is veiled; one cannot prove that the person in 13:26 is different from the person in 13:23. It is not impossible that the disciple lying close to Jesus—the one whom Jesus loved—is authorially related to the one to whom Jesus gave the unleavened bread he had dipped. Is this an authorial way of symbolically indicating that the Betrayer and Beloved are not categorically distinct?

Finally, the exegete and historian must conclude that it is unlikely the author of the GosJn thought he had given the impression that the Beloved Disciple is to be confused with Judas Iscariot. Another reason he is not a viable candidate is because chapter 21 salutes the Beloved Disciple as the honored witness of the gospel, whereas Judas is not present within early Christianity to write what might be called the *magnum opus* among all the gospels.

Andrew, Simon Peter's Brother (Lützelberger)

In the same year that Bruno Bauer, famous for arguing that Jesus never existed, published his *Kritik*, in which he claimed that the GosJn was composed by a Christian poet, E. C. J. Lützelberger argued that the Beloved Disciple was Andrew, the brother of Peter.[259] He subjected the traditions that place the apostle John in Ephesus to the acids of historical criticisms, ultimately rejecting their validity. Among other arguments he pointed out that Clement lauded Peter and Paul, but does not mention the apostle John.[260] Lützelberger was convinced that the author of the GosJn was not the Beloved Disciple, but another person. In fact he was a Samaritan who migrated during the Bar Kokhba revolt from Palestine to Mesopotamia. The GosJn was written sometime later in Edessa.

Here are Lützelberger's arguments that Andrew is the Beloved Disciple: Andrew is one of the two former disciples of John the Baptist. He is the first to recognize and to confess that Jesus is the Messiah (1:41). Andrew is a special disciple whom other disciples must consult, as we know from chapter 12. Philip informs Andrew of the desire of the Greeks to meet Jesus. The struggle between the Beloved Disciple and Peter has its natural explanation in the recognition that Andrew and Peter are brothers

---

[259] E. C. J. Lützelberger, *Die kirchliche Tradition über den Apostel Johannes und seine Schriften in ihrer Grundlosigkeit* (Leipzig: F. A. Brockhaus, 1840).

[260] Ibid., 170.

(1:40). It is therefore obvious that the Beloved Disciple is not the apostle John but Andrew: "Demnach ist also der geliebte Jünger des Herrn nicht Johannes, sondern Andreas."[261]

This hypothesis is not impossible. Andrew is a former follower of John the Baptist. He finds his brother Simon Peter, and brings him to Jesus. And to Andrew the narrator gives the first confession by a follower of Jesus: "We have found the Messiah (which means Christ)" (1:41). But, if the anonymous disciple of 1:35-42 is to be identified with the Beloved Disciple, then the one hypothesis dismissed would be Andrew, since he is identified as the other of the two.

Philip (Boismard)

The distinguished Johannine expert at the Ecole Biblique in Jerusalem, M. É. Boismard, is persuaded that Philip may be the Beloved Disciple.[262] The first one to whom Jesus calls "Come and see" (1:39) is Andrew and his anonymous companion. They follow Jesus. Boismard offers "cette conjecture: le compagnon anonyme d'André et le disciple anonyme que Jésus aimait ne font qu'un; c'est 'celui qui témoigne de ces faits et qui les a écrits' (Jo., 21.24)."[263] He acknowledges that such a conjecture is not thoroughly convincing. He continues to argue, with much more confidence, that if a name may be given to this anonymous disciple it is surely not John the son of Zebedee but Philip. Here are his arguments: (1) Andrew and Philip often appear together in the GosJn and thus must have been closely linked (see 6:5-9, 12:20-22). (2) In the list of the apostles their names appear together (Mk 3:18, Acts 1:13). (3) Along with Peter they are from the same village, namely Bethsaida (1:44). Thus, not exactly equating the Beloved Disciple with Philip, Boismard is more intent on identifying the anonymous disciple in chapter 1 with Philip: "Il est donc préférable, ou de laisser le compagnon d'André à son anonymat, ou de voir en lui l'apôtre Philippe, lié d'amitié à André."[264]

Very interesting in this hypothesis is the perception that Philip and Andrew are associated in close harmony in the GosJn and are from the same city. Obviously one of the former followers of John the Baptist was Andrew. Attractively pointed out by Boismard is the fact that Jesus tells the two followers of the Baptist, who ask him "where are you staying," to "Come and see." These are obviously highly charged symbolic words. It

[261] Ibid., 205. It is important to note that he wrote a book focused on early traditions of the apostle John, not a monograph on the identity of the BD.

[262] Boismard, M.É., *Du Baptême à Cana (Jean 1.19-2.11)* (Paris: Cerf, 1956) see esp. 72-73.

[263] Ibid., 72.

[264] Ibid., 73.

is thus impressive to observe that the first two declarations in the GosJn are by Andrew, who states to Peter, "We have found the Messiah," and Philip, who tells Nathanael, "We have found him of whom Moses in the Law and the prophets wrote, 'Jesus, the son of Joseph, who is from Nazareth'" (1:45). The case for Philip being the anonymous companion of Andrew in 1:35-40 is the possibility that 1:43 is a later redactional insertion; it introduces Philip, suggesting that he had not yet been earlier introduced to the reader. But although Thyen defends this possibility, it is purely conjectural and without any textual base or link with other clearly redacted passages.[265]

Nathanael (Gutjahr, Spaeth, Rovers)

According to M. H. Shepherd, in *The Interpreter's One-Volume Commentary on the Bible*, some scholars have concluded that Nathanael is the Beloved Disciple: "Others believe him (Nathanael) to be the elusive 'beloved disciple' of the gospel." He continued, by contending that if Nathanael is not the Beloved Disciple, "the most likely alternate name for him would be Thomas—a nickname that means 'Twin.'"[266] While it would have been enlightening to hear more of his thoughts on Thomas, our attention is now on his comment that scholars have concluded that Nathanael is the Beloved Disciple, for only after extended research did I find a scholar who concluded that the Beloved Disciple is Nathanael. The search was extensive and at one point seemed to be fruitless.

Scholars have argued that Nathanael is an unknown disciple, judged him to be only a symbol of an ideal Israelite, and claimed that he is either Bartholomew or Matthew.[267] But, we are interested in who concluded Nathanael is the Beloved Disciple.

When he reviewed the early hypotheses, Bauer did not mention that a scholar had suggested Nathanael.[268] In his "Who was Nathanael?" R. B. Y. Scott also did not mention this hypothesis.[269] When discussing John the

---

[265] See Thyen in *L'Évangile de Jean*, 275: "Es scheint mir fast *sicher*, dass dieser Vers 43 zu dem Zweck interpoliert worden ist, den einen der beiden Erstberufenen zum Anonymus zu *machen*" (italics his). Notice how he continues: "Ohne Vers 43 sind Andreas und Philippus die beiden vom Täufer an Jesus gewiesenen ersten Jünger."

[266] M. H. Shepherd, "The Gospel According to John," *The Interpreter's One-Volume Commentary on the Bible*, ed. C. M. Laymon (Nashville/New York: Abingdon, 1971) 707–28; cf. 711.

[267] Hanhart is convinced "that Nathanael equals Matthew" (*Studies in John*, 22–46; esp. 25).

[268] W. Bauer, *Das Johannes-Evangelium* (Handbuch zum Neuen Testament 6; Tübingen: J. C. B. Mohr, 1933) 173–75.

[269] R. B. Y. Scott, "Who was Nathanael?" *The Expository Times* 38 (1926–1927) 93–94.

son of Zebedee (128–55) and Thomas (166–87), E. G. Kraeling, in *The Disciples*, never suggested that anyone has identified Nathanael with the Beloved Disciple, yet he discussed the Beloved Disciple at length under John but not once under Nathanael.[270] In his "The Representative Figures of the Fourth Gospel,"[271] and again in "Nathanael," in *The Anchor Bible Dictionary*, R. F. Collins did not mention any scholar who connects Nathanael and the Beloved Disciple.[272] When reviewing the hypotheses presented for the identification of the Beloved Disciple, J. Kügler mentioned John the son of Zebedee, a pseudepigraphical character, the Presbyter John, John Mark, Matthias, the Rich Young Ruler, Judas (not Iscariot [14:22]), and Lazarus. No mention was made of Nathanael, but then his list was not exhaustive (as we see in this section of the monograph). Should we conclude that Shepherd, who was Hodges Professor of Liturgics at the Church Divinity School of the Pacific (Berkeley), was mistaken, or that he meant to write "Lazarus"? Phone calls to other scholars in the field of Johannine studies confirmed my impression—no one has apparently concluded that Nathanael is the Beloved Disciple.

Perhaps we should continue on this path in the search of the identity of the Beloved Disciple, since Hengel also reports that scholars have attempted to prove that the Beloved Disciple was "Nathanael."[273] He refers the reader to Kragerud's monograph, but the latter presents no evidence that a scholar has opted for Nathanael as the Beloved Disciple.[274]

In the seventh edition of *Einleitung in das Neue Testament* (1931), A. Jülicher discussed the identity of the Beloved Disciple. This distinguished German New Testament expert suggested that he is one of the disciples mentioned in the GosJn at 21:2, offering the opinion that perhaps "Nathanael or one of the two anonymous disciples" could be the Beloved Disciple.[275] Jülicher did not think that Nathanael was the Beloved Disci-

---

[270] E. G. Kraeling, *The Disciples* (Chicago/New York: Rand McNally & Company, 1966); on the BD see especially "John in the Fourth Gospel" on 130–36.

[271] R. F. Collins, "The Representative Figures of the Fourth Gospel—I," *The Downside Review* 94 (1976) 26–46; "The Representative Figures of the Fourth Gospel—II," *The Downside Review* 94 (1976) 118–32.

[272] R. F. Collins, "Nathanael," *The Anchor Bible Dictionary* (1992) 4.1030–31.

[273] Hengel, *Question*, 78, 196; *Die johanneische Frage*, 215.

[274] Kragerud, *Lieblingsjünger*, 42–46.

[275] A. Jülicher, *Einleitung in das Neue Testament*, rev. with E. Fascher (Grundriss der Theologischen Wissenschaften 3.1; Tübingen: Mohr [Siebeck], 1931) 401. This opinion was Jülicher's and not Fascher's; see Jülicher, *An Introduction to the New Testament*, trans. J. P. Ward (London: Smith, Elder, & Co., 1904) 410–29.

ple. As we have already seen, he concluded that an unknown disciple of the apostle John wrote the GosJn and conferred upon his teacher the title "Beloved Disciple."

In 1904 F. S. Gutjahr argued that if one worked from the Synoptics and the GosJn it is possible to identify the Beloved Disciple, who is clearly the author of the GosJn; he could well be John the son of Zebedee. If one searched for the identity of this figure within the GosJn, however, it becomes highly unlikely that the Beloved Disciple could be John: "Working through the GosJn alone one is led most easily to Nathanael."[276] Jesus greeted him with honor (1:47ff). This disciple appears in the beginning and end of the gospel (chapters 1 and 21). Gutjahr did not settle on the identification of Nathanael as the Beloved Disciple, for he moved on from these brief comments to Lazarus who is also a possibility.[277]

In 1868 H. Spaeth, a Pfarrer in Gründelhardt in Würtemberg, presented his research on Nathanael in an attempt to understand how the GosJn took literary shape.[278] His work is impressive. He is imaginative, brilliant, and independent; but at the same time he is gifted philologically. He observes that Nathanael is a proper name that appears only in the GosJn. He points out his prominence in the opening of the GosJn and Jesus' high salute of him, ἴδε ἀληθῶς Ἰσραηλίτης ἐν ᾧ δόλος οὐκ ἔστιν (1:47). Nathanael's confession distinguishes him favorably within the gospels. He is the first disciple in the GosJn to have the appropriate faith.[279] The Evangelist has represented John the son of Zebedee (who does not otherwise appear in the GosJn) by the name Nathanael. The latter etymologically means "God's gift." The word play is attractive.[280] Since "Nathanael Johannes wäre,"[281] it is necessary to see how he appears throughout the GosJn. He is indeed the "Busenjünger." "Nathanael-Johannes" is symbolically painted by the Evangelist as the "Lieblingsjünger."[282] That means the Beloved Disciple is a human in whom there is no falsehood ("ein Mensch ohne Falsch"), indeed a spiritual person ("Geistes-

---

[276] F. S. Gutjahr, *Die Glaubwürdigkeit des Irenäischen Zeugnisses über die Abfassung des Vierten Kanonischen Evangeliums* (Graz: Leuschner & Lubensky's, 1904) 184.

[277] Also see Macgregor, *The Gospel of John*, 45–46.

[278] H. Spaeth, "Nathanael: Ein Beitrag zum Verständniss der Composition der Logos-Evangeliums," *Zeitschrift für wissenschaftliche Theologie* 11 (1868) 309–43.

[279] Ibid., 322.

[280] Ibid., 327: "Nathanael ist der von Gott Geschenkte, bezeichnet also Johannes als den Jünger, welchen der Sohn in besonderem Maasse als einen ihm von dem Vater Gegebenen anerkennt."

[281] Ibid., 340.

[282] Ibid., 342.

menschen")[283] who enables us to be united with the revelation made known through Jesus. Regardless of how scholars judge Spaeth's identification of the Beloved Disciple, it is a pity that they have missed his insights and philological connections. His work has not been cited by those who will write on the Beloved Disciple for the next 120 years.

In 1888, twenty years later, M. A. N. Rovers did conclude that Nathanael is to be identified as the Beloved Disciple. He noted that only seven disciples are named in the GosJn: Andrew, Peter, Philip, Nathanael, Thomas, Jude (the brother of James), and Judas Iscariot.[284] He then concluded that Nathanael—"den van God gegevene"—the Israelite in whom there is no guile, according to Jesus, the one to whom Jesus has promised a vision of the Son of Man "is waarschijnlijk 'de disciple, dien Jezus lief had.'"[285]

A case can be made for Nathanael. He was a real person of history, even if he is mentioned only in the GosJn (1:43-51, 21:2). He knew Jesus from the beginning. Jesus calls him, perhaps employing a revelatory formula derived from Psalm 32:2, an Israelite in whom there is no guile or deceitfulness (רמיה).[286] And, later, Jesus promises him an apocalyptic vision that is reminiscent of Jacob's dream in Genesis 28:12 (and the account in the pseudepigraphical work called the *Ladder of Jacob*).[287] Nathanael makes the first confession, and it is indeed impressive: "Rabbi, you are the Son of God! You are the King of Israel!" (1:49). He appears to be learned (perhaps a case may be made that because he was under a fig tree he had been a scribe or studying with one; cf. Mic 4:4, Zec 3:10; and *Midrash Rabbah*, Eccles 5.11, *b.Erub* 54a).[288] He was devout and perceptive, and he saw the resurrected Jesus (21:2). It might be appropriate to find in the Beloved Disciple one whose name meant "God (אל) has given (נתן)." Nathanael could possibly make a good candidate for the Beloved

---

[283] Ibid., 342.

[284] M. A. N. Rovers, *Nieuw-Testamentische Letterkunde* (Hertogenbosch: Gebroeders Muller, 1888) 172.

[285] Ibid., 172.

[286] Note the excellent translation of the NRSV to Psalm 32:2, "Happy are those to whom the LORD imputes no iniquity, and in whose spirit there is no deceit."

[287] The links between this document and the GosJn have not been adequately explored, and remain virtually unperceived. See *The Old Testament Pseudepigrapha*, vol. 2.

[288] See the comments by Brown, *Gospel*, 1:83. A. Spaeth (then Professor of Hermeneutics and NT Exegesis at Lutheran Seminary, Philadelphia) contended that Jesus set "his own seal and approbation on Nathanael's confession "as He did on later occasions with Peter and Thomas" (*Annotations on the Gospel According to St. John* [New York: The Christian Literature Co., 1896] 23).

Disciple; however, we really know very little about him, and he is conspicuously absent in the second half of the GosJn (13-20).

Lazarus (Kreyenbühl, Kickendraht, Griffith, Draper, Lewis, Filson, J. N. Sanders, Eckhardt, Brownlee, Léonard, Eller, Nepper-Christensen, Stibbe)

Biographical Sketch: Some leading experts have contended that the Beloved Disciple is Lazarus, who is from Bethany, which is just east of Jerusalem over the Mount of Olives (11:1).[289] This mysterious person is mentioned only in the GosJn, and in only two chapters of it. He is an enigmatic figure who does not even move about in the shadows of other passages in the New Testament, including the Synoptic Gospels (Matthew, Mark, and Luke) and Acts. He is introduced in the Johannine narrative in words addressed to Jesus, "Lord, behold, he whom you love is sick" (11:4). His sickness, which may have been leprosy,[290] was severe;[291] he died. Jesus wept (11:35). Lazarus had been dead four days, and Martha, his sister, warned that there would be a foul stench (11:39). The tomb, which was in a cave, was opened by removing the stone. Jesus prayed to the Father, and then cried out in a loud voice to Lazarus, "Come out."

---

[289] Brown (*Gospel*, 1:422) rightly connects this Bethany with modern El Azariyeh (from La zār which = Lazarus); it is not Bethany beyond the Jordan and east of Jericho as in GosJn 1:28 (*pace* Haenchen, *John* 2:56). Probably 1:28 "beyond the Jordan" was added to distinguish this Bethany from the town common in early Christian tradition in which Jesus often stayed during his trips to Jerusalem (see Mk 11:11, 14:3).

[290] See D. P. Wright and R. N. Jones, "Leprosy," *The Anchor Bible Dictionary* (1992) 4.277-82. I wish to express appreciation for many informative discussions on leprosy in antiquity to Joe Zias of the Rockefeller Museum in Jerusalem.

[291] If Lazarus was a leper as was Simon (Mk 14:3, Mt 26:6), then Bethany (in which Simon the leper lived) might have been a colony for lepers. That would fit perfectly the rule for a leper colony east of Jerusalem as specified in the Temple Scroll (see 11QTemple 46.16-18). This Dead Sea Scroll has the following: "And you shall make three places towards the east of the city (Jerusalem), separated from each other, into which the lepers shall come (באים המצורעים; 46.18)." For the Hebrew see Y. Yadin, ed., *The Temple Scroll* (Jerusalem: Israel Exploration Society, 1983) 2:200. Yadin was convinced that the Temple Scroll, which informs us for the first time that there was a leper colony east of Jerusalem, helps explain Jesus' actions. He stayed with Simon the leper (Mark 14:3). Yadin with erudition speculated that "Jesus had not happened by chance to find himself in the house of a leper, but had deliberately chosen to spend the night before entering Jerusalem in this leper colony, which was anathema both to the Essenes and the Pharisees" (*The Temple Scroll: The Hidden Law of the Dead Sea Sect* [London: Weidenfeld and Nicolson, 1985] 177).

Lazarus came out of the tomb, and "many of the Jews" believed in Jesus (11:45); but some Judaeans, especially the ruling authorities, plotted his death (12:10).

In 1900 J. Kreyenbühl in a lengthy presentation sought to discern the identity of the Beloved Disciple. He concluded that he was a Palestinian Jew (pace Scholten)[292] and that the author of the GosJn uses "the disciple whom Jesus loved" as a self-designation (Selbstbezeichnung). He cannot be one of the sons of Zebedee, because they are not evident in the GosJn. The author's mysterious self-designation is Lazarus.[293] Only Lazarus is designated as "him whom Jesus loved." Thus "the Lazarus pericope is a self-admission or self-disclosure of the author of the GosJn." He represents himself as the object of resurrection through Christ's spirit or as a person in whom Christ's spirit confronts death and experiences eternal life.[294]

In 1914 K. Kickendraht, without knowing about Kreyenbühl's work, argued that the Beloved Disciple was Lazarus.[295] Virtually no one who has argued for this identification seems to know about Kreyenbühl's or Kickendraht's work. Kickendraht argued that Lazarus is the Beloved Disciple because he appears at the midpoint of the gospel and just before the mention of the Beloved Disciple, who is not one of the Twelve. He is the disciple whom Jesus loved. As one resurrected by Jesus he amply symbolizes Jesus' words, "he who believes in me shall live."

In the 1920/1921 edition of The Expository Times B. G. Griffith (unaware of Kickendraht's article) suggested that the Beloved Disciple should be identified as Lazarus. He pointed out that Lazarus would fit the three requirements for identifying the Beloved Disciple: of all the disciples Lazarus would be in the best position to have known Jesus' secrets (13:22-24), he could have been known to the High Priest (18:15), and his home would have been near Jerusalem so he could take Jesus' mother there (19:26-27).[296] In addition Griffith brings forth four additional points in

[292] See Scholten, "Is de vierde evangelist een Jood?" in Het Evangelie naar Johannes, 438-40; see the German translation, "Ist der vierte Evangelist ein Jude?" in Das Evangelium nach Johannes, 412-15.

[293] Thus Kreyenbühl in 1900 claimed that Lazarus was the BD; hence, Fenton in 1970 was not completely accurate when he wrote that the suggestion that Lazarus was the BD was "first made sixty years ago" (The Gospel According to John, 12).

[294] J. Kreyenbühl, "Der Verfasser des Evangeliums," Das Evangelium der Wahrheit: Neue Lösung der Johanneischen Frage (Berlin: C. A. Schwetschke und Sohn, 1900) 146-369; see esp. 151-52, 156-62.

[295] K. Kirkendraht, "Ist Lazarus der Lieblingsjünger im vierten Evangelium?" Schweizerische Theologische Zeitschrift 31 (1914) 49-54.

[296] If 19:26-27 is taken literally, then it would take less than two hours to walk from Golgotha (which is most likely the massive stone highlighted in the

favor of Lazarus' candidacy: he would have lived "in the atmosphere of 'understanding'" (that is, Lazarus would have been a member of the household in which the ointment was placed on Jesus' feet [12:1-4]); he lived near Jerusalem, and it was in his home that Jesus was well received; he looked into the tomb and believed immediately because he knew about death; one should expect Jesus' disciples to assume Lazarus would not die before Jesus returned.[297]

Two articles responding to Griffith praised him. H. M. Draper wrote to *The Expository Times*, concluding that "this may prove to be one of the most important discoveries of the day, and go far in solving the authorship of the Fourth Gospel."[298] Likewise, F. W. Lewis was convinced that "the points mentioned by Mr. Grey Griffith are capable of even more emphasis than he has placed upon them." He did, however, demure on several accounts: The reference to "another disciple" of 18:15 does not refer to the Beloved Disciple. Verse 21:24 refers to the whole of the GosJn; "it is the work of Lazarus issued (and perhaps edited) by the apostle John—or that other John, beloved of critics." The Beloved Disciple was not one of the Twelve; his *"relation to Jesus centred and was contained in this one thing: personal affection."*[299]

A third article published in *The Expository Times* was flatly critical and unappreciative of Griffith's gentle suggestions. Advocating that the

---

Church of the Holy Sepulchre) to Bethany (which is across the Kedron Valley, past the Mount of Olives, and over the rise towards the East). That would have been considered a short journey in antiquity.

[297] B. G. Griffith, "The Disciple Whom Jesus Loved," *Expository Times* 32 (1920–1921) 379–81.

[298] H. M. Draper, "The Disciple Whom Jesus Loved," *The Expository Times* 32 (1920–1921) 428–29. Among Draper's insights is the perception of the possibly high social standing of the sons of Zebedee: "We are told that Zebedee not only had his sons to assist him in fishing, but also 'hired servants,' which seems to indicate a higher social position than the other fisherman-disciples. Moreover, the request of Zebedee's wife concerning her two sons is just what we might have expected from a loving mother who moved in a higher social sphere than did the families of the other disciples" (429). It is important to observe how sociology (or a social description of ancient societies) was about to become important in the field of Christian origins; but due to social crises around the world (esp. the stock market crash and WW II), it did not begin until about 1970. At that time the American Academy of Religion invited numerous scholars to seek to discern how and in what ways sociological insights and methodology would help improve historical research; among those chosen along with me were J. Z. Smith, L. Keck, J. Gager, and W. Meeks.

[299] F. W. Lewis, "The Disciple Whom Jesus Loved," *The Expository Times* 33 (1921–1922) 42 (italics his). Lewis went on and—as we have seen—identified Lazarus as the Rich Young Ruler.

Beloved Disciple is surely John the son of Zebedee, H. Rigg presented his four reasons why the Beloved Disciple cannot be identified with Lazarus: it is impossible that Lazarus, whom the chief priests want to put to death, could move freely about the courtyard; Lazarus' name never appears in the short lists of disciples close to Jesus (Mk 14:33); Lazarus is introduced as "he whom (Jesus) loved" but Mary and Martha are also described as loved by Jesus; Lazarus is not mentioned beside Mary, Jesus' mother in the Acts account (1:13-14).[300]

In 1949 F. V. Filson, who knew the arguments by Kreyenbühl and Eisler, contended that the Beloved Disciple is to be identified as Lazarus.[301] He began (and indeed concluded) by emphasizing that the scholar must focus only upon the GosJn in search of the identity of the Beloved Disciple, that in the past errors were made by looking outside of the GosJn either elsewhere in the New Testament or in Patristics. In 1962 he summarized his position in *The Interpreter's Dictionary of the Bible*. One can discern that at least seven points were impressive to him: (1) When read by itself, without reference to early traditions or the other gospels, the indelible conclusion is that the Beloved Disciple is Lazarus. He is the only man the GosJn indicates is loved by Jesus. (2) According to 13:23 the Beloved Disciple shares a meal with Jesus, and the "alert reader can hardly avoid identifying him with Lazarus unless he knows another answer from some other source." (3) Since Lazarus lived near Jerusalem, he could easily have taken Jesus' mother to his own home, as Jesus urged him to do from the cross. (4) It is entirely fitting for the GosJn, which has life through Christ as its theme, to have Lazarus as its witness. (5) It is "likewise fitting" for Lazarus to be the "first to recognize the risen Lord." (6) To identify Lazarus as the Beloved Disciple gives an attractive unity to the GosJn. (7) For Filson the Beloved Disciple is the way the author of the GosJn refers to himself.[302]

E. L. Titus responded to Filson's article, claiming that the hypothesis was unpersuasive. He criticized Filson for overlooking, "among other things, the possibility that Lazarus was a creation of the gospel writer."[303] The author of the GosJn combined the Mary and Martha story in Luke 10:38-42 and the parable of the rich man and Lazarus of Luke 16:19-31 in

[300] H. Rigg, "Was Lazarus 'the beloved disciple'?" *The Expository Times* 33 (1921–1922) 233–34.

[301] F. V. Filson, "Who Was the Beloved Disciple?" *Journal of Biblical Literature* 68 (1949) 83–88.

[302] F. V. Filson, "Beloved Disciple," *The Interpreter's Dictionary of the Bible* (1962) 1.378–79. Also, see Filson, "Author of the Fourth Gospel," *A New Testament History* (New Testament Library; London: SCM Press, 1965) 372–73.

[303] Titus, *Journal of Biblical Literature* 69 (1950) 323.

order to create—for "symbolic purposes"—an historical character. As mentioned earlier, Titus concluded that the Beloved Disciple is Matthias (Acts 1:15-26).

During the 1953 meeting of the *SNTS*, J. N. Sanders read a paper on "the historicity of the family at Bethany, Martha, her sister Mary, and their brother Lazarus, of whom the Fourth Evangelist says that Jesus 'loved' them, $\dot{\eta}\gamma\dot{\alpha}\pi\alpha$."[304] He was convinced that 11:5 was "a pointer to the identity of the Beloved Disciple ... as none other than Lazarus."[305] In 1957 Sanders picked up the theme again, arguing that if "then it is granted that the beloved disciple was a real person, and further that he was distinct from John of Ephesus, the likeliest candidate is Lazarus."[306] In 1968 B. A. Mastin completed and edited the commentary on the GosJn by J. N. Sanders. The latter presented reasons why he was convinced the Beloved Disciple should be identified with Lazarus: First, 11:5 clearly states that Jesus "loved" Martha, her sister, and Lazarus. Second, since Lazarus had already died, one can imagine the belief developing that he would not die again, and that fits nicely with the confusion over the death of the Beloved Disciple (21:22). Third, Lazarus lived in Judea, and if he were the Beloved Disciple this oddity would be explained. Fourth, Lazarus as the Beloved Disciple would explain the "centrality of the raising of Lazarus in the scheme of the Gospel." Fifth, since "Lazarus had not been called to be a disciple, he could have" taken Jesus' mother to his home. Sanders argued, "I do ... happen to believe that Lazarus was raised from the dead, and to accept him as the Beloved Disciple."[307] Many of his comments were written against the backdrop of contemplating that the Beloved Disciple must be either John the son of Zebedee or Lazarus.

Sanders concluded that Lazarus' memoirs lie behind the GosJn. The author of the GosJn, however, was John Mark who preserved these memoirs of the Beloved Disciple.

In 1961 K. A. Eckhardt stressed the point that since the Beloved Disciple is intentionally anonymous in the GosJn, he cannot be identified with anyone named in that gospel. In his view that point eliminates Peter, Andrew, Philip, Nathanael, Thomas, Judas Iscariot, and the other Judas. He disagreed with Filson that the author introduced himself as the Beloved

---

[304] Sanders, "'Those Whom Jesus Loved' (John XI.5)," *New Testament Studies* 1 (1954–55) 29–41; see esp. 29.

[305] Ibid., 33.

[306] J. N. Sanders, "Who Was the Disciple Whom Jesus Loved?" *Studies in the Fourth Gospel*, ed. F. L. Cross (London: A. R. Mowbray, 1957) 72–82; cf. 82.

[307] Sanders, *The Gospel According to St. John* (London: Adam & Charles Black, 1968) 29–32.

Disciple,[308] arguing rather that the author used the memoirs of the Beloved Disciple, who is Lazarus. And there is more: Lazarus is the name John the son of Zebedee received after Jesus raised him from the dead.[309] As Paul once referred to himself in the third person (2Co 12:1-5), so the author of the GosJn continuously referred to himself in the third person.[310]

In 1972 W. H. Brownlee, influenced by Filson and his own reading of the GosJn, contended that the Beloved Disciple is none other than Lazarus.[311] He pointed out that all clues "point only to Lazarus" for the following reasons: The Beloved Disciple and Lazarus were singled out as loved by Jesus. Both were prominent at the Last Supper and the special supper mentioned in 12:1-2. When the Beloved Disciple takes Jesus' mother to his home, the attractiveness of Bethany is obvious because Bethany is not far from Golgotha (I would estimate about a 90-minute walk). As the Beloved Disciple, Lazarus would be one with experience of the meaning of the grave clothes and "instantly recognize there in the still-rolled cocoon-like garments the clear proof of a super-natural resurrection."[312]

In 1983 J.-M. Léonard reported that the distinguished scholar O. Cullmann, near the end of 40 years of teaching at the Faculté protestante de théologie de Strasbourg, concluded that the Beloved Disciple is most likely Lazarus. I know of no publication in which Cullmann defended or even introduced this hypothesis, and it would not follow from Cullmann's contention that the Beloved Disciple appears in GosJn 1. As we saw in the previous pages, Cullmann concluded that the Beloved Disciple was a real human but that his identity is lost.

Léonard—perhaps because Cullmann never published his support for Lazarus as the Beloved Disciple—attempts to follow this suggestion with

---

[308] K. A. Eckhardt, *Der Tod des Johannes als Schlüssel zum Verständnis der Johanneischen Schriften* (Berlin: Walter de Gruyter & Co., 1961) 28.

[309] Ibid., 21–22.

[310] Cullmann rightly pointed out that Eckhardt's hypothesis is too complicated and speculative: "The fact that the same disciple is mentioned by name in ch. 11 whereas elsewhere he remains anonymous seems to me to present a serious difficulty for this hypothesis, but it cannot be ruled out altogether" (*The Johannine Circle*, 77). Cullmann was also right to stress that the identity of the BD cannot be solved by importing information from the Synoptics. One of the weaknesses in Eckhardt's work is that he missed Filson's point (emphasized independently in the opening pages of the present monograph) that the GosJn is the only source for discerning the identity of the BD.

[311] Brownlee, W. H. "Whence the Gospel According to John?" in *John and the Dead Sea Scrolls*, ed. J. H. Charlesworth (COL; New York: Crossroad, 1990) 166–94; see esp. "Who Was the Beloved Disciple?" 191–94.

[312] Ibid., 192.

particular attention to Jesus' words to Mary in chapter 19. When Jesus tells the Beloved Disciple to take his mother home, the house must be nearby since there is insufficient time for a journey with the Sabbath about to begin. No better place is known from the GosJn except the home of Lazarus in which Jesus' mother will also receive the support and assistance of both Mary and Martha.[313]

In 1987 V. Eller in his *The Beloved Disciple* explored the name, story, and thought of the Beloved Disciple. He was so convinced that the Beloved Disciple must be Lazarus that he concluded, "if it is not Lazarus, then we have not been given a ghost of an idea about who it might have been. Lazarus fits better than any other possible candidate."[314] It is noteworthy to report that Eller did not study the works of scholars in the field, and he did not consider other candidates such as Thomas.

In 1990 Nepper-Christensen concluded his study of the Beloved Disciple by identifying him with Lazarus. He examines each of the disciples named in 21:2 and finally must conclude that this verse and this chapter cannot lead us to the identity of the Beloved Disciple. He is, however, to be identified in chapters 11 and 12. The answer to our question is found in the words of Mary and Martha to Jesus (11:3). Lazarus is the one Jesus loved and hence the Beloved Disciple. Moreover, 11:1-44 helps clarify the meaning of Jesus' words concerning the belief in the Johannine Community that the Beloved Disciple would not die (21:23).[315]

In 1992 M. Stibbe's *John as Storyteller: Narrative Criticism and the Fourth Gospel* appeared.[316] In this monograph Stibbe concluded that Lazarus is the Beloved Disciple, and John the Elder is the Evangelist. The eyewitness material from Lazarus was transmitted as "a primitive, written ur gospel."[317] Stibbe contends that "the eye-witness tradition of Lazarus" is the "primary source" behind a portion of the GosJn.[318]

In 1993 T. L. Brodie discussed the presentation of the Beloved Disciple in 13:23 and the last reference to Lazarus in 12:17. He perceived a "continuity" in the way they are introduced to the reader. He discerned that "the phraseology used to describe the reclining Lazarus (v. 2) finds its nearest equivalent in the reference to the reclining beloved disciple

---

[313] J.-M. Léonard, "Notule sur l'Évangile de Jean: Le disciple que Jésus aimait et Marie," *Etudes Théologiques et Religieuses* 58 (1983) 355–57.

[314] V. Eller, *The Beloved Disciple* (Grand Rapids: Eerdmans, 1987) 73; see also 53.

[315] Nepper-Christensen, *Dansk Teologisk Tidsskrift* 53 (1990) 93–96.

[316] M. Stibbe, *John as Storyteller: Narrative Criticism and the Fourth Gospel* (SNTSMS 73; Cambridge: Cambridge Univ. Press, 1992).

[317] Ibid., 81.

[318] Ibid., 80.

(13:23)." These two figures are not to be identified, however; they depict interwoven fates and suggestions about love.[319]

In chapter 5 below, I discuss the major reasons why Lazarus cannot be the Beloved Disciple. Briefly, I argue that the epithet does refer to a real person, but Lazarus may be a narrative fiction. The Beloved Disciple is the model disciple of Jesus, yet Lazarus is never called a disciple,[320] and he does and says nothing. Thinking about the narrative flow of the GosJn, Hugh Anderson, formerly head of the New Testament Department, New College, the University of Edinburgh, wrote me on 10 October 1994, that the "thought that Lazarus out of his stinking grave clothes should recline by Jesus at the Last Supper seems to be grossly offensive." Also, recognizing that resuscitation is not resurrection, Anderson continues, "Lazarus, though he is brought back from the dead, must die again and so while he points forward to the resurrection, it is as a foil to the risen Christ who will never die."

John Mark (Völter, Wellhausen, Weiss, Parker, Johnson, Marsh, Eckle)

In 1904 and again in 1907 Völter suggested that the Beloved Disciple is to be identified with John Mark of Acts 12.[321] He claimed to have been able to show that behind "dem Lieblingsjünger desselben niemand anders als Johannes Markus zu verstehen ist."[322] He was also convinced that the author of the GosJn added to Jesus' teaching and tradition a mixture of Paul and Philo. His position became more complex in 1907, when in *Mater Dolorosa und der Lieblingsjünger des Johannesevangeliums* he argued that in chapters 1–20 the Beloved Disciple is John Mark, but in chapter 21 this figure is fused with the portrait of the Presbyter John.[323]

In the first decade of this century the famous J. Wellhausen argued that the Beloved Disciple is none other than John Mark. He argued that Jesus' mother was a widow and had only one son. Knowing this, Jesus at the cross presented her to a disciple who took her εἰς τὰ ἴδια. That means this disciple, the adopted son of Mary, took her to his home, which must be in Jerusalem. He is thus no Galilean and cannòt be John the son of

---

[319] T. L. Brodie, *The Gospel According to John: A Literary and Theological Commentary* (New York/Oxford: Oxford Univ. Press, 1993) 387, 407.

[320] This point I now observe was made by Fenton in *The Gospel According to John*, 12.

[321] Völter, *Die Offenbarung Johannis* (Strassburg: J. H. Ed. Heitz [Heitz & Mündel], 1904); and Völter, *Mater Dolorosa und der Lieblingsjünger des Johannesevangelium* (Strassburg: J. H. Ed. Heitz [Heitz & Mündel], 1907).

[322] Völter, *Die Offenbarung Johannis*, 55–56.

[323] Völter, *Mater Dolorosa und der Lieblingsjünger des Johannesevangeliums*, 16–23.

Zebedee. He is rather John Mark whom we know about from Acts 12:12.[324]

In 1917 J. Weiss, Professor of Theology in Heidelberg, wrote a widely-influential book, *Das Urchristentum*. He stressed that the GosJn is not present to us in its original form, but is heavily edited.[325] He contended that chapter 21 was an appendix, written after the death of the author of the GosJn. The editor added 13:23, 19:26f, 35, and 20:1-10. Also, 1:40-42 and 20:24-29 come from the hand of the editor. Weiss concluded that it is conceivable the author himself was most likely a Jerusalemite, perhaps John Mark. He was convinced that the author and editor belonged to the same circle in Asia Minor, and that one can understand the GosJn only with the recognition that he and his readers knew the first three gospels.[326]

In 1960 P. Parker argued that John Mark wrote the GosJn and that he was, therefore, the Beloved Disciple. As he did when he listed the reasons why the Beloved Disciple cannot be the apostle John, he lists the reasons why this epithet aptly fits John Mark. Here are his reasons *in nuce*:

(1) John Mark lived in Jerusalem.
(2) He was of a priestly family.
(3) He was "a person of means."
(4) The Last Supper may have been in his home, and as the host and BD he would have the seat of honor.
(5) He was a companion of Paul, and that explains some so-called Pauline ideas in the GosJn.
(6) Paul links Mark and Luke which explains the Lucanisms in the GosJn.
(7) Mark was originally a Judaizer, and that fits the GosJn (7:22ff.)
(8) Mark's missionary work was with Diasporic Jews.
(9) He was a companion of Peter.
(10) Mark was Peter's interpreter.
(11) He wrote after Peter's death (according to Papias).
(12) Mark could have met Alexandrianism in Jerusalem.
(13) He is placed in Ephesus (1Ti 1:3, 2Ti 1:18; 4:12)

---

[324] J. Wellhausen, *Das Evangelium Johannes* (Berlin: Georg Reimer, 1908) 87–88; see esp. 88, "den Schriftsteller selber, Johannes Markus, erkannt und ihn zum Lieblingsjünger Jesu erhoben."

[325] J. Weiss, *Das Urchristentum* (Göttingen: Vandenhoeck & Ruprecht, 1917) 611: "Das Werk ist nach unserer Auffassung nicht in ursprünglicher Gestalt, sondern überarbeitet auf uns gekommen."

[326] Weiss, *Das Urchristentum*, 612.

Impressive are his observations that Papias' words about Mark writing the Gospel of Mark "do not fit our Second Gospel at all." They do, however, "describe the Fourth Gospel."[327]

In the 1965/1966 volume of *The Expository Times*, without knowledge of the thesis put forward by Wellhausen and other scholars who concluded that the Beloved Disciple is John Mark, L. Johnson argued that "John Mark is exclusively the only man of whom we have record who with any likelihood fits into the picture of the Beloved Disciple." John Mark, mentioned in Acts 12, lived in Jerusalem, and that accords well with the account of Jesus' friend in Jerusalem who would help to arrange the Passover meal (Mark 14:13-15). It also fits nicely with John 19:27, which teaches us that "the Beloved Disciple had a house in Jerusalem to which he took the mother of Jesus after the crucifixion on the Friday afternoon."[328] The extent to which his argument can be sustained will depend on the exegesis of the passages in which the Beloved Disciple appears.

Responses in *The Expository Times* were not favorable.[329] Johnson replied by affirming, somewhat categorically, that the Beloved Disciple took Jesus' mother to "his own house" (19:27). For him that means sure knowledge (his "we know") that since she was taken to John Mark's house, where the Last Supper was celebrated (cf. Acts 1), the Beloved Disciple must be John Mark.[330]

We turn now to P. Parker who has influenced or stimulated both Brown and Schnackenburg. Each of these commentators offer the opinion that Parker published the most complete lists of objections against the hypothesis that the apostle John was the author of the GosJn.[331] Parker in fact presented twenty-one reasons why the author of the GosJn cannot be the apostle John (see the Preface of the present book).[332]

---

[327] Parker, "John and John Mark," *Journal of Biblical Literature* 79 (1960) 97–110; cf. 103.

[328] L. Johnson, "Who Was the Beloved Disciple?" *The Expository Times* 77 (1965–1966) 157–58.

[329] See J. R. Porter, "Who Was the Beloved Disciple?" *The Expository Times* 77 (1965–1966) 213–24. D. G. Rogers, "Who was the Beloved Disciple?" *The Expository Times* 77 (1965–1966) 214. Rogers states that the BD could be Joseph Justus or Matthias, but he opts for John the son of Zebedee.

[330] Johnson, "The Beloved Disciple—A Reply," *The Expository Times* 77 (1965–1966) 380.

[331] Brown, *Gospel*, 1:xvii; Schnackenburg, *St. John*, 1:92.

[332] Parker, "John the Son of Zebedee and the Fourth Gospel," *Journal of Biblical Literature* 81 (1962) 35–43. When he published this article, Parker was on the editorial committee of the *JBL*; and it is indeed a splendid article.

In his commentary of 1968 J. Marsh offered his opinion regarding the identity of the Beloved Disciple. He based his conclusion upon a study of Parker's article and on a study of the key passages in the GosJn. He wrote, "the possibility that John Mark was the beloved disciple has much to commend it." John Mark would have "a background of piety and culture that could, under proper stimuli, become the author of so surpassing a work as the Gospel according to St. John." Here are the points that impressed him: John Mark has the requisite name. "He lived in Jerusalem, was of a priestly family, and therefore possessed a good knowledge of the Temple. He was wealthy, and it is possible, if not indeed probable, that the Last Supper was held in his parental home (cf. Acts 12[12ff])." Marsh continued, that he also "knew the controversy about Judaizing, and had taken part in it; he was influenced by Paul, and associated with Paul and Luke (Acts 12[25]; 13[5,13]; 15[37ff]), whose gospel approximates more to John than either Mark or Matthew."[333] He concludes that John Mark was an "interpreter" of Peter, which fits nicely the relation between the Beloved Disciple and Peter in the GosJn.

In the following section Marsh seems to take back the certainty of his position. The claim that John the Elder, mentioned by Papias, is the Beloved Disciple has little to commend it. But, as "for John Mark, there seem no strong reasons against identifying him with the beloved disciple." Then again, however, "no positive evidence can be offered for the conjecture." In fact, "no certain hypothesis can be put forward on the basis of the evidence available." In summation, the "identity of the author (that is the beloved disciple) must remain hidden."[334]

In 1991 in his *Den der Herr liebhatte: Rätsel um den Evangelisten Johannes*, W. Eckle argued that the Beloved Disciple should be identified with John Mark.[335] Influenced by the work of Johnson and Parker, he is convinced that the name of the Beloved Disciple never appears in the GosJn, so one must look outside the document to discover his name.[336] Working from Mark, he is convinced that the Beloved Disciple is the "other disciple" of chapter 18.[337]

Goguel argued that if John Mark is the Beloved Disciple of the GosJn, it is difficult to comprehend the ancient tradition that Mark is the author of "the Gospel According to Mark," which is so different from the

---

[333] J. Marsh, *Saint John* (The Pelican Gospel Commentaries; Harmondsworth, Middlesex: Penguin Books, 1968) 24.

[334] Marsh, *Saint John*, 25.

[335] Eckle, *Den der Herr liebhatte: Rätsel um den Evangelisten Johannes*, 213–17.

[336] Ibid., 213.

[337] Ibid., 140–41.

GosJn.[338] Advocates of John Mark as the Beloved Disciple were aware of this criticism; usually they deny that the Gospel of Mark was composed by John Mark. Actually there is, in my judgment, no compelling reason to suggest that John Mark wrote anything, either within or without the New Testament.

Judas, Jesus' Brother (J. J. Gunther)

In 1980 and 1981 J. J. Gunther presented three articles in which he defended, *inter alia*, the hypothesis that the Beloved Disciple "was a brother of Jesus and the last to join the Twelve but ranked first (20:4, 8) in true discipleship."[339] Pointing out what is common coin, namely that the Beloved Disciple was closer to Jesus and understood him better than any other disciple including Peter, Gunther is convinced that as "a close confidant he was more spiritually akin to Jesus than was any other."[340] The Beloved Disciple was able to outrun Peter "because of his youth."[341] He was able to recognize Jesus on the shore of the Sea of Tiberias because of the miraculous catch of fish and his intuitive insight.

Gunther contends that the Beloved Disciple is both apologist and interpreter for the Johannine Community. He cannot be John the son of Zebedee; moreover, Irenaeus thought that the Beloved Disciple was John the Elder (but dropped the unflattering title).[342] That two disciples are presented as anonymous in 21:2 serves to surround the Beloved Disciple with mystery. The Beloved Disciple obtains custody of Jesus' mother, who symbolizes Israel, and that suggests he was associated with "Hebrew Christians" in Alexandria, Palestine, or Mesopotamia.[343] He was a member of the Twelve, but one of the least known members, since "we must assume that Jesus esteemed him enough to include him among the Twelve or perhaps to leave directions that he take Iscariot's place."[344]

Turning to the Synoptic Gospels, Gunther fills out his portrait of the Beloved Disciple. According to Luke, the names of the last three members of the Twelve, not counting Judas, are James, Simon, and Judas (Lk 6:12-16 and par. [Aland 49]).[345] These are the names of Jesus' brothers (Mk

---

[338] Goguel, *Le Quatrième Évangile*, 346.

[339] J. J. Gunther, "The Relation of the Beloved Disciple to the Twelve," *Theologische Zeitschrift* 37 (1981) 129–48; cf. 129.

[340] Ibid.

[341] Ibid., 132.

[342] Gunther, "Early Identifications of Authorship of the Johannine Writings," *Journal of Ecclesiastical History* 31 (1980) 407–27; see esp. 426.

[343] See also Gunther's "The Alexandrian Gospel and Letters of John," *Catholic Biblical Quarterly* 41 (1979) 596–99.

[344] Gunther, *Theologische Zeitschrift* 37 (1981) 142.

[345] I have attempted to simplify his presentation of this data.

6:3 [James, Joses, Judas, Simon]). Gunther is convinced that Judas of James (who is also Thaddaeus and Labbaeus), the Lord's brother and bearer of the hypocoristic names Thaddaeus (from *tad* "breast") and Labbaeus (from *leb* "heart"), is the Beloved Disciple. This identification is camouflaged because of the intentional anonymity of the GosJn and the confusion of the Encraties, who mixed Judas Thaddaeus (Jesus' brother) with Judas Didymus Thomas (supposedly Jesus' spiritual twin).[346] He asks, "Who but a brother could receive the special attention of Jesus without violating the other disciples' sense of propriety and equity?"[347]

John the Apostle (MacFarlane, Lofthouse, viz. Strauss, Macdonald, Westcott, Godet, Chapman, Nunn, Bernard, Hoernle, Schlatter, Strachan, Morris, Bruce, Hendriksen, Barrett, Braun, Tasker, Strathmann, de Boor, Smalley, Crane, Michaels, Carson, Voigt, Kaufman, Manns, Schmithals, Whitelaw)[348]

As is well known, and thus needs little demonstration, most scholars who write on the GosJn have traditionally concluded, usually without any independent research, that the Beloved Disciple is obviously John the son of Zebedee.[349] The position—really an assumption—which identifies the Beloved Disciple with John the Apostle appears in the precritical period

---

[346] Gunther, "The Meaning and Origin of the Name 'Judas Thomas'," *Le Muséon* 93 (1980) 113–48. The concept of the "twin" is very important in world myths and religions, especially in Zurvanisim (in which Ahura Mazda and Angra Mainyu were twin sons of the one great God Zurvan) and among native Americans in southwest America (notably the Navaho). See Campbell, *The Hero*, 70, 132; Boyce, *Zoroastrianism*, 96–99 (for Zurvanite texts); Klimkeit, *Gnosis*, 83, 215–16 (in which we hear about Mani's heavenly twin [*narjamig*]). Also, see the discussion of "twins" in C. G. Jung, et al., *Man and his Symbols* (New York: Doubleday Dell, 1964) 105–07, 116, 125.

[347] Gunther, *Theologische Zeitschrift* 37 (1981) 148.

[348] It should not be necessary to list all the scholars who defended what was for virtually twenty centuries the consensus. Thus, for example, de Solages concluded that the author of the GosJn is the Beloved Disciple who is none other than John the son of Zebedee. See Mgr. de Solages, *Jean et les synoptiques* (Leiden: Brill, 1979). His book was centered on the relation of the GosJn and the Synoptics. While I disagree with de Solages that the BD is John the son of Zebedee, I am in full agreement with him that simple solutions are the most appealing, and that the author of the GosJn knew, but did not depend on, the Synoptics as sources. I am convinced that the author of the GosJn derived his data—at least some of the Jesus traditions—from the BD whom he claimed was indeed an eyewitness to Jesus.

[349] A significant list is found in D. J. Hawkin's article, "The Function of the Beloved Disciple Motif in the Johannine Redaction," *Laval Théologique et Philosophique* 33 (1977) 135–50, in his first note.

and is common coin in "Sunday-school-type" literature. In 1835 (the same year as D. F. Strauss's magisterial study of Jesus) in a little booklet bound with "*The Beloved Disciple*" on the spine, members of the American Sunday-School Union were informed about the identity of the Beloved Disciple: "It is John."[350] In 1855 J. MacFarlane issued a book whose title reveals the conclusion: *"The Disciple Whom Jesus Loved": Being Chapters from the History of John the Evangelist.*[351] In a subsequent book J. Culross issued a similar devotional work titled *John, Whom Jesus Loved.*[352]

As W. F. Lofthouse stated in his *The Disciple Whom Jesus Loved*, "from about A.D. 175 to 1800 the apostolic authorship [of the GosJn] was never seriously denied or impugned."[353] As is well known, the dam holding back critical historical work broke with the founding of the Tübingen school headed by F. C. Baur, who concluded that the GosJn could not have been written by the apostle John because it reflected the developments of the second century and was composed after 160.[354] The influence of the Tübingen School was unprecedented in the study of the GosJn. G. Volkmar, Professor of Theology in the Universität Zürich, for example, concluded (in a scathing attack on Tischendorf's conservatism) that the GosJn reflects "der katholischen Zeit," mirrors the "antignostische Schwarmgeisterei des Montanismus," and thus dates from the later part of the second century C.E.[355] Here, therefore, only a few representative voices will be heard defending the position that the GosJn was written by John the son of Zebedee.

In 1835 D. F. Strauss, who was the first New Testament expert to publish a major work on the historical Jesus, advanced the perception of the multivalent nature of "myth," and dismantled many cherished idols. He argued somewhat polemically, in the Preface to volume one, that in contrast to the previous studies of Jesus, from either supranaturalist or naturalistic methodology, he would approach the history of Jesus from the mythical, which meant that "every part of it is to be subjected to a critical

---

[350] [P. Beck], *The Beloved Disciple: The Life of the Apostle John* (Philadelphia: American Sunday-School Union, 1835) 3.

[351] J. Macfarlane, *"The Disciple Whom Jesus Loved": Being Chapters from the History of John the Evangelist* (Edinburgh: Paton and Ritchie, 1855).

[352] J. Culross, *John, Whom Jesus Loved* (London: Morgan and Scott, n.d.).

[353] W. F. Lofthouse, *The Disciple Whom Jesus Loved* (London: Epworth Press, 1936) 16.

[354] F. C. Baur, *Kritische Untersuchungen über die kanonischen Evangelien ihr Verhältniss zu einander, ihren Charakter und Ursprung* (Tübingen: Ludw. Fr. Fues, 1847) 327–89. See esp. 328.

[355] G. Volkmar, *Der Ursprung unserer Evangelien nach den Urkunden, laut den neuern Entdeckungen und Verhandlungen* (Zürich: J. Herzog, 1866) 18–21.

examination, to ascertain whether it have not some admixture of the mythical."[356] At the age of only twenty-seven Strauss was certainly deeply religious, industrious, and focused; and he was bolstered in his fresh and daring work by the conviction that more erudite scholars were not able to the task because they were not liberated "from certain religious and dogmatical presuppositions." Strauss was convinced that he had been liberated' from such distorting feelings and thoughts "by means of philosophical studies."[357] At that time he contended that the GosJn cannot have been written by the apostle John.[358]

In the second edition of 1836 he reiterated his position with little modification. As Strauss wrote in the Preface to the second edition, a "thorough revision" was impossible "in view of the short intervening time and my current circumstances, which are unfavorable to sustained scholarly studies." The date is 23 September 1836.[359]

In the third edition of 1838 he retreated from his brashness against the pressure of adverse criticisms from scholars and the public. He drew attention to the Greek circle (griechischen Entstehungsgebiete) from which the GosJn derives and raised the question whether the apostle John, who was certainly not a Greek, can really be the author of the GosJn.[360] He urged his readers to consider how an apostle could have presented such an "unhistorical" account of the relationship between Jesus and John the Baptist,[361] and how the apostle John could have neglected to mention the apostolic significance of his brother, James, who is so prominent in the Synoptics.[362] He suggested that the reference to the Beloved Disciple in 21:24 may be added by another author (ein Zusatz von fremder Hand). The comment in 19:35 must indicate that the Beloved Disciple actually saw the lance being thrust into Jesus' side (so kann damit zwar nur der Lieblingsjünger gemeint sein). This verse also seems to make a distinction between the witness and the author of the GosJn. The confession by the

---

[356] See D. F. Strauss, "Preface to the First German Edition," in *The Life of Jesus Critically Examined*, ed. P. C. Hodgson and trans. G. Eliot (Philadelphia: Fortress, 1972 [from the 4th ed. of 1840 and first published in English in 1892]) li.

[357] Ibid., lii.

[358] As is well known but often treated too cavalierly, Strauss changed his position on the authenticity of the GosJn through the editions of the *Das Leben Jesu*.

[359] D. F. Strauss, "Preface to the Second German Edition," in *The Life of Jesus Critically Examined*, lvi.

[360] D. F. Strauss, *Das Leben Jesu kritisch bearbeitet* (Tübingen: C. F. Osiander, 1838 [3rd ed.]) 1:625.

[361] Ibid., 626.

[362] Ibid., 627.

Beloved Disciple in 21:7 could just as well have been made by one of
"those of Zebedee" as by one of the two anonymous disciples mentioned
in 21:2.[363]

In the Preface to the third edition of his *Das Leben Jesu*, Strauss
made a particular point of explaining why one of the major changes in his
work concerned the authorship of the GosJn. Note these words:

> The changes offered by this new edition are all more or less related to
> the fact that a renewed study of the Fourth Gospel, on the basis of de
> Wette's commentary and Neander's *Leben Jesu Christi*, has made me
> again doubtful of my earlier doubt concerning the authenticity and
> credibility of this Gospel. It is not that I have become convinced of
> its authenticity, merely that I am no longer certain of its inauthenti-
> city.[364]

Strauss's shift to a more conciliatory and conservative approach to the
GosJn is because of "ein erneuertes Studium des vierten Evangeliums,"
found in particular in the publications by de Wette and Neander. Hence,
Strauss doubts his former doubts: "mir die früheren Zweifel an der Aecht-
heit und Glaubwürdigkeit dieses Evangeliums selbst wieder zweifelhaft
gemacht hat."[365]

In the fourth edition of 1840 he returns to his earlier position on the
GosJn. In the Preface, dated 17 October 1940, he states that "this last
revision" will not contain "any essential alterations." That is not true as
he himself goes on to admit. He confesses that his third edition "contained
too much of compliance," and that he "had lost sight of the subject itself,"
so that the changes "had evidently done myself an injustice."[366]

After rhetorically discussing "the Fourth Evangelist" as if he were
the apostle John,[367] Strauss presents his objections to the apostolic authorship of the GosJn. Ten interrelated points may be discerned:

---

[363] Strauss: "Verset 7, soit Jean nécessairement; ce pourrait être aussi bien
Jacques ou un *des deux autres disciples*, ἄλλοι ἐκ τῶν μαθητῶν δύο, mentionnés
verset 2" (*Vie de Jésus, ou examen critique de son histoire*, trans. E. Littré
[Paris: Librairie de Ladrange, 1839 (from the 3rd ed.)] 1:589 [italics his]).

[364] Trans. P. C. Hodgson; see *The Life of Jesus Critically Examined*, lvii.

[365] Strauss, *Das Leben Jesu*, 1:v.

[366] Trans. G. Eliot in *The Life of Jesus Critically Examined*, lviii.

[367] Strauss, *The Life of Jesus Critically Examined*, 326–29. Note in
particular: "But these advantages of Peter are in the fourth gospel invalidated in
a peculiar manner, and put into the shade, in favour of John" (328). And: "but
in the fourth, John is placed under it (the cross), and is there established in a
new relation to the mother of his dying master" (329).

(1) We "have no absolute proof from the contents of the fourth gospel" that the epithet the Beloved Disciple applies to the apostle John.

(2) There is nothing narrated in the GosJn of the apostle John; the actions and sayings of the Beloved Disciple do not correspond to those of John in the Synoptics.

(3) The Beloved Disciple mentioned in 21:7 does not have to be John; he may be James or one of the anonymous disciples.

(4) GosJn 21:24 may be "an addition by a strange hand."

(5) Only the Beloved Disciple is described as present at the cross, but the third-person speech—"his testimony is true"—may not refer to John but to any eyewitness (cf. 1:14,16).

(6) The apostle John would not have presented "so unhistorical a sketch of the Baptist as that in the fourth gospel."

(7) The apostle John would not have neglected "the well-founded claims of his brother James."

(8) That the apostle John would refer to himself as "the disciple whom Jesus loved" should be "considered as an offence against modesty."

(9) This epithet is "far too laboured and embellished" for an apostle, since such a person "would, at least sometimes, have simply employed his name."

(10) A "venerator of John, issuing perhaps from one of his schools," could have naturally honored his teacher with "this half honourable, half mysterious manner."[368]

Subsequently Strauss argued at length that the sayings of Jesus in the GosJn are not those of a Palestinian Jew but of an Alexandrian Greek.[369]

In the separate work of 1864 Strauss returned also to his original position. In this book, *Das Leben Jesu für das deutsche Volk bearbeitet*, Strauss contends that the GosJn is not apostolic.[370] It is indicative of the climate, both within the church and within the academy, that Strauss felt forced to blunt his critical insights. Nevertheless, his *Das Leben Jesu* was a "watershed in the development of a critical method for the study of the Gospels."[371] In summation, Strauss's pioneering work certainly stimulated

---

[368] Strauss, *The Life of Jesus Critically Examined*, 329–30.

[369] Ibid., 381–86.

[370] See Strauss, *A New Life of Jesus*, 2 vols. (London: Williams and Norgate, 1865). Here I am indebted to P. C. Hodgson's comments in Strauss, *The Life of Jesus Critically Examined*, xliii.

[371] P. B. Hodgson, in Strauss, *The Life of Jesus Critically Examined*, xvii.

other liberal New Testament experts to question the apostolic origin of the GosJn; but he should be studied within the continuing force of the advocacy of the apostolic authorship of the GosJn. He was forced to alter his comments on the GosJn in the third edition, which was widely influential.[372]

James M. Macdonald of Princeton Theological Seminary studied the life and writings of the apostle John. He died before his research could be published, but the work was edited by the Dean of Chester, J. S. Howson and appeared in 1877 as a massive 436-page work titled *The Life and Writings of St. John*. It is a landmark publication with a detailed study of Roman history. Macdonald concluded that the Beloved Disciple was the apostle John who wrote the GosJn at Ephesus in 85 or 86 C.E.[373] As other scholars of his time, Macdonald relied heavily on what he described as "the unanimous testimony of antiquity." He rightly perceived that the author of the GosJn wrote primarily for those who "were ignorant of the customs of the Jews" in ancient Palestine, and from a perspective "of things as long past and viewed from a distance."

In 1882 the highly acclaimed scholar B. F. Westcott focused his attention on the authorship of the GosJn and the identity of the Beloved Disciple. The former Lord Bishop of Durham argued that a careful study of the indirect evidence, all the passages in which the Beloved Disciple appear, leads to the conclusion "that the fourth gospel was written by a Palestinian Jew, by an eye-witness, by *the disciple whom Jesus loved*, by John the son of Zebedee."[374] He had argued that the Beloved Disciple must be one of the three intimate associates of Jesus, namely Peter, James, or John. Peter is eliminated because the Beloved Disciple is presented along side of, and often in opposition to him. James cannot be the Beloved Disciple who wrote the GosJn, because he was martyred early. We are thus left only with John who must be the Beloved Disciple.

This logic was persuasive for virtually a century to numerous critics, most of whom were either persuaded by Westcott's prestige and clarity, or because they did not wish to challenge a revered tradition which dates from the beginnings of Christianity. In *The Beloved Disciple*, A. E. Garvie rightly pointed out the weaknesses of Westcott's argument:

---

[372] I have easy access to the third edition in German and French, but the first edition is virtually inaccessible.

[373] J. M. Macdonald, "St. John Writes the Fourth Gospel, Date, Design, and Contents," *The Life and Writings of St. John*, ed. J. S. Howson (New York: Scribners, Armstrong & Co., 1877) 268-77.

[374] B. F. Westcott, *The Gospel According to St. John* (London: John Murray, 1882) xxiv–xxv (italics his).

> There is nothing in all these references that shuts us up to the conclusion that the beloved disciple was one of the three intimates, even one of the Twelve, even a companion of Jesus in Galilee. Thus Bishop Westcott's last link is not only severed; it does not exist at all.[375]

In addition, it is important to point out that Westcott came to the GosJn assuming incorrectly that the Synoptics contain the key for unlocking the identity of the Beloved Disciple.

In 1886 Godet presented one of the most thorough reports on scholarly suggestions of the identity of the Beloved Disciple. Despite the numerous reasons to reject the traditional hypothesis, Godet amassed the evidence to prove that the Beloved Disciple is none other than John the Apostle. In fact John wrote three works: the GosJn, the first epistle, and Revelation.[376]

On May 29, 1907, the Vatican responded to the mounting attacks upon the thesis that John the son of Zebedee wrote the GosJn. The biblical commission pontificated that the GosJn was composed by the apostle John, as the Holy Fathers attested and as sound historical research proved:

> ... ex S. S. Patrum ... testimoniis et alllusionibus quae, cum ab Apostolorum discipulis vel primis successoribus derivasse oportuerit, necessario nexu cum ipsa libri origine cohaerent ... ex publico usu liturgico inde ab Ecclesiae primordiis toto orbe obtinente; praecindendo ab argumento theologico, tam solido argumento historico demonstretur Ioannem Apostolum et non alium quarti Evangelii auctorem esse agnoscendum.[377]

What is singularly missing in these criteria, and recognized now as essential by the leading Roman Catholic biblical exegetes is the criterion of detailed exegetical research, which is "disinterested" and inductive, focused on the GosJn.

In 1911 J. Chapman, in his *John the Presbyter and the Fourth Gospel*, stated he was "entirely certain" that the Beloved Disciple is the author of the GosJn (and of the *Apocalypse of John*).[378] In 1927 H. P. V. Nunn defended the traditional view that the author of the GosJn and the Beloved Disciple is John the son of Zebedee, who was not martyred in Palestine but moved to Asia.[379] Nunn also argued (quite remarkably) that archaeo-

---

[375] Garvie, *The Beloved Disciple*, 226.

[376] Godet, *Commentary on John's Gospel*, 29, 47–53.

[377] For the text see Colson, *L'Énigme du disciple que Jésus aimait*, 6–7.

[378] J. Chapman, *John the Presbyter and the Fourth Gospel* (Oxford: Clarendon Press, 1911) 87.

[379] H. P. U. Nunn, *The Son of Zebedee and the Fourth Gospel* (London: S.P.C.K., 1927, 1932) 112, 128.

logical drawings in Roman catacombs prove that the GosJn was known "in Rome long before the middle of the second century."[380] In 1928 J. H. Bernard claimed that the Beloved Disciple was John the son of Zebedee, Jesus' maternal cousin. He rightly saw that the Beloved Disciple is one of the disciples mentioned in 21:2; but he concluded that there "can be no reasonable doubt that the name of the Beloved Disciple was John, and therefore Thomas and Nathanael are excluded."[381] In 1931 E. S. Hoernle claimed that the GosJn is composite with one papyrus scroll being the "*testimony of John, the Disciple of the Lord.*"[382]

In 1937, which was a year of severe struggle in Germany, A. Schlatter wrote *Kennen Wir Jesus?* This devotional guide revealed that Schlatter held virtually the same opinion on the authorship of the GosJn as did the later Strauss, also a Tübingener. Schlatter's exegesis of 20:9 revealed not only that he contended, perhaps uncritically, that the Beloved Disciple was John the Apostle, but also that John now believed in Jesus' resurrection as he stood in the empty tomb.[383]

In 1925, in 1941, and then again in 1946, R. H. Strachan, Professor of New Testament Language and Literature at Westminster College, Cambridge, was convinced that the Beloved Disciple is the apostle John. In 1925 he wrote that "it is impossible to doubt that the Evangelist does identify himself in some real fashion with the Apostle, in these references to the Beloved Disciple."[384] In 1941 he announced being "certain" that the Beloved Disciple was "John, son of Zebedee."[385] He contended that "in all probability, of the two disciples mentioned in i.35-40, one of which is unnamed, the latter must be John."[386] The "another disciple" in 18:15-16 cannot be the Beloved Disciple.[387] He was convinced that another person authored the GosJn. This author used the epithet for an "old friend" who

---

[380] Ibid., 84.

[381] J. H. Bernard, "John the Apostle was the Beloved Disciple," *Gospel According to St. John*, 2 vols., ed. A. H. McNeile (Edinburgh: T.& T. Clark, 1928) 1:xxxiv–xxxvii.

[382] E. S. Hoernle, *The Record of the Loved Disciple Together with the Gospel of St. Philip Being a Reconstruction of the Sources of the Fourth Gospel* (Oxford: Blackwell, 1931) 80 (italics his).

[383] A. Schlatter, "Johannes Glaubte im leeren Grab Jesu," *Kennen Wir Jesus?: Ein Gang Durch ein Jahr im Gespräch mit Ihm*, with a preface by H. Stroh (Stuttgart: Calwer Verlag, 1980 [4th ed.]) 418–20.

[384] R. H. Strachan, *The Fourth Evangelist: Dramatist or Historian* (London: Hodder and Stoughton, 1925) 47.

[385] Strachan, *The Fourth Gospel: Its Significance and Environment* (London: Student Christian Movement Press, Ltd., 1941, 1946) 82.

[386] Ibid., 82.

[387] Ibid., 84–85.

"stood in a very intimate relationship to Jesus, was regarded as a disciple who understood the mind of Jesus, and had His confidence in a very special degree."[388] He also conjectured that

> the Beloved Disciple must also have been an intimate friend of the author of the Gospel, and that the Evangelist owed to him—as Philemon did to Paul—'his own soul'. He had been his own intimate friend and teacher, whose deep spiritual insight and knowledge of Jesus had aroused a kindred experience in the heart of his friend.[389]

Another valid insight is his claim that the Beloved Disciple functioned "to secure the validity and authority of the Gospel itself."[390] In 1971 L. Morris and in 1983 and 1992 F. F. Bruce, both with less assertiveness, also concluded that the Beloved Disciple was probably the apostle John.[391]

In 1954 W. Hendriksen published an erudite study of the GosJn.[392] He showed unusual ability with ancient texts and citations in manuscripts, and was convinced that the author of the GosJn is the Beloved Disciple. This individual knew Jesus better than other members of the Twelve, was a trustworthy eyewitness of Jesus' life beginning with the time of John the Baptist (1:35, 40), and was a converted Palestinian Jew who did not write at a time long removed from the events. The author of the GosJn is John the son of Zebedee and Salome (Mk 1:19; 16:1), and "he styles himself 'the disciple whom Jesus loved' (12:23)."[393] He wrote sometime "between 80 and 98." Hendricksen was convinced that "the presbyters at Ephesus appended" the words of 21:24.

In 1955, in his first edition and in 1978 in his second edition, C. K. Barrett published his reflections on the GosJn. He concluded that the Beloved Disciple is indeed John the son of Zebedee. His methodology and perspective are informed, refined, balanced, and impressive. Barrett is convinced that the author of the GosJn knew at least one of the Synoptics, and that the lack of support for the GosJn in the second century "makes it impossible to believe that it had been published with the full authority of apostolic authorship."[394] After stressing that the gospel is itself anony-

---

[388] Ibid., 83.

[389] Ibid.

[390] Ibid.

[391] Morris, *Gospel According to John*, 8–30. Bruce, *The Gospel of John*.

[392] W. Hendriksen, "Authorship, Date, and Place," *A Commentary on the Gospel of John*, 2 vols. (London: Banner of Truth Trust, 1954, 1959) 1:3–31. See also 2:245.

[393] Ibid., 1:29.

[394] C. K. Barrett, *The Gospel According to St. John* (Philadelphia: Westminster, 1978 [2nd ed.]) 115.

mous, Barrett argues that the Beloved Disciple was present at the Last Supper and thus probably a member of the Twelve, that he was close to Peter and Jesus' mother, and that he was not simply an ideal figure. These three valid (and in my judgment accurate) claims lead him to conclude "that the author of the gospel, whoever he may have been" identified "the disciple whom Jesus loved," as "John, the son of Zebedee and one of the Twelve."[395]

Barrett is impressed with the brilliance of the author of the GosJn, which does not mean he claims the gospel is far removed from so-called heresy or Gnosticism. For him the author, a Jew, who had no "first-hand knowledge of conditions in Palestine," was a "Christian theologian with a profound and penetrating understanding of his material."[396] Though "here and there behind the Johannine narrative there lies eye-witness material," the Hellenisitic evidence in the gospel "suggests that the final editor of the gospel was not an eye-witness."[397] He means the Evangelist (not an alleged editor who added chap. 21). This person revered the Beloved Disciple, John the son of Zebedee, and based his writing on his ostensible eyewitness account.[398]

In 1959 F.-M. Braun, pleased with Barrett's solution,[399] argued that the Beloved Disciple was not the author of the GosJn, but the eyewitness source for the author.[400] He originated the tradition, and he was John the son of Zebedee.[401] The apostle John, who is known traditionally to be of a priestly family, let Peter into the high priest's courtyard; and he is the Beloved Disciple since he is the habitual companion of Peter in the GosJn and in Acts.[402] After his death an author, perhaps one of his students, looked back on him as Jesus' Beloved Disciple.[403]

---

[395] Ibid., 117.

[396] Ibid., 120.

[397] Ibid., 123.

[398] Barrett emphasizes that the author of the GosJn used sources, some of which were written. He does not, however, affirm that the Beloved Disciple left written sources for the Evangelist to use. I am convinced that Barrett is correct in both judgments.

[399] J.-M. Braun, "Le disciple que Jésus aimait," *Jean le théologien et son évangile dans l'église ancienne* (Études bibliques; Paris: Gabalda, 1959) 301–330; see esp. 305.

[400] See Braun, *Jean le Théologien: Sa théologie—Le mystère de Jésus-Christ* (Études Bibliques; Paris: Gabalda, 1966) 226.

[401] Braun, *La mère des fidèles: Essai de théologie johannique* (Cahiers de l'Actualité Religieuse; Paris: Casterman, 1954) 9.

[402] F.-M. Braun, *Jean le théologien: Les grandes traditions d'Israël et l'accord des écritures selon le quatrième évangile* (Études Bibliques; Paris: Gabalda, 1964) 93.

[403] F.-M. Braun, *Jean le théologien et son évangile dans l'église ancienne*, 396–97.

In 1960 R. V. G. Tasker contended that chapter 21, with the possible exception of 21:25,[404] was composed by "the author of the rest of the book." He was in unquestionable agreement with the verdict of Archbishop William Temple: "I regard as self-condemned any theory about the origin of the Gospel which fails to find a very close connection between it and John the son of Zebedee."[405] It is self-evident that such a position can be found if one is intent on finding it in the GosJn; but are these words of sensitivity and openness to what may be found in a complex literary masterpiece?

In 1972, however, Braun was much more certain about the functions of the Beloved Disciple than of his identity. He even called the claim that the Beloved Disciple was the apostle John an example of romantic reconstruction, "nous n'aurions pas besoin de cette interprétation romancée des données évangéliques pour savoir que son livre conserverait sa valeur."[406]

In 1963 H. Strathmann was convinced that few words were necessary to prove that the Beloved Disciple was clearly John the son of Zebedee. He was certain that "den Jünger, den Jesus lieb hatte" was "kein anderer" than the apostle John. He finds the criticisms of this traditional position "unverständlich."[407]

In 1973 W. de Boor stated that it was clear that the Beloved Disciple was not merely a symbol, but represented a real person of the apostolic period. He had no doubt that in a refined manner the author of the GosJn reveals to his readers that he is none other than the apostle John. Also, the fact that Peter and John work in tandem, according to Acts and Galatians 2:9, combined with the close relationship of Peter and the Beloved Disciple, indicates that the latter is most likely John.[408]

In 1978 S. S. Smalley concluded that he had found no reason to deny that the Beloved Disciple was John the son of Zebedee. He argued that there are three stages in the composition of the GosJn. First, the apos-

---

[404] This verse is omitted in Codex Sinaiticus, the original hand.

[405] R. V. G. Tasker, *The Gospel According to St. John: An Introduction and Commentary* (Leicester: Inter-Varsity Press; Grand Rapids: Eerdmans, 1960 [repr. 1994]) 11.

[406] Braun, *Jean le théologien: Sa Théologie—Le Christ, notre Seigneur* (Études Bibliques; Paris: Gabalda, 1972) 72, n. 33. (It is significant that this statement is hidden within a footnote.) See also p. 19.

[407] Here he cites Eduard Meyer approvingly. See H. Strathmann, *Das Evangelium nach Johannes* (Das Neue Testament Deutsch 4; Göttingen: Vandenhoeck & Ruprecht, 1963) 20.

[408] W. de Boor, "Wer schrieb dieses Buch über Jesus?" *Das Evangelium des Johannes* (Wuppertaler Studienbibel; Wuppertal: Brockhaus, 1973 [3rd ed.]) part 1, 15–20.

tle John, "who was the beloved disciple" moved from Palestine to Ephesus, where he handed on Jesus traditions orally to a disciple or disciples (much as by tradition Peter did to Mark). Second, his disciple or his disciples wrote down the traditions "preserved by the beloved disciple." Third, the first draft, after the death of the Beloved Disciple, was published in a "finally edited version" of the GosJn. It now included the Prologue, which was based on a community hymn, some editing (esp. in chapters 6, and 14–17), and the Epilogue (chapter 21). Smalley concluded, "If the beloved disciple's witness lies behind the Gospel's production, and others were responsible for its actual writing, the work retains its apostolic character, and the particular features of its composition and history are explained."[409]

Over ten years later, in 1994, when Smalley published his study on the Revelation of John, he argued that this book belongs to the Johannine Community and that its literary products were in the following chronological order: Revelation, the Gospel of John, and the Epistles of John.[410] He is convinced that John the Apostle moved from Palestine to Ephesus in the 50s with his followers. There are not two Johns in Ephesus. John the Elder never existed; he is an error by Eusebius. John the Apostle wrote Revelation in "the middle months of AD 70, under Vespasian." Revelation is thus "a valuable early witness to the history of the community gathered around the beloved disciple." The latter was John the Apostle, who taught his followers the Jesus tradition. One of his students, "the fourth evangelist or evangelist, then began to formulate this tradition within the Johannine circle, for purposes of worship and instruction." Thus the author of the GosJn is not the apostle John, but the latter is the Beloved Disciple.

In 1980 T. E. Crane, in a book on the Beloved Disciple, claimed that the GosJn contained the apostle John's spiritual teaching.[411] In 1985 and again in 1989 J. R. Michaels apparently vacillates between the Beloved Disciple being John the son of Zebedee or some anonymous disciple.[412] He suggests that while the arguments for identifying the Beloved

---

[409] S. S. Smalley, *John: Evangelist and Interpreter* (Nashville: Thomas Nelson Publishers, 1978) 119–21.

[410] S. S. Smalley, *Thunder and Love: John's Revelation and John's Community* (Milton Keynes: Nelson Word Ltd., 1994) see esp. 38–40, 48–50, 66–69.

[411] T. E. Crane, *The Message of Saint John: The Spiritual Teaching of the Beloved Disciple* (New York: Alba House, 1980).

[412] In 1989 M. Làconi pointed to ancient Christian tradition and contended that the claim that the apostle John is the author of the GosJn and the BD is "presumibilmente su buone basi" ("La testimonianza del 'discepolo che Gesù amava,'" in *Il racconto di Giovanni* [Assisi: Cittadella Editrice, 1989] 6–7; see esp. 6).

Disciple with John are "impressive," the author of the GosJn left him anonymous "and the commentator has no choice but to respect his anonymity."[413] It thus appears that Michaels changed his mind on the identity of the Beloved Disciple.

In 1991 in his important commentary on the GosJn, D. A. Carson concluded that "the internal evidence is very strong, though not beyond dispute, that the beloved disciple is John the apostle, the son of Zebedee."[414] He confronted the argument that the Evangelist would not have referred to himself as "the disciple whom Jesus loved" and advised that such reasoning "should be abandoned." He advised that "when a New Testament writer thinks of himself as someone whom Jesus loves, it is *never* to suggest that other believers are *not* loved, or are somehow loved less." He continued to affirm that the apostle John is both the Beloved Disciple and the Evangelist: "if the Evangelist is someone other than John the son of Zebedee, his failure to mention the apostle John by name, when he mentions so many others, is even more difficult to explain."[415]

In 1991 G. Voigt saw that the Beloved Disciple could not be simply an ideal figure, because such an ideal writes no book (as demanded by 21:24), cannot die and cause a crisis (as is required by 21:23), has no eyes with which to witness Jesus' death (as is obvious from 19:35), and cannot sustain a heated rivalry with a real historical person named Peter (as is apparent throughout the GosJn). The Beloved Disciple is to be recognized as the John whose authority lies behind the GosJn.[416] At this point many scholars will feel that Voigt's critical review was initially insightful, but in the end shortsighted.

Also in 1991 P. S. Kaufman wrote *The Beloved Disciple: Witness Against Anti-Semitism*. While his main purpose was to reveal that the passion narrative in the GosJn is the least hostile to the Jews and the priestly

---

[413] I have the impression that Michaels favors John in his Introduction (2–4) but shifts to anonymity in his commentary (249) (*John* [New International Biblical Commentary; Peabody, Mass.: Hendrickson Publishers, 1984, 1989 (repr. 1993)]).

[414] D. A. Carson, *The Gospel According to John* (Leicester: Inter-Varsity Press; Grand Rapids: Eerdmans, 1991) see esp. 75–77. See Carson's earlier, "Historical Tradition in the Fourth Gospel: After Dodd, What?" in *Gospel Perspectives: Studies of History and Tradition in the Four Gospels*, ed. R. T. France and D. Wenham (Sheffield: JSOT Press, 1981) 83–145.

[415] At this point I wonder how he knows so much about John the Apostle. Has he read the GosJn in light of the Synoptics? If so, has he really heard the voice of the Evangelist above the other voices?

[416] G. Voigt, "Der 'Lieblingsjünger,'" *Licht-Liebe-Leben: Das Evangelium nach Johannes* (Biblisch-theologische Schwerpunkte 6; Göttingen: Vandenhoeck & Ruprecht, 1991) 17–19.

establishment, he evidenced that he had read widely and carefully many of the arguments pertaining to the identity of the Beloved Disciple. He inclined to the opinion that the Beloved Disciple is John the son of Zebedee. Six observations may be obtained: (1) The Beloved Disciple was a real person. (2) He was most likely a follower of the Baptist. (3) Hence, he would have been with Jesus from the beginning. (4) John was not from a poor family and therefore uneducated. (5) He could have written the simple, Semitically influenced, Greek found in the GosJn. (6) The reticence to speak about James and John the sons of Zebedee by name may well derive from a "reticence to speak of his own family, rather than ignorance."[417]

F. Manns also published in 1991 his claim that the Beloved Disciple is to be identified with John the Apostle. He rightly saw that this epithet represents a real historical person. He is the model disciple, because he never abandoned his master, and arrived at spiritual perception rapidly and profoundly.[418]

As we have seen, each of the categories under which we have organized the hypotheses of scholars is usually complex. And so it is with those who conclude that in some ways the Beloved Disciple is the apostle John. Schmithals, for example, concludes that the editor who added the Beloved Disciple passages is the author who shifted the anonymity of the GosJn so that the work is attributed to one of Jesus' disciples. He argues further that the "LJ-Redaktion" attributes the GosJn to the apostle John.[419]

In 1993 a book appeared that bears no earlier date. It must be a reprint, not acknowledged, of a work that antedates 1917, when the author died. The author T. Whitelaw (1840–1917) concludes that the author, and the Beloved Disciple must be John the son of Zebedee. Many of the points made and the presuppositions held are now recognized to be impossible; among them would be the conclusion that the author of Revelation "must have composed" the GosJn.[420]

---

[417] P. S. Kaufman, *The Beloved Disciple: Witness Against Anti-Semitism* (Collegeville, Minn.: The Liturgical Press, 1991) see esp. 31–35.

[418] F. Manns, "Le disciple que Jésus aimait," *L'Evangile de Jean à la lumière du Judaïsme* (Studium Biblicum Franciscanum Analecta 33; Jerusalem: Franciscan Printing Press, 1991) 87–89.

[419] Schmithals, "Die Lieblingsjünger-Redaktion," *Johannesevangelium und Johannesbriefe*, 249: "Es ist also die LJ-Redaktion, die das JohEv, bis dahin eine anonyme Schrift, dem Apostel Johannes zuschreibt."

[420] T. Whitelaw, *Commentary on John* (Grand Rapids: 1993 [sic]) xxiv-xxxiv. On the back of the title page is found only "Originally published: Gospel of St. John. Scripture Truth Book Company." The impression may be given that the ideas found in this book of 1993 represent the latest research. The book does contain a mine of valuable information.

These publications are significant. They clarify that the identification of the Beloved Disciple as John the Apostle is still current (if not popular among many influential Johannine specialists). They also—and to me far more importantly—help indicate that the Beloved Disciple was most probably a real person who was an eyewitness to Jesus' life and teachings.

The arguments against the contention that the Beloved Disciple is the apostle John, however, are numerous and, in my judgment, undermine the hypothesis. John the son of Zebedee was a familiar name to Christians around the end of the first century. Would it have been necessary to append a chapter to the Fourth Gospel in order to claim that he was a person whose testimony was accurate?

Also, does the temperament of John mirror the image of an ideal disciple, like the Beloved Disciple? Long ago Macgregor pointed out that what "we know of the temperament of the son of Zebedee reflects little either of the nature we would look for in one deemed worthy of such peculiar intimacy with Jesus, nor of the spirit of the Gospel to which tradition has attached his name." This John, the son of thunder, did have the reputation of being caught up in egocentric quarrels for power, as well espousing an unloving request to have fire rain down on inhospitable Samaritans.[421]

Surely, one of the main reasons that chapter 21 was added to the gospel was to commend the witness of the Beloved Disciple. His witness was "true" (21:24). As Painter states,

> Perhaps the most damaging evidence against the traditional view of authorship is to be found in Jn 21:24. Had Jn the Apostle been the author it is unlikely that this would not have been known or that he would need anyone to defend the veracity of his witness.[422]

Before leaving the arguments for and against the hypothesis that the Beloved Disciple is John the son of Zebedee, which is not today unthinkable, let me point to three arguments not yet used in favor of that position. First, the title given to a Mount Athos Manuscript of Revelation (namely Hoskier's 236 or Gregory's 1775) identifies the author, who is John the Apostle, as the "bosom friend" of Jesus, Christ's beloved, and the adopted son of Mary: Ἡ ἀποκάλυψις ... ἐπιστηθίου φίλου, ... ἠγαπη-μένου τῷ Χριστῷ, Ἰωάννου τοῦ Θεολόγου, ... Θετοῦ δὲ υἱοῦ τῆς Θεοτόκου Μαρίας, καὶ υἱοῦ Βροντῆς.[423] These three epithets reveal that the copyist thought John the Apostle was the Beloved Disciple.

---

[421] See Macgregor, *The Gospel of John*, xlv.
[422] Painter, *Quest*, 91.
[423] See Metzger, *The Text of the New Testament*, 205.

Second, an addition of John 17:26 in a codex of the GosJn in the archives of the Templars of St. John of Jerusalem in Paris is interesting. According to it, the resurrected Jesus instructs his disciples that "John shall be your father, till he shall go with Me into the paradise."[424] More attention should be given to what is contained in the manuscripts themselves. The additions are often interesting, even if they preserve only the reflections of highly trained scribes who reveal the teachings of their own contemporaries.

Third, among the early Irish Apocrypha are texts about the Beloved Disciple. These celebrate John the Apostle as the Beloved Disciple, which in Irish is *Eoin Bruinne* ("John of the Breast" which derives from Jn 13:25). In one of the episodes John, the son of Zebedee, is heralded to be "a god in a human body." Then unbelievers are convinced by his powers and build "a beautiful lofty church in honour of the eloquent beloved John." In a fragment of an apocalypse words are quoted by "John, the eloquent Beloved Disciple."[425]

In the Preface we presented Parker's list of reasons why the Beloved Disciple cannot be the apostle John. This position may seem new to those who have depended on the commentaries by Brown and Schnackenburg. Thus it is pertinent to remember that already in 1820, K. G. Bretschneider strenuously resisted the consensus that the Beloved Disciple is John the son of Zebedee. He pointed out that this person is never named in the GosJn—not even in chapter 21:

> Hoc enim proprium est quarto evangelio, quod Joannes apostolus nullo in loco nominatur, sed ubique lectori conjectura relinquitur, an de hoc Apostolo velit cogitare, nec ne. Etenim vel simpliciter ὁ ἄλλος μαθητής[426] appletatur ut cap. I, 35-41. XVIII, 15. XX, 3.4.8., vel formula ὁ μαθητὴς ὃν ἠγάπα ὁ Ἰησοῦς[427] insignitur.[428]

Finally, the arguments against John the son of Zebedee as the author of the GosJn were succinctly summarized by Nunn, who endeavored sub-

---

[424] See B. Pick, *The Extra-Canonical Life of Christ* (New York/London: Funk & Wagnalls, 1903) 279.

[425] M. Herbert, and M. McNamara, "Texts Relating to the Beloved Disciple," *Irish Biblical Apocrypha* (Edinburgh: T & T Clark, 1989) 89-98, 180-81.

[426] Bretschneider missed two accents in the Greek; it is corrected.

[427] He missed four accents in the Greek; they are corrected.

[428] Bretschneider, *Probabilia de evangelii et epistolarum Joannis, apostoli, indole et origine* (Leipzig: Jo. Ambros. Barthii, 1820) 110.

sequently to answer each of them.[429] In his *The Son of Zebedee* he listed them:

> (1) If the Evangelist had been one of the Twelve, he would not have spoken of himself as the "Beloved Disciple," while another disciple, outside the number of the Twelve, might with perfect propriety refer to one of the Twelve as such.
>
> (2) John, the son of Zebedee, had not the education and training which would have fitted him to write such a book as the Fourth Gospel.
>
> (3) His character, as described by the Synoptists, does not seem suitable to the author of such books as the Gospel and the First Epistle.
>
> (4) It is difficult to understand how the son of a Galilean fisherman was "known to the High Priest" and able to gain admission to his house on an important occasion.
>
> (5) It is unlikely that he had a house in Jerusalem.
>
> (6) His lack of interest in the Galilean ministry, and his concentration on the Judean ministry, are best explained by supposing that he was not with the Lord in Galilee, but only in Jerusalem.[430]

Our exegesis of the passages in which the Beloved Disciple is mentioned and of the passages in which an anonymous disciple conceivably might be this individual,[431] as well as the full study of the drama and flow of the narrative in the GosJn leaves us with the impression that each of these objections against the authorship of the GosJn by the apostle John still remains.[432]

John the Elder (F. von Hügel, Bousset, Burney, Dibelius)

In 1911 F. von Hügel argued that in chapters 1–20 the Beloved Disciple is certainly never identified and may well be "only ideally, mystically true." In chapter 21 the Beloved Disciple seems to be identified; he cannot be John the son of Zebedee, "else why, now he is dead and gone, not proclaim" it? The Beloved Disciple seems to be the Elder John and that attribution "would not violate the literary ethics of those times."[433] In 1912 W. Bousset too argued that the Beloved Disciple

---

[429] Nunn's answers to each of the six objections to the possibility that the GosJn was written by the apostle John are found in *The Son of Zebedee*, 130–32.

[430] Nunn, *The Son of Zebedee*, 130.

[431] See respectively my chapters 2 and 6.

[432] Also see Parker's list of objections against the apostle John hypothesis; these are found in my Preface.

[433] F. von Hügel, "John, Gospel of St," *The Encyclopaedia Britannica* 15 (1911) 452–58; cf. 457.

cannot be John the son of Zebedee, despite the late-second century patristic evidence. He is most likely the Presbyter John.[434]

In 1922 C. F. Burney studied the language of the GosJn and concluded that it had been originally written in Aramaic. Since the author of GosJn was versed in rabbinic methodology and knew the *Biblia Hebraica*, he thus cannot be the apostle John. He was rather John the Elder, who had been educated in Jerusalem in rabbinic thought and was of a priestly family.[435]

In 1929 M. Dibelius also suggested that the Beloved Disciple was to be identified with the Presbyter John.[436] The sons of Zebedee were martyred in Jerusalem. The Presbyter John meets the requirements of the Beloved Disciple; he was of a later generation than the apostles, and was not martyred, but a "pupil of the Lord." Polycrates' report that the John of western Turkey was of a priestly family may be combined with the impressions in the GosJn that the Beloved Disciple was of a priestly family in Jerusalem, and so could take Jesus' mother to his home and let Peter into the high priest's area.[437]

Dibelius does present a possible interpretation of Polycrates' report. Here is the comment by Polycrates, around 190 C.E.:

ἔτι δὲ καὶ Ἰωάννης ὁ ἐπὶ τὸ στῆθος τοῦ Κυρίου ἀναπεσών· ὃς ἐγενήθη ἱερεὺς τὸ πέταλον πεφορηκὼς (18), καὶ μάρτυς καὶ διδάσκαλος· οὗτος ἐν Ἐφέσῳ κεκοίμηται.[438]

---

[434] W. Bousset, "Johannesevangelium," *Die Religion in Geschichte und Gegenwart* 3 (1912) cols. 608–36; see esp. col. 612.

[435] Burney, *The Aramaic Origin of the Fourth Gospel* (Oxford, Clarendon Press, 1922) 139–41.

[436] R. H. Charles did not seek to discern the identity of the BD, but he contributed significantly to the search for the identity of the author of the GosJn. Charles concluded that the ApJn and the GosJn were clearly written by different authors (because of style and language), and that John the Apostle was martyred before 70. The GosJn, and the three epistles of John, were composed by John the Elder, who conceivably was the pupil of John the Apostle. The ApJn was composed by a Palestinian prophet who migrated to Asia Minor. See Charles, *The Revelation of St. John* (ICC; Edinburgh: T. & T. Clark, 1920) 1:xxxviii–l.

[437] M. Dibelius, "Johannesevangelium," *Die Religion in Geschichte und Gegenwart* 3 (1929) cols. 349–63; see esp. col. 362.

[438] Polycrates, "Fragmenta," *PG* 1 (1857) col. 1360. ET = "Yet also John who reclined on the chest of the Lord, who was priest [who wore] the golden plate, [was] also a witness [or martyr] and teacher; this one is buried in Ephesus." Brown, *Gospel*, 1:xcvii, suggests that while "the information of Polycrates that John was at Ephesus may warrant some confidence, the information about John's priesthood may well be a deduction from the passage we are considering." Brown refers to the meaning of GosJn 18:15-16 (see my chapter 6).

The Bishop of Ephesus did not identify the "John,"[439] so the reference may be to any one named John, including John the son of Zebedee or the Elder John.

John the Elder Blended with John the Apostle (Uechtritz, Streeter, Hengel)

In 1876 F. Uechtritz, a layman, published a work which he could not revise due to an illness from which he never recovered.[440] He argued that the author of the GosJn could not be John the Apostle.[441] The Beloved Disciple was a real historical person and no "Phantasiegebild."[442] He is to be identified with the anonymous disciple of chapters 1 and 18, and he is a member of the Twelve.[443] The author of the GosJn was a Jerusalemite, but he was not a member of the Twelve.[444] He cannot be identified for certain, but it is likely that he is John the Elder, who portrayed John the Apostle as the Beloved Disciple.[445] The early scholars of the Church did not err in seeing John the Elder as John the Apostle; these two figures— the Ephesian John and the apostle John—blended into one John who may be judged rightly to be a witness and an "apostle."[446]

In 1924, and in the subsequent editions of *The Four Gospels* up until 1951, B. H. Streeter concluded that the author of the GosJn was the Elder John and that he called John the son of Zebedee the "Beloved Disciple."[447] He claimed that nowhere in the GosJn is there a suggestion that the author is the apostle John. The author clearly distinguished himself from the "Beloved Disciple" whom he greatly admired in 21:24. The "Beloved Disciple" is portrayed by the author of the GosJn as an apostle "transfigured into the ideal disciple."[448] Obviously, the apostle John is the Beloved Disciple; that becomes evident when one looks at the three apostles closest to Jesus. According to Mark they are Peter, James, and John.

---

[439] Most scholars have tended to conclude that the apostle John is intended by Polycrates. Note Godet, *Commentary on John's Gospel*: "John, the last survivor of the apostolate, had left in the Church of Asia the impression of a pontiff whose forehead was irradiated by the splendor of the holiness of Christ" (50).

[440] F. Uechtritz, *Studien eines Laien über den Ursprung, die Beschaffenheit und Bedeutung des Evangeliums nach Johannes* (Gotha: F. Andreas Perthes, 1876) vi.

[441] Ibid., 53.

[442] Ibid., 54.

[443] Ibid.

[444] Ibid., 543–44.

[445] Ibid., 214, 546–48.

[446] Ibid., 550.

[447] Streeter, *The Four Gospels: A Study of Origins* (London: Macmillan, 1924, 1951 [7th imp.]) 430–61.

[448] Ibid., 432.

The former is portrayed pejoratively in the GosJn, and James was martyred too early to be thought of as tarrying until the Lord returns. Hence, only the apostle John is a viable candidate for the Beloved Disciple.[449] From Papias and the Johannine epistles we learn that the author of the GosJn is none other than the Elder John.[450]

From 1985 to 1989 M. Hengel lectured on "the founder and head of the Johannine school" and finally published his conclusions. Unlike Uechtritz, Hengel is an internationally acclaimed scholar, and he is convinced that the Beloved Disciple, as the editor of the GosJn in chapter 21 claimed, is to be identified with the author of the GosJn. He is John the Elder whom the early church confused with John the son of Zebedee. Rightly pointing out that the author of the GosJn "incorporated some powerful opposition" to Docetism in his work, Hengel is convinced of the narrative coherence of the author's gospel and that he knew, and sometimes was directly influenced by the Synoptics (but in "a very free manner").[451] Perceiving that the Beloved Disciple must be not only an ideal figure, but also a real historical person, Hengel points out that Peter and Timothy are not only historical persons, but also ideals, and that a fictive character can neither die and be lamented nor write a gospel as the editor claimed.[452]

Astutely sensitive to philology, Hengel demonstrates that the Jewishness of the founder and of his school is evident in his title. He is not called in good Greek ὁ πρεσβύτης or ὁ γέρων. His title is ὁ πρεσβύτερος, which is the usual Septuagint translation of זָקֵן,[453] 'of ripened (old) age,' which denotes an experienced and prudent elder.

Hengel speculates on the identity of the Beloved Disciple, but admits he is moving out onto "the thin ice of hypotheses which are difficult to prove."[454] Observing that the GosJn places "special and deliberate stress on the southern province and the capital," and the "'aristocratic' character" of the gospel, Hengel derives the impression that its author was from "the upper class in Jerusalem." The title of the GosJn and the attribution of authorship to him in 21:24 indicate that the author was called "John." The Beloved Disciple is thus John the Elder. The link with John the son of Zebedee is also significant; note these words by Hengel:

---

[449] Ibid., 432–33.

[450] For a scathing—indeed unfair—critique of Streeter, see Nunn, *The Son of Zebedee*, 70–106.

[451] Hengel, *Question*, 91.

[452] Ibid., 78–79.

[453] The translators of the LXX chose 127 out of 178 occurrences to translate זָקֵן as ὁ πρεσβύτερος.

[454] Hengel, *Question*, 124.

Given the unique way in which the figures of John son of Zebedee and the teacher of the school and author of the Gospel are deliberately superimposed in a veiled way, it would be conceivable that with the 'beloved disciple' 'John the elder' wanted to point more to the son of Zebedee, who for him was an ideal, even *the* ideal disciple, in contrast to Peter, whereas in the end the pupils impressed on this enigmatic figure the face of *their* teacher by identifying him with the author in order to bring the Gospel as near to Jesus as possible.[455]

The gospel's connection with the apostle John, the traditions about John the Elder, and the historical and symbolical nature of the Beloved Disciple are thus combined by Hengel. The Beloved Disciple, indeed the Elder John who may have lived from 15 to 100 C.E., wrote the GosJn intending to recast the Beloved Disciple so that he resembled John the son of Zebedee. His students, however, portrayed their own teacher, the Elder John, as the Beloved Disciple.[456]

One of the Two Anonymous Disciples Noted in 21:2 (Brown, Schnackenburg)

The weaknesses of the hypothesis that the Beloved Disciple was John the son of Zebedee have been gradually recognized by experts on the Fourth Gospel who once espoused this view. Paramount among such scholars are Schnackenburg and Brown.[457]

As most readers of this monograph surely know, both Schnackenburg and Brown changed their minds on the identity of the Beloved Disciple. Once they concluded that the Beloved Disciple is the apostle John. Now each, independently, concludes that he is to be identified with one of the anonymous disciples noted in 21:2. This position is similar to the one held by scholars who conclude that the Beloved Disciple is "A Real Human Whose Identity is Lost" (see the discussion at the beginning of this chapter).

In his first volume of *The Gospel According to St. John*,[458] which appeared in German in 1965, Schnackenburg confronted the question of

---

[455] Ibid., 131–32.

[456] Consult the German here; Hengel, *Die johanneische Frage*, 321. For a critique of Hengel's position, see D. Muñoz León, "Juan el presbítero y el discípulo amado," *Estudios Bíblicos* 48 (1990) 543–63.

[457] Lindars also seemed to advocate that the BD is one of the anonymous disciples mentioned in 21:2. See Lindars, *The Gospel of John*, 33. The position also may be attributed to K. Grayston, *The Gospel of John* (Philadelphia: Trinity Press International, 1990) 111.

[458] The title page does not contain the dot after St., but it sometimes appears on covers.

the authorship of the GosJn. He made the important point that the GosJn "cannot simply be treated as the work of an author in the modern sense."[459] He first discusses the external evidence regarding the authorship of the GosJn, and concludes that tradition clearly indicates "that the Apostle St. John wrote the Fourth Gospel."[460] Recognizing that the apostle John cannot be the author of the GosJn if he was martyred, he points out the weaknesses (but not the strengths) in the traditions,[461] and concludes that "the hypothesis of the martyrdom of the Apostle John may be pigeonholed without misgivings."[462] Schnackenburg turns to the internal evidence and cautions that "the personal element cannot be entirely excluded from the verdict on the particular issues."[463] He begins with the Synoptics and then goes to the GosJn. He disassociates himself from the "conservative defenders of the authorship of the son of Zebedee."[464] Influenced by Braun's arguments in *Jean le Théologien*, he concludes that the apostle John is the witness of the GosJn but that the Evangelist, with considerable independence and skill, wrote the document.[465] The Beloved Disciple is the circumlocution the disciples of the apostle John (and the Evangelist) used to refer to him.[466]

In the third volume of *The Gospel According to St. John*, which appeared in German in 1975, Schnackenburg (on 375–88) again discusses the identity of the Beloved Disciple. He has changed his mind; he no longer thinks the Beloved Disciple is the apostle John. To see why and in what ways he changed we need to turn to his study of 1970 titled "Der Jünger, den Jesus liebte." Most importantly he no longer relies heavily on external evidence: "Die altkirchlichen Zeugnisse ... reichen nicht weiter zurück als bis etwa 180 n. Chr. und zeigen einen deutlichen Hang zur Lebendenbildung."[467] He continues to side with the scholars (like Harnack and Streeter) who contend that the Beloved Disciple represents a real historical person. Against Bultmann and especially Kragerud, he rightly argues that 21:24 seems to demand a historical witness.[468]

---

[459] Schnackenburg, *St. John*, 1:75.

[460] Ibid., 85.

[461] For my discussion of the martyrdom of the apostle John see chapters 4 and 5.

[462] Schnackenburg, *St. John*, 1:88.

[463] Ibid., 92.

[464] Ibid., 104.

[465] In contrast to Braun, Schnackenburg attributes "a far greater independence" to the Evangelist (*St. John*, 1:101).

[466] Ibid., 103.

[467] He thus clearly distances himself now from Braun, and states so in a footnote (Schnackenburg, "Der Jünger," 97).

[468] Schnackenburg rightly asks of Kragerud: "Was ist in ihnen an Tradition verarbeitet, und warum wurde die Tradition in dieser Weise aufgenommen und

He shifts his research so that it is focused on an exegesis of the GosJn. He examines each passage in which the Beloved Disciple appears, and is convinced that he is perhaps meant in chapter 18 but not in chapter 1. He discusses each disciple named in the GosJn. In particular he notes that Thomas is influential in gnostic circles and in Syria; he also was of "special interest" to the Johannine Christians.[469] The Beloved Disciple, however, is not to be associated with a disciple named in the GosJn. He is an historical person who remains anonymous and does not belong to the Twelve.[470] In summation,[471] the Beloved Disciple is not one of the Twelve, but perhaps an unknown Jerusalem disciple who witnessed the last events of Jesus' life.

In 1975 Schnackenburg nuanced his position in the third volume of his commentary. He expresses the reasons he must differ from the conclusions presented by Kragerud, Bultmann, Mahoney, and Thyen who concluded that the editor of chapter 21 interpolated all the Beloved Disciple passages. Of Thyen he states that the argument fails to convince at the "passage where Thyen claims to demonstrate it, namely, 13:21-26." Of Mahoney he rejects the position that the Beloved Disciple is primarily or only a literary function.[472] He stresses that because of the closeness in thought and literary style, the editor of chapter 21 had "a rather close contact with the evangelist" (as we argue in our exegesis).[473] That means the editor would not have been mistaken about the identity of the Beloved Disciple. It is unlikely that he would have made "a historical person out of a symbolic figure" (*pace* Bultmann).[474] Exceedingly important is his comment that the Beloved Disciple

> was not introduced in order to *find* a person of authority for the gospel, but in order to endorse his already *existing* authority in the congregation, to maintain it after his death and to commend the written gospel as his everlasting testimony.[475]

In my judgment this perception is exactly on target.

Note now how he distinguishes his position in 1975 from those of previous years. He "abandoned" his dependence on "tradition" and the

---

weitergebildet?" ("Der Jünger," 99).

[469] Schnackenburg, "Der Jünger," 116-17.

[470] Ibid., 117.

[471] I am indebted here to his summary of his 1970 position; it is found in *St. John*, 3:381.

[472] Ibid., 377.

[473] Ibid., 379.

[474] Ibid., 379.

[475] Ibid., 380.

opinion that the Beloved Disciple "was to be regarded as the Apostle John," because of the "internal evidence" in the GosJn. While in 1970 he had still held to the link between tradition and exegesis, he was "unwilling to separate" the Beloved Disciple from the Evangelist.[476] He now maintains (rightly in my opinion) that the Evangelist is not to be confused with the witness, the Beloved Disciple. He revises his own thesis so that the Beloved Disciple is "the authority who stands behind the gospel," but the GosJn was written by another person "connected" with the Beloved Disciple. The author was

> possibly an educated Hellenist of Jewish origin, an exceptional theologian, who took up the tradition of the beloved disciple while also using other sources, interpreted them theologically, and put them together into a gospel which was to serve the Johannine Church and, over and above it, persons of that period who were seeking.[477]

This scenario is conceivable; but it leaves us with two anonymous individuals who cannot be located in the history of early Christianity. Most importantly, in my judgment, Schnackenburg is correct to see the Beloved Disciple as one of Jesus' followers, one of his disciples who witnessed his life.[478]

In his two influential volumes on the GosJn, Brown contended that the Beloved Disciple and author was the apostle John. In 1966 the evidence external to the GosJn is summarized as follows: "it is fair to say that the only ancient tradition about the authorship of the Fourth Gospel for which any considerable body of evidence can be adduced is that it is the work of John son of Zebedee."[479] Then Brown contended that the hypothesis that the apostle John is the author of the GosJn was "gradually returning in favor."[480] After examining the internal evidence, he presented this conclusion:

> When all is said and done, the combination of external and internal evidence associating the Fourth Gospel with John son of Zebedee makes this the strongest hypothesis, if one is prepared to give credence to the Gospel's claim of an eyewitness source.[481]

---

[476] See Schnackenburg, "Der Jünger," 114–15 and *St. John*, 3:381.

[477] Schnackenburg, *St. John*, 3:381.

[478] Of course, as will become even more clear, I became convinced that the BD witnessed more of Jesus' life than just the events beginning with GosJn 13 (see chapter 6). Frankly, this was a startling discovery for me.

[479] Brown, *Gospel*, 1:xcii.

[480] Ibid., xvii.

[481] Ibid., xviii.

Brown meant that the apostle John was thus the Beloved Disciple. He admitted that there were clear difficulties in identifying John the son of Zebedee with the Beloved Disciple; but these are not so extreme as those facing other hypotheses, for example, "if he is identified as John Mark, as Lazarus, or as some unknown."[482]

Brown is always an independent and nuanced scholar.[483] When he concludes that the apostle John wrote the GosJn he distinguishes between "author" and "writer." The apostle John authored the GosJn, but he may not have written it with his own hand. Brown thus contends that John is the apostolic witness of the GosJn: He is the Beloved Disciple.[484]

In his subsequent *The Community of the Beloved Disciple*, which was published in 1979, thirteen years after the first volume of his commentary, it is evident that Brown's research and thinking had evolved to the point that he had grown to distrust his previous conclusion. The Beloved Disciple is "obviously the hero" of the Johannine community,[485] but note these words:

> I am inclined to change my mind (as R. Schnackenburg has also done) from the position that I took in the first volume of my AB commentary identifying the Beloved Disciple as one of the Twelve, viz., John son of Zebedee.[486]

Why did he change his mind? Earlier he had begun with the external evidence, and in light of it and with one eye on the Synoptics he began to probe the GosJn itself. Note his change in methodology. Formerly he had "insisted" on "the combination of external evidence and internal evidence which made this the strongest hypothesis."[487] He came to recognize that "the external and internal evidence are probably not to be harmonized."[488]

Brown continues (rightly) to claim that it is "quite implausible" that the Beloved Disciple is "purely fictional or only an ideal figure."[489] He

---

[482] Ibid., xcviii.

[483] Note in particular how he astutely distinguishes between "author" and "writer": "in considering biblical books, many times we have to distinguish between the *author* whose ideas the book expresses and the *writer*" (*Gospel*, 1:lxxxvii [italics his]).

[484] Brown's position does not demand that "John physically wrote the Gospel or gave it its relatively smooth Greek phrasing. The Gospel claims that the BD was the source of its tradition, and that is what concerns us here" (Ibid., 1:xcviii).

[485] Brown, *Community*, 31.

[486] Ibid., 33.

[487] Ibid.

[488] Ibid., 33–34.

[489] Ibid., 31.

finally came to the conclusion that the Beloved Disciple cannot be the apostle John. He was instead one of the anonymous disciples noted in 12:2.

It is interesting to observe how Brown's insights tend to affirm the hypothesis that Thomas is the Beloved Disciple. He points out that "the Beloved Disciple remains with Jesus." He is the "Disciple par excellence" and closer to Jesus "both in life (13:23) and in death (19:26-27)."[490] This valid insight would be even sharper if Thomas were recognized as the Beloved Disciple, since he enters the story with the paraenesis to follow Jesus ultimately, even if it meant to die with him (11:16). What does Brown say about Thomas? Although in his commentary he spoke disparagingly about Thomas, these are his words in *The Community of the Beloved Disciple*:

> In fact, Thomas's delayed confession of Jesus as "My Lord and my God" may be paradigmatic of the fuller understanding of Jesus' divinity to which, John hopes, the Apostolic Christians may ultimately be brought.[491]

Would it not fit nicely if Thomas were then the Beloved Disciple whom, according to Brown, is "the Disciple par excellence, the Disciple whom Jesus loved."[492] If that were the case, then Thomas and the Beloved Disciple would be one and the same, and the paradigm for authentic discipleship, according to the Johannine Community.

There is much to commend the conclusion that the Beloved Disciple is anonymous. He may well be one of the unnamed disciples mentioned in 21:2. On the one hand, this conclusion does nothing to lift the veil of anonymity and mysteriousness from the Beloved Disciple; and surely that goal is the main reason scholars have searched for some insight into the identity of the Beloved Disciple, who was certainly a real person.[493] On the other hand, to conclude that he is one of the anonymous disciples mentioned in 21:2 is to support the insight (which is valid) that he was a real person and an eyewitness to what was recorded—at least the events described beginning with chapter 13. It is exceedingly important to perceive

---

[490] Ibid., 84.

[491] Ibid., 85.

[492] Ibid., 84. See also Brown, *The Churches the Apostles Left Behind* (New York: Paulist Press, 1984), esp. 84, n. 120. See esp. "The Heritage of the Beloved Disciple in the Fourth Gospel: A Community of People Personally Attached to Jesus," 84–101; and "The Heritage of the Beloved Disciple and the Epistles of John: A Community of Individuals Guided by the Paraclete-Spirit," 102–23.

[493] See the comments by Painter, *Quest*, 91.

that the Beloved Disciple, according to the GosJn, is a real historical person and the source of some of the traditions in it that go back to an eyewitness, indeed one of Jesus' disciples.[494]

3.2 CONCLUSION

The review of publications in which the search for the Beloved Disciple is significantly dominant or advanced has been revealing; it has intermittently even been astounding. There is an incredible variety of suggestions. Some of them are arrestingly creative.

Studying the publications on the Beloved Disciple leaves me with some key questions: Why have we New Testament specialists habitually not consulted the brilliant thinkers who mastered theological language and wrote world-shaping commentaries on the GosJn, such as Augustine, Luther, and Wesley? After mastering the issues raised by the primary text, why have we frequently written without thoroughly examining the publications of others who also have devoted themselves to identifying the Beloved Disciple? Conversely, why have we in exegesis too frequently been influenced by misunderstandings in works by influential pioneers in biblical criticism? Why do we, when confronted with perplexing passages, tend to turn prematurely from a textual enigma to a commentator's dogma?

We New Testament scholars are trained in philology, which is necessary because we must master the Greek and other languages in which the Jesus traditions are transmitted. That also means a focus on not only classical culture, but also on the Semitic world. Is it because of the way we New Testament scholars were trained that the publications reviewed sometimes tend to indicate a deficient understanding of symbolical language? Too frequently lost from view is the profundity, even subtlety, of Johannine symbolism. In the search for the identity of the Beloved Disciple, the focus has habitually veered away from the GosJn in which, and only in which, the identity of the Beloved Disciple may be discovered. Perhaps the most impressive fact is that while scholars have endeavored to prove that the Beloved Disciple is Paul, Matthias, John Mark, the Rich Young Ruler, the apostle John, Nathanael, or Lazarus, no one exegetically focused on the GosJn has explored the possibility that the Beloved Disciple may be Didymus Thomas.[495]

---

[494] See Brown, *Gospel*, 1:xciii.

[495] This is especially striking to me, since I reviewed the work of scholars only after completing an exegesis of the BD passages in the GosJn. After months of uninterrupted reading of what others had thought, I must admit worrying that someone would already have made the identification that gradually became attractive to me. Finally, I discovered that two scholars, both working on the Nag Hammadi tractates, had made this identification; but they either assumed it

We end this review of hypotheses regarding the identity of the Beloved Disciple with amazement at the brilliance and creativity of dedicated and gifted scholars. There is certainly no consensus in the field regarding the identity of the Beloved Disciple. Who may he be?[496] Let us continue our explorations which have already indicated that Thomas is probably the Beloved Disciple.

---

to be self evident (deductively) or did not develop it fully. Neither based his work on an exegesis of the GosJn. The two scholars are P. de Suarez, *L'Évangile selon Thomas* (Éditions Métanoïa; Marsanne: Éditions Métanoïa, 1974) 260–61; and H.-M. Schenke, "The Function and Background of the Beloved Disciple in the Gospel of John," in *Nag Hammadi, Gnosticism, and Early Christianity*, ed. C. W. Hedrick and R. Hodgson, Jr. (Peabody, Mass.: Hendrickson, 1986) 111–25.

[496] I am convinced that there is a consensus among Johannine experts that the Beloved Disciple is an epithet for a real historical person.

CHAPTER 4

Fresh Insights Suggesting that Thomas Is the Beloved Disciple

Twelve additional insights which are exegetically based indicate that the most likely candidate for the Beloved Disciple is Thomas. The *first*, and most decisive, indicates that Thomas must have knowledge possessed only by the Beloved Disciple; according to the narrator only the Beloved Disciple sees the thrust of the lance (19:32-35). Yet Thomas, whom the narrator otherwise does not indicate could have known about Jesus' thoracic wound, demands to see and put his hand into it (20:25). The *second* pertains to the link between the Beloved Disciple and Judas Iscariot; and these may imply that the former is Thomas. The *third* concerns martyrdom. Neither Thomas nor the Beloved Disciple were martyred, yet the narrator may imply that the former and the latter were faithful to Jesus unto death, by on the one hand exhorting martyrdom, and on the other being the only disciple with Jesus until the end. The *fourth* discloses that both the Beloved Disciple passages and the Thomas story in 20:24-29 were added to the developing GosJn by the Evangelist, perhaps in the second edition. The *fifth* concerns the framing of "the Twin" in the narrative of the GosJn, which indicates that Thomas and the Beloved Disciple are linked by the way they are introduced in the gospel. The *sixth* focuses on the disciples of Jesus, among whom is the Beloved Disciple. The *seventh* indicates that the repetitions and formulae indicate to the reader that the Beloved Disciple is Thomas. The *eighth* picks up Minear's insight regarding the Benjamin motif behind the portrayal of the Beloved Disciple and reveals a little known fact about Thomas. The *ninth* brings out the identity between Thomas and the Beloved Disciple that is apparent narratively in the Book of Glory and the portrayal of each as the ideal student. The *tenth* is a technical, sequential literary device that through ambiguity, misunderstanding, and clarification gradually reveals that the Beloved Disciple is Thomas. The *eleventh* is a grand *inclusio* in which a follower of

John the Baptist witnesses to Jesus, then is disclosed to be the Beloved Disciple, and finally is revealed to be none other than Thomas. The *twelfth* clarifies that the Beloved Disciple, if he is Thomas, follows the Jewish regulations for purification, and thus serves as the ideal disciple for those Johannine Christians who wish to continue in observing Jewish rules and customs.

The name "Thomas" deserves discussion. From Hebrew and Aramaic-speaking circles prior to 135 C.E. there is insufficient data to conclude that תאום, which means "twin," was a *nomen proprium*. In Syriac-speaking Christianity, of course, it was a well-known name, because of the New Testament texts in Syriac in which Thomas, called Judas Thomas, appears in Semitic form. The old Hebrew translations of the New Testament represent the name as טומא//ס,[1] תומאס, תומה, תומוס, or תומאס.[2] The Greek equivalent, or translation, of tᵊ̄ômâ is Δίδυμος (which appears in GosJn at 11:16, 20:24, 21:2). This Greek noun was a *nomen proprium* in Greek-speaking communities. The author of John repeatedly translates the meaning of the name into Greek: Θωμᾶς ὁ λεγό-μενος Δίδυμος (11:16, 21:2; cf. 20:24).[3] Unlike the names Lazarus (i.e., Eleazar) and Nathanael, Thomas is not theophoric; it is, however, hypocoristic, and ancient traditions connect him with Jesus (if not his twin in blood then in looks or spirituality).[4] There are abundant early Christian traditions that would lend credence to the conclusion that Thomas is indeed the Beloved Disciple. We now turn to the eleven additional exegetical indications that the Beloved Disciple is most likely Thomas.

4.1 THE BELOVED DISCIPLE, THOMAS, AND THE PIERCED SIDE

The first additional reason the Beloved Disciple appears to be none other than Thomas should be persuasive to those who have an open mind and seek to discern who may be the Beloved Disciple. There are numerous steps that help explain this discovery, which came at the very end of my

---

[1] G. Howard, *The Gospel of Matthew according to a Primitive Hebrew Text* (Macon, Ga.: Mercer, 1987) 42.

[2] See the facsimiles of Hebrew manuscripts from 1668 and 1805 in J. Carmignac, ed., *Evangiles de Luc et de Jean traduits en hébreu en 1668 par Giovanni Battista Iona retouchés en 1805 par Thomas Yeates* (Turnhout: Brépols, 1982) ad loc. cit.

[3] See the comments by Brown in *Gospel*, 1:424.

[4] In some Syriac texts "Thomas" is a hypocorism, or pet name, for Jesus' brother, his twin by birth. A helpful discussion of the name "Thomas" and the importance of the Thomas traditions and compositions is found in Gunther, "The Meaning and Origin of the Name 'Judas Thomas,'" *Le Muséon* 93 (1980) 113–48.

exegetical study of the Beloved Disciple passages in the GosJn. According to 20:25 Thomas desires to place his hand into Jesus' side (εἰς τὴν πλευρὰν αὐτοῦ).

This observation leads one to question, Why would Thomas want to place his hand in Jesus' side? How is this action possible or conceivable? The immediate context indicates that an unnumbered and unnamed group of disciples, hidden behind closed doors, see Jesus. He shows them his hands and his side. The narrator does not inform his reader who was present to see these marks of crucifixion. He reports only that Thomas was not there, thereby shifting the spotlight onto him. Then the Evangelist mentions that these disciples inform Thomas, "We have seen the Lord" (20:25). That is all the narrator has them state to him. His response is startling and revealing. Not knowing that they know about the wound in Jesus' side, and not being informed by them of any of the wounds, he refuses to believe their claim that they have "seen the Lord" unless specific criteria are fulfilled.[5] He specifies these criteria for believing them: to see in Jesus' hands the print of the nails, to place his finger in the nail marks, *and to place his hand in Jesus' side.*[6] How does he know about this wound? A first-century Jew could be expected to know about wounds to feet and hands, but the final request by Thomas is exceptional. As far as I know, the wound in Jesus' side is the only unique wound he suffered, and it is reported only by the author of the GosJn. Who saw this wound?

Only the Beloved Disciple saw it, according to the narrative flow of chapter 19. If the reader assumes that Mary Magdalene saw it, she has not communicated this information to Thomas; moreover, the narrator disqualifies her from possessing such knowledge because she encountered the risen Jesus and mistook him for the gardener. The disciples have not informed Thomas that Jesus has a wound in his side. Yet Thomas's question discloses that he knows this oddity. How does he know?

If we are to stick to the narrative, we cannot conclude that he could have heard it from Jesus' mother, her sister, Mary the wife of Clopas, Joseph of Arimathea, or Nicodemus. One could speculate that they may have seen the wound, but the narrator does not tell that to the reader; and

---

[5] I have profited in my understanding of this pericope from conversations with Walt Weaver, and I am grateful to him for insights and enthusiastic support of my hypothesis.

[6] This account does not neatly correspond to the wounds suffered by Jehohanan, which is the name of the only person who was crucified in antiquity whose remains have been found. His ankles were nailed to the cross, but his hands may have been tied to the horizontal bar. See J. Zias and Charlesworth in *Jesus and the Dead Sea Scrolls*, 273-89. (Also see the first two illustrations; the correct recreation is on the left side and above the caption at the bottom of the page.)

to make such a claim runs the risk of eisegesis. Most importantly, each of these individuals exits from the story before the final scene in which Thomas makes his request (20:19-31).

How would Thomas know that something had happened to Jesus' side during his crucifixion? There is no mention of Jesus' side being wounded in the New Testament, except in the GosJn 19:32-35 (cf. 20:20). And according to chapter 19 the only male disciple mentioned present at the crucifixion is the Beloved Disciple. The narrator clarifies that he—and only he—saw the soldier thrust the lance into Jesus' side (19:35) and the Evangelist editorially emphasizes that "his witness is true." Then with a typical but meaningful redundancy, the Evangelist writes, "and he knows that he tells the truth—that you may also believe." The redundancy drives the point home; the reader is to have no doubt about the accuracy of this aspect of Jesus' death.

Morris comprehended the narrative of Thomas's request to put his hand into Jesus' side. The request does not present Thomas in a pejorative light. He wrote that Thomas is probably not one who had a skeptical mind, but one who "was so shocked by the tragedy of the crucifixion that he did not find it easy to think of its consequences as being annulled."[7] Let us continue with the recognition that Thomas's request is understandable and indeed admirable.

According to 19:34 one of the soldiers "with a spear pierced his side" (λόγχῃ αὐτοῦ τὴν πλευρὰν ἔνυξεν). The aorist of νύσσω employed by the author denotes the action of nudging, piercing, pricking, or stabbing someone with something. Sometimes, as most likely here in the GosJn, it denotes an action intended to discern if someone is dead (as in the roughly contemporaneous Plutarch, *Cleom.* 37,16), or to wake someone up from sleep (as with Peter, according to Acts 12:7 in MSS D and gig, who was "being nudged" [νύξας] on his side by an angel).

Who saw a soldier stab Jesus' side? Studies on the GosJn have failed to recognize and emphasize that only one person was present to see it; according to chapter 19 it is the Beloved Disciple. This becomes clear when we approach the GosJn with narrative exegesis and attend to the flow of the drama.

Readers indwelling the story are enticed to reflect on the psychic effect of this scene. Should they not imagine how traumatic it must have been for one of Jesus' followers to witness the piercing of his side? For one of Jesus' disciples it would have been an horrific moment: seeing in a land promised to Abraham and his descendants but now occupied by Romans, a pagan mutilate the side of the corpse of a Jew, especially a revered teacher.

---

[7] L. Morris, *The Gospel According to John* (Grand Rapids: Eerdmans, 1971) 852.

The author of the GosJn makes it pellucidly obvious that *the only disciple* to witness this event is Jesus' intimate and sensitive student, the Beloved Disciple. His Jewish consciousness would have been indelibly marked and his psyche scarred by this event. After stressing in 19:35 that the Beloved Disciple did witness the piercing of Jesus' side, the Evangelist adds authorially that his witness is true (cf. 19:35 and 21:24).[8] According to the narrative the only disciple to see the mutilation of the corpse (which causes extensive uncleanness according to Mishnah Ohalot 1:1–2:3) by a spearhead (which according to Mishnah Kelim 11:8 is unclean) is none other than the Beloved Disciple. For a religious Jew, like any of Jesus' disciples, the mutilation of a corpse by a pagan soldier would have been incomprehensibly shocking.[9]

Within chapter 20 Thomas's desire to see Jesus' pierced side makes little sense. Indeed, in the context of this chapter Thomas's demand to place his hand in the wound in Jesus' side defies explanation. In fact, the narrator does not describe Thomas's putting his hand in Jesus' side according to the GosJn.

He does touch the resurrected body, according to some of the early scholars of the church,[10] and especially to a later second-century apocryphal work which has been called "the most Johannine of Christian dialogues in the context of the development both of the dialogue and of the

---

[8] R. L. Sturch correctly concludes that Westcott's goal to prove that the Evangelist is the apostle John because of the eyewitness quality of the GosJn "cannot in fact be achieved" (324). Sturch also rightly points out the uniqueness of 19:35. In this verse we have the Evangelist or the Beloved Disciple's overt claim to be present and to witness the thrust of the spear. Either this is the truth or a deliberate lie. The former is alone probable; Sturch contends, "I can make sense of the language of this verse only on the assumption that the witness referred to is the Evangelist himself" (324). As demonstrated in chapter 1, I distinguish between the BD and the Evangelist; only the former is the "eyewitness." It is not so easy to move from narration to history; yet there are reasons to conclude that the BD could well have actually been present at the crucifixion. See Sturch, "The Alleged Eyewitness Material in the Fourth Gospel," *Studia Biblica 1978*, ed. E. A. Livingstone (JSNT Supplement Series 2; Sheffield: JSOT Press, 1980) 313–27.

[9] This dimension of the GosJn has been missed by commentators, who have habitually been understandably interested in the sacramental meaning of the αἷμα and ὕδωρ which is said to have flowed from Jesus' side (19:34).

[10] Cyril of Jerusalem, for example, states that Thomas thrust his hand into Jesus' side (καὶ θωμᾶς ὁ βαλὼν τὴν χεῖρα εἰς τὴν πλευρὰν αὐτοῦ). *Cath. Lec.* 13.39. For the Greek text see W. C. Reischl -J. Rupp, *Cyrilli Hierosolymarum archiepiscopi opera quae supersunt omnia* (Hildesheim: Olms [original is from Munich, 1860]) 102.

church order genre."[11] In it both Thomas and Peter can say "we touched him that we might truly know whether he had risen in the flesh." In this document, called the *Epistle of the Apostles (Epistula Apostolorum)*, we find the following words before the cited quotation:

> That you may know that it is I, put your finger, Peter, in the nail-prints of my hands; and you, Thomas, put your finger in the spear-wounds of my side; but you, Andrew, look at my feet and see if they do not touch the ground. (11–12, from the Coptic)[12]

Peter and Thomas are singled out to verify Jesus' wounds.[13] Why were they put in central focus to verify Jesus' physical resurrection? Is it because the author of this apocryphal work, who obviously knew and was dependent upon the GosJn, perceived that Thomas was the Beloved Disciple; moreover, that he and Peter had run to the empty tomb and gone home, *not knowing* the Scriptures that he must rise from the dead? Did he—like the editor who added chapter 21—wish to remove the narrative ambiguity of 20:1-10? If so, then he surely assumed that Thomas was the Beloved Disciple.

Turning from this apocryphal work, which is more of an apocalypse than an epistle, and which is certainly anti-gnostic and anti-docetic, we now return to the GosJn with this question: Why did Thomas want to view and touch Jesus' wounded side, and why did the Evangelist not clarify whether Thomas did touch Jesus? The narrator informs the reader that some disciples told Thomas only, "We have seen the Lord" (ἑωράκαμεν τὸν κύριον. 20:25). They did not explain to him, at least not according to chapter 20, that Jesus had shown "them his hands and his side" (20:20). The narrator does not explain in 20:19-22 anything about Jesus' side. What was so unique about it and what is the function of this aspect of the story in the drama of the GosJn?

To answer these questions the reader must remember 19:34-35, and that means confronting again the Beloved Disciple, who is not only the "true" witness to this episode, but the witness who alone authenticates the Johannine claims. According to chapter 19 the BD is the sole witness to the claim that a soldier thrust a spear into Jesus' side. Thomas would have

---

[11] J. Hills, *Tradition and Composition in the "Epistula Apostolorum"* (Harvard Dissertations in Religion 24; Minneapolis: Fortress, 1990) ix.

[12] Elliott, *The Apocryphal New Testament* (Oxford: Clarendon, 1993) 563.

[13] As Lietzmann argued long ago, the author of the *Epistula Apostolorum* mixed so-called orthodox opinion and gnostic thought to indicate not only the "bodily character of the Risen Lord," but also "the deity of the logos." Lietzmann, *The Founding of the Church Universal*, trans. B. L. Woolf (London: Lutterworth Press, 1938 [3rd ed. rev. 1953]) 93.

had to obtain this information from him; he could not have learned it from Mary Magdalene, who, we have already observed, is the only person according to the narrative who could possibly have seen the wound and who has not already exited from the story.[14] Even though she was at the scene of the crucifixion (19:25), there is no narrative word that she saw this act; and she may have left Golgotha before this alleged event occurred (19:34). She surely shows no indication that the gardener she meets near the site of the crucifixion has any crucifixion marks. If Jesus' side had been wounded and if he were clothed then she would not have observed the wound in his side; but that pericope is notoriously a *non sequitur* to 20:1-10 in which Jesus' burial clothes are left in the not-so-empty tomb. Nevertheless, the point is certain: Mary Magdalene does not observe any marks of crucifixion on Jesus' "body"; the narrator again bewitches us here as we seek to discern the varied traditions and tensions in chapter 20.

She does not talk with Thomas. How does he know about the wound in Jesus' side? Is it not odd that Thomas never meets and talks with the Beloved Disciple who alone could have informed him? Is that because Thomas is the hypocorism of the honorific epithet, the Beloved Disciple? I think such a conception should be given deep consideration.

It has become very strange to read that Thomas demands to see and touch Jesus' wounded side. Why?

The most viable explanation is to assume that Thomas had witnessed this aspect of the crucifixion, which is described in chapter 19. If he had witnessed this deed, it is obvious that he would have been traumatized by it; and the piercing of the side is the one image that seems to stand out for Thomas ($\dot{\epsilon}\grave{\alpha}\nu\ \mu\grave{\eta}\ \ddot{\iota}\delta\omega\ ...\ \kappa\alpha\grave{\iota}\ \beta\acute{\alpha}\lambda\omega\ \mu o\upsilon\ \tau\grave{\eta}\nu\ \chi\epsilon\hat{\iota}\rho\alpha\ \epsilon\acute{\iota}\varsigma\ \tau\grave{\eta}\nu\ \pi\lambda\epsilon\upsilon\rho\grave{\alpha}\nu\ \alpha\dot{\upsilon}\tauο\hat{\upsilon}$). It is apparent that Thomas may have been at Jesus' crucifixion, but why did the author of the GosJn not mention that he was there? Or is it probable that he was present as the Beloved Disciple? J. H. Bernard, in his classical study of the GosJn, rightly (and apparently alone among the commentators) perceived this aspect of the GosJn: "Thomas is represented as knowing of the lance-thrust in Jesus' side, which suggests that he was a witness of the Crucifixion."[15]

---

[14] To suggest that the pagan soldier could be the witness is so preposterous that it should be relegated to a footnote. Anyone who would suggest that avenue for Thomas's knowledge is far removed from the *Tendenzen* and symbolisms of the Evangelist and his world.

[15] Bernard, *Gospel According to St. John*, 2 vols. (Edinburgh: T. & T. Clark, 1928) 2:682. Bernard could not entertain the possibility that Thomas is the Beloved Disciple, because he assumed, as did virtually every commentator when he wrote (1928), that John is without question the BD. See his "John the Apostle was the Beloved Disciple," in 1:xxxiv-xxxvii; see esp. xxxvii on which we read, "There can be no reasonable doubt that the name of the Beloved Disciple was John, and therefore Thomas and Nathanael are excluded."

Bernard is perspicacious. Thomas could have been present as the Beloved Disciple.

Why does the author of the GosJn indicate this need of Thomas's? Perhaps because seeing someone alive again who had been crucified would not clinch an argument against synagogal Jews that the crucified person is none other than Jesus of Nazareth. Hearing Mary Magdalene's account and affirming it verbatim opens one to the charge of believing in apparitions, or succumbing to self-generative visions of angels (20:11-12). The unique feature of Jesus' crucifixion, according to the GosJn, needs to be perceived. Seeing the wound must also be accompanied with the knowledge obtained by touching it; otherwise it is possible one's eyes are generating a mirage due to hallucination or some other psychic or emotional condition. In chapter 20 we find the narrative working on two fronts: the time of Jesus and the time of the Evangelist.[16] Nothing less than the validity of Jesus and the Johannine Community is at stake here.

During the time of the composition of the GosJn (circa 65 to 100) thousands of Jews had been crucified in ancient Palestine. According to Josephus five hundred persons a day were crucified on the circumvallation ramp that enclosed Jerusalem before 70 C.E. Hence, by 85 C.E. the claim that one who had been crucified had been seen alive again does not indicate that the person is none other than Jesus son of Joseph.

For the Johannine Christians, and even more so for their antagonists in the synagogue nearby, there was only one persuasive answer to the charge that Jesus' followers had succumbed to apparitions, illusions, angels, or visions of someone who had been crucified. It is the reliable witness of the authority behind the GosJn, indeed the true witness—Thomas as the Beloved Disciple—that the resurrected person seen was not someone else "resurrected" from the dead according to the GosJn,[17] but Jesus and no one else. Thomas claims to have seen in the resurrected body the one distinguishing mark of Jesus' crucifixion. He had seen in the

---

[16] As Smith points out, "the narrative operates at two levels, that of Jesus himself and that of the Johannine Christians and community. To elucidate John's theology means not to destroy his narrative, but to show how its theological emphases arose from and relate to the emergence of the Christian community on Martyn's second level." Smith, of course, is referring to the pioneering and paradigmatic research published by J. L. Martyn, especially his *History and Theology in the Fourth Gospel*, which has clearly helped us in our explorations (D. M. Smith, *The Theology of the Gospel of John* [Cambridge: Cambridge Univ. Press, 1995] xi).

[17] I am not convinced that the distinction we scholars make between resuscitation in the case of Lazarus and resurrection in the case of Jesus was clearly drawn by the contemporaries of the Johannine School.

resurrected body the thoracic wound that corresponded precisely with what he had observed as the Beloved Disciple, when a soldier thrust his spear into Jesus' body, indeed his corpse, during the last moments it dangled from the cross.

Hence, it seems possible, indeed probable, that the author of the GosJn portrays Thomas (in his honorific epithet as the Beloved Disciple) seeing Jesus' side gouged by a soldier's spear and then witnessing (in his hypocoristic name as Thomas) that the resurrected Lord was none other than the crucified Jew named Jesus son of Joseph. Both the crucified Jesus and the resurrected Lord had the one distinguishing mark: a wound in the side caused by a spear. It seems that these observations—especially the final one—help to clinch the argument that Thomas is the Beloved Disciple.

Finally, we must return to a question asked previously. Why did Thomas not touch Jesus' body, according to the narrative? Perhaps it was to emphasize the Johannine truth that resurrection faith is not the goal but the means of the affirmation that Jesus is the Christ, the Son of God, the One from above. Are Jesus' words to Thomas, "be not unbelieving (or faithless), but believing (or faithful)" meant to warn him (and the reader) not to succumb to Docetism or cling to physiological proofs for Christological development? If so, then the narrative of 20:27 harmonizes with Jesus' words to Mary Magdalene: "Do not touch (or hold) me" (20:17). The risen Lord is indeed none other than Jesus son of Joseph, but a resurrection has occurred; it is not a resuscitation. What Thomas sees and is invited to touch occurs within a narrative that stresses not a physically wounded body, but a Johannine truth: the *continuity* of the risen one with the crucified one, and the fact that he is the bearer of *life* so that "believing you may have life ($\zeta\omega\grave{\eta}\nu$) in his name" (20:31).

4.2 THE BELOVED DISCIPLE AND JUDAS ISCARIOT

The second of the additional reasons why the Beloved Disciple may be Thomas derives from a study of the various ways the narrator has presented him in tandem with Judas Iscariot, who—as we have seen—is considered the Beloved Disciple by more than one scholar (see chap. 3).[18] Only Judas Iscariot (6:71) and Thomas (20:24) are clearly designated as

---

[18] I cannot agree with W. E. Sproston who contends, "No gospel paints a blacker portrait of Judas Iscariot than the Fourth Gospel" (307). There are actually two portraits of Judas in the GosJn; one is rather positive as we see in chapter 13, in which all his co-disciples (including the BD) think he leaves the Last Supper to fulfill Jesus' will (as he does in the sense of the economy of salvation and determinism apparent in the GosJn). W. E. Sproston, "Satan in the Fourth Gospel," *Studia Biblica 1978*, 307-11. (This study is short and perfunctory.)

members of the Twelve (Peter belongs to this group only by inference; cf. 6:67-68). It seems apparent that the author of the GosJn intended to communicate something important to the reader by revealing the names of only two of the Twelve. We should explore the rhetorical meaning of this dimension of the GosJn. Obviously, Judas and Thomas are related in the mind of the author of the GosJn because only they are singled out as members of the Twelve; but how does the Evangelist conceptually link them?

Likewise, the author of the GosJn thinks paradigmatically, with groups of contrarieties like the following: above versus below, believing versus not-believing, seeing versus being blind, life versus death (having life versus perishing), understanding versus misunderstanding, darkness versus light (and the full light-darkness paradigm).[19] He is the New Testament theologian who thinks dualistically and does so *par excellence*. Hence, if Judas Iscariot is the betrayer, then his opposite might be the beloved.

In addition, the dualism in the Twelve would be represented by the only two people clearly cast as belonging to the Twelve; namely, Judas Iscariot and Thomas. It becomes apparent then that the author of the GosJn clearly portrayed the former as the betrayer and may have considered the latter as the Beloved Disciple. The major contrasting pair would then be Judas the betrayer versus Thomas the Beloved Disciple. This concept fits nicely within the narrative of the GosJn in which dualistic, usually complimentary, pairs are well known. This literary feature appears significantly in chapter 1: John the Baptist's two disciples who follow Jesus (1:35), Andrew and Simon Peter,[20] Philip and Nathanael,[21] and perhaps "John" in 1:1-35 may conceivably refer to two different men.[22] Then in chapter 11 we hear about Mary and Martha. Nicodemus and Joseph of Arimathea also seem to be a pair. There are two angels in the tomb (20:12). And in an intriguing way Peter and the Beloved Disciple constitute a pair (especially in 20:1-10 and 21:1-23).

Among the disciples at the Last Supper, Jesus' betrayer is known to only two individuals: Judas and the Beloved Disciple; and so they seem to be subtly contrasted. On the one hand, Judas Iscariot is portrayed as the

[19] See my discussion of Johannine dualism in *John and the Dead Sea Scrolls*; see esp. 76-89.

[20] In some pericopes Philip and Andrew seem to form a pair (see 12:20-22).

[21] Since we are focusing on the GosJn we cannot add James and John the sons of Zebedee. According to this gospel their names are not given; and we cannot even discern the number or gender of "those of Zebedee."

[22] The list would grow if we included the Synoptics. See E. J. Goodspeed, "The Apostolic Pairs," in *The Twelve: The Story of Christ's Apostles* (Philadelphia: John C. Winston Company, 1957) 14-32.

devil (6:70; cf. 13:2);[23] on the other hand, the Beloved Disciple fulfills many of the functions of the Spirit of Truth, the Holy Spirit, the Paraclete (chapters 14–16).[24] During his agony on the cross Jesus has been abandoned by the betrayer, namely Judas, one of the Twelve. He is supported by only one disciple, the Beloved Disciple. If he is Thomas, then Jesus is supported by the only other member of the Twelve whom the narrator names. This insight depends on the prior conclusion that the Beloved Disciple is Thomas.

Finally, Judas and the Beloved Disciple tend to represent two opposites. Perhaps they are paradigms for "those who do not believe" and "those who do believe." Although only implied, there can be little doubt that the Evangelist held that Judas represents those who walk in darkness, while the Beloved Disciple is a paradigm for those who walk in the light. The latter are Sons of Light (12:36),[25] because they belong to the Light, that is Jesus. Culpepper perceived this contrariety that unites Judas and the Beloved: "Judas is related to the children of the devil, who hate and kill, in much the same way as the Beloved Disciple is related to the children of God, who are marked by love (cf. 1 John 3:10)."[26] This link is forged permanently if the Beloved Disciple is then Thomas, who is the leader of the disciples (11:16) and the one who makes the concluding and dramatic confession in 20:28, which is anticipated by the incipient resurrection belief of the Beloved Disciple in 20:8 which culminates in his confession in 21:7.

One of the Twelve is Judas, who is the betrayer. In contrast, one of the Twelve is Thomas, who presents the paradigmatically acceptable confession: and as the model for questioning and then confessing, he is in harmony with the ideal disciple, who is the Beloved Disciple. We have already seen that the Beloved Disciple is assumed by the Evangelist to be one of the Twelve (chap. 2). Using the information provided by the Evangelist, he is thus either Peter, Judas, or Thomas. Peter is impossible, because they appear on stage together at the Last Supper and running

---

[23] See also the reference to Satan (13:27), "the ruler of this world" (12:31; 14:30; 16:11), and "the Evil One" (17:15 [if that is the intended meaning]).

[24] As Culpepper stated, "The Beloved Disciple is not the Paraclete, of course, but he has embodied the Paraclete for others and shaped their understanding of the work of the Holy Spirit in their midst" (*Anatomy*, 123).

[25] As most experts now admit, this *terminus technicus* is inherited from the Dead Sea Scrolls in which "Sons of Light" is defined, developed, and applied to explain the origin (4Q186), character and destiny (1QS 3.13–4.26) of the members of the יחד. See Charlesworth's chapter in the D. M. Smith Festschrift, ed. C. C. Black and A. Culpepper, and to be published by Westminster/John Knox Press.

[26] Culpepper, *Anatomy*, 124.

together to the tomb. Judas is not a possible candidate because the narrator portrays him as one in whom Satan has entered. Thomas is the only choice. These reflections certainly add credence to our hypothesis. The Beloved Disciple may well be Thomas.

4.3 THE BELOVED DISCIPLE AND THOMAS'S CALL TO MARTYRDOM

The supplementary chapter to the GosJn reveals the anguish in the Johannine Community over the death of the Beloved Disciple. Many reasons for this trauma have been examined. Some of Jesus' words ostensibly meant to the Johannine Christians that the Beloved Disciple was not to die until Jesus returned (the Parousia). But he died. Hence, Jesus' words, the certainty, and indeed the validity of the witness of the Beloved Disciple has been undermined, even shattered. Can another tremor for the splitting of the Community be the loss of faith in the Beloved Disciple?

Now we need to confront another major dimension of the earth-shaking event. The Johannine Community knew Peter had been martyred—as we surely know from 21:18-19. In fact, the earliest documentary evidence for his martyrdom is chapter 21; he was crucified: "but when you grow old, you will stretch out your hands, and another will encircle[27] you and take you where you do not wish to go" (21:18). Then the editor added his own explanation: "This he [Jesus] said, giving a sign by what manner of death he would glorify God."[28] The Greek ἐκτείνω ("to stretch out") has the connotations of crucifixion (ἐκτείνας σεαυτὸν ὡς οἱ ἐσταυρωμένοι in Epictetus 3.26.22); but it also denotes the extension of one's self in prayer (as in 4Mac 4:11).[29] Hence, with *double entendre* the editor signifies how Peter, through crucifixion, will honor God as if in prayer through crucifixion.

As we know from the paintings in the second-century Roman catacombs, from the *Odes of Solomon* (27:1-3, 35:7, 42:1-2), from Revelation 20:4-6,[30] from Tertullian,[31] and from works of early Christian art

---

[27] The Greek ζώννυμι denotes to be girded; that is, encircled with a belt or waist cloth.

[28] This is a very symbolical sentence and can be translated only idiomatically.

[29] 4Mac 4:11 ὁ 'Απολλώνιος ... τὰς χεῖρας ἐξέτεινεν εἰς τὸν οὐρανὸν καὶ μετὰ δακρύων τοὺς Εβραίους παρεκάλει ὅπως περὶ αὐτοῦ προσευξάμενοι τὸν οὐράνιον ("At that Apollonius ... stretched out his hands to heaven and with tears entreated the Hebrews to pray to heaven for him").

[30] According to this passage in Rev 20:4, only those who have been martyred—that is "have been beheaded" for their witness to Jesus as Lord—will be allowed to reign with him in the millennium.

[31] Nos vero non attollimus tantum sed etiam expandimus et *dominicam passionem modulantes* et orantes confitemur Christo; *De Orat.* 14.

(like the Lia Lungara Sarcophagus)[32] the orante was both a means of prayer and a symbol of Jesus' crucifixion.[33] A striking parallel to the symbolism of John 21:18-19 is in *Ode of Solomon* 27:1-3, which depicts Christian prayer as a somatic reenactment of crucifixion:

> I extended my hands
> And hallowed my Lord,
> For the expansion of my hands
> Is his sign
> And my extension
> Is the upright cross.

This observation is singularly important for us in the present focused question of why the Johannine Community was shaken by the death of the Beloved Disciple. According to chapter 21, his major rival, Peter, had been martyred. He, however, had only passed away. The importance of martyrdom in and around 100, when chapter 21 would have probably taken final shape, is well known and needs only a succinct illustration.

Ignatius of Antioch yearned for martyrdom, and his prayers were answered in Rome (cf. Eusebius, *HE* 3.36). He urged the Roman Christians to let him "be eaten by the beasts" (ἄφετέ με θηρίων εἶναι Βοράν [*Rom* 4.1]). He even prayed for martyrdom (ὀναίμην τῶν θηρίων τῶν ἐμοὶ ἡτοιμασμένων καὶ εὔχομαι σύντομά μοι εὑρεθῆναι [*Rom* 5.2]).

This criterion for ideal discipleship does not fit the demise of the Beloved Disciple. How can he possibly continue to be the model for us? those members of the Johannine Community who defined ideal discipleship with martyrdom may have thought. As Martyn has shown, the synagogal Jews may well have martyred some Jews who belonged to the Johannine Community.[34] There can be no doubt that he is correct in interpreting 16:2 to refer to Jews not only casting out of their synagogue other Jews who are now in the Johannine Community, but also killing them:

> I have told you these things (that the world will hate you) to keep you from being shaken in your faith. They are going to excommunicate you from the synagogue. Indeed the hour is coming when the man who puts you to death will believe that in doing so he is offering an act of service to God! (16:1-2).[35]

---

[32] See the photograph and informative discussion in *Encyclopedia of Early Christianity*, ed. E. Ferguson, et al. (New York/London: Garland Publishing, Inc., 1990) 662-64.

[33] See D. Plooij, "De 'Oranten' Houding in de Oden van Salomo," *Theologisch Tjidschrift* 45 (1911) 449-62.

[34] Martyn, "Persecution and Martyrdom," *The Gospel of John in Christian History*, 55-89; also see his *History & Theology in the Fourth Gospel*, 64-91.

[35] Martyn, *The Gospel of John in Christian History*, 56.

Now, it is significant to wonder what some Johannine Christians living in a community experiencing the martyrdom of some of its members would think when they realized that unlike other members of their community— and unlike Peter and others—the Beloved Disciple did not receive this glory (as the early Christians termed the witnessing dimension of martyrdom). The author of the GosJn could not recast history and falsify the culmination of the earthly life of the Beloved Disciple. His credibility would be rightly questioned if the Beloved Disciple did not die a martyr's death, yet he nevertheless portrayed him as a martyr like Jesus and Peter.[36]

What could he do? He could portray the Beloved Disciple as the herald who exhorted the other disciples to face martyrdom. What better way to portray him than as one who enters on the scene of the drama, the narrative of the GosJn, as the spokesman who leads in being willing to die for Christ. Yes, that would be the only answer.

Thus, Thomas would be the Beloved Disciple. As he is introduced by name for the very first time and placed on center stage, the spotlight is cast upon him. He appears alone of the *dramatis personae* capable of leadership. He exhorts his fellow disciples to follow Jesus back into Judea, even if it means martyrdom: "Thomas, called the Twin, said to his co-disciples, 'Let us also go, that we may die with him' (ἵνα ἀποθάνωμεν μετ' αὐτοῦ"; 11:16). As A. Smith argued, "The disciples followed Thomas, who for the moment had become the leader."[37] R. F. Collins also rightly stresses that "11:16 presents Thomas as the courageous one and as a leader among the disciples of Jesus."[38] Carson likewise points out Thomas's "raw devotion and courage."[39] By recognizing that Thomas is the Beloved Disciple, the reader can comprehend that although this individual did not die a martyr's death, he can remain the ideal disciple because he willingly faced martyrdom for Jesus, the Christ.[40] Furthermore, if Thomas is the Beloved Disciple, only he was beside Jesus when he died.

[36] See Eckhardt, *Der Tod des Johannes*, 12–16.

[37] A. Smith, *The Twelve Christ Chose* (New York: Harper, 1958) 98.

[38] Collins, *These Things Have Been Written* (Louvain: Peters, 1990; Grand Rapids: Eerdmans, 1991) 36–37. Collins points to Mark 14:29 and parallels in which "Peter is presented as the disciple who is ready to follow Jesus unto death" (37, n. 101). Has the author of the GosJn been reacting to an oral tradition that depicted Peter as the leader exhorting martyrdom with Jesus and that transferred the tradition to his favorite, Thomas and the BD?

[39] Carson, *The Gospel According To John*, 410.

[40] I cannot agree with Carson that Thomas's call to be willing to die with Jesus is "shot through with misunderstanding and incomprehension" (*The Gospel According to John*, 410). I would concur that Thomas depicts the ideal disciple who is growing in understanding, which will explode fully developed in chapter 20.

We may now turn to a final point regarding martyrdom. Late second-century eastern Christians, and subsequent generations, attributed martyrdom to Thomas and composed acts in his name to commemorate his martyrdom. Do they undermine the possibility that Thomas is the Beloved Disciple, or are these traditions etiological legends?

The earliest record clarifies that Thomas was not martyred. In the second century, Heracleon pointed out that Levi, Matthew, Philip, and Thomas never "confessed" before the magistrates; therefore, they were not martyred (Clement, *Stromata* 4.9). Is rivalry between the East and West apparent in Heracleon of Rome's insinuation that Thomas is superior to Peter who was martyred (see chap. 8)?[41]

The major point now is to observe that Heracleon preserves an apparently reliable and certainly early tradition that Thomas "had died a natural death."[42] Hence, Thomas can fit the mold of the Beloved Disciple according to chapter 21.

The reverse, however, may well be the case for the apostle John, as many experts have shown (including Schwartz, Wellhausen, Moffatt, Charles, and Burney).[43] Galatians 2:9 may indicate that the apostle John was still alive when that epistle was composed, and Acts 12:2 may suggest that only James had been martyred by "Herod."[44] Mark 10:35-40, however, may well preserve an early tradition that both James and John the sons of Zebedee were martyred by approximately 70 C.E.;[45] it implies that

[41] This is an obscure passage in Clement of Alexandria; for a good discussion see E. H. Pagels, *The Gnostic Gospels* (New York: Random House, 1979) 96-97.

[42] P. Carrington, *The Early Christian Church* (Cambridge: Cambridge Univ. Press, 1957) 2:262.

[43] See Braun, *Jean le Théologien*, 375-85, 407-11. Braun contends that the apostle John was not martyred. Nunn likewise attempted to show that the apostle John was not martyred. See his "Was John the Son of Zebedee a Martyr?" in *The Son of Zebedee*, 1-53. Colson reviews the traditions and adds credence to the possibility that the apostle John had been martyred. See his *L'Énigme du disciple que Jésus aimait*, 66-84.

[44] It is purely speculative to conjecture that Acts 12:2 originally read ἀνεῖλεν δὲ 'Ιάκωβον καὶ τὸν ἀδελφόν. There is no manuscript evidence for this reading.

[45] Schnackenburg concludes that Mark 10:39 is not a *vaticinium* of James and John's martyrdom; it only indicates the "suffering which awaits all disciples of Jesus" (*St. John*, 1:87). I prefer the exegesis of G. Quispel, who presents further convincing evidence from the Aramaic Church, including the Manichean Psalms (PsB 148,22), that both of the sons of Zebedee were martyred ("The Fourth Gospel and the Judaic Gospel Tradition," in *Manichaica Selecta*, ed. A. van Tongerloo and S. Giversen [Manichaean Studies 1; Louvain: International Association of Manichaean Studies, 1991] 289-93).

both of them will drink the cup which Jesus will drink and be baptized with the baptism with which he was baptized.[46] It is further possible that not only Peter and James, but also John and Andrew were known to be martyrs by the author of Mark 13:3-13; this section has Jesus tell "them" (apparently these four) that they will be brought to trial and delivered up (Mk 13:11).

The common opinion among many scholars that the apostle John was not martyred may be misleading.[47] It is not clear that the comment by Eusebius (*HE* 3.1.1) that John the Apostle lived to a very old age in Ephesus, according to Gregory Harmatolus, is to be taken as one of the *bruta facta*.[48] Also possibly misleading is the report of Polycrates, the Bishop of Ephesus at the close of the second century. He claimed that John the Apostle was a witness (a "martyr") and a teacher, who reclined on the Lord's bosom (at the Last Supper) and "fell asleep at Ephesus."[49]

Second-century accounts must not be treated cavalierly. Although Papias' books are still lost, he seems to have reported that John had been martyred.[50] Philip Sidetes recorded from Papias' second book the report that John and James were martyred by Jews.[51] Georgius Harmartolus also reported that Papias knew that John had been martyred;[52] and adds that the polymath Origen, in his comments on Matthew, recorded that John had been martyred.[53] It is also significant that Heracleon can report that Thomas was not martyred, but remains silent about his hero John.[54] The

---

[46] Matthew in 20:23 does not contain the baptism metaphor; Luke does not preserve the saying. Some attempts to prove that John was not martyred assume such arguments are proved by the "fact" that only James is said to be martyred by Herod according to Acts 12:2. The historical reliability of Acts has been severely questioned, and John may have been martyred *at another time and place* (perhaps by "Jews" as some early scholars of the church maintain). Hence, the arguments against John's martyrdom are not convincing.

[47] Schnackenburg, *St. John*, 1:88, concludes that the apostle John was not martyred.

[48] See the Greek text in Kürzinger, *Papias von Hierapolis*, 118.

[49] See Nunn, *The Son of Zebedee*, 5.

[50] For a rebuttal of this view see Nunn, *The Son of Zebedee*, 13.

[51] Παπίας ἐν τῷ δευτέρῳ λόγῳ λέγει, ὅτι Ἰωάννης ὁ θεολόγος καὶ Ἰάκωβος ὁ ἀδελφὸς αὐτοῦ ὑπὸ Ἰουδαίων ἀνῃρέθησαν. *Historia christiana, Epitome*, Codex Baroccianus 142; for the full citation see Kürzinger, *Papias von Hierapolis*, 116.

[52] Παπίας ... ὅτι ὑπὸ Ἰουδαίων ἀνῃρέθη· (Georg Hamartolus, *Chronicon*, Codex Coislinianus 305, fol. 204r).

[53] ὡς ὅτι μεμαρτύρηκεν Ἰωάννης (*Chronicon,* Codex Coislinianus 305, fol. 204r). See Kürzinger, *Papias von Hierapolis*, 118.

[54] This was pointed out long ago by R. H. Charles, *Revelation*, 1:xlvi–xlvii.

martyrdom of John is apparently celebrated in some early calendars (viz. the Calendar of Carthage of 505 C.E.).[55]

These observations leave us with two conclusions. First, John the Apostle is not a good candidate for the Beloved Disciple, because he was martyred,[56] and the Appendix to the GosJn implies that the Beloved Disciple did not, in contrast to Peter, suffer martyrdom. Second, Thomas, like the Beloved Disciple, was not martyred, and is thus a prime candidate for this figure. Perhaps the Evangelist portrayed Thomas as the bold one who exhorted willingness to follow Jesus until the end, and appeared alone at the foot of the cross as the Beloved Disciple, in order to answer a charge that he could not be an ideal witness because he had not been martyred.

4.4 THE EVANGELIST'S SHAPING OF TRADITIONS

Johannine specialists have always known that the Evangelist inherited sources which he shaped or edited. Building upon the best critical research, Fortna suggests which words have been added during the editorial work of the Evangelist. He contends that the Beloved Disciple passages and the story of Thomas's questioning in 20:24-29 were contributed to the story of the GosJn by the Evangelist.[57] This suggestion is far more persuasive than relegating all such pericopes to a later redactor. I am convinced that both the Beloved Disciple passages and the Thomas pericopes were added to pre-Johannine tradition by the Evangelist.

---

[55] The date is Dec 27, but the person who is called John is "S. John Baptist." Are two men named John confused? "Yes" was the answer of Charles; see his *Revelation*, 1:xlvii. Earlier F. C. Burkitt discussed the martyrdom of John. He also answered affirmatively, and he pointed to the Syriac Calendar of Edessa (dated to 411 C.E.) and which for Dec 27 commemorates the martyrdom of the two sons of Zebedee, James and John. Burkitt, who did not tell us his reflections on the identity of the BD, offered the odd suggestion that the author of the GosJn, "before he became a Christian, must have belonged to the Sadducean party, to have been indeed himself a Priest" (p. 248). Burkitt, *The Gospel History and its Transmission* (Edinburgh: T. & T. Clark, 1911 [3rd ed.]) 247–56.

[56] See the discussion esp. by E. Schwartz, *Ueber den Tod der Söhne Zebedaei* (AGWG N.F. 7.5; Berlin: Weidmannnsche Buchhandlung, 1904). He claimed that μένειν in 21:23 meant sleeping in the grave and was therefore "als Ersatz für das Martyrium ... dem Lieblingsjünger zu Teil geworden" (49). Schwartz concluded on the basis of Papias and other earlier reports, the following: "Als historische Thatsache muss demnach angesehen werden, dass Jakobus und Johannes im Jahre 43 oder 44 auf den Befehl des Königs Agrippa hingerichtet sind" (5).

[57] R. T. Fortna, *The Fourth Gospel and its Predecessor* (Philadelphia: Fortress Press, 1988) 187–200.

If he added not only the passages about the Beloved Disciple, but also the story of the questioning-then-confessing Thomas, then in what ways has he related these two? How did he perceive them; can we be certain he distinguished them?

Fortna sees them as separate individuals, but his words come very close to indicating what I take to be the true intention of the Evangelist, that they are two aspects of one and the same person. Fortna perceptively sees that after Thomas questions and makes his confession, the Evangelist has Jesus pronounce a "benediction upon the faith of those like the beloved disciple but with even less to rely on."[58] Fortna intends to contrast the Beloved Disciple and Thomas, but in expressing his position he stimulates thoughts on the possibility that they are not only related, but also identical.

Subsequently, Fortna points out that in contrast to "the Gospel of Signs," the Evangelist does not stress Jesus' resurrection; he makes it "only an occasion for Johannine explanations of the role of the beloved disciple ... and especially for the all-important and crowning Johannine episode of questioning Thomas (20:24-29), both figures having to do with the themes of knowing and validly believing."[59] Fortna rightly portrays both men as leading and ideal figures: Thomas is not a doubter; he is a questioner (see not only 20:24-25, but also 14:5, which Fortna seems to imply belonged to the Signs Source).[60] These are exceedingly important insights; they correct the commentators' concerted attempts to prove that 20:8 must refer to resurrection faith. And thus these reflections build on our previous exegetical work.

Fortna's brilliant reflections open the door for grounding speculation that the Evangelist did relate the functions of the Beloved Disciple and Thomas. Both figures illustrate the Evangelist's concept of knowing and believing. The author has added to his sources one figure: the Beloved Disciple, who is unmasked as Thomas the Twin. This person is the model disciple. I am convinced that as the Beloved Disciple did not believe Mary Magdalene's report about the removal of Jesus' corpse and his only incipient belief in Jesus' resurrection at the empty tomb, so he—as Thomas—would not believe the reports of others. Not only in 20:8 (the BD ἐπίστευσεν), but also in 20:25 (Thomas states "οὐ μὴ πιστεύσω") the verb "to believe" appears unaccompanied by an object; and, moreover, both may well refer to believing the reports of fellow followers of Jesus.

The Beloved Disciple did not need a confrontation with the resurrected Jesus to substantiate or shore up his faith. His believing did not

[58] Ibid., 194.
[59] Ibid., 214.
[60] Ibid., 194. On this page he contends that the figure of Thomas is "from the source."

need such other-worldly assurances. He did not hold a "faith," but espoused a "believing," which was a dynamic process of growing founded on the knowing that Jesus is truly the One who has been sent by the Father.

Finally, these exegetical comments reveal more clearly that Thomas was not "unbelieving" *in Jesus*, according to 20:25; he did not believe the amazing claim of his fellow disciples that Jesus had been physically raised from the dead. Jesus encourages him to cease this "unbelieving" in 20:27. As the Beloved Disciple he believed in Jesus, which did not entail any belief in Jesus' physical resurrection from the dead; as Thomas, he later believes in Jesus' physical resurrection. We need to contemplate the possibility that the Evangelist has introduced not two but one person: the Beloved Disciple who is Thomas.

4.5 FRAMING DIDYMUS NARRATIVELY

The author's use of "the Twin" in the narrative of the GosJn indicates that he seems to identify Thomas with the Beloved Disciple. Five disciples are introduced in the opening of the gospel (1:35-51): two anonymous disciples (one of whom is disclosed to be Andrew), Simon Peter (Cephas), Philip, and Nathanael.[61] Judas Iscariot is introduced by name at the close of Jesus' teaching about the bread of life with an editorial comment that follows upon the desertion of many of Jesus' followers (6:71). Women are introduced, but none is called a $\mu\alpha\theta\eta\tau\acute{\eta}\varsigma$. In fact in chapters 1–20, the Second Edition of the GosJn, only three persons are called a $\mu\alpha\theta\eta\tau\acute{\eta}\varsigma$: Judas Iscariot (in 12:4), the Beloved Disciple (beginning in 13:23), and Joseph of Arimathea (in 19:38).[62] This fact is rather outstanding, because $\mu\alpha\theta\eta\tau\acute{\eta}\varsigma$ appears in the GosJn 78 times,[63] and the author states that Jesus made many disciples (4:1).

What does stand out is the way the author introduces Thomas in chapter 11 and then features him in chapter 20. Between these two pericopes he frames the narratives that feature the Beloved Disciple. The narrator's repetitive words (names, nouns, verbal forms, prepositional phrases, and clauses) form a framework for the perception of the central

---

[61] This passage may well explain why the Talmud reports that Jesus had five disciples.

[62] The editor of the GosJn who appended chapter 21 added more names in 21:1-2: Simon Peter, Thomas, Nathanael, those of Zebedee, and two others who remain anonymous. They may be "seven," but that will depend on the number of "those of Zebedee."

[63] In Matthew, Mark, and Luke, $\mu\alpha\theta\eta\tau\acute{\eta}\varsigma$ appears respectively the following number of times: 73, 46, and 37.

character, the Beloved Disciple.[64] Within the sophisticated and symbolically advanced theological climate of the Johannine School, the *mimesis* of Jesus' words from the trustworthy witness and the salvific efficaciousness of this heavenly wisdom would stimulate reflection and discussion on the cosmological and transcendent dimension of the anonymous one.[65] One salubrious effect would be the unity of narrative, time, and "beloved" with the source of love. It is probably by careful design that the author introduces the Beloved Disciple at the beginning of the Book of Glory and during a meal, as Jesus begins to say "farewell."[66] It is also apparently significant that the Farewell Discourses are adumbrated in the one key question asked by Thomas, that is the way to the Father: "How can we know the way?" (14:4) Jesus' words echo this theme: "I go the Father" (14:28); "I go to the Father" (16:10); "I came from before the Father and have come into the world; again I leave the world and go to the Father" (16:28); "I am coming to you, Holy Father, keep them ..." (17:11; cf. 17:13).

The Evangelist thematically links the Beloved Disciple with the Paraclete,[67] and then stresses that he will abide. The editor later brings out what was felt in the Johannine Community with a Johannine key word μένειν (21:22).[68]

---

[64] See S. Talmon, "The Presentation of Synchroneity and Simultaneity in Biblical Narrative," *Scripta Hierosolymitana* 27 (1978) 9–16; and B. O. Long, "Framing Repetitions in Biblical Historiography," *Proceedings of the Ninth World Congress of Jewish Studies* (Jerusalem: World Union of Jewish Studies, 1986) Division A, 69–76.

[65] For a discussion of Auerbach's *Mimesis*, see L. Alonso-Schökel, "Erzählkunst im Buch der Richter," *Biblica* 42 (1961) 143–72.

[66] With chapter 13 the Evangelist begins a section that is clearly, as F. F. Segovia states, "distinguished from what precedes and what follows" (*The Farewell of the Word: The Johannine Call to Abide* [Minneapolis: Fortress, 1991] 3). Segovia argues that chapters 13–17 in the GosJn constitute "a large narrative section in which a Jesus who is aware of his impending death proceeds to bid farewell to his disciples in the context of a last meal with them" (2). I am convinced, however, that 15–17 were a later addition to the GosJn. But that does not mean the Evangelist, who may have added them, was unaware of the unity of time, place, and characters in this section. In my judgment Segovia misses a rare opportunity to contrast the Beloved with the Betrayer at the Last Meal with the One from Above.

[67] The BD functions at times as another Paraclete in many ways, as experts (esp. Culpepper) have demonstrated. Perhaps it is important to stress again that although chapters 15 through 17 were added later, they were written and added to the GosJn by the Evangelist. The setting is the Last Supper in which the BD is obviously in center focus.

[68] According to Morganthaler, μένειν occurs 40 times in the GosJn but only 3, 2, and 7 times respectively in Matthew, Mark, and Luke.

The verb μένειν is a Johannine technical term, as is well known. What is not so evident is the fact that the Beloved Disciple will remain and so will only a few of Jesus' disciples. The conceptual links between "go away" and "remain" and the semantic domains that they reveal theologically can here only be noted briefly. The anonymous one, the Beloved Disciple, will remain (1:38, 39; 21:22, 23). The anonymous one, the Beloved Disciple, does not go away, as do many of Jesus' disciples (6:66). Note the way the author shapes Jesus' question to him (and the other members of the Twelve): θέλετε ὑπάγειν; (6:67). He does not go away; he remains. Note how the editor expresses this thought, again put into the mouth of Jesus and as a question: θέλω μένειν ... (21:23).

In the Johannine Community the theological meaning of "go away" or "remain" probably had dynamic social aspects. Not only during the life of Jesus, but also during the life of the Johannine Community, some went away while others remained. The schism has shaped not only the Johannine epistles, but also the GosJn, especially in the additions of chapters 15–17. Singularly important within this atmosphere is the emphasis upon the fact that the Beloved Disciple is *one who remains*. That is the mark of the trustworthy witness, the ideal disciple.

Having perceived the importance of ὑπάγω in the light cast by the theologically pregnant μένειν, we can now see how the author subtly may reveal that Thomas is the Beloved Disciple. Rather than ὑπάγω—"go away"—Thomas leads his co-disciples paraenetically with the word ἄγωμεν, "let us go." They are to *go with Jesus*. Thomas's first words on center stage are from Jesus' mouth; he has just said to his disciples ἄγωμεν.

The next time Thomas speaks, he asks where Jesus is going; the verb is from ὑπάγειν (14:5). The verb has again immediately before been used by Jesus: ὑπάγω (14:4). Once again Thomas's words come from Jesus' own previous saying. Readers are in the process of learning, if they had not known previously (from living in the Community or reading the GosJn before) that Thomas and the other disciples are on the way to the Father; they will not ὑπάγειν, that is "go away" (6:67). What is singularly important about Jesus' question in 6:67 is that it is addressed not to "disciples" but only to the Twelve. That means that although the Evangelist is addressing twelve people, only three are identified by name in the GosJn: Judas, Peter, and Thomas. Although Thomas has not yet been introduced in the narrative, that is by name, he is obviously present in 6:67. That is possible not only because the reader will comprehend that he is one of the Twelve, but also because he is the Beloved Disciple.

The author of the GosJn is clearly interested in Thomas the Twin (and only he employs the term "Twin").[69] Thomas appears for the first time in 11:16; in fact, he explodes into the narrative as the leader of his co-disciples, exhorting them to follow Jesus even if it means death.[70] Note the formula θωμᾶς ὁ λεγόμενος Δίδυμος. This exact phrase is repeated again *only* in 20:24.[71] Within the intervening passages the Beloved Disciple is introduced. Note the framing of the Beloved Disciple:

θωμᾶς ὁ λεγόμενος Δίδυμος (11:16)
εἷς ἐκ τῶν μαθητῶν ... ὃν ἠγάπα ὁ Ἰησοῦς (13:23)
καὶ τὸν μαθητὴν παρεστῶτα ὅν ἠγάπα (19:26)
τὸν ἄλλον μαθητὴν ὃν ἐφίλει ὁ Ἰησοῦς (20:2)
θωμᾶς δὲ εἷς ἐκ τῶν δώδεκα ὁ λεγόμενος Δίδυμος (20:24)

Observe that the repeated clause "he who is called Twin" frames the presentation of Thomas and the Beloved Disciple.[72] The repetition and *inclusio* seem to be literary devices, which have syntagmatic value,[73] to shape the reader's understanding of the Beloved Disciple.[74]

But more is dexterously concealed by these words and their place in the narrative. It is significant that the Beloved Disciple is introduced at the

[69] The Evangelist mentions Thomas six times (plus the name "Thomas" appears in 21:2). Matthew, Mark, and Luke mention him only once each (Mt 10:3, Mk 3:18, Lk 6:15). The author of the GosJn calls Thomas a Twin in 11:16 and 20:24 (cf. 21:2).

[70] The response of the reader, it seems to me, is supposed to be one of admiration: this is the ideal disciple; indeed, Thomas understands Jesus and follows him, regardless of the costs. On "reader-response criticism" see, among other main publications, M. A. Powell, *What is Narrative Criticism* (Minneapolis: Fortress, 1990) 16–18. Characteristically Roman Catholic exegetes tend to denigrate Thomas; for example, Collins, referring to 11:16 and 14:5, contends that "Thomas ... epitomizes both the bravado and the ignorance of the disciples" (*These Things Have Been Written*, 37).

[71] The editor of chapter 21 uses it in 21:2.

[72] For a discussion of the biblical art of repetition see R. Alter, *The Art of Biblical Narrative* (New York: Basic Books, 1981) 88–113.

[73] That is, the value of the BD is obtained by perceiving the chain-like order of what has preceded and followed it. For a discussion of this literary device, see D. Patte, *What is Structural Exegesis* (Philadelphia: Fortress, 1976) 25.

[74] For a discussion of these narrative techniques see J. C. Exum, "Promise and Fulfillment: Narrative Art in Judges 13," *Journal of Biblical Literature* 99 (1980) 43–59. Also see J. Muilenberg, "A Study in Hebrew Rhetoric: Repetition and Style," *Congress Volume* (Supplements to Vetus Testamentum 1; Leiden: Brill, 1953) 97–111 [no editor clarified]. As Muilenberg states, "Repetition ... serves ... to center the thought ..." (99).

beginning of a meal.[75] Within the Book of Glory the linguistic formula εἷς ἐκ τῶν plus μαθητῶν or δώδεκα appears only in 13:23 and 20:24.[76] Apparently by this formula the author is linking conceptually the Beloved Disciple and Thomas. And, as Fenton stated, the author of the GosJn used recurring devices to frame or highlight a thought.[77]

After reading the GosJn, and hearing it read out loud over and over,[78] these phrases, especially in an eastern oral culture, would have become mnemonic formulae.[79] As Thomas is "one of the Twelve" so the Beloved Disciple is "one of the disciples." The repeated prepositional phrase εἷς ἐκ τῶν plus "disciple" or "Twelve" appears to be the author's means of identifying the Beloved Disciple as Thomas without giving away the anonymity. This narrative technique allows him to use a symbol that transcends not only the narrative, but also the fundamental concepts of place and time. Hence, the Beloved Disciple can be a model of ideal discipleship for all who wish to follow Jesus but cannot "see" him as did the Beloved Disciple (viz. 19:35, 20:8), and within the narrative, Thomas (20:27-29). The author also ostensibly chose "disciple" instead of "Twelve" to define the Beloved Disciple for the same reason: to allow the historical figure to be also symbolical for Christians of the future.

Finally, the introductions of Thomas and the Beloved Disciple are placed not in some insignificant place in the GosJn, but in the center of the gospel. We can learn from those scholars who have endeavored to claim that Lazarus is the Beloved Disciple. One of their most insightful comments was the place in which Lazarus is introduced. It is in chapter 11; yet he is not mentioned after chapter 12. Kickendraht argued that Lazarus is to be identified as the Beloved Disciple because he is introduced in the core section of the GosJn.[80] Filson also stressed the argument that the Beloved Disciple was introduced in the center of the GosJn:

---

[75] See W. J. Ong, *Orality and Literacy: The Technologizing of the Word* (London/New York: Routledge, 1982) 34.

[76] The Book of Glory is a rhetorical unit, and within this literary block the authoritative figure is surely Jesus, supported by his twin, Thomas, the Beloved Disciple. See a discussion of similar rhetorical techniques in B. L. Mack, *Rhetoric and the New Testament* (Minneapolis: Fortress, 1990) see esp. 21-24.

[77] J. C. Fenton, *The Gospel According to John in the Revised Standard Version* (New Clarendon Bible: New Testament; Oxford: Clarendon Press, 1970) 19.

[78] As is well known, reading in antiquity meant reading aloud. I have observed this phenomenon in public today in Israel, Jordan, Turkey, Greece, Italy, and Egypt.

[79] See Ong, *Orality and Literacy*, 33-36.

[80] Kickendraht, "Ist Lazarus der Lieblingsjünger im vierten Evangelium?" *Schweizerische Theologische Zeitschrift* 31 (1914) 49-54.

> When the first readers had completed what we call ch. 11, which
> makes clear Jesus' love for Lazarus, and ch. 12, in which the risen
> Lazarus shares a significant meal with Jesus, they went immediately
> to ch. 13. Here, in 23, they found a mention of "the disciple whom
> Jesus loved," and he was eating with Jesus.[81]

Any weight in the argument of Kickendraht and Filson here is even more
appropriate for Thomas as the Beloved Disciple. Not only Lazarus (not
categorized as a disciple), but also Thomas is introduced in chapter 11;
moreover, unlike Lazarus, he is called a disciple (11:16) and speaks in
chapters 11 and 14 (14:5).

It does seem significant that the author of the GosJn *introduces*
Jesus' *disciples* in chapter 1, except for Judas who is introduced in chapter
6, Thomas in 11,[82] and the Beloved Disciple in chapter 13. Then Thomas
asks the key Johannine question in chapter 14 ($\pi\tilde{\omega}\varsigma$ $\delta\upsilon\nu\acute{\alpha}\mu\epsilon\theta\alpha$ $\tau\grave{\eta}\nu$ $\grave{o}\delta\grave{o}\nu$
$\epsilon\grave{\iota}\delta\acute{\epsilon}\nu\alpha\iota;$). And in the first edition of the GosJn (before the addition of
chapters 15–17) the next episode is the crucifixion and resurrection
(chaps. 18–20) in which the leading disciple is the Beloved Disciple,[83]
until Thomas reassumes the lead role in the rest of chapter 20 as he had
been in chapter 11. These narrative highs, and the sequence in which the
major characters are introduced in the drama, strengthen the suggestion
that the Beloved Disciple is Thomas.

4.6 THE DISCIPLES OF JESUS

Five Disciples. In chapter 1 the reader is given the impression that
Jesus had five disciples. After meeting Andrew and the Beloved Disciple
the reader is introduced to Simon Peter, Philip, and Nathanael. Thus,
according to *a tradition* preserved in the opening chapter of the GosJn,
Jesus had five disciples.

The editor who added the Appendix also must have thought that
Jesus had five disciples. He adds "those of Zebedee" to the list (21:2).
Despite the number represented by "those" the tradition inherited had only
five disciples: Peter, Thomas, Nathanael, and two anonymous disciples.

---

[81] F. V. Filson, "Who Was the Beloved Disciple?" *Journal of Biblical
Literature* 68 (1949) 85.

[82] Lazarus is also introduced in chapter 11, but the author does not inform
the reader that he is a disciple.

[83] I doubt that the intention of the author of the GosJn was to elevate Judas
Iscariot in that role. The fluctuating concatenation between Betrayer and Beloved
is exceedingly intriguing. I have no doubt that he was playing with the vast similarities in the Betrayer and Beloved (or as Aristotle pointed out centuries before
him, in any contrariety there is essentially more in common than antithetical).

According to our interrogative exploration the Beloved Disciple is among the special five, and this is apparent in chapters 1 and 21. In chapter 1 he is the anonymous former follower of the Baptist. In chapter 21 he is Thomas who as the Beloved Disciple makes the confessional identification, "It is the Lord."

The tradition that Jesus had five disciples thus seems to have been inherited by the Evangelist and by the editor of chapter 21. It is independently preserved, albeit within rabbinical anti-Christian polemics in the Talmud.[84] In a Baraita of the Babylonian Talmud in Sanhedrin 43a we read that "Jesus had five disciples: Mattai, Naqai, Netser, Buni, and Todah," לישו [מ. לישו הנוצרי] מתאי נקאי [מ. נקי מתי] נצר [מ>] ובונה [מ. בוני] ותודה. While it seems clear that the Baraita is legendary, the tradition of Jesus' having five disciples was probably not invented by rabbinic Jews,[85] and while the Evangelist knows about twelve disciples, he seems to preserve a tradition that Jesus had five disciples.[86] I am convinced that the issue is not so much whether the Baraita is dependent upon the GosJn as it is how and in what ways both documents have inherited this tradition. The link here between Talmudic tradition and Johannine tradition is even more intriguing when we observe that both witness to another tradition: that Jesus was crucified before the Passover meal (and the eve of the Sabbath).[87] What is crucial now for our search is to recognize how the Evangelist, as redactor of pre-Johannine traditions, seems to be highlighting Thomas, and perhaps indicating that he is the Beloved Disciple.

Thomas the Seventh. It is interesting to observe that in chapters 1–5, after five disciples are introduced to the reader, there is a long pause;[88]

---

[84] See J. Maier, *Jesus von Nazareth in der Talmudischen Überlieferung* (Erträge der Forschung 82; Darmstadt: Wissenschaftliche Buchgesellschaft, 1978) see esp. "Die fünf Jünger" (232–35). See D. Goldenberg's claim that Maier's argument that there are no authentic Tannaitic Jesus-passages reflects his "apologetic wishes," and ignores important manuscript discoveries ("Once More: Jesus in the Talmud," *Jewish Quarterly Review* 73 [1982] 78–86).

[85] J. Z. Lauterback defends the opposite interpretation, advocating that the Baraita lists only five names because the "author or authors of this legend may not have heard or known of more than five," or that "these five disciples were regarded as the most prominent" ("Jesus in the Talmud," in *Jewish Expressions on Jesus: An Anthology*, ed. T. Weiss-Rosmarin [New York: KTAV, 1977] 1–98; see esp. 82–83).

[86] Is it possible that the tradition which represented Johanan ben Zakkai, the distinguished student of Hillel and Shammai, having five students has helped shape Jesus traditions in the Talmud? Note Aboth 2:8, "Five disciples had Johanan ben Zakkai" (חמשה תלמידים היו לרבן יוחנן בן זכאי).

[87] See the additional Bariata in b.San 43a: "On the eve of the Passover they hanged Yeshu [of Nazareth]." See J. Klausner, *Jesus of Nazareth: His Life, Times, and Teaching*, trans. H. Danby (New York: Macmillan, 1929) 27.

[88] There is no meaning in the fact that Judas, the sixth disciple introduced

then Judas is introduced as the Betrayer (6:70-71). He is categorized as a member of the Twelve,[89] but he is number six, the Semitic number for imperfection. As the Betrayer he is the murderer (the sixth command-ment); as the evil one he is the serpent who was created on the sixth day; as "sixth" he may represent four (the human's world) plus two (human enmity to God).[90]

The symbolism—or at least some of it—would probably not have been lost within the Semitic environment of the Johannine School, since within the Bible one group of writings stand out as unusually important in the search for the symbolic meaning of numbers;[91] it is the writings from the Johannine School. Not only in Revelation (esp. in 13:18),[92] but also in the GosJn (notably in 21:11)[93] numbers clearly have symbolic meaning. Hence, the GosJn stands between the "Old Testament," in which numbers have a restricted or ambiguous symbolic meaning, and Rabbinics, in which numbers take on consecutively more symbolic value.

Numbers were thus more significant for the Johannine School than we scholars have so far perceived. It is indicative of our slowness here (due perhaps to the excessive and absurd use of numerology by the crack-pots) that we miss the symbolism of Judas as sixth on stage, but stress the symbolic meaning of his going out from Jesus' circle into the night ($\mathring{\eta}\nu$ $\delta\grave{\varepsilon}$ $\nu\acute{\upsilon}\xi$. [13:30]).

After Judas the next disciple named is Thomas, and he and Judas are the only two disciples the narrator specifies are members of the Twelve. He is the seventh disciple named in the GosJn. If numerology is important for introducing Judas Iscariot, it may be significant for introducing Tho-mas, who is the seventh named. As is well known, this is the number of perfection. Note how the narrator inserts the names of Jesus' disciples into the story:

(1) an anonymous follower of the Baptist
(2) Andrew

---

in the GosJn, is presented in chapter 6. Some medieval readers, when the chap-ters were added, may have thought otherwise.

[89] When twelve is divided it symbolically denotes imperfection; the twelve tribes were divisive. Judas divides the Twelve; he is a devil (6:70). I am con-vinced that there a pejorative stance is taken by the Johannine School against the concept of the Twelve. There are hints in that direction through the *Tendenzen* of the GosJn (see chapters 7, 14).

[90] See E. W. Bullinger, *Number in Scripture* (Grand Rapids: Kregel Publi-cations, 1967, 1993) 150–57.

[91] See J. J. Davis, *Biblical Numerology* (Grand Rapids: Baker, 1968, 1992).

[92] The number of the beast is 666.

[93] Jesus' disciples catch 153 fish.

(3) Simon Peter
(4) Philip
(5) Nathanael

These names are presented in 1:35-51. An interval separates this pericope from the passage in which an additional name of a disciple is clarified. Nicodemus is presented to the reader in chapter 3; but he is never called a disciple, even though he defends Jesus against the charges of the crowd in 7:35. Nicodemus is described as "a ruler of the Jews" (3:1) and "a teacher of Israel" (3:10). The name of an additional disciple appears in chapter 6: (6) Judas Iscariot. It is significant that he is described as follows: $\varepsilon\hat{\iota}\varsigma\ \delta\iota\acute{\alpha}\beta o\lambda\acute{o}\varsigma\ \dot{\varepsilon}\sigma\tau\iota\nu$ (6:70). There is another long interval before the reader hears about the name of another disciple. Then the reader is told that Thomas speaks for his co-disciples ($\sigma\upsilon\mu\mu\alpha\theta\eta\tau\alpha\hat{\iota}\varsigma$ [11:16]); he is thus a disciple: (7) Thomas. Is it not imperative to discern if Thomas is seventh in order because he is the perfect disciple? No number is so symbolically important and pervasive in Semitic numerology as "seven." The seventh day of the week mirrors the day when God perfected, completed, and blessed his acts of creation (Gen 2:1-3). It is the day of rest: Sabbath (השבת). That Thomas is the seventh character who enters the Johannine drama could reveal him to be the Beloved Disciple.[94]

The Beloved Disciple Is Introduced. The introduction of the Beloved Disciple at the beginning of the account of the Last Supper in chapter 13, the first chapter in the second half of the book, is startling. J. L. Staley indicates the narrative force of the introduction:

> By introducing an unnamed character into this intimate setting with the phrase "one whom Jesus loved," the narrator raises all kinds of questions for the implied reader. Since this person is also described as "reclining on Jesus' breast," and is known to Peter (v 24), he must be counted among the disciples (v 5), and must have shared the companionship of Jesus and the other disciples for some time.[95]

---

[94] If one wanted to continue the search for other disciples, it is conceivable that twelve are mentioned in chapters 1-21: (8) Joseph of Arimathea (who is a disciple according to 19:38); (9) and (10) those of Zebedee (who may perhaps be the two sons); (11) and (12) the two anonymous disciples. The problem with this neat arrangement may be that a Judas who is not Iscariot appears in 14:22 and the scene seems to continue that of the Last Supper (13:1-30). The response is obvious: he is not called a disciple.

[95] J. L. Staley, *The Print's First Kiss: A Rhetorical Investigation of the Implied Reader in the Fourth Gospel* (SBL Dissertation Series 82; Atlanta: Scholars Press, 1988) 108.

Especially appealing is the perception that the Beloved Disciple has been present already in the narrative.[96] Implied readers would most likely not think that the Beloved Disciple is a "new recruit" or owner of the house (as advocates of John Mark have argued [as we saw in chap. 3]); they would have assumed that the Beloved Disciple is Jesus' special disciple and a confidant of Peter.

The narrator thus brings heightened mystery to this setting. The reader is prompted to ponder which of the disciples, already named, is the Beloved Disciple. In the flow of a narrative, the most likely answer is the disciple who has been named and has acted prominently in the preceding scene. If so, then the Beloved Disciple seems to be Thomas. He enters the drama as a leader of the Twelve and exhorts his co-disciples to follow him (11:16). Then the narrator presents the episode about Lazarus, his resuscitation and its effects (11:17-55), the pre-Passover meal in Bethany (12:1-11), the triumphal entry into Jerusalem, and Jesus' teachings about his passion and the coming judgment (12:12-50). Thus the narrator sets the stage for the entrance of the Beloved Disciple: in Jerusalem, at Passover time, and at the commencement of his Book of Glory. Convincing proof that exegesis leads us to conclude that the author is subtly revealing that Thomas is the Beloved Disciple is the lengthy "aside" about Lazarus, which separates the introduction of one disciple, Thomas, from another, "the disciple whom Jesus loved." It is tempting to seek to prove that the Lazarus episodes are intrusive additions to a smoothly flowing narrative; but I think the disruption is intentional, otherwise the identity of the Beloved Disciple might be too obvious.

In this regard, and in search for the identity of the Beloved Disciple, a remark by Segovia is of assistance. He comments that in the room in which the special meal is taking place (the Last Supper) there are the following disciples mentioned: "Judas Iscariot; Simon Peter; the disciple whom Jesus loved; Thomas; Philip; and the other Judas."[97] That adds up to six disciples, which would be a most inappropriate number symbolically for this special meal. The summation indicates either that one disciple is not named, thereby bringing us to the perfect number (7), or—more likely—that one of the disciples is mentioned twice, but only once named, in the list; and that would leave us with the appealing number "five" which is a positive symbol, among other things representing the Penta-

---

[96] If I am correct on the possible identity of the BD, then he was introduced by name in chapter 11 (but only the members of the Johannine Community and those taught within it would be able to discern this fact).

[97] F. F. Segovia, *The Farewell of the Word: The Johannine Call to Abide* (Minneapolis: Fortress Press, 1991) 3.

teuch and the division of the Psalter. That is precisely our solution: Judas Iscariot, Peter, Philip, and the other Judas cannot be identified with the Beloved Disciple without doing violence to the narrator's art. The opposite is true if Thomas is the Beloved Disciple.

Let us contemplate who may be the Beloved Disciple.[98] He is one of the disciples named. He cannot be Judas Iscariot who leaves the room and who, as the Betrayer, is the symbolical counterpart to the Beloved Disciple.[99] He cannot be Peter, who is contrasted with and appears alongside of the Beloved Disciple. That leaves us with only three candidates: Thomas, Philip, and the other Judas. Only one of these is dominant in the narrative. Again we are led, by the subtle symbolism of the Evangelist, to Thomas. As indicated repeatedly, he is most likely the Beloved Disciple.

4.7 REPETITIOUS FORMULAE: THE READER MEETS THE DISCIPLES

In the first book, "The Book of Signs" (1–12), the reader is twice taken to the Bethany which is across the Jordan. In the first episode the reader is introduced to all the disciples (except Judas Iscariot and Thomas). According to 1:28, "Bethany across the Jordan where John was baptizing" is the locale in which "two" disciples begin to follow Jesus; they formerly were disciples of John the Baptist.

The first of these is named: he is Andrew, Peter's brother (1:40). The second one is unnamed. Many Johannine experts claim—rightly in my judgment—that he is the Beloved Disciple (see chap. 6). The place in which Jesus stays is formulaic and charged with theological language; his first two disciples ask him, ποῦ μένεις; (1:38).

The next time the reader is introduced to a disciple it is in chapters 10 and 11, except for Judas who, according to the Johannine School, is not really one of Jesus' own, because Jesus lost none of those given to him, and because if he had been one of Jesus' group he would have remained (as the Community said about the schismatics).[100] Thus, in chapter 10 the reader is again taken to the same locale: across the Jordan where John was baptizing (10:40). Here Jesus is said to remain; the reader will remember the technical terms and especially καὶ ἔμεινεν ἐκεῖ (10:40).[101]

---

[98] When Judas leaves the room the number drops to four, a symbolically positive number; hence, the number cannot have been seven. When he leaves that would leave us with that horrible number "six."

[99] Nevertheless, some experts have argued (in an oddly persuasive way) for identifying Judas with the BD (see chapter 3).

[100] Is it not conceivable that the author probably says things like "Jesus chose the Devil" to make his readers think and to keep somewhat veiled the identity of the BD?

[101] W. J. Ong rightly urges us to enrich exegesis with the obvious

In this locale the reader is introduced to Thomas (11:16). Since Jesus has only five disciples (if we focus on those mentioned in 1:35-51) the implied reader, who is attentive to learn what other members in the Johannine School know, may recognize that the anonymous one, the Beloved Disciple, is Thomas. That is, in chapter 1 the Beloved Disciple appears as an anonymous disciple; but when the reader is again taken to Bethany, she is informed that Jesus has a disciple named Thomas who is the leader of the disciples. If Jesus has only five disciples, then Thomas must be the anonymous disciple of chapter 1, who is most likely the Beloved Disciple. The Bethany episodes seem to strengthen this hypothesis.

We have lately focused on the narrative techniques of repetition and connecting narrative by formulae. Note how the author may present the reader with clues that the Beloved Disciple is Thomas:

1:28	10:40
πέραν τοῦ Ἰορδάνου,	πάλιν πέραν τοῦ Ἰορδάνου
ὅπου ἦν ὁ Ἰωάννης Βαπτίζων.	ὅπου ἦν Ἰωάννης τὸ πρῶτον Βαπτίζων
1:38	10:40 (cont.)
ποῦ μένεις;	καὶ ἔμεινεν ἐκεῖ.
1:40	11:16
anonymous one (BD) introduced	Thomas the Twin introduced

The words πάλιν and τὸ πρῶτον are not necessary to link these two episodes, but perhaps the author imagined some readers might miss his intention; that is, 1:28 and 10:40 are certainly linked. From that obvious linguistic, symbolic, and narrative fact, I am convinced that the author is apparently hinting that Thomas is the Beloved Disciple. He cannot be too obvious.

The importance of μένειν in the GosJn is evident both to the early readers of the GosJn and to the readers of recent monographs. In fact the verb appears three times in 1:38-39. The two first disciples will *remain* with Jesus, which links again the anonymous one with the Beloved Disciple, who will *remain* (21:22, 23).

---

importance of memory in oral cultures. See his "The Psychodynamics of Oral Memory and Narrative: Some Implications for Biblical Studies," in *The Pedagogy of God's Image: Essays on Symbol and the Religious Imagination* (The College Theology Society Annual Publications [1981]; Chico, Cal.: Scholars Press, 1982) 55–73. Although not focused on the GosJn, W. H. Kelber's work is full of insights on orality. See his *The Oral and Written Gospel* (Philadelphia: Fortress, 1983).

Additional clues that Thomas "the twin"—that is, one of *two* who are related—is the Beloved Disciple may be found in two separate verses. In 1:35-40 "one of the two" (εἷς ἐκ τῶν δύο) who followed Jesus is Andrew; the other is the Beloved Disciple. He is thus the "second" one; is it not impressive that Thomas is called the "Twin" (Δίδυμος = תאום) only in the GosJn, and in 11:16 (when he is introduced), 20:24, and 21:2? Is it not impressive that in the Appendix Thomas is named *second* in the list, and after Peter (with whom the BD is almost always related narratively)? Surely these repetitions (not redundancies) have meaning, since the GosJn has come to us from a school of brilliantly trained Jews. That is, while one author has given us the first two editions of the GosJn, he reflects the research and reflections on symbolical theology of the Johannine School (which has inherited the genius of many Jews, including probably the Essenes, the great Jewish authors in Early Judaism). The Evangelist loved paronomasia, as is well known from his use, e.g., of ἄνωθεν, ὕδωρ ζῶν, φῶς καὶ σκοτία, ἀποστέλλω, and ὑψόω. He has also used Δίδυμος in two ways, *double entente:* to signify Thomas as the Twin and to clarify that he is the "second" mentioned in the GosJn, both in 1–20 and in 21.

These reflections may lead to further speculation that may have heuristic value. As Jesus is the "twin" of John the Baptist (in the sense of leading a baptist movement as did the Baptist [3:22, 4:1]),[102] so Thomas the Twin—as the Beloved Disciple—is the twin of Jesus. Both John the Baptist (1:7) and the Beloved Disciple "witness" to Jesus (19:35, 21:24).[103]

Further proof that Thomas is the Beloved Disciple (and additional evidence that this anonymous one cannot be Lazarus) is what the author attempts to do, *inter alia*, in his second edition, when he adds chapters 15–17. Knowing that those who were acquainted with the Beloved Disciple are dying, and more importantly that new members of the Community never knew him (because he has died), the Evangelist clarifies not only that the Beloved Disciple certainly was present at the Last Supper, but that he was with Jesus *from the beginning*. Jesus says to those with him at the Last Supper—remember the Beloved Disciple is lying close to him—"and you also are witnesses, because you have been with me from the begin-

---

[102] Surely there can be little doubt today that 4:2 is redactional. It reflects the historical settings of Matthew and Luke (harmonization and the tendency to deny that Jesus was baptized by John) and the latter apocryphal gospels (removing Jesus from the influence of John and needing to be baptized).

[103] On the witnessing of the Baptist see E. Harris, "John and his Witness," *Prologue and Gospel: The Theology of the Fourth Evangelist* (JSNT Supplement Series 107; Sheffield: Sheffield Academic Press, 1994) 26–62; and R. F. Collins, *John and His Witness* (Zacchaeus Studies: New Testament; Collegeville: Glazier, 1991).

ning (ὅτι ἀπ᾽ ἀρχῆς μετ᾽ ἐμοῦ ἐστε" [15:27]). Those words, *ex ore Christi*, solidify the argument that the Beloved Disciple is present anonymously in 1:37-40.[104]

Jesus' claim that those with him, especially the one so close to him, are his witnesses (καὶ ὑμεῖς δὲ μαρτυρεῖτε [15:27]) are significant. They become words that will ring in the readers' ears when they are told that the Beloved Disciple is the only *witness* (καὶ ὁ ἑωρακὼς μεμαρτύρηκεν, [19:35]) of Jesus' physical death. The force of this claim is strengthened when the implied author states "his witness is true" (καὶ ἀληθινὴ αὐτοῦ ἐστιν ἡ μαρτυρία [19:35]).

Then in 21:24 the redactor who added the Appendix emphasizes that οἴδαμεν ὅτι ἀληθὴς αὐτοῦ ἡ μαρτυρία ἐστίν. How would the Johannine Christians "know that his witness is true"? Note the flow of the narrative: The Beloved Disciple alone sees the thrust of the lance. Two days later the resurrected Jesus shows some disciples, but not Thomas, his hands and side. They inform Thomas only that they "have seen the Lord"; the narrator does not have them inform Thomas of the wound in Jesus' side. Thomas exclaims that he will not believe them until he sees the wounds in Jesus' hands (or wrists), places his finger in the nail marks, and his hand in his side. According to the narrative, the disciples must have been shocked and wondered how Thomas knew about the wound in Jesus' side. They may well have thought this information was unique to them. Thomas has privileged knowledge (in a way reminiscent of the *Transitus Maria*).

Eight days later Jesus reappears in the story and permits Thomas to touch him and put his hand in the side wound. The narrator does not clarify whether Thomas does so, but in all the resurrection narratives in the GosJn and even elsewhere in the intracanonical gospels only he is allowed this special permission to touch the resurrected Jesus (contrast the *Epistula Apostolorum*). The Johannine Christians founded their believing and knowing on the true witness of the Beloved Disciple, who as Thomas was permitted to touch Jesus, and through that epithet is described as lying on the bosom of Jesus (13:23), as Jesus is in the bosom of the Father (1:18).

There is an appealing harmony and unity in the oneness with which the witness is proclaimed to be "true" (5:32, 19:35, 21:24), and in which it is embodied, through the Beloved Disciple (Thomas) in the oneness of God the Father (much like the metaphor of the vine in GosJn 15). Thus, "we know that his witness is true" (21:24) was possible, because of the phenomenological and organic link that unites believers with the Beloved Disciple (Thomas), who functioned among them as the Paraclete, and through him with Jesus who is in the Father (1:18, 17:20-26). Also, at

---

[104] Obviously this monograph was not written from page 1 to the end. Chapter 6 was written; then the whole work was rewritten and edited.

least some of the Johannine Christians would have been able to collaborate the Beloved Disciple's witness. At least some of them had also witnessed aspects of Jesus' life, and Andrew was also with Jesus during the time that he was a baptizer. Hence, recognizing the Beloved Disciple as Thomas helps explain why the Johannine Christians could proclaim that they knew ὅτι ἀληθὴς αὐτοῦ ἡ μαρτυρία ἐστίν.

The Johannine narrator is thus not only subtly revealing that the Beloved Disciple is Thomas, but also unifying the narrative in the progression of those who witness. The Johannine Christians can claim that the witness of the Beloved Disciple is "true," because of the following progression: I witness to the Father who sent me (Jesus, according to 5:35-37), he witnesses to me (the BD according to 19:35 and probably 5:35), and the Beloved Disciple's colleagues know that his witness to Jesus as the One sent by the Father is true (21:24).

In many and subtle ways the Evangelist seems to be using repetitions and presenting formulae to introduce the *dramatis personae* and to develop the characters. In the process we may have detected clues that help us in discerning the identity of the Beloved Disciple. He appears to be Thomas.

4.8 THOMAS AND BENJAMIN

As we saw in chapter 3 of this monograph, Minear pointed out striking and impressive links between the tradition of Benjamin, especially his blessing from Moses in Deuteronomy 33, and the presentation and portrayal of the Beloved Disciple. It seems evident that the Beloved Disciple was presented by the Evangelist to the Jewish trained readers as one who obtained Moses' blessings. The introduction of the Beloved Disciple in GosJn 13 is reminiscent of Moses' blessing on Benjamin in Deuteronomy 33:12:

> The beloved of the Lord rests in safety—
> the High God surrounds him all day long—
> the beloved rests between his shoulders. (NRSV)

It is attractive to think that the Evangelist portrayed the Beloved Disciple (ὃν ἠγάπα ὁ Ἰησοῦς) as resting in the bosom of Jesus (ἀνακείμενος ... ἐν τῷ κόλπῳ τοῦ Ἰησοῦ) because of such Benjaminite traditions (Ἠγαπη-μένος ὑπὸ κυρίου κατασκηνώσει [LXX]). They were certainly alive in Judaism prior to 135 C.E. as we know from the Testaments of the Twelve Patriarchs, which may contain traditions that influenced the Evangelist and which may in its final form have absorbed ideas developed from the GosJn and from extracanonical writings.[105] Did the Evangelist borrow

---

[105] The T12P must not be used as if they do not contain Christian expan-

from the Benjamin traditions the contention that at the "consummation of the ages" (ἕως συντελείας τῶν αἰώνων) shall arise "the beloved of the Lord," (ἀγαπητὸς κυρίου [TBen 11:2]) who "shall be written of in sacred books" (καὶ ἐν βίβλοις ἁγίαις ἔσται ἀναγραφόμενος [TBen 11:4])?[106] That conclusion is certainly at least conceivable.

In the little known *Gospel of the Twelve Apostles*, Thomas is presented as the apostle who is from the tribe of Benjamin (Syriac = *wt'wm' mn šbṭ' dbnymn*).[107] No other member of the Twelve is from that tribe. That tradition, which is difficult to date, indicates that only Thomas is a Benjaminite.

The Beloved Disciple does seem to incorporate Benjamin traditions. The fact that Thomas is portrayed in some Syriac texts as of the tribe of Benjamin not only strengthens the possibility of such a typology, but it also may help to galvanize the link between the Beloved Disciple and Thomas.

4.9 THE BOOK OF GLORY AND THE IDEAL STUDENT

Chapter 13 of the GosJn begins the "The Book of Glory," which comprises chapters 13–20, as many leading experts on the gospel have demonstrated (namely Bultmann,[108] Brown,[109] Schnackenburg,[110] and Smith[111]). In fact this insight has been recognized for decades, for as M. Goguel, Professeur á la Sorbonne, stated, "C'est par l'épisode des pieds lavés que

---

sions or editing. See M. de Jonge, *Studies on the Testaments of the Twelve Patriarchs* (SVTP 3; Leiden: Brill, 1975).

[106] See Testament of Benjamin in the T12P; here I follow Kee in *OTP* 1. 828. For the Greek see M. de Jonge, *The Testaments of the Twelve Patriarchs: A Critical Edition of the Greek Text* (PVTG 1,2; Leiden: Brill, 1978).

[107] For the English and the Syriac see J. R. Harris, ed., *The Gospel of the Twelve Apostles* (Cambridge: Cambridge Univ. Press, 1900) ad loc.

[108] Bultmann divided the GosJn into "The Revelation of the ΔΟΞΑ To The World" (chapters 1–12) and "The Revelation of the ΔΟΞΑ Before the Community" (chapters 13–20). See Bultmann, *John*.

[109] Brown began his second volume with chapter 13, which he titled "The Book of Glory" (*Gospel*, vol. 2). For his rationale for dividing the GosJn into two parts, The Book of Signs (1:19–12:50) and the Book of Glory (13:1–20:31), see 1:cxxxviii–cxxxix and 2:541–42.

[110] Schnackenburg divides the GosJn into "Jesus reveals himself to the world" (chapters 1–12) and "Jesus in the Circle of his Own" (chapters 13–20). He advises that "the evangelist opens a new part of the gospel in Chapter 13" (*St. John*, 3:1).

[111] Smith divides the GosJn into the "public ministry" (chapters 2–12) and "a final Jerusalem period in which Jesus appears principally with his disciples" (chapters 13–20) (*John*, 11).

s'ouvre la dernière partie de l'évangile constituée par le récit de la dernière soirée qui sert de cadre auz suprêmes entretiens de Jésus avec ses disciples."[112] The identity of the Beloved Disciple may be disclosed skillfully in this section in which Jesus is portrayed showing his love for his disciples. The identity of the Beloved Disciple becomes apparent if we apply a mathematical formula which seeks to find the equation between an anonymous disciple and a leading character in the Book of Glory. In fact the drama of the GosJn centers upon the introduction of the Beloved Disciple during the very scene in which the Betrayer is unmasked and exits into the dark of night.

Only three disciples are revealed to be members of the Twelve, according to the GosJn: Thomas, Judas, and by implication, Peter. Surely the identity of the Beloved Disciple should be one of these three (see chap. 2.3).

At the beginning of GosJn 13 only three male figures among the disciples loom large on center stage; they are the Beloved Disciple, Judas, and Peter. Thomas will take on significant roles in the Book of Glory. He will thus be a prime candidate for the Beloved Disciple. Nicodemus and Joseph of Arimathea must be eliminated because the Evangelist makes it clear that they were not full and public disciples of Jesus (and of these two only Joseph of Arimathea is called a "disciple" [19:38]). Applying the mathematical formula means that *prima facie* Judas = Judas, Peter = Peter, and we are to search for the final equation, the Beloved Disciple = whom? Thus we need to search afresh for the identity of the Beloved Disciple. Our quest will be guided by the insight articulated by J. N. Sanders in 1953:

> That the Beloved Disciple should be identifiable among the *dramatis personae* of the Gospel seems to be demanded by the emphasis laid upon his testimony, since an anonymous and unidentifiable witness is a contradiction in terms.[113]

Who are the *dramatis personae* in chapters 13–20? Since our task is to discover the identity of a male disciple of Jesus—the anonymous Beloved Disciple—then we should seek to discern if he might be one of the leading male characters, namely *Peter, Judas Iscariot, or Thomas.* Let us examine the opening of this second half of the GosJn.

In chapter 13 only three leading disciples are introduced, and in this order: First, the spotlight moves past *Judas Iscariot*, Simon's son (13:2),

---

[112] M. Goguel, *L'Église primitive* (Paris: Payot, 1947) 494.

[113] Sanders, "'Those Whom Jesus Loved' (John XI.5)," *New Testament Studies* 1 (1954–55) 33.

to indicate he will loom large in this chapter, and goes directly to Jesus who is about to wash his disciples' feet, expressing his absolute love for them (13:1).[114] Jesus' actions here may symbolize for the Evangelist and his Community the salvific nature of the sacraments,[115] which have in common the need for cleansing and purification.[116] With foreknowledge he seems to be forgiving each of his disciples of the weaknesses they will reveal as the drama continues;[117] and such forgiveness includes Judas, whose feet he has washed (13:11),[118] but whose foot (i.e., heel [13:18; Ps 41:10]) will be raised against him. According to the author of the GosJn Jesus has prior knowledge of all that is to occur (13:3), but Jesus must say to the disciples, "What I am doing you do not know now, but you will know after these things" (13:7). Despite the disciples' actions in the following scenes, Jesus loves them εἰς τέλος (13:1).

Jesus comes to Simon *Peter* who refuses to have his feet washed until he begins to understand the symbolism of the act (13:8-9). *Judas* is again subtly swept before the mind of the reader (13:11), as Jesus explains the meaning of his action.

Then the subject turns to the identity of the Betrayer, and for the first time the reader is introduced to the *Beloved Disciple*, as the leading disciple and Jesus' confidant (13:21-26). The pericope shows the triumvirate of *Beloved Disciple, Peter, and Betrayer (Judas)*. Peter must ask the Beloved Disciple regarding the identity of the Betrayer. The reader has the knowledge that others are present at the Last Supper, but only three are

[114] Goguel accurately represented Jesus' action: it was "un exemple d'amour et d'humilité" (*L'Église primitive*, 369).

[115] At least eleven interpretations, all which have some anchor in exegetical observations, have been offered of the meaning of the footwashing. See G. Richter, *Die Fusswaschung im Johannesevangelium* (Regensburg: Friedrich Pustet, 1967) and W. Lohse, *Die Fusswaschung (Joh 13.1-20): Eine Geschichte ihrer Deutung* (Ph.D. Dissertation, the Friedrich Alexander Universität, Erlangen and Nürnberg, 1967). A succinct and insightful discussion, with additional bibliography, is found in J. C. Thomas, *Footwashing in John 13 and the Johannine Community* (JSNT SS 61; Sheffield: JSOT Press, 1991, 1993).

[116] Haenchen, who contended that behind chapter 13 lies an "old source," contrasted John and Judaism: "The footwashing is the great token of love. Instead of the Jewish concept of 'covenant with god,' its 'meaning' is Jesus' love for his 'own'" (*John 2*, 105).

[117] Note 13:18, "I know whom I have chosen"; subsequently Jesus states that he knows what is in the future (13:19).

[118] As J. C. Thomas states, "No doubt Judas had been bathed and received the footwashing" (*Footwashing*, 113). Thomas, however, does not see that the Evangelist apparently conceives of Jesus forgiving Judas of what he is about to do.

mentioned: the Beloved Disciple, Peter, and Judas. This is significant when it becomes apparent that Nathanael, Philip, and even Lazarus have already been given prominent roles in the first half of the GosJn. The Evangelist prefers during the drama of the Last Supper to focus on only three: *the Beloved Disciple, Peter, and Judas.*

The significance of chapter 13 needs to be highlighted. This chapter, and not chapter 9 as some scholars have indicated, is the pivotal (and perhaps most important) chapter in the GosJn. It begins the second half of the GosJn, "the Book of Glory." It is no accident that the Beloved Disciple is introduced at this point, since he will serve to witness to the glory of God's Son. In contrast to the entrance of the Beloved Disciple, *Judas* now exits into the night. The stage is well lit, and the action has prepared the reader for Jesus to introduce his new commandment (13:31-35). It is defined by Jesus' own action—"as I have loved you"—which was demonstrated by Jesus' servile lowering of himself to demonstrate his love (13:1) by washing the feet of his disciples.

Chapter 14 will have only one leading character: *Thomas.* He asks the key question in the GosJn: "How can we know the way?" (13:5). Jesus honors him by revealing that he is the way, truth, and life. The brilliance of Thomas's question is clarified by Philip's inane demand, "Lord, show us the Father, and it shall be satisfying to us" (14:8). This lack of perception and appreciation by Philip is shocking in light of what has transpired in the previous scene (chapter 13). Philip receives a well deserved rebuke from Jesus. The episode indicates that Thomas is a major character and action will swirl around him again, as it does in four verses in chapter 20 (20:24, 26, 27, 28). In contrast, Philip will now depart from the narrative of the GosJn with Jesus' lament, "Have I been with you so long, and still you do not know me, Philip?" (14:9). Thus, Philip exits from consideration as the Beloved Disciple.

The centrality of Thomas's question is often missed. It is not only framed by Philip's following question which leads to his embarrassment, but by Peter's preceding question which leads Jesus to predict that Peter will deny him. Note the narrative flow:

Peter's question (13:36-37)	Jesus' prediction of Peter's denial (13:38)
Thomas's question (14:1-5)	Jesus' blessing on Thomas (14:6-7)
Philip's question (14:8)	Jesus' rebuke to Philip (14:9-11)

Thus Thomas represents the ideal *student*, which is highly significant when we perceive that the GosJn comes to us from a Johannine *School.* Far from being "the figure of ignorance,"[119] he is one who knows the lim-

---

[119] These are the words of Collins, who continues to contend that "Thomas

its of his own knowledge and those in his group. Thomas knows that Jesus is going somewhere and perceives that this is something of singular importance; but he—as the model student—knows that he needs further knowledge. Thus he is portrayed focusing his mind on the key question to ask, and the narrator depicts him as the spokesman for the disciples.

Thomas admits, "Lord, *we* do *not know* where you are going" (14:5). Then out of this knowledge and perception of its limits, on behalf of the group, and as the model spokesman he asks, "How can we know the way?" (πῶς δυνάμεθα τὴν ὁδὸν εἰδέναι; [14:5]). Upon hearing this astute question,[120] Jesus blesses Thomas, speaks directly to him, and delivers one of the great *theologoumena* of the GosJn, "I am the way, truth, and life."[121] Then he blesses Thomas and those he represents (the verbs are in the second person plural)[122] with the words, "henceforth you know him (= the Father) and have seen him" (14:7).

The recognition that the Beloved Disciple is the founder of the Johannine *School*, that he appears in an intimate relationship with Jesus in chapter 13 when Jesus and his "students" celebrate a meal at Passover time,[123] and that he readily recognizes the meaning of events (the open tomb in chapter 20) and persons (Jesus in chapter 21) indicate that he, like Thomas, is the model student. Both, in the words of Philo of Alexandria, exhibit in the narrative the hallmark of the model student, "a voluntary and spontaneous eagerness to learn" (ἐθελουργῷ καὶ αὐτοκελεύστῳ προθυμίᾳ χρώμενος,).[124] Voluntary and spontaneous recognition is depicted in

---

... epitomizes both the bravado and the ignorance of the disciples" (*These Things Have Been Written*, 37).

[120] Schnackenburg refers to "Thomas's uncertain question," and then goes on to rightly accentuate Jesus' "extremely important revelation" (*St. John*, 3:64).

[121] Cf. τὰ θεολογούμενα in Plutarch, 2.421e. I use this technical term here not in the sense of "discourses" on the gods, but to denote a brilliant (revelatory) theological insight by the Evangelist.

[122] Each is in a verbal form that is the second person plural.

[123] Obviously the meal is not the Passover Meal, but all meals at Passover time, which encompasses more than one night and had deep theological meaning, as indeed did all meals celebrated by devout Jews. See Charlesworth's discussion of the proto-rabbinic prayer called "Grace After Meals," in his "A Prolegomenon to a New Study of the Jewish Background of the Hymns and Prayers in the New Testament," *Early Judaism and Its Modern Interpreters*, ed. R. A. Kraft and G. W. E. Nickelsburg (Philadelphia: Fortress; Atlanta: Scholars Press, 1986) 265–85. Also, see J. Neusner's discussion of prayers before and after meals, according to Mishnah Berakhot, in *Introduction to Rabbinic Literature* (ABRL; New York: Doubleday, 1994) 134–41.

[124] Philo, On the Change of Names, 270. I am here following the superb translation of C. D. Yonge in *The Works of Philo: Complete and Unabridged* (Peabody, Mass.: Hendrickson, 1993). The Greek is from Colson and Whitaker in the LCL, *Philo*, 5:280.

Thomas's exhortation in chapter 11 and question in chapter 14; the same applies to the Beloved Disciple in his voluntary rush to the tomb and spontaneous believing at the tomb, which is emphasized in his quick perception in 21:7.

Thomas and the Beloved Disciple are also linked narratively through Jesus' devotional affection for them. The Evangelist honors Thomas by depicting Jesus speaking to him and giving to him the theological epitome: "I am the way, the truth, the life," and allowing him all his requests and returning again for him and him alone (20:26-29). The same applies to the Beloved Disciple: The devotional affection is obvious not only in the words "the disciple whom Jesus' loved," but in the opening scene in which the Beloved Disciple is introduced, with words reminiscent of Jesus' introduction to the reader as the Logos (1:18); he is lying in the bosom of Jesus (13:23). Both Thomas and the Beloved Disciple are thus the disciples who are devotionally and affectionately linked with Jesus; they are the students from which the succession of discipleship is forged from Jesus to all Johannine Christians, for whom the Evangelist has Jesus pray to the Father that they may be one (17:21). Here we see how the Evangelist represents some of the uniqueness of the Palestinian Jesus Movement in contrast to Rabbinics with which it has so much in common:[125] Jesus' students are united to him (esp. chapters 15-17); rabbinic students are united by Torah taught by a Rabbi.[126]

[125] Again I wish to point out that despite the vast difference between Johannine Christianity and Hinduism, a close parallel here is found in Hinduism. Like the Johannine Jesus, the Bhagavad-Gita's Krishna exhorts his beloved disciples to be united with him, "Mentally resign all your action to me. ... Be united always in heart and consciousness with me" (S. Prabhavananda and C. Isherwood, *The Song of God: Bhagavad-Gita*, 128).

[126] Similar thoughts and conclusions were articulated long ago by A. Schlatter in his *Die Theologie des Neuen Testaments* (Stuttgart: Calver, 1909) 1:123–24; these were reiterated as definitive by R. Riesner in *Jesus als Lehrer* (WUNT 2.7; Tübingen: Mohr [Siebeck], 1984) 417. This conclusion is not monopolized by so-called conservative scholars. Bultmann stressed essentially the same point when he pointed out that Jesus' words were collected not because of their didactic value; they were collected because they were "his, the coming king's, words" (*Theology of the New Testament*, trans. K. Grobel [New York: Scribner's Sons, 1951] 1:47). See Bultmann, *Theologie des Neuen Testaments* (Tübingen: Mohr [Siebeck], 1984 [9th ed.]) 50: "Wenn man seine Worte sammelt, so geschieht das nicht nur wegen ihres Lehrgehaltes, sondern weil es seine, des künftigen Königs, Worte sind." See the finally chiseled reflections by B. T. Viviano, *Study as Worship: Aboth and the New Testament* (SJLA 26; Leiden: Brill, 1978) 1.

Most importantly, both Thomas and the Beloved Disciple witness to Jesus as the way, the truth, and the life. Thomas grounds Christian faith in a believable and trustworthy, though nonemotionally generative report that Jesus as resurrected Lord is continuous with the crucified one. The GosJn is grounded on the trustworthiness of the Beloved Disciple's witness.

These observations cumulatively raise the question of the background of these portrayals. At Qumran we find a teacher (the Righteous Teacher [מורה הצדק]) who has didactic functions; but he is not portrayed with a model student. Also, even though there is an interesting link between the Qumranites' faithfulness to the teachings of the Righteous Teacher (ואמנתם במורה הצדק [1QpHab 8.2-3]) and the Beloved Disciple's faith, we do not find an ideal student portrayed in the Dead Sea Scrolls.

The earliest "scholar" *qua* scholar was probably Jesus ben Sira. Although he had students, there is no evidence of an ideal student—no Beloved Disciple—presented in Sirach. Hillel too was a gifted luminary and had brilliant students, but there is no presentation of a special, beloved disciple.[127]

Post-70 Rabbinics preserve for us accounts of Rabbis and their students; and it may be here that we find the closest parallel to the Johannine portrayal of Jesus,[128] his group of disciples, and a disciple whom he loved.[129] For the Rabbis study was worship; a case can even be made that study is superior to worship since studying תורה means indwelling God's word and will, but worship may devolve into self-centered discourse.[130]

---

[127] The study of Hillel is notoriously difficult. The rabbinic texts tell us, it seems, more about the Hillelites than Hillel.

[128] S. Sandmel's warning against parallelomania is often misunderstood. He knew well that links and similarities are evident above all in "parallels," but he bewailed those students of religion who see verbal parallels and do not comprehend the different contexts and meanings ("Parallelomania," *Journal of Biblical Literature* 81 [1962] 1-13). He stressed the "extravagance" by which "scholars" jump from alleged parallels to positing a "literary connection flowing in an inevitable or predetermined direction." In fact Sandmel encouraged the study of parallels between the documents in the New Testament and Jewish sources, "especially in the case of the Qumran documents."

[129] Of course, Ahiqar's life and career comes to mind. He was "a wise and skillful scribe" (Col. 1.1), and he had a favorite student, Nadin. The latter was Ahiqar's nephew and adopted son; however, he was treacherous and devised a plot against Ahiqar. Nadin cannot be a model for the BD. See J. M. Lindenberger in *OTP* vol. 2. Very close to the Johannine BD is Aboth 4:12, "Let the honor of your disciple be as dear to you as your own (יהי כבוד תלמידך חביב עליך כשלך)."

[130] See B. T. Viviano, *Study as Worship*.

Reminiscent of the Evangelist's claim that believing in Jesus as "the Christ, the Son of God" is the position that "the more study of Torah the more life" (מרבה תורה מרבה חיים [Aboth 2:8]). The Rabbis' disdain for those who were not preoccupied with Torah study,[131] reflected in the cursing of an Am ha-aretz "even if he is a saint,"[132] may help us comprehend the saying in the GosJn, "But this crowd, who do not know the Torah (τὸν νόμον),[133] are accursed" (7:49). Along with Ben Sira, Qumran,[134] and Rabbinics, the Johannine School depicts learning as occurring under the tutelage of a great teacher who has students, who learn from him and from each other.[135] As J. Lightfoot noted in 1859,[136] Johanan ben Zakkai honored Eliezer ben Erech upon the latter's brilliant exegesis by kissing his head (j.Hagig 77.1); likewise Rabbi Abba praised his prize student, R. Levi, by kissing his head (j.Hor 48.3).

These rabbinic parallels are highly significant for perceiving the concept of "the disciple whom Jesus loved." In the end, however, one has to admit that there is no clear parallel. Hillel had no ideal or model student who is portrayed as the Beloved Disciple; and that seems surprising

---

[131] Note b.Kuddushin 40b, Socino ed., 202, in which this question was raised: "Is study greater or practice (תלמוד גדול או מעשה)?" The great Akiba answered that Torah study was superior: נענה רבי עקיבא ואמר תלמוד גדול. Viviano rightly points out that the conclusion, which has "all" (כולם) supporting Akiba's answer, indicates that the decision represents "a majority vote and hence normative" (*Study as Worship*, 105).

[132] Viviano turns our attention to b.Pesahim 49b and especially Pirke de Rabbenu ha-Kadosh, ed. Schoenblum, 21b: "R. Simeon b. Yohai said: "An Am ha-aretz, even if he is pious, even if he is a saint, even if he is honest, cursed be he to the Lord, the God of Israel" (*Study as Worship*, 42).

[133] As is well known, νόμος does not adequately represent תורה (which certainly is not "law"); and knowing that τὸν νόμον in 7:49 indicates Torah, I have avoided the term "law," or even "Law."

[134] Note 1QS 6.1-8 in which Torah study was advocated and practiced day and night: "And where there are ten (members) there must not be lacking there a man who studies the Torah day and night" (1QS 6.6). Trans. Charlesworth, *Rule of the Community*, 27.

[135] The same phenomenon is presented in the Gospel of Matthew which comes to us from the School of Matthew. See the informative study by S. Byrskog, *Jesus the Only Teacher: Didactic Authority and Transmission in Ancient Israel, Ancient Judaism and the Matthean Community* (CB NT Series 24; Stockholm: Almqvist & Wiksell International, 1994).

[136] J. Lightfoot, *A Commentary on the New Testament from the Talmud and Hebraica* (Peabody, Mass.: Hendrickson, 1989 [1859]) 2:429. Lightfoot was convinced that the apostle John was the Beloved Disciple, and that he received this epithet because "John had promised that he would take care of Christ's mother after his death" (2:430).

when it becomes obvious that the Bêt Hillēl, "the House of Hillel," became a dynasty which lasted until 425 C.E.[137] Shammai also did not have a disciple who is similar to the portrait of the Beloved Disciple. Both these sages taught Joḥanan ben Zakkai;[138] he is their protégé, but he is neither portrayed as their model student nor as the beloved student. He also was neither appointed to office nor signaled out as a successor.[139] The Johannine concept of the Beloved Disciple as one who is in the bosom of Jesus and performs some of the functions of the Paraclete is clearly foreign to Rabbinics.[140] One reason could well be the paucity of narrative (hagadah) in Rabbinics.[141]

These traditions show only that the GosJn is to be studied within the history of Judaism, and that the Beloved Disciple is, so to speak, Jesus' protégé. There is no clear parallel that I can find to the Johannine emphasis on the revelatory aspect of Jesus' teaching and the depiction of an intimate student, who is the one the teacher "loved."[142] Thus, the portrayal of the Beloved Disciple and Thomas in the GosJn is not only dependent on Jewish traditions, which stretch back to Elijah and Elisha, to Moses and Joshua, and even to Abraham, whom Philo depicts as God's "perfect disciple,"[143] but also is impressively original. These brief forays into Jewish models for the Beloved Disciple and Thomas ultimately leave us with a better perception of the ways the Evangelist may have identified them.

The place of women in the GosJn also seems to serve to identify the Beloved Disciple with Thomas. As scholars have attempted to show,

---

[137] See E. E. Urbach, *The Sages: Their Concepts and Beliefs* (Jerusalem: Magnes, 1979) 593–99.

[138] Note m.Aboth 2:9, רבן יוחנן בן זכאי קבל מהלל ומשמאי. See S. R. Hirsch, *Chapters of the Fathers*, trans. G. Hirschler (Jerusalem: Feldheim, 1967, 1989) 28.

[139] The problem of succession after Gamaliel II allowed for the recognition of Bar Kokhba as patriarch. See Urbach, *The Sages*, 604.

[140] Consult Urbach, "The Internal Relations in the Academies of the Sages," *The Sages*, 620–30.

[141] There was sufficient, even abundant data, for the Rabbis to expand the story of a Sage, like Honi, into a life. They did not. Why, and how do such questions help us understand the formation of Johannine theology? See the helpful thoughts by J. Neusner in *Why No Gospels in Talmudic Judaism?* (BJS 135; Atlanta: Scholars Press, 1988).

[142] Billerbeck is impressively silent on the possibility of a rabbinic parallel to "the disciple whom Jesus loved" (*Kommentar zum Neuen Testament aus Talmud und Midrasch*, H. L. Strack and P. Billerbeck [Munich: Beck, 1983 (8th ed. of the 1924 work)] 2:559).

[143] Philo, On the Change of Names §270.

women are closely aligned with Jesus in this gospel.[144] Mary Magdalene, like the Beloved Disciple and Thomas, looms large in the GosJn, not only in contrast to the Synoptics but in the narrative of the gospel. Note the way she is woven within the flow of the narrative of chapter 20: Mary Magdalene runs to Peter and the Beloved Disciple, they enter and exit the tomb (and Peter exits the drama), she reappears without explanation, and then Thomas is again dominant and closes chapters 1–20. Mary Magdalene, not the Beloved Disciple, is the first to see the resurrected Jesus and believe in his resurrection (see chap. 2.1); yet, like the Beloved Disciple, she is a challenge to traditions associated with Peter.[145]

Returning to the drama of the Last Supper we note that in 14:22 an obscure character—"Judas (not Iscariot)"—asks another question: "Lord, how is it that to us you will manifest yourself, and not to the world?" The question is answered in an oblique manner by Jesus. It is not clear who this person is; but according to the Old Syriac Gospels—which contain far more valuable data than scholars have lately been willing to allow—he is Thomas.[146]

No characters appear on stage in chapters 15 through 17. When Jesus is alleged to have said "I chose you" (15:16) the reader has no clue to whom he is referring. The commandment to love as Jesus has loved is harshly re-presented as "You are my friends if you do what I command you" (15:14). Jesus' critique—"none of you asks me, 'Where are you going?'" (16:5)—not only contradicts Thomas's question in 14:5 but is addressed to no one in particular. The anonymity of the individuals Jesus is addressing is obvious from 16:17, "Some of his disciples said to one another ...." The anonymity is evident again in 16:29, "His disciples said ...." Who are they? How many are they? The sentence in 17:12, "and none of them is lost except the son of perdition," is anonymous (although the reader might be expected by now to know that Judas Iscariot is the "son of perdition"), and it clashes with other passages in the GosJn (viz. 6:37). In contrast to the other chapters in 13–20, 15–17 shows no interest in the identity of the characters in the drama. It is as if during 15–17 the stage is covered by a curtain so that Jesus can deliver long orations. I take this discovery as additional evidence that these chapters were later added

[144] See esp. E. Schüssler Fiorenza, *In Memory of Her: A Feminist Theological Reconstruction of Christian Origins* (New York: Crossroad, 1983). Also see the following: R. J. Karris, "The Women in John's Gospel," *Jesus and the Marginalized in John's Gospel* (Collegeville: Glazier, 1990) 73–95; M. Scott, *Sophia and the Johannine Jesus* (JSNT SS 71; Sheffield: JSOT Press, 1992).

[145] Also see Fiorenza, *In Memory of Her*, 332; and Scott, *Sophia*, 229.

[146] I present the full evidence in chapter 7, "The Johannine School and the School of Thomas."

to the GosJn. There is no interest in the Beloved Disciple in chapters 15 through 17.

The curtain goes up again with chapter 18. Of the three main characters highlighted in chapter 13—*the Beloved Disciple, Peter, and Judas*—two are in spotlight on center stage. *Judas* comes with a band of armed men to Jesus' secret place in a garden across the Kidron Valley. *Peter* asserts himself by cutting off the ear of Malchus, the high priest's slave. Surprisingly no other disciples are named. The armed group returns to the court of the high priest. Peter and another disciple follow at a discreet distance. Could the other disciple known to the high priest be Judas, or is he simply anonymous (see chap. 6)? During Jesus' interrogation by Annas, Peter is the focus of attention. He thrice denies he is one of Jesus' disciples.

According to chapter 19 Jesus is taken to Golgotha. The disciples are conspicuously absent. The only male disciple at the crucifixion is *the Beloved Disciple* (19:25-27). He and he alone serves as the witness to Jesus' physical death. Then out of the shadows onto center stage comes a secret disciple of Jesus; he is named Joseph of Arimathea (19:38). He has an associate named Nicodemus. The drama of Jesus' earthly life ends with two mysterious male figures hastily burying his corpse. Moreover, they are merely secret followers of Jesus, and only one of them is called a disciple. The reader wonders where Jesus' disciples are. Except for the Beloved Disciple (and Joseph of Arimathea perhaps) all abandoned him. They allowed someone else to bury his corpse. At least Jesus did not suffer the fate of Pompey, whose corpse was abandoned with none to bury him (Psalms of Solomon 2).[147]

Chapter 20 is climactic. In it there are three main characters. Upon hearing the report of Mary Magdalene, *Peter and the Beloved Disciple* race to Jesus' tomb. They go home not perceiving the meaning of Scripture (as we saw in chap. 2).

All the other disciples remain anonymous so that one hero can receive the final culminating moment. *Thomas* is the hero. The author of the GosJn uses Thomas to undergird the fact that belief in Jesus' resurrection is not because of a wishful desire to trust the reports or beliefs of others. He questions the possibly energetic and self-serving apparition of his fearful comrades. He does not believe the report of his friends, who are anonymous in chapter 20. They are simply "disciples" (20:18, 19), "other disciples" (20:25), or Jesus' "disciples" (20:26).

The Book of Glory ends with only two people on center stage (the disciples recede into the background): Jesus and *Thomas* (20:26-29). Can

---

[147] Psalms of Solomon 2:27, "His body was carried about on the waves in much shame, and there was no one to bury (him), for he (God) had despised him with contempt" (R. B. Wright in *OTP* 2.653).

a gifted dramatist like the Evangelist conclude the final act without high-lighting the model student on center stage with the one great teacher? If the GosJn is a developing drama, then no other than Thomas can be the Beloved Disciple.

Does this insight not seem conclusive in retrospect? Only three male characters dominate the Book of Glory: *Peter, Judas, and Thomas.* And each of these, and only these three, are distinguished as members of the Twelve. Another anonymous figure intermittently dominates the center of the stage: the Beloved Disciple—the ideal and model disciple of Jesus. He is most likely one of these three.

Which one is he? Let us apply the mathematical formula. He cannot be Peter, because he is repeatedly contrasted with him. He cannot be Judas, since he is distinguished from him in chapter 13. The Betrayer may occasionally imitate Jesus' beloved, but he cannot be the Beloved.

Only one person is left: Thomas, who is the disciple to whom the author gives the final scene. He speaks and utters the climactic confession ὁ κύριός μου καὶ ὁ θεός μου. The mathematical formula of the Book of Glory indicates that the Beloved Disciple is to be identified with the hero Thomas. Obviously, this equation may be as startling to critics today as it was common knowledge to the members of the Johannine Community who knew the identity of the Beloved Disciple.

4.10 A TECHNICAL AND SEQUENTIAL LITERARY DEVICE

We have been observing that the identity of the Beloved Disciple seems to be revealed subtly and progressively within an intricately composed, and expanded, literary creation.[148] Regarding the GosJn, I. de la Potterie offers the following insight:

> A text is not simply a collection of words, but a unity, a living organism. That being the case, a text should be interpreted as a "whole," as a totality. The characteristic of a living organism is that all its parts contribute to its life.[149]

Within the GosJn a trifold literary device helps to present the in-depth meaning to the reader. The technical, sequential literary device is

[148] I am aware that my exegesis is built upon a comprehension of the GosJn that is almost a polar opposite to Bultmann's composition theory. I am convinced that the GosJn is far more unified than Bultmann could admit. For a discussion of the growing recognition of more unity in the GosJn, see Culpepper, *Anatomy*; Hengel, *Die johanneishce Frage*, and Kügler, "Das Johannesevangelium als einheitlicher Text," *Der Jünger, den Jesus liebte*, 18–24.

[149] I. de la Potterie, *The Hour of Jesus: The Passion and the Resurrection of Jesus According to John* (Middlegreen, Eng.: St. Paul Publications, 1989) 20.

ambiguity, followed first by misunderstanding, and then by clarification.[150] The following examples alone must suffice before we use this literary device to perceive how the author of the GosJn may progressively disclose the identity of the Beloved Disciple. Note the following:

(1) ambiguity	Jesus said, "Destroy this temple, and in three days I will raise it up." 2:19
misunderstanding[151]	The Judeans think Jesus is speaking about the Temple. 2:20
clarification	The Evangelist states Jesus spoke about his own body as a temple. 2:21
(2) ambiguity	Jesus tells Nicodemus that he must be born anew. 3:3
misunderstanding	Nicodemus asks how a human can enter again into the womb. 3:4
clarification	Jesus explains that one must be born of water and spirit. 3:5
(3) ambiguity	Jesus tells the Samaritan woman he has "living water." 4:10
misunderstanding	She states he has no means to draw water from the well. 4:11
clarification	Jesus explains that he has salvific water. 4:14
(4) ambiguity	Jesus states that Lazarus has fallen asleep. 11:11
misunderstanding	His disciples think Lazarus is sleeping. 11:12
clarification	The Evangelist explains that Jesus meant Lazarus was dead. 11:13-14
(5) ambiguity	Jesus tells Martha that Lazarus will rise again. 11:24
misunderstanding	Martha mistakes him to mean at the Endtime. 11:24
clarification	Jesus states he is the resurrection and will raise Lazarus immediately. 11:25
(6) ambiguity	Jesus tells Peter if he does not wash his feet he has no part in him. 13:5-6
misunderstanding	Peter urges Jesus to wash his feet, hands, and head. 13:9

[150] In the following I am indebted to the reflections by J. C. Fenton in *John*, 19–22. He rightly states that one of "the most frequent" of the Evangelist's literary techniques is "the sequence Ambiguity, Misunderstanding, Clarification" (19).

[151] On this literary technique in the GosJn see especially H. Leroy, *Rätsel und Missverstandnis: ein Beitrag zur Formgeschichte des Johannesevangeliums* (Bonn: P. Hanstein, 1967).

clarification	Jesus clarifies that Peter does not need a bath. 13:10[152]
(7) ambiguity	Jesus tells his disciples they know him and have seen the Father. 14:7
misunderstanding	Philip asks Jesus to show them the Father. 14:8
clarification	Jesus tells Philip that one who has seen him has seen the Father. 14:9

The above examples help clarify the first part of the trifold literary technique. The "ambiguity" is not because of some obscurity or opaqueness; it is because a word has two or more meanings. As the author of the GosJn had a gift with *double entendre* (viz. ἄνωθεν in chapter 2 and ὑψόω in chapter 12), so he used the rhetoric of ambiguity to allow Jesus' words to admit of more than one meaning. One is literal, the other symbolical.

---

[152] The passage 13:1-30 is ingeniously structured. It is shaped by an *inclusio*: a reference to Judas Iscariot opens (13:1-2) and closes (13:18-30) the pericope. What has been missed by the commentators is the fact that the Evangelist portrays Jesus washing his disciples' feet which certainly includes Judas's feet (which obviously had heels), and then concluding this pericope by indicating that the act fulfills Scripture, specifically the prophecy that one at the Last Supper would raise "his heel" (τὴν πτέρναν αὐτοῦ) against him (Ps 41:9). Knowing this fact (since he knew all that would happen [see 2:25; 13:3, 11, 18]), Jesus washes Judas's feet (13:2-5). That is, he washes the heels of the one prophesied to raise his heel against him. Does this act suggest he is purifying Judas—that is forgiving him of what Jesus knows he is about to do? Is that not the God portrayed by the Evangelist? Is he not the God who forgives all, including Judas, who in terms of the divine economy must hand Jesus over (recall the arguments of the exegetes who concluded that Judas Iscariot is the BD [see chap. 3])? When the Devil entered into the human Judas (13:27)—εἰσῆλθεν εἰς ἐκεῖνον ὁ σατανᾶς—did he not leave his chiefdom and enter into the world of flesh? If so, did he not then enter into the real in which the Logos (the Creator) had also entered, since the Logos had become "flesh" (1:14)? Does that not mean the Evangelist was suggesting that harmony is returned to creation not by conquering the Devil in battle (contrast 1QM and Rev), but by conquering him through divine incarnate love? This exegesis is persuasive to me because of the unified narrative, the positive portrayal of Judas (at least before the redaction of 13:29), Jesus' love of his own εἰς τέλος (13:1 [a *double entente*]), Jesus' final word from the cross: τετέλεσται (19:30), and the etymological meaning of 1:5 (the darkness could not put down the Light). How could the Evangelist, who portrayed the triumphant Jesus exalted on the cross, have him promulgate that "it is finished" if he thought Satan and Judas marred or threatened the cosmic harmony? I think the Evangelist is contemplating an arresting idea: Jesus' finishing act means that Satan is no longer the ruler of this world and that Judas is forgiven. Contrast Brown, *Gospel*, 2:568-71; Haenchen, *John 2*, 109-10.

The person who misunderstands assumes the first and misses the second meaning.

Another example of this literary technique may be found in chapter 5; and if so, it pertains to the Beloved Disciple. In 5:31-40 the verb "to witness" and the noun "witness" appear no less than eleven times.[153] Note in particular 5:32, "There is another who witnesses concerning me, and I know that the witness which he witnesses concerning me is true." Surely the concentration of this verb and cognate noun in one pericope is not mere coincidence; as we have seen, the author of the GosJn used language carefully and symbolically. The repetitious use of this verb and noun most likely point to the witness behind the gospel, the witness who is trustworthy; and that is the Beloved Disciple.

Jesus is pointing to his special witness, and he affirms that the witness of this person is "true" (ἀληθής). This comment reminds the attentive reader who ponders over the meaning of this symbolic literary work of two passages: 19:35 in which the Evangelist affirms that the witness of the Beloved Disciple is "true" (ἀληθῆ), and 21:24 in which the redactor confirms that the Beloved Disciple's witness (the "one who has been witnessing to these things") is "true" (ἀληθής).

An additional clue that the Beloved Disciple is implied as a witness to Jesus in 5:31-40 is the comment in 5:36. In this verse the Evangelist has Jesus state that the witness to him is greater than John's witness; the link between the Beloved Disciple and John the Baptist seems to be intentional here, and it is singularly significant that his witness exceeds that of John. Is that because he clearly followed Jesus and witnessed to all "these things" (see the eleventh additional exegetical reason which follows the present one)?

A final clue that 5:31-40 may contain, *inter alia*, a reference to the witness of the Beloved Disciple may be the use of "another" (ἄλλος) in 5:32. The "other" who witnesses to Jesus, and whose witness is "true," is linked with the fourfold use of ἄλλος in chapter 20 (20:2, 3, 4, 8). In our exegesis of this passage we discovered that the author was clearly referring to the Beloved Disciple by the use of ἄλλος.

These exegetical reflections help us perceive a hidden structure in the GosJn. The trifold literary technique that molds so many pericopes in the GosJn also shapes the full living gospel itself; but since the arena moves from those within the narrative to those reading it from outside (even if in the Johannine Community) the technique needs some alteration. The shift, of course, is from movement towards a person within the narrative to meaning directed to a reader. Note this outline:

---

[153] Often translators seek to vary translations and employ "to testify" and "testimony."

ambiguity　　　　　　Jesus states he has "another" witness to him and his witness is true. Then Jesus makes an oblique reference to John the Baptist, announces his special witness is not from man and is superior to that of John. He then declares that his works and Scriptures witness to him (5:31-39).

misunderstanding　　Thomas and Lazarus are introduced in chapter 11; but only the latter is defined as (the?) one Jesus loved (11:3, 5, 36). The chief priests see Lazarus and Jesus as the dangerous pair; they seek to kill each of them (and no others even though Thomas is called "the Twin" in 11:16).[154]

clarification　　　　The anonymous disciple is the disciple who formerly followed John the Baptist. He is "the disciple whom Jesus loved"; he is close to Jesus at the Last Supper. He takes Jesus' mother as his own. He sees Jesus' physical death; and as Thomas he witnesses Jesus' physical resurrection.

There appears to be a movement in the GosJn from the Beloved Disciple's anonymity (thus ambiguity) to his identification; that narrative clarification has been assumed as an axiom by all who have sought to identify him with John the son of Zebedee, Lazarus, or another person in the GosJn.[155] The trifold formula demands that only in the final stage does the clarification become evident to one who has understanding (one who knows); and that would mean in the culminating scene, which is clearly dominated by Thomas. If the clarification comes at the end (as in so many literary masterpieces), and if the final scene is dominated only by Thomas, then only he can really be a candidate for the identity of the Beloved Disciple.

---

[154] The Evangelist does not clarify that Lazarus is a witness to Jesus; that would undermine his apparent attempt to portray Lazarus as the wrong choice as the BD. The closest he comes to declaring Lazarus is a witness is the statement at the end of 12:11; that is, on account of Lazarus many of the Judaeans were "believing in Jesus." Another aspect of misunderstanding is the failure to perceive that "Twin" is meaningful, signifying either Jesus' physical twin (as in some Syriac writings) or Jesus' spiritual twin (perhaps along the lines of another Paraclete).

[155] And as stated in the beginning of this monograph, the BD must be mentioned by name in the GosJn; otherwise the Evangelist could not be faithful to the knowledge in the Johannine School, the fact that he knows who he is, and his intent to portray the BD as a real person with a proper name.

What is not clear is the second factor; that is, does the Lazarus story function as a dimension of misunderstanding in the GosJn? Perhaps as evidence of this possibility are the numerous gifted scholars who have attempted to demonstrate that Lazarus is the Beloved Disciple (see above, chap. 3). In seeking to discern the trifold structure of the gospel itself, we must take the vantage point of *the implied reader*. The second part of the tripart literary technique of the author of the GosJn, moreover, is the least precise (as a careful study of the eight passages previously noted reveals). Thus, it is easy to see how readers may misperceive Jesus' love for Lazarus with his attachment to "the disciple whom he loved." The former is affection; the latter is much more. It includes discipleship and trust-worthy witness from the time he and Jesus were together with John the Baptist in the wilderness through the agony of the passion to the palpable evidence of Jesus' physical resurrection. Because the Beloved Disciple's witness is trustworthy, the reader can trust Jesus' words. Perhaps to signal that Lazarus is not "the disciple whom Jesus loved," despite being labeled one whom Jesus loved, the Evangelist did not call him a "disciple," or give him an action or saying.

The clarification that the narrative structure of the GosJn implies that Thomas is the Beloved Disciple becomes less opaque. He is "another" disciple according to chapter 20. His witness is true. He had a significant link with John the Baptist, yet in the eyes of the Evangelist he was super-ior to John the Baptist. And since he was sent by one sent from above, namely John the Baptist, his witness cannot be labeled only "human."

The trifold sequential literary technique is one way the author of the GosJn apparently attempted to disclose in subtle ways the identity of the Beloved Disciple.[156] But he was writing, at this level, for those in his cir-cle of influence who understood and were trained in symbolism and liter-ary techniques.[157] The cumulative thrust of his employment of the tripart literary device and the over-all structure of the GosJn enhances the pro-bability that the Beloved Disciple is Thomas.

4.11 THE GRAND INCLUSIO

As many scholars have shown, there is a grand *inclusio* between chapters 1 and 20. An unperceived dimension of the *inclusio* is between 1:19-34 and 20:26-31.

---

[156] The identity of the BD must not be revealed, otherwise the whole pur-pose of the anonymity or ambiguity at the beginning would be aborted. Here we might think about the beginnings of the early Christian use of *disciplina arcana*.

[157] Some readers would not need to know the identity of the BD; all they needed to be assured was that the witness of the BD was trustworthy and truth-ful. The author states that explicitly, and as we have seen more than once (19:35, 21:24).

In 1:19 we are confronted with ἡ μαρτυρία τοῦ Ἰωάννου. This form is almost always taken to be a subjective genitive; the witness comes from John. More probably, the phrase is also an objective genitive. The witness is about John the Baptist's witness to Jesus.

Who would be the one who makes such a witness in 1:19-28? It is surely one of the followers of John the Baptist. Could he be the Beloved Disciple, who was formerly one of the followers of John the Baptist, as we shall see in the study of 1:35-42 (see chap. 6)? The witness is not by but about John the Baptist; hence, the inquisitors ask him σὺ τίς εἶ? In 1:23 we find a report on the self-identification of John the Baptist. He is "a voice crying in the wilderness." The allusion is to Isaiah 40:3, which was a significant verse to many early Jews, as we know assuredly from the Rule of the Community.[158]

Next comes the witness of John the Baptist to Jesus in 1:29-32. With these verses we observe a significant problem. Why is there apparently a gross redundancy in the beginnings of verses 31 and 33? Note how each begins:

31 κἀγὼ οὐκ ᾔδειν αὐτόν, ἀλλ᾽
33 κἀγὼ οὐκ ᾔδειν αὐτόν, ἀλλ᾽

This outstanding redundancy cannot be unintentional even though the Evangelist is one of the most repetitive authors in the New Testament; it seems to be intentional, otherwise it would be thoughtlessly repetitive and verbose. Since our author is a gifted linguist, it must be an intentional repetition. The commentators have not helped us solve this problem.[159]

Could the Evangelist intend to indicate that two different speakers are involved? That would certainly solve the problem. This solution seems attractive when we ask who said, "he who sent me to baptize with (ἐν) water, that one said to me (ἐκεῖνός μοι), 'He on whom you might see the spirit descend and remain upon him, this is he who baptizes with (ἐν) the Holy Spirit'" (1:33). The usual assumption is that God spoke these words to John the Baptist, perhaps because of ὁ πέμψας με; that is, God is he who sends in the GosJn. Hence, Bultmann blatantly states "God who had sent him, had also told him the sign by which he should recognize the

---

[158] See 1QS 8.12-14 which is discussed and translated in Charlesworth, *The Dead Sea Scrolls: Hebrew, Aramaic, and Greek Texts with English Translations*, vol. 1, ad loc. cit.

[159] Schnackenburg, *St. John*, 1:304, judges that in 1:31 John the Baptist witnesses to Jesus' prerogative of baptizing with the Spirit and in 1:33 to his person. Despite his valuable comments about the OTP and 1QS 4, he does not point out the redundancy. Brown, *John*, 55-57 does not discuss the redundancy.

Christ."[160] And Schnackenburg is of the opinion that "John here appeals to his personal mission from God."[161] Brown writes, "John the Baptist is one to whom the word of God has come (Luke iii 2)."[162]

But, either the commentators have missed the real problem, or there are serious problems with their interpretations. John the Baptist is one sent (ἀπεσταλμένος) from God (1:6). But that does not mean he cannot send forth a disciple to baptize. The author of the GosJn, in 17:18, has Jesus pray to God, "As you have sent (ἀπέστειλας) me into the world, so I have sent (ἀπέστειλα) them [his disciples] into the world." Obviously, the author of the GosJn could also have portrayed John the Baptist, who is one sent by God, as one who sends his disciples forth to baptize.

The exegesis of the specialists proceeds from an assumption. They do not adequately observe the redundancy between verses 31 and 33, and they do not ponder the possibility that another speaker could be intended in verses 33 and 34. Problematic, of course, is Καὶ ἐμαρτύρησεν Ἰωάννης which begins what is now verse 32. It does seem to govern the words from 32 to 34, and it seems out of place; it should have been placed at the beginning of 1:29. As Bultmann perceived, "The new start in v. 32 and the repetition of the κἀγὼ κτλ. in v. 33 are surprising. Clearly v. 32, which alongside v. 33b is quite superfluous, is an insertion from the Synoptic tradition, after which the editor takes up the κἀγὼ again, in order to establish the connection with what follows."[163] Perhaps 32 through 34 should be translated as follows:

> And John witnessed, saying: "I saw the spirit descending as a dove from heaven and remain upon him." (His disciple also witnessed thus:) "I also did not know him (Jesus), but he (John the Baptist) who sent me to baptize with water, that one said to me, 'He on whom you might see the spirit descending and remain on him, this is he who baptizes with the Holy Spirit.' And I have seen and have witnessed (in the following account) that this is the Son of God."

This translation is novel and literal, and while it solves some problems it assumes, along with many Johannine experts, that the present text of the GosJn has undergone massive editing, especially in chapter 1.[164] Perhaps we are catching a glimpse into the first edition of the GosJn.

---

[160] Bultmann, *John*, 92.

[161] Schnackenburg, *St. John*, 1:304.

[162] Brown, *Gospel*, 1:57.

[163] Bultmann, *John*, 85. Bultmann's keen exegetical eye is outstanding.

[164] See especially Bultmann, *John*, 84–85. Bultmann was influenced by the insights of Wellhausen, Spitta, Goguel, and Hirsch.

Let us now confront the obvious objection that there is no smooth transition in 1:33. How would the reader know that another speaker is introduced? Does this observation and question demolish the hypothesis we are now exploring? No, the Evangelist is gifted in jolting the reader with inelegant transitions, as in 3:16 and between chapters 5 and 6.

In the development of the drama, the Beloved Disciple—who is one of the Baptist's followers, as most experts have shown (see chap. 6)—enters his first scene mysteriously and quietly. He is without voice or name. Unlike others, notably Andrew, he will not even make a declaration. Thus, with a gentle brush the Evangelist paints a mere shadowy figure; he is the Beloved Disciple. During the drama of the gospel his identity will be revealed, but only to those who are in the Community and who know and believe (unlike Nicodemus, the Samaritan woman, and others who *misunderstand*).

The ostensibly rough transition in 1:33 is intended to jar the reader who knows. It is very similar to a linguistic phenomenon in the *Odes of Solomon*. In the *Odes* there is an unmistakable move from the Christian Odist to the Christ. The latter speaks through the Odist. There is no formula or mark of any kind in the manuscripts to indicate that at a certain point the words are *ex ore Christi*. Note, for example, the following:

7   And peace was prepared for you,
      Before what may be your war.

    (*ex ore Christi*)[165]
8   Hear the word of truth,
      And receive the knowledge of the Most High. (Ode 8:7-8)

The *Odes of Solomon*, which date from the same time and probably same locale as the GosJn (perhaps in its second edition), help us to understand the linguistic phenomenon of what appear to us today as abrupt transitions. The Christians who chanted the *Odes* knew when the thought elevated to become words as if from the mouth of Christ. (The link with early Christian prophecy which goes back to "thus, saith the Lord" of the Israelite prophets is obvious.)

The transition in the *Odes* and the GosJn is a poetic or narrative jolt. It seems to be significant, arresting the attention of attentive readers and prompting them to ponder what is occurring in the poem or narrative.[166] Thus, the Evangelist appears to be introducing the Beloved Disciple with a gentle nudge to the reader.

---

[165] I have added this parenthetical comment to aid the reader.

[166] My arguments here, which date back into the sixties, are now supported by M. Lattke in "Dating the Odes of Solomon," *Antichthon* 27 (1993) 45–59.

The present exegesis solves another problem with the assumed meaning of verse 33; that is the appearance of ἐκεῖνός μοι.[167] The words "that one"—which is usually left untranslated—seem to point back to 1:8 in which John the Baptist is ἐκεῖνος. Hence, "that one" does not denote God;[168] it signifies John the Baptist. Thus the words "he who sent me to baptize with water, that one said to me" refer to John the Baptist, and they are words from one of his disciples. Thus the repetition is intentional and the "that one" is a key to the interpretation. These are the words of one of John's disciples.

This interpretation also solves a major problem in Johannine studies. There is only one witness to Jesus' baptism according to the usual exegesis of the GosJn. As is well known—especially from studies on the apocryphal book of Susanna—Jewish culture demanded two witnesses, usually males, to confirm the veracity of an account.[169] The author of the GosJn knew this well and demonstrated it in his treatment of the visit to the tomb (obviously Jesus' corpse was no longer inside as Peter and the BD affirmed);[170] and he cited the Jewish norm for forensic rhetoric: καὶ ἐν τῷ νόμῳ δὲ τῷ ὑμετέρῳ γέγραπται ὅτι δύο ἀνθρώπων ἡ μαρτυρία ἀληθής ἐστιν (8:17). Hence, two independent male witnesses are needed to prove that Jesus is from above; miracles, signs, and appeals to "Scripture" or "God" are not admissible in the Jewish court.[171] The Evangelist, as is well known, wrote a gospel that is shaped by Jewish forensic rhetoric and by the desire to obtain self-understanding in a polemical ambience with Jews who have expelled members of the Johannine Community from the synagogue.[172]

About the same time as the GosJn reached the form as we know it today, with chapter 21 but without 7:53–8:11, an apocalypse was being

---

[167] Because of the necessary accents in "that one" I have also presented the pronoun.

[168] 1:18 does not belong to the context. "That one" in 2:21 refers to Jesus who cannot be both subject and object of the sentence now examined.

[169] There is no need here to demonstrate once again the well-accepted fact that the GosJn is shaped by forensic rhetoric. Aristotle's work on rhetoric and other rhetorical studies were known to most literate people like those in the Johannine School.

[170] As we saw earlier, the witness of a woman, Mary Magdalene, needed to be substantiated by the independent witness of two males.

[171] Of course, according to 5:33-36 the Evangelist is breaking the usual norm; he lets works and the Father serve as witnesses to the fact that "the Father has sent me."

[172] As Collins states, the opening of the GosJn "seems to suggest that the Evangelist's readers are about to look in upon a courtroom drama" (*John and His Witness*, 9).

composed in a Jewish community that shared the early rabbinic ideals and perspectives of the synagogal Jews. In this work, the *Apocalypse of Baruch*, we find a stark contrast to *1 Enoch* 42 in which we read that "Wisdom could not find a place in which she could dwell"[173] on earth and so returned to heaven. The author of the *Apocalypse of Baruch* states that Wisdom is "in us" (*whkmt' mitrt' d'it bn*)[174] and "will support us" because "we" are those who "received the Law from the One."[175] The Jews of this apocalypse stress that they are the people of "the Name," because they are blessed since "we did not mingle with the nations (*dl' 'thltn b'mm'*)."[176]

The contrast with the Johannine Community is obvious and helps us understand, or at least imagine, the strife between the Johannine Jews and the synagogal Jews. The Johannine Christians would reply to such claims that Jesus is the Logos, who is to be seen in terms of Wisdom and thus speaks with the formula $\dot{\varepsilon}\gamma\grave{\omega}$ $\varepsilon i\mu i$;[177] that they are one in Jesus, the vine; and that Jesus was before Abraham (8:58), and superior to Moses through whom God did give the Torah: "For the Law was given through Moses; grace and truth came through Jesus Christ" (1:17). They would also argue that they are blessed and do mingle with all others. In the time when the Johannine School was seeing the final edition of the GosJn, as Peter Brown states, Christian groups were defined as the assemblies in which "Jews and former pagans, men and women, slaves and free" came together.[178] If Brown is correct in claiming that "Small study-circles were the powerhouses of the Christian culture of the second and third century,"[179] then the first of these was probably the School of John. The scholars in it had to struggle against virtually insurmountable odds to sustain their claims that appeared illogical and mad to so many. This task was all the more thwarted by their absence of power, since after 70 C.E. it seems obvious that power, not rhetoric, was often the operative means to winning a social or political argument.[180]

---

[173] 1En 42:1; *OTP* 1.33 [Isaac].

[174] The Syriac is from S. Dedering, ed., *Apocalypse of Baruch* (The Old Testament in Syriac 4.3; Leiden: Brill, 1973) 24.

[175] 2Bar 48:24; *OTP* 1.636 [Klijn].

[176] 2Bar 48:23; *OTP* 1.636 [Klijn].

[177] Whiteley argues that the Evangelist "took over from the wisdom writers the 'I am' formula, which is an extension of Prov. 8.30, 'I was beside him as a master-builder'" (*ANRW* II.25.3, 2487).

[178] P. R. L. Brown, *The Body and Society: Men, Women and Sexual Renunciation in Early Christianity* (Lectures on the History of Religions N.S. 13; New York: Columbia Univ. Press, 1988) 49.

[179] Brown, *The Body and Society*, 104.

[180] See P. R. L. Brown, *Power and Persuasion in Late Antiquity: Towards a Christian Empire* (Madison, Wis.: Univ. of Wisconsin Press, 1992): "Power, not persuasion, remains the most striking characteristic of the later Roman

Hence, the Evangelist would not be oblivious to the fact that the descent of the dove upon Jesus, symbolizing the descent of the Spirit upon Jesus and its remaining upon him,[181] *must be witnessed by two males.* According to the exegesis presented here, this eschatological epoch was confirmed in the author's mind (and most likely in the Community) by the witness of the one sent by God, John the Baptist, and by his special disciple. Could he be the trustworthy witness that validates the GosJn? Could this disciple be none other than the Beloved Disciple? The apparent answer to each is "yes."

Our exegesis of chapter 1 solves two problems: First, the redundancy between 1:31 and 1:33 is explained to be a judicious rhetorical use of repetition.[182] Second, perceiving that in 1:33 it is a disciple of John the Baptist who is speaking solves the need for two witnesses of Jesus' empowerment by the Spirit: two men guided by God (they were sent) witness this empowering of Jesus; two men witness to the claim that Jesus is thus the bearer of the Holy Spirit (ὁ βαπτίζων ἐν πνεύματι ἁγίῳ).

Finally, another problem seems to be solved. In 1:35 a *nomen regens* seems otiose, according to the customary interpretation that takes 1:29-34 to denote the report of John the Baptist. Scribes have even had difficulty with this proper name; ὁ Ἰωάννης appears as Ἰωάννης in Papyrus 75 and some other manuscripts. If 1:34 contains the words of a disciple of John the Baptist, then the shift back in 1:35 to John the Baptist is clarified by the appearance of ὁ Ἰωάννης. The first conclusion is that a disciple of John the Baptist has spoken the words in 1:33-34.

Who is this prized disciple of John the Baptist? A key seems to be in the words which, according to our exegesis, were said by him. He states in 1:34, κἀγὼ ἑώρακα καὶ μεμαρτύρηκα ὅτι οὗτός ἐστιν ὁ υἱὸς τοῦ θεοῦ. According to my understanding of the GosJn these words mean, "And I have seen and have witnessed [in the following account] that this is the Son of God." Has our gifted author left a clue as to who is the one who has spoken these words? The answer lies in the formula and *terminus technicus* in this verse. And we have seen how often the author of the GosJn uses repetitious words and phrases, even clauses as a literary technique.[183] They point ahead to two verses: 19:35 and 20:26-31.

Empire in all its regions" (7).

[181] See *Odes of Solomon* 24.

[182] This linguistic device is typical of refined Semitic philology; and 1:31-33 reflects the Semitic use of ἐν (not in water but the Semitic dative of means with ב).

[183] As Fenton noted, "it is possible to detect recurring devices which he uses; and the frequency with which they occur in the Gospel suggests strongly that they are part of the author's technique, not the record of an eye-witness reporting what happened." *John*, 19.

Who then is the speaker of the words in 1:34? If he is not John the Baptist then who is he? In 19:35 we find the linguistic formula again: καὶ ὁ ἑωρακὼς μεμαρτύρηκεν. The significance of this formula (ὁράω plus μαρτυρέω) is evident in the GosJn. It appears only in 1:34 and 19:35—and in 3:11 and 3:32 in which it refers first to Jesus' words and then to Jesus himself.

In 1:34 the verb form is the perfect in the first person pronoun singular; in 19:35 it is the perfect in the third person pronoun singular. Both verbs mean "have seen and witnessed."[184] Apparently the author has linked not only the verses, but also the speakers (either intentionally or subconsciously); the same person seems to be intended. Who is the speaker? It has been clarified in the exegesis of this passage (see chap. 2.1). The final passage, that is 19:35, indicates that he is the truthful witness of the GosJn; he is the Beloved Disciple. The second conclusion is that the person of 1:34-35 and 19:35 is none other than the former follower of John the Baptist who is called "the disciple whom Jesus loved."

Can we learn who he is? Studying the formula and the technical term leads us on to 20:26-31. In this passage we find ὅτι ἑώρακάς με in 20:29. Obviously Jesus is speaking to Thomas; and his words bring to memory the disciples' report to Thomas: ἑωράκαμεν τὸν κύριον in 20:25. The third conclusion is that the former prized disciple of John the Baptist is the Beloved Disciple, who is unmasked in the final scene as Thomas.

Further evidence that John the Baptist's disciple, the Beloved Disciple, is none other than Thomas is the use of the aforementioned formula (ὁράω plus μαρτυρέω) in the GosJn:

> 1:34 κἀγὼ ἑώρακα καὶ μεμαρτύρηκα
> 3:11 ὃ ἑωράκαμεν μαρτυροῦμεν
> 3:32 ὃ ἑώρακεν καὶ ἤκουσεν τοῦτο μαρτυρεῖ
> 19:35 ὁ ἑωρακὼς μεμαρτύρηκεν

This formula appears only in these four verses in the GosJn.[185] The formula applies to a disciple only in the first and last passages. In the middle two occurrences it applies to Jesus. The Beloved Disciple, that is Thomas, and Jesus are thus linked. Thomas—and only he—is called "the Twin" (ὁ λεγόμενος Δίδυμος) in 11:16, 20:24, and 21:2. The Beloved Disciple—Thomas—is Jesus' spiritual twin because of his witness. He is the twin witness.

---

[184] The difference between first and third person discourse seems to be explained by the different contexts.

[185] The verb ὁράω appears with μαρτυρέω also in 5:37; but in that verse the formula does not appear. In 5:37 Jesus states that his Father who bears witness to him, has a "form you have never seen."

A study of 5:32 and 21:24 helps secure the hypothesis that the Beloved Disciple is Thomas. In 5:32 Jesus states ἄλλος ἐστὶν ὁ μαρτυρῶν περὶ ἐμοῦ. This study of "the other" disciple in the GosJn showed that in chapter 1 he is the Beloved Disciple. In this section we have discovered that the witness of 1:34 is none other than the Beloved Disciple. Could Jesus be referring here to the silent anonymous one who has been watching Jesus, beginning from the time the Spirit descended upon him? The rest of 5:32 clarifies that the answer is affirmative. It continues, *ex ore Christi*, καὶ οἶδα ὅτι ἀληθής ἐστιν ἡ μαρτυρία ἣν μαρτυρεῖ περὶ ἐμοῦ. Jesus affirms, as does the author of the GosJn in chapters 19 and 21 (as we have seen), that the witness of the Beloved Disciple, Thomas, is true.

The formula (to see and to witness) reappears in the Johannine corpus in 1 John 1:2. In this passage the members of the Johannine Community state that they have seen with their own eyes (1:1) that which "was from the beginning." They then state καὶ ἑωράκαμεν καὶ μαρτυροῦμεν. They are able to proclaim that they have seen and have witnessed to the truthfulness of the witness recorded in the GosJn; and that is because of the trustworthy witness of the Beloved Disciple whose identity some members of the Community knew. Once again the formula is linked with the Beloved Disciple since not all members of the Community, if 1 John postdates the GosJn, would have known the Beloved Disciple who has died (as we know from GosJn chapter 21).

We can conclude by observing the *inclusio* that unites the proem of the Logos Hymn and the Epilogue of 20, which has only been partially perceived by Johannine experts, who have understandably focused only on the Logos as θεός and Thomas's crowning confession of the resurrected Jesus as θεός.[186] As Strachan demonstrated long ago, indeed in 1925, the GosJn "ends, as it began, with an act of creation"; that is, Jesus as the Christ "breathes into His disciples Life, the Holy Spirit."[187]

But there is much more that harmonizes the beginning with the ending of the GosJn. The *inclusio* between 1:19-34 and 20:26-31—the opening and closure of the GosJn—becomes evident when 1:34 and 20:31 are compared. The former is the witness of John the Baptist's disciple (the Beloved Disciple who is Thomas) that Jesus is ὁ υἱὸς τοῦ θεοῦ. The latter is the culmination of the GosJn (without the Appendix) in which Thomas, the Beloved Disciple, makes the grand and closing confession, after which the author urges the reader to believe that Jesus is ὁ χριστὸς ὁ υἱὸς τοῦ θεοῦ. Here we have the reappearance of the *terminus technicus* noted earlier when discussing 1:34, κἀγὼ ἑώρακα καὶ μεμαρτύρηκα ὅτι οὗτός ἐστιν ὁ υἱὸς τοῦ θεοῦ.

---

[186] See Bultmann, *John*, 698-99; Ashton, *Understanding*, 265-66; Fenton, *John*, 206; I. de la Potterie, *The Hour of Jesus*, 190.
[187] Strachan, *The Fourth Evangelist*, 17.

Finally, if the Beloved Disciple, Thomas, witnesses to everything significant in the life of the One from above, the Son of God, this would surely include witnessing the fact that the Logos was united with Jesus, and that means witnessing the descending of the Spirit from above to remain on Jesus. It would continue to include all the events of Jesus' life through to his passion and physical resurrection; thus we now can understand a perplexing phrase in the Appendix. This was written by a member of the Johannine Community who most likely knew the identity of the Beloved Disciple and who, moreover, would have heard about his former life with John the Baptist and then Jesus. In 21:24 he stated concerning the Beloved Disciple the following: Οὗτός ἐστιν ὁ μαθητὴς ὁ μαρτυρῶν περὶ τούτων. According to our exegesis he did indeed witness to these things, and indeed beginning from the time of John the Baptist.[188]

4.12 PURIFICATION

The twelfth insight clarifies that the Beloved Disciple, if he is Thomas, follows the Jewish regulations for purification, and thus serves as the ideal disciple for those Johannine Christians who wish to continue in observing Jewish rules and customs. The Beloved Disciple comes to the tomb before Peter, but he does not enter it (20:5). As suggested elsewhere in this book, he does not go into the tomb because of the defiling nature of a corpse. He eventually enters the grave (20:8) and becomes ritually impure; he must therefore purify himself for a specific amount of time. He thus goes home because he is a danger to himself and to the other disciples.[189]

According to the widely followed norms for purification, observed in most sectors of Early Judaism, he must purify himself for *seven days* (Nu 19:14-15; Eze 44:26; cf. b.Moʿed Qatan 15b). The *Temple Scroll* stipulates that a Jew, like the Beloved Disciple, who has been defiled by a corpse or where a corpse has been (as in a "grave" [50.4-6]), remains unclean for seven days (*Temple Scroll* 49.5-7; 50.1-6).[190] He must purify

---

[188] This is a well-known formula used in the early Palestinian Jesus Movement; it needs no demonstration again. Also as so many excellent exegetes have demonstrated, the final verses in chapter 21 refer to the entire good news from God preserved in the GosJn. See e.g., Schnackenburg, *St. John*, 3:373; Burge, *Interpreting the Gospel of John*, 42.

[189] I am well aware that Peter was also contaminated when he entered the tomb, but we certainly know that he cannot be the BD. All that we know assuredly is that Peter also goes home. As is evident to readers of this monograph, to be impure is to be in danger of condemnation for oneself and to all others.

[190] As one would expect, the compilers of the *Temple Scroll* depended on Numbers but expanded the wilderness concept from "tent" to "house."

himself, otherwise he is unclean (טמא הוא [50.7]) and will contaminate all who touch him (50.8). After purifying himself with water (and immersions in the mikveh) he will be clean again after the seventh day (וביום השביעי [49.18]), in the evening (לערב [49.20])[191] when the sun sets (50.8-16).

We know that the Evangelist was well-versed in Jewish rules for purification and other Jewish laws (see 2:6, 7:22-23 [which reports the Jewish custom which allows circumcision on the Sabbath]; 8:17); hence it seems that the narrator has the Beloved Disciple go home to purify himself after entering the grave. He remains unclean and at home following the precepts for purification.

What has not yet been observed is the fact that the narrator has him, as Thomas, reenter the narrative at the proper time. He appears *precisely eight days later* (μεθ᾽ ἡμέρας ὀκτὼ πάλιν [20:26]); that is, eight days after the Beloved Disciple finally entered the tomb and became ritually impure by Jewish law. The narrator specifically signals the reader that Thomas was not present when Jesus first appeared to the disciples (20:24). If he were ritually impure, then it is understandable why he could not be present. Thus the Beloved Disciple, who is Thomas, reappears only after the completion of the *seven-day period* specified in the Tanach or Old Testament and in Jewish rules for purification from contamination upon entering a tomb.[192] This exegesis clarifies for the first time why the Beloved Disciple must go home, why Thomas is not present when Jesus appears for the first time to some disciples, only reappears after the com-

---

[191] Of course, לערב can also denote "towards the time of sunset."

[192] Another interesting insight that some Johannine Christians may have made is that circumcision was performed on the eighth day (Ge 17:12); that would be seven days after the male baby had been polluted by blood at birth. According to the *Odes of Solomon* the Odist was circumcised by the Holy Spirit: "For the Most High circumcised me by his Holy Spirit" (11:2). Since these *Odes* were obviously known by some Johannine Christians—if only by later generations—then we may perceive how some of them may have understood why the narrator did not need to have Thomas present when Jesus gave the Holy Spirit to the disciples when he first appeared to them (21:22). Thomas reappears on the eighth day and as the BD will perform some of the functions of the Paraclete who is closely associated with the Holy Spirit (see GosThom 53 which disparages physical circumcision but lauds "circumcision in Spirit"). In this connection it is informative that Philo, in discussing the meaning of "the eighth day" in Gen 17:12 declares that "Israel" means "seeing God" (QuesGen 2.49). This etymological meaning cannot derive from ישראל since that means "El persists"; but Philo's exegesis may help us understand how Johannine Christians could move from Thomas's circumcision to his ability to see Jesus as God and then to utter the climactic confession.

pletion of seven days, and—most importantly for our present search—why it is evident that the Beloved Disciple is none other than Thomas. In addition, for the Jews in the Johannine Community who eagerly wish to continue attending synagogal services and observe Jewish customs and laws for ritual purity, Thomas as the Beloved Disciple looms large as the model disciple.

4.13 SUMMARY

We have examined twelve additional exegetical insights which indicate that the most likely candidate for the Beloved Disciple is Thomas. The first, and most decisive, insight is the narrator's indication that Thomas must have knowledge possessed only by the Beloved Disciple. Thomas knows, without being told by anyone, what only the Beloved Disciple witnessed at the foot of the cross.[193] The most attractive exegetical explanation for this fact is that the Evangelist wrote with the knowledge that the Beloved Disciple was Thomas.

The second insight suggests, *inter alia*, that the relation between the Beloved Disciple and Judas Iscariot indicated that both belonged to the Twelve, and thus the Beloved Disciple is either Peter (impossible), Judas (incredible), or Thomas (probable). The third concerns martyrdom and the link between Thomas's exhortation to die with Jesus and the portrayal of the Beloved Disciple who alone is present at Jesus' death. The fourth insight discloses that both the Beloved Disciple passages and the Thomas story in 20:24-29 were added to the developing GosJn by the Evangelist, perhaps in the second edition. Thus both were on the mind of the Evangelist as he was editing his work; hence, we should ponder how and what ways he may have identified them.

The fifth insight concerns the framing of "the Twin" in the narrative of the GosJn which indicates that Thomas and the Beloved Disciple are linked by the way they are introduced in the gospel. The sixth focuses on the disciples of Jesus, among whom are Thomas and the Beloved Disciple; it may be significant that Thomas is the "seventh" disciple to enter the narrative, and that he is the disciple introduced before the disclosure of the existence of the Beloved Disciple. The seventh observation is that the repetitions and formulae indicate to the reader that the Beloved Disciple may be Thomas. The eighth picks up Minear's insight regarding the Ben-

---

[193] The narrator does not state that the women were still at the site of the crucifixion. They may have remained until the corpse was mutilated, or they could have left when Jesus died, or earlier when the throes of death were too horrific. What is important is to focus on what the narrator states: the BD saw it, and the Evangelist stresses that his witness is true (an unusual dimension of the narrator, at least up to this point).

jamin motif behind the portrayal of the Beloved Disciple and reveals a little known fact about Thomas which clearly ties him with Benjamin and perhaps thus with the Beloved Disciple. The ninth brings out the identity between Thomas and the Beloved Disciple that is apparent narratively in the Book of Glory and the portrayal of each as the ideal student. The tenth is a technical, sequential literary device that through ambiguity, misunderstanding, and clarification gradually reveals that the Beloved Disciple could well be Thomas. The eleventh is a grand *inclusio* in which a follower of John the Baptist witnesses to the descent of the Spirit upon Jesus, then is disclosed to be the Beloved Disciple, and finally seems revealed to be none other than Thomas. The twelfth indicates that the narrative of chapter 20 is clarified by the recognition that the Beloved Disciple goes home because of ritual defilement and reappears eight days later as Thomas. Thus the most representative conclusion is that the hypocoristic name "Thomas" identifies the epithet "the Beloved Disciple."

4.14 CONCLUSION

This intensive study of the GosJn assumes the new look on the GosJn. It has come to us from a Jewish group of brilliant, highly trained, and industrious scholars who may, under the leadership of the Beloved Disciple, have founded a Johannine School in which lived and worked some of the most sophisticated "converted" Pharisees, Samaritans, and Essenes—the great minds of Early Judaism.[194] Faced with the loss of Jesus, the confusion over the meaning of some of his teachings, the guidance of the Beloved Disciple (as if he were the Paraclete)[195] and then his faith-shattering death, these Jewish intellects began to fashion an unusually complex yet intertwined symbolic literary masterpiece. With a perspicacity fired by rejection from fellow Jews and the defection of loved companions, the Johannine crucible would be heated; from it an unusual genius emitted sparks that Christians have come to cherish as inspired. The author pointed to the Beloved Disciple as the trustworthy witness of everything salvific, from Jesus' empowering by the Spirit from above to his final blessing before returning above.

These exegetical insights are not like twelve links in a chain. That would mean that if one is weak the chain would break and be worthless.

---

[194] Brown points out that there were probably Samaritan converts in the Johannine Community. See Brown, *The Community*, 23; *The Churches the Apostles Left Behind*, 103. On the Essenes, see the contributions to Charlesworth, ed., *John and the Dead Sea Scrolls*, and my essay in the D. M. Smith Festschrift (in press).

[195] As Brown states, the Johannine Christians were not as traumatized by the fact that Jesus had not yet returned, because "in a very real way he has returned in and through the Paraclete" (*Community*, 13).

They are rather like narrative windows through which one may peer into the thought-world of the Johannine Community. If only one of these apertures is transparent, that is sufficient; then the examiner may perceive the actions and words of the individual who was celebrated by Johannine Christians as Jesus' Beloved Disciple. The viewer will have successfully obtained a glimpse of Thomas moving about as the Beloved Disciple; the task of identifying the person behind the epithet will have been completed.

CHAPTER 5

Evidence and Speculation as to Who Is Not the Beloved Disciple

5.1 EVIDENCE SUGGESTING LAZARUS IS NOT THE BELOVED DISCIPLE

What case can be brought forward to suggest, or demonstrate, that Lazarus is not the Beloved Disciple? How impressive is the case for Lazarus?

First, Lazarus says nothing in the GosJn. How can he be identified with the Beloved Disciple, if the latter, as most exegetes agree, is a model for discipleship?

Second, Lazarus does nothing in the GosJn. How can he be defended as the Beloved Disciple? Surely, as Bacon stated long ago, the Beloved Disciple is a "type of true discipleship."[1] Is it not obvious that true, or ideal,[2] discipleship, according to the author and editor of the GosJn, demands not only speaking, but also acting on behalf of Jesus? The answer obviously needs no demonstration; it is clear from reading passages like "A new commandment I give to you, that you love one another, as I have loved you. ... By this all will know that you are my disciples" (13:34-35).

Third, Lazarus is never called a disciple in the GosJn. He is not named among the disciples who see the resurrected Jesus (20:19-22); he is not even named among the disciples who are present beside the shore of the Sea of Tiberias (21:2). It is, of course, conceivable that he is one of the two anonymous disciples; but to mount such an argument would sound like special pleading.

---

[1] Bacon, *The Fourth Gospel in Research and Debate: A Series of Essays on Problems Concerning the Origin and Value of the Anonymous Writings Attributed to the Apostle John* (New York: Moffat and Yard, 1910) 301.

[2] See Bacon, *The Fourth Gospel,* 320-21.

Fourth, Lazarus is introduced for the first time in chapter 11 and not mentioned again after chapter 12. Why does the narrator not describe or imply that Lazarus was present at the Last Supper, witnessed the crucifixion, and went to the tomb? Would it not be easy to imagine Lazarus standing before Jesus' tomb, and thinking about how he had also been wound in linen? Why does the Evangelist not bring Lazarus back again for a confrontation with death, now being experienced by Jesus in the tomb?

How can Lazarus be the witness to "these things" of 21:24 when he is not said to be present during the crucial events in Jesus' life? The narrator does not describe Lazarus as being present at the baptism, Last Supper, crucifixion, or resurrection.

Fifth, Lazarus is not known in the GosJn except in two contiguous chapters. He is not mentioned anywhere in the NT except in the GosJn.[3] This fact has prompted many critics to question his existence. As scholars we cannot appeal to the criterion of multiple attestation; there is no evidence outside the GosJn that there was a man named Lazarus of whom Jesus was ostensibly fond. As D. M. Smith states, "we cannot prove that John did not invent any number of the characters in the Gospel, about whom we know nothing either from the Synoptics or from any other source."[4] Recently B. Byrne in *Lazarus: A Contemporary Reading of John 11:1-46* points out that 11:1-46 looks like "a skillfully constructed dramatic narrative," and that the Evangelist may be expanding the traditions that lie behind Luke 10:38-42, by making Mary "simply the foil for Martha," and Luke 16:19-31, which is the parable of the Rich Man and Lazarus.[5] It is true that the tradition behind the Lucan parable may have helped shape the idea that Lazarus had died from leprosy and that resuscitation or resurrection would not prompt believing in the Johannine sense.[6] Schnackenburg may be correct that behind the Lazarus story lies "a miracle story

---

[3] Perhaps more than any other story in the New Testament, the Johannine pericope stimulated early Christian artists; it became one of their favorite themes. The resurrection of Lazarus is celebrated in third-and-fourth-century catacomb paintings, carved ivory sarcophagi, and early Christian objects made of precious commodities. For a discussion and illustrations, see R. M. Jensen, "The Raising of Lazarus," *Bible Review* 11 (1995) 20–28, 45.

[4] Smith, *John*, 42.

[5] As Brown states, to solve problems by contending that the Lazarus story is a "fictional composition based on Synoptic material" generally presupposes that the Evangelist is "reshuffling" traditions obtained from the Synoptics. As he rightly judges, this approach to the GosJn has not been "found to be successful elsewhere in the Gospel" (*Gospel*, 1:428).

[6] I agree with Lindars that there is insufficient evidence "to think of a Synoptic-type miracle story overlaid with Johannine reflection" (*The Gospel of John*, 383).

from the σημεῖα-source" which was heavily reconstructed by the Evangelist: "the supreme revelation of Jesus as the life-giver is balanced by the determination of unbelief to destroy him."[7] But I am persuaded that Meier is probably correct to think about a pre-Johannine story that was in a "fluid" state.[8] In any case, it is wise to resist the temptation to posit that the account is a literary creation by the Evangelist.

Sixth, we know so little about Lazarus. How can he be the Beloved Disciple if the latter is to be the paradigm for beloved discipleship? How can he be the founder of the Johannine School if he is portrayed so cryptically in the GosJn? There is no evidence that Lazarus believes in Jesus.

Seventh, if we are to take the narrative seriously, as experts in narrative theology point out, then it is difficult to imagine Lazarus outrunning Peter to the empty tomb only a few days after being raised from the dead.[9] To imagine such actions is to ask the reader to believe more than is believable—a reminder of how significant Questioning Thomas is to the narrative.

Eighth, to argue that "the disciple whom Jesus loved" must be Lazarus because the narrator says that Jesus "loved" him (11:3, 36) is myopic. The narrator clarifies that Jesus also loved Mary and Martha (11:5), and that he loved all his disciples εἰς τέλος (13:1). The Evangelist even stresses that Jesus' new commandment exhorts all his disciples to love one another *as he had loved them* (13:34). The narrator has not said that Jesus loved only Lazarus; he has carefully balanced the description of "the disciple whom Jesus loved" within the broader perspective that Jesus loved all his disciples perfectly. Hence, the statement in 13:3 does not indicate that Lazarus is the Beloved Disciple.

Many experts have advocated identifying the Beloved Disciple with Lazarus, but he is not really a strong candidate for this honorific epithet. I thus concur with Brown,[10] Byrne,[11] Culpepper,[12] Grassi,[13] Schnackenburg[14] and most Johannine experts that Lazarus cannot be identified as the

---

[7] Schnackenburg, *St. John*, 2:345.

[8] J. P. Meier, *A Marginal Jew: Rethinking the Historical Jesus*, 2 vols. (ABRL; New York: Doubleday, 1991) 2:819.

[9] Eller is convinced that Lazarus is the BD and claims that "Lazarus *and* Peter ... race each other to the tomb" (*The Beloved Disciple*, 71).

[10] Brown, *Community*, 34.

[11] Byrne, *Lazarus*, 93.

[12] Culpepper, *Anatomy*, 141.

[13] Grassi also adds that the Lazarus hypothesis fails to convince because it is not supported by ancient tradition; and while the BD is compared or contrasted with Peter, this literary phenomenon does not pertain to Lazarus (*The Secret Identity of the Beloved Disciple*, 12).

[14] Schnackenburg, *St. John*, 3:385.

Beloved Disciple. Most of the arguments amassed in favor of Lazarus, however, would also fit an eyewitness who was Jesus' confidant and devoted to him.

5.2 SPECULATIONS THAT THOMAS IS NOT THE BELOVED DISCIPLE

To be thorough we should also ask the following: How significant a case may be mounted against the hypothesis that Thomas is the Beloved Disciple? Here are sixteen major objections that might be suggested.

First, students of the GosJn will note that Thomas is never called "the disciple whom Jesus loved." That is, of course, correct. But then no disciple—indeed no one—is declared by the narrator to be the Beloved Disciple. The task before us is to seek to discern if his name can be found in the GosJn, while admitting that no solution can be without some scholarly speculation.

Second, some experts who have attempted to identify the Beloved Disciple may claim that Thomas is not obviously "the disciple whom Jesus loved." They may contend that he must be Lazarus because the one Jesus raised from the dead is introduced with the requisite formula: His sisters sent to Jesus, saying, "Lord, he whom you love is ill" (11:3).

How devastating is this evidence against identifying Thomas as the Beloved Disciple? Looking on this data alone, one must admit that Lazarus looks more promising than Thomas as the Beloved Disciple. But as Johannine experts have shown for decades, no verse in the GosJn should be interpreted in isolation from other passages in the GosJn.[15] The words of Solotareff are important: "Paul Diel was able to show ... that mythical symbolism stemmed from an intuitive and imaged introspection.... In times when mythical symbols were intuitively felt and understood, they had an evocative power arousing an emotion springing from the depths of the human psyche."[16]

The author of the GosJn did not write a biography of the Beloved Disciple; he enmeshed in his gospel the witness of the Beloved Disciple. The narrative serves to define the fundamental thought adumbrated in the symbol which is multivalent. Building upon the insight of Solotareff, it is important to perceive that the author of the GosJn employed mythical

---

[15] See especially the major commentaries by Brown, Haenchen, and Schnackenburg. Though too shaped by Greek mentality and mythology and too imbued with modern psychological method, Diel's book on the GosJn is full of precious insights. For example: "The intention of the Evangelist himself is to lead the reader in search of the deep meaning underlying the seemingly miraculous narrative" (3); see Diel with J. Solotareff, *Symbolism in the Gospel of John*, trans. N. Marans (San Francisco: Harper & Row, 1988).

[16] Solotareff, *Symbolism in the Gospel of John*, vii.

symbols, especially those which are grounded in historical reality like the Beloved Disciple, so that they would be intuitively felt and comprehended. The anonymity of this ideal disciple gave it an evocative power which awakened and aroused the reader to contemplate the claims of the GosJn.

Furthermore, these words "he whom you love" are attributed to Lazarus' sisters; they are not canonized as coming from Jesus. He does not call Lazarus the disciple whom he loves; and it is stated in 11:5 that Jesus "loved (ἠγάπα) Martha, her sister, and Lazarus." A case against Thomas thus cannot be sustained by an exegesis of 11:3. Finally, Jesus gives his disciples "a new commandment" to love one another "as I have loved you" (καθὼς ἠγάπησα ὑμᾶς). Thus, Lazarus is not the only one Jesus loved. And in favor of Thomas over Lazarus is the observation that he, and not Lazarus, is called not only a disciple, but also one of the Twelve.

Third, Thomas cannot be the Beloved Disciple, some experts might add upon hearing the previous discussion, because Thomas is not even said to be "loved" by Jesus; hence, how can he be "the disciple whom Jesus loved"? That same criticism would be placed against John the son of Zebedee and all other candidates, with the exception of Lazarus. It does not seem to be a significant objection in light of the fact that Jesus makes it clear, as has been already stated, that he loves all his disciples. That is the basis of his new commandment.

Fourth, some critics may suggest that Thomas cannot be the Beloved Disciple because only the latter is from Judea. Is this not special pleading? The claim that the Beloved Disciple must be from Judea is based on the dismissal of the report in chapter 21, and a myopic focus on where he is explicitly present; that is, at the Last Supper, the crucifixion, and the empty tomb.[17] Yet, there are numerous reasons to conclude, as have many experts on the GosJn, that the Beloved Disciple is the anonymous former follower of John the Baptist mentioned at the beginning of the GosJn (see chap. 6). It is disappointing to observe how the claim that the Beloved Disciple must be from Judea has been passed from one commentator to another.

The narrator explicitly states that the time was the Passover Festival. It was a mandatory pilgrimage to Jerusalem for all devout Jews.[18] The

---

[17] The claim that the BD must be from Judea has influenced the experts who have argued that he is John Mark. Thus, Parker contended that "Jerusalem and its environs ... was indeed his home" (*JBL* 79 [1960] 97). The same methodology characterizes those who contend he must be Lazarus. Hence, Grassi concludes that he "was from Judea, probably Jerusalem" (*The Secret Identity of the Beloved Disciple*, 115).

[18] According to Lk 2:41-43 Jesus went to Jerusalem "every year" to celebrate Passover.

edict in Deuteronomy was honored and observed by early Jews like Jesus and his followers:

> Three times a year—on the Feast of Unleavened Bread, on the Feast of Weeks, and on the Feast of Booths—all your males shall appear before the Lord your God in the place that He will choose. [Dt 16:16; Tanakh]

As S. Safrai points out, the Passover pilgrimage in the first century and before 70 C.E. "has no measure" (Peah 1:1); which means it can be observed each Passover (Tanhuma, *Tetsaveh* 13), less frequently, or only once in a lifetime.[19] For the devout Galilean Jew, pilgrimage to Jerusalem at Passover time was thus an aspect of social obligation.[20] This aspect of Judaism was well known to the Evangelist and his Community, not only because he was well versed in Jewish traditions, but also because he gives prominence to the Jewish feasts.[21]

The Holy City is where religious Jews massed at this time of year. Hence, for example, Simon of Cyrene may have come to Jerusalem from northern Africa to celebrate Passover. Philo came from Alexandria to Jerusalem in order to offer prayers and sacrifices, quite possibly at Passover time (*De Providentia* 2.64). Thus when we consider that the time and setting during which the scenes in the GosJn 13–20 are staged is Passover and Jerusalem, then we should be cognizant that then and there Judeans were outnumbered in the Holy City. Attention is usually directed to the fact that while most of these were pilgrims, many also were merchants and soldiers.[22]

---

[19] See the popular article by Safrai titled "Pilgrimage in the Time of Jesus," *Jerusalem Perspective* (September/October 1989) 3–4, 12.

[20] For the social dimensions of pilgrimage see V. Turner, "Pilgrimages as Social Processes," *Dramas, Fields, and Metaphors: Symbolic Action in Human Society* (Ithaca/London: Cornell Univ. Press, 1974) 166–30.

[21] Only in the GosJn do we find mention of Tabernacles (7:2), Dedication (10:22), and an unspecified "feast of the Jews" (5:1). In the GosJn we have a clear reference to Passover, but in the GosJn it appears both at the beginning and the end of the gospel (chapters 2 and 13–20). G. A. Yee rightly claims that "these feasts had an important place in the piety of" the Johannine Community (*Jewish Feasts and the Gospel of John* [Wilmington, Del.: Glazier, 1989] 27). Still challenging and full of heuristic insights is the claim by A. Guilding that the GosJn in chapters 13–20 reflects the "entire *lectionary* year" and includes thus Passover, Rosh ha-Shana, Tabernacles, Dedication, and Purim (*The Fourth Gospel and Jewish Worship: A Study of the Relation of St. John's Gospel to the Ancient Jewish Lectionary System* [Oxford: Oxford Univ. Press, 1960] see esp. 49).

[22] Still valuable is M. P. Charlesworth's succinct "The Trade of the Empire: Trade and Travel," *The Roman Empire* (London: Oxford Univ. Press,

Galileans like Thomas would be present in great numbers, especially if Feldman is correct that "we must assume that most of the pilgrims came from the Land of Israel itself."[23] The author of the GosJn makes this rather clear himself: "Now the Passover of the Jews was at hand, and many went up from the country to Jerusalem before the Passover, to purify themselves" (11:55). Many of those who "went up from the country" would denote Galileans, since Galilee, according to Josephus, was one of the most heavily populated areas in ancient Palestine (*Life* 235).

During the three or four days covered by the time from the Last Supper to the surprising discovery of the empty tomb, many of Jesus' Galilean disciples, especially those who belonged to the Twelve, would most likely be in Jerusalem with Jesus. Hence, it is unpersuasive, to say the least, to claim that the Beloved Disciple must be a Judean because the setting of chapters 13 through 20 is in Judea.[24]

In fact, if statistics have been employed to demonstrate that the Beloved Disciple must be a Judean, then it is necessary to point out that most of the people in Jerusalem during the time of the Last Supper, the crucifixion, and discovery of the empty tomb were not Judeans. We have evidence that visitors at Passover flocked to Jerusalem from Arabia, Asia Minor, Cyprus, Cyrene, Egypt, Ethiopia, Gaul and Germany, Greece, Mesopotamia, Parthia, Rome, Syria, and elsewhere.

The so-called Triumphal Entry, that is Palm Sunday (12:12-18), assumes that large crowds are pouring through the gates of Jerusalem from the East (as well as the South, West, and North). We know that at Passover time Jerusalem more than doubled in size, due to the appearance of Jewish pilgrims,[25] and from the influx of Roman troops needed to keep peace and order at the peak time of messianic expectation (when Jews celebrated God's deliverance from Egypt and from oppression in "our"

1951) 119–34. Especially intriguing is his comment about commerce from East to West, and notably from Damascus, Berytus, Apamea, Byblus, and China (126–31).

[23] L. H. Feldman, *Jew and Gentile in the Ancient World: Attitudes and Interactions from Alexander to Justinian* (Princeton: Princeton Univ. Press, 1993) 23.

[24] Moreover, we must not forget that we are working primarily with narration.

[25] Four sources record the number of pilgrims in Jerusalem for Passover: Rabbinics (b.Pes 64b; LamR 1.2), Josephus' account of lambs slain (*War* 6.420–31; cf. *War* 2.280), Josephus' account of people trapped in Jerusalem when the Great Revolt of 66 began at Passover time (*War* 6.420; 7.210-15), and Tacitus (*Hist* 5.13). The numbers are ridiculously inflated, but the ratio still would produce an increase of two times, or more, the population of Jerusalem.

time). These facts are indisputable and have been clarified in the publications of numerous scholars, especially by J. Jeremias and E. Sanders (Christians) and S. Safrai and L. H. Feldman (Jews).[26]

Is it not axiomatic that one simply cannot ignore any part of the GosJn in developing or defending an hypothesis? Chapter 21 is an appendix to the GosJn, but it is not from some maverick who knows nothing about the origins of this gospel. His use of words ties him with the group who has helped shape the GosJn. His task seems to have been to represent the Johannine Community in defense of the trustworthiness of the Beloved Disciple, the source of the gospel. In addition, Judea and Galilee, as we have shown previously, are not isolated antagonistic regions as some scholars assumed earlier. The data in the GosJn do not demand the assumption that the Beloved Disciple must be a Judean.

Finally, to claim that the Beloved Disciple must be from Judea because he appears for the first time in the GosJn in Jerusalem overlooks many verses in the GosJn. For example, the Beloved Disciple must not be delinquent in fulfilling what are requisites for a disciple. According to 15:27[27] Jesus calls those disciples who are with him at that moment his "witnesses." That is singularly important because the Beloved Disciple is singled out as the witness of this gospel. Note, now, the criterion according to this verse: "because from the beginning ($\ddot{o}\tau\iota$ $\dot{\alpha}\pi$' $\dot{\alpha}\rho\chi\tilde{\eta}\varsigma$) you have been with me." If that is taken in its strict sense, it would mean from the time Jesus was leading a baptist movement, either independently or as a disciple of John the Baptist (see chap. 6); if not, then it means since his ministry in Galilee when he called for the first time someone to follow him, namely Philip, who then shared his discovery with Nathanael (1:43-51).

These observations tend to suggest that the Beloved Disciple was a Galilean, since he was with Jesus during the Galilean ministry. A prime

---

[26] J. Jeremias, *Jerusalem in the Time of Jesus*, trans. F. H. and C. H. Cave (Philadelphia: Fortress, 1969). E. Sanders, "The Common People: Daily Life and Annual Festivals," *Judaism: Practice and Belief 63 BCE – 66 CE* (London: SCM; Philadelphia: Trinity Press International, 1992) 119–45; S. Safrai, "The Temple and the Divine Service," in *The Herodian Period*, ed. M. Avi-Yonah and Z. Baras (The World History of the Jewish People 1.7; New Brunswick, 1975) 282–337. L. H. Feldman, *Jew and Gentile in the Ancient World*, see esp. "Contacts Between Jews and Non-Jews in the Land of Israel," 3–44.

[27] Chapter 15 belongs to a series of chapters (15–17) that most likely are additions to the "first" edition of the gospel. It thus cannot be dismissed as irrelevant. The author of these chapters, who is most likely the same person as the author of the gospel, knew the Johannine Community, and surely lived within it. That means he knew the identity of the Beloved Disciple, because later (when chapter 21 was added) the community was shaken by his death.

candidate would thus be the Galilean Thomas, whom we can imagine went up to Jerusalem at Passover time to celebrate the continuing triumph and promise of the God of Israel.

Fifth, some experts may point out that the Beloved Disciple at the empty tomb "saw and believed" (20:8) in Jesus' resurrection, and that later Thomas was not present and resisted any belief in the resurrection of Jesus. I have tried to point out that an exegesis of 20:1-10 indicates that the Beloved Disciple did not necessarily believe that Jesus was raised from the dead; he could have believed many things, including the possibility of what Mary Magdalene had reported; that is, that the tomb was empty (20:8). He did so because along with the other disciples he "as yet did not know the scripture, that he (Jesus) must rise from the dead" (20:9). Consequently, the narrator has the Beloved Disciple go home, as did Peter (20:10). That interpretation certainly explains why he, but not necessarily Peter, was absent when Jesus appeared to some disciples (20:19-23). Hence, the Beloved Disciple, as Thomas, can well be intended to deliver the climactic confession of the GosJn. That would certainly help prove that Thomas, as the Beloved Disciple, is the paradigm for Johannine discipleship.

Not only the Beloved Disciple before the empty tomb, but also Thomas before convincing proof of Jesus' resurrection are linked together by the narrative of the gospel; both refuse to jump quickly to the conclusion that Jesus must have been raised by God. They stand out together, and as one person, against the picture of pious individuals who may appear as soft and unreflective and too eager to believe anything that might save them. Hence, Thomas, the real hero of the GosJn, is a very attractive candidate for being the Beloved Disciple.

Sixth, New Testament scholars may be persuaded that Thomas is a minor figure in the New Testament and in the origins of Christianity since Thomas appears only once in each of the Synoptics (Mt 10:3, Mk 3:18, Lk 6:15) and only one time elsewhere in the New Testament (Acts 1:13). Similarly, they may bring into focus the fact that while the Beloved Disciple appears for the first time in chapter 13, Thomas appears already in 11:16. Furthermore, they may wish to stress that Thomas comes into view again only at 14:5, except for chapter 20 (20:24, 26, 27, 28) and 21 (21:2). Some critics may use these statistics to argue that Thomas is a minor figure, and that Lazarus is more prominent in the GosJn.

This claim would be hard to sustain, but it is presupposed in some monographs. We must not forget that Thomas is on center stage at the conclusion of the original form of the GosJn; that is, at the culmination of chapter 20. Thomas alone dominates the final scene, and as we have seen, he has already played a significant role in the GosJn.

Seventh, perhaps an argument will be presented that claims Thomas cannot be the Beloved Disciple because he is not present when Jesus is described as breathing on the disciples and empowering them with the Holy Spirit (20:22). It is conceivable that the sons of Zebedee were present, perhaps Lazarus, and even Peter; but Thomas is explicitly excluded.

What answer can be given? Narrative theology will point out that the scene is thereby set for Thomas's experience of the physically resurrected Jesus and his magisterial confession. Hence, it is not so important that he is present when Jesus says "Receive the Holy Spirit," to the disciples. What *is* important is that he is present to have a personal encounter with the risen Jesus. Thomas and Mary Magdalene are signaled out for this special attention in John's story. Would not such special attention make better sense if Thomas was the ideal disciple; that is, the Beloved Disciple?

One has to admit, however, that Thomas is not blessed in the GosJn; to attempt to mount that claim would do violence to 20:27-29. The greeting by Jesus to the disciples, "Peace to you," (20:26) certainly includes Thomas, but in light of its Semitic meaning, שלום לכם, specifically "hello," (heard today in Israel each day),[28] it is not wise to attempt to claim that with these words Jesus is blessing the disciples, including Thomas. But then Jesus also does not bless Lazarus (unless he is assumed to be present in 20:19-23). Either the Johannine Community did not need to have Thomas blessed because they knew he was the Beloved Disciple, or they were being faithful to tradition and history (as in the reporting of Judas's betrayal, the disciples' inability to believe, and in the final death of Jesus).

Here we might fruitfully entertain consideration of Thomas—as the Beloved Disciple—and his role in fulfilling many of the functions of the Paraclete. If he was thus, like Jesus, one who functions like the Paraclete, who is not easy to distinguish from the Holy Spirit, then it might not be necessary to describe him receiving the Holy Spirit. Let us explore this idea further.

There is another answer to the conceivable objection that the Beloved Disciple cannot be Thomas because he was not present when the resurrected Jesus says to some disciples, "Receive the Holy Spirit" (20:22). According to the GosJn the Holy Spirit (that is the Paraclete, the Spirit, or the Spirit of Truth) will supply those who believe in Jesus with living water (7:39), counsel them (14:16), be present among them

---

[28] Brown (*Gospel*, 2:1035) does not intend to suggest that the greeting was intended to bless Thomas; but he does rightly point out that "Peace to you" is "not to be mistaken for an ordinary greeting." The narrative dimension and theological perspective of the author, who is after all writing a gospel, must not be forgotten.

(14:17), teach them (14:26), help them remember Jesus' teachings (14:26), witness to Jesus (15:26), judge the world (16:7-8), and guide Jesus' disciples into all truth (16:13). Each of these functions are fulfilled by the Beloved Disciple, especially the middle four: being present, teaching them, aiding them to remember, and especially witnessing to Jesus. Hence, it is possible to respond that the reason the author of the GosJn did not need to depict Thomas receiving the Holy Spirit is because as the Beloved Disciple he was the embodiment of the Paraclete, the Spirit of Truth. If Thomas is the Beloved Disciple, then he is the only disciple who does not need to be present to receive the Holy Spirit, the Paraclete. As Culpepper states, the Beloved Disciple "has embodied the Paraclete for others. In him, belief, love, and faithful witness are joined. He abides in Jesus' love, and the Paraclete works through him."[29]

The link between the Beloved Disciple, indeed Thomas, and the Paraclete becomes even more impressive when attention is given to Jesus' prophecy that "the Paraclete will remain with you forever ($\varepsilon i\varsigma\ \tau\grave{o}v\ \alpha i\hat{\omega}v\alpha$, 14:16)." If the Beloved Disciple functioned after Jesus as the Paraclete, then it is understandable why Johannine Christians were disturbed that he did not remain for ever.[30] The trauma caused by the death of the Beloved Disciple whom the Johannine Christians thought would not die because of Jesus' words concerning him (21:22-23) may be understood in light of 14:16. The link is forged when it becomes obvious that the Beloved Disciple and the Paraclete are the witnesses to Jesus (compare 15:26 and 21:24).

Eighth, perhaps some critics will contend that Thomas is not a candidate for the Beloved Disciple because he was resistant to belief. They may point to the clear meaning of 20:25 in which Thomas states, "I will not believe." Surely, this is not unintentional or a mistake by the author of the GosJn. Is it not probable that he wanted to stress that the Johannine Community was not a sect of apocalyptic enthusiasts who easily believe even the absurd? The polemical ambience of the GosJn leads one to imagine that the synagogal Jews were lambasting the Johannine Christians for believing nonsense. Thomas stands out as the hero who does not believe easily; he needs solid and convincing evidence. The author of the GosJn was warning against soft-headedness or letting the wish become the father of the thought. Furthermore, Thomas does not disbelieve Jesus; he disbelieves his co-disciples whom he may well have thought were creating illusions because of their fear.

---

[29] Culpepper, *Anatomy*, 123–24. Grassi quotes these words of Culpepper to make his valid point that chapters 14 through 17 reveal "a striking parallel between the function of the Holy Spirit and the beloved disciple" (*The Secret Identity of the Beloved Disciple*, 82).

[30] Also see my reflections on the GosTh Log. 1, 13, and 108 in chapter 7.

He and his community were against those who let the will to believe create resurrection claims. As Jews they surely knew the Wisdom tradition, and perhaps some synagogal Jews cast up at them that they were simple people who believe everything. Perhaps the following was hurled at the Johannine Christians:

> A simple person believes anything;
> A clever man ponders his course. (Pr 14:15; TANAKH)

Such an embarrassing charge would not have been the monopoly of Jews. As G. W. Bowersock has recently emphasized, "Among the most conspicuous features of the fiction of the Roman empire, not only the prose romances but the mythological confections as well, is resurrection after death in the original body."[31] The Johannine Christians were confronted with the exasperating fact that their claims were articulated by ill-trained "Christians," and virtually indistinguishable from such absurdities as the myth that Zamolxis (Zalmoxis) "had died ... only to be resurrected and become, as a result of this miracle, regarded as a divinity."[32] Although resurrection belief was affirmed in the Amidah (the so-called Eighteen Benedictions) and may well have been professed by the synagogal Jews,[33] most contemporaries of the Evangelist would have agreed with Aeschylus' Apollos that "there is no resurrection ($οὔτις ἔστ᾽ ἀνάστασις$)."[34]

How could the Evangelist then distinguish between "apparent death" (*Scheintod*) and his kerygma about Jesus, the Son of God? What reply would the Johannine Community make to such charges and opinions? The answer may well lie in the story of Thomas, the accurate witness to Jesus,

---

[31] G. W. Bowersock, "Resurrection," *Fiction as History: Nero to Julian* (Sather Classical Lectures 58; Berkeley/London: Univ. of California Press, 1994) 99–119; cf. 99.

[32] Bowersock, *Fiction*, 100.

[33] Amidah 2,

> You [are] mighty: humbling the haughty ones,
> Powerful: calling to judgment the violent ones,
> Life of Eternity: causing the dead to rise;
> Causing the wind to blow and the dew to fall,
> Sustaining the living, reviving the dead.
> As in the twinkling of an eye, causing salvation to shine for us.
> Blessed are you, O Lord, who revives the dead.

The phrases most important are מקים מתים, מחיה המתים, ברוך אתה יי מחיה המתים. For the Hebrew see S. Schechter, "Genizah Specimens," *Jewish Quarterly Review* O.S. 10 (1898) 654–59.

[34] I am appreciative to Bowersock for this data; see Aeschylus, *Eumenides* 647–48.

who resisted easy belief, whether before an empty tomb (20:1-10), from claims that angels had been seen in the tomb (20:12), from the testimony of a woman (20:17-18), or the ecstatic enthusiasm of other disciples (20:24-25). The narrator thus allows Thomas to stand for reliable belief. He is confronted by the risen Lord (20:26-28). He makes the resounding confession (20:28), and becomes the basis for the blessing on those who must rely on him. He is thus a trustworthy witness.

Thomas was not an enthusiast who was easily persuaded by second-hand evidence. He pondered his course, and slowly came to believe that Jesus was alive again—and palpably alive, not just as a disembodied spirit. Why do others believe in Jesus' resurrection? They believe because of the validity of the Beloved Disciple's witness (21:24). Their believing is not primarily a resurrection belief; it is believing that Jesus is the Christ, the Son of God (20:30-31).[35] This believing is a process, a journey as Moloney has shown.[36] Believing is anchored in witnessing—now expressed in writing (20:31, 21:24). All of this is driven home, especially if Thomas is perceived to be the Beloved Disciple.

Ninth, some experts may be persuaded that Thomas is not a viable candidate because Jesus publicly criticized him. One of the harshest interpretations of Thomas is presented by G. J. Riley in his informative and erudite *Resurrection Reconsidered: Thomas and John in Controversy*.[37] He contends that as "a character in John, Thomas is cast as one who is wrong, ignorant and unbelieving."[38]

---

[35] These words may derive ultimately from the putative Signs Source, but in their present context they do color the message of the GosJn. This gospel was directed primarily to members of the Community who had questions and had been confronting sociological and ideological (especially Christological) problems. In my judgment, although the GosJn has been used for over eighteen hundred years as a missionary tract, its author did not intend it to win converts. Perhaps the aorist (as an inceptive aorist) in 19:35 and 20:31 is the first evidence of the GosJn as a missionary document. We must remember that the aorist may also be an aorist perfectum, and like the present tense, denote that the GosJn was written to deepen the readers' understanding and process of believing.

[36] Moloney rightly stresses the dynamic nature of the journey of believing in the GosJn; but he uses the word "faith" which does not occur in the GosJn, and he tends to conclude that the journey leads from unbelief to belief in Jesus' resurrection. If faith in the GosJn is primarily resurrection faith, then what has happened to the abiding significance of 1:14, 3:16, and 20:31? See Moloney's articles in *Australasian Catholic Record* 59 (1982) 417–32 and in *Studia Biblica 1978*, 185–213.

[37] G. J. Riley, *Resurrection Reconsidered: Thomas and John in Controversy* (Minneapolis: Fortress, 1995).

[38] Riley, *Resurrection Reconsidered*, 79.

According to some translations, verse 20:27 does *apparently* portray Jesus lambasting Thomas. According to the RSV the words mean "do not be faithless, but believing." This translation is the one developed by Schnackenburg, who (like Bultmann) presents a black picture of Thomas.[39] According to the NRSV the words are more accurately translated "Do not doubt but believe"; but "doubt" does not accurately represent *apistos* and may have appeared under the distorting myth of Doubting Thomas. The Greek ἄπιστος denotes that Thomas is confronted with what is not easy to believe; hence, "unbelievable, unbelieving, incredible, faithless, untrustworthy." It might be interesting to think about replacing Doubting Thomas with Incredible Thomas (and the paronomasia would have been seen immediately by the Evangelist).

If 20:27, especially the adjective *apistos* denotes Thomas's unfaithfulness or unbelieving—indeed doubting—nature, then one can see why Thomas is not a very attractive candidate for the Beloved Disciple. According to the Greek, however, Jesus urges Thomas, in a personal dialogue with him,[40] not to be *apistos* but *pistos*: (καὶ μὴ γίνου ἄπιστος ἀλλὰ πιστός.). Here we are confronted with a semantic field of meaning. This tight lexical unit must be observed in translating.[41] A translator should stay within the same range of the meaning of one word: either "be not unfaithful but faithful," or "be not unbelieving but believing." The latter semantic domain is represented in the translation of the Revised English Bible.[42]

Also, the semantic domain from *apistos* to *pistos* is introduced and governed by the alpha privative. The same noun appears twice, except in the first occurrence it has "the oldest form of the special negative"; that is, the prefix *a*, which has the effect of reversing the primary meaning of the noun and creating a negative denotation.[43] Hence, Thomas is to move

[39] Schnackenburg, *St. John*, 3:332.

[40] In some ways the dialogue is reminiscent of Jesus' private conversation with the BD in 13:25-26.

[41] Our lexicons have lumped together too many diverse meanings and based citations on criteria that are not integrated. See now the lexicon based on semantic domains: J. Louw and E. A. Nida, editors, *Greek-English Lexicon of the New Testament Based on Semantic Domains* (New York: United Bible Societies, 1988) 1:370–71, under 31.35 πιστεύω and 31.39 ἀπιστέω.

[42] "Be unbelieving no longer, but believe." See *The Oxford Study Bible: Revised English Bible with the Apocrypha*, ed. M. J. Suggs, K. D. Sakenfeld, and J. R. Mueller (New York: Oxford, 1992) 1392.

[43] As we know from the Mycenaean Linear B (the earliest examples) and Homer, the original form of the negative was apparently ἀ(ñ) (Sanskrit *a*[*n*] and Latin [*in-*]). As in ἄπιστος the derivation in Greek was almost always from adjectives, which had originally a good sense so that the prefix introduced a deprecatory sense. It is interesting that in Greek, as with English *un*worthy and

from not-believing to believing. Since the context pertains to Jesus' physical resurrection, then the transformation would be from not-believing the other disciples' report of Jesus' physical resurrection to believing through his own experience of a bodily resurrected Jesus. Thomas sees palpable evidence of Jesus' physical resurrection and does not need to confirm it by touching, as he had requested (20:24-25). Hence, the narrator is drawing attention not so much to a physically resurrected body as to the fact of continuity between the crucified and the resurrected one.

Anderson rightly urges us to meet Thomas "on his own ground," and to comprehend that Thomas is "certainly not charged with being faithless, *because he has seen*, answers, without ever 'touching' Jesus, with the sublimest confession of faith possible for the Evangelist, recalling as it does the Prologue (1:1), 'My Lord and my God' (20:27-28)."[44]

Let us now turn to the lexical meaning of the noun with the alpha privative. The Greek noun, *apistos*, pertains to not being believable. What does Jesus urge Thomas to do? He exhorts him to begin believing that something is trustworthy and true. What is the content of believing in Jesus' words?

Thomas had said earlier in 20:25 that he was not willing to base his belief in Jesus' *physical resurrection* on other disciple's reports. He would not be dependent on too enthusiastic impressions which may be fostered by dreams and fears, even if they are defended by revered colleagues. Hence, it is obvious that Jesus reveals himself to Thomas and exhorts[45] him not to continue in his unbelief of what the other disciples had claimed. Thomas's confession in Jesus' physical resurrection is founded on what he has now experienced.

Thomas's position in the gospel thus becomes less vague. Also, the content of belief in 20:24-29, but not earlier in 20:8 or later in 20:30-31, becomes more clear. We do not know what Thomas had been believing before he sees the resurrected Jesus. He came to the disciples so there is

---

German *un*gut, the prefix was not added to negative terms (e.g., there is no "unwicked" or "unschlecht"); This insight led A. C. Moorhouse to ponder on the possibility that "what is 'good' (desirable, proper) provides a standard, from which what is 'bad' is a departure; so that, while 'bad' is a departure from 'good', the converse does not apply" ("Negative Composition in Indo-European and Greek," *Studies in the Greek Negatives* [Cardiff: Univ. of Wales, 1959] 41–68; cf. 62).

[44] Anderson, ed., *The New Testament in Historical and Contemporary Perspective* (Oxford: B. Blackwell, 1965) 52, 54; cf. also Anderson, *Jesus and Christian Origins: A Commentary on Modern Viewpoints* (New York: Oxford Univ. Press, 1964) 236-37.

[45] The present subjunctive γίνου with μή forbids continuing to believe that something is not true.

no reason to conclude that he apostacized or was "unbelieving" or "faithless." What could he have believed? He could have been the embodiment of believing as the Evangelist stressed from chapters 1 through 19, namely that Jesus is the One from above, that Jesus is the Son of God, the one who has been sent by the Father who sends. He may have even believed in Jesus' resurrection from the dead.

What he did not believe is clear: he did not believe his colleagues' report that Jesus had been *physically resurrected*. That is the focal point of the narrative in 20:19-29. Thomas thus stands tall as the gospel reaches its conclusion. He is a beacon against the docetic tendencies that have split the Johannine Community, causing a schism. Believing in the resurrected Jesus, he acknowledges him as Lord and God.

The verse 20:27 was quoted by Theophilus of Antioch (whom Eusebius reported became bishop of Antioch [in 169 C.E.]); but he did not disparage Thomas. Urging his associates with the words μὴ οὖν ἀπίστει, ἀλλὰ πίστευε (14),[46] Theophilus confesses, "I too did not believe that the resurrection would take place, but now that I have considered these matters I believe." Why? Because he "encountered" the truth that was found in the "sacred writings of the holy prophets," which is reminiscent not of 20:27—which contains Jesus' words to Thomas—but of 20:9. And that verse, as is so obvious now (see chap. 2), indicated that the Beloved Disciple (as well as Peter) did not comprehend the meaning of the Scriptures that Jesus must rise from the dead. Does the exegesis of Theophilus of Antioch suggest not only admiration for Thomas, but possibly some association between him and the Beloved Disciple?

Tenth, these observations bring up a major, perhaps the singularly most telling argument against the hypothesis that Thomas is the Beloved Disciple: he is Doubting Thomas. Those who will not read this monograph carefully but who hear that I have claimed that Thomas is the Beloved Disciple may show their distance from the exegesis of the GosJn and reject a position they have not thoroughly examined. Perhaps they may guffaw with the exclamation: How can anyone really take seriously the possibility that Doubting Thomas can be the Beloved Disciple? We should expect such cavalier nonchalance from dilettantes, because they have habitually vilified Thomas in lectures and sermons.

Serious exegetes, nevertheless, may point back to scholars like Heitmüller, who disparaged Thomas and contrasted him with the Beloved Disciple. Note Heitmüller's claim that the former is at the bottom and the latter is at the top of the ladder of faith in the GosJn:

---

[46] R. M. Grant, *Theophilus of Antioch: Ad Autolycum* (Oxford: At the Clarendon Press, 1970) 18-19.

> Am höchsten steht der Lieblings-Jünger, der ohne weiteres glaubt, als
> er den Herrn nicht im Grabe findet. Ihm steht am nächsten Maria,
> derren Glaube aus ihrer innigen Beziehung zu Jesus erwächst. Die
> Jünger müssen sehen. Am tiefsten steht Thomas, der mit groben
> Händen tasten will.[47]

As I have endeavored to show in the section on exegesis, the Beloved Disciple may begin to believe (incipient aorist) in the resurrection of Jesus before the empty grave and its contents. He believes fully in Jesus' physical resurrection as Thomas before the risen Lord.

It is precisely this imagined group who disparages "doubting" Thomas which nevertheless knows and uses quotations that represent an antithetical view. They are fond of a verse from Alfred Lord Tennyson's *In Memoriam* (Part 96, Stanza 3):

> There lives more faith in honest doubt,
> Believe me, than in half the creeds.

Equally essential for authentic faith is the period of personal doubt, reflected poignantly in J. Bailey's *Festus: A Country Town*: "Who never doubted never half believed."

Nevertheless, we must confront a major objection against the candidacy of Thomas, that is the claim that he cannot be the Beloved Disciple because he is renowned as "Doubting Thomas." The author of the GosJn wants his readers to believe (indeed *believe* is a key term in this gospel), and doubting Jesus in any way is not a conceivable category for the Beloved Disciple.

What answer is possible? Surely, Thomas has been stigmatized by a most inappropriate label. Jesus, as a Jew, urged his listeners to question. Thomas stands out as a paradigm against those who believe virtually anything, and against the enthusiasts who have marred the development of Christianity from the earliest days until the present. Thomas is a disciple whose speech and action show that eagerness to believe too easily can be confused with a penchant for being duped and tricked. Jesus repeatedly warned against those who were spiritually blind and did not struggle to see the inviting evidence (cf. GosJn 9). Bernard correctly stressed that the author of the GosJn did not teach "that a facile credulity is a Christian virtue; and Thomas was not wrong in wishing for some better proof of his Master's Resurrection than hearsay could give."[48] Hence, Thomas is not a Doubter; he is a Questioner. He is not a dreamer; he is a realist.

[47] Heitmüller, *Die Schriften des NT*, 4:179.
[48] Bernard, *Gospel According to St. John*, 2:684.

The objection of scholars on this point, however, must be taken seriously and fully confronted. It is deeply ingrained in our consciousness. Let us confront it. In western culture Thomas is known as Doubting Thomas. John Calvin, perhaps letting his personal austerity and occasional vindictiveness appear, disparaged Thomas. For Calvin he was "not only slow and reluctant to believe, but even obstinate." He continued by referring to Thomas's

> dullness of apprehension, and that his stupidity ... was astonishing and monstrous; for he was not satisfied with merely beholding Christ but wished to have his hands also as witnesses of Christ's resurrection. Thus he was not only obstinate, but also proud and contemptuous in his treatment of Christ.[49]

Surely these words are more indicative of Calvin and his concern for believers in sixteenth-century Geneva than of the intention of the Evangelist in the first century. This insight becomes obvious when we observe how Calvin continues hermeneutically and homilectically.

Such vitriolic words are not always typical of western scholars. Observe the following note by John Wesley who celebrated the continuing dynamism of Thomas's believing: "Thomas ... acknowledges Him to be the Lord, as he had done before." Wesley interprets the Thomas pericope so that Thomas moves beyond affirming Jesus' physical resurrection ("and to be risen") to confessing "His Godhead; and that more explicitly than any other had yet done. And all this he did without thrusting his hand into His side."[50] Unfortunately, Wesley's exegesis is atypical of our culture. The pejorative portrayal of Thomas follows *de règle* of western scholarship. The consciousness of the West is imbued with Judas as the Betrayer and Thomas as the Doubter. Note these representative comments by the leading commentators on the GosJn:

> The doubt of Thomas is representative of the common attitude of men, who cannot believe without seeing miracles (4.48). (Bultmann, John [1964, 1971] 696)

> And so it seems that Thomas is to be reprimanded on two counts: for refusing to accept the word of the other disciples, and for being taken up with establishing the marvelous or miraculous aspect of Jesus' appearance. Scholars such as B. Weiss, Lagrange, and Wendt think that it was on the first score that Jesus accused him of being a disbeliever. However, Jesus' words in 27 challenge Thomas only on the second count. (Brown, *Gospel* [1966, 1971] 2:1045–46)

---

[49] Calvin, *Commentary on the Gospel According to John*, 2:274–75.
[50] Wesley, *Explanatory Notes upon the New Testament*, 387.

> Jesus' words which repeat what Thomas said to his fellow disciples, must have struck home to the doubter.... So he perceives himself to have been seen through and is put to shame by the goodness of Jesus who fulfills his challenging wish. (Schnackenburg, *St. John* [1975, 1987] 3.331)

Thomas is "convinced in shame," according to Bultmann.[51] But that exegesis raises problems, as Bultmann himself admits. He continued: "Does not the reproach that falls on Thomas apply to all the other disciples as well? All of them indeed, like Mary Magdalene, believed only when they saw."[52] Hence, it seems to follow from Bultmann's own brilliant reflections on the narrative of the GosJn that Thomas was not convinced in shame.

Bultmann's brilliance comes out again when he states that Thomas "has not been chosen for the role of the doubter because of his name."[53] The Greek noun *didymos* may mean "double" as well as "twin." Hence, one is prompted to jettison the conclusion that "the Twin" is a doubter (that is of double mindedness).

Apparently, in the exegesis of 20:27 Schnackenburg, when he uses the word "shame," reads the GosJn in the light of Bultmann's commentary. The word "shame" is inherited from Bultmann. From reading most of the leading commentaries, we are left with a clear portrait of Thomas. He is a disbeliever, a shameful doubter. We are left with a Doubting Thomas. This portrait is deeply ingrained in teaching and preaching, perhaps because of the need to have a clear pedagogical and homiletical model for disbelief. However, it is time to stress that *there is no evidence in the Greek that Thomas ever doubted Jesus in any way.*

Is Thomas portrayed as a "doubter" in the GosJn? As A. Smith rightly warned, epithets like "doubter" are colorful, but they "can completely distort a person's true character."[54] How can the great doubter be also the consummate confessor in this narrative? How can one be publicly reprimanded by Jesus, and in the same scene, present what Ashton calls "the resounding affirmation"?[55]

In the entry on Thomas in the *Anchor Bible Dictionary* R. F. Collins, while describing him as a courageous leader in 11:16, points to his bravado and misunderstanding. He concludes that the Evangelist chose

---

[51] Bultmann, *John*, 694.

[52] Ibid., 696.

[53] Bultmann, *John*, 694.

[54] A. Smith, "Doubting Thomas," *The Twelve Christ Chose* (New York: Harper & Brothers, 1958) 94–108; cf. 95.

[55] Ashton, *Understanding*, 246.

Thomas "to dramatize disbelief of the group."[56] According to Collins he is "faithless," and so Jesus chides and reproaches him.[57] It will not be easy to change the minds of those who subliminally have assumed that Thomas is everywhere and always "Doubting Thomas."

They can support their opinion on an exegesis of 20:29, according to which Jesus may have reprimanded Thomas for his unbelief. Note these words by Haenchen: "The Fourth Gospel expresses its critique of the story of Thomas and the faith of Thomas in John 20:29."[58] G. R. Osborne refers to "Thomas's cynicism" and his "stubborn refusal to believe."[59]

The words of Jesus to Thomas are "Because you have seen me have you believed? Blessed are those who have not seen and (yet) believe." The first statement may in fact not be a question; it may simply state the obvious that Thomas saw and then believed.[60] There is no rebuke here. There is also no reason to assume that only those who have not seen will be blessed. That interpretation would exclude from the blessing at least Mary Magdalene and the disciples mentioned who were present and saw the risen Jesus and believed (20:19-23). The flow of the narrative does not indicate that the author is portraying Jesus as rebuking Thomas.

The picture of Thomas in early Christianity is often poorly conceived; on the one hand with a disparaging brush, and on the other hand with attractive emphasis. For example, Gregory the Great, in his homily on John 20:19-29, opined that "Thomas's lack of faith did more for our faith than did the faith of the disciples who believed" (*Hom.* 26 in *Evang*; PL 76.1202).[61] This is somewhat contradictory. Much better, and more responsively sensitive to philology, social context, and the narrative of the GosJn, would be this: Thomas's phenomenological founding of belief easily did more for our faith than did the unconstrained faith of some disciples. This exegesis seems to be represented in Carson's impressive *The Gospel According to John*. He rightly emphasizes that "Thomas' faith is not depreciated," and that Jesus blesses those "who, in part because they read of Thomas' experience, come to share Thomas' faith."[62] Missing in

---

[56] A similar view is presented by Collins in his article on the disciples in the GosJn that was published in *The Downside Review* 94 (1976) 125.

[57] R. F. Collins, "Thomas," *Anchor Bible Dictionary* (1992) 6.528-29.

[58] Haenchen, *John 2*, 215.

[59] G. R. Osborne, "John's Resurrection Narrative," in *The Resurrection Narratives: A Redactional Study* (Grand Rapids: Baker, 1984) 171.

[60] Note the translation in Hoskyns and Davey: "Jesus saith unto him, Because thou hast seen me, thou hast believed; blessed are they that have not seen, and yet have believed." E. C. Hoskyns, *The Fourth Gospel*, ed. F. N. Davey (London: Faber and Faber, 1947 [2nd ed.]) 539.

[61] See E. LaVerdiere, in *Encyclopedia of Early Christianity*, 899.

[62] Carson, *The Gospel According to John*, 660.

other commentaries is the proper accent: "Jesus immediately (if implicitly) praises him (Thomas) for his faith."[63]

In my judgment Carson rightly perceives that the Beloved Disciple was one of the Twelve and the eyewitness for the GosJn. But Carson is too committed to the traditional view that the Beloved Disciple must be the apostle John to recognize that he has almost affirmed the position that the Beloved Disciple is Thomas. Carson makes two comments that almost open this vista for him. He rightly claims that "Thomas ... 'saw and believed,' to use the language applied to the beloved disciple (v. 8)." He then perceives that Jesus "foresees a time when he will not provide the kind of tangible evidence afforded the beloved disciple and Thomas."[64]

Bruce also rightly saw the intention of the Evangelist. Thomas was "not impressed" by the reports of others. He may well have thought that they "might have succumbed to wishful thinking, but he was not to be taken in." Thomas knew "what imagination was capable of" and "illusions were not unknown." Bruce perceived correctly: "He has come to be known as 'doubting Thomas,' but he was not really any more doubting than the others." For those exegetes and commentators who want to conclude that Thomas, unlike the other disciples of Jesus, was a doubter, the following words by Bruce are helpful: "Thomas was no different from the other disciples in this respect: they did not believe until they saw: if they believed a week earlier than Thomas, that was because they saw a week earlier than he."[65]

Jesus does not rebuke Thomas. As Culpepper states, he is "the clear-eyed realist." Thomas serves as a paradigm against unrealistic idealism (e.g., Docetism and apocalyptic eschatology). Culpepper rightly concludes that he is "more than a doubter."[66] R. Brownrigg perceptively sees that Thomas was an absolutely practical man. He continues by stating that Thomas did not believe the other disciples, perhaps because "he felt they had succumbed to wishful thinking or had seen a ghost."[67]

Thomas also becomes a paradigm for confronting one of the dangers threatening the Johannine Community. Within his polemical ambience—especially the castigations received from fellow Jews—the author of the GosJn wants to warn his community against other-worldly apocalypsology and eschatologically unbridled excitement.[68] Against some Jewish apoca-

---

[63] Ibid., 658.

[64] Ibid., 659.

[65] Bruce, *The Gospel of John*, 393–94.

[66] Culpepper, *Anatomy*, 124.

[67] R. Brownrigg, *Who's Who in the New Testament* (New York: Oxford, 1993) 272.

[68] See the contributions in the following major works: D. Hellholm, ed., *Apocalypticism in the Mediterranean World and the Near East* (Tübingen: Mohr [Siebeck], 1983); J. J. Collins and Charlesworth, eds., *Mysteries and Revela-*

lyptists contemporaneous with him, the Evangelist warns that no one has ever seen God (1:18) or the Father (6:46), and that no one has ascended into heaven (3:13).[69] As N. A. Dahl pointed out, the author of the GosJn warns against visions and theophanies, and directs a polemical note against any who would make "the patriarchs and prophets heroes of mystical visions of the heavenly world."[70] Hence, Thomas serves as a warning; he is the paradigm of virtue. That is perhaps why the editor, who added chapter 21, lists him second only to Peter. The narrator seems to be saying that the believer should be like Thomas, a realist, and not duped by eager believers and auto-genetic apocalyptic visionaries. Brownrigg rightly states that "Thomas was that loyal and practical, down-to-earth, 'seeing-is-believing' disciple of Jesus, whose doubts of the Resurrection dissolved in the presence of his risen master."[71]

The Evangelist knew that there was explosive resistance—especially among the powerful and influential Jews who controlled the synagogue—to the proclamation that the crucified one was the resurrected one, even if this claim had already proved to possess unusual generative power.[72] As Morris contended, "Thomas makes abundantly clear, the appearances were not at first welcomed." Morris continues with important imaginative reflections: Thomas may have been "so shocked by the tragedy of the crucifixion that he did not find it easy to think of its consequences as being annulled."[73]

Is it not exegetically sound to conclude that Thomas's attitude and preoccupation with Jesus' wounds is precisely because he (as the Beloved Disciple) still had seared in his memory the sight of Jesus' sufferings and death on the cross, and the resulting mutilation by a spear-jabbing soldier? Brownrigg comes very close to being the only one to have seen this possi-

---

tions: Apocalyptic Studies Since the Uppsala Colloquium (JSPS 9; Sheffield: Sheffield Academic Press, 1991).

[69] Of course the discontinuity with 14:9 may be explainable by appealing to the good news of the incarnate Logos. The duality of identity and distinction between Jesus and God is a dynamic aspect of Johannine Christology.

[70] N. A. Dahl, "The Johannine Church and History," in The Interpretation of John, ed. J. Ashton (Issues in Religion and Theology 9; London: SPCK; Philadelphia: Fortress, 1986) 137. The article appeared originally in 1962.

[71] R. Brownrigg, The Twelve Apostles (New York: Macmillan, 1974) 177.

[72] W. A. Meeks writes that "one of the most powerful symbols that has ever appeared in the history of religions" is the claim that God's Son, the Messiah, had been crucified (The First Urban Christians: The Social World of the Apostle Paul [New Haven/London: Yale Univ. Press, 1983] 180).

[73] L. Morris, The Gospel According to John (Grand Rapids: Eerdmans, 1971) 852–53.

bility: "In that moment Thomas must have seen both the body on the cross, hanging by hands and feet, the side opened by the soldier's spear, *and* his living friend and master. As these two figures fused together, so Thomas leapt the gap between loyalty to a friend and adoring faith in God himself."[74] This effect would suggest that Thomas is the Beloved Disciple who experienced this horrible scene.

The passage in 20:26-29 does not denigrate Thomas. It ultimately elevates him, and it leads to the great confession given only to him at the culmination of the gospel. Jesus does not reprimand Thomas. A. Smith studied the figure of Thomas and found that he has been woefully misperceived. Note Smith's words:

> I disliked Thomas at the start. But to live with him in imagination is to replace one's impression of a man who knows all and believes nothing with that of a very human and very courageous spirit, whose example lifts one's soul like music to the light.[75]

Thomas represents the realistic follower of Jesus who grounds belief in trustworthy reality. He did not base his faith on hearing another's report; as Philo stated "seeing" is superior to "hearing."[76] Thomas is thus a symbol for those who do not let desire dictate belief. He requests to experience only what the other disciples claim to have seen, and—moreover—to touch the risen Lord, upon seeing his wounds from the crucifixion (20:24-24).[77] Thomas stands out as representative of the disciples. I think Bultmann is correct, then, in stating that as "the miracle is a concession to the weakness" of humans, so "is the appearance of the Risen Jesus a concession to the weakness of the disciples."[78] In this way we grasp how very

[74] Brownrigg, *Who's Who in the New Testament*, 272.

[75] Smith, *The Twelve Christ Chose*, 95.

[76] "It is possible to hear the false and take it for true, because hearing is deceptive (ὅτι ἀπατηλὸν ἀκοή), but sight, by which we discern what really is, is devoid of falseness (ἀψευδὲς δ' ὅρασις,)." Philo, *On Flight and Finding* 208. Of course, it is sometimes possible to discover the opposite view. The gnostic Theodotus apparently thought that hearing is superior to seeing: "the ears are more sceptical than the eyes (ὅτι ὦτα τυγχάνει ἀπιστότερα ὀφθαλμῶν)." *Excerpta ex Theodoto* 5.1. See R. Casey, ed. and trans., *The Excerpta ex Theodoto of Clement of Alexandria* (London: Christophers, 1934) 42.

[77] Bultmann held that "Thomas demanded no other proof than Jesus had freely offered the others (v. 20)." *John*, 696. Thomas had requested more; he wanted to place his finger in the mark of the nails, and to place his hand in Jesus' side (20:25). In *John 2*, p. 212, Haenchen rightly sees, contra Bultmann, that "the request of Thomas stands out from what was granted to all eyewitnesses."

[78] Bultmann, *John*, 696.

human and courageous was Thomas.

Thomas's confession sets the tone for Jesus to bless "those who have not seen and yet believe" (20:29). Thus, narrative exegesis of chapters 1–20 shows how Thomas becomes the means for the great blessing on all those who believe that Jesus is the One sent from the Father (see 7:28, 12:44-46) and the Son of God (3:16-18, 20:31). The blessing on "those who have not seen" is also an indication that the GosJn is speaking to those who are far removed in time from the historical Jesus.

R. J. Cassidy, who attempts to understand the GosJn without thinking about 21 as an appendix, argues that the author of the GosJn "regards Jesus' encounter with Thomas as the culminating scene of the body of the Gospel." In the following paragraph he continues: "In and of itself Thomas' memorable confession of belief and allegiance supports the interpretation that this is indeed to be regarded as the Gospel's culminating scene." Cassidy claims the drama's culmination provides "readers of the Gospel with a sense of closure and satisfaction."

Cassidy rightly sees that Thomas's confession forms an *inclusio* with the opening of the GosJn: "In effect, then, the evangelist can be seen to fashion a powerful 'inclusio' from 1:1 to 20:28 of the Gospel." Hence, *Thomas is not a doubter.* He brings the GosJn to its highest point; he is the only disciple who fully grasps the origin and meaning of the Son. Only he "comes to believe in him fully." Thomas alone affirms Jesus as "my Lord and my God."[79]

We should not conclude this discussion focused on the claim that Thomas is the Doubter without exploring again the semantic domain that links Thomas and the Beloved Disciple (especially in 20:28 and 21:24). The resurrected Jesus tells Thomas that he has believed ($\pi\epsilon\pi\iota\sigma\tau\epsilon\upsilon\kappa\alpha\varsigma$). The perfect tense denotes not only completed action, but also that the action continues; hence Thomas has fulfilled what Jesus had required and he continues in it. The continuing effect of this verb defines Thomas: he is the paradigm of believing. And this elevated status has been bestowed on him by Jesus after the resurrection.

The verb is extremely important in its fundamental meaning and in the narrative of the GosJn. Semantically, "to believe" means something quite different from the denotation "to inculcate a viewpoint" (as with $\xi\chi\omega$, $\lambda o\gamma\iota\zeta o\mu\alpha\iota$, and $\phi\rho o\nu\epsilon\omega$). It also has the connotation of possessing confident trustworthiness.[80] Narratively, "to believe" in Jesus as the One from above means to be united with the One from above, the Son, the Way, the Life, and the Truth (see GosJn 15-17).

---

[79] R. J. Cassidy, *John's Gospel in New Perspective: Christology and the Realities of Roman Power* (Maryknoll, N.Y.: Orbis Books, 1992) 71-72.

[80] See the pertinent discussion in Lou and Nida's *Greek-English Lexicon*, 1:370.

Like the Beloved Disciple, Thomas is the hero of the GosJn. Like the Beloved Disciple, Thomas is celebrated to be faithful and trustworthy. As A. Smith judged, Thomas is not the Doubter, he "was really one of the most loyal and steadfast apostles among the Twelve."[81] Is it not now more apparent that in the eyes of the author and editor of the GosJn the Beloved Disciple has a "twin": Thomas? Are they not to be, therefore, identified?

It is time, after two thousand years, to clean the portrait of Thomas. It is well past time to remove Thomas's persona from the pillory. The Evangelist portrayed Thomas as the hero of his gospel. Thomas was a leader; he urged Jesus' disciples to follow his example and be willing to go again into Judea, even if it meant dying—that is being martyred—with Jesus. As I have attempted to show in *Jesus Within Judaism*,[82] Jesus knew he was a prophet who had been sent to Jerusalem, perhaps to be persecuted and stoned. He was like his former colleague or teacher, John the Baptist, who was beheaded, and Honi, a Galilean miracle worker who had been stoned outside the walls of Jerusalem. He imagined he was facing the probability of stoning. Thomas is the only disciple who perceived that Jesus' course would demand his death; and he courageously exhorted his fellow disciples, "Let us go, even we [fellow disciples], in order that we may die with him" (11:16).

Thomas, finally, is the *realist* who stands firmly against *wishful* believing. Does the Thomas pericope function as the narrator's answer to the polemical barbs from the synagogal Jews who were constantly defaming other Jews in the Johannine School and Community, vilifying them for believing a crucified Jew who thought he was the Messiah, the Jews' Savior, and had been raised from the grave? Did the synagogal Jews ostracize what they considered wayward Jews with the castigation that they held this absurd, incredibly outlandish belief because Jesus' tomb was empty, a silly woman of ill repute had initiated a resurrection claim, and weak-minded, self-serving, fearful disciples of this possibly well-meaning teacher claimed, under perhaps a self-generative and hopeful emotional vision, that they had even seen him in a resurrected body? Surely it is easy to imagine the synagogal Jews shouting down the Jews in the Johannine Community with words such as "Unheard of, impossible!"

Such imaginative reflections are not so far afield when we recall the previous bitter rivalry between two leaders of the same party, the Zealots, namely John of Gischala and Simon Bar Giora, in Jerusalem during the Great Revolt (66–70 C.E.); the much later infrastructural animosity within

---

[81] Smith, *The Twelve Christ Chose*, 95.
[82] Charlesworth, *Jesus Within Judaism*, 153.

the rabbinic academies and the schisms among the circles of the Sages;[83] and especially the fratricide indicated by GosJn 16:2. The GosJn mirrors the efforts to obtain some normative self-understanding by the two Jewish groups that survived the holocaust of 70, the followers of Hillel and the followers of Jesus. It is within this ambience that we are to understand the rhetoric of the final chapter of the GosJn, chapter 20,[84] in which the scholars in the Johannine School attempted to write a gospel which was an erudite and well-crafted *apologia* for Johannine faith. Within such a milieu and the narrative context of the text, it becomes more obvious how the two heroes, the Beloved Disciple and Thomas, are really one person, the model for Johannine discipleship.

Thomas, therefore, would be the Evangelist's answer to such a public scandal. Thus, Thomas is not a doubter; he is the reliable *realist* in the GosJn. He is no duped enthusiast; he is the self-reflective and thoughtful, even courageous, leader. He is the hero to whom the narrator gives the final scene and allows him to dominate it. To him, and to him alone, is given the stirring words in the climactic scene: "My Lord and my God."

These comments are necessary because Thomas has been disparaged by highly influential commentators. Haenchen has no doubt that the Evangelist uses Thomas to disclose "faith that originates in that way is of little value," and that Thomas in 11:16 is blind "to the power of Jesus."[85] Collins is convinced that Thomas "epitomizes both the bravado and the ignorance of the disciples."[86] Lindars claimed the Evangelist "makes him represent doubt concerning the Passion and Resurrection (14.5; 20.24-9)."[87] Schnackenburg is persuaded that Thomas is a type of "one blind to faith and of one with a weak faith to whom belief in its wholeness will be granted as a gift only by Jesus himself, and that, after the resurrection."[88]

---

[83] The President of the Israel Academy, E. E. Urbach, discusses "the tension and clashes between the Exilarchs and the heads of the academies," and the "very rivalry between the authorities" (*The Sages: Their Concepts and Beliefs* [Jerusalem: Magnes Press, 1971]; see esp. 602–03).

[84] If Essenes are now working in the Johannine School, as seems obvious to some experts, then we might do well to consider not only their influence on the growing restriction of the exhortation to love one another so that it meant only a fellow Johannine Christian, but also their influential ability with polemics and their long-standing skill in labeling all others as Sons of Darkness, so that Jesus can call "Jews" the children of the Devil (cf. GosJn 8:44). For the insight that Essenes were probably living in the Johannine Community, see Charlesworth's contribution to the D. M. Smith Festschrift (in press).

[85] Haenchen, *John 2*, 60.

[86] Collins, *These Things Have Been Written*, 37.

[87] Lindars, *The Gospel of John*, 392.

[88] Schnackenburg, *St. John*, 3:329.

Bultmann opined that Thomas had to be "convinced in shame."[89] Brown speaks about Thomas's "obstinacy," claims that we "can tell that the Johannine writer disapproves of Thomas' demand" and contends that "Thomas is to be reprimanded on two counts: for refusing to accept the word of the other disciples, and for being taken up with establishing the marvelous or miraculous aspect of Jesus' appearance."[90] Stibbe depicts Thomas as "a rash pretender to martyrdom," and is convinced of his "false bravado" in chapter 11, his "misunderstanding" in chapter 14, and that the "false bravado and misunderstanding have progressed to 'unbelief'" in chapter 20.[91]

How can Thomas appear so pejoratively in the commentaries, and yet be the Evangelist's choice for the final scene and for the climactic confession? It is time to stop pillorying Thomas. In my judgment, after twenty centuries we are finally free to acknowledge that Thomas, the hero of the GosJn, is none other than the Beloved Disciple.

Eleventh, some scholars may reject the hypothesis that Thomas is the Beloved Disciple because, in their view, he asks "stupid" questions as in 14:5. In fact, beginning in the second century it was the institutional church which warned Christians that they should not ask questions. To ask is to question, even doubt, the authority of the church in having all the answers. The early centuries also are full of examples that priests are not supposed to question traditions, scriptural or ecclesiastical. Tertullian excoriated the heretics because they asked questions. True Christians must eschew questioning; they must not be like Thomas who even "doubted." Tertullian, when he was deeply orthodox and ecclesiastical, argued that the rule of Christ raised "no other questions than those which the heresies introduce and which make men heretics."[92] It is no wonder, therefore, how Thomas was turned from the questioning disciple to the Doubter. Yet, we must wonder, is that the Thomas intended in the GosJn?

According to the GosJn 14:5, Thomas does ask, "Lord, we do not know were you are going; how is it possible to know the way?" This is surely not an idiotic question. Instead, it shows discernment. As A. Smith pointed out in his excellent study of Thomas, this question portrays the realist in Thomas.[93] It is the practical mind facing a mystical demand. It is the man who lives in a hostile phenomenal world trying to grope his way into the noumenal world of faith. It is the man of common sense con-

[89] Bultmann, *John*, 694.

[90] Brown, *Gospel*, 2:1045–46.

[91] Stibbe, *John*, 206.

[92] Tertullian, *De Praescr.* 13. I am grateful to my colleague Elaine Pagels for pointing me to this passage. See her *The Gnostic Gospels*, 109.

[93] Smith, *The Twelve Christ Chose*, 98.

fronted with uncommon knowledge. Like Thomas, the reader is to seek to ask questions, especially those relating to "the way" Jesus has revealed. Thomas's insightful question contrasts with Philip's, which did not please Jesus.

Thomas's interrogative sets the stage for one of the most profound sayings of Jesus, which in the Vulgate, as Swete pointed out, is presented in beautiful alliteration: "Ego sum Via et Veritas et Vita."[94] It is the way back to the Father—indeed, one of the major themes of the GosJn. Thomas is not an ignorant disciple who asks stupid questions; he is the one disciple to whom the narrator gives the insightful question which is one of the hallmarks of the GosJn.

If the Johannine Community is actually a *School*, then Thomas is the model for the ideal student.[95] As Brownrigg stated, "It was not as though the others knew any more than Thomas, but he was not the sort to let his master get away with something that he, Thomas, did not understand."[96] Does that not encapsulate a model student in Early Judaism and Rabbinics? To ask hard questions of a teacher is not to embarrass a Rabbi; it is to honor him. Throughout the GosJn, Jesus is not portrayed as one who is a dictator forcing his disciples to understand him. He is one who elicits questions and is eager for his disciples to ask serious questions. That is in fact at the heart of the truly Jewish Jesus. He chides them for not asking enough questions (16:5) and urges them to "ask ... so that your joy may be full" ($\alpha i \tau \epsilon \hat{\imath} \tau \epsilon$ ... $\emph{\iota} \nu \alpha$ $\dot{\eta}$ $\chi \alpha \rho \grave{\alpha}$ $\dot{\upsilon} \mu \hat{\omega} \nu$ $\mathring{\eta}$ $\pi \epsilon \pi \lambda \eta \rho \omega \mu \acute{\epsilon} \nu \eta$ [16:24]).

Perhaps Penfield's poem, *My Name is Thomas*, might help to cast Thomas in the light intended by the author of the GosJn:

> As Life
> Made Peter rash, it made me over cool.
> I seldom spoke.
> I had to think a proposition through.
> And Peter's quick, enthusiastic jump
> To optimistic ends would rouse my blood.
> How could he know so surely at the start

---

[94] H. B. Swete, *The Last Discourse and Prayer of Our Lord* (London: Macmillan, 1913) 17.

[95] I have no doubt that in the Johannine School rhetorical techniques were taught, or at least discussed, that the "Old Testament" was studied, that pre-Johannine traditions (Jewish and Christian) were reworked, and that teaching was paramount. A contemporaneous model, which may well have been known to the Johannine Christians, is the School of Paul. See E. A. Judge, "The Early Christians as a Scholastic Community," *Journal of Religious History* 1 (1960) 4–15, 125–37; and Meeks, *The First Urban Christians*, 82–83.

[96] Brownrigg, *Who's Who in the New Testament*, 272.

> The truth that life reveals but by degrees?
> My colder logic had to prove each step.
> I held that faith was deeper tested so,
> And lent a calmer courage to one's deeds.[97]

Such an attitude of inquisitive learning fits well within the Jewishness of the GosJn, its ambience, and especially the Johannine School. The rivalry between Peter and Thomas in this poem is reminiscent of the narrative tension between Peter and the Beloved Disciple.

This observation might well elicit the complaint that while Peter and the Beloved Disciple are presented in tension and sometimes even as rivals, with the latter always coming off superior, the narrator never portrays Peter and Thomas in an adversarial way. Is it not evident that Peter and Thomas are never presented in such a way that the latter is superior to the former? Does this claim invalidate the candidacy of Thomas?

The answer is "no." Thomas and Peter are indeed once presented in tension, in a way somewhat reminiscent of the "rivalry" between the Beloved Disciple and Peter. Peter asks, "Lord, where are you going?" ($\pi o \hat{v} \, \upsilon \pi \alpha \gamma \epsilon \iota \varsigma$; 13:36). Strikingly similar words are attributed by the narrator to Thomas, and less than eight verses later: "Lord, we do not know where you are going ($\pi o \hat{v} \, \upsilon \pi \alpha \gamma \epsilon \iota \varsigma$;); how can we know the way?" (14:4). Both Peter and Thomas are given the exact same words: $\kappa \acute{v} \rho \iota \epsilon$, $\pi o \hat{v}$ $\upsilon \pi \alpha \gamma \epsilon \iota \varsigma$; (13:36) $\kappa \acute{v} \rho \iota \epsilon$ ... $\pi o \hat{v} \, \upsilon \pi \alpha \gamma \epsilon \iota \varsigma \cdot$ (14:5). The narrator must have intended some comparison to be seen by the attentive reader.

Indeed, he seems to be denigrating Peter and elevating Thomas. Peter's question receives Jesus' response that he "cannot follow" Jesus now and a warning that he will deny him. Thomas's question receives one of the highest *theologoumena* in the GosJn: "I am the way" (14:6) and the promise that "henceforth you know" my Father and "have seen him" (14:7). Thus, the narrator portrays Thomas in a way that should remind the reader of the Beloved Disciple; both are contrasted to and presented as superior to Peter. The objection to Thomas's candidacy becomes another insight to support it.

Twelfth, specialists who are convinced that the Beloved Disciple must be Lazarus, and not Thomas, may wish to point out a problem in the presentation of the "disciple whom Jesus loved." They might stress that Thomas is presented in chapter 11 along with Lazarus, then the Beloved Disciple is introduced in chapter 13, Thomas is mentioned again in chapter 14, then the Beloved Disciple again in chapter 19 (at the cross), then Thomas again in chapter 20. Furthermore, in chapter 21 Thomas is named and then the Beloved Disciple is described in the boat on the Sea of

---

[97] As quoted by A. Smith in *The Twelve Christ Chose*, 101.

Tiberias. Critics pushing Lazarus as the Beloved Disciple may find that mixing of presentations of Thomas and the Beloved Disciple proves that Thomas cannot be the Beloved Disciple.

They may smile at what they are convinced is a contrastingly neat presentation of Lazarus. He is introduced in chapter 11 as the one whom Jesus loved, dominates chapters 11, appears in chapter 12, and then exits so he can reappear as "the disciple whom Jesus loved" is introduced in chapter 13 (which, of course, begins the second half of the GosJn). These experts may feel contented that just as Lazarus exits by name from the scenes of the GosJn, the Beloved Disciple, a Judean, dominates subsequently at the Last Supper, the cross, and the empty tomb. This hypothesis does present a neat order of appearances; but perhaps it is persuasive primarily to those who have already concluded that the Beloved Disciple must be Lazarus.

Lazarus supporters will be dismissed, furthermore, by those scholars who advocate a link between the Beloved Disciple and the "other disciple" who appears before and after the two chapters in which Lazarus is named (that is, in GosJn 1 and 18). Such experts do have on their side the observation that the Beloved Disciple and "the other disciple" are linked in chapter 20:2, "the other disciple, the one whom Jesus loved" (see chap. 6).

The main question from the Lazarus supporters may be simplified: Is it not obvious that only Lazarus can be the Beloved Disciple because of his presentation in relationship with the Beloved Disciple, and does not this one observation disprove the attempt to identify Thomas with the Beloved Disciple? Is an answer possible?

It is. Recognize that the relationship of Lazarus with the Beloved Disciple would thus be rather simple, and perhaps too neat to be convincing. The attempt to prove that the Beloved Disciple must be Lazarus may well seem unpersuasive because Lazarus simply exits and there is no reason to think that he reappears as the Beloved Disciple. In fact, that is the exegesis suggested by most leading commentators.

The author of the GosJn might not want to make a simple presentation of the one he wants to keep anonymous, except to those who have insight (or private knowledge of the identity of the Beloved Disciple). He is gifted in bringing *dramatis personae* on and off the stage, as is particularly attractive with Nicodemus, Jesus' mother, Mary Magdalene, and Peter.

The anticipated criticism from the Lazarus supporters has opened my eyes to a possible unrecognized chiasm in the GosJn. It is apparent to me now that the author of the GosJn has a sophisticated schema in mind by the way he has presented Thomas as the Beloved Disciple. Note the sequence:

Chapter	Thomas mentioned at the	the BD is present at the
11	death of Lazarus	
13		Last Supper
14	Last Supper, asks for "Way"	
19–20[98]		crucifixion and empty tomb
20	sight of Jesus, confession	

The sequence has a surprising order: As we shall see, it is the famous chiastic ABCB′A′ which X. Léon-Dufour and Brown find elsewhere in the GosJn, in 6:36-40.[99] Perhaps the chiasm has gone unnoticed because this rhetorical aspect of ancient writings is known but seldom studied,[100] because it has been too frequently misused, because of a failure to perceive that it unites prose (and not only poetry), and because it almost always has been understood to unite, with inversion and balance, only words or sentences in sequence.

Chiasmus also unites entire literary works, bringing out their narrative unity.[101] For example, N. W. Lund thought that Revelation and Philemon were constructed chiastically.[102] Numerous experts have shown that whole psalms are constructed chiastically, and Y. T. Radday demonstrates it is not merely an artificial device, but "a key to meaning" that unites

---

[98] An objection that these episodes are in two different chapters misses the following points: there were neither chapters nor verses when the author and the editor worked; the close proximity of 19:35 (in which the BD claims to be a trustworthy eyewitness) to 20:2 (the mention of the BD); and the crucifixion and empty tomb are conceivably one scene (the death of Jesus).

[99] X. Léon-Dufour, "Trois Chiasmues Johanniques," *NTS* 7 (1961) 249-55; Brown, *Gospel*, 1:274. Brown is critical of Léon-Dufour's arrangement; but he affirms that verses 6:36-40 "may have a history of their own," that "these verses have their own organization," and that they present a chiastic structure.

[100] See the survey of chiasm throughout ancient literatures in the studies edited by J. W. Welch titled *Chiasmus in Antiquity: Structures, Analyses, Exegesis* (Hildesheim: Gerstenberg Verlag, 1981).

[101] See the 1992 preface by D. M. Scholer and K. R. Snodgrass to N. W. Lund's valuable *Chiasmus in the New Testament: A Study in the Form and Function of Chiastic Structures* (Peabody, Mass.: Hendrickson, 1992) vii-xxi. Also see the studies on chiasm by the following: C. H. Talbert, *Literary Patterns, Theological Themes, and the Genre of Luke-Acts* (Society of Biblical Literature Monographs Series 20; Missoula: Scholars Press, 1974); D. J. Clark, "Criteria for Identifying Chiasm," *Linguistica Biblica* 35 (1975) 63-72; A. Stock, "Chiastic Awareness and Education in Antiquity," *Biblical Theology Bulletin* 14 (1984) 23-27; R. E. Man, "The Value of Chiasm for New Testament Interpretation," *Bibliotheca Sacra* 141 (1984) 146-57.

[102] Lund, *Chiasmus in the New Testament*, passim.

narratives, and entire books.[103] As N. W. Lund, R. A. Culpepper, and others have clarified, chiasmus is a literary tool used by the author of the GosJn. F. Ellis and C. H. Talbert have argued that the GosJn is structured according to chiasm,[104] In fact, the Prologue of the GosJn is structured according to chiasmus.[105]

The chiasm which seems to unite Thomas and the Beloved Disciple is as follows:

A   Thomas's exhortation to die with the Lord
  B   BD's presence at the Last Supper (beginning of passion)
    C   Thomas's question of the way
  B'   BD's presence at the crucifixion and open tomb (culmination of passion)
A'   Thomas's confession to the living Lord.

Obviously in such a chiastic structure the emphasis falls on the central member "C" (which in technical jargon is in climactic centrality). Thus the accent falls upon the question: "Thomas said to him [Jesus], 'Lord, we do not know where you are going; how is it possible to know the way?'" (14:5). This is surely central, not only to this chiastic structure, but also to the GosJn. Jesus is now able to announce, "I am the way, the truth, and the life." The exhortation in the GosJn is to call the believer to follow Jesus, who is sent from above (he is the only Son sent from the Father). Jesus is on his way back to the Father. Thomas is on center stage to ask the central question: "How can we know the way?" That is, what is the way to the Father, who has sent you? In the Johannine Community (or School) this was most likely the focal question (in contrast to Socrates' "know thyself"). Thomas's question is framed also by his exhortation to die with Jesus and his confession: "My Lord, and my God."[106]

Thirteenth, perhaps some experts on Christian origins may feel reticent to perceive the Beloved Disciple as Thomas because they assume the

[103] Y. T. Radday, "Chiasmus in Hebrew Biblical Narrative," in *Chiasmus in Antiquity*, 50–117.

[104] F. Ellis, *The Genius of John* (Collegeville: Liturgical Press, 1984); Talbert, "Artistry and Theology: An Analysis of the Architecture of Jn 1,19–5,47," *Catholic Biblical Quarterly* 32 (1970) 341–66.

[105] N. W. Lund, "The Influence of Chiasmus Upon the Structure of the Gospels," *Anglican Theological Review* 13 (1931) 42–46; R. A. Culpepper, "The Pivot of John's Prologue," *New Testament Studies* 27 (1980/1981) 1–31. J. Staley, "The Structure of John's Prologue: Its Implications for the Gospel's Narrative Structure," *Catholic Biblical Quarterly* 48 (1986) 241–64.

[106] It is possible that the Appendix, chapter 21, forms a chiastic structure with chapter 20: ABB'A', with the appearance of the BD, Thomas, Thomas, and the BD.

latter, and not the former was martyred. What is the evidence of Thomas's martyrdom? It seems relatively clear that 21:22-23 indicates both that the Beloved Disciple has died and that the author of this section cannot appeal to his martyrdom. In this case Peter seems to come off better than the Beloved Disciple, since the former's crucifixion in Rome has most likely affected the choice of words in 21:18-19.

Thomas's alleged martyrdom is clearly known. His bones were revered in Edessa, and his shrine outside the walls of this city were accorded magical powers. St. Ephraem, in *Carmina Nisibena* (42), records an early tradition:

> The devil wailed ... I stirred up Death that I might slay the Apostles.... The Apostle [clearly Thomas] whom I slew in India has come before me to Edessa.... The coffin of Thomas has slain me.[107]

The tradition of Thomas's martyrdom is also found in the apocryphal work titled *The Acts of Thomas*. Note in particular chapter 168:

> And when he [Thomas] had thus prayed he said to the soldiers, "Come here and accomplish the commandments of him who sent you." And the four came and pierced him with their spears, and he fell down and died.[108]

If this tradition is accurate, and if the Beloved Disciple did not suffer martyrdom, as suggested by the GosJn, then it would be unlikely that Thomas can be seen as the Beloved Disciple.

However, the traditions about Thomas's martyrdom are apocryphal, legendary, and tell us more about the need of Edessan Christians for apostolic authority. They are certainly far too late to help us in the search for the identity of the Beloved Disciple in the GosJn. That gospel took final shape around 100 C.E. and Ephraem lived in the fourth century C.E. The *Acts of Thomas* dates from the third century. In the period between the writing of the GosJn before 100 C.E. and the composition of these Syriac texts circa 150 C.E. the apostles were being shrouded with fabulous legends. According to Hegesippus almost all the apostles were martyred; this report tells us more about the needs of second-century Christian communities than it does about the possible identity of the Beloved Disciple. In summation, there is no reason to think that Thomas was martyred. He

---

[107] See the discussion in J. B. Segal, *Edessa: 'The Blessed City'* (Oxford: Clarendon Press, 1970) 175.

[108] J. K. Elliott, ed., *The Apocryphal New Testament: A Collection of Apocryphal Christian Literature in an English Translation* (Oxford: Clarendon, 1993) 510.

continues to loom large in the search for the identity of the Beloved Disciple.

Fourteenth, many critics will undoubtedly claim that Thomas cannot be the Beloved Disciple, because this epithet is simply a symbol and does not represent an historical figure. They may claim that he represents only an idea or a concept. Many New Testament scholars may be drawn over to this possibility since there seems to be a growing penchant to see the Gospels and Acts as only literature without any historical facts. For me, however, proclamation and history are inseparable in the New Testament documents. In the GosJn apologetics and polemics are anchored in sociological crises. The Beloved Disciple cannot be merely a literary typos; chapter 21 in the GosJn shows that he was a figure known to the Johannine Community (see chap. 1.2).

As we have attempted to show in the previous pages, chapter 21, which may be an appendix but must be incorporated in any search for the identification of the Beloved Disciple, clarifies that this person was a real historical individual. The commentators, and most of the authors of the major monographs on the Beloved Disciple, have demonstrated that the author of the GosJn and the editor of chapter 21 present us with a real historical figure, whose death shocked the Johannine Christians and shook their faith. The ones who have given us the GosJn are gifted linguistically and were masters of symbolism. They certainly knew that Peter, Judas Iscariot, and Thomas were not only symbolical figures, but also historical individuals. Symbolical theology was grounded in historical reality.

To claim that the Beloved Disciple is only a symbol undermines the whole thrust of Johannine theology: Jesus was real; the Logos became flesh. The GosJn anchors and gives meaning to symbolism by presenting, sometimes through the rhetoric of irony, the incarnation of the One sent from above.

Fifteenth, exegetes familiar with the GosJn may well claim that the author and editor of the gospel never mentioned the name of the Beloved Disciple. They may claim that this individual is always anonymous in the GosJn, even though the members of the Johannine School (and some in the Johannine Community) knew his identity. They may ask why I assume the name is given in the GosJn.

The answer should begin with another question: Why should one assume the name does *not* appear in the GosJn? That is an equally awkward position, yet both may be defended from a careful exegetical study of the GosJn. Furthermore, to contend that the name is never supplied does not mean the Evangelist did not know the identity of the Beloved Disciple. As most Johannine experts have attempted to show, the Evangelist knew the identity of the Beloved Disciple and diligent study might well disclose his perspective. I have come to recognize that the Evangelist slowly unravels the enigma of the identity of the Beloved Disciple. He seems to do so with refined narrative art.

I did not assume that the name must be found in the GosJn, but I discovered that there is a progressive disclosure from chapters 1 to 20. At first the Beloved Disciple is mentioned only anonymously; he is a former follower of John the Baptist. At the Last Supper he is revealed partially with the words, "the disciple whom Jesus loved." This epithet continues to be used in chapters 19 and 20. Finally, in chapter 20 the Beloved Disciple "sees and believes." He goes home. The rhetoric of suspense demands that he return. The Evangelist skillfully narrates that only Thomas is clearly stated not to be present when Jesus appears to the "disciples." He later demands to see the marks of crucifixion and specifically the wound in the side, which was witnessed only by the Beloved Disciple. Thus, as the Beloved Disciple, and before the risen Jesus, he can present the culminating and supreme confession. That is why I think his name is given in the GosJn. It is not an unexamined presupposition; it is an exegetical discovery that attends to the narrative art of the GosJn.[109]

Sixteenth, some New Testament experts may argue that the Beloved Disciple cannot be Thomas because the former, but not the latter, was perfect. It is certainly true that the Beloved Disciple represents the ideal follower of Jesus, but that hardly exhibits perfection. In the GosJn no one who was a real person of history was perfect or walked always in the light. The author of the GosJn makes it pellucidly clear that Jesus alone is from above. All others are from below. No follower of Jesus was ideal like the Beloved Disciple, which has led some experts to slip into the fallacy of thinking that this figure is only a symbol. As so many experts have stressed, John the son of Zebedee was never seen as perfect; he is fallible and flawed. To appeal to Lazarus as perfect is to confront the fact that no action or word can be seen in a pejorative way since he does and says nothing according to the GosJn. Moreover, inaction or lack of full action (as with Nicodemus and Joseph of Arimathea, and with the early responses by the man born blind in chap. 9) is condemned by the author of the GosJn.

The Syriac Gospel of the Twelve Apostles helps clarify Thomas's place in early Christian lore. He is from the tribe of Benjamin (Syriac = *wt'wm' mn šbt' dbnymn*).[110] That means he is from the same tribe as Jere-

---

[109] Of course, I have continuously contended that one should not go to the Synoptics or elsewhere to interpret the GosJn; thus, if the name is not given in the GosJn, we have no other place to look. So, I looked through the GosJn and was astonished to discover that the BD is Thomas.

[110] See fol. 48 a of the Syriac in J. R. Harris, ed., *The Gospel of the Twelve Apostles* (Cambridge: Cambridge Univ. Press, 1900).

miah (Jer 1:1) and Paul (Ro 11:1, Php 3:5).[111] He is one of the Twelve to whom Jesus "promised thrones that they may judge Israel." Hence, Thomas should not be assumed to be one unworthy of being the Beloved Disciple; he was one who was ideal, courageous, and faithful, finally supplying the supreme confession.

The disciples are Sons of Light, but they lack perception and understanding. The author of the GosJn does not show the disciples growing in perception and understanding. They do not know, for example, that Jesus has food from above (4:32, cf. 3:4, 4:10-11, 4:22, 7:29, 8:14-15, 19:54-55). Their understanding comes, as Bultmann showed, only after he has returned to the Father (14:15-24, 16:7, 25-33, esp. 20:9).[112] As at Qumran the cosmic spirit, the Spirit of Truth, abides among and within them (14:17); but also as at Qumran, the Sons of Light are not one hundred percent light (as we shall see). Jesus' disciples are men of slow understanding and defective in faith, even during the Last Supper conversations with their master.[113] The connection in these passages between ignorance and darkness is not explicit, but it is implied; as Sons of Light the disciples are not full of light. As R. H. Lightfoot stated, "even among the twelve evil is at work."[114]

As has been demonstrated by many specialists, the anthropology of the GosJn has been influenced, in ways not yet clear, by the concepts uniquely developed in the Dead Sea Scrolls. As in the Scrolls (1QS 3.13-4.26) so in the GosJn there are two types of people, and these are defined in terms of the light-darkness paradigm. From the Qumran Scrolls the author of the GosJn probably inherited the *terminus technicus* "the Sons of Light." This is well known and widely acknowledged.[115]

What is not so obvious is the observation that clearly at Qumran and very nuanced in the GosJn is the conception that the Sons of Light have portions of darkness. According to the Qumranic 4Q186 all Sons of Light have portions of light and darkness. The most perfect ones have eight

[111] Is it possible that since he was considered to be from the tribe of Benjamin, like Jeremiah, Thomas represented a rejection of Zion theology (as we find in Isaiah) and an emphasis on the traditions of the Exodus, Covenant, and Conquest? If so, then it is understandable how he, with these universal models of redemption, became the saint of the East. For a discussion of the Benjamin traditions see G. von Rad, *Old Testament Theology*, trans. D. M. G. Stalker (New York: Harper & Row, 1965) 2:192.

[112] Bultmann, *John*, 195.

[113] See Schnackenburg, *St. John*, 3:207.

[114] R. H. Lightfoot, *St. John's Gospel: A Commentary*, ed. D. F. Evans (Oxford: Clarendon Press, 1956) 70.

[115] See, e.g., the contributions in Charlesworth, ed., *John and the Dead Sea Scrolls*.

scoops of light and one of darkness (4Q186 2). All Sons of Light need to be purified of their darkness by study, dedication, meditation, purification, and especially by the purifying of the Holy Spirit (see 1QS, CD, 1QH, 11QTemple). This idea may well be reflected in the GosJn, but it is presented in narrative form, so that Peter, Thomas, and others show both traits of light and darkness. The author of the GosJn apparently alludes to this concept, with an intentional paronomasia among the words "bathed," "washed," and "cleansed," when he portrays Jesus washing his disciples' feet. He is made to say "The one having bathed has no need, except to have his feet washed; but he is wholly cleansed; and you are cleansed ones" (13:10). This is surely an acted parable with deep spiritual symbolic meaning, disclosing, among other insights perhaps, that the Sons of Light need to be purified of their darkness.

As at Qumran (1QS 10-11, 1QH 3-5) so in the GosJn, God is portrayed as the One who purifies—in the GosJn he is the vine dresser who prunes the vine, the disciples. Jesus' disciples are Sons of Light, they are with him who is the Light; they are "not of the world" but called "out of the world" (15:19, 17:6) so that Jesus can send them "into the world" (17:18). Bultmann correctly stressed that the fundamental meaning of the world in the GosJn is darkness;[116] hence the disciples are called by Jesus to follow him and no longer "walk in darkness" (8:12). As in the Dead Sea Scrolls, in which a concept of predestination is developed in a unique way in Early Judaism,[117] so in the GosJn the Sons of Light are the ones God has elected.[118] As at Qumran, so it seems that in the Johannine Community the Sons of Light, because of the portions of darkness in them, sometimes err and walk in the ways of darkness.

Thomas, as all Jesus' disciples, walks not only in the light, but also in the darkness. The author of the GosJn in 2:25 claims that Jesus knew what was within the human (αὐτὸς γὰρ ἐγίνωσκεν τί ἦν ἐν τῷ ἀνθρώπῳ). Jesus knew the dual nature and the struggle between the forces of light and darkness in each human. Thomas, and every human, has one goal: to ascend to the light and to follow Jesus, the Light, who has returned to the Father to prepare the Way for the Sons of Light. He has sent the Paraclete, the Spirit of Truth, the Holy Spirit, to cleanse them of the darkness that remains in them. Thomas, who is on the way of becoming a purified Son of Light (12:36), remains the ideal candidate for the Beloved Disciple.

[116] Bultmann, *Theology of the New Testament*, trans. K. Grobel (New York: Charles Scribner's Sons, 1955) 2:15.

[117] See my discussion in the introduction to H. Ringgren's *Faith of Qumran* (COL; New York: Crossroad, 1995) xi, xx-xi.

[118] See Schnackenburg, *St. John*, 2:264.

CHAPTER 6

The Beloved Disciple
and "the Other"

In two chapters in the GosJn the Beloved Disciple is conceivably present through a reference to a disciple who is also anonymous. Our task is now to seek to discern if the anonymous disciple in chapters 1 and 18 might be the Beloved Disciple, as Kragerud, Cullmann, Brown, and numerous Johannine experts have concluded.[1] As in previous examinations, we will benefit from a sensitivity to the narrative and drama of the GosJn and the formulae that might connect an anonymous disciple with the Beloved Disciple explicitly mentioned in chapters 13, 19, and 20 (and in the Appendix). As D. M. Smith stated, we are invited by the "simple yet mysterious character of Johannine language" to pause and reflect, then "to inquire about and explore its meaning."[2]

The connection between an anonymous disciple—"another disciple"—and the Beloved Disciple is made explicit in chapter 20. Disturbed by what she has seen, Mary Magdalene runs to communicate this information to Peter and "another disciple" (καὶ πρὸς τὸν ἄλλον μαθητήν). This "other disciple" is then specified as the one ὃν ἐφίλει ὁ Ἰησοῦς (20:2). Thus, the exegete of the GosJn should seek to discern if earlier the

---

[1] Kragerud, *Lieblingsjünger*, 12–13, and 19–21; Cullmann, *The Johannine Circle*, 77–78; Brown, *Community*, 31–34; Brown, *Gospel*, 1:73; 2:822. Brown is clear that chapter 1 refers to the BD (32–33); he is hesitant about that identification in chapter 18 ("Obviously no certain solution is possible" [823]). I agree with Brown on chapter 1, but am convinced that chapter 18 does not refer to the BD. J. A. T. Robinson saluted Cullmann and Brown's judgment on the identity of the anonymous disciple in chapters 1 and 18 (*The Priority of John* [London: SCM Press, 1985] 109).

[2] Smith, *Johannine Christianity: Essays on Its Setting, Sources, and Theology* (Columbia, S.C.: Univ. of South Carolina Press, 1989) 186.

Beloved Disciple is presented simply as "another disciple" or with a similar expression. As Neirynck states, 20:2 has been "the main argument" for claiming that the "another disciple" of 18:15-16 is none other than the Beloved Disciple.[3]

While chapter 20, the original ending of the GosJn, suggests a link between "the other disciple" and the Beloved Disciple, chapter 21, the Appendix to the GosJn, presents a contradictory insight. In 21:2 the reader is introduced to two anonymous disciples of Jesus (καὶ ἄλλοι ἐκ τῶν μαθητῶν αὐτοῦ δύο.). We obtain a major insight from this verse in light of the subsequent drama in which it becomes clear that the Beloved Disciple is included in the list of disciples given in 21:2. Distinguished scholars, notably Brown and Schnackenburg, have now concluded that the Beloved Disciple is one of the anonymous disciples of 21:2. If that is the case, then the Beloved Disciple may be hidden elsewhere in the GosJn behind the concept of "other."

But another observation must also be made. Since there are two "other" disciples that are anonymous in 21:2, both of them cannot be the Beloved Disciple. Hence, there is at least one disciple who is anonymous in the GosJn who cannot be the Beloved Disciple. That means references in the GosJn to "other" or "another" do not necessarily mean the Beloved Disciple.[4] Hence, we can now explore the passages in the GosJn in which "other," "another," or some striking anonymity occurs, being warned that the mere appearance of "other" or "another" may, but does not necessarily, represent the Beloved Disciple. The key chapters are 1 and 18.

6.1 THE ANONYMOUS DISCIPLE IN CHAPTER ONE

Who is the anonymous disciple in 1:35-40? It is difficult to imagine that the author of the GosJn, who worked within a community that could well be designated a "school" (and which the BD most likely founded),[5] has failed to give the disciple's name, because he has forgotten it.[6] There must

---

[3] Neirynck, "The 'Other Disciple' in Jn 18,15-16," *Ephemerides Theologicae Lovanienses* 51 (1975) 113–41; see esp. 136.

[4] Culpepper, who has made numerous contributions to an elucidation of the identity of the BD, concludes from focusing only on 20:2 (and not seeing the importance of 21:2) that we should "treat John 18:15-16 as a scene involving the Beloved Disciple" ("Beloved Disciple: The Apostle in the Fourth Gospel," in *John, the Son of Zebedee: The Life of a Legend* [Studies on Personalities of the New Testament; Columbia, S.C.: Univ. of South Carolina, 1994] 56–88; see esp. 58).

[5] As Culpepper shows in *The Johannine School*, and discussed earlier.

[6] See Kragerud's judicious comments in *Der Lieblingsjünger im Johannesevangelium*, 13.

be another symbolical meaning. The reader is invited to seek the identity of the anonymous one; neither the qualifying phrase "the one whom Jesus loved," nor the term ἄλλος appears in this section to designate the anonymous disciple. In this passage we find the phrase εἷς ἐκ τῶν δύο. This seems to be a formula; it is the same phrase with which the Beloved Disciple is clearly mentioned in chapter 13; he is εἷς ἐκ τῶν μαθητῶν αὐτοῦ. This phrase, εἷς ἐκ τῶν, is a favorite for the author of the GosJn; it is found in the following passages:

εἷς ἐκ τῶν δύο	1:40 [= an anonymous disciple]
εἷς ἐκ τῶν μαθητῶν	6:8 [= Andrew]
εἷς [ἐκ] τῶν μαθητῶν	12:4 (ἐκ is suspect [= Judas Iscariot])[7]
εἷς ἐκ τῶν μαθητῶν	13:23 [= BD]
εἷς ἐκ τῶν δούλων	18:26 [= an anonymous slave]
εἷς ἐκ τῶν δώδεκα	6:71 [= Judas Iscariot]
εἷς ἐκ τῶν δώδεκα	20:24 [= Thomas][8]

The phrase εἷς ἐκ τῶν is not *prima facie* evidence that the Beloved Disciple is in the mind of the author in 1:40. But, it is significant that only the Beloved Disciple (13:23), Andrew, Judas Iscariot, and Thomas along with the anonymous disciple of 1:40 are disciples who are so introduced in the GosJn.

Numerous questions arise as this list is studied. How significant is it that one of the slaves is presented in the narrative by this phrase?[9] Is there any importance in the observation that Andrew is associated with the one mentioned in 1:40 and the person designated by the phrase in its next occurrence (in 6:8)? If the Beloved Disciple is the anonymous one of 1:40, then why does he not appear again with Andrew in the GosJn? Were they not close, having once been the only two of John's disciples who followed Jesus?[10]

---

[7] The ἐκ does not occur in some early and noteworthy witnesses to the Greek New Testament. For full evidence and an assessment, see B. M. Metzger, *A Textual Commentary on the Greek New Testament* (London/New York: United Bible Societies, 1994 [2nd ed.]) 201.

[8] In 12:2 Lazarus is described as εἷς ἦν ἐκ τῶν ἀνακειμένων. In 13:21 Judas Iscariot is presented as εἷς ἐξ ὑμῶν.

[9] On slavery within Judaism see the subsequent footnote to the slave who is named Malcus. For an understanding of slavery in the Roman world I have benefited from A. Kirschenbaum, *Sons, Slaves and Freedmen in Roman Commerce* (Jerusalem: Magnes; Washington, D.C.: Catholic Univ. of America Press, 1987).

[10] Also, if the BD is Thomas, then it is strange that Andrew is not linked with him in other pericopes in the GosJn. Note how Andrew and Philip are presented together in 12:21-23; does it not seem strange that Andrew does not

What suggestions are stimulated by reflections on this list? If Thomas is the Beloved Disciple, then it is significant that the anonymous one in 1:40, the Beloved Disciple in 13:23, and Thomas himself are presented with this phrase. That amounts to three out of the five undisputed uses of the formula to designate one of Jesus' disciples. The last two occurrences of the formula are associated with the Twelve; moreover, only disciples who are most likely, or clearly are (Judas and Thomas), members of the Twelve are designated by the phrase. These insights might add additional strength, if any is needed, to our conclusion that the Beloved Disciple was one of the Twelve (see chap. 2.3).

Focusing upon 1:40 we learn that the author of the GosJn mentioned two disciples who left John the Baptist and began to follow Jesus; one of them is revealed to be Andrew, but the other disciple is not named. Who could he be? Can we find additional support for the hypothesis that this anonymous disciple is the Beloved Disciple?

There is indeed another link between the mention of the two former disciples of the Baptist and the first clear presentation of the Beloved Disciple. Note the use of ἦν in 1:40 and 13:23; the asyndeton with ἦν "is the most obvious linguistic similarity between both" passages, according to F. Neirynck.[11] Here are the verses presented in which ἦν appears at the beginning of a sentence but without an accompanying connective with what proceeded:

> ἦν Ἀνδρέας ... εἷς ἐκ τῶν δύο τῶν ἀκουσάντων παρὰ Ἰωάννου (1:40)
> ἦν ἀνακείμενος εἷς ἐκ τῶν μαθητῶν αὐτοῦ (13:23)

In these two passages we have the asyndetic use of ἦν, the formula—εἷς ἐκ τῶν—and the genitive of person (Ἰωάννου and αὐτοῦ). This forges a strong link between the Beloved Disciple and the anonymous one who formerly followed John the Baptist.[12] The asyndetic use of ἦν appears only in 1:40 and 13:23; and that is highly significant since ἦν appears at the beginning of sentences in the Johannine narrative 36 times, but only in

---

appear with Thomas or the BD? Philip, but not Andrew, may be presented in close relation with Thomas in 14:4–14:8. While these questions may remain puzzling from a narrative exegesis of the GosJn, they can be explained by the social context of the GosJn. The Johannine Community founded its belief on the witness of the BD; it was not interested in explaining the relation between the BD and the other former followers of John the Baptist.

[11] F. Neirynck, "The Anonymous Disciple in John 1," *Ephemerides Theologicae Lovanienses* 66 (1990) 25.

[12] Asyndeton is possibly a Semitism, and may reflect an Aramaic source at this point. See C. F. Burney, *The Aramaic Origin of the Fourth Gospel* (Oxford: Clarendon Press, 1922) 150–51.

1:40 and 13:23 is it—as H.-J. Kuhn pointed out—"completely asyndetic."[13] We have thus found impressive philological evidence to suggest
that the anonymous disciple of 1:40 is most likely the Beloved Disciple.[14]
That is, through linguistic subtleties the narrator is linking the introduction
of the Beloved Disciple in chapter 13 with the introduction of Jesus' first
disciple, who seems also to be the Beloved Disciple.[15]

Let us remember that a first-time reader of the GosJn would have no
reason at all to think that chapter 1 refers to the Beloved Disciple.[16] The
question then becomes refined: Is that identification intended by the author
of the GosJn or in his thought, and would members of the Johannine
Community (or School) who knew the identity of the Beloved Disciple
recognize immediately that he was meant by the ambiguity of this pericope? If the Beloved Disciple is intended by $εἷς ἐκ τῶν δύο$ in 1:40, then it
becomes clear why in chapter 21 Peter must be told by Jesus to follow
him and not the Beloved Disciple, who in 1:37 is said to "follow" Jesus.

Evidence that the anonymous disciple in 1:35-42 may be the
Beloved Disciple is found in our research on the question whether the
Beloved Disciple was a member of the Twelve (see chap. 2.3). We
learned that there is impressive evidence in the GosJn that the Beloved
Disciple was one of the Twelve. Most importantly for us now, is the
recognition that Jesus had said to the Twelve that they had been with him
from the beginning ($ἀπ' ἀρχῆς μετ' ἐμοῦ ἐστε.$ [15:27]). Thus, it seems
to follow that the Beloved Disciple was mentioned in chapter 1 and was
present at the *beginning of Jesus' ministry*. It would then seem evident
from our previous research that he is not one of the disciples named in
chapter 1, namely Andrew, Simon Peter (Cephas), Philip,[17] or Nathanael.

[13] H.-J. Kuhn, *Christologie und Wunder: Untersuchungen zu Joh 1,35-51*
(Biblische Untersuchungen 18; Regensburg: Verlag Friedrich Pustet, 1988) 106.

[14] The linguistic link does not prove that the Beloved Disciple is to be seen
in chapter 1. Hence, Neirynck admits that there "are real resemblances between
1,40 and 13,23," but he concludes that chapter 1 does not contain a reference to
the BD (*Ephemerides Theologicae Lovanienses* 66 [1990] 27, 36).

[15] For a guide to scholars' opinions on whether the BD is meant by the
anonymous disciple in chapter 1, see F. Neirynck, "The Anonymous Disciple in
John 1," *Ephemerides Theologicae Lovanienses* 66 (1990) 5-37. Neirynck concludes that Kuhn is wrong: Kuhn's parallels "are unable to support the identification of the anonymous in 1,35-39 as the Beloved Disciple" (36).

[16] Schnackenburg is convinced that the identification of the anonymous
disciple in chapters 1 and 18 with the BD is "fragwürdig" and so does not
include these chapters in his search for the identity of the BD ("Der Jünger,"
100).

[17] Boismard concludes that the anonymous disciple is Philip (*Du Baptême à
Cana: Jean 1.19-2.11* [Paris: Cerf, 1956] 72-73). Philip and Andrew do appear
together in the Johannine narrative (6:5-9, 12:21-22). Colson was also convinced
that the "compagnon d'André, dans cette page de la vocation des premiers disci-

Thus it becomes more conceivable that the Beloved Disciple would be the unnamed disciple of 1:35-42.

Cullmann was convinced that the Beloved Disciple is the anonymous one of chapter 1. He pointed to two factors. First, both the Beloved Disciple and the unnamed former follower of John the Baptist are anonymous. We saw that, in light of chapter 21, this anonymity is not sufficient evidence to clinch the argument.

Cullmann had a second point: the Beloved Disciple and the anonymous one of chapter 1 are "*set alongside Peter.*"[18] His comment here is insightful. The anonymous former follower of the Baptist is presented in the narrative before Peter, and before his companion, Andrew, proceeds to find his brother and bring him to Jesus. Andrew's brother was Peter, whose name Jesus changed to "Cephas."[19] Thus, as in almost all of the passages in which the Beloved Disciple appears, he is superior to Peter; the same seems to be the case, albeit less strikingly, in chapter 1. The anonymous disciple appears and follows Jesus before Peter is even introduced into the narrative.

The anonymous disciple, and former follower of the Baptist, is the first disciple introduced to the reader. That observation should add credence to the proposition that he is the hero of the GosJn, the Beloved Disciple. If Thomas is the Beloved Disciple then he is the disciple who appears in the first and final scenes. The dramatic skill of the Evangelist becomes even more impressive with this observation, and the development of the drama is one from anonymity to identity of the leading character.[20]

This conclusion would indicate that Andrew and the Beloved Disciple were formerly disciples of John the Baptist. The scenario fits well with the inordinate emphasis placed on John the Baptist in the opening of the GosJn; that is, if the witness behind the GosJn was the Beloved Disciple, a former follower of John the Baptist, then it is understandable why John the Baptist looms so importantly in the GosJn, and why Jesus is portrayed as leading a baptist movement beside and in association with John the Baptist in this gospel.

---

ples, pourrait donc bien être l'apôtre Philippe" (*L'Énigme du disciple que Jésus aimait*, 14).

[18] Cullmann, *The Johannine Circle*, 72.

[19] Jesus certainly did not change a disciple's name to "the one whom I love." But, he could have changed the BD's name to Thomas, in the sense that he is Jesus' spiritual twin, who will function as the Paraclete after Jesus returns to his Father.

[20] I exclude for the moment Jesus as the dominant character in the GosJn; that is obvious, but I think it is best to focus on supporting characters as we seek to discern the identity of the hero.

Similar reasoning persuaded Eller in his *The Beloved Disciple* to conclude that the Beloved Disciple is the anonymous one of 1:35-42. He is impressed by the disruption of the Prologue by two intrusive comments. In 1:6-8 and 1:15 the Evangelist presents John the Baptist to make the point that while John was a true servant of God, he was not the Word or the Light. The *Tendenz* of the passages regarding John the Baptist convinces Eller that it represents the Beloved Disciple's self-justifying *apologia pro vita sua*. Eller contends that the passages about John the Baptist mirror the fact that the Beloved Disciple "had probably come under criticism—his Jewish enemies even accusing him of being a fence-jumper and traitor for the way in which he had deserted the Baptist in order to join Jesus."[21] Perhaps Eller is correct, but Bretschneider's argument of over a hundred years ago is still persuasive;[22] that is, the references to John the Baptist in the GosJn are shaped by a rivalry between followers of Jesus and followers of John the Baptist.[23] That is, the GosJn reflects a polemic between those who claimed that Jesus is the One sent by God and those who argued that the One is John the Baptist.[24]

Eller's argument is, nevertheless, somewhat persuasive, and his position and Bretschneider's insight, which I take to be valid, are not necessarily incompatible. The assumption that the Beloved Disciple, the witness behind the GosJn, was once a follower of the Baptist helps explain otherwise disruptive passages, like 3:25-30, which chronicle a debate between disciples of John the Baptist and another Jew over purification.

---

[21] Eller, *The Beloved Disciple*, 50.

[22] K. G. Bretschneider, *Probabilia de evangelii et epistolarum Joannis, apostoli, indole et origine* (Leipzig: Jo. Ambros, Barthii, 1820). See esp. his comments on 5: "Chapters 1:7-8, 15, 19-28, 30-36, 3:25ff., 5:33-37, and 10:41ff show that the author of the GosJn was writing against the followers of John the Baptist *(baptistae discipulis opposita esse)*."

[23] The Mandaeans are offshoots of either a pre-Christian group somehow associated with John the Baptist or a divergent type of Christianity. In either case the Baptist plays a significant role and "John the Baptist's Prayer" is found in the Mandaean Prayerbook. See E. S. Drower, *The Canonical Prayerbook of the Mandaeans* (Leiden: Brill, 1959) 315-16. I am persuaded that this Prayer of the Baptist most likely does not derive from him; it seems more likely that it may have been composed to fulfill the need for such a prayer in light of Lk 11:1, where Jesus' disciples asked him, "O Lord, teach us to pray, as also John taught his disciples."

[24] W. Baldensperger's insight is also found in his *Der Prolog des vierten Evangeliums: sein polemisch-apologetischer Zweck* (Freiburg: J. C. B. Mohr [Siebeck], 1898) 71-74. His position is generally endorsed by J. Thomas, who stated that the "quatrième évangile fournit un argument indirect, mais solide, de l'existence de la secte des Johannites" (*Le mouvement baptiste en Palestine et Syrie* [Gembloux: Duculot, 1935] 109).

In *Jesus im Horizont der Evangelien* Ruckstuhl explains why he is convinced that the Beloved Disciple is to be identified with the anonymous disciple of 1:35-42. Especially insightful is his perception of an *inclusio* ("eine absichtliche Rahmung")[25] between chapters 1 and 21. In 1:35 an anonymous disciple, the Beloved Disciple, is introduced; then a disciple, revealed to be Andrew, is given a significant action (1:40-42). In 21:2 two anonymous disciples are mentioned, and then a disciple, revealed to be the Beloved Disciple, is given a significant declaration (21:7).

This *inclusio* would have been provided by the editor who added chapter 21, in my opinion. But this editor belonged to the Johannine Community and was very familiar with Johannine language and symbolism (see my chap. 2 and the introduction to the exegesis of 13:23-26). I agree with Ruckstuhl that chapters 1 and 21 frame the introduction and exodus of the Beloved Disciple. The *inclusio*, I am convinced, may be explained as follows: In chapter 1 the anonymous former follower of the Baptist, the Beloved Disciple, is introduced and follows Jesus who invites him to "come and see" (1:37-39). In chapter 21 the name of the Beloved Disciple is subtly introduced in the list of disciples. If he is Thomas, then as the Beloved Disciple (21:7) he alone sees that the stranger on the shore is Jesus, and exclaims "It is the Lord" (21:7).

The connection between 1 and 21 would not be lost on the reader,[26] who was taught or learned from studying the GosJn that in the first episode the Beloved Disciple is accompanied by Andrew—the brother of Peter—and in the final scenario he is accompanied by Peter—the brother of Andrew. Moreover, in the first part of the *inclusio* Andrew exclaims to Peter: εὑρήκαμεν τὸν Μεσσίαν (1:41); and in the second part of the *inclusio* the Beloved Disciple exclaims to Peter: ὁ κύριός ἐστιν (21:7). Finally, the framing seems to be molded with actions occurring with water in the background or foreground. Indeed, the movement Christologically is from background (Messiah, and the water of Bethany)[27] to foreground (the Lord, the Sea of Tiberias in the promised land),[28] so that Peter is des-

[25] Ruckstuhl, *Jesus im Horizont der Evangelien*, 392.

[26] The GosJn was probably directed to Christians who sought the deeper meaning of God's good news about Jesus. In the GosJn the Greek is bewitchingly simple, but the message is profoundly deep.

[27] There must be water in Bethany beyond the Jordan because "John was baptizing" there (1:28). The original readers of the GosJn probably knew the meaning of the geography in it; which is not always to be dismissed as mere symbolism since some of the sites have now been shown to be factual (see Brown, *Gospel*, 1:45).

[28] A Joshua-Jesus typology may well be in the mind of our author; that is, as Joshua led the people of Israel into the Promised Land, so Jesus leads those who believe in the One from above into the land of eternal life, paradise (cf. OdesSol 11).

cribed as jumping into the sea (21:7). Hence, while "Messiah" is tied to early Jewish theology and needs to be translated in 1:41, "Lord" moves the good news out beyond such boundaries (since the Greeks have come, and wish to see Jesus, and so signal that Jesus' hour has come [12:20-23]). Perceiving the *inclusio* between 1:35-42 and 21:1-8 helps to strengthen the hypothesis that the Beloved Disciple is intended in the former pericope. Thus, far from being concretely and theologically uninteresting as Lorenzen claimed, 1:35-42 initiates a dramatic presentation of the Beloved Disciple that shows what is real, living, and dynamic faithfulness to the One who is from above.[29]

The importance of perceiving the Beloved Disciple within the baptist circles becomes even more clear in the exegesis of 1:14, "and the Word became flesh." When did this occur? As C. H. Talbert has shown,

> the most attractive time when the divine power of the Logos was manifest in the truly human Jesus was at his baptism. As we have endeavored to show elsewhere in this monograph, the Beloved Disciple probably saw this monumental event. He and John the Baptist were the *two male* witnesses of this epochal moment.[30]

As we endeavored to demonstrate in the preceding chapter, two male witnesses are needed to prove the claim that the Spirit descended and remained on Jesus. This requirement is fulfilled if the Baptist and his protégé both witness it independently. Also, the witness needs to be the trustworthy witness of the GosJn, the Beloved Disciple.

C. H. Clergeon astutely points to the parallelism and linguistic link between chapter 1 and 19 focusing upon 1:34 and 19:35. In both cases the reader is presented with an individual who sees and witnesses. He claims that "les textes du début et ceux de la fin se correspondent étroitement."[31] He then proceeds to conclude that the author's name is probably "John" since in the parallel to 19:35 the anonymous one is John the Baptist:

> On peut effectivement se demander si le nom de l'évangéliste n'est pas livré indirectement, de façon discrète, à l'aide du parallélisme.

---

[29] Lorenzen, *Lieblingsjünger*, 45: "Der andere, anonym gebliebene Jünger bleibt sachlich und theologisch uninteressant, and es besteht kein Anlass, ihn mit dem Lieblingsjünger zu identifizieren bzw. anzunehmen, dass der Evangelist ihn mit dem Lieblingsjünger identifiziert habe."

[30] Talbert, "'And the Word Became Flesh': When?" in *The Future of Christology* [the L. E. Keck Festschrift], ed. A. J. Malherbe and W. A. Meeks (Minneapolis: Fortress, 1993) 43–52.

[31] C. H. Clergeon, "Le quatrième évangile indique-t-il le nom de son auteur?" *Biblica* 56 (1975) 32–36; cf. 35.

> Comme le premier témoignage au début de l'évangile, le témoignage
> final que lisent les chrétiens a été apporté par un homme 'dont le nom
> était Jean.'"[32]

I doubt that the Evangelist was discreetly hiding the name "John," but the
evidence is strongly in favor of the exegesis which indicates that the
Beloved Disciple is implicit in chapter 1.

Grassi is so convinced that the Beloved Disciple knew Jesus when he
led a baptist movement in the wilderness that he paints a scenario that
reminds me of the romance in modern Jesus' novels; but it may not be far
from the truth. Note his comments in *The Secret Identity of the Beloved
Disciple:*

> As a young lad he met Jesus by the Jordan River with John the Bap-
> tist, whose close disciple and protégé he had been. The beloved disci-
> ple was from Judea, probably Jerusalem. ... During the time John and
> Jesus were together by the Jordan, a deep bond of teacher/disciple
> grew up between the two. Jesus adopted the youngster as his own son
> in a strong affectionate relationship. (115)

Since the fact that the Beloved Disciple is mentioned anonymously in
chapter 1, and that he was a former follower of John the Baptist may well
lead to such historical imagining, we dare never forget that our evidence,
the text, cannot substantiate such a clear vision of the past. The picture,
nevertheless, is certainly intriguing.

In *The Community of the Beloved Disciple*, Brown speaks to the
objection that the Beloved Disciple cannot be the unnamed disciple of
1:35-42 because he is not called "the disciple whom Jesus loved."[33] His
response also helps explain why he was beloved by Jesus. Here are his
words:

> The unnamed disciple of chap. 1 was not *yet* the Beloved Disciple
> because at the beginning of the Gospel story he had not yet come to
> understand Jesus fully—a christological development that would place
> a distance between him and the other named disciples of chap. 1 and
> would bring him uniquely close to Jesus. Consonant with the theory
> that the Gospel is giving us an insight into Johannine ecclesiological
> growth, I think it no accident that the Beloved Disciple makes his
> appearance by name only in "the hour" (13:1) when Jesus, having
> loved his own, "now showed his love for them to the very end." This

---

[32] Ibid., 36.

[33] Culpepper, however, is convinced that there is no suggestion that 1:35-42
refers to the BD (*John, the Son of Zebedee*, 59).

does not mean that this Disciple was not present during the ministry, but that he achieved his *identity* in a christological context.[34]

These insights and mature reflections are helpful; but if the Beloved Disciple is concealed as the anonymous one of 21:2 then we do not see a clear development of an anonymous disciple in the GosJn. If, however, he is identified with a named disciple—Thomas, for example—then an ecclesiological development can be followed and become a paradigm for others' growth, a requisite for the Beloved Disciple who is indeed the model for ideal discipleship.

Note how such a development springs out of the Johannine narrative and drama, if the Beloved Disciple is Thomas. The disciple appears in the very first scenes as a follower of John the Baptist; but he is anonymous. The superiority of Jesus over John, one who is also sent into the world, is clarified by the Beloved Disciple's witness recorded by the author of the GosJn. He then as Thomas, the leader of the Twelve, exhorts his fellow disciples to be willing to die with Jesus. Then he is called the Beloved Disciple at the beginning of the Last Supper, reclining on Jesus' chest in a position of authority and honor. He thus appears as "the disciple whom Jesus loved" immediately after an action of love—Jesus' washing the feet of his disciples—and before the only new commandment: Jesus' paraenesis to love as he has shown how to love.

During the Last Supper the Beloved Disciple asks Jesus the central question for discipleship—"O Lord, we do not know where you are going; how can we know the way ($\tau\dot{\eta}\nu$ $\dot{o}\delta\dot{o}\nu$ [14:5])?" Next, he is shown as the only disciple standing at the cross beneath Jesus. He has followed Jesus until the end. He is the only disciple with Jesus when he dies; thus he alone obeys the exhortation in 11:16, his first words in the GosJn. The narrator describes him alone observing how the soldier's lance is thrust into Jesus' side. Three days later he hears Mary Magdalene's report to him and Peter and runs to the tomb. He sees and believes; and he goes home.

Later his fellow disciples inform him, "We have seen the Lord" (20:25). He answers that he will not believe such possibly hope-generated faith. He must see and verify (touch) the lance wound that would distinguish Jesus from anyone else. He knows that aspect of the crucifixion only because he alone witnessed it. Then eight days later, when he is with his fellow disciples, he sees the risen Jesus with the requisite wound. He does not touch Jesus. Jesus urges him no longer to distrust the reports of others regarding his resurrection, but to believe because he has seen for himself. He then—on center stage and in the spotlight with Jesus alone—

[34] Brown, *Community*, 33.

presents the climactic confession: "My Lord and my God." That scenario presents us with an impressive development.

The Beloved Disciple's (Thomas's) faithful following and continuous believing cannot be shattered by the possibility that someone has stolen Jesus' corpse. It is dynamic, growing faith, and is not eager to believe easily or from possibly weak-minded claims of close friends. His development in the GosJn, his faithfulness, his constant witness, his questioning, and his refusal to be swayed by the claims of others portray Thomas as the model disciple. Thus it becomes clear why he is probably designated by the author of the GosJn, and the Community (or School), as the disciple whom Jesus loved.[35]

6.2 WHO IS THE "OTHER DISCIPLE" IN CHAPTER 18?

John 18:15-16 is the other passage in which an anonymous disciple appears who is to be identified with the Beloved Disciple, according to the informed opinions of experts.[36] Those who defend this identification are usually scholars who have held that the Beloved Disciple is John the son of Zebedee; these opinions date back to John Chrysostom and Jerome.

According to the narrative, Peter follows Jesus along with "another disciple" (ἄλλος μαθητής). Peter must remain outside because only the "other disciple" was allowed to enter; and that is because "he was known to the high priest" (18:15). Then the "other disciple" (18:16) who was "known to the high priest" (18:16) went out, spoke to the maid who kept the door, and she brought Peter into the court of the high priest. The redundancy and ambiguity in this pericope is as striking as the dramatic color and verisimilitude of chapter 18. As Dodd stated, "This vivid narra-

---

[35] S. van Tilborg in *Imaginative Love in John* (Biblical Interpretation Series 2; Leiden: Brill, 1993) 88, rightly points to the "poly-interpretable" dimensions of 1:35-40. The Evangelist and the editor who added chapter 21, who seems to remove some of the secrecy surrounding the identity of the BD, apparently do not intend to reveal the identity of the BD, except to those who are growing in believing and knowing the inner message of the One from above.

[36] W. Heitmüller, *Die Schriften des NT* (Göttingen: Vandenhoeck und Ruprecht, 1918) 1:168. Dibelius concluded that the anonymous disciple in chapter 18 should be identified with the BD (*From Tradition to the Gospel*, 216–17). Neirynck published a most impressive defense for the hypothesis, *Ephemerides Theologicae Lovanienses* 51 (1975) 113–41. A good portion of Eckle's *Den der Herr liebhatte* is an attempt to show that the BD is meant in chapter 18 (see 8–19, 42, 64–65, 140–41). Most Johannine experts (rightly in my opinion) reject this identification, including Schnackenburg (*St. John*, 3:235) and Lindars (*The Gospel of John*, 548). Augustine (*Tract* 118.2), Bernard (*Gospel According to St. John*, 2:593), and Brown (*Gospel*, 2:823) hold the opinion that the evidence is too ambiguous for identification.

tive, every step of which is clear and convincing, is either the product of a remarkable dramatic *flair*, or it rests on superior information."[37]

Is the Beloved Disciple the "another disciple" in this scene?[38] Five factors may be brought forward in favor of that identification.[39] *First*, he is called ἄλλος μαθητής as in 20:2. Some early manuscript witnesses, such as ℵ² C L Θ and others,[40] indicate that the Beloved Disciple is intended by placing the definite article before "other disciple" (καὶ ὁ ἄλλος μαθητής). This reading is found in John Chrysostom, Cyril, and the Textus Receptus. Thus, "the other disciple" would seem to be the Beloved Disciple. It is obvious that in 20:2 the Beloved Disciple is "*the* other disciple." Neirynck is convinced that the parallels between 18:15-16 and 20:3-10 show that the Beloved Disciple is meant, and that the Evangelist himself added both passages.[41]

How impressive is this evidence? The variant reading in 18:15 probably reflects the guesswork of scribes who lived hundreds of years after the composition of the GosJn.[42] Also, as we noted at the outset, anonymity or the appearance of "another disciple" was not a factor obviously in itself in favor of an identification with the Beloved Disciple. Hence, the variant reading and the linguistic similarity between 18 and 20 is not impressive enough to warrant the conclusion that the Beloved Disciple is meant in not only 20, but also 18.

[37] Dodd, *Historical Tradition in the Fourth Gospel*, 86.

[38] Lindars concluded that 1:35 and 18:15-16 do not refer to the BD (*The Gospel of John*, 31–32).

[39] S. van Tilborg argues that 18:15-16 may well point in "the direction of the beloved disciple"; but he judges the passage to be "poly-interpretable" and considers it "proper to leave it that way" (*Imaginative Love in John*, 93–94).

[40] See the *apparatus criticus* (308) in Nestle-Aland, *Novum Testamentum Graece* XXVII.

[41] Neirynck, *Ephemerides Theologicae Lovanienses* 51 (1975) 138–41. He is also persuaded that in both passages the source is a "Synoptic Peter story and the role of Peter is duplicated and superseded by the ἄλλος μαθητής" (138). Also, see Neirynck's "Note sur Jn 20, 1-18," *Ephemerides Theologicae Lovanienses* 62 (1986) 404. I agree with Neirynck that both 18:15-16 and 20:1-10 seem to come from the same layer and that it is the author's work. Cp. Brown, who judges that "the other disciple" is from a source and "the one whom Jesus loved" is an editorial insertion (*Gospel*, 983). It is not easy to distinguish between sources, traditions, the author's first edition, the second edition, and the work of an editor like the one who added chapter 21. I harbor the opinion that the author in his second edition may have added some of the references to the BD.

[42] As Schnackenburg states, the definite article "is secondary from a text-critical point of view, and is evidence of the early trend to identify him with the 'disciple, whom Jesus loved' (13:23)" (*St. John*, 3:235).

The text has "another disciple." It does not have " the other disciple." As Tasker points out, the "very fact, however, that the author does not use the latter description here would appear to indicate that the disciple 'known to the high priest' was a different person."[43] Hence, the variant indicates that the text probably does not denote the Beloved Disciple.

Second, the Greek of 18:15 is ambiguous; according to the NRSV, it means "Simon Peter and another disciple followed Jesus."[44] This would indicate that the two disciples *together* followed Jesus; and that could suggest that the other disciple was the Beloved Disciple. This translation also gives the impression that the anonymous disciple seems to know that Peter is outside, which would indicate that he came to the courtyard together with Peter.[45]

As we shall see, however, the Greek of 18:15-16 is ambiguous, and 18:15 means literally, "Simon Peter went along with Jesus and another disciple." The latter noun, however, is in the nominative case as is "Simon Peter"; it cannot mean that the anonymous one was with Jesus.

Third, "another disciple" may denote the Beloved Disciple since he is in association with Peter as in 13:23-26, 20:2-10, 21:7, and 21:20-23. Kragerud judged the scene in chapter 18 to be one characteristic of the Beloved Disciple, especially in his relationship with Peter.[46] Haenchen also concluded that "another disciple" denoted the Beloved Disciple. He reasoned that the designation "Beloved Disciple" was not used here by the author because it would comport "poorly with the position of someone known to the high priest." Also, "the superiority of the 'other disciple' over Peter" comes "fully into view."[47] Neirynck and Culpepper speculate that as in other pericopes where the Beloved Disciple is clearly present, so in 18:15-18, where he is to be recognized, he has "precedence over Peter";[48] that is, he has "some priority or advantage over Peter."[49]

Does the relation between the "another disciple" and Peter in chapter 18 seem reminiscent of the way the Beloved Disciple and Peter relate

---

[43] R. V. G. Tasker, *The Gospel According to St. John* (Leicester: Intervarsity Press; Grand Rapids: Eerdmans, 1994 [1960]) 199.

[44] This is not a good translation; it suggests that the verb "followed" is in the plural and that the two disciples went together. The verb tense is imperfect, third person singular.

[45] This does not represent the Greek, which means literally, "Peter followed Jesus, and another disciple (did also)." The singular verb denotes that Peter followed alone and that another disciple also followed, but how and in what proximity to Peter is not indicated.

[46] Kragerud, *Lieblingsjünger,* 26.

[47] Haenchen, *John 2,* 167.

[48] Neirynck, *Ephemerides Theologicae Lovanienses* 51 (1975) 141.

[49] Culpepper, *John,* 62.

in pericopes in which they are obviously present? Where is the polemical tension between the other disciple and Peter that so characterizes the rivalry between the Beloved Disciple and Peter? As Bultmann pointed out, the Beloved Disciple is probably not intended by the pericope in chapter 18, because what is conspicuously missing is the portrayal of a rivalry between Peter and the Beloved Disciple.[50] In this pericope the other disciple and Peter have a close relationship that even seems intimate within a polemical ambience.[51]

Fourth, the narrative would move more smoothly if the "other disciple" were the Beloved Disciple so that this disciple, clearly identified as the Beloved Disciple, can be present at the crucifixion and witness Jesus' death (19:25-27). One reason Brown gives for the possibility that the anonymous disciple is the Beloved Disciple is that he "must have followed Jesus during the passion because he appears at the foot of the cross in xix 25-27."[52] Thus, the Beloved Disciple would be a witness to the events of the Passion.[53]

To this argument Brown subsequently (and rightly in my opinion) raises a major objection, "if this 'another disciple' was known to the high priest, can he be the Beloved Disciple?[54] Would it not be also known that he was the favorite of Jesus and how then could he be admitted to the high priest's palace without question when Peter was interrogated?"[55]

It is true that Polycrates, according to Eusebius (*H.E.* 5.24), argued that the author of the GosJn "wore the sacerdotal plate." But, is this tradi-

---

[50] Bultmann, *John*, 645. Bultmann concluded that the "other disciple" "cannot be divined."

[51] Brodie also points out that Judas is "often grouped with Peter (6:68-71; 13:1-11, 21-30)" (*The Gospel According to John*, 529).

[52] Brown, *Gospel*, 2:822.

[53] The BD is clearly at the cross. Why then does he not remain to help bury Jesus' corpse? Is the author constrained by history? Is there some narrative or theological meaning we have missed here? If he returns to his home with Jesus' mother, then why does the narrator give the impression that Mary Magdalene comes to where Peter and the BD are residing alone? The BD is at the cross and then again at the empty tomb. Does that suggest a theological link between cross and resurrection that would be missing if the BD was at the cross, burial, and then empty tomb? We have seen that the narrator wanted to stress Jesus' physical death and bodily resurrection and gave that witness to the BD who is Thomas. How does this insight help answer the present query?

[54] Even more damaging is the claim that the apostle John would have been known to the high priest. As Parker stated, still "more decisively, at Acts 4:5-23 the high priest and all his court treat the apostle John as a total stranger" (*Journal of Biblical Literature* 81 [1962] 42).

[55] Brown, *Gospel*, 2:822.

tion historically reliable? Thornecroft contends it is and urges scholars to give it "more serious attention";[56] but does it not suggest an early Christian scholar's attempt to explain that John the Apostle is both the author of the GosJn and the Beloved Disciple, and that, therefore, he must be the anonymous disciple of chapter 18? Polycrates assumed that the author of the GosJn was John and the Beloved Disciple.[57]

Cumulatively there are abundant reasons to doubt that the anonymous disciple of chapter 18 is to be identified as the Beloved Disciple. The valid insights presented above certainly undermine the hypothesis that the "other disciple" of chapter 18 is to be identified with the Beloved Disciple.[58]

Fifth, the narrative does suggest that the anonymous disciple is physically closest to Jesus during the questioning before Annas.[59] In contrast to Peter, he does not deny Jesus. These observations imply, according to Culpepper, "the faithfulness of the Beloved Disciple in contrast to Peter's failure."[60]

Do they? Culpepper's suggestions follow a subjunctive: "If we identify the other disciple as the Beloved Disciple ...."[61] This may indicate deductive logic, which will prove an hypothesis and not seek to move interrogatively towards an understanding of the text. Culpepper obviously is aware of this, and has used the words to clarify a possible position that he later affirms; but in the process he apparently does not see that the anonymous disciple cannot be simultaneously admired by Jesus and by the high priest (as we shall see).

In chapter 18 the anonymous disciple's function is not to appear faithful or as one who does not deny Jesus. He neither speaks up nor defends Jesus in any way when he is slapped; that is neither faithfulness nor a model for true discipleship since the author of the GosJn decries secret discipleship (as in the case of the blind man of chapter 9 and Nicodemus). He is present in the narrative to let Peter in and so provides for the opportunity for Peter to deny Jesus three times. These actions pose

[56] Thornecroft, *Expository Times* 98 (1986–1987) 138.

[57] See the comments of Smalley, *John: Evangelist and Interpreter* (Nashville: Thomas Nelson, 1978) 69; and Barrett, *The Gospel According to St. John* (1958 ed.) 84.

[58] Colson rightly points out that this other disciple "n'est sûrement pas Jean de Zébédée" (*L'Énigme du disciple que Jésus aimait*, 15; also see 96–97).

[59] Although Caiaphas was high priest that year (18:13), Jesus is taken before Annas; hence the scene from 18:13 to 18:24 depicts Jesus before Annas, who was of the high priestly family.

[60] Culpepper, *John*, 62.

[61] Ibid.

grave difficulties for one who wishes to see the anonymous one as the Beloved Disciple, the model of discipleship.

Undermining further the hypothesis that the Beloved Disciple is the anonymous disciple of chapter 18 are the following additional observations: There seems no reason to question the presence of the Beloved Disciple in the garden across the Kidron in which Jesus is betrayed by Judas; and the narrator does not say that Jesus' disciples fled, which would be inappropriate for the Beloved Disciple. Readers may have assumed he heeded Jesus' words to Peter, that the action of Judas and the soldiers in some way fit the divine plan "which the Father had given" to Jesus (18:11). He is then not needed by the narrator until it is necessary to have him as the trustworthy witness observing his master's physical death on the cross. That requisite looms large when we recall that the Johannine Community is devastated by a schism, which was motivated in at least some ways by docetic tendencies (one aspect of which was the denial that Jesus died on the cross, because he was God and could not suffer; cf. *ActsJn*).[62]

Long ago Stanton shared an observation that is equally true today. Many experts, including Culpepper,[63] seem to evidence a desire to have the Beloved Disciple present at the "trial" so that it comes from a reliable witness and so that the witness can move through the narrative to the foot of the cross. In 1920 Stanton wrote, "It seems to me that supporters of the traditional view of 'the beloved disciple' have been led to identify the disciple who introduced Simon Peter into the high priest's palace with him from a desire to fill in as much as possible their picture of him; and that other writers have followed suit without sufficiently considering the question."[64] Thus, there are numerous reasons to doubt the suggestion that the "another disciple" of 18:15 is the Beloved Disciple.[65]

Who then could this other disciple be? Bernard[66] said, if we must guess, he is perhaps Nicodemus or Joseph of Arimathea; E. A. Tidall sug-

---

[62] According to the *Acts of John* 97, John is told by Jesus in a cave on the Mount of Olives that he is being crucified "below in Jerusalem" for the ordinary people.

[63] Culpepper, *John*, 58, 62–63. Culpepper comes so close to perceiving the problems in identifying 18:15 with the BD; but he seems to be intent on filling in the picture of the BD so as to "strengthen the credibility of the Beloved Disciple," and to move him through the Passion Narrative so that he can be there at the cross.

[64] Stanton, *The Gospels as Historical Documents*, 3 vols. (Cambridge: Cambridge Univ. Press, 1903–1920) 1:143.

[65] Earlier in chapter 3 we saw that Parker pointed out that it is not possible to believe that John (or the Beloved Disciple I might add now) could have been known to high priest (*The Journal of Biblical Literature* 81 [1962] 42).

[66] Bernard, *Gospel According to St. John*, 2:593–94.

gested that he is Nicodemus.[67] While Nicodemus—or Joseph of Arimathea for that matter—would have easily moved freely within the court of the high priest, as does the "other disciple," he does not appear in the Johannine narrative in any anonymous fashion or with the phrase ἄλλος μαθητής. He is not present during the passion but only after Jesus has been crucified (19:39).

Most importantly, there is no evidence in the Johannine narrative that Nicodemus went to the garden across the Kidron after the Last Supper. Hence, he could not have followed Jesus out of the garden (18:15), since those who went there were only "his disciples" (18:1);[68] and as we have seen, that seems to denote, and perhaps exclusively, only the Twelve. We need to look for another more viable candidate for the anonymous disciple of chapter 18.

Could the "other disciple" be Judas Iscariot as scholars from the early 1700s to the present have argued (J. C. Mercken in 1730,[69] E. A. Abbott at the beginning of this century, and Brodie recently)?[70] Bernard scoffed at Abbott's suggestion, dismissing it with this remark: "But that Judas should *wish* to introduce Peter, or that Peter would have tolerated any advances from him or accepted his good offices, is difficult to believe."[71]

This disdain for Judas more accurately reflects developed Christian theology than the Johannine narrative. During the Last Supper Jesus and Judas seem to be involved in some secret plan (chap. 13), and as Brodie points out "in 13:21-30 there is a certain interchangeability between the beloved and the traitor."[72]

---

[67] E. A. Tidall, *ET* 28 (1916-1917) 283-84; I am indebted to Brown (*Gospel*, 2:822) for this information.

[68] There is certainly no reason to imagine that he went with the band of soldiers and officers to arrest Jesus.

[69] J. C. Mercken, *Observationes criticae in Passionem Jesu Christi*, trans. into Dutch by F. Kuijpers (*Oordeelkundige Aanmerkingen over het Heylig Lijden van Onzen Heere Jesus Christus* [Dordrecht, 1730]) 531: "Want wie van de Discipelen was aan den Hoogenpriester bekent dan Judas?" I am grateful here to the unusually thorough and erudite article by Neirynck titled "The 'Other Disciple' in Jn 18,15-16," *Ephemerides Theologicae Lovanienses* 51 (1975) 113-41.

[70] E. A. Abbott, *ET* 25 (1913-1914) 149-50. Abbott, "The Disciple that was (R. V.) 'Known unto the High Priest,'" *The Fourfold Gospel* (Diatessarica 10.2; Cambridge: Cambridge Univ. Press, 1914) Appendix II, pp. 351-71. Also see the reference to Abbott in Bernard, *St. John*, 2:593. Brodie, *The Gospel According to John*, 529-60.

[71] Bernard, *The Gospel According to St. John*, 1:593.

[72] Brodie, *The Gospel According to John*, 529.

Narrative art is effective when it corresponds with historical veri-similitude. Hence, Judas is with the band of soldiers when they take Jesus. The soldiers and others then go to the house of the high priest. There is no suggestion that Judas has left this band of soldiers. He would not have been considered one of Jesus' disciples to the soldiers or to the high priestly family with whom he had devised the plot. If Iscariot means "man from Kerioth,"[73] then he is the only one of the Twelve who is from Judaea; he could then have known (and been known by) the high priest. If Jesus chose him to be the one who was the treasurer of the Jesus group, then he probably had some experience with money in the past; and that suggests some elite level in society which would most likely have brought him into rather close contact with society's leaders like the high priest.

The Greek γνωστὸς τῷ ἀρχιερεῖ of 18:15 ("known to the high priest") does not indicate a mere acquaintance. It denotes an intimate relationship such as with relatives.[74] The similar phrase in 18:16 ὁ γνωστὸς τοῦ ἀρχιερέως ("the one known by the high priest") indicates that they knew each other rather well. The verbal form γνωστός with either the dative (τῷ [18:15]) or genitive (τοῦ [18:16]) indicates intimate friend-ship;[75] in the Septuagint it corresponds to the Hebraic form מְיֻדָּע (Puʿal participle of יָדַע)[76] which denotes a close friend or intimate companion.[77]

---

[73] See Joshua 15:25. Billerbeck, *Kommentar zum NT*, 1:537, and Dalman, *Jesus-Jeshua*, 28–29, support this interpretation. Is there any connection between the Johannine narrative and Kerioth as denoting Jerusalem, as in the Targums? If traditions in the GosJn indicate that Judas was from Jerusalem, then his connection with the high priest may be even more significant. Are we to think about a disciple of Jesus coming from the wealthy upper city of Jerusalem, as revealed now by stunning archaeological discoveries?

[74] See the judicious philological comments by Bruce, *The Gospel of John*, 345, who rightly warned that we must avoid the ready conclusion that the anonymous one of chapter 18 is the BD (344). Carson presents the evidence against identifying the anonymous disciple as the BD, but suggest "tentatively" that he may be (*The Gospel According to John*, 581–82).

[75] Strachan rightly pointed out from a philological study of γνωστός in the LXX that this disciple "must have had a fairly intimate standing with Caiaphas and his entourage" (*The Fourth Gospel: Its Significance and Environment*, 84).

[76] Note the following: Psalm 55:14, "but it is you ... my companion, my friend" (וּמְיֻדָּעִי; καὶ γνωστέ μου [LXX 54:14]); sweet was our friendship" [TANAKH]; and 2Kings 10:11 which refers to King Ahab's intimates or confi-dants (וּמְיֻדָּעָיו; καὶ τοὺς γνωστοὺς αὐτοῦ). In the Qumran Scrolls we find an emphasis upon ידע and its cognates; but the closest to the Puʿal participle is וְעִם ידעים (1QH 11.14 "and with them who know") and וְהַידעים (1QSa 1.28 "and the knowledgeable ones"). See also Barrett's important philological discussion in *The Gospel According to St. John*, 525.

[77] Psalm 41:9 ("Even my bosom friend in whom I trusted, who ate of my bread, has lifted the heel against me" [NRSV]) has been taken to be behind the

The anonymous disciple is thus a close friend of the high priest; that raises a question, not heard for a long time, but articulated in the beginning of the nineteenth century, when Kuinoel wrote, "Quomodo Iohannes potuit amicus esse Iesu et Caiaphae?"[78]

The anonymous one cannot be simultaneously a friend of Caiaphas and of Jesus (certainly not as the model disciple, "the disciple whom Jesus loved") as Jesus stands bound before Annas. The evidence does not lead us to accept the hypothesis of Burkitt, Strachan, and Whiteley that the Evangelist was "originally a member of the Sadducean party";[79] but it does seem to follow that Judas alone remains as the most viable candidate among the disciples for such a relation with the high priest.

Hence, Schnackenburg is correct in rejecting the suggestion that chapter 18 refers to the Beloved Disciple. He argues that the anonymous disciple's "acquaintance with the high priest ... would also be astonishing for a close intimate of Jesus." He continues by claiming that "it remains quite incomprehensible why the evangelist did not speak here also of 'the disciple whom Jesus loved' if he was that 'other disciple.'"[80]

Why would Peter allow Judas to let him into the high priest's court? That was Bernard's objection against Judas being identified as the ἄλλος μαθητής. The prima facie answer is because Peter was curious and wanted to find out what was going to happen to Jesus. Moreover, we must not import a later portrait of Peter back into the Johannine narrative. In chapters 1 through 20 the narrator does not portray Peter as a discerning disciple; he seems rather confused and often lost. He exits the drama ignorant and without confessing any belief (20:1-10). He is also impetuous, rushing into the tomb and diving into the Sea of Tiberias; hence, his actions near the courtyard should not be portrayed out of character as one who carefully reviews a situation.

---

account of Judas's betrayal. That conclusion is sound; but the Greek is not etymologically related to γνωστός: ὁ ἄνθρωπος τῆς εἰρήνης μου, ἐφ᾽ ὃν ἤλπισα (Ps 40:10 [LXX]).

[78] C. T. Kuinoel, *Commentarius in Libros Novi Testamenti Historicos* (Leipzig: Iohannem Ambrosium Barth, 1825) 3:676. Kuinoel examined the arguments in favor of Judas being the anonymous disciple of 18:15. He concluded that the many scholars who had argued for John the son of Zebedee were correct (cum veterum). He doubted that Peter would be in the company of Judas.

[79] Burkitt, *The Gospel History and Its Transmission*, 248; Strachan, *The Fourth Gospel: Its Significance and Environment*, 86. Whiteley, "Was John Written by a Sadducee?" *Aufstieg und Niedergang der Römischen Welt* II.25.3. (Berlin: Walter de Gruyter, 1985) 2481-2505. See esp. "The B.D. Died While Finishing John: He Was a Sadducee," on 2492-2502.

[80] Schnackenburg, *St. John*, 3:235.

Most importantly, the text does not state that the mysterious disciple opened the door for Peter. Schnackenburg does not accurately represent the text when he states that the anonymous disciple "leads him (Peter) into the high priest's court-yard."[81] Rather, the anonymous disciple ordered the portress, which is noteworthy,[82] to open the door to Peter so he could enter the courtyard of the high priest. The narrative does not suggest that Peter asked or received any favor from the anonymous disciple. There is no dialogue or interchange between Peter and the anonymous disciple. The reader is not even told that Peter knew that the maid opened the door to him because of the initiative of the anonymous disciple.

The narrator does not even suggest that the maid knew that the anonymous disciple and Peter were more than acquainted with each other. The narrator does not imply that she comprehended that both were "disciples" of Jesus. Sometimes translations camouflage the actor. The anonymous disciple goes outside the court of the high priest; he speaks to the woman in charge of the door. She brings Peter inside.[83]

Misunderstandings also arise from the invalid assumption that Peter and the anonymous disciple arrive together at the residence of the high priest. This is inaccurate as we shall see.

We have focused on why Peter would relate to Judas. Another question also should be raised: Why would Judas want Peter to enter τὴν αὐλήν, that is the open courtyard? The author does not inform the reader, but some reflections are possible because of the dynamic drama. Judas knew it was cold and may have wanted Peter to come into the courtyard where there was a fire. But, there are even more important reasons why Judas may have wanted to bring Peter inside.

In the garden Jesus and Judas never relate; they do not even speak to one another. Peter acts and is reprimanded publicly by Jesus. What would Peter be thinking? Is it conceivable that he thought Judas and Jesus were developing some schema? The last words of Jesus to Judas were at the Last Supper, and some of the disciples—possibly therefore Peter—thought

[81] Schnackenburg, *St. John*, 3:235.

[82] We should expect a male to be controlling or guarding the door to the courtyard of the high priest, especially at night and during the charged atmosphere of Passover. The Syrus Sinaiticus has "the man keeping the door" (*lntr tr*ʿ) and later "the handmaid of the man keeping the door" (*ʾmth dntr tr*ʿ). See Lewis, *The Old Syriac Gospels*, ad loc. cit.

[83] The ambiguity in the Greek third person singular is clarified by the Arabic Diatessaron; it has the third person singular *feminine*. See Ciasca, *Tatiani Evangeliorum Harmoniae Arabice*, ad loc. cit. Syrus Sinaiticus has "male porter" so the Semitic verb form will be of no help with this particular problem. Indeed, the male porter brought in (Aphael, 3rd person masculine singular) Peter: *w 'lh lšmʿwn*.

that Judas was carrying out Jesus' orders. We know little about the motives of Judas or of Peter; hence, the narrator does not obviously portray Judas and Peter on opposite sides of the struggle. In fact, the theological thrust of the Johannine passion is that Judas the Betrayer, Peter the Denier, the soldiers, officers, high priests, and Pharisees are on one side; on the other is Jesus as the only One from above. He alone is to be captured and bound (18:8). He alone stands before Annas, Caiaphas, and Pilate. He carries his own cross and is "exalted" upon it. The author of this narrative joins Judas and Peter in predetermined action; hence, there is no reason to wonder why Judas would have asked for Peter to enter the courtyard.

Judas is not condemned in the GosJn by Jesus or Peter. He is one of the Twelve (6:71), has a sophisticated place of honor at the Last Supper, and is an officer of the group (12:6). Although it is said that Judas had concern for the poor (perhaps from a putative source), the narrator disparages any good motives in Judas (12:6). There is an intriguing air of complicity between Jesus and Judas during the Last Supper, and Judas is the only one who is reported explicitly to eat during the Last Supper—he received (that probably means ate) the morsel (τὸ ψωμίον). No one at the Last Supper (including the BD), knew the meaning of Jesus' words to Judas. Some of the disciples assume he is following Jesus' orders, which were perhaps to buy what was necessary for Passover or to distribute some money to the poor (13:27-30). He subsequently appears in the garden with a band of soldiers and officers. He says nothing. He does nothing. As W. Klassen noted, what is "striking here is the mechanical behavior Judas displays."[84] Unfortunately, even scholars who advocate studying the GosJn in terms of its own traditions and *Tendenzen* tend to read the Passion Narrative in light of what they have learned from the Synoptics. They especially sometimes import knowledge about Judas obtained from Matthew and Luke. Judas in the GosJn is not the Judas in the Synoptics.

Judas is a most mysterious character in the GosJn. The author of the GosJn allows him only one sentence ("Why was this perfume not sold for 300 denarii and given to the poor" [12:5])? As Peter is portrayed as a man of specious speech with hesitant action, Judas is a man of elusive action with few words. It is as if Judas is portrayed as a son of darkness,[85] a shadowy character who is seldom heard but darts on stage with ambiguity from unlit corners.

We have seen that some New Testament exegetes concluded that Judas is none other than the Beloved Disciple (see chap. 3). How strong is the evidence that he could be the "another disciple" of chapter 18?

---

[84] W. Klassen, *Anchor Bible Dictionary* (1992) 3.1095.

[85] The term "Sons of Light" appears in the GosJn, but another Qumranic

The Judas hypothesis increases in possibility when one approaches the text with narrative exegesis, asking how the narrator imagined the actions and sayings of the leading characters. Let us begin with imagining how the narrator would have intended the actions of "another disciple" if he were the Beloved Disciple.

If the Beloved Disciple were the anonymous disciple of 18:15, then the narrator has marred an otherwise stunningly dramatic and pictorial story. When Jesus tells the arresting mob—the most dangerous sociological institution[86]—to "let these men go" (18:8), he leads the reader to imagine that the Beloved Disciple, along with the other disciples in the garden, will now disappear at this point from the narrative.[87] He thus cannot be the anonymous disciple who enters the courtyard with the soldiers.

Why did the high priest not interrogate Jesus' faithful witness, when Jesus asked them to question those who heard him (18:21)? If the Beloved Disciple is implied to be present, then it is unthinkable that the narrator would allow an officer to slap Jesus and depict him standing nonchalantly nearby. The theological implication of 18:36 is that since Jesus' disciples are not "of this world" they are not present to fight against temporary rulers of this world; hence, the reader receives the impression that Jesus' faithful disciples, including the Beloved Disciple, are not present during these scenes.

Upon arriving at the courtyard Peter remains *outside* the central scene, *warming himself with Jesus' adversaries* beside a charcoal fire.[88] The drama of the stunningly clear narrative becomes obfuscated if the anonymous one is the Beloved Disciple. Peter is not supported by the presence of the ideal disciple; amidst antagonists and adversaries he denies his Lord. The logic of the narrative demands that Peter sinks because of surrounding darkness. The weight of the Betrayer along with Jesus' enemies overwhelm him.

The flow of the narrative is not improved if we assume the Beloved Disciple continues to be present from the garden to the cross. There is no reason to assume that because he was at the crucifixion he must have been

---

term, the "Sons of Darkness," does not.

[86] The crowd or mob was what the Romans and sacerdotal aristocracy feared most. It had no published agenda, no history, and no one with whom a governor could negotiate. New Testament research can be enriched by such sociological studies as G. Le Bon's *The Crowd: A Study of the Popular Mind* (New York: Viking Press, 1960).

[87] Peter seems to be up front with Jesus, the disciples behind; hence, he alone will continue with Jesus, the mob (and Judas within it).

[88] I am convinced the gifted narrator of the GosJn intended some paronomasia here.

following Jesus each step of the way. The so-called trial before the high priest and Pilate was private and behind closed doors;[89] the crucifixion was public and outside the city (18:17-20). Crucifixion was not instantaneous. It took hours in the case of Jesus. The Beloved Disciple is not shown at the beginning of the crucifixion. Along with the women he appears at the scene of the crucifixion only after Jesus has carried his own cross through the mob of Roman soldiers and Judeans from the Gabbatha to Golgotha, and only after the crosses are raised for the three who were crucified. Only after the work of the soldiers is completed and they are dividing between them Jesus' garments and casting lots for his tunic, is the reader informed that the Beloved Disciple was at the foot of the cross.[90] The tendency of the narrative is to place the Beloved Disciple near the end of the crucifixion so that he can witness the thrust of the lance into Jesus' corpse.

The developing plot indicates that Judas Iscariot is most likely the "another disciple" who was with the band of soldiers. Note these developments: Judas is clearly in the garden across the Kidron; and he came with the soldiers. Judas would have been known to the high priest (18:15), because he apparently—although this is only implied—colluded with the high priest; he came to the garden having procured a band of soldiers and some officers "from the chief priests and Pharisees" (18:3 [see also 11:45-57]). There is no reason to doubt that Judas remains with these soldiers and officers and returns to the court of the high priest with them. The last words from the narrator about Judas is that he was "with them" ($\mu\varepsilon\tau$' $\alpha\dot{\upsilon}\tau\hat{\omega}\nu$ [18:5]); that is, Judas is with the band of soldiers and officers from the high priest and Pharisees.

Confusion has been caused by translations of 18:15-16. Note the NRSV:

> Simon Peter and another disciple followed Jesus.[91] Since that disciple was known to the high priest, he went with Jesus into the courtyard of the high priest, but Peter was standing outside at the gate. So the

---

[89] It is misleading to call the "trial" an examination "before the Sanhedrin" as did Bultmann in his *John*, 641.

[90] Brown (*Gospel*, 2:841) points to 16:32, which contains Jesus' word that all his disciples will be scattered and he will be left alone. This saying is contradicted by the appearance of the BD at the foot of the cross. If Judas is the anonymous disciple of chapter 18 then there are three disciples who conceivably did not forsake Jesus, at least in the garden: Peter, Judas, and the Beloved Disciple (who is, according to my research, Thomas).

[91] This sentence incorrectly suggests "they" followed; but the verb in the Greek is in the singular.

other disciple, who was known to the high priest, went out, spoke to the woman who guarded the gate, and brought Peter in.

The translation of the opening of this episode is better in the RSV (2nd edition), "Simon Peter followed Jesus, and so did another disciple." The author neither states nor implies that Peter and "another disciple" *together followed* the band. The verb is not in the plural.[92] It is singular: Ἠκολού-θει; he, Simon Peter, followed Jesus.[93]

The beginning of verse 16 is better in the NRSV, "*but* Peter was standing outside," than the RSV (2nd edition), "*while* Peter stood outside at the door." The question which is raised, however, is whether the author intends the action of the anonymous disciple and Peter to be simultaneous? That is not inconceivable, but the text, perhaps disturbed by some tension between tradition and redaction, seems to denote some sequence. The verb is singular, followed by a subject, then καί and another subject; this syntax denotes, unlike one plural verb, that Peter acted independently of the "other disciple."

Peter had just cut off the ear of a member of the band of soldiers and officers; and they are armed (18:3). Are we to conclude that the narrator intended for the reader to imagine Peter following closely behind them? While the scene is depicted in the darkness of night there is some light flickering from the lanterns and torches of the militant band, and Jesus is subdued and in custody. Would they not have seen Peter? Would they not have driven him off or even attacked him? In the dark in the garden with the light from lanterns and torches, Peter is active, lunging forth at the band with a sword (18:10). Later when he is standing by the fire he may still have a sword, because Jesus told him to put it in its sheath (18:11). Surely the statement that the armed mob "drew back and fell to the ground" (18:6) at Jesus' word, "I am he," is Christology directing narrative. Does it hide the fact that there was a "scuffle" or fight in the garden? Is that why no one in the crowd seemed to be certain that Peter

---

[92] Of course, a singular verb with one subject followed later by another subject is a Semitism. A fresh example of this philological norm (two singular subjects with a singular verb) is in CD 5.17: עמד משה ואהרן (contrast CD 5.20). It is thus not unthinkable in New Testament Greek. In 18:1 we have the same syntax as in 18:15; there is a singular verb, εἰσῆλθεν, with a nominative, αὐτός (denoting Jesus), followed by another subject, also in the nominative: "into which he entered and his disciples."

[93] Culpepper asks, "Is it credible that Peter, who had just slashed off the ear of the high priest's servant at the arrest scene, would allow Judas to accompany him?" (*John*, 58). He misses the meaning of the Greek here, and follows too closely the NRSV (which was his choice for biblical quotations [see p. xiv]).

had dealt the severe blow to Malchus, supposedly a mere slave but conceivably a Hebrew who was in slavery to the high priest?[94] Or, are we to assume that the crowd is a mob which is disoriented? Would that make sense when it is guided by soldiers following out the commands of priestly authorities?

Would Peter not have been remembered and in danger? He is apparently recognized by a servant of the high priest who saw him in the garden, "Did I not see you in the garden with him?" (18:26). The scenes subsequent to Peter's following the band depict him being identified three times; each time he saves his life by lying (denying he is Jesus' disciple). Narrative exegesis, grammar, and syntax indicate that the author did not mean to portray Peter following closely behind the band and along with the anonymous disciple.[95]

These reflections lead me to think it is best to take 18:15 to mean that Peter came after Jesus,[96] as had "another disciple" earlier. Indeed, not only the drama, but also the Greek of 18:15 suggests that Peter arrived at the abode of the high priest after the anonymous disciple; the latter "*entered along with Jesus* (καὶ συνεισῆλθεν τῷ Ἰησοῦ) into the courtyard of the high priest.*" Thus, the anonymous disciple enters with Jesus. Perhaps the following translation conveys the drama imagined by the narrator:

> Simon Peter followed Jesus, and (so had) another disciple. But that disciple was known to the high priest, and so with Jesus he entered into the courtyard of the high priest. However Peter stood before the door outside. Therefore, the other disciple who was known by the

---

[94] Bernard claimed that "an injury to a slave would not excite much interest; had Peter struck one of the officials, it would have been a different matter" (*St. John*, 2:598). That is true only to a certain extent. Slaves of high priests were no ordinary slaves, and slaves were often highly valued. Proof is evident in the Mishnah in which, *inter alia*, we read about Gamaliel's slave, Tabi, who was a reputed scholar (m.Suk 2.1). The argument that first-century Jews did not have slaves, and certainly not fellow Jews was demolished by E. E. Urbach in his *The Laws Regarding Slavery* (New York: Arno Press, 1979). For *halakoth* regarding Hebrew slaves owned by Jews, see esp. m.Maaser Sheni 4.4 (slaves are sometimes called "bondsmen" or "bondswomen"), m.Kidd 1.2; b.Kidd 14b–15a (a Baraita); m.Sotah 3.8 (a man may sell his daughter and a man may be sold). For an informed discussion of Josephus, *Ant* 16.1.1, see Urbach, *Slavery*, 19–22.

[95] Hence, I must disagree with Schmithals, who states that "zunächst folgen beide Jünger Jesus nach," and concludes that 18:15-16 refers to the BD who continued to follow Jesus all the way to the cross ("Die Lieblingsjünger-Redaktion," *Johannesevangelium und Johannesbriefe*, 227).

[96] There is no theological meaning of ἀκολουθέω in 18:15; Peter proceeds to deny Jesus.

high priest went out and spoke to the woman door keeper and she
brought Peter inside.

Since Jesus entered with the band of soldiers who had arrested him, the
anonymous disciple must have also been in that group. The probability
that he is Judas seems rather likely. He was the only disciple who is seen
moving within the band of soldiers and officers.[97]

How did he know that Peter was outside? Had he seen him following at a distance? Did he catch a glimpse of Peter through the gate? Did
someone comment that another disciple was outside? We can only guess;
the narrator has not told the reader. It is unlikely that he intended us to
think that Peter came to the courtyard simultaneously with the anonymous
disciple. Verses 15 through 18 are not well constructed as are the other
verses of this pericope, and there is reason to think of both mixed sources
and some editorial alterations (perhaps by the Evangelist himself).[98]

The meaning of "therefore" ($o\tilde{v}\nu$) in verse 16 is unclear ("Therefore,
the other disciple ... went out and spoke to the woman door keeper"); all
we are told is that the anonymous disciple somehow knew that Peter was
outside and instructed the maid to open the door so he might enter. The
"therefore" that begins 18:17 is even more problematic (and is ignored by
the translators of the NRSV). Because of what she observed about the
anonymous disciple or from what he had instructed her, "therefore," she
asked Peter if he was not also a disciple of Jesus. What is the reader to
think? Is she thinking that Peter is like the other disciple? She and the servants and officers who are warming themselves near Peter are not alarmed
by him or by the other disciple. What is the narrator intending?

Surely, the impression is given that Peter and the anonymous disciple are not adversaries. We are left with Judas as the most likely candidate
for the anonymous disciple; and Peter seems to be his usual vacillating
self—so he denies Jesus repeatedly. The drama presents us with Jesus
accompanied by two disciples: the Betrayer and the Denier. Peter comes
off so poorly in chapters 1–20 that it is obvious why he needed to be reinstated in chapter 21.

[97] It is now obvious that I disagree with Brown, who contended that "there
is no evidence that the Fourth Evangelist is thinking of the disciple as Judas in
the description of 15-16" (*Gospel*, 822).

[98] See the reflections by Bultmann who correctly perceived that the author
of the GosJn inherited "a source of his own" (643) and that as we have it now it
is marred by redactional insertions and glosses that show some misunderstandings (*John*, 643–45). Lorenzen, who works with the probability that 18:15b and
16 are Johannine redactions or a pre-Johannine source, concludes that the anonymous disciple of chapter 18 is the BD because of editorial insertions (*Lieblingsjünger*, 49–53).

The maid who was in charge of the door did not think the anonymous disciple was loyal to Jesus or related to him, because she takes orders from him as Jesus moves under guard into the high priest's offices. Then she becomes suspicious that Peter was one of Jesus' disciples. This episode alone indicates that the anonymous disciple cannot be the Beloved Disciple; he must be one who was thought no longer to be Jesus' disciple—and that fits only Judas in this narrative.

This passage, 18:15-18, may reflect two sources, one about Peter and another about Judas. Two authorial hands seem to be suggested by the following: the third person singular verb with Peter followed by another noun in the nominative singular ("and another disciple"), two different ways of referring to the maid in charge of the door: τῇ θυρωρῷ in 18:16 and ἡ παιδίσκη ἡ θυρωρός in 18:17; the use of ἐκεῖνος first for the anonymous disciple (18:15) and then for Peter (18:17); the two different expressions γνωστὸς τῷ ἀρχιερεῖ in 18:15 and ὁ γνωστὸς τοῦ ἀρχιερέως in 18:16. All of these problems disappear if a putative source (or traditions) and redactions are separated as follows:[99]

Putative Petrine Source	**Redaction [with early traditions]**[100]
Ἠκολούθει δὲ τῷ Ἰησοῦ Σίμων Πέτρος	καὶ ἄλλος μαθητής. ὁ δὲ μαθητὴς ἐκεῖνος ἦν γνωστὸς τῷ ἀρχιερεῖ καὶ συνεισῆλθεν τῷ Ἰησοῦ εἰς τὴν αὐλὴν τοῦ ἀρχιερέως
ὁ δὲ Πέτρος εἱστήκει πρὸς τῇ θύρᾳ ἔξω.	ἐξῆλθεν οὖν ὁ μαθητὴς ὁ ἄλλος ὁ γνωστὸς τοῦ ἀρχιερέως καὶ εἶπεν τῇ Θυρωρῷ καὶ εἰσήγαγεν τὸν Πέτρον.
λέγει οὖν τῷ Πέτρῳ ἡ παιδίσκη ἡ θυρωρός· μὴ καὶ σὺ ἐκ τῶν μαθητῶν εἶ τοῦ ἀνθρώπου τούτου; λέγει οὐκ εἰμί. εἱστήκεισαν δὲ οἱ δοῦλοι καὶ οἱ ὑπηρέται ἀνθρακιὰν πεποιηκότες, ὅτι ψῦχος ἦν, καὶ ἐθερμαίνοντο· ἦν δὲ καὶ ὁ Πέτρος μετ᾽ αὐτῶν ἑστὼς καὶ θερμαινόμενος.	ἐκεῖνος·

[99] Using the traditions in Syrus Sinaiticus, M. Black argues for an Aramaic source behind the GosJn at this point. Black, *An Aramaic Approach to the Gospels and Acts* (Oxford: At the Clarendon Press, 1967 [3rd ed.]) 258–59.

[100] Some of these traditions are most likely originally about Judas. They reflect more than one source.

This suggestion is entirely hypothetical; at best it suggests the isolation of a Petrine source behind the GosJn. At least the putative Petrine source is cohesive and has its own integrity and flow.

The mixture of redaction with early traditions, which constitute the Greek in the right column, is far from satisfactory. There are some Johannine terms and expressions that suggest the hand of the author of the GosJn; note these observations: ἄλλος with μαθητής is not found in Matthew, Mark, or Luke, but it is often in the GosJn (18:15, 20:2, 3, 4, 8; cf. ἄλλοι and the plural "disciples" in 20:25, 21:2, 8); the demonstrative pronoun ἐκεῖνος appears more often in the GosJn than in any other writing in the New Testament (54/23/33/70/22); γνωστός in the New Testament appears only in the GosJn and only in chapter 18 (in the two appearances above); συνεισέρχομαι in the New Testament is found only in the GosJn, and only twice (6:22 and 18:15), each time it is in the form συνεισῆλθεν.

I have the impression that the author of the GosJn, who was editing sources and oral traditions,[101] knew that the anonymous disciple was Judas; but he did not want his readers to think of Judas here.[102] The passion was a spiritual war. Judas represented the devil (Satan); he could not also appear as a human, moving freely in the high priest's courtyard and helping Peter.[103] The Greek of 18:15-18 is admittedly not easy to understand.[104] That is why some Greeks radically reshaped the text. In the sixth

---

[101] If one is disturbed by two anonymous disciples in the passion narrative, this factor may account for it. Personally, I am convinced that the original readers knew the identity of the BD; hence, he would not count as an anonymous disciple in the narrative.

[102] Earlier, in chapter 12, the author separates Judas's only words in the GosJn (12:5) from Jesus' answer to him (12:7) by a denigrating and clearly editorial comment: "This he (Judas) said, not that he cared for the poor but because he was a thief, and as he had the money box he used to take what was put into it" [RSV, 2nd edition]. The author wants to separate Judas from Jesus; even in the garden when Jesus is arrested, Jesus and Judas do not interact.

[103] Jesus alone is arrested. Peter is not arrested, although a reader might have expected him to be at least taken as a prisoner. Note the importance of 11:50 and 18:11. The Johannine drama reveals only one dynamic leader. Only Jesus is in charge. His disciples are not by any means dynamic followers or leaders who should also be arrested. The model of Jesus as a charismatic leader is most persuasive, as Hengel has shown, following Weber's paradigm; see Hengel, *The Charismatic and His Followers*, trans. J. C. G. Greig (Edinburgh: T. & T. Clark, 1987).

[104] There are many fewer problems with Syrus Sinaiticus. The Greek of p^{66} is impressive; it does not contain the redundant and intrusive clause in 18:15. That text even clarifies an attractive chiasm: Simon Peter, the anonymous disciple, Peter, the anonymous disciple, Peter. The emphasis is certainly upon Peter.

century Ammonius presented the following text: Συνεισῆλθεν ὁ Ἰωάννης τῷ Ἰησοῦ μετὰ τοῦ ὄχλου ἀγνώστως καὶ τότε ὡς γνωστὸς εἶπε τῇ θυρωρῷ καὶ εἰσήγαγε τὸν Πέτρον.[105] Assuming that the text here refers to the Beloved Disciple and that he is the apostle John, Ammonius depicted him entering with Jesus and with the crowd who were ignorant that he was Jesus' favorite disciple. Ammonius has changed the text of the GosJn; and his alterations warn us against reading the text according to a preconceived notion.

It is difficult to understand how the Beloved Disciple could enter into the courtyard with Jesus and not be recognized as Jesus' favorite disciple. It is also hard to comprehend how he could have been intimately known to (and by) the high priest. As Hengel states, it is not possible to associate in one disciple both friendship with the high priest and "the one whom Jesus loved."[106] It thus seems virtually impossible that the Evangelist intended the Beloved Disciple to be seen as the anonymous disciple of chapter 18.

With Judas the situation is entirely different. He could have been well known to the high priest; he had procured soldiers and officers from him (18:3). The woman in charge of the door to the high priest's courtyard would have recognized him from his earlier visits and ostensibly warm welcome from the high priestly family who were eager, according to the Evangelist, to get rid of Jesus (GosJn 11:45-53, 57). It is thus easy to comprehend why Judas was allowed to enter with Jesus—he was, after all, returning to the high priest with the one whom he had been sent out to arrest. He would not have been suspicious as Jesus' disciple; and he would not have been threatened or threatening as is the case with the Beloved Disciple. It is easy to understand why the portress perceived him, Judas, as an authority figure and obeyed, without question, his command (εἶπεν) to open the door to Peter. Her question to Peter also is cast in a different, less confusing, light; she may assume that he is with Judas and one who had also deserted Jesus.[107]

---

[105] See Ammonius of Alexandria' fragments in J. Reuss, ed., *Johannes-Kommentar aus der griechischen Kirche* (TU 89; Berlin: Akademie-Verlag, 1966) 339 [frag. 579].

[106] Hengel, *Die johanneische Frage*, 216.

[107] The reader is not told what Peter's reaction was to Jesus' rebuke of him in the garden. Jesus orders Peter neither to discard his sword nor fight with it; he is to put it back "into its sheath" (18:11). Readers might have the impression, especially if they were militant revolutionaries, that Peter could well have felt betrayed by Jesus. Peter, the reader may assume, was not only curious but confused. What was to be the next act? Are Judas and Jesus planning something that will need his action?

If Judas is the "another disciple" of 18:15 then we can observe some strikingly similar functions between the actions, and at times inactions, in 18:1-11 and in 18:15-18. Both Judas and the "another disciple" know something important. Judas knew the place where Jesus and his disciples customarily withdrew. The other disciple was known to and by the high priest. In both cases the knowing is one of familiarity; Judas was customarily familiar with the garden place and the "another disciple" was apparently intimately familiar with the high priest. Both initiate the action that sets the stage for monumental deeds. Judas initiates the confrontation in the garden; the other disciple initiates the act of opening the door for Peter. One leads to arrest, the other to denial. Both remain in the shadowy background. Judas and the other disciple relate respectively to Jesus or Peter in indirect ways and only through intermediaries. The "action" of Judas and the "another disciple" occurs within circumscribed space, within a garden, which would most likely have stone borders and barriers, and within a closed courtyard.[108] The lanterns and torches of the armed mob (including some officers) in the first scene are paralleled by the fire made by officers in the second scene. These observations strengthen the hypothesis that one author has composed both narratives, and that he is describing the same disciple; that is the "another disciple" seems to be Judas.

Additional observations undergird this supposition.[109] Jesus enters the garden and so do his disciples; another disciple enters with Jesus into the courtyard. Judas was standing ($\varepsilon\iota\sigma\tau\eta\kappa\varepsilon\iota$) with the mob (with them, $\mu\varepsilon\tau$' $\alpha\upsilon\tau\omega\nu$); Peter was standing ($\varepsilon\iota\sigma\tau\eta\kappa\varepsilon\iota$) outside the door of the courtyard. Later, Peter, servants, and officers were standing by the charcoal fire; the author states that Peter was standing with them ($\mu\varepsilon\tau$' $\alpha\upsilon\tau\omega\nu$). Jesus' thrice repeated "I am" ($\varepsilon\gamma\omega$ $\varepsilon\iota\mu\iota$ [18:5, 6, 8])[110] contrasts with the

---

[108] I have no doubt that the perennial (and perhaps primordial) myth of a threshold, a guardian, watcher (or watchers) of established bounds and barriers, and a passage or gate to an area that is of the unknown in which there are lurking dangers helped shape the story in chapter 18 and may have unconsciously been a guiding impulse or image in the mind of the author. Peter enters the gate, proceeds beyond the barriers, enters a place that contains the unknown and the unfamiliar, indeed the hostile. He is cold and the area is dark. His danger is obvious as he three times denies his relation with Jesus. For a discussion of the myth of the threshold guardian see Campbell, The Hero, 82, 97, and 99.

[109] A similar stratum seems also to be reflected in Peter's striking of the high priest's slave in 18:10 and the officer of the high priest's striking of Jesus in 18:22.

[110] This highly symbolic expression is typically Johannine and recalls God's disclosure of his name to Moses.

thrice denier's "I am not" (οὐκ εἰμί [notice no "ego" for Peter]).[111] From beginning to end the noun ἀρχιερεύς and its cognates sew the narrative's fabric tightly together.

The recognition that Judas is the ἄλλος μαθητής of 18:15 helps us understand 18:14. The narrative function of this verse is frustratingly ambiguous: "It was Caiaphas who had given counsel to the Jews that it was expedient that one man should die for the people" (18:14, RSV [2nd edition]). Why would Caiaphas, the high priest when Jesus was crucified, be portrayed by the author of this gospel as one who advocated the position that Jesus will die to save "the people"?

Three steps help clarify this verse. First, Ἰουδαῖοι in the GosJn does not always denote "Jews"; it sometimes—as in this verse—denotes "Judeans." This is by no means a novel idea;[112] it is stressed by experts.[113] Hence, Caiaphas addresses these words to Judeans (compare 18:14 with 11:45-53).

Second, in the present narrative "Judeans" may well include a disciple named Judas, who (as we saw) is most likely from Judea. It is interesting to ponder if some Semitic author, perhaps the author of the GosJn himself, saw paronomasia here: Ἰούδας ("Judas") like Ἰουδαία ("Judea") derives from יהודה. Narrative exegesis indicates that Judas may well have considered that Jesus is the one man who should die ὑπὲρ τοῦ λαοῦ. Obviously, this noun, *laos*, is a highly charged theological term. It may well

---

[111] By the comment "no 'ego' for Peter" I mean that according to this narrative he has no integrity, no center.

[112] See esp. U. C. von Wahlde, "The Johannine 'Jews': A Critical Survey," *New Testament Studies* 28 (1982) 33-60; Smith, "Judaism and the Gospel of John," in *Jews and Christians: Exploring the Past, Present, and Future*, ed. J. H. Charlesworth with F. X. Blisard and J. S. Siker (New York: Crossroad, 1990) 76-99; Culpepper, "The Gospel of John as a Threat to Jewish-Christian Relations," in *Overcoming Fear Between Jews and Christians*, ed. J. H. Charlesworth with F. X. Blisard and J. L. Gorham (Philadelphia: The American Interfaith Institute; New York: Crossroad, 1992) 21-43. Also see M. Lowe, "Who Were the *Ioudaioi*?" *Novum Testamentum* 18 (1976) 101-30. Finally, see the appreciative and critical response to Lowe by Ashton ("The Identity and Function of the *Ioudaioi* in the Fourth Gospel," *Novum Testamentum* 27 [1985] 40-75; *Understanding*, 132-37).

[113] That does not mean Ἰουδαῖοι in the GosJn always means "Judeans"; sometimes it certainly refers to "Jews." The Passover is not a Judean feast; it is a Jewish feast (11:55). That Ἰουδαῖοι means "Judeans" or "Judean leaders" is palpably obvious from any careful study of 11:54. Jesus does not go away from the "Jews" (RSV, 2nd edition). He goes away from the Judeans and Judea ("from there") to Ephraim, surely a Jewish town. Contrast the comments by Brown, *Community*, 41.

denote "Israel" (cf. 18:35). With this meaning clarified, the narrative is no longer marred by a confusing verse and a *non sequitur*. As interpreted, it now flows smoothly: the "another disciple," Judas, carries out *the divine plan* which had been articulated by none other than the high priest, the one whom Jews acknowledge knows God's plan and will. Verse 14 leads into 15.

Third, since 18:14-15 points to Judas as the "another disciple," then the reference in 18:14 to Caiaphas' counsel in 11:49-52 takes on added meaning and helps fill in a missing piece in the Johannine puzzle of Jesus' passion. Was Judas, a Judean, intended by the author to be among the Judeans (11:45) present when Caiaphas made his recommendation, which is defined as prophecy by the author (11:51)? If not, Judas could well have heard about it and been influenced by it. Thus, the meaning of the following verse is less opaque: "The chief priests and the Pharisees gave orders that if any one might know where he (Jesus) was he should disclose (it), so they could arrest him" (11:57). Judas is clearly the one who disclosed this information to the high priests and the Pharisees; and the author apparently intends for the reader to learn that he heard this order either directly or indirectly. This section (11:45-57) strengthens the suggestion that not only 18:14, but also 18:15 refer to Judas as the "another disciple." Prior to 18:14 Judas had shown the representatives of the chief priests and Pharisees (18:3) the place in which Jesus often retreated with his disciples (18:2). Thus, 18:14 refers back to 11:49-57 and 18:1-11 so that Judas is most likely the "another disciple" who entered the high priest's courtyard with Jesus (18:15).

Finally, the theological tendency (*Tendenz*) of the author of the GosJn helps us understand Judas's ambiguous character. The Passion Narrative in the GosJn harmonizes with the perspective of the Prologue (1:1-18). That is, Jesus is from above (8:23); he is Light (8:12, 9:5) which cannot be conquered by darkness (1:5). He carries his own cross,[114] and is "exalted" on it.[115] In the GosJn Jesus is entirely in charge of his destiny. Jesus even knows his "betrayer" and chooses him to carry out the preordained salvific drama. Jesus is cognizant of what is to befall him.

With this scenario is there any real place for betrayal? Why are Judas's actions never sinister? Why do some of Jesus' disciples during the Last Supper assume Judas exits to do Jesus' will? Why is it possible to think that Peter and Judas are close even after the arrest in the garden?

---

[114] This perspective is unique to the author of the GosJn.

[115] In the GosJn the Greek verb ὑψόω always refers to Jesus' exaltation on the cross; this *terminus technicus* is frequently (3 out of 5 occurrences) linked with a "title," "the Son of Man"; this may well suggest a source emphasized by the author of the GosJn (see 3:14 [*bis*], 8:28, 12:32, 34).

Why are Judas's sinister actions—well known by at least 85 C.E.—so surprisingly "curtailed"? Why is there no description of a plot between Judas and Jesus' enemies, especially the sacerdotal aristocracy? Why is there no mention of, or aside to, the tradition of 30 pieces of silver or a kiss in the garden?[116] Why is there no indication of what happens to Judas?[117]

To what extent has the gifted symbolic author who has given us this masterpiece presented a "betrayer" who is Jesus' "beloved"? Under the influence of Qumranic dualism (esp. 4Q186) have some members of the Johannine School reflected on the betrayer (i.e., darkness) in every beloved (or Son of Light; see 12:36), and have they influenced Johannine phrasing?

Are we to think about a Christ Jesus who never ceased loving Judas? Is that the meaning of the statement in 13:2, "Jesus knew that his hour had come ... he loved (his own) until the end (εὶς τέλος)."[118] According to the GosJn Jesus taught his disciples to love others as he loved them. Does the narrative of the GosJn not show us the Light from above who continued to love Peter, the denier, and Judas, the betrayer?

Jesus stressed a new commandment based on his *love of his disciples*; that would mean he loved both the Beloved Disciple and the Betrayer. And he continued loving both. Is this not the perfect paradigm for loving?

Does the Johannine *narrative* not show us a Judas who was especially loved by Jesus? He is portrayed sitting so close to Jesus at the Last Supper that the Master can reach over and hand him the morsel to eat. According to the story in the GosJn, Jesus must have loved Judas in a special way; he asked him to be in charge of the money. Has the author of the GosJn not depicted Jesus entrusting the group's money to a disciple who is trusted, even beloved? To what extent is the author of the GosJn, or an author of a source he inherits,[119] turning around a prismatic ideal that reflects divine truths; that is the betrayer was always Jesus' beloved?

---

[116] The apparently late addition of the name of the slave, Malchus, is all the more striking if the GosJn shows developed Christian hermeneutics. Such additions to the gospel story should also be evaluated in light of what seems to be "omitted" from the Jesus traditions.

[117] In contrast to the narrative in Matthew, Judas does not hang himself. In contrast to Luke and other early Christian authors, he does not burst from swollen sin.

[118] There can be little doubt that the author of the GosJn has used εὶς τέλος with a *double entendre*.

[119] This possibility looms large in light of the observation that the author of the GosJn adds (perhaps in the second edition) comments that portray Judas pejoratively. Surely 12:6 is editorial and reflects the perspective of the Evangelist. There has been an informative debate between Neirynck and Borgen on the author of the GosJn's use of oral or written traditions. I tend to side with

The "another disciple" of 18:15 is probably to be identified as Judas. This tradition, however, was inherited by the author of the GosJn. He certainly would not have created such a story and most likely would not want to stress to his readers that the ἄλλος μαθητής was Judas.

Borgen. The author of the GosJn inherited and interpreted oral and written traditions that are not to be labeled "Synoptic." See Borgen, "The Independence of the Gospel of John: Some Observations," in *The Four Gospels: 1992 [Festschrift Frans Neirynck]*, ed. F. Van Segbroeck, et al. (Leuven: Leuven Univ. Press, 1992) 3:1815-33. [This important collection of essays in honor of Neirynck came to my attention when this monograph was virtually completed.]

CHAPTER 7

The Johannine School and the
School of Thomas

In our attempt to identify the Beloved Disciple we have followed the faint footprints left by him in the narrative of the GosJn. As Robinson Crusoe from one footprint left in the sand became convinced that there was another human on the island, so we from traces left in the Johannine narrative became convinced of the identity of the Beloved Disciple.

We have circled around and intermittently entered briefly into the Johannine School. In this "School" the document we know as the "Gospel According to Saint John" took shape. From sources (esp. the Signs Source, and most likely the memoirs and living oral traditions of the Beloved Disciple) the "First Edition," and then the "Second Edition" (which included expansions, some of which we can isolate, specifically 1:1-18, 4:2, and chapters 15-17) appeared within the Johannine Community. Finally, this core was expanded by an editor (chapter 21). Much discussion has been devoted to the appropriateness of the noun *School*. That seems justified if we keep in mind that we should think about "schools" in antiquity, as Culpepper has urged us to do in his *The Johannine School*. Moreover, we should allow for the fluidity among the social structures, needs, and purposes of each school, and the sociological model of groups that are not schools, in which devotees come together to share in their search for meaning (as in the Buddhist and Hindu shrines).

What has not been adequately questioned is the adjective "Johannine." Do we know that this book, the GosJn, originally was intended as the "Gospel According to Saint John"? Or, did later Christians put that title on it to insure the power—indeed infallible apostolicity—of its message?

Who is the "John" of the Gospel According to John? If "John the son of Zebedee" never is mentioned by name in the GosJn, not even in chapter 21, then why was this gospel attributed to him? The name Ἰωάν-

360

νης appears frequently in the GosJn, but only in the Book of Signs (chaps. 1–12) and always it refers to John the Baptist. His name appears no less than eight times in chapter 1 alone; and usually it is accompanied with an emphasis on his witness to Jesus. It may well be that in some early circles, before 125 C.E., the name "John" meant John the Baptist. A remnant of this tradition may well be preserved in Clement of Alexandria (c. 150– c. 212) who talks about "John" in such a way that he represents the GosJn: "Do you not know that John also invites us to salvation and becomes wholly a voice of exhortation? ... Who then is John? Allow us to say, in a figure, that he is a voice of the Word (φωνὴ τοῦ λόγου), raising his cry of exhortation in the desert."[1]

Scholars have emphasized that Thomas, and neither John the Baptist nor John the son of Zebedee, looms large as the hero of the GosJn. It is to him, and to him alone that the culminating and elevating confession is given in confrontation with the risen one. The preceding explorations and discussions have raised, for the first time from an exegesis of the GosJn, the possibility that the eyewitness behind the writing of the GosJn, the Beloved Disciple, is to be identified with Thomas. This equation raises a major series of questions focused on the following query: How and in what ways was the so-called Johannine School (a scholars' construct) related to the well-known School of Thomas? Did the School of John merely influence the School of Thomas? Was the Johannine School in its earliest years in ancient Palestine, before it ostensibly moved to Ephesus, known by some Christians as the School of Thomas? From whence does the School of Thomas come? How do we scholars find data to help us approximate informed responses to such questions?

As scholars have indicated for decades, and specialists on early Syriac and Gnosticism have demonstrated,[2] there was a major school in the East; it was called "the School of Thomas."[3] From this school, which was centered in but not limited to Edessa, issued such writings as the *Gospel of Thomas*, the *Acts of Thomas*, the *Minor Acts of Thomas*, the "Book of Thomas," the *Consummation of Thomas*, the *Infancy Gospel of Thomas*, and the *Martyrdom of Thomas* (but not the *Apocalypse of Thomas*).[4]

---

[1] For the Greek and ET see Clement of Alexandria, *Exhortation to the Greeks*, ed. and trans. G. W. Butterworth (LCL 92; Cambridge, Massachusetts: Harvard, 1982) 22–23.

[2] See Pokorný, *Řecké dědictví v Orientu (Helénismus v Egyptě a Sýrii)* (Prague: Oikúmené, 1993). This major introduction deserves to be translated into English.

[3] See the succinct summary in Layton, "The School of St. Thomas," *The Gnostic Scriptures* (Garden City, N.Y., 1987) 359–409.

[4] For bibliography on these publications see Charlesworth with J. Mueller, *The New Testament Apocrypha and Pseudepigrapha: A Guide to Publications, With Excursuses on Apocalypses* (The American Theological Library Association

Another early work bearing the name of Thomas is the *Book of Thomas the Contender*, which is preserved only in the Nag Hammadi Codices.[5] In the *Acta Apostolorum Apocrypha* are traditions pertaining to and stressing the importance of Thomas; and these may also reflect the interest in Thomas of the School of Thomas.[6]

The School of Thomas was one of the most influential of the early Christian schools. Its links with Judaism and ancient Palestine are evident. These have been intimated, indeed at times affirmed, in various ways by such leading experts as J. C. L. Gibson,[7] A. F. J. Klijn,[8] G. Quispel,[9] H. Koester,[10] J. B. Segal,[11] J. Neusner,[12] R. Murray,[13] B. Layton,[14] E. Yamauchi,[15] and Pokorný.[16] There can be no doubt that Thomas was considered the most important disciple of Jesus in Syria; these traditions very early spread from there to the East (especially India) and to the West (especially Egypt). The interest in Thomas is found in the Thomas compositions and in the Codex Curetonianus recension of the Old Syriac Gospels

---

Bibliography Series 17; Metuchen, N.J./London: Scarecrow Press, Inc., 1987) ad loc. cit.

[5] For bibliography on the Nag Hammadi Codices see the superb periodical publications by D. M. Scholer (the most recent "Bibliographia Gnostica" is "Supplementum XXII") which are published in *Novum Testamentum*. The latest is in *NovT* 36 (1994) 58–96.

[6] See especially the *Acts of Thomas*. Consult now P.-H. Poirier, *La Version copte de la prédication et du martyre de Thomas* (Subsidia Hagiographica 67; Brussels: Société des Bollandistes, 1984).

[7] J. C. L. Gibson, "From Qumran to Edessa," *New College Bulletin* [Edinburgh] 2 (1965) 9–19.

[8] A. F. J. Klijn, *Edessa: Die Stadt des Apostels Thomas*, trans. M. Hornschuh (Neukirchener Studienbücher 4; Neukirchen-Vluyn: Neukirchener Verlag des Erziehungsvereins, 1965).

[9] Quispel, *Gnostic Studies II*, passim, et 15, 128.

[10] H. Koester in *Trajectories Through Early Christianity* (Philadelphia: Fortress, 1971) see esp. 129–34.

[11] Segal, *Edessa: 'The Blessed City'* (Oxford: Clarendon Press, 1970) see esp. 30.

[12] J. Neusner, *Aphrahat and Judaism* (Leiden: Brill, 1971).

[13] R. Murray talks about "a reliable consensus ... forming on the Judaeo-Christian origin of Syriac Christianity, if not on where its first main centre lay" (*Symbols of Church and Kingdom* [Cambridge: Cambridge Univ. Press, 1975] 4, 8).

[14] Layton, *Gnostic Scriptures*, 364.

[15] E. Yamauchi, "The Syriac Evidence," *Pre-Christian Gnosticism* (Grand Rapids: Eerdmans, 1973) 84–100.

[16] Pokorný, *Píseň o Perle: Tajné knihy starověkých Gnostiků* (Prague: Vyšehrad, 1986).

(the *Evangeliôn da-Mĕpharrĕshê*)[17] in which at GosJn 14:22, Thomas is identified as Judas[18] Thomas (*ʾmr lh ihwdʾ tʾwmʾ*; contrast Syrus Sinaiticus: *ʾmr lh tʾwmʾ*).[19]

The Thomas traditions are early. This fact is unassailable, even though the conversion of Edessa and the place of Thomas in Edessan writings date no earlier than the fourth century, and is simply an example of the pervasive attempt to ground a nation's Christianity on the missionary activity of one of the Twelve. This perception is amply demonstrated by W. Bauer's significant work titled *Orthodoxy and Heresy in Earliest Christianity*.[20]

The connection between Adiabene and Palestine is well known; this province was farther to the East than Edessa where the School of Thomas

---

[17] See J. H. Charlesworth, "Semitisms in the New Testament and the Need to Clarify the Importance of the Syriac New Testament," in *Salvacion en la Palabra: Targum, Derash, Berith: Homenaje al Profesor Alejandro Diez Macho*, ed. Domingo Munoz Leon (Madrid: Ediciones Cristiandad, 1986) 633–38.

[18] Klijn shows that "Thomas" in Johannine circles was an epithet for "twin," because the *Acts of Thomas* is really the Acts of Judas since in the oldest Syriac manuscript (5/6th cent. C.E.) the leading character is Judas, and because Jesus appeared as a "twin," that is as Judas, according to early Syriac Christology ("John XIV 22 and the Name Judas Thomas," in *Studies in John Presented to Professor Dr. J. N. Sevenster* [Supplements to Novum Testamentum 24; Leiden: Brill, 1970] 88–96 [no editor given]).

[19] In preparing a new critical edition of St. Catherine's Monastery Codex Syriacus (MS Sin. Syr. 30) I have chosen the title Syrus Sinaiticus. In fact, this is the way Harnack referred to this manuscript. See Harnack, *The Mission and Expansion of Christianity in the First Three Centuries*, 2:144. For the Syriac of 14:22, see the critical apparatus (ad loc. cit.) in F. C. Burkitt, ed., *Evangelion Da-Mepharreshe: The Curetonian Version of the Gospels*, 2 vols. (Cambridge: Cambridge Univ. Press, 1904) and in A. S. Lewis, ed., *The Old Syriac Gospels or Evangelion Da-Mepharreshê* (London: Williams and Norgate, 1910).

[20] Unfortunately, Bauer used terms like "orthodoxy" and "heresy" for a period of history in which there was no "orthodoxy" and hence no "heresy." He also miscast the advent of Christianity in many regions and often missed the kernel of history in legends. For example, he judged the Abgar legend to be "pure fabrication" (11). But, Syriac experts today acknowledge that behind the fiction is some reliable historical information (as W. S. McCullough suggested in his *A Short History of Syriac Christianity to the Rise of Islam* [Scholars Press General Series 4; Chico, Cal.: Scholars Press, 1982] 24). See Bauer, *Orthodoxy and Heresy in Earliest Christianity*, ed. R. A. Kraft and G. Krodel (Philadelphia: Fortress, 1971). Murray also points out, and correctly, that there is a consensus that Syriac Christianity was formed out of Judaeo-Christianity, that there is some historical value in some traditions preserved in the *Doctrine of Addai*, and that Bauer's work suffers from excesses and a "trace of romantic idealization of early" so-called heretics (*Symbols of Church and Kingdom*, 4–6).

settled and became one of the great schools in antiquity.[21] The kings and queens of the province of Adiabene converted to Judaism before the destruction of Jerusalem in 70 C.E., and their presence in the Holy City at that time is attested today by the impressive rock-hewn tombs on Saladin Street in Jerusalem, and also perhaps by the remains of palaces south of the Temple Mount.[22] The caravans and the pilgrims, especially at the time of the mandatory pilgrimages, would have linked Adiabene with Palestine. Many would have stopped at Petra, whose monumental tombs and buildings are now dated to the first century C.E.[23] The connection between the School of Thomas and Palestine seems also confirmed by the prominence of Tobias "from Palestine" in the accounts of the conversion of Edessan pagans to Christians.

The School of Thomas is related in some ways with the putative Johannine School and both of them show some influences from Qumran and Persia.[24] Christianity was present in Edessa (= Orhay, and modern Urfa) by about 130 at least, although the early Edessan compositions exaggerate the early nature of the connections with Palestine and Jesus.[25] Second-century Edessa was a melting-pot for creative ideas from both West (especially Rome) and East (including Turfan and Canton) and a caravan-stop for merchants conveying silk, spices, incense, and jewels from East to West. Scholars like Bardaisan were apparently influenced by

[21] Segal points out that in the first century there "was constant traffic between Edessa and Adiabene, through Nisibis" (*Edessa*, 30).

[22] It is well accepted today that at least one aspect of Kahle's thesis regarding the origins of the Peshiṭta is correct. He correctly perceived that the Peshiṭta was produced probably by Jews in Adiabene.

[23] See G. W. Bowersock, *Roman Arabia* (Cambridge: Mass./London: Harvard Univ. Press, 1983, 1994) 12–14, 58–62. Also see the studies assembled in *Petra und das Königreich der Nabatäer*, ed. M. Lindner (Munich: Delp, 1980 [3rd ed.]).

[24] See esp. Quispel, "Qumran, John and Jewish Christianity," in *John and the Dead Sea Scrolls*, 137–55. For thirty years I have argued that Zurvanism, an early form of Zoroastrianism, influenced Qumran. See *John and the Dead Sea Scrolls*, esp. xv. For additional reading on Zurvanism see G. Widengren, *Iranische Geisteswelt von den Anfängen bis zum Islam* (Baden-Baden: Holle Verlag, 1961) 79–93; and A. Hultgård, "Mythe et histoire dans l'Iran ancien: Cosmogonie et l'histoire du monde," in *Recurrent Patterns in Iranian Religions: From Mazdaism to Sufism*, ed. Gignoux (Studia Iranica. Cahier 11; Paris: Association pour l'avancement des études Iraniennes, 1992) 37–56. For a general overview of Iranian influences on proto-gnostic and gnostic works, see K. Rudolph, *Gnosis: The Nature and History of Gnosticism*, trans. R. McL. Wilson (San Francisco: Harper, 1984) 59–67.

[25] Christianity may have come to Edessa from Adiabene.

the GosJn—he advocated a Logos Christology[26]—but it is not certain, as H. J. W. Drijvers stated, that he was a "Christian" (whatever that might mean then and there).[27] Both ancient traditions now edited and apostolic legitimacy now serving the Edessan church are reflected in the pseudonymous "Letter of Christ to Abgar."

In the study of Christian origins we can no longer simply ignore Gnosticism,[28] Mandaeanism,[29] Manichaeism,[30] and Nestorianism[31]—each

[26] The appearance of the concept and *terminus technicus* Logos does not in and of itself suggest, let alone prove, knowledge of the GosJn. B. M. Metzger argues that Justin knew the GosJn because of his references to "the *logos*"; and he concludes that "the idea that Christ was the only-begotten Son seems to have been derived from the Fourth Gospel" (*The Canon of the New Testament* (Oxford: Clarendon Press, 1987, 1992) 146–47. This conclusion is entirely possible, but the Logos concept goes back to Heraclitus, and both Philo and the author of Poimandres present a logos concept that is strikingly similar to that of the GosJn 1:1-18. For example, Philo refers to the Logos as God, second to the Father: τὸν δεύτερον θεόν, ὅς ἐστιν ἐκείνου λόγος (Greek frag. no. 62; LCL 401, 203). The "divine Word" is High Priest and God's First-Born (*On Dreams* 1.215). Also, see *On Dreams* 1.230, καλεῖ δὲ θεὸν ... λόγον, ... Finally, see Poimandres, which is close to the time when the GosJn reached its final editions with the Appendix. Note, in particular the claim that the Word is associated with Light and is called Son of God, and that the Word created all things (*CH* 1).

[27] H. J. W. Drijvers, *Bardaiṣan of Edessa* (Studia Semitica Neerlandica; Assen: Van Gorcum & Co., 1966) 220–24.

[28] For translations, see esp. Robinson, ed., *The Nag Hammadi Library*; Layton, *The Gnostic Scriptures*; Klimkeit, *Gnosis on the Silk Road*.

[29] See esp. M. Lidzbarski, *Das Johannesbuch der Mandäer: Einleitung, Übersetzung, Kommentar* (Giessen: Töpelmann, 1915 [reprinted in 1966]), Lidzbarski, ed., *Ginza: Der Schatz oder das grosse Buch der Mandäer* (Göttingen: Vandenhoeck & Ruprecht, 1925), E. S. Drower, *The Mandaeans of Iraq and Iran* (Oxford: Clarendon, 1937), Drower, *The Canonical Prayerbook of the Mandaeans* (Leiden: Brill, 1959), W. Foerster and R. McL. Wilson, eds., *Gnosis: A Selection of Gnostic Texts;* Vol. 2: *Coptic and Mandaean Sources* (Oxford: Clarendon, 1974). Also see Rudolph, *Gnosis*, 343–66.

[30] Esp. see I. Gardner, ed., *The Kephalaia of the Teacher* (Nag Hammadi and Manichaean Studies 37; Leiden: Brill, 1995). Among the abundance of works on Manichaeism see Jes Asmussen, *Manichaean Literature* (Delmar, New York: Scholars' Facsimiles & Reprints, 1975); G. Widengren, ed., *Der Manichäismus* (Wege der Forschung 168; Darmstadt: Wissenschaftliche Buchgesellschaft, 1977); S. N. C. Lieu, *Manichaeism in the Later Roman Empire and Medieval China: A Historical Survey* (Manchester: Manchester Univ. Press, 1985); L. Cirillo, ed., with A. Roselli, *Codex Manichaicus Coloniensis* (Studi e Richerche 4; Rome: Marra Editore Cosenza, 1984 [notably the articles by J. Maier and L. Loenen]); A. van Tongerloo and Søren Giversen, eds., *Manichaica Selecta* (Manichaean Studies 1; Louvain: International Association of Manichaean Studies, 1991); J. C. Reeves, *Jewish Lore in Manichaean Cos-*

of these were once powerful and influential.[32] The GosJn may not be "gnostic"; but it certainly is related to the world-wide interest in knowing (gnosis) and is, in my judgment, proto-gnostic.[33]

The so-called eastern gnostic texts (which often celebrate Mani) are now available in a convenient format thanks to H.-J. Klimkeit.[34] In these documents the name of Thomas is conspicuously absent, and the Beloved Disciple is never mentioned.[35] This fact is surprising because of the crucifixion texts or hymns,[36] the eastern provenience of the documents, and the fact that Mani called his *Twin* "the Paraclete."[37]

Much earlier than the spurious "Letter of Christ to Abgar," and free from the full-blown gnostic myth, as G. Quispel has shown,[38] is the *Gos-*

---

mogony: Studies in the Book of Giants Traditions (Monographs of the Hebrew Union College 14; Cincinnati: Hebrew Union College Press, 1992).

[31] See L. Abramowski and A. E. Goodman, *A Nestorian Collection of Christological Texts* (Cambridge: Cambridge Univ. Press, 1972). Also see S. A. Harvey, "Nestorianism," in *Encyclopedia of Early Christianity*, 644-47 (and the following entry on "Nestorius") and the bibliography cited by her. Refreshing and insightful is Crown Prince El Hassan Bin Talal's *Christianity in the Arab World* (Royal Institute for Inter-Faith Studies; Amman: Arabesque, 1994).

[32] An important, but little known, work is E. Lupieri's *I Mandei: Gli ultimi gnostici* (Biblioteca di cultura religiosa 61; Brescia: Paideia Editrice, 1993).

[33] It is not gnostic because, *inter alia*, the Evangelist employs the verb "to know" more frequently than any other intracanonical evangelist, but he never uses the noun γνῶσις. In fact, according to Morgenthaler, the verb γινώσκειν appears only 12 times in Mk, 20 and 28 times in Mt and Lk respectively, but 56 times in the GosJn.

[34] H. J. Klimkeit, *Gnosis on the Silk Road: Gnostic Texts from Central Asia* (New York/San Francisco: Harper, 1993).

[35] I do not think it is justifiable from scholarly research to restore lacunae as in the "Crucifixion Hymn" 5: "... and send word to Simon and [John and James and the] other [disciples of the Lord] that the Lord [has risen]. [And he on the] right side said, ..." See Klimkeit, *Gnosis on the Silk Road*, 70-71. The restoration, based on GosJn 20, assumes that the Beloved Disciple is the apostle John. How are we to know that the words circumscribed by brackets did not once contain the name of Thomas?

[36] See esp. the Crucifixion Hymns and texts in Klimkeit, *Gnosis on the Silk Road*, 70-75.

[37] See the Coptic *Kephalaia* 14,29-15,24. A convenient English translation is found in Klimkeit, *Gnosis on the Silk Road*, 2-3.

[38] Quispel rightly points out that "the gnostic myth is absent in the *Gospel of Thomas*" ("Das Lied von der Perle," *Gnostic Studies II* [Uitgaven van het Nederlands Historisch-Archaeologisch Instituut te Istanbul 34.2; Istanbul: Nederlands Historisch-Archaeologisch Instituut te Istanbul, 1975] 122-41; see esp. 125).

pel of Thomas. It is the one apocryphal book that powerfully challenges, in the judgment of many specialists, the shape of the closed canon.[39] Its traditions and some of its sayings have a long history which pulls us back into the first century.

In the *Acts of Thomas* is preserved another early composition, which is clearly independent of it as the manuscripts demonstrate.[40] It is an early hymn (a ψαλμός according to its Greek text) called "The Hymn of the Pearl." It is surely not "gnostic" but proto-gnostic in the sense that it antedates the second-century gnostic systems that appear near the end of the career of the genius Valentinus. As Layton indicates, it is like "a figurative fairy tale or folktale," which preserves a "Hellenistic myth of the human soul's entry into bodily incarnation and its eventual disengagement from the body."[41] It is similar to the books of Wisdom in ancient Israel in that it embodies the ancient lore of the human's search for meaning and self-understanding.

The Hymn of the Pearl clearly antedates the *Acts of Thomas*, as the content of the work and the style of the Syriac indicate,[42] and as most scholars now recognize. The date of composition is a subject of debate; but it certainly antedates 165 C.E. when the Parthians lost control of the area in which the School of Thomas was located. It may even date back— perhaps in any earlier form—into the first century C.E.[43] A. Adam dates

[39] See the mature reflections by Metzger in "Is the Canon Open or Closed?" in *The Canon*, 271-75.

[40] See the discussion by P.-H. Poirier who clarifies the manuscript evidence for the Hymn of the Pearl. It is not in Greek MS P (*Parisinus Graecus* 1510 of the 10th cent. C.E.) nor in some other manuscripts; and it is in only one of the six Syriac manuscripts (e.g., it is only in BM Add. 14645 fols. 30va–32ra of 936 C.E. [which is reproduced in Poirier's book]). See Poirier, *L'Hymne de la Perle des Actes de Thomas: Introduction, Texte, Traduction, Commentaire* (Homo Religiosus 8; Louvain-La-Neuve: [Institut Orientaliste de l'Université Catholique de Louvain-la-Neuve], 1982) see esp. 181–84.

[41] Layton, *The Gnostic Scriptures*, 366.

[42] The wandering saint of the Thomas works (esp. the *Acts of Thomas*) and the journeying prince of the Hymn of the Pearl both set out from Mesopotamia.

[43] Segal insightfully states that the Hymn of the Pearl (which he calls the Hymn of the Soul) "probably derives from a Syriac source and was composed not later than the first century A.D." (*Edessa*, 31). A. Adam is convinced that the Hymn of the Pearl was composed in the first century C.E., but before Christianity shaped Edessa (*Die Psalmen des Thomas und das Perlenlied als Zeugnisse vorchristlicher Gnosis* [Beihefte zur Zeitschrift für die neutestamentliche Wissenschaft 24; Berlin: Alfred Töpelmann, 1959] 60, 75). The early traditions in the Hymn of the Pearl are obvious; they have even led G. Widengren to date the hymn before 150 B.C.E. ("Der iranische Hintergrund der Gnosis," *Zeitschrift für Religions- und Geistesgeschichte* 4 [1952] 97-114).

the composition to the period 50–70 C.E.,[44] but that seems too early, except for traditions preserved within it.

According to the *Acts of Thomas*, Judas (the earliest form of the name which later becomes Judas Thomas), like his Master (his "twin"), remains silent during his trial and is the object of people's worship (106). In prison when he is asked by other prisoners to pray for them, he chants the "Hymn of the Pearl." Later Christians may have seen reflections of the Beloved Disciple in the account of the youth who attaches himself to "Judas."[45] The youth was fair, lovable, and became "Judas's" (καὶ συνό-μιλον αὐτὸν ἔσχον, καὶ φίλον καὶ κοινωνὸν τῆς ἐμῆς).[46]

What is the relation between the Johannine School and the School of Thomas? The relationship has virtually never been seen, and therefore commentators and scholars have not asked this question. Schnackenburg has come very close to discussing this question, and his comments should be incorporated now for reflection. He speculates that "the Johannine tradition, originating in Palestine, was subjected to Syrian influences before it reached Asia Minor (Ephesus), where it was fixed and edited."[47] I have no doubt that the GosJn originated in ancient Palestine and that very early so-called Syrian influences shaped the Johannine traditions. Schnackenburg continues in the subsequent volume of his commentary on the GosJn:

> The prominence of Thomas may derive from the fourth gospel's connection with Syria (cf. vol.1, 150–52); the Acts of Thomas and Gospel of Thomas probably come from Syria, where this apostle was particularly venerated. In the Syrian tradition, however, he is known as Judas Thomas and Didymus, while in the fourth gospel "Judas, not Iscariot" is distinguished from him (14:22). Probably the Thomas tradition developed in Syria in two directions, one in the Johannine circle, in which he is less prominent than other disciples and is the type of the disciple who takes a long time to understand, and one in Gnostic circles, where he is regarded as the recipient of secret revelations. The Johannine portrait of the disciple is definitely the earlier stage, and the basis for the later development of the Gnostic cult. A third strand is constituted by the missionary tradition, according to which Thomas brought the gospel to India. The Johannine tradition is

---

[44] A. Adam, *Die Psalmen des Thomas*, 59.

[45] The quotations warn that although Judas is chanting the hymn, the original does not name the one who goes in search of the pearl. Like the Beloved Disciple, the actor is anonymous.

[46] The Greek is provided for convenience of comparison with the GosJn, although the original work, like the *Acts of Thomas*, was composed in a Semitic language. For the Greek of the Hymn of the Pearl see Adam, *Die Psalmen des Thomas*, 84–90.

[47] Schnackenburg, *St. John*, 1:152.

the earliest layer and shows independence of the Gnostic tradition, a fact which is not without importance for an assessment of the inter-relation of the two.[48]

Schnackenburg is not merely speculating. He has focused on a detailed exegesis of the GosJn with remarkable insight.

Unfortunately, his exegesis is marred by disparaging thoughts about Thomas in the GosJn. How can Schnackenburg, after living with the GosJn for decades, judge that Thomas is "less prominent than other disciples" in the "Johannine circle"? According to the GosJn we do not hear the names of James and John the sons of Zebedee; and in fact they are virtually absent (see chaps. 2.1 and 3). We do not know the names of the "Twelve." We know only that Judas Iscariot and Thomas are assuredly in this group, but we are not even sure if it constitutes the elite group of disciples (see chap. 2.3). Furthermore, how can Schnackenburg claim that Thomas "is the type of the disciple who takes a long time to understand?" Has he taken that idea from the GosJn or from a desire to distance the GosJn from Gnosticism?

The quotation from Schnackenburg has been highlighted not because of the imperfections in it, in my view, but because of his perspicacious insight into Christian origins. Yes, the School of Thomas did apparently develop in two directions by the middle of the second century C.E. One may be seen in the GosJn and the other in the *Gospel of Thomas*. These are roughly contemporaneous gospels and both preserve traditions that are very early, even going back to Jesus himself, albeit in later edited forms. Either the School of Thomas developed primarily out of Johannine traditions, or there was a first-century circle of Thomas traditions that influenced in different and independent ways the GosJn and the early Thomas compositions. The period covered by the shaping of the GosJn and also by the completion of the *Gospel of Thomas* allows for more than one level, or direction, of relationship.

Let us now delve deeper, in a preliminary way, into the School of Thomas. Five early Christian compositions bear the name of Thomas, who is almost always called Thomas, Judas the Twin. Thomas is the twin of Jesus. Obviously some early Syriac scholars developed this idea from the GosJn in which Judas who is not Judas Iscariot is mentioned in 14:22 (Ἰούδας, οὐχ ὁ Ἰσκαριώτης). This verse in the Old Syriac Gospels, as we saw earlier, appears not as merely Judas, but as "Judas Thomas." The early tradition is also found in the Abgar legends.

---

[48] Schnackenburg, *St. John*, 2:327.

7.1 GOSPEL OF THOMAS

The apocryphal work titled the *Gospel of Thomas* was probably composed in Greek before circa 140 C.E.[49] It is not a gospel but, as Koester states, the *incipit* suggests the title "Thomas's Book of Secret Sayings."[50] It contains 114 sayings of Jesus, but it is not to be confused with Q (the source of Jesus sayings used by Mt and Lk).[51] Scholars are no longer in consensus that it is gnostic. In fact, although some scholars have disparaged the literary products of the School of Thomas as "gnostic," Layton is surely correct to judge that "the Thomas literature shows no unmistakable signs of being Valentinian or classically gnostic." Notice how he continues:

> Instead, it presupposes only an uncomplicated Hellenistic myth of the divine origins of the self; conceives of god as unitary; does not discuss the alleged error of wisdom; puts no stress on revisionistic retelling of the myth of Genesis; and does not teach about an ignorant maker of the world.[52]

These valid and erudite insights succinctly help define the School of Thomas.

Our present task is to seek to discern how and in what ways the *Gospel of Thomas* and the GosJn—or the traditions preserved in them—may be related, and how this helps us evaluate the possibility that in the GosJn Thomas may in fact be the Beloved Disciple. Research on the *Gospel of Thomas* has been characterized by a blind focus only on the Synoptics, with little or no mention of the GosJn. Notice how the following excellent books and monographs center discussion only on the Synoptics: W. Schrage, *Das Verhältnis des Thomas-Evangeliums zur synoptischen Tradition und zu den koptischen Evangelienübersetzungen*,[53] and C. M.

---

[49] H. Koester is of the opinion that the GosTh "may have been composed as early as the end of the 1st century" (*Ancient Christian Gospels: Their History and Development* [Philadelphia: Trinity Press International; London: SCM, 1990] 21).

[50] Koester, *Ancient Christian Gospels*, 21.

[51] Too often scholars have insinuated that the GosTh is like Q; but as R. McL. Wilson pointed out long ago, this gospel "should not be linked with Q" (*Studies in the Gospel of Thomas* [London: Mowbray, 1960] 143). The GosTh is both like and unlike Q; that is, it is a sayings source, but it has a distinctly different theological outlook and comes from another social milieu.

[52] Layton, *The Gnostic Scriptures*, 360.

[53] Berlin: Verlag Alfred Töpelmann, 1964. Schrage's excellent study mentions the GosJn only in connection with Log. 1 (cf. GosJn 8:52); see 28.

Tuckett, *Nag Hammadi and the Gospel Tradition: Synoptic Tradition in the Nag Hammadi Library.*[54] H. Montefiore's and H. E. W. Turner's *Thomas and the Evangelists* is about only the Synoptic Evangelists.[55] R. McL. Wilson's *Studies in the Gospel of Thomas* is concerned with Synoptic parallels to the *Gospel of Thomas.*[56] Since there are no parables in the GosJn, the striking links between the *Gospel of Thomas* and the GosJn are not considered in the many books on Jesus' parables that include the Thomas traditions; hence J. D. Crossan's *In Parables* does not even include the GosJn.[57]

Of the 357 publications on the *Gospel of Thomas* in German, French, English, Latin, Japanese, Spanish, Swedish, and less familiar languages like Serbo-Croatian that I have cited, many feature the parallels between the Synoptics and the *Gospel of Thomas.* Not one monograph, however, is devoted to a study of the GosJn and this apocryphal gospel.[58] The impression is that J. Leipoldt's[59] and R. M. Grant's[60] judgment serves as a consensus; they concluded that in contrast to the Synoptics, the GosJn has few parallels in the *Gospel of Thomas.* There is reason to question such a consensus.

It is well known that the Gospel of Thomas and the GosJn share the same ethos.[61] It is not so much the matter of which gospel influenced the other,[62] as it is that both preserve and highlight strikingly similar tradi-

---

[54] Edinburgh: T. & T. Clark, 1986. On 186 Tuckett lists the passages cited from the GosJn, so he does not ignore it altogether.

[55] H. Montefiore, H. E. W. Turner, *Thomas and the Evangelists* (SBT 35; London: SCM, 1962).

[56] R. McL. Wilson, *Studies in the Gospel of Thomas* (London: Mowbray, 1960).

[57] J. D. Crossan, *In Parables* (San Francisco/Cambridge: Harper & Row, 1973, 1985). Crossan's *Four Other Gospels* (Minneapolis: Winston, 1985) discusses the independence of the GosTh by comparing it only with the Synoptics; see esp. 36–37.

[58] J. H. Charlesworth, *The New Testament Apocrypha and Pseudepigrapha: A Guide to Publications, with Excursuses on Apocalypses,* see 374–402.

[59] J. Leipoldt, in *Koptisch-gnostische Schriften aus den Papyrus-Codices von Nag-Hammadi* (Hamburg-Bergstedt, 1960).

[60] R. M. Grant, *The Secret Sayings of Jesus According to the Gospel of Thomas* (London, 1960).

[61] The most striking literary parallels are with Mt, then Lk, less with Mark, and very few with the GosJn. The links with the GosJn are more in terms of the proto-gnostic social environment and are ideological. For a chart of some parallels between the GosTh and the GosJn, see J. Doresse, *L'Évangile selon Thomas* (Paris: Éditions du Rocher, 1988 [2nd ed.]) XV; 209–15.

[62] J. Meier argues against those who have claimed far too much for the apocryphal writings (in my opinion he has written a marvelous book, but in this area he tends to overreact). *A Marginal Jew: Rethinking the Historical Jesus,* 2

tions.[63] For example, note these sayings that are unique to the *Gospel of Thomas* and the GosJn (italics are added to clarify possible links [allowance must be made both for the differences between Coptic and Greek and for striking similarities diminished because the original Aramaic is not available]):

GosTh[64]	GosJn
Whoever discovers the meaning of these sayings *will not* taste (*jitpe*) *death*. Log. 1[65]	If *any one* keeps my word he will never *taste* (γεύομαι) death. 8:52
There is *light within*	... the *light* is not *within* him. 11:10[66]
	The *light* is *in* you
a man *of light*,[67] .... Log. 24	... become Sons *of Light*. 12:35-36

---

vols. (The Anchor Bible Reference Library; New York: Doubleday, 1987, 1994) see esp. vol. 1, chap. 5 "The *Agrapha* and the Apocryphal Gospels."

[63] See the debate among specialists; see esp. Brown, "The Gospel of Thomas and St. John's Gospel," *New Testament Studies* 9 (1962/1963) 155-77; Brown, "Gnosticism," *Gospel*, 1:lvii-lvi; S. L. Davies, "Thomas and John," in *The Gospel of Thomas and Christian Wisdom* (New York: Seabury, 1983) 106-16.

[64] Translations from the Coptic of the GosTh and from the Greek of the GosJn are my own, but I am appreciative of other translations, namely the following: A. Guillaumont, et al., *The Gospel According to Thomas* (Leiden: Brill; London: Collins, 1959); T. O. Lambdin in *The Nag Hammadi Library in English*, ed. J. M. Robinson (New York: Harper & Row, 1977); B. Layton, *The Gnostic Scriptures* (Garden City, N.Y.: Doubleday, 1987); R. W. Funk, R. W. Hoover, et al., *The Five Gospels: The Search for the Authentic Words of Jesus* (New York: Macmillan, 1993) 471-532.

[65] For a discussion of Log. 1 and GosJn 8:52, which concludes that the former may be earlier, see E. Gillabert, Bourgeois, Y. Haas, *Évangile selon Thomas: Présentation, traduction et commentaires* (Paris: Dervy-Livres, 1985) 156. In contrast, Schrage makes some stylistic and textual observations that raise the possibility that the GosTh is here dependent on the GosJn, although the εἰς τὸν αἰῶνα of the GosJn has a secondary character. Schrage, *Das Verhältnis*, 28-30.

[66] Cf. GosJn 8:12 and 9:5.

[67] Unfortunately for a closer link with the GosJn, this expression in the GosTh cannot be translated "a son of light." The Sahidic and Boharic versions have a literal translation of GosJn 12:36, and each is different from the GosTh Log. 24. The *termini technici* "Sons of Light" and "Sons of Darkness," which scholars have rightly traced to Essene creative thought, appears in the *Kephalaia* in a way strikingly similar, and perhaps influenced by, the Qumran *War Scroll*. See, e.g., *Kephalaia* 58,1-60,12, in which we find the following: "The sons of light waged five [war]s against the sons of darkness. The sons of light [humili-

There will be days when	
you will seek me	*You will seek me*
(*and*) *you will not find me.*	*and you will not find me.* 7:34
Log. 38	
I am the one who *comes from* what	Jesus, knowing that the *Father*
is Undivided. I was granted some	had given all *things* into his
of the *things* of my *Father.*[68]	hands, and that he had *come*
Log. 61[69]	*from* God and was going to God
	.... 13:3
I will *destroy* [this] *house, and no*	*Destroy this temple, and* in three
one will be able to rebuild *it* ...	days I *will* raise *it* up. 2:19
Log. 71	
[your] *governors* ...	*Pilate* says to him,
they [shall] not be able to know	"What is
the *truth* (*tme*).[70] Log. 78	*truth* (ἀλήθεια)?"[71] 18:38
Whoever *drinks* from my mouth	If any one thirst, let him come to
will become like *me*; I myself	*me* and *drink*. He who believes
shall become that person, and the	in *me* ... "Out of his heart shall
hidden things shall be revealed	flow rivers of living water."
to him.[72] Log. 108	7:37-38

ated the s]ons of darkness in them all" (I. Gardner, *The Kephalaia of the Teacher* [Nag Hammadi and Manichaean Studies 37; Leiden: Brill, 1995] 62). Also see the expressions "the sons of the Darkness" who are contrasted to "the sons of the Day" in *Hymn to the Third Messenger as Sun God* (Parthian) and "All you sons of [Darkness] ..." on a Parthian amulet; see Klimkeit, *Gnosis on the Silk Road*, 58, 164. Clearly, not only the GosJn, but also Qumranic documents (or early Jewish documents found in the Qumran caves) like the *Book of the Giants* were preserved by Mani and his followers; hence, Manichaeism can no longer be ignored in seeking to understand the first century.

[68] For a different translation see Gillabert, et al., *Évangile selon Thomas*, 346.

[69] See J. Sell, "Johannine Traditions in Logion 61 of the Gospel of Thomas," *Perspectives in Religious Studies* 7 (1980) 24–37.

[70] The noun in the Coptic [*netn*]r̄rōou, "[your] governors," derives from *rro*; it corresponds to many Greek nouns, including ἄρχων and ἡγούμενος. Both of these were used in antiquity (from Polybius to the Oxyrhynchus Papyri) to denote the Roman governor (*praefectus*). The Roman governor during Jesus' ministry was only Pilate who served from 26 to 36; hence, this parallel is impressive. Pilate was called a "prefectus" as we know from the first-century inscription. For a facsimile, see Charlesworth, *Jesus Within Judaism*, illus. 10.

[71] Coptic *tme* corresponds to ἀλήθεια. Also see GosJn 8:32, "You shall know the truth and the truth shall make you free."

[72] Some experts point not to GosJn 7:37-38 but to 6:53 and see "une tonalité différente, une réalité identique à celle du logion 108." They also express some loss for words: "Arrivé au logion 108, le commentateur souhaite déposer la plume, laisser un grand blanc et s'abîmer dans une profonde

This is merely a selected list of parallel sayings of which some have not been seen before by specialists; it is abbreviated from a more extensive collection.[73] For our present purposes it is necessary, however, to dig deeper into the first parallel. It is significant and may help us in the search for the identity of the Beloved Disciple.

According to GosTh Log. 1, the disciple who finds the meaning of Jesus' words "will not taste death" (*fnajitipe an m̄pmou*). According to Log. 108, Jesus explains that "whoever drinks from my mouth"[74] will "become as I am and I myself will become he." This seems to indicate that a disciple will be Jesus' spiritual twin. Also in Log. 108 is Jesus' word that this disciple will receive a revelation of the secret meaning of Jesus' words. According to Log. 13, Thomas knows the meaning Jesus sought; consequently, Jesus replies that he is no longer Thomas's master. Jesus then states that Thomas has drunk from the spring he has measured out, thus fulfilling the requirement of Log. 108 which also stipulated that such a disciple would receive the revelation of the hidden meaning of Jesus' words. These reflections seem to indicate that Thomas "will not taste death," because he understands the meaning Jesus intended. These three logia, seen together, seem to indicate that Thomas is Jesus' twin, Didymos Judas Thomas (Log. 1), and that he "will not taste death."

So interpreted, these logia are strikingly similar to traditions in the GosJn; and they build upon the common theme of not tasting death (Coptic *jitpe* = γεύομαι). The redactor who added chapter 21 to the GosJn refers in 21:23 to a saying that spread abroad among some Christians that the Beloved Disciple would not die (οὐκ ἀποθνῄσκει = *namou an* [in the Sahidic NT]). Is it possible to find a Christian community, which the redactor might know and would consider "abroad," in which there is a tradition that a favorite disciple of Jesus would not die? Indeed, these criteria are fulfilled when Log. 1 is perceived along with Log. 108 and Log. 13 in the *Gospel of Thomas*. As we have seen they indicate symbolically that Thomas was not to taste death. These insights certainly raise an intriguing link between GosJn 21 and the *Gospel of Thomas*.

We scholars have not been successful in finding the logion that the redactor of GosJn 21 knew was disturbing the Johannine Christians. It is clearly a traditional saying of Jesus that had been interpreted to mean that

---

prosternation" (Gillabert, et al., *Évangile selon Thomas*, 256).

[73] Compare also the following: Log. 27 with GosJn 9:14-16; Log. 28 with GosJn 1:9-14; Log. 31 with GosJn 4:4.

[74] Compare GosJn 7:37, "Jesus stood up and proclaimed saying, 'If one is thirsty let him come to me and drink.'"

the Beloved Disciple would not die. Apparently the Thomas traditions antedate the addition of chapter 21 and help us comprehend the claim that Thomas will not taste death (see chap. 2.1). In this research we have thus uncovered evidence that suggests the redactor of the GosJn knew that the Beloved Disciple was Thomas.

Moreover, the traditions seem to be contemporaneous with the writing of the second edition of the GosJn. Jesus' treatment of Thomas in Log. 13 is strikingly similar to his way of relating to the Beloved Disciple in GosJn 13:23-26. According to Log. 13, after Thomas's confession, Jesus takes him aside and shares with him some secret knowledge. Thomas does not share the knowledge with his co-disciples. Similarly, in the GosJn 13 Jesus whispers to the Beloved Disciple the knowledge he had requested (13:25). The Beloved Disciple does not share this information with his co-disciples, and not even with Peter, even though he had raised the question at the outset (13:24). The portrayal of Thomas in the *Gospel of Thomas* is sometimes stunningly similar to the narrative portrait of the Beloved Disciple in the GosJn. Cumulatively we have seen that in the first century C.E. and in the GosJn there is considerable evidence that the Beloved Disciple is none other than Thomas.

While the Synoptics portray a Jesus who looks to the future coming—or at least fulfillment—of God's Kingdom, both the *Gospel of Thomas* and the GosJn stress its present—realizing—reality.[75] They also contain ideas and perspectives that are either incipiently gnostic or proto-gnostic.[76] Yet, neither is to be branded as "gnostic." It is not helpful to simply state that all these links are unimpressive because the *Gospel of Thomas* dates from around 140 and is "uncanonical." It contains traditions that go deep into the first century C.E.,[77] was written when there was no canon (let alone a closed one),[78] and the linguistic and conceptual links

---

[75] This fact has been pointed out often. Note, for example, R. Grant and D. N. Freedman, *The Secret Sayings of Jesus* (New York: Barnes & Noble, 1960, 1993) 113-14. Metzger clarifies that the most numerous parallels between the GosTh and the GosJn chiefly relate to "Jesus' conversation with the woman of Samaria (chap. iv) and the Farewell Discourses in chaps. xii-xvii." He also notes that in both "the presence of divine wisdom" is the "true destiny of human existence" (*The Canon*, 85).

[76] Brown also judges the GosTh as "incipiently Gnostic" (*Gospel*, 1:liii).

[77] For a discussion of traditions preserved with less redactional alteration, and independent of the intracanonical gospels, see Charlesworth, "Jesus, the Nag Hammadi Codices, and Josephus," *Jesus Within Judaism*, 77-102; idem, "Gesù, i codici di Nag Hammadi e Giuseppe Flavio," *Gesù nel giudaismo del suo tempo* (Piccola biblioteca teologica 30; Turin: Claudiana, 1994) 103-32.

[78] See B. M. Metzger, *The Canon of the New Testament: Its Origin, Development, and Significance* (Oxford: Clarendon, 1987, 1992).

between it and the GosJn are complex and do not lend themselves to a facile theory of literary dependence.[79]

As the GosJn presents Thomas as the one true disciple who grasps who Jesus is—confessing him in the grand climax as Lord and God—so the *Gospel of Thomas* elevates Thomas above all the apostles. The author of this work has Jesus tell Thomas, "I am not your master (*anok pekcah an*), because you have drunk, you have become drunk from the bubbling spring which I have measured out" (Log. 83).

In the *Gospel of Thomas* the apostle Thomas is portrayed as Jesus' twin (Log. 1). This links the work with the GosJn which is the only document in the New Testament in which Thomas is called the "twin" (11:16, 20:24, 21:2). A spiritual twinship is most likely meant (and this tradition has been kept alive not only within Syriac Christianity, but also within the Russian Orthodox Church). If Thomas is the Beloved Disciple in the GosJn, then it is easy to understand why Leonardo da Vinci in his painting of the Last Supper places Thomas in the seat of the Beloved Disciple.[80] The traditions certainly do not prove that Thomas made his way to India within a few decades of Jesus' life,[81] but they do preserve evidence that some Christians held that Thomas was indeed the Beloved Disciple.[82]

Thus there is an organic relation between the GosJn and the *Gospel of Thomas*. As eminent scholars have stated for years about this apocry-

---

[79] See Charlesworth and C. A. Evans, "Jesus in the Agrapha and Apocryphal Gospels," in *Studying the Historical Jesus: Evaluations of the State of Current Research* (New Testament Tools and Studies 19; Leiden: Brill, 1994) 479–533.

[80] See the comments by H. Mc. Ross, *Thirty Essays on the Gospel of Thomas* (Longmead, Shaftsbury: Element Books, 1990) 40–47.

[81] Without a sufficiently critical sifting of complex traditions Ross comes to the conclusion that Thomas reached Muziris (now Cranganore) on the Malabar Coast of southwest India by 52 C.E., before which he compiled his gospel, none other than the *Gospel of Thomas* within 20 years of Jesus' life and within Palestine (*Thirty Essays on the Gospel of Thomas*, 47).

[82] Long after this monograph was in final draft, I found Ross's book and his comments led me to de Suarez's *L'Évangile selon Thomas* (Marsanne: Éditions Métanoïa, 1974), who on 260–62 claims that Thomas is the BD. He suggests that GosJn 21:20 should be translated so that παραδίδωμι is understood to mean "to transmit" tradition. We evaluated this possibility during our discussion of Judas as a candidate for the BD (see chapter 3). Hence, de Suarez translates 21:20 as follows: "Seigneur, quel est celui qui transmet ton (enseignement) à la postérité" (261)? While καὶ ὁ γράψας ταῦτα of 21:24 can be translated "et qui les a transcrites," the translation of 21:20 is unconvincing. No arguments clarify why he thinks the BD is Thomas. de Suarez simply declares, "sous la dénomination du *disciple que Jésus aimait* Jean rend à Thomas la première place" (260) [italics his].

phal work, "While more of its materials come from Matthew and Luke than from John, its point of view is more like that of John."[83] It would not be surprising to see that both works shared the same milieu (broadly speaking, the eastern provinces).

7.2 INFANCY GOSPEL OF THOMAS

This apocryphal work was composed sometime in the late second century. Although Jesus does seem to possess perfect knowledge, he is not presented as a gnostic teacher, and a developed gnostic metaphysical soteriology is not presented. In this work the apostle Thomas is the one who speaks in the very first line: "I, Thomas the Israelite, announce and make known to you all ...."[84] Thomas is thus the one who reveals knowledge to all regarding Jesus' childhood. The account is disappointing, even disgusting, in that it portrays Jesus as mean, hateful, condescending, indeed the *enfant terrible*. For example, he is said to have called the son of Annas an "insolent" and "godless ignoramus." At Jesus' command he withers into an old man near death (InfGosTh 3). In the next section a child bumps Jesus as he is running; Jesus curses him and he dies.

The GosJn has clearly influenced this apocryphal aberration. Note the following ideas in the *Infancy Gospel of Thomas*. Jesus says, "I come from above (ἐγὼ ἄνωθεν πάρειμι) to curse them and I call them to the things above (καὶ εἰς τὰ ἄνω καλέσω) as he who sent me (ὁ ἀποστείλας με) ordained for your sakes" (8:1; Greek A).[85] According to another Greek text, Jesus again speaks in ways shaped by the GosJn, "You speak what you know, but I understand more than you; for before the ages I am (πρὸ γὰρ τῶν αἰώνων εἰμί)" (6:2; Greek B). This agraphon is probably developed from GosJn 8:58. In summation, the *Infancy Gospel of Thomas* is significantly influenced by the GosJn; but the GosJn was not *the only gospel* in the School of Thomas. This apocryphal work also shows influences from all the intracanonical gospels.

7.3 THE BOOK OF THOMAS THE CONTENDER

This work is difficult to date, but it must antedate 350 (the age of the Nag Hammadi manuscript). The apocryphon also postdates the *Gospel of Thomas*, since 138:1-2 ostensibly knows about it. As in the GosJn, so in the

---

[83] Grant and Freedman, *The Secret Sayings of Jesus*, 116.

[84] See Elliott, *The Apocryphal New Testament*, 75.

[85] The Greek is from C. Tischendorf, *Evangelia Apocrypha* (Leipzig: Avenarius et Mendelssohn, 1853) ad loc. cit. The Johannine portion of Jesus' words is missing in the Syriac. See W. Wright, *Contributions to the Apocryphal Literature of the New Testament* (London: Williams and Norgate, 1865) ad loc. cit.

Book of Thomas the Contender, the premier disciple is Thomas. Its author has Jesus say to Thomas, "you are my twin and true companion" (138.7).

In the *Book of Thomas the Contender* we find surprising support for the hypothesis that Thomas is the Beloved Disciple. In the GosJn the Beloved Disciple is distinguished as the only disciple at the cross; it is to him and to him alone that Jesus says that he is to behold Jesus' mother as his own (19:27). Jesus tells the Beloved Disciple, "Behold your mother!" Does that not mean he becomes Jesus' adopted brother in a sibling way? In the *Book of Thomas the Contender* Jesus tells Thomas, "you are going to be called my sibling" (138:10).[86] That verse begins with "inasmuch as," which apparently derives from an exegesis of GosJn 19:27, and so identifies the Beloved Disciple under the cross as Thomas. If so, this exegesis reveals that at least some scholars in the School of Thomas perceived the Beloved Disciple as none other than Thomas. Thomas, especially in the East, is often portrayed as Judas Didymus, that is Jesus' twin brother, because of an exegesis of GosJn 14:22. This insight is highly significant, for in the *Acts of John* the Beloved Disciple is portrayed as John the son of Zebedee, as we should expect.[87]

7.4 ACTS OF THOMAS (HYMN OF THE PEARL, MARTYRDOM)[88]

The *Acts of Thomas* (περίοδει θωμᾶ) is so late that we should expect that it reflects knowledge of all the intracanonical gospels; perhaps a Diatessaron was quoted.[89] This is highly significant, since a case can be made for the possibility that Tatian based his harmony on the GosJn, which may

---

[86] Layton, *The Gnostic Scriptures*, 403.

[87] It is very interesting to observe that when early Christian scholars assume that John is the Beloved Disciple because he is the one who sat at table upon Jesus' breast (89), he is then sometimes confused with Thomas. Indeed, in the *ActsJn* Jesus confronts John with words taken from Jesus' words to Thomas according to the GosJn 20:27, "John, be not unbelieving, but believing" (ActsJn 90). Has a tradition that identifies Thomas as the Beloved Disciple caused this confusion in the *Acts of John*?

[88] The *ActsTh* is clearly composite. See Y. Tissot, "Les Actes de Thomas, exemple de recueil composite," in *Les Actes Apocryphes des Apôtres* (Publications de la faculté de théologie de l'Université de Genève 4; Geneva: Editions Labor et Fides, 1981) 223–32.

[89] See Klijn, *The Acts of Thomas: Introduction, Text, Commentary* (Leiden: E. J. Brill, 1962) 17. It is astounding that some scholars speak or write as if we know what was in Tatian's harmony. The task of reconstructing it is difficult. See G. Quispel, *Tatian and the Gospel of Thomas* (Leiden: Brill, 1975). Also see the reviews of this complex book by B. M. Metzger in *JTS* 27 (1976) 479–81, and by H. Quecke in *Biblica* 57 (1976) 444–46.

have commenced it.[90] I thus agree with Metzger that Tatian "gave to his harmony the chronological framework of the Fourth Gospel (but without following it slavishly), into which the Synoptic accounts are fitted."[91]

The *Acts of Thomas* must antedate Epiphanius (315–403) who refers to it.[92] But, it is impressive to observe that this apocryphal work is imbued with the GosJn.[93] In chapter 10 the apostle Thomas begins a prayer with words right out of the GosJn: "My Lord and my God, who ...." The words Ὁ κύριός μου καὶ ὁ Θεός μου in Acts of Thomas 10,[94] are, of course, right from the GosJn 20:28: ἀπεκρίθη θωμᾶς καὶ εἶπεν αὐτῷ· ὁ

[90] According to A. Ciasca, the Arabic Diatessaron began with, "In principio erat Verbum, et Verbum erat apud Deum, et ipsum Verbum Deus est" (*Tatiani Evangeliorum Harmoniae Arabice* [Rome: Ex Typographia Polyglotta, 1888]; using his Latin rendering). The Arabic Diatessaron has unwisely been ignored in recent Diatessaronic studies (see Baarda, *Early Transmission*, 173), and the elusive harmony of Tatian was probably compiled from more than four gospels of which the dominant one may have been the GosJn. See J. H. Charlesworth, "Tatian's Dependence Upon Apocryphal Traditions," *Heythrop Journal* 15 (1974) 5–17. T. Baarda is one of the premier experts on the Diatessaron; see esp. his *The Gospel Quotations of Aphrahat, The Persian Sage: Aphrahat's Text of the Fourth Gospel*, one volume and an appendix (Amsterdam: Krips Repro B.V. Meppel, 1975). Also see Baarda, *Early Transmission of Words of Jesus; Thomas, Tatian and the Text of the New Testament*, ed. J. Helderman and S. J. Noorda (Amsterdam: VU Boekhandel/Uitgeverij, 1983); and W. L. Petersen, *The Diatessaron and Ephrem Syrus as Sources of Romanos the Melodist* (Ph.D. diss., Rijksuniversiteit te Utrecht 1984) esp. 14–17, 32, 35. Against the widespread opinion that one may simply pick up the Diatessaron and read it, Petersen rightly warns that "the most fundamental problem has been determining to the satisfaction of all scholars precisely which readings are Diatessaronic, and which are not" (37).

[91] Metzger, *The Canon*, 114–15. I remember well the enjoyable times Metzger and I shared with Kurt Aland, Matthew Black, and other greats who participated in the *SNTS* Diatessaron Seminar, which I helped co-convene; and I am most grateful to each of them for the insights they shared with me about the Diatessaron.

[92] For the Greek and an astute discussion see Klijn, *The Acts of Thomas*, 21.

[93] This is not to neglect the fact that the GosJn was exceedingly influential in the West. R. C. Hanson judges that "Irenaeus can be regarded as the first great theologian produced by the Christian church. Henceforward it can almost be said without exaggeration that Christianity will be Johannine Christianity" (*The Cambridge History of the Bible*, ed. R. Ackroyd and C. F. Evans [Cambridge: Cambridge Univ. Press, 1970] 1:426).

[94] C. Tischendorf, *Acta Apostolorum Apocrypha* (Leipzig: Avenarius et Mendelssohn, 1861) 198.

κύριός μου καὶ ὁ θεός μου. Also, in both documents the speaker is clearly Thomas.[95]

The *Acts of Thomas* take us into the East where the Apostle Thomas was considered Judas Thomas and Jesus' twin brother. What is not so clear, but suggestive, is the portrayal of Thomas, the *Twin*, as also the one who is in the *bosom* of Jesus, and thus the Beloved Disciple (from GosJn 13:23). In the *Acts of Thomas* a large serpent and later a colt of an ass herald Thomas as "the twin brother of Christ" (ATh 31 [by a serpent] and 39 [by a colt]). In some eastern circles Thomas was assumed to be Jesus' bosom friend and the Beloved Disciple of the GosJn. A key to unlocking this tradition is the enigmatic Coptic noun *saiš*. W. E. Crum took this noun to denote an "incorporeal being accompanying man, 'double' [?]."[96] This meaning can be refined. G. Widengren discerned that *saiš* meant "pair-companion"; that is, the heavenly counterpart to each person.[97] In the *Manichaean Psalmbook* this Coptic noun sometimes clearly denotes "Christ,"[98] as in "your Light-Familiar, Christ" (42.22), "Jesus," as in

---

[95] The *Apocalypse of Thomas* is a very late work. It is most likely attributed to the Thomas who was one of the leading disciples of Mali. It is based on RevJn (esp. chapters 5–8). It should not be confused with the products of the School of Thomas. The "Thomas" of the Psalms of Thomas is also not Didymus Thomas, but one of the first disciples of Mali who died in 276. T. Säve-Söderbergh rightly concluded, "I am convinced that the original version of the Psalms of Thomas was composed by Mali's disciple and should consequently be dated to the last quarter of the 3rd century" (*Studies in the Coptic Manichaean Psalm-Book* [Uppsala: Almqvist Wiksells Boktryckeri AB, 1949] 156). Hence, the Thomas who is also behind the *Apocalypse of Thomas* must not be confused with the Thomas who is prominent in the GosJn.

[96] W. E. Crum, *A Coptic Dictionary* (Oxford: Clarendon Press, 1939) 374.

[97] G. Widengren, *The Great Vohu Manah and the Apostle of God* (Uppsala: Uppsala Universitets Årsskrift 1945:5; A.-B. Lundequistska Bokhandeln, 1945) 25. Note esp. his comment on 37: "To be able to make this progress the soul needs a companion, *parvānaɣ*, and a guide, *rāhnimūðar*, who shows it the way leading to its salvation, *buxtan*." The *saiš* is thus one's own "companion or helper." The links with the earlier concept of the Helper in the OdesSol are interesting. For a succinct and reliable introduction, with texts, to the setting of the Manichaeans, see Widengren, ed., *Iranische Geisteswelt von den Anfängen bis zum Islam* (Baden-Baden: Holle Verlag, 1961); cf. also *Encyclopedia Iranica* and Les *Cahiers de Studia Iranica*.

[98] The Coptic word *saiš* appears in the *Manichaean Psalmbook* in the following passages (cited according to page and line): 40.16 (two kinds), 56.12 (*bis*; linked with "Paraclete"), 19.22 ("my Familiar"), 42.22 ("your Light-Familiar, Christ"), 138.24 ("the Familiar"), 139.5 (the "blessed Familiar"), 139.12 ("the Beloved Familiar [or Twin]"), 146.53 ("your unfailing Familiar"), 166.34 (Jesus is "the Familiar of the Wise One"), 111.15 ("his perfect Familiar, the Holy Wisdom"), 217.4 ("his Familiar").

"Jesus ... Familiar of the Wise one" (166.34), and "Wisdom," as in "his perfect Familiar, the holy Wisdom (*tsophia*, σοφία [111.15]).[99] It must be remembered that this psalmbook shows deep influences from the GosJn. For example, it refers frequently to "the Paraclete," which comes directly or indirectly from the GosJn.[100] Thus Johannine influence, coupled with the connection between "Twin" and the place of the Beloved Disciple at the Last Supper (in the bosom of Jesus), seems evident in G. Bornkamm's comment that the meaning of *saiš* is not only "Twin" or "Twin-Companion," but also "Bosom Friend."[101] One obtains the impression that the GosJn has been interpreted so that Thomas, the Twin, is the Beloved Disciple, who was in the bosom of Jesus (GosJn 13:23). In fact, in the *Manichaean Psalmbook* we confront the phrase "the Beloved Twin" (*psaiš emmerit*), which may well reflect the assumption that Thomas is both the Twin of Jesus and the Beloved Disciple.

7.5 THE SCHOOL OF THOMAS AND THE GOSJN

Shaping the School of Thomas is the GosJn.[102] The dominance of Thomas within the so-called canon only in the GosJn makes this rather understand-

---

[99] C. R. C. Allberry, ed., *A Manichaean Psalm-Book* (Manichaean Manuscripts in the Chester Beatty Collection; Stuttgart: W. Kohlhammer, 1938) vol. 2, part 2. One of the most beautiful passages is 19.22-28:

I was gazing at my Twin-companion (*apasaiš*) with my eyes of light,
    beholding my glorious Father, he who waits for me forever,
    opening before me the gate up to the height.
I spread out my hands, praying unto him.
I bent my knees, worshipping him also,
    that I might remove from myself the image (εἰκών) of the flesh (σάρξ),
    and take off from me the form (σχῆμα) of humanity.
[Psalms of the Bema]

My translation is based on the Coptic, and influenced by Allberry's excellent rendering.

[100] See Allberry, ed., *A Manichaean Psalm-Book*, vol. 2, part 2, 46*-47*. See esp. 36.8 to 38.13, in which "Paraclete" appears no less than 17 times. Mani is portrayed as both "the Paraclete" and "the Spirit of Truth who has come out fro[m the Father]" (36.9). The source is obviously the GosJ.

[101] G. Bornkamm in *New Testament Apocrypha* (1965 ed.) 2:441. Of course, it is also conceivable that "Bosom Friend" implies no connection with the GosJn and is only a generic way of referring to one's heavenly twin. But the connection between the texts we are examining and the GosJn suggests a link here between Thomas the Twin and the Twin as denoting the bosom companion.

[102] As Irenaeus reported, the "gnostics" chose the GosJn as their own, to the exclusion of almost all of the other intracanonical gospels (*Adv. Haer.* 5-7). See Pagels' discussion, *The Johannine Gospel in Gnostic Exegesis*: Heracleon's commentary on John (Nashville: Abingdon Press, 1973) 16-17.

able; indeed it is to be expected. What is surprising is the evidence that the School of Thomas perceived Thomas to be none other than the Beloved Disciple. As in the GosJn Jesus is portrayed as revealing his secrets only to the Beloved Disciple with whom he is intimate, so in the School of Thomas Jesus' secrets are known only to Thomas. As is well known, the *Gospel of Thomas* begins, "These are the secret words which the living Jesus spoke and Didymus Judas Thomas wrote [them down]" (80.10).[103]

Decades ago scholars categorized the products of the School of Thomas as unsophisticated popular lore. Now we know, as H. J. W. Drijvers states, that "they came into being in a learned milieu, to which symbolism and typology were familiar and in which a certain form of biblical exegesis had already developed."[104] Klijn also points out that a writing that represents the so-called Johannine School, namely the *Odes of Solomon*, is the Syriac work that has the most parallels with the *Acts of Thomas*. Pointing to "striking agreements" Klijn concludes that while the *Acts of Thomas* embodies later Syriac theology, the Christology in the Odes and the Acts "remains the same."[105] It is in such an ambience that an insightful perception of Johannine symbolism could—and did—develop.

These reflections on the School of Thomas raise a question: Why did the "church fathers" not perceive that Thomas was the Beloved Disciple? Is the answer not so obvious? The GosJn was not considered authoritative or "canonical" by the early scholars of the church because its apostolic origins were disputed and especially because the gnostics adopted it as their special gospel. For example, Irenaeus was disturbed that the "heretics"—that is the gnostics—had chosen the GosJn as their own because of their metaphysical theology.[106] As is common knowledge, the earliest commentary on the GosJn was by the Valentinian gnostic Heracleon (c. 160–180).[107] Were the so-called church fathers not blinded by the brilliance of gnostic speculation on the GosJn that was often, but not always, aberrant?

---

[103] See the facsimile in *The Facsimile Edition of the Nag Hammadi Codices: Codex II* (Leiden: Brill, 1974) ad loc. cit.

[104] H. J. W. Drijvers in *New Testament Apocrypha*, ed. E. Hennecke, W. Schneemelcher, and trans. under the editorship of R. McL. Wilson (Cambridge: James Clarke & Co. Ltd; Louisville: Westminster/John Knox Press, 1992 [rev. ed.]) 2:327.

[105] Klijn, *The Acts of Thomas*, 49.

[106] See Pagels, *The Johannine Gospel in Gnostic Exegesis*, 24.

[107] Pagels, *The Johannine Gospel in Gnostic Exegesis*, see esp. 16: "Given their theory of revelation, it is no wonder that gnostic theologians are the first known authors to have produced exegetical commentaries on the 'evangelistic and apostolic sayings' (CJ Frag 16)."

How could the early scholars of the church see that Thomas was the Beloved Disciple while they were struggling for existence and combating the gnostics who were threatening Christian theology with Docetism and wild mysticism? How could they see that Thomas was the Beloved Disciple when the GosJn was being interpreted in gnostic ways and when Thomas was being heralded as the great gnostic?

7.6 THE DIVERSITY IN GNOSTICISM

We must remember that some of the gnostics produced masterpieces like the *Gospel of Truth*. Many were great scholars; and as K. Froehlich states, biblical interpretation owes a "considerable debt" to the Christian Gnostics (who were certainly quite diverse).[108] Gnosticism, that is the metaphysical and soteriological systems clearly evident by the middle of the second century C.E.,[109] probably should not be considered a "movement."[110] The diversity among the so-called gnostics is too diverse for such a neat category.[111] To what extent can we learn from them,[112] and perhaps with some of them contemplate the truth that Thomas is the Beloved Disciple?

[108] K. Froehlich, *Biblical Interpretation in the Early Church* (Philadelphia: Fortress, 1984) 11.

[109] It is not possible to define Gnosticism. It can be described as follows: Gnosticism should be differentiated from Proto-Gnosticism (early forms of spirituality that are heavily used by the gnostics, notably the GosJn and the Odes of Solomon) and Pre-Gnosticism (early traditions and texts that are not in any way gnostic but were heavily used by the gnostics, as for example the writings in the TANAKH). A world-wide concern for personal and salvific knowledge antedates Gnosticism; it may be called "gnosis." See similar attempts at some description in U. Bianchi, ed., *Le Origini dello Gnosticismo* (Studies in the History of Religions 12; Leiden: Brill, 1970) esp. xxvi.

[110] Although H. Jonas used the term "movement" he described the "manifoldness of sectarian doctrines," and warned that "Gnosticism" is not easy to define and can be only representatively presented. See his masterful *The Gnostic Religion: The Message of the Alien God and the Beginnings of Christianity* (Boston: Beacon Press, 1963 [2nd ed.]) esp. 31-37.

[111] As K. Rudolf warns, the variety of gnostic speculations can be "confusing and discouraging" (*Gnosis: The Nature and History of Gnosticism*, trans. R. McL. Wilson [San Francisco: Harper & Row, 1984] 53). See the similar comments by Winterhalter, *The Fifth Gospel* (San Francisco: Harper & Row, 1988) 1.

[112] Almost all of the Nag Hammadi Codices were originally composed in Greek and show us much more than ideologies in Egypt; some of the documents were composed in Syria or not far from the Jordan. See J. M. Robinson, ed., *The Nag Hammadi Library in English*, 12.

We would also do well, as scholars who are living on a small globe which has suffered from western parochialism, to remember two additional points. First, most of the people described as present in Jerusalem at Pentecost were from the East: Parthians, Medes, Elamites, Mesopotamians, Cappadocians, Asians, Judeans, and Arabs (Acts 2:9-11). Second, Eusebius lists first among Jesus' "holy apostles and disciples" Thomas; and "according to tradition he obtained by lot Parthia" (θωμᾶς μέν, ὡς ἡ παράδοσις περιέχει, τὴν Παρθίαν εἴληχεν, [HE 3.1.1]). Why did Eusebius, who was working in early fourth-century Caesarea,[113] mention Thomas first, and before such pillars of the church as Peter and Paul? Is it not conceivable that in ancient Palestine Thomas was highly revered?

7.7 THE ORIGINAL TITLE OF THE GOSJN

Finally, one more question: Was the GosJn always titled "The Gospel According to Saint John"? The answer seems to be "no." Even Hengel, who makes a magnificent case for the position that the GosJn was not given its present title "at a later date," must admit that there was a time when the work was probably anonymous, or at least not yet circulating under the name of "John." He argues that this gospel was labeled the Gospel According to John "by the pupils of the head of the school when they edited it after the death of their master and circulated it in the communities."[114] Hengel reiterates his position, clarifying that "the attribution in the title of the Gospel, euangelion kata Iōannēn, was added only after the author's death, by his pupils."[115] This position allows for a time when the GosJn was not clearly related to "John" or associated by a title with him.

Indeed, the earliest copy of the GosJn, Papyrus 52 (John Rylands MS 457) preserves the top margin where one might expect an identifying title to appear (as with Syrus Sinaiticus). No title is associated with this writing; therefore, C. H. Roberts had to painstakingly identify the recto and verso as containing words from what we call the GosJn.[116] If this document is dated to roughly 125 C.E. then we might not be wrong to assume that the title was not then part of the text.

---

[113] K. Lake thought (on the basis not only of contextual, but also textual evidence) that the HE went through four editions beginning in 311 and continuing until 323. Here he is indebted to E. Schwartz. See Lake, Eusebius: The Ecclesiastical History (LCL 153; Cambridge, Mass.: Harvard; London: William Heinemann, 1965) xx–xxi.

[114] Hengel, Question, 74; Question, 205.

[115] Hengel, Question, 75; Die johanneische Frage, 205–06 (in a slightly different form).

[116] See C. H. Roberts, An Unpublished Fragment of the Fourth Gospel (Manchester: Manchester Univ. Press, 1935). See the facsimile of both recto and verso of the titleless Ryl. Bk. 457 facing the title page.

If Hengel is correct that the disciples of the Beloved Disciple added the title, then at the beginning it did not have the title "the Gospel According to Saint John." What was its title? Could the first edition of the GosJn have had another name? Or, was it as yet anonymous? Did the schism, which vivisected the Johannine Community, cause the dissemination of the so-called "Gospel According to Saint John" under another name?[117] We now know that the term *gospel* did not have its technical meaning of a written work, as in the *Gospel* of John, until after approximately 150 (probably due to the stimulus of Marcion). E. F. Osborn has argued persuasively that Justin Martyr used a harmony, which seems to have been an oral form of the Synoptic gospels; and—most importantly—Justin referred not to "gospels" but to "memoirs of the apostles."[118] It can also be added, as J. N. Birdsall showed, that Justin quoted from so-called apocryphal works "as possessing a status equivalent to that which was later defined as scripture."[119] That would be very interesting in light of Peter Brown's claim that Justin "may well have been the first to introduce the notion" of heresy into Christian literature.[120]

It is obvious that the titles prefixed to the GosJn grew from the second to the fifth century, but we have virtually no evidence to discern what title or titles were used to identify what we call the Gospel of John prior to approximately 125.[121] Papyrus Bodmer II (P 66) of circa 200 is rare in that it contains the superscription of the GosJn in the upper margin.[122]

Koester has shown that the "gospels" did not receive titles from the beginning. Hence, for our purposes this demonstrates the fallaciousness of the argument which proceeds from the assumption that since the work is called the Gospel According to John, the author must be the son of Zebedee.

Note Koester's major points: (1) Early Christian missionaries borrowed from imperial propaganda the meaning and use of the word $\varepsilon\dot{v}\alpha\gamma\gamma\dot{\varepsilon}\lambda\iota o\nu(\omega\nu)$. (2) Paul used the word *gospel* to denote what is universally preached and not a written document. (3) Ignatius of Antioch in about 110 C.E. employed *gospel* to represent the preaching about Jesus Christ.

---

[117] It is conceivable that the schismatics gave the gospel a name different from the one used by the Johannine Community.

[118] E. F. Osborn, *Justin Martyr* (BHTh 47; Tübingen: Mohr [Siebeck], 1973) esp. 121.

[119] Birdsall in *The Cambridge History of the Bible*, 1:337.

[120] Brown, *The Body and Society*, 104.

[121] See B. M. Metzger, *The Text of the New Testament* (New York/Oxford: Oxford Univ. Press, 1968 [2nd ed.]) 26, 205.

[122] See the facsimile in K. Aland and B. Aland, *The Text of the New Testament* (Leiden: Brill; Grand Rapids: Eerdmans, 1987) Plate 22.

(4) The deutero-Pauline epistles employ the term *gospel* to signify what Paul had proclaimed. (5) The author of the *First Epistle of Clement* (c. 96) did "not know or use a written gospel." (6) The roughly contemporaneous *Epistle of Barnabas* contains the word *gospel*, but it denotes "oral proclamation." (7) In the *Didache*, which may date anywhere from the late first to the late second century C.E., *gospel* seems to denote Jesus' preaching (ὡς ἐκέλευσεν ὁ κύριος ἐν τῷ εὐαγγελίῳ αὐτοῦ [8.2]). (8) In the *Shepherd of Hermas* (c. 100) the noun *gospel* and its cognate verb do not appear. (9) Polycarp around the middle of the second century wrote a *Letter to the Philippians*; in it the word *gospel* does not appear. (10) The so-called *Gospel of Thomas* has only a colophon that clarifies that designation; but the opening of the work indicates that this writing is really "Thomas' Book of Secret Sayings." (11) The alleged *Gospel According to Mary* (Coptic Papyrus Berolinensis 8502) three times utilizes the word *gospel*, but each time it signifies "the message of the disciples." (12) The *Gospel of Truth* of the mid second century C.E. is "not a writing that belongs to the gospel literature; but it is a homily or meditation." In this work *gospel* denotes "the message of salvation." (13) In the Nag Hammadi collection of writings *gospel* is utilized "as a designation of a written source for the first time in the *Treatise on the Resurrection*, which must be dated at the end of the 2nd century."[123] (14) Most importantly for us, in the GosJn neither the noun τὸ εὐαγγέλιον nor the cognate verb εὐαγγελίζεσθαι appears, illustrating that "the beginnings of the Johannine community lay outside of the scope of the Pauline mission area."[124]

The researches and reflections summarized reveal that we cannot facilely conclude that from the beginning the gospels, especially the GosJn, received titles. The GosJn, therefore, may not have been described as a gospel, or as a "Gospel According to John." Thus, we should not unreflectively suppose that the Beloved Disciple must be a certain "John" because of the title given to the book, which does not derive from the author.

Thus there is impressive evidence that the word *gospel* did not have its technical meaning until late in the second century C.E. and that "the gospels" were sometimes originally called "memoirs." Did the Johannine schismatics, which may have been the larger portion of a once united community, take with them a work they considered the "Memoirs of Thomas" (ἀπομνημονεύματα θωμᾶ)?

This exploration of the earliest corridors of Christianity and an attempted reconstruction of first-century Christian traditions helps clarify

---

[123] Koester, *Ancient Christian Gospels*, 23.
[124] Ibid., 9; the summary above is taken from pp. 4–43.

the importance of Thomas before 140 C.E. Many of the fresh insights help clinch the argument that the hero of the GosJn, the Beloved Disciple, would make imminent sense as Thomas in such early Palestinian traditions. The rivalry between him and Peter now takes on historical meaning. As Käsemann argued, "Whatever may be the significance of the Beloved Disciple elsewhere, it is obvious that he obscures the significance for the Church of the Prince of the Apostles. Peter no longer towers above the disciples, as is shown in exemplary fashion in 20.21."[125] In light of the new insights derived from following the footprints of the Beloved Disciple in text, tradition, and history we may ask: To what extent can we conclude that the Beloved Disciple represented the East, Peter the West?[126]

7.8 SUMMARY AND CONCLUSION

In summation, the earliest form of the GosJn—perhaps the "First Edition" and maybe other writings later incorporated into the "Second Edition" (i.e., the Logos Hymn)—may have taken literary shape in Palestine (as M. E. Boismard argues),[127] conceivably in Jerusalem and later in Transjordan (as Cullmann contended),[128] perhaps in Syria and Transjordan (as G. Richter concludes),[129] or in northern Transjordan (as K. Wengst argues).[130] From these eastern areas the Thomas tradition moved further eastward towards Edessa. Perhaps the Johannine School, which may have been heralded by some Christians as the Thomas School, may have moved to Ephesus, possibly after the Jews in it were expelled from the synagogue (cf. the works by Brown and Martyn).

[125] E. Käsemann, *The Testament of Jesus*, trans. G. Krodel (Philadelphia: Fortress, 1968) 29.

[126] See chapter 8, below. Although he thought John the son of Zebedee was the Beloved Disciple, Agourides rightly saw that the "emphasis on the superior authority of the beloved disciple as against Peter's is meant only to counteract ideas relating to Peter's prestige and Peter's superior authority. These ideas were based on a misunderstanding of the Synoptic tradition within certain Christian circles in the province of Asia" ("Peter and John in the Fourth Gospel," *Studia Evangelica* 4 [1968] [= TU 102] 3-7; cf. 7).

[127] M. E. Boismard, *L'Evangile de Jean* (Paris: du Cerf, 1977).

[128] Cullmann, *Der johanneische Kreis*.

[129] Richter, "Präsentische und futurische Eschatologie im 4. Evangelium," in *Gegenwart und Kommendes Reich: A. Vögtle Schulergabe*, ed. Fiedler and D. Zeller (Stuttgart: Katholisches Bibelwerk) 117-52.

[130] K. Wengst, *Bedrängte Gemeinde und verherrlichter Christus: Der historische Ort des Johannesevangeliums als Schlüssel zu seiner Interpretation* (Biblisch-theologische Studien 5; Neukirchen-Vluyn: Neukirchener, 1983 [2nd ed.]).

Thomas thus becomes a key for unlocking some of the mystical insights in the GosJn. Seeing him as the Beloved Disciple helps us overcome much of the fragmentation and preoccupation with sources or editorial alterations that have hindered us from perceiving the narrative harmony and beauty of this great work of literature (see also chap. 4).[131] We more perceptively comprehend the Semitic argument of the GosJn with the unifying *inclusio*: John the Baptist—and his special disciple (the BD)—opens the drama, and Thomas, the Beloved Disciple, closes it.[132] This great drama moves majestically from chapter 1 in which we find the Baptist's confession, "Behold, the Lamb of God," in 1:29, and the confession of his disciple (the BD): "And I have seen and have borne witness that this one is the Son of God," in 1:34 through to the final chapter which contains the grand finale of Thomas's confession, "My Lord and my God" in 20:28. Both confessions are echoed in the original conclusion: "these things are written that you may continue believing that Jesus is the Christ, the Son of God, and that believing you may have life in his name" (20:31).

The Thomas connection—that is, his identification as the Beloved Disciple—helps us comprehend more fully the origins of Christianity and the early rivalry between Rome and Jerusalem, or Peter and the Beloved Disciple (see chap. 8). As A. Harnack stated long ago, from "the close of the first century the Roman church was in a position of practical primacy over Christendom."[133] In the GosJn through the rivalry between Peter and the Beloved Disciple (who is Thomas), and in the Thomas School, we may feel such pressure from Rome.

It is more likely that Thomas became so prominent in Syria, west as well as east, because he was already prominent in circles that shaped the GosJn, than it is that he was insignificant in the GosJn and became significant only later. It is also apparent that the Thomas traditions began in or near Palestine and spread from there to the East as well as to Egypt. At

---

[131] For an approach that also seeks to recover the harmonious unity of the GosJn but which seems at least at times to deprecate the historical-critical approach to the GosJn, see T. L. Brodie, *The Quest for the Origin of John's Gospel: A Source-Oriented Approach* (Oxford: Oxford Univ. Press, 1993) see esp. 21, 149–55.

[132] See the brilliant comment about Semitic writing according to which the author "proceeds not by exhausting topics successively but with frequent *inclusio,* circling round on itself like a conversation round a fire, gradually advancing and going deeper" (Murray, *Symbols of Church and Kingdom,* 2).

[133] A. Harnack, *The Mission and Expansion of Christianity in the First Three Centuries,* trans. J. Moffatt (London: Williams and Norgate; New York: G. Putnam's Sons, 1908) 1:485.

the center of these traditions stands the so-called Gospel According to St. John in which Thomas is the one who is prominent. Thomas and the Beloved Disciple are the heroes of the GosJn; they are, in fact, the hero.

CHAPTER 8

The Beloved Disciple and Peter: A Rivalry Between East and West?

As we have seen in the *Forschungsbericht* (chap. 3), for well over a century scholars have observed in the GosJn some subtle polemical relation between the Beloved Disciple and Peter.[1] Once experts saw the rivalry as hostile in which Peter is embarrassed and the Beloved Disciple lauded. Now it is imperative to inculcate the scholarly perception that the narrator of chapters 1 through 20 and the author who added chapter 21 support Peter, but elevate the Beloved Disciple over him. Only the Beloved Disciple has special knowledge; only he is "the disciple whom Jesus loved." Peter is not a hero of the GosJn: he denies Jesus, and he exits the drama ignorant and without a confession. No matter how reinstated Peter might be according to the author of chapter 21, he is not Jesus' Beloved Disciple.

Perhaps the relation between the Beloved Disciple and Peter might be explained in the following fashion. In chapters 1 through 20 Peter has access to Jesus through the Beloved Disciple who is said to be within Jesus (13:23) as Jesus, as the Logos and Only God, is within God (1:18). In chapter 21 Peter is reinstated from his fallen state due to the denials. Jesus empowers Peter and then calls him to follow him (21:19, 22). Peter is elevated by Jesus, but he does not enjoy the close relation the Beloved Disciple has to the Lord. Peter's understanding is limited and Jesus' final word to him is not flattering (21:22). The witness of the GosJn and its validity does not rest upon Peter; it is grounded solely on the truthfulness of the witness of "the disciple whom Jesus loved."

---

[1] Some scholars have exaggerated the tension between the BD and Peter. It is not overt, and Peter neither is presented as the disciple who denied Jesus, nor is he the Evangelist's bête noire.

Johannine scholars today tend to concur regarding the portrayal of the relation between the Beloved Disciple and Peter. In *Peter and the Beloved Disciple: Figures for a Community in Crisis*, K. Quast, accurately reports that

> A consensus has developed that sees the evangelist portraying a rivalry between Peter and the Beloved Disciple in which Peter is subordinated to the hero of the Fourth Gospel because of the insight and intimacy the Beloved Disciple shares with Jesus.[2]

The rivalry, which I deem to be more subtle than Quast's words suggest, mirrors some social struggle. It has been variously explained by Brown, Bultmann, Cullmann, Gunther, Neirynck, Minear, and Quast.

While scholars rightly see the tension between the Beloved Disciple and Peter as indications of social conflicts or stress-points within the Johannine Community, I have become impressed with a possible global perspective mirrored in the GosJn. Peter obviously represents the West. The Beloved Disciple, if he is Thomas, certainly symbolizes the East. Hence, the GosJn, at the end of the first century C.E., may reveal a global tension within Christendom. If so, it was one in which, at least within the GosJn, both Peter and Thomas (that is the Beloved Disciple) are honored and invested with authority by the risen Christ (which is perhaps the main function of the GosJn in chapter 21). I am convinced that what the Evangelist attempted to achieve in chapters 15 through 17 within the Johannine Community—that is, to bring unity within the group—the author of chapter 21 later strove to achieve for the universal church.

The rivalry between groups within earliest Christianity is well known. The Pauline epistles (including the post-Paulines) and the Epistle of James represent two different definitions of Christian faith, especially in relation to the continuing efficaciousness of Torah and the relation between righteousness and soteriology. Second Peter seems to be a "correction" of Jude and its appreciation for and dependence upon so-called pseudepigraphical compositions.[3] Although the Tübingen School in the nineteenth century exaggerated these early conflicts and distorted them through an imposition of Hegelian philosophy,[4] the differences within earliest Christianity and the search by "Christians" for a normative self-definition is well known and insightfully articulated by the MacMaster group

---

[2] K. Quast, *Peter and the Beloved Disciple* (Journal for the Study of the New Testament, Sup. Ser. 32; Sheffield: JSOT Press, 1989) 7.

[3] See G. W. MacRae's "Foreword" to the *OTP*.

[4] Among the many surveys on this subject the most recent is by W. Baird titled *History of New Testament Research;* see volume one: *From Deism to Tübingen* (Minneapolis: Fortress, 1992) esp. 258–69.

and by Brown and Meier.[5] What is newly discovered, therefore, is not a tension within the Johannine Community, or between rival Christian groups. What is new is that the search for the identity of the Beloved Disciple seems to disclose a global rivalry for supremacy: Peter in the West and Thomas in the East.[6] While Peter clearly represents Rome, Thomas may represent various communities (due no doubt to the crises of 66–70 [74] and 132–35 C.E. [the great Jewish revolts against Rome and the end of the history of Ancient Israel]).[7]

8.1 REHEARSING THE EVIDENCE WITHIN THE GOSJN

It is impressive to recognize that almost everywhere in the GosJn the Beloved Disciple appears in contrast to Peter. The author has Peter ask the Beloved Disciple for information at the Last Supper, signifying not only the more honored position of the Beloved Disciple, but also his superior access to Jesus and possession of knowledge. Racing to the empty tomb, the Beloved Disciple arrives first, Peter second. Moreover, while the Beloved Disciple is said to see and believe, nothing similar is said about Peter. Ignorant of the Scriptures concerning Jesus Christ, they both return home (see chap. 2.1).

In the Appendix Peter leads the disciples on a fishing expedition. The Beloved Disciple is the only disciple who recognizes that the stranger on the shore is Jesus. Peter thence immediately springs into the water to get to Jesus. Subsequently, Peter is questioned by Jesus—indeed commissioned by him—only to be apparently embarrassed by Jesus when he asks about the Beloved Disciple.

There is an attractive pattern in the dramatic interplay between the Beloved Disciple and Peter in the Book of Glory (chaps. 1–20). Note this drama:

[5] See the MacMaster volumes ed. E. P. Sanders, et al., titled *Jewish and Christian Self-Definition* and published by Fortress Press. Also see R. E. Brown and J. P. Meier, *Antioch and Rome: New Testament Cradles of Catholic Christianity* (New York: Paulist Press, 1983). In the previous chapters, especially under "The Johannine School and the School of Thomas" (chap. 7), I have cited numerous publications that have helped me comprehend the complex social world within and without the Johannine Community.

[6] A. Feldtkeller insightfully draws attention to rivalry between "thomanischem Christentum und petrinischem Christentum." See his *Identitätssuche des syrischen Urchristentums* (Novum Testamentum et Orbis Antiquus 25; Göttingen: Vandenhoeck & Ruprecht, 1993).

[7] R. J. Cassidy insightfully points out that Johannine theology has been shaped by Roman hostility to Christians (*John's Gospel in New Perspective: Christology and the Realities of Roman Power* [Maryknoll, N.Y.: Orbis, 1992]).

Chapter	Drama
1	the BD (an anonymous disciple) sees the Spirit descending on Jesus (after the BD, Peter follows Jesus)
13	the BD is at the Last Supper and Peter asks him for information
19	the BD, the only disciple at the crucifixion, witnesses the Spirit leave Jesus
20a	the BD outruns Peter to the empty tomb
20b	the BD (= Thomas) alone talks with the resurrected Jesus

The interweaving of narratives in which the Beloved Disciple (= Thomas) and Peter appear is attractive: the Beloved Disciple alone, the Beloved Disciple with Peter, the Beloved Disciple alone, the Beloved Disciple with Peter, and finally the Beloved Disciple alone. The only disciple to witness the descent and ascent of the Spirit is the Beloved Disciple. There is also an *inclusio* that connects the entrance and exodus of the Beloved Disciple in the Johannine narrative. The first episode is a revelation to the Beloved Disciple who sees the Spirit descending and remaining on Jesus. The final episode centers upon an intimate and personal conversation between the Beloved Disciple (as Thomas) and Jesus, who has been resurrected.

The Johannine narrative is thus like a memorable and exquisitely composed fugue that possesses two major mutually dependent notes.[8] The main note is the Beloved Disciple. He weaves forward in the Johannine drama, bouncing off the other major tone, the often forceful and quick Peter. The drama moves forward majestically with contrapuntal force. The notes resonate together and then gradually build up into the finale, the confession by the Beloved Disciple, now unveiled as Thomas the Twin, before the risen Jesus, who is—following the grand *inclusio*—triumphantly revealed as identified with God.

It is clear that Peter was the figurehead of western Christianity and Thomas the spokesman of eastern Christendom in the second century (see the preceding chapter). To what extent is Thomas disparaged in the West? Are there innuendoes that some early Christian experts in the West knew that Thomas was the Beloved Disciple, or argued against other Christians who professed that identification? The search for clues amidst the debris of antiquity and the power of the Roman church has been tedious but surprisingly rewarding. Since our search will be for the identity of the

---

[8] A. van Aarde offers some help here in understanding narrative. He writes, that as "soon as a narrative has been written, the text is divorced from its historical writer and it functions as a closed narrated·world with its own architectonic design with intrinsic harmonious characteristics" (*God-With-Us: The Dominant Perspective in Matthew's Story* [Pretoria Hervormde Teologiese Studies, Supplementum 5; Pretoria: Univ. of Pretoria, 1994] 89).

Beloved Disciple, no mention will be made of the authors and documents that make no claim about the identity of the Beloved Disciple but *only presuppose* that John the Apostle is the author of the GosJn (hence, e.g., there is no discussion of the so-called *Muratorian Canon* and Clement of Alexandria).[9]

8.2 ADVOCATES FOR THE APOSTLE JOHN AS THE BELOVED DISCIPLE

Writings or individuals, some who or which were highly influential in early Christianity, identified the Beloved Disciple with John the son of Zebedee. They are the *Gospel of Gamaliel* (impossible to date, but prior to the sixth century), Origen (c. 185–c. 254), Dionysius of Alexandria (d. c. 264), the Pseudo-Clementine letters (early 3rd cent.), Hippolytus (c. 170–236), Tertulian (c. 160–c. 225), Polycrates (late 2nd cent.), Irenaeus (c. 130–c. 200), Papias (c. 60–130), and conceivably the author of the GosJn chapter 21 (c. 90–100). I am presenting the data in reverse chronological order so that we can trace the portrayal of Thomas back in time, and indeed pick up any faint traces of pro-Roman scholars stressing that the Beloved Disciple must be John the Apostle and cannot be Thomas. The exploration proceeds with the recognition of what J. Pelikan has rightly called the search for normative self-understanding within a world sharply divided. It is "not between Rome and Jerusalem, but chiefly between Rome and 'Syria,' that the dichotomy of East and West manifested itself."[10]

1. Gospel of Gamaliel (pre-6th cent.)

It is not easy to find the evidence we are seeking. For example, in early Coptic accounts of Jesus' passion there are passages that indicate Christian scholars are assuming that "John" is the Beloved Disciple. In the

---

[9] The often polemical relation between East and West is not always evident, and early Christianity must not be portrayed as divisive so that there are two polar opposites. Bardaiṣan of Edessa, for example, did portray the East as Light (*nwhr'*) but the West was not Darkness; it was Wind (*rwḥ'*), which was the only instigator of creation. For the texts and discussion see H. J. W. Drijvers, *Bardaiṣan of Edessa* (Studia Semitica Neerlandica 6; Assen: Van Gorcum, 1966) 98–99, 138–39.

[10] J. Pelikan, "The Two Sees of Peter: Reflections on the Pace of Normative Self-Definition, East and West," in *Jewish and Christian Self-Definition: The Shaping of Christianity in the Second and Third Centuries*, ed. E. P. Sanders (Philadelphia: Fortress, 1980) 57–73. He identifies the sees of Peter as Rome and Antioch (and before each of them, Jerusalem). That perspective may help us understand why, especially in chapter 21, Peter is recognized to be leader and receives the ecclesiastical commission.

Coptic fragments of the passion often called the *Gospel of Gamaliel*, which were perhaps written in Coptic sometime before the sixth century,[11] we have abundant evidence that its author was heavily influenced by the GosJn. Numerous passages in the GosJn are quoted (e.g., 6:15, 14:31, 19:5) or alluded to (the attempt to make Jesus a king [cf. GosJn 6:15], Judas who cheats [GosJn 12:6], a dialogue between Christ and Pilate [cf. GosJn 18:28-38] and Pilate's words "Ecce homo"). Thomas is addressed by Jesus who urges him to touch his wounds and even see the wound in his side. In fact, in the *Gospel of Gamaliel* the GosJn is cited as "the Gospel."

Most important in our search for the identity of the Beloved Disciple is fragment 15. According to it Jesus addresses his mother. Jesus instructs her: "Do not doubt that I am your son." Note the next words, "It is I who placed you into the hands of John (*etootf niōhannēs*) when I was hanging on the cross."[12] Clearly this apocryphal text shows that in Egypt, if this text was composed in Coptic, the Beloved Disciple is assumed to be John (most likely the son of Zebedee).[13]

2. Origen (c. 185–c. 254)

According to Eusebius (*HE* 6.25.9) the great biblical scholar, Origen of Alexandria and Caesarea Maritima, thought that John was the Beloved Disciple. Origen taught that the author of the GosJn was John, the one "who leaned back on Jesus' breast," which is clearly the description of the anonymous Beloved Disciple (chaps. 13, 21).

3. Dionysius of Alexandria (d. c. 264)

Dionysius succeeded Origen as head of the Alexandrian Cathetical School. He was also Bishop of Alexandria. He agreed with his teacher, Origen, concerning the identity of the Beloved Disciple. According to

---

[11] See the comments by M.-A. van den Oudenrijn and A. de Santos Otero in *New Testament Apocrypha*, ed. W. Schneemelcher and trans. R. McL. Wilson (Cambridge: James Clarke & Co.; Louisville: Westminster/John Knox, 1991 rev. ed.) 1:558–60.

[12] See E. Revillout, *Les apocryphes coptes: Publiés et traduits* (Paris: Fages, 1904) part 1, p. 54.

[13] Elliott in *The Apocryphal New Testament*, 163, unfortunately, and obviously inadvertently, misleads one who is searching for the identity of the Beloved Disciple. He incorrectly reported, in his summary of the fragments published by Revillout, that in Coptic Fragment 13 Jesus addressed Thomas "reminding him of the signs of the crucifixion." That would mean Thomas was the Beloved Disciple who had seen Jesus' crucifixion and could be reminded of what he had seen. The Coptic, however, has only "if you wish to see," not let me remind you of what you saw.

Eusebius (*HE* 7.24.6-26) he was a perspicacious New Testament critic. He argued that the author of the Apocalypse of John cannot be John the Apostle, because the character, style, and language of this Apocalypse is distinguishable from that of the GosJn. The apostle John did write the GosJn and the First Epistle of John. The author of these last two mentioned works, moreover, is none other than "the disciple loved by the Lord (τὸν ἠγαπημένον ὑπὸ τοῦ κυρίου μαθητὴν [*HE* 7.25.12]) ... he who leaned back on his breast, the eyewitness and hearer of the Lord" (*HE* 7.25.12).

4. The Spurious Clement Epistles on Virginity (early 3rd cent.)

These two letters are pseudonymous, and they are really one document that dates from the first half of the third century.[14] In chapter 6 the author declares that John the Apostle is the greatest man born of a woman, because he was a virgin. He is the Beloved Disciple who reclined on Jesus' bosom (GosJn 13 and 21). The author exhorts his readers to imitate John, "the ambassador of the Lord."

5. Hippolytus (c. 170–236)

In the fragmentary letter of Hippolytus, quoted in the section on exegesis, we noted that he assumed John was the Beloved Disciple. Now, we need to stress that Hippolytus also had a very high regard for Thomas. According to him, Jesus selected Thomas, when "his disciples were in doubt." He "called Thomas to him," in order "to show that the same (body) had been raised which had also died."[15] In this letter Hippolytus did portray Thomas in a very exalted position among the disciples, but he did not suggest that Thomas was the Beloved Disciple.

Is it not possible that Hippolytus, the great theologian of the Roman Church in the early third century, was able to hold independent ideas—especially in contrast to the fiery positions of leading Roman scholars prior to him—because he was, at least for a part of his life, anti-Pope? He did attack Popes Zephyrinus, Callistus, Urban, and Pontianus. He even announced that Pope Callistus (217–22) was a heretic. As one immune to Roman control and indeed free of the pro-Roman propaganda of the second century, did Hippolytus inherit and emphasize a very early pro-Thomas tradition? It is becoming more evident that these questions are not only warranted but perhaps should be answered in the affirmative.

---

[14] See the discussion and bibliography given by J. Quasten, *Patrology* (Utrecht-Antwerp: Spectrum; Westminster, Md.: Newman, 1962) 1:58–59.

[15] Hippolytus, apud Theodoret, Second Dialogue ἀσύγχυτος [*Works* 4.88]. See the translation and notes in ANF 5, p. 240.

6. Tertullian (c. 160–c. 225)

The Father of African Christianity and the first great Latin scholar, in his early polemical writing titled *De praescriptione haereticorum*, argued that the Roman church alone, as evident in the episcopal succession, inherited the true tradition and the key for interpreting Scripture. In chapter 22 Tertullian indicated that John the Apostle was the Beloved Disciple. John is the one who reclined on Jesus' breast. He is the only one to whom Jesus disclosed the identity of the Betrayer. He is the one to whom Jesus entrusted his mother as a son. Obviously, Tertullian cannot debase Thomas as he did Marcion and Valentinus (chap. 30), because he was one of Jesus' twelve disciples to whom Jesus revealed the truth and who faithfully, sufficiently, and fully transmitted it to "the whole church" (chaps. 21–27).

7. Polycrates (late 2nd cent.)

The Bishop of Ephesus, Polycrates, argued against Pope Victor I, Bishop of Rome, regarding the day on which the annual celebration of Jesus' resurrection was to be held. Defending a tradition that some early church scholars claimed went back to the apostle John, Polycrates held to the ancient tradition: the fourteenth day of Nisan, according to the Jewish calendar. This custom, Quartodecimanism, Polycrates defended in a letter to Pope Victor. In it he referred to the great luminaries (μεγάλα στοιχεῖα) in Asia who observed Easter on this day and not on the preceding or following Sunday. Pope Victor excommunicated Polycrates and threatened "to cut him off from the common unity in the dioceses of all Asia (τῆς Ἀσίας πάσης)" (Eusebius, *HE* 5.24.9). This Pope even prepared letters announcing that all the Christians in the East "were absolutely excommunicated" (Eusebius, HE 5.24.9). Though following Victor's rule for observing Easter, Irenaeus urges him not to excommunicate Christians for following an ancient custom. According to Eusebius Irenaeus deserved his name: Καὶ ὁ μὲν Εἰρηναῖος ... εἰρηνοποιός, τοιαῦτα ὑπὲρ τῆς τῶν ἐκκλησιῶν εἰρήνης παρεκάλει (*HE* 5.24.18).

This letter of Polycrates reveals the growing power of Rome. In it Polycrates, Bishop of Ephesus, refers to the apostle John, who "sleeps at Ephesus" (Eusebius, *HE* 5.24.4). He clearly affirms the tradition that John is the Beloved Disciple, relying on the descriptions in the GosJn, chapters 13 and 21: ἔτι δὲ καὶ Ἰωάννης ὁ ἐπὶ τὸ στῆθος τοῦ κυρίου ἀναπεσών, (Eusebius, *HE* 5.24.3; see also *HE* 3.31.3).

8. Irenaeus (c. 130–c. 200)

Irenaeus, who (as is well known) is a major witness for the composition of the GosJn (*Adv.Haer.* 2.22.5; 3.3.4), repeatedly refers to "John, the disciple of the Lord." Irenaeus believed John the Apostle was the

Beloved Disciple. He was the anonymous one who rested on Jesus' breast, and wrote the GosJn while living in Ephesus (*Adv.Haer.* 3.3.1; Eusebius, *HE* 5.8.4).

9. Papias (c. 60–130)[16]

The writings of Papias of Hierapolis—his five books[17]—are lost. We must reconstruct his thoughts from citations in other writings. Papias apparently pushed John the son of Zebedee as the Beloved Disciple, because he ostensibly knew and heard him.[18] If Papias was not only a student[19] of John the Evangelist, but also intimate with him, "the Beloved Disciple," as Anastasius of Sinai reported,[20] then he would most likely advocate that this John, and not others—whether John the Elder or Thomas—was Jesus' Beloved Disciple. Although Papias never states clearly that John the son of Zebedee is the Beloved Disciple, that tradition is associated with him,[21] and indeed a ninth-century Vatican manuscript refers to Papias as one who knew that John wrote the GosJn. It even refers to Papias as "a beloved disciple of John."[22]

10. The Author of the GosJn, Chapter 21 (c. 90–100)

The author who appended chapter 21—whatever he may have thought was the truth—may conceivably have intended to insinuate that the Beloved Disciple was John the son of Zebedee. The name of this disciple is not given anywhere in the GosJn, but he probably appears anonymously as one of "those of Zebedee" in 21:2. Why did the author of chapter 21

---

[16] The citations from texts are taken from J. Kürzinger, *Papias von Hierapolis und die Evangelien des Neuen Testaments* (Eichstätter Materialien 4; Regensburg: Verlag Friedrich Pustet, 1983).

[17] Irenaeus, *Adv.Haer.* 5.33.4: *sunt enim illi quinque libri conscripti*; Eusebius, *HE* 3.39,1: Τοῦ δὲ Παπία συγγράμματα πέντε τὸν ἀριθμὸν φέρεται; Philip Sidetes, *Historia christiana, Epitome* in Codex Baroccianus 142: Παπίας ... πέντε λόγους κυριακῶν λογίων ἔγραψεν.

[18] Irenaeus, *Adv.Haer.* 5.33.4: *Ioannis auditor*; Jerome, *De viris illustribus* 18: *Papias, Iohannis auditor*. Philip of Side in his *Historia christiana, Epitome* in Codex Baroccianus 142: Παπίας Ἱεραπόλεως ἐπίσκοπος, ἀκουστὴς τοῦ θεολόγου Ἰωάννου γενόμενος.

[19] Jerome, *Ep.* 75,3: *et Papiae, auditoris euangelistae Iohannis* ....

[20] Anastasius of Sinai, *Considerations on the Hexaemeron* 1: τοῦ Ἱεραπολίτου, τοῦ τῷ ἐπιστηθίῳ φοιτήσαντος.

[21] Anastasius of Sinai, *Considerations on the Hexaemeron*, 1. He reported that Papius was close to John the Apostle, "him who leaned on Christ's bosom," that is obviously the Beloved Disciple.

[22] Ex codice Vaticano (olim Alexandrino, nunc) Reginensi lat. 14: *discipulus Iohannis carus*.

add those belonging to Zebedee to the disciples named in the GosJn? It may be to shift subtly the identity from another, whoever he may be, to John the son of Zebedee. This may also be one of the results caused by the exodus of the Johannine Community from ancient Palestine to western Turkey (Asia Minor). It would fit harmoniously with the elevation of Peter, and his commissioning, which are clarified only in the Appendix of the GosJn.

I am more persuaded that the mention of "those of Zebedee" is to harmonize the GosJn with the Synoptics. It thus is not an attempt to shift the identity of the Beloved Disciple from some disciple to John the son of Zebedee. Other harmonizing tendencies of the author of the Appendix, who unlike the author of 1–20 knew the Synoptics and wrote in light of them, are the addition of resurrection appearances in Galilee, the appearance of the resurrected Jesus to Peter, the reinstatement of Peter and a more positive attitude to him, and a subtle move to add more disciples to those noted or named in 1–20 so that one could imagine that Jesus did have twelve disciples.

8.3 EVIDENCE SOME BELIEVED THOMAS WAS THE BELOVED DISCIPLE

Documents indicating that John the Apostle is the Beloved Disciple appear along with other writings that present the reader with other options. These works are seldom cited or studied, and some are virtually unknown.

1. Assumption of the Virgin (Transitus Mariae)

The Latin text of the *Assumption of the Virgin (Transitus Mariae)*[23] is known through Pseudo-Melito. In it we find some refreshing data that is undigested in Beloved Disciple research. The history of the transmission of traditions in this apocryphon is unknown. The text is preserved in numerous languages and various recensions, so it is impossible, without a critical edition and focused research upon it, to ascertain the antiquity of its traditions. But C. Tischendorf was certainly correct in judging the apocryphon to be not medieval, but a monument from early Christianity.[24] It

---

[23] For bibliography see Charlesworth with Mueller, *The New Testament Apocrypha and Pseudepigrapha*, ad loc. cit.

[24] C. Tischendorf concluded that the *Dormitione Mariae*, another name for the work, "non ad medii aevi sed antiquitatis Christianae monumenta certum est ...." He dated it to the fourth century (*Apocalypses Apocryphae* [Leipzig: Druckerei Lokay, 1866; repr.: Hildesheim: Georg Olms Verlagsbuchhandlung, 1966] xxiv).

may date from sometime around the fourth century.[25] It is a virtually unknown document.[26]

The author assumes that the Beloved Disciple is John the Evangelist. The passage in GosJn 19, according to which the Beloved Disciple receives Jesus' mother as his own, is clearly etched into the drama of this apocryphon in chapter 2:

> Jesus Christ ... saw standing beside the cross his mother and John the evangelist, whom he loved more than the other apostles because he alone of them was a virgin in body. To him therefore he committed the charge of the holy Mary saying to him, "Behold your mother," and to her, "Behold your son." From that hour the holy mother of God continued in the especial care of John as long as she endured the sojourn of this life.[27]

We should probably assume that "John" is John the son of Zebedee and not the Elder John (John Mark is out of the question). It is interesting that the author of this work thought Jesus loved the Beloved Disciple "more than the other apostles," and that his special affection for him was because he "was a virgin in body." Such passages in the text reflect the doctrinal disputes from the second to the fourth centuries,[28] and are too doctrinal for significant insight in our search for the identity of the Beloved Disciple, except for the following passage.

A conflicting tradition seems to be buried within a section of this apocryphon. It is, however, only in one recension of the *Transitus Mariae*, Manuscript A, ed. by Tischendorf and trans. A. Walker, M. R. James, and Elliott.[29] The passage is significantly absent in Latin Manuscript B, the Syriac texts,[30] the Greek text, the Coptic text, and the recen-

---

[25] Elliott judges that the story originated "in apocryphal literature from about the fourth century onwards" (*The Apocryphal New Testament*, 691).

[26] See M. Erbetta, *Gli Apocrifi del Nuovo Testamento* (Turin: Marietti, 1975) 1.2:407–632. *The Assumption of the Virgin (Transitus Mariae)* is not contained in Hennecke and Schneemelcher, eds., *New Testament Apocrypha*, ed. and trans. R. McL. Wilson.

[27] Elliott, *The Apocryphal New Testament*, 709.

[28] See P. Brown, *The Body and Society: Men, Women, and Sexual Renunciation in Early Christianity*.

[29] C. Tischendorf, "Transitus Mariae. A," *Apocalypses Apocryphae*, 113–23; A. Walker, "The Passing of Mary," in *Ante-Nicene Fathers*, 8:592–94; M. R. James "The Assumption: Narrative by Joseph of Arimathaea," *The Apocryphal New Testament* (Oxford: At the Clarendon Press, 1924) 216–18; Elliott, "The Assumption of the Virgin," *The Apocryphal New Testament*, see "Narrative by Joseph of Arimathaea," 714–16.

[30] See W. Wright, ed., *Contributions to the Apocryphal Literature of the New Testament* (London: Williams and Norgate, 1865). Wright referred to three

sion called "The Discourse of Theodosius." Our focus will be on the recension, Latin Manuscript A, which contains a long narrative regarding Thomas. He receives from the Virgin Mary her girdle and alone sees her assumption into heaven. James associated the text with the relic of Prato, and offered the opinion that "the prominence given to this incident is another indication that we have here a mediaeval Italian composition, not earlier, I imagine, than the thirteenth century."[31]

The text in its present form is late, but many questions abound: What is the date of the Thomas traditions? Why are they preserved in this apocryphon? What social world do they represent? How are they to be judged in light of the first and second-century Thomas traditions? At this period in our research it would be wise neither to ignore completely the forces represented by this Thomas story nor to claim the traditions may be traced back into the earliest origins of Christianity. We may now turn to some intriguing Thomas traditions.

According to the "Narrative by Joseph of Arimathea" within the *Assumption of the Virgin*, at the death of Mary the disciples were dispersed over the earth (section 5). All the disciples, except Thomas, arrive on clouds (*prima facie* the author would have included Judas, but then he presents a list of disciples that does not include him and is rather unique). The prominence of the apostle John is evident: he is named first in the list. After the disciples place Mary's corpse in the tomb, angels take it to heaven—but the apostles are ignorant of what has been happening.

At this point in the narrative "the most blessed Thomas" (*beatissimus Thomas*) appears suddenly. He alone sees (*vidit*) the ascension of "the most blessed body" (*beatissimum corpus*). This is surely reminiscent of pericopes in the GosJn which attribute to the Beloved Disciple alone special knowledge (chap. 13) and perception (chaps. 20 and 21). Thomas alone calls to her for mercy. She throws down to him her "girdle" (*zona* [from ζώνη]), with which the apostles had encircled her body when they placed it in the tomb.[32] He receives this special gift from her and goes to the Valley of Josaphat.

"editions or redactions" of this apocryphal work in Syriac, and judged that it was "most probably a production of the latter half of the fourth century" (7). The Thomas traditions are conspicuously absent in the Syriac recensions.

[31] James, *The Apocryphal New Testament*, 218. Elliott (*The Apocryphal New Testament*, 691) passed on James's judgment: "(Tischendorf's Transitus A is a late Italian fiction attributed to Joseph of Arimathea)."

[32] Compare this narrative to the *Testament of Job* 46–50 in which Job's three daughters receive "multicolored cords," representing an inheritance greater than that which the sons received. These cords, worn on the breast, will protect the women from "the enemy" all the days of their lives.

Now the rivalry between Peter and Thomas surfaces (and it is similar to the rivalry between Peter and the Beloved Disciple in the GosJn):

> When he had greeted the apostles, Peter said, "You have always been obdurate and unbelieving (*Vere semper durus et incredulus fuisti*), and so the Lord has not suffered you to be at his mother's burial." He smote his breast and said, "I know it and I ask pardon of you all," and they all prayed for him.[33]

This account is simply embellished legend based on the GosJn 20, but did these Thomas traditions originate in Italy in the thirteenth century?

The next sentences reveal something different. Obviously testing the other disciples who are all (including John) inferior to him in this special knowledge, Thomas asks them where the Virgin's body is buried (*Ubi posuistis corpus eius?*). They inform him that it is in the sepulcher. As the reader already knows, they are mistaken. Thomas is quick to correct them. He informs them:

> "The body which is called most holy is not there (*Non est ibi corpus quod dicitur sanctissimum*)." Then the blessed Peter said to him, "Formerly you would not believe in the resurrection of our Master and Lord at our word (*credere noluisti nobis*), unless you went to touch him with your fingers, and see him. How should you believe us (*quomodo credes nobis*) that the holy body is here (*hic esset*)?" Still he went on saying, "It is not here." Then, as if in anger (*quasi irati*), they went to the sepulcher, which was a new one hollowed out in the rock, and took away the stone, but they did not find the body. And they did not know what to say, being vanquished (*victi erant*) by Thomas's words. (MS A 19)

This is remarkable. It not only shows dependence on the GosJn; it also discloses a struggle by some group of Christians with the rank of Thomas. The tension between Thomas and Peter is more exacerbated than that between the Beloved Disciple and Peter in the GosJn. Peter is deliberately set up as the fall-guy. The reader knows the truth, but Peter is given words of attack against Thomas. They make him look foolish in the eyes of the reader. Peter castigates Thomas unjustly. Peter and the other disciples are even said to have become angry. Thomas wins on all accounts. The story concludes with a very high opinion of Thomas.

What social tensions does the book mask? Thomas explains to the ignorant disciples (including John and especially Peter) that he had been brought to the Mount of Olives while he was saying mass in India, and

---

[33] Elliott, *The Apocryphal New Testament*, 715.

how he had seen Mary's ascension. Thomas then shows them Mary's girdle, with which they had encircled her, and which she had given only to him. Notice the disciples' response. They all asked his pardon, "because of the benediction which the blessed Mary had given him" (*omnes beato Thomae propter benedictionem, quam dedit illi beata Maria*). All the disciples bless Thomas for an additional reason, "because he had seen the most holy body going up into heaven" (*et propterea quod vidit corpus sanctissimum celos ascendere*).

The disciples ask Thomas's pardon. He blesses them by quoting from Psalm 133:1, which ends with a celebration of unity. Like the author of the GosJn when he added chapters 15–17 and the editor of the GosJn who appended chapter 21, the author of this apocryphon appeals for unity.

What do these traditions reflect about early Christianity and about the place of Thomas in Christendom? Obviously, the author of Manuscript A reflects a picture of Thomas that portrays him as an unparalleled hero among the Twelve. In the conclusion, Thomas is impressively elevated. He obtains the power of Mary's girdle. He is the one all the disciples turn to for forgiveness.[34] He blesses them, calling for unity and harmony among the Christian brethren.

Most importantly for our search to identify the Beloved Disciple, there are unmistakable innuendoes that Thomas had been considered, by someone, as the Beloved Disciple, since he is identified narratively with sections of the GosJn in which the Beloved Disciple alone is the dominant figure (as we saw in chap. 2.1). For example, Thomas assumes the Beloved Disciple's place in the GosJn by alone perceiving (Mary this time and not Jesus), by his special relation with Jesus' mother (from GosJn 19), and by the rivalry with Peter. How are we to evaluate these insights in the search for the identity of the Beloved Disciple? No sure answers will be forthcoming until we have critical texts of this apocryphon, a careful analysis of the Thomas traditions in Manuscript A, and a better understanding of the reason Peter and the other disciples tend to disparage Thomas, until it is clear to them, as to the reader, that he is superior to them.

2. Gospel of the Twelve Apostles

This work is virtually unknown. It is not to be confused with works of similar title. It is not to be equated with the apocryphon Origen called τὸ ἐπιγεγραμμένον τῶν Δώδεκα εὐαγγέλιον (*in Luc. hom.* 1).[35] It is also none of the following: the Kukean Gospel of the Twelve, the *Gospel of the Twelve Apostles* ed. J. R. Harris, the *Ebionite's Gospel of the Twelve*,

---

[34] The Joseph traditions may have helped shape the narrative here.

[35] See Hennecke and Schneemelcher, eds., *The New Testament Apocrypha*, ed. McL. Wilson, 1:374.

the *Memoria Apostolorum* mentioned in 440 C.E. by Turribius of Astorga, and the Manichean *Gospel of the Twelve*.[36] The work titled the *Gospel of the Twelve Apostles* is a melange of sixteen Coptic fragments of various dates.[37]

In the Coptic apocryphal so-called *Gospel of the Twelve Apostles*,[38] fragment 2, Thomas is the leading actor with Jesus. Thomas assists in the multiplication of the loaves and fishes. One should not base a reconstruction of Jesus' time on this apocryphon because it is late and out of touch with ancient Palestine. For example, it calls the hill of Bethany "the mountain of Bethany" (*ptoou nbethunia* [A² p. 27]), which seems to derive from a misunderstanding of the same area called the "Mount of Olives" (*montem oliveti*).[39] Thomas confesses his unbelief (*etbe tamnt apistos* [A³ p. 19]).[40] The author does not call Thomas the "Beloved Disciple"; in fact he calls John "my love" (*pamerit*).

Nevertheless, the stress is on Thomas, who is the major interlocutor with Jesus in the account of the resurrection of Lazarus. Jesus calls not only Lazarus, but also Thomas *pašbēr*, "my friend."[41] Since the noun *šbēr* often represents φίλος, *pašbēr* may be translated "my beloved." Surely this possibility suggests that some Christians were thinking Thomas was the Beloved Disciple.

Jesus urges Thomas to ask everything that might come into his mind. Jesus honors Thomas for wanting to know about the resurrection of the body. Repeatedly Jesus urges Thomas, "Come with me, Didymus." Conflating the accounts of the GosJn in chapters 11 and 20, the author has Jesus tell him, "O Thomas, you have searched for the signs of the resurrection; come and I will show them to you in the tomb of Lazarus" (A² p. 28). Jesus salutes Thomas with the words that it is good (*kalōs*; καλός) that he searched for the signs of resurrection (A² p. 26). There is certainly

[36] See Hennecke and Schneemelcher, eds., *The New Testament Apocrypha*, 1:374–82. Also see the discussion of Manichaeism in chapter 7.

[37] For the text see A. Baumstark, "Les apocryphes coptes," *Revista bíblica* N.S. 3 (1906) 245–65; Ladeuze, "Apocryphes evangéliques coptes: Pseudo-Gamaliel, Évangile de Barthélemy," *Revue d'histoire ecclésiastique* 7 (1906) 245–68; Hennecke and Schneemelcher, eds., *The New Testament Apocrypha*, 1:382.

[38] The text has not been translated into English. It is not presented in the standard editions of the New Testament Apocrypha.

[39] The transliteration of Coptic is not vocalic; it is simple. It is understandable that one who did not know Jerusalem and its environs might misunderstand the expression "Mount of Olives" which is simply a rise to the east of Jerusalem beyond the Kedron Valley.

[40] The Coptic represents, of course, the ἄπιστος of GosJn 20:27.

[41] The Coptic noun *šbēr* often was used to represent the Hebrew חבר.

no "doubting Thomas" here; and the tradition is also represented in the *Acts of Thomas* in which Thomas rejects any claim that he was a doubter: "But this I say not as one doubting ...."[42]

Jesus with a joyous voice speaks to Thomas and allows him to remove the stone from before the tomb of Lazarus (A³ p. 19). The entire work, "the Resurrection of Lazarus," is obviously an apocryphal expansion of the GosJn. The author in fact quotes passages from the GosJn; for example, he has Jesus say, "I am the resurrection and the life" (*anok pe tanastasis auō pōnah* [A² p. 26]) which is directly from John 11:25 (the Sahidic NT is virtually identical to the Coptic of A² p. 26).[43]

The prominence of Thomas in the Coptic apocryphal *Acts of the Apostles* is very close to the status of the Beloved Disciple. Later in this apocryphon (at A⁹ p. 66) the Father (*peiōt*)—that is God—is alleged to have said to Thomas (*thōmas*), "My elect one, your faith (*tekpistis, πίστις*) shall become an eagle of light (*nouaetos* [ἀετός] *nouoein*) which shall soar over all lands until they [the inhabitants of all lands] believe in the name of my son through you (*hitootk*). Amen" (A⁹ p. 66). In light of the portrayal of Thomas in this apocryphon, are we to imagine that this work preserves a defense of Thomas as the Beloved Disciple? Who then (that is, what Christian group) would be disparaging him, and why?

3. Cassiodorus' Fragment of Clement Alexandrinus

The sixth-century Cassiodorus (c. 485–c. 580) was a Roman. After failing to found a theological school in Rome after the model of Alexandria, he established an academy at Vivarium. Cassiodorus translated into Latin works by Clement of Alexandria (c. 150–c. 215). Some of these writings of Clement are preserved only in Cassiodorus's fragments. One of them is apparently authentic and exceedingly important in our search for the identity of the Beloved Disciple.

The fragment is from Clement of Alexandria's commentary on the *First Epistle of John* (1:1). In it Clement explains his understanding of 1:1, which states "that which was from the beginning ... we have touched with our hands." Clement took this verse to mean someone touched the resurrected Jesus Christ. He was aided in this exegetical move by the reference in 1:1 to logos: Ὅ ἦν 'ἀπ' ἀρχῆς ... καὶ αἱ χεῖρες ἡμῶν ἐψηλάφησαν περὶ τοῦ λόγου τῆς ζωῆς.

---

[42] ActsTh 167; see Drijvers in *New Testament Apocrypha*, 2:404.

[43] See *The Coptic Version of the New Testament in the Southern Dialect Otherwise Called Sahidic and Thebaic* (Oxford: Clarendon Press, 1911) 3:186. Contrast the Bohairic version which is more idiomatically Coptic; see *The Coptic Version of the New Testament in the Northern Dialect Otherwise Called Memphitic and Bohairic* (Oxford: Clarendon Press, 1898) 1:472.

Clement then refers to some traditions he has received. According to them, John the Apostle touched the body of Jesus: "It is accordingly related in traditions, that John, touching the outward body itself, sent his hand deep down into it, and that the solidity of the flesh offered no obstacle, but gave way to the hand of the disciple."[44] How early is this tradition? Does it go back into the first decades of the second century, or even earlier?

What is the meaning of this odd statement? Apparently there is confusion between the apostles John and Thomas. Only the latter, according to the GosJn, desired and was invited to place his hand in Jesus' side. He did not do so, according to the GosJn, but we have already seen apocryphal and church traditions in which he did touch Jesus' resurrected body (see chap. 4).

This fragment is exceptional. The author of this tradition inherited by Clement attributes to John this action. Yet, John is not named in the GosJn. He does nothing and says nothing. In fact he does not even appear in the Johannine drama of chapters 1–20. The action attributed to him by Clement would be appropriate for only one disciple: Thomas. How did this tradition become confused?

It appears that someone, thinking John was the Beloved Disciple, found a reference to the Beloved Disciple touching Jesus, and equated the action of the anonymous one with John. If so, then it seems that originally the tradition Clement preserves made sense only because its author had concluded that the Beloved Disciple was none other than Thomas. That is, someone earlier than Clement knew that Thomas was the Beloved Disciple and recorded how the Beloved Disciple touched Jesus' body. Later Christians assumed incorrectly that the Beloved Disciple was John and transferred to him traditions earlier associated with Thomas as the Beloved Disciple.

Clement saw a reference to the Beloved Disciple's touching Jesus and assumed, incorrectly, that John had done so. If this passage was in some gnostic or proto-gnostic work, it is understandable why Clement might have been attracted to it. Unlike Irenaeus and Hippolytus, he was not a polemicist against the gnostics. With them he affirmed that gnosis—spiritual enlightenment—was the paramount means to Christian perfection. With them, or some of them, he perceived that ignorance was more evil than sin.

This great teacher, Clement, taught Origen and perhaps Hippolytus. His erudition is well known. He was the author of three of the great early

---

[44] See W. Wilson, "Fragments of Clemens Alexandrinus," *The Ante-Nicene Fathers*, ed. A. Roberts and J. Donaldson (Grand Rapids: Eerdmans, 1975 [the original date in the 19th cent. is not given]) 2:571, n. 1; the translation is on p. 574.

classics of the church: λόγος ὁ προτρεπτικὸς πρὸς Ἕλληνας (*Exhortation to the Heathen*), παιδαγωγός (*Instructor*), and στρωματεῖς (*Stromata*). It is apparent that he preserved traditions once espoused by Christians who "knew" that the Beloved Disciple was Thomas.

As so many other early gifted scholars, Clement was so preoccupied with defending the faith, establishing the institution, and clarifying the vast needs of Christians who needed instruction on how to act at feasts and how to laugh,[45] and even facing martyrdom, that he did not have sufficient time for disinterested scholarly reflection on the symbolic meaning of the GosJn.[46] The Appendix of the GosJn apparently misled him, and of course he needed the witness of an apostle to secure the foundations of the faith. No candidate was better suited for this task than the apostle John, especially in light of the lore about him circulating thanks to Polycarp and Papias.

Papias, Clement, Irenaeus, and others were forced to defend the legitimacy of the "Gospel According to Saint John." Many pre-Nicene critics did not consider it reliable and authentic; it was tainted by the interpretations found in Heracleon's Ὑπομνέματα. Other Valentinians and numerous gnostics almost caused the GosJn to be cast into the rubbish heaps of condemned literature. The Appendix to the GosJn apparently helped save the reputation of the GosJn. The irony is that it misled experts in the search for the identity of the Beloved Disciple. In *The Secret Identity of the Beloved Disciple* Grassi pens these choice insights:

> The end of the eclipse of the beloved disciple turns out to be a surprise: as a result of the gospel Appendix, the letters, and the *misidentification with John the apostle*, the book inspired by the beloved disciple was considered "safe" enough to be received into the canon of the official books of the church. If the eclipse had not occurred, the beloved disciple's work might have been permanently lost or reduced to a part of the unapproved apocryphal New Testament literature gathering dust in large tomes. As a result, the beloved disciple's work has remained with us. (125, italics mine)

The Evangelist is a genius who can be subtle. He did not need to remove the attractive veil of anonymity from the Beloved Disciple because his readers knew whom he intended, but he had not intended someone to add a misleading Appendix to his second, and final, edition.

---

[45] See *Instructor* 5.4–5.

[46] Clement, of course, did focus on the symbolic meaning of poetry, philosophy, and theology. See *Stromata* 5.8–10.

4. Coptic Irenaeus

A virtually unknown Coptic collection of early traditions contains a passage in which Thomas is highlighted.[47] Within it there is a reference to an otherwise unknown argument by Irenaeus (c. 130–c. 200). In a prolix style typical of Irenaeus, we learn that when Jesus was crucified Thomas was not present (*mmau an pe nje thōmas*).[48] Thus, the other disciples must inform him about the lance (*nlongkhē* = λόγχῃ of GosJn 19:34)[49] that was thrust into Jesus' side. What is behind Irenaeus' polemic? Against whom is he directing this lambaste? It is certainly not against the tradition that when Thomas was martyred a lance was thrust into him in a manner reminiscent of the account of Jesus' crucifixion only in the GosJn (ActsTh 168,[50] and ψαλμοὶ Σαρακωτῶν 27–30).[51] Irenaeus's polemic must have to do with the identification of the disciple who witnessed Jesus' crucifixion.

[47] This lost fragment of Irenaeus is not reproduced or noted in the standard collection of Irenaeus' fragments. I could not find it in the following: Lagarde's edition (n. 48 below) is of 1886, so the fragment of Irenaeus will not be cited in A. Roberts and J. Donaldson, eds., "Fragments from the Lost Writings of Irenaeus," in *Ante-Nicene Christian Library* (Edinburgh: T. & T. Clark, 1869) 2:158–87; but it should have been cited and excerpted in Irenaeus, *Contre les hérésies*, ed. A. Rousseau and L. Doutreleau (Sources Chrétiennes 210; Paris: Cerf, 1974). They focused only on the Latin, and the fragments extant in Greek, Armenian, and Syriac.

[48] P. de Lagarde, ed., *Catenae in Evangelia Aegyptiacae Quae Supersunt* (Göttingen: Prostant in Aedibus Dieterichianis, 1886) 230.

[49] The Irenaeus Coptic fragment which has *nlongkhē hen pefsphir* is closer to the Bohairic New Testament (*m̄pefsphir n̄teflogkhē*) than to the Saihidic New Testament (*m̄pefspir n̄oulogkhē*).

[50] "And the four came and pierced him with their spears, and he fell down and died" (Elliott, *The Apocryphal New Testament*, 510).

[51] See C. R. C. Allberry, ed., "ψαλμοὶ Σαρακωτῶν," *A Manichaean Psalm-Book* (Stuttgart: Kohlhammer, 1938) part 2, 133–86. Allberry could not discern the meaning of the "Psalms of Sarakōtōn" (xxi–xxii). The Greek Σαρακωτῶν looks very much like the Hebrew צדקות and the confusion between ר and ד is frequent in Semitic (Hebrew, Aramaic, and Syriac) manuscripts. Thus, these may be "Psalms of the Righteous Ones." In any case, the celebration of Thomas in lines 27 to 30 of this Coptic Psalter is significant. He dies on a cross (σταυρός) and soldiers pierce him with a lance (λόγχη). The link with the GosJn is obvious; only in it do we find the use of λόγχη, and only in the passage which depicts the BD observing Jesus' death (19:34-35). It is true that it appears in a variant to Mt 27:49, but surely this is an intrusion from the GosJn. On behalf of the textual critics who have given us the *NTG*, Metzger rightly offers this judgment: "It is probable that the Johannine passage was written by some reader in the margin of Matthew from memory ... and a later copyist awkwardly introduced it into the text" (*A Textual Commentary on the Greek New Testament*, 71). What is important is to observe that the variant is found in the

What is the meaning of this fragment for us? Since the fragment is obviously conceived in terms of the GosJn, in which alone the thrust of the lance is noted, then we should concentrate our attention there. According to the GosJn, the Beloved Disciple was the only male disciple said to be present at the crucifixion. Only he saw the lance thrust into Jesus' corpse (see chap. 2.1). Why would Irenaeus deny that Thomas was present?

That question demands a reconstruction of the second century that is presently impossible. An attempt, however, is surely possible: Irenaeus engaged in polemics against gnostics, and those he thought were gnostics; he wrote *A Refutation and Subversion of Falsely So-Called Knowledge*. It is likely that Irenaeus, *inter alia*, was arguing against "Christians" who claimed that Thomas was present at the crucifixion and saw the thrust of the lance. Have we not found additional evidence that some early Christians contended Thomas was the Beloved Disciple who saw the lance thrust into Jesus' side and was the only "true" witness to it?

If so—and the answer in my judgment is affirmative—then they correctly understood what Johannine Christians knew. That is, they understood the intention of the author, if not necessarily the final editor, of the GosJn. They knew the identity of the Beloved Disciple: he is Thomas.

Have we made a significant discovery? The powerful bishop of Lyons, in France, was a spokesman for the West. Although little is known of his life, it is evident he studied in Rome. He advocated the supremacy of Rome and the apostolic succession preserved continuously only there (*Adv. Haer.* 3.3.2-4); but this is now wisely seen as pro-Roman propaganda, thanks especially to the research of Bauer.[52]

Such arguments, like the present one by Irenaeus, explain why scholars sometimes call him the first Catholic theologian. He bewailed Christians who were so "Judaic" that they revered Jerusalem (*Adv. Haer.* 1.26.2). That is astounding, given that the drama of salvation he so loudly proclaimed was from ancient Palestine. Indeed, Jesus' crucifixion and resurrection are placed in Jerusalem by his major gospel, the GosJn. His comment is understandable when we remember his context: Rome was supreme; Jerusalem had long ago been razed, and Aelia Capitolina had been erected over the ruins.

---

oldest and most important uncials, and—more importantly for us now—that these Coptic Psalms, which Allberry dates to about 340 C.E. (p. xx), indicate that Thomas is the one who experienced the trust of.the "lance" as had the BD in the GosJn.

[52] Bauer, *Heresy and Orthodoxy in Earliest Christianity*, 229-31 (but much of Bauer after those pages is in great need of revision).

His rejection of ideas popular in the East is significantly obvious: he lambasted any who abstained from eating animals, and he accosted Tatian (*Adv. Haer.* 1.28.1, 4.23.1-8), the compiler of the magnificent harmony (inappropriately labeled Diatessaron as if it were compiled from only four gospels in Greek). He attacked what he judged to be Christian aberrations in the East.

It is conceivable then that Irenaeus' fragment, preserved only in Coptic, significantly assists us in the search for the identity of the Beloved Disciple. It is likely that Irenaeus knew that some Christian scholars assumed Thomas was present at the crucifixion because he was the Beloved Disciple.

Less *prima facie* conceivable would be the claim that the alleged "heretics" thought Thomas represented the invisible Decad, because he was not present when Jesus appeared to the other disciples, who would be ten in number. Yet, that is precisely what Irenaeus reported about them (perhaps the Marcosians; see *Adv. Haer.* 1.18.3). He assumed the Beloved Disciple was John the son of Zebedee, since he wrote, "John, the disciple of the Lord, who also had leaned upon his breast, did himself publish a gospel during his residence at Ephesus in Asia" (*Adv. Haer.* 3.1.1).

Irenaeus is not only *defensor fidei*; he is defender of Rome and the West. His heroes are Peter (who represents Rome), John (who is the author of his favorite gospel), Matthew (whom he thought composed the first intracanonical gospel), and Paul (the missionary to the Gentiles, esp. in Rome; see *Adv. Haer.* 3.21.3; cf. 3.1.1).

8.4 CONCLUSION

Our search for the identity of the Beloved Disciple has been challenging. We seem to see a veil being lifted from some phases of early Christianity. We periodically witness a Roman celebration of John as the Beloved Disciple. The increasingly powerful bishopric of Rome will allow no divergent opinions or traditions regarding the identity of the Beloved Disciple. Rome is struggling to control what is true and whose witness is trustworthy. Intermittently we catch a glimpse of the attempt, often emanating from Rome, to elevate John and denigrate "Doubting Thomas." That would be ironic if the author of the GosJn concealed Thomas as the Beloved Disciple and presented him as the one true witness to Jesus' life, teaching, crucifixion, and resurrection.

The rivalry between Thomas and Peter is mirrored in much of the literature we have just reviewed. Thomas is the hero of the East; Peter tends to represent the Pope in Rome. As the West tended to disparage Thomas (considering him the "Doubter"), so the East, especially in gnostic circles, contended that Peter was the worst obfuscator (*Adv. Haer.* 3.12.9).[53]

These conflicts were developing while "Christianity" tried to obtain some normative self-definition, as it perceived itself, at times, as a little ship on a tossing sea whipped by powerfully destructive winds. R. Mac-Mullen has warned us that too often we scholars have packed antiquity into neatly arranged and acceptable categories, because the tidy mind abhors the chaotic scene in which the drama of early Christianity took place. Despite the title of his book, *Paganism in the Roman Empire*, he wisely warns about the way we have arrogantly labeled non-Christian people and works as "paganism."

Most importantly, MacMullen points out that Christians were put on the defensive because they committed the one unforgivable sin; they were deserters from their spiritual home, Judaism. Indeed, reviewing the early apocryphal writings churns up vast amounts of distasteful anti-Jewish sentiment. Porphyry, Hesiod, and the vast majority of ancients—including those who composed Jewish, Pythagorean, Christian, and other forms of pseudepigrapha—celebrated the past as paradigmatic. As MacMullen points out, "innovation in itself was not only painful but bad."[54]

Such thoughts about so-called paganism, binding tradition, and creative innovation pour over me when I sit on benches at Gamla, stand near an archaeologist's balk in Sepphoris, see the sun set from Hippus, walk through the columnated streets of Jerash and Scythopolis, and worship on the Mount of Olives or in St. Catherine's Monastery. Not only I, but also those who were there long ago, revered traditions and the patriarchs and sought to comprehend how life is possible in a world all too often out of control. Hence, the celebration of Thomas, John, or whoever was the Beloved Disciple is to be perceived in terms of those in the Johannine School who were celebrating traditions, and creating new ones, about the One from above, and adhering to the one disciple, the Beloved Disciple, whom they revered and knew was trustworthy.

Our depiction of early Christianity appears to be in line with the best reconstructions now available. In the beginning there was no harmony and concord within the Palestinian Jesus Movement (PJM). Right from the beginning the tensions and differences that had previously separated Jews, even Shamites from Hillelites, produced clashes not only among "converted" Jews in this new (but ill-defined) Jewish sect, but also with once despised "pagans" who espoused the innovatively new faith. Dunn correctly points to the considerable diversity within Christianity from the

[53] See Pagels, *The Johannine Gospel in Gnostic Exegesis*, 13.
[54] R. MacMullen, *Paganism in the Roman Empire* (New Haven/London: Yale Univ. Press, 1981) 3.

inception of the PJM,[55] and C. C. Hill rightly seeks to discern how diverse were the Hellenists and Hebrews not only against each other but within themselves.[56]

Bauer did not exaggerate when he wrote, "Rome shows itself to be controlled and motivated more by a strong desire for power than by the sense of brotherly love and by a selfless sense of duty."[57] He was perceptive. *1 Clement* does reveal that Rome was imposing its might upon Corinth. It is not from an individual; it is from the church in Rome. About the time the GosJn was finally edited and the Appendix was in place,[58] emissaries were sent from Rome (τοὺς δὲ ἀπεσταλμένους ἀφ' ἡμῶν [*1Clem* 65.1]) to Corinth to stress the point, developed from 1 Corinthians that "love allows no schism" (ἀγάπη σχίσμα οὐκ ἔχει [*1Clem* 49.5]). By the middle of the second century, Rome was imposing its interpretations and ecclesiastic powers on the East, as we know, *inter alia*, from Eusebius about the disputes over the time of Easter noted in the above discussion on Polycrates (*HE* 5.24.1-18). As Brown points out, the little groups of Christians were eking out existence in a world where the rhetoric and the art of persuasion had been replaced by force and intimidation.[59]

We thus obtain an enlightened perspective on Christian origins. The West, represented by Peter, was in a polemical relation with the East, represented by Thomas (or Judas Thomas). It is tempting, but unwise, to seek some confirmation for our reconstruction in two sources which refer to a "Judas." Around 380 C.E., in his commentary on the Revelation of John, Tyconius (d. c. 400), who supported the Donatists, stated that the "Church of Judas" has always been opposed to the "Church of Peter."[60] Tyconius, whom Augustine admired and quoted in his *De Doctrina Christiana*, probably taught that the Church must be a universal one encom-

---

[55] J. D. G. Dunn, *Unity and Diversity in the New Testament: An Inquiry into the Character of Earliest Christianity* (London: SCM, 1977) 275.

[56] C. C. Hill, *Hellenists and Hebrews: Reappraising Division Within the Earliest Church* (Minneapolis: Fortress, 1992).

[57] Bauer, *Orthodoxy and Heresy in Earliest Christianity*, 97.

[58] K. Lake dated *1 Clement* to the last decade of the first century, or at least between 75 and 110 C.E. Lake, *The Apostolic Fathers* (LCL 24; Cambridge, Mass./London: Heinemann, 1912, 1965) 1:4.

[59] Brown, *The Body and Society*, 5-115. See esp. Brown, *Power and Persuasion*, 7: "Power, not persuasion, remains the most striking characteristic of the later Roman Empire in all its regions."

[60] See K. B. Steinhauser, *The Apocalypse Commentary of Tyconius: A History of its Reception and Influence* (European University Studies Series 23, no. 301; Bern/New York: Peter Lang, 1988). Also see W. H. C. Frend, *The Donatist Church: A Movement of Protest in Roman North Africa* (Oxford: Clarendon Press, 1952) esp. 315-32.

passing the entire earth.[61] Similar views about a rivalry between "Peter" and "Judas" were articulated by the Donatist Petilian of Constantine about twenty years later (c. 400).[62] In most passages the "Judas" is obviously a *typos* for betrayers.[63]

Is it possible that occasionally a confusion arises among the Donatists between "the betrayer Judas" and "the doubter Judas Thomas"? The latter would denote the church in the East. I am convinced this is not a profitable search. Augustine did condemn "all schismatics" and labeled them those who commune with Judas (*On Baptism, Against the Donatists* 8.25). But even here he is focusing his attention on the Donatist schism in the African Church. Hence, references around 400 to a schism categorized as headed by "Judas" does not help us with the rivalry between "Peter" and "Judas Thomas."

We have been reviewing evidence that the obvious polemics of the second and later centuries—the tension between the West and the East— apparently can be traced back to communities that antedate 100 C.E. If the reconstruction offered here is on target, then some perplexing questions may be answered. After citing Tyconius's comment about the rivalry between the churches of Peter and Judas, W. H. C. Frend of Cambridge University pondered how ideas "prevalent in Palestine in the first century B.C." had "so great an effect on North African Christian thought."[64] Christendom in the East and West was not separated; it was linked in many ways, including polemics.

We have also seen that Rome's (or the West's) emphasis that John the son of Zebedee was the Beloved Disciple and the author of "the Gospel According to St. John" undermined and tended to vanquish other rival opinions. These rival opinions were surely discordant to the Roman position, but they may have been more reliable. Yet pro-Roman Christian scholars also ironically, sometimes inadvertently, preserved faint echoes from those who held to an ancient tradition that the Beloved Disciple was Thomas the Twin. Hence, our surprising discovery from an exegesis of the GosJn seems confirmed by the remnants of documents from the second century; the Beloved Disciple is most likely Thomas, the Twin.

---

[61] See Bright, *The Book of Rules of Tyconius: Its Purpose and Inner Logic* (Christianity and Judaism in Antiquity 2; Notre Dame: Univ. of Notre Dame Press, 1988) 11.

[62] See Augustine, *Contra Litteras Petiliani*, 2.8., 2.11., 2.18, 2.19. Also see W. H. C. Frend, *Martyrdom and Persecution in the Early Church* (Oxford: Blackwell, 1965) 61, 77.

[63] The Donatists called themselves "saints" and their Christian opponents "betrayers" (*traditors*; see 2.109).

[64] Frend, *Martyrdom and Persecution in the Early Church*, 61.

CHAPTER 9

The Gospel of Thomas and Thomas as the Beloved Disciple

The preceding discussions illustrate that there are numerous and complex ties between the *Gospel of Thomas* and the GosJn. The historical and ideological relations between these two early gospels are intriguing; but, as of the present, they have not been sufficiently explained.[1] Has no Coptic expert working on the apocryphal *Gospel of Thomas* contemplated the possibility that the Beloved Disciple in the GosJn is to be identified with Thomas?

9.1 P. DE SUAREZ'S EXEGESIS

Two experts in Gnosticism, working on the *Gospel of Thomas*, have indeed claimed that the Beloved Disciple in the GosJn is Thomas. In 1974 de Suarez contended that "sous le dénomination du *disciple que Jésus aimait* Jean rend à Thomas le première place ...."[2] His initial observations are that Thomas appears more frequently in the GosJn than in the Synoptics, and that in the GosJn he is introduced as "Thomas called the Twin." Hence, in the GosJn Thomas is much more of an imposing figure than he is in the Synoptics.

Most importantly, he defends the claim that κύριε, τίς ἐστιν ὁ παραδιδούς σε; (21:20) means "Lord, who is the one who will transmit

---

[1] As mentioned earlier, in *Resurrection Reconsidered: Thomas and John in Controversy* (Minneapolis: Fortress, 1995), Riley rightly sees the important relationships that unite the GosJn and the GosTh; but he sees them in a polemical relationship. This interpretation is primarily because of his denigrating opinion of Thomas, which is not supported by an exegesis of the GosJn.

[2] P. de Suarez, *L'Évangile selon Thomas*, 260.

(your teaching) to posterity?"[3] Is this translation likely?

Obviously, παραδίδωμι is sometimes employed as a *terminus technicus* for "transmitting," as we know from 1 Corinthians 11:23, "I also transmitted (παρέδωκα) to you." The Greek here in Paul's letter is shaped by Semitics, which he knew well. Evidence of Paul's rabbinic training is his use in 1 Corinthians of the *termini technici* for reception and transmission of oral tradition; "he received" (קבל) and "he transmitted" (מסר) tradition. These terms are found in the earliest rabbinic documents. Note, e.g., Pirke Aboth: "Moses received (קבל) Torah from Sinai and he transmitted it (ומסרה) to Joshua" (m.Ab 1.1).

But that is not the issue here, despite de Suarez' exegesis. Does ὁ παραδιδούς σε; mean "Who shall transmit you?" or "Who shall betray you?" Obviously, de Suarez opts for the former, but his exegesis is exceedingly dubious. The verb preceding the phrase κύριε, τίς ἐστιν ὁ παραδιδούς σε; in 21:20 clarifies the context. It is the aorist εἶπεν, "he said (or had said)," which points the reader back to chapter 13 in which the Beloved Disciple was first introduced under this epithet. There is no room for doubting that the author of chapter 21 is introducing "the disciple whom Jesus loved" not in terms of when he last appeared in the narrative (i.e., in 20:8), but in terms of when he is first introduced in the narrative, specifically in 13:23 (see chap. 2.1).

That context assuredly concerns which disciple will *betray* Jesus. In 13:21 Jesus announces that one of his own will "betray me" (παραδώσει με.). The meaning cannot be "transmit me"; that is illogical in terms of the Greek, and betrayal is certain because the literary context continues to specify that "Satan" now enters into the betrayer, namely Judas Iscariot (13:27).

It is also evident that the quotation attributed to the Beloved Disciple in 21:20 is anchored in the pericope which describes Jesus' last meal with his faithful followers: "Turning, Peter sees the disciple whom Jesus loved following [them]; he [was the one] who during the supper had lain on his chest (στῆθος) and had said, 'Lord, who is it that is going to betray you?'" (compare 20:20 with 13:25). In chapter 13 we are told about *Jesus' betrayal*, and not about the transmission of Jesus' teachings.

P. de Suarez seems to be reading the GosJn in light of his own understanding of the *Gospel of Thomas*. Also, the tendency to avoid the

---

[3] "Seigneur, quel est celui qui transmet ton (enseignement) à la postérite?" (*L'Évangile selon Thomas*, 261. In examining the authors who concluded that Judas Iscariot is the BD we confronted the claim that παραδίδωμι meant "hand over" and not "betray." The Greek verb means "hand over," "entrust," "betray," and "transmit." It is the literary context and the immediate syntax that is the guide to which of these meanings is intended by an author.

prima facie meaning of ὁ παραδιδούς σε with its obvious contextual meaning of betraying seems to be indicative of the possibility that de Suarez has imported gnostic teaching and understanding into the GosJn[4] In Gnosticism, especially among the Cainites, Judas Iscariot is sometimes portrayed as the hero of the gospel (not the betrayer). Some gnostics claimed, according to Irenaeus, that Judas Iscariot "alone was acquainted with the truth."[5]

Furthermore, some words in de Suarez's translation are not in the Greek of 21:20. His translation demands adding the following words: "your teaching" (enseignement) and "to posterity" (à la postérité). Greek can often be frustratingly cryptic, and frequently words—especially verbs—must be supplied in order to provide an acceptable modern translation. But, these additions in modern translations are usually implied by the syntax and grammar of the ancient Greek. To add nouns—and two of them in succession—and to suggest all commentators have missed the meaning of the Greek in 21:20 is hardly persuasive.

P. de Suarez is also convinced that 21:24 means the following: "This is the disciple who has witnessed these things and who has transcribed them, and we know that his witness is true."[6] While this translation is not impossible, it does not represent the fundamental meaning of γράψας, which denotes "writing"; and it seems conceivable that his suggested translation is rooted not in philology, but in his interpretation of

---

[4] I am persuaded that the GosJn, like the OdesSol, is proto-gnostic; that is, it is not gnostic, but contains ideas and phrases that will later receive a gnostic meaning, and that some phrases may well have an *incipient* gnostic meaning. Contrast K. Rudolph, who thinks the GosJn is "gnostic" (*Gnosis: The Nature and History of Gnosticism*, trans. R. McL. Wilson [San Francisco: Harper, 1984] 305). I thus cannot accept the thorough-going gnostic interpretation of the GosJn found in L. Schottroff's *Der Glaubende und die feindliche Welt: Beobachtungen zum gnostischen Dualismus und seiner Bedeutung für Paulus und das Johannesevangelium* (WMANT 37; Neukirchen: 1970). It is surprising that Schottroff's work is not cited in the commentaries by Lindars, Haenchen, Schnackenburg, or Carson. An apology for reading the GosJn in terms of the traditions and ideas found in the Nag Hammadi Codices has been provided by Robinson in the Foreword to Haenchen's *John 1*, pp. ix–xiii. In contrast to Robinson's position, I agree with Hengel that the Nag Hammadi Codices help clarify "der nicht-gnostische Charakter" of the GosJn (*Die johanneische Frage*, 46). One of the finest scholars of Gnosticism, G. MacRae, rightly stated that "John did not intend his work to be gnostic; his emphasis on the real humanity of Jesus rules that out" (*Invitation to John*, 20).

[5] Irenaeus, *Against Heresies* 1.31.1; see Layton, *The Gnostic Scriptures*, 181.

[6] "C'est ce disciple qui témoigne de ces choses et qui les a transcrites, et nous savons que véridique est son témoignage" (*L'Évangile selon Thomas*, 261).

21:20.[7] That is, the choice of "transmit" has colored the meaning of "transcribe." Thus, while Thomas appears to be the Beloved Disciple in the GosJn, and de Suarez deserves credit for perceiving this hypothesis, his argument is not firmly grounded in an exegesis of the GosJn.[8]

9.2 H.-M. SCHENKE'S INSIGHTS

In 1986 H.-M. Schenke, the distinguished Professor of New Testament Literature and Theology at the Humboldt University in Berlin, published his thoughtful reflections on why he has concluded that the Beloved Disciple in the GosJn is none other than Thomas. In contrast to my focused search for the identity of the Beloved Disciple by means of an exegetical study of the GosJn, Schenke seeks to understand "the function and background of the Johannine Beloved Disciple with the help of the gnostic parallels found in the Nag Hammadi documents and related texts."[9]

He astutely points out that in both the *Book of Thomas the Contender* and the GosJn, Jesus' "dialogue partner(s) frequently misunderstand him."[10] Schenke is thus interested in solving "one of the great puzzles in the mysterious Fourth Gospel," by studying the Beloved Disciple in light cast upon him (or it) "from outside the Gospel of John and Johannine research."[11] Our methodology and goal is thus quite distinct; but one of our conclusions is identical: we concur that the Beloved Disciple in the GosJn is none other than Thomas.

---

[7] The Greek verb γράφω can mean "scratch, draw, mark, inscribe, prescribe," and especially in the NT "write." I cannot find evidence that it obtained by 100 C.E. the derivative meaning "to transcribe." I would expect that meaning to be located in the Greek verb γραμματεύω which denotes what a scribe does; but this verb does not appear in the NT; and although γραμματεύς appears frequently in Mt, Mk, and Lk (respectively 22, 21, and 14), it never appears in the GosJn. This fact is interesting; I am convinced that the Evangelist deliberately avoids certain nouns (like "knowledge" and "faith") and that the avoidance of "scribe" may well be intentional. Did the Evangelist wish to disassociate his School from the rabbinic scribes?

[8] P. de Suarez appeals in his argument to Mt, Mk, and the GosTh; but that breaks the rule which is stressed in most recent publications: We must listen to the GosJn, and to it alone, if we want to hear its voice.

[9] H.-M. Schenke in *Nag Hammadi, Gnosticism, and Early Christianity*, ed. C. W. Hedrick and R. Hodgson, Jr. (Peabody, Mass.: Hendrickson, 1986) 111.

[10] Schenke, *Nag Hammadi*, 112. For a better understanding of misunderstanding in the GosJn I am indebted to H. Leroy, *Rätsel und Missverständnis: Ein Beitrag zur Formgeschichte des Johannesevangeliums* (BBB 30; Bonn: Hanstein, 1968). See the helpful insights on misunderstanding by Smith in *The Theology of the Gospel of John* (Cambridge: Cambridge Univ. Press, 1995) 113–15.

[11] Schenke, *Nag Hammadi*, 115.

In the preceding chapters it is obvious that I can agree with Schenke on the following points: the GosJn 21 is "redactional"; the Beloved Disciple is the witness behind the GosJn, not the Evangelist;[12] and the GosJn cannot be portrayed "as a whole" and seen as "guaranteed by a historically trustworthy person or regarded as written by an eyewitness."[13] But, I am not as convinced as he is that "certain parts of it" are not so categorized and historically trustworthy.

It should also be obvious that my exegesis leads me to agree with Schenke, broadly speaking, about the strata in which the Beloved Disciple appears. I have become convinced that the Evangelist, not the editor who added chapter 21, is the one who added *some* of these references to the Beloved Disciple in the second edition of the GosJn. While I am persuaded that there are abundant reasons to suspect that 4:2 was added in the second edition,[14] I have found no reason to conjecture that 13:23 and 20:2 are secondary additions (see chap. 2.1).[15] Moreover, to claim that only "whom Jesus loved" in 13:23 and "the one whom Jesus loved" in 20:2 are added, leaves us with a mutilated text, unsupported by textual variants, which mars the narrative by putting stress respectively on the ambiguous "one of the disciples" and "other disciple."

I am convinced, therefore, that Schenke stresses quite rightly that "the extent of the material ascribed to the redactor is increasing to such an extent that the evangelist is about to disappear."[16] Thus he disagrees with those scholars (viz. Thyen) who ascribe all the Beloved Disciple passages to a later redactor. Thus, he cautions that "one ought not to assign more of the Beloved Disciple passages to the redactor than is absolutely necessary."[17] I fully agree.

What difference is there fundamentally between Schenke and me? It is considerable at one point. I find it difficult to agree with Schenke that

---

[12] Schenke contends that the author of chapter 21 "blatantly and recklessly identified the Beloved Disciple as the author of the Gospel" (*Nag Hammadi*, 116).

[13] Ibid.

[14] GosJn 3:22 clearly states that Jesus "baptized" ($\dot{\varepsilon}\beta\dot{\alpha}\pi\tau\iota\zeta\varepsilon\nu$) and 4:1 refers to Jesus baptizing. This could have been embarrassing to Johannine Christians who did not want to subsume Jesus categorically with or under the Baptist. Hence, 4:2 was added: "(although Jesus himself did not baptize, but only his disciples)."

[15] Verses 19:26 and 27 may, however, be redactional. If so, then 19:34 and 35 are also later additions by the same author. They do not have to be additions by a "redactor"; they may well be additions by the Evangelist during the editing of a previous edition. Thus they could be additions by the Evangelist to a second edition.

[16] Schenke, *Nag Hammadi*, 117.

[17] Ibid., 118.

the Beloved Disciple "is a redactional fiction who functions to give the Fourth Gospel the appearance of being authenticated and written by an eyewitness."[18] He argues (also contrary to Thyen) that "the Beloved Disciple passages are only a simple fiction of the redactor."[19] Although the Evangelist may well employ the Beloved Disciple, who does function narratively as the trustworthy eyewitness, to prove the historical claims in the GosJn, I have no doubt that "the disciple whom Jesus loved" represents a real person (see chap. 1.2). As most scholars have concluded, chapter 21 cannot be ignored, and it indicates that the Beloved Disciple has died. Moreover, his death has caused misunderstandings and a loss of confidence in him, in his witness (as we also know from 19:35), and even in the infallibility of Jesus' message. All these points developed out of the exegetical studies in the previous chapters (see esp. 1, 2, 4, and 6).

Perceptively eschewing any importance the so-called *Secret Gospel of Mark* may have for solving the riddle of the identity of the Beloved Disciple, Schenke contends for a starting point. It is "the assumption that the redactor in modeling the fictitious Beloved Disciple had in view a special legendary disciple-figure of Jesus who, advanced in years, had died a natural death and about whom various legends had arisen."[20] Schenke thus sets out to see if, perchance, this disciple's name can be discerned.

He rejects Mary Magdalene, although like the Beloved Disciple she is portrayed as more beloved than any other disciple in the *Gospel of Philip* 55b and the *Gospel of Mary* 17–18,15. He likewise rejects the candidacy of James, the brother of Jesus, even though sometimes in the Nag Hammadi Codices he appears like the disciple whom Jesus loved (cf. esp. *Gospel of Thomas* Log. 12).

Finally, Schenke comes to Judas Thomas. He is seen to embody "'the Beloved Disciple' idea." According to the *Gospel of Thomas* only Thomas knows the appropriate confession (Log. 13a). Thomas is even "more suggestive for the 'Beloved Disciple'" in the *Book of Thomas*; in it "the framework for the first part of its paraenetic materials is a revelation discourse delivered by Jesus to Thomas (138,4-21)."[21] Thomas's superiority to Peter, which clearly is evident in the extracanonical Thomas compositions, aligns Thomas with the portrait of the Beloved Disciple in the GosJn.

The GosJn 19:26-27 finally obtains its full meaning when one observes that the Thomas traditions portray Thomas as Jesus' real brother. Schenke thus asks,

[18] Ibid., 116.
[19] Ibid., 119.
[20] Ibid., 121.
[21] Ibid., 123.

> Here the question suggests itself whether Judas Thomas, the most mysterious of all the brothers of Jesus, might not have been the historical model (in terms of history of tradition) for the Beloved Disciple figure of the Fourth Gospel. In other words, has the redactor of the Fourth Gospel made use of one of the versions of the Thomas legend? This seems to be particularly plausible if Johannine Christianity be localized in Syria, which is otherwise known as the home of the Thomas tradition.[22]

To bolster his argument, Schenke points out that these extracanonical texts represent Jesus promising Thomas that he would not die, but would remain until he returned (at the second coming). Such an interpretation is supported by an exegesis of the *Gospel of Thomas*, especially of Logia 1, 13b, 18, and 108. Both of them promise to Thomas, either directly or by implication, that he will not die.

Schenke considers a possible objection: If the Beloved Disciple is Thomas, then does that not create a duplicate in the GosJn? As he points out, this is not a viable objection. He comments that the redactor could "have done it without realizing it; or, he could have done it deliberately and, for that very reason, have chosen the mysterious paraphrase."[23] He also points out that Thomas also appears in two roles in the *Gospel of Thomas*. He is the alleged author (incipit) and a disciple in the report (Log. 13).

Since I concur with Schenke on the identity of the Beloved Disciple, I may be permitted an additional comment on the ostensible objection of duplication in the GosJn. If the references to the Beloved Disciple do not come solely from the hand of the redactor, but also from the Evangelist, then some duplication is understandable. Second, duplication was never seen to be a problem for those who advocated other hypotheses which demanded that the Beloved Disciple is also a person mentioned by name in the GosJn—which, indeed to me, is imperative if we are to identify by name the Beloved Disciple. Here we need only recall the arguments for Lazarus and others named in the GosJn (see chaps. 3 and 5). Only from the GosJn should we expect to learn the name of the Beloved Disciple in the GosJn.

9.3 THE GOSJN AND THE EARLIEST THOMAS TRADITIONS

The Thomas traditions outside the GosJn are important. They cannot all be relegated as post-Johannine creations, dependent on the portrayal of Thomas in the GosJn. In the first century the Thomas traditions were not

---

[22] Ibid., 123–24.
[23] Ibid., 124–25.

absorbed totally or exclusively by the Evangelist who wrote the GosJn. The fluidity of traditions, especially oral ones, were not exhausted when an intracanonical author cited a few of them. Some continued on and shaped compositions of a later date; others shaped documents now lost. Many, as Papius and Tatian seem to indicate, were never captured in written form. A witness to this living phenomenon is, of course, the Evangelist, who in 20:30 warned all readers that he (or she) had not recorded all the "Christian" traditions known to him (or her).

Syria, broadly defined as it was in the last decade of the first century C.E., or somewhere in or near ancient Palestine,[24] seems to be the setting for the shaping of the GosJn and the earliest Thomas compositions.[25] This geographical insight, shared by many experts, adds credence to the suggestion that the Beloved Disciple is Thomas.[26] Thus, the extracanonical Thomas traditions, though present in post-Johannine compositions, may preserve the end of a conduit that goes back to traditions, less elaborate and less developed, that were contemporaneous with and even earlier than the present work called the Gospel According to John.

Scholars working outside the GosJn on compositions in the Nag Hammadi Codices and in the New Testament Apocrypha and Pseudepigrapha have independently concluded that the Beloved Disciple in the GosJn is Thomas. Our exegesis centered on the GosJn has led us to the same conclusion. Surely, this novel hypothesis should be taken seriously. Is Thomas not the best candidate for the Beloved Disciple?

---

[24] Topographical research in this area, especially in regions controlled by the Nabataeans, has been astounding in the past two decades. I have profited greatly from such publications as R. Wenning's "Die Dekapolis und die Nabatäer," *ZDPV* 110 (1994) 1–35.

[25] As J. Robinson pointed out long ago, the provenience of the GosJn has shifted "from Alexandria or Asia Minor to Syria" (*Trajectories Through Early Christianity* [Philadelphia: Fortress, 1971] 233). Koester rightly stated thirty years ago that Thomas may well have been the disciple who was the missionary to Edessa; at least it is evident that "Thomas was the authority for an indigenous Syrian Christianity even before the formation of noticeable orthodox influence in this area" (*Trajectories*, 133).

[26] Koester stresses (rightly in my opinion) that "the significance of Thomas for the Eastern Church argues for an east-Syrian origin of the Gospel of Thomas" (*Ancient Christian Gospels: Their History and Development* [Philadelphia: Trinity Press International; London: SCM, 1990] 80).

CHAPTER 10

Conclusion

10.1 CONFIRMATION AND VERIFICATION

The following insight is impressive: according to the Johannine narrative, the Beloved Disciple confirms Jesus' death and Thomas verifies Jesus' resurrection (see chaps. 2, 4). In both passages the author of the GosJn stresses the *physical* aspect of the event in the sense that his resurrection was no purely spiritual experience or emotional hallucination. The Beloved Disciple witnesses Jesus' crucifixion (19:26); of him the author reports, "He who saw it has borne witness. His testimony is true; and he knows that he tells the truth" (19:35). What the Beloved Disciple witnessed was that when a soldier pierced Jesus' side with a spear, "blood and water" came out (19:24). The narrator leaves the reader with no doubt that Jesus really died, and that Jesus' death was not faked or only illusory (as in the *Acts of John* 97).[1]

In a similar way, Thomas does not see a mirage or vision of Jesus. He refuses to believe his colleagues' report; he demands to see the marks of crucifixion, especially the wound in the side caused by the lance. Standing before the resurrected Jesus, he is shown the marks of crucifixion—and these wounds are described as belonging to the resurrected Jesus only in John, chapter 20.[2]

According to the Johannine narrative only one disciple, the Beloved Disciple, sees (i.e., witnesses) the lance enter Jesus' corpse. Although the narrator does not identify the witness of 19:35 as "the disciple whom

---

[1] According to the ActsJn Jesus says to John, who is distressed when he sees Jesus suffer on the cross, "John, for the people below in Jerusalem I am being crucified and pierced with lances and reeds and given vinegar and gall to drink" (K. Schäferdieck in Schneemelcher, ed., *New Testament Apocrypha*, 2:184).

[2] The variant in Mt 27:49 is an intrusion from the GosJn.

422

Jesus loved," it seems relatively obvious that he is the one intended. He is the only male disciple described as present at the crucifixion (see chap. 2). And the formulaic claim that "his witness is true" links 19:35 with 21:24 in which the Beloved Disciple is certainly meant (cf. 5:32).

The narrator indicates that Thomas is not informed of this event by anyone. Indeed, to conclude that anyone—Jesus' mother, the soldier, the two men who buried him—informed Thomas of the thoracic wound, would be impossible in terms of narrative criticism. That is to say, the text does not allow the exegete to draw such conclusions. Since only the Beloved Disciple witnessed the thrust of the lance, only he could report it to Thomas; but he exits in 20:10. The corpse is buried before it is seen by the disciples; and after they see the resurrected Jesus, they merely say to Thomas, "we have seen the Lord"; they do not describe the resurrected Jesus for him. If he is Thomas, then all these problems are solved.

Thomas knows this one distinguishing mark of Jesus' crucifixion. How is that possible? The best, indeed the only explanation, is that he saw it *as the Beloved Disciple*. Although both the Beloved Disciple and Thomas are dominant in the narrative, they never meet and never talk to each other. Is that observation not revealing in the honest search for the identity of the Beloved Disciple? That they would converse with each other would be impossible if they are the same person. Since that is now becoming rather obvious, then Thomas knows what to ask to distinguish Jesus' resurrected body from others. He knows precisely how he died, because he had witnessed it as the Beloved Disciple.

The conceptual link between what the Beloved Disciple witnessed at Golgotha and what Thomas saw in Jerusalem is significant. It also has a sociological and Christological function. The claim in a *physical* death and a *physical* resurrection would be powerful blasts against the docetists who were undermining the faith of the Johannine Community. These pseudo-Christians, in the judgment of the Evangelist and author of chapter 21, caused the schism which is so clearly reflected in the Johannine Epistles and in the addition of chapters 15-17. The latter chapters were added to stress unity, either just before or just after the schism.

Hence, the literary genius who wrote the GosJn presents the Beloved Disciple so as to stress the "fleshly" existence of Jesus both before and after the resurrection. His witness is trustworthy. It grounds the trustworthiness and fundamental solidarity of the community's beliefs.

In the New Testament only Thomas makes a *personal* confession when confronted by a physically resurrected Jesus. Using personal pronouns, he is depicted as uttering the final words of a disciple in the GosJn: "My Lord, and my God." Thomas verifies the Beloved Disciple confirmation; both serve as witness. Thomas's grounding of believing in careful reflection and pragmatic observations illustrates the *continuity* between the crucified one and the Resurrected Lord.

10.2 NARRATIVE AND HISTORY

While it is apparent that a case can be made for identifying the Beloved Disciple with Thomas, it is far from evident how the exegete can move from narrative to history. Is it possible to move from our Greek text back into some historical context? Few critics will conclude that we have been working only within the Johannine School, which is behind the GosJn, and most will agree that in many places it is obvious that we have moved further back into the first century C.E.

Are we able to see back through redaction and traditions into the life of a disciple called Thomas? To what extent can we today trust his account of Jesus' life and words? Obviously, we are not left only with tradition or redaction. There can be no doubt that both are "historical," but can tradition be traced, with some reliability, to the period before Jesus' crucifixion? That seems to be the central question that has intermittently been posed by our research up until now.

It surely deserves exploration with the same thoroughness and carefulness as our search for the identity of the Beloved Disciple. We will need to struggle with the evaluation of tradition within redaction. As D. M. Smith stated, "The Johannine community conceived of itself as linked directly to Jesus and the original circle of disciples through the Beloved Disciple, however that linkage may have been understood and whatever may be its validity as a historical claim."[3] Our task is not so much to test the claim of the Johannine Christians; it is to sift the claims and the insights to see how and in what ways they transport us back into the period before Easter, when over there and back then action swirled around "Jesus son of Joseph" (6:42).

A consensus exists among experts that the Johannine Christians lived in a Community which linked itself directly to Jesus and the original disciples through the Beloved Disciple. The agreement is world-wide and virtually unanimous, but this unanimity must not be confused with the search for the identity of the Beloved Disciple. There is certainly no agreement about whether he was really an eyewitness to Jesus' life and teaching. The validity of the traditions associated with him is also *sub judice*. This monograph contributes to the clarification of these issues, but it attempts only to suggest, with as much insight and force as data will permit, to resolve a dilemma of nearly two millennia: Who is the Beloved Disciple?

---

[3] D. M. Smith in *The New Testament and its Modern Interpreters*, ed. E. J. Epp and G. W. MacRae (SBL The Bible and Its Interpreters; Philadelphia: Fortress; Atlanta: Scholars Press, 1989) 285.

Obviously, we are much closer to Jesus' life and teaching with the realization that Thomas is the Beloved Disciple than we are with the conclusion that the latter is merely an ideal figure or a literary fiction. Even if we were left with the latter option, we would have some insight into the Johannine Community and its struggle for self-understanding and legitimation in confrontation with synagogal Jews, docetic Christians, the early gnostics, and the powerful western Peter establishment. Perhaps within the Johannine School we find some traditions, obviously in edited form, that derive ultimately from the man of Nazareth. In searching for the identity of the Beloved Disciple—and certainly if we are correct that this technical phrase represents the eyewitness record of the disciple Thomas—we are freed from our western parochialism to another time and another place, from which many of our values, beliefs, and dreams derive.

10.3 A COMPARISON

In summation, it might prove helpful to compare my position with that of Brown, who incidentally came to the end of his *The Community of the Beloved Disciple* by contrasting his viewpoint with Cullmann's position.[4] Obviously, in many ways my own reconstruction is similar to Brown's perception. We both share the following conclusions: The identity of the Beloved Disciple was well known to the Johannine Community; the members of that Community and the author or editor of the GosJn saw him as the founder of the Community and the trustworthy witness of Jesus' life and teachings. The Beloved Disciple is the anonymous one of chapter 1, and he was formerly a disciple of John the Baptist. There is a historical core to the GosJn, which has been exposed from excavations, not only archaeological, but also textual. The Beloved Disciple cannot be the author of the GosJn; it cannot have been written by an eyewitness of Jesus' life and teaching. The GosJn took shape over decades; there were editions and additions. These reflect struggles with synagogal Jews and with other Jewish Christians. The Beloved Disciple is a real person and one of Jesus' disciples.

My disagreement with Brown is primarily on the identity of the Beloved Disciple; and since that is the focal purpose of this monograph, the difference is not unimportant. Brown now thinks the Beloved Disciple is one of the anonymous disciples of 21:2. He speaks pejoratively of Thomas. For me, Thomas is the hero of the GosJn, the one who boldly exhorts his fellow disciples to follow Jesus even if it means martyrdom. He asks the key question, which elicits Jesus' disclosure of the way to the One above.

---

[4] With Brown I eschew the distorting labels like "heterodox Jews" which Cullmann used.

10.4 A FRESH APPROACH

Thomas refuses to believe lightly or accept what may be enthusiastic and wishful beliefs even if they are espoused by his close associates and friends. He alone confesses affirmatively before the One who is from above and now free from this constricting life. This confession is a personal affirmation that is the culmination of this brilliantly composed dramatic and symbolic masterpiece. For me, Thomas well deserves the title "the Beloved Disciple." No doubter he—he is "the disciple whom Jesus loved." Even if Thomas refused to believe his possibly too enthusiastic co-disciples, and that denotes "doubting," then let us not forget the profound truth in Miguel de Unamuno's *The Agony of Christianity*: "A faith which does not doubt is a dead faith."[5]

Long ago the German genius, Goethe, wrote of a thinker who lived long before him. Of Copernicus, Goethe offered these arresting reflections:

> The world had scarcely become known as round and complete in itself when it was asked to waive the tremendous privilege of being the center of the universe. Never, perhaps, was a greater demand made on [humankind]—for by this admission so many things vanished in mist and smoke! What became of Eden, our world of innocence, piety and poetry; the testimony of the senses; the conviction of a poetic—religious faith?[6]

Something creative, and anything against the stream of scholarship will seem threatening. It is all too frequently unwelcome. Change can be too difficult.[7]

Did the author of the GosJn intend to portray the Beloved Disciple as the model of faithful discipleship and Thomas as the paradigm of unfaithful discipleship? That is the implication I have found in many of the distinguished commentaries on the GosJn.

---

[5] M. Pepper, ed., *The Harper Religious & Inspirational Quotation Companion* (New York: Harper & Row, 1989) 156.

[6] The original has "mankind." See R. B. Downs, *Books that Changed the World* (New York: The New American Library, 1956) 141.

[7] When I originally wrote these words, and before six months of polishing this monograph, I was convinced that no scholar would react positively to my suggestion, which seemed "outlandish" at times. Now, I am buoyed up by the positive support I have received privately from Hugh Anderson, Peder Borgen, John Meier, Hans Martin Schenke, Moody Smith, and Walter Weaver. Each began with serious reservations, but after listening to my questions and search for answers, each offered helpful advice, and—most importantly—voiced support and approval of some of my exegetical moves.

Did the Johannine narrator intend for the reader to conclude that one of the Twelve was in fact a doubter? Did he portray a "Doubting Thomas"? Experts have suggested that the Beloved Disciple is Andrew, Ananda, Apollos, Benjamin, John Mark, John the Apostle, John the Elder, Judas Iscariot, Judas James' brother, Lazarus, Matthias, Nathanael, Paul or a Paulinist, Philip, the Rich Young Ruler, an unknown disciple, one of the anonymous disciples of 21:2, or a purely symbolic literary figure.[8] No scholar before me has attempted to argue and demonstrate with exegesis focused on the GosJn that the Beloved Disciple is to be identified as Thomas.

But, what if it is true? How would Johannine studies and Christian origins appear then?

10.5 A UNIFIED STORY

When one contemplates that the Beloved Disciple is Thomas, then the unifying harmony of the Johannine narrative springs to life. An anonymous follower of John the Baptist appears on stage. He follows Jesus. He is the Beloved Disciple, that is "the disciple whom Jesus loved"; but not yet—at least not clearly according to the flow of the narrative. In contrast to Andrew (1:41) the narrator gives him no confession. He is depicted as quietly observing and compiling a trustworthy witness. His commitment is apparently couched in Andrew's first person plural discourse: "we have found the Messiah" (1:41). Another disciple at this stage apparently must speak for him.

The former follower of the Baptist stands on center stage without name and without voice. With the rhetoric of suspense, the author entices the reader to wonder: Who is this former follower of the Baptist?

Thus the narrative continues. Other disciples—like Philip (1:45), Nathanael (1:49), and Peter (6:79)—come forth with too ready a confession, or a confession that is not complete, joined with inappropriate (or misleading) titles, and perhaps perfunctory or without critical reflection. The Johannine narrator is warning the reader about being too eager or ready to confess or to use titles that may not be suitable for Jesus. By this means the narrator seems to be indicating that titles do not define Jesus; he defines them.

---

[8] The widespread opinion that until recently virtually all New Testament scholars thought that the Beloved Disciple was John the son of Zebedee is simply inaccurate. This opinion may derive from classes in which professors use primarily the commentaries by Brown and Schnackenburg and point out that each of them changed their minds from concluding that the BD is John the Apostle to holding that the BD is one of the anonymous disciples of 21:2.

The One from above provides the meaning to well-known titles;[9] and so the Beloved Disciple is presented in the narrative watching, pondering, and being present so that he can provide for later readers of the GosJn the faithful witness. He will speak in the final dramatic scene, after he has observed all. Having followed Jesus from the time he was with John the Baptist until after his resurrection, the Beloved Disciple has been the trustworthy witness of "these things" from the beginning (21:24).

In a string of confessions the first is often the least apposite and the last the most representative. For example, in the Gospel of Thomas the apostle Peter "confesses" first and Thomas last. Peter says to Jesus that he is "like a righteous ($\delta\iota\kappa\alpha\iota\circ\varsigma$) angel ($\mathring{\alpha}\gamma\gamma\epsilon\lambda\circ\varsigma$)"; Thomas says he is incapable of saying whom Jesus is like (GosTh Log. 13). Thus, not only in the Gospel of Thomas, but preeminently in the GosJn, Thomas is presented in the honorific role of articulating the perfect confession. According to the Johannine narrator, Thomas is alone with Jesus in the grand finale and in the spotlight. He speaks to the resurrected Jesus: $\mathring{\text{o}}$ $\kappa\mathring{\upsilon}\rho\iota\acute{\text{o}}\varsigma$ $\mu\text{o}\upsilon$ $\kappa\alpha\grave{\iota}$ $\mathring{\text{o}}$ $\Theta\epsilon\acute{\text{o}}\varsigma$ $\mu\text{o}\upsilon$.

Chapter 1, especially 1:35-40, receives exegetical meaning from chapter 20, notably 20:26-29. The *inclusio* between 1:50 and 20:29 is evident in the repetition of technical terms "seeing" and "believing"; both times the terms are placed by our author on the lips of Jesus.

The Beloved Disciple appears in the opening and closing chapters, specifically 1 and 20. In chapter 1 he has no name and he does not speak. In chapter 20, in my opinion, he is presented with a name; and this time he speaks. The confession is by a named disciple; the confession is personal. Thomas brings all human dialogue to closure and fruition: "My Lord and My God!" (20:28).

The Beloved Disciple enters for the first time on stage without voice and without name. He exits as the story is complete with voice and name. The disciple who utters the grand confession is Thomas. The silent one speaks. The drama is complete.

10.6 THE EIGHT CRITERIA

Let us now summarize our discoveries. We recognized that eight criteria would help us in the search for the Beloved Disciple. How does Thomas fulfill each of them?

The first criterion is *love*. Thomas enters the Johannine drama with the paraenesis to his fellow disciples, "Let us also go, so that we may die with him" (11:16). Thomas is willing to lay down his life for Jesus. After presenting again his new commandment "to love one another as I have

---

[9] Again it is helpful to remember that "Logos" never appears after the Prologue, and that the Evangelist never clearly states that Logos is a title for Jesus.

loved you" (15:12; cf. 13:34) Jesus adds, "Greater love no one has than this, that one lay down his life for his friends (τῶν φίλων)" (15:13). As the Beloved Disciple, Thomas is the only male disciple described as present when Jesus dies; therefore, he alone fills this requisite. The concept of "love" in the GosJn should not be reduced to the absurd claim that Jesus loved "only" Lazarus; "love" is an action on behalf of others, as illustrated by Jesus' washing of his disciples' feet. The love of Thomas for Jesus is evident in his life as reflected in the story: exhorting the disciples as their leader to be willing to follow Jesus until the end, asking the most insightful question, and finally grounding resurrection belief as a trustworthy witness. As the Beloved Disciple is unafraid and standing beneath the cross, so later Thomas is not said to be hiding and afraid with a group of unnumbered and unnamed disciples somewhere in Jerusalem. Both—apparently as one character in the grand drama of salvation—have appeared openly in the world, witnessing to events. As "the disciple whom Jesus loved" Thomas rejoins the other disciples; then Jesus returns so that they and Thomas can share a *personal and final intimate* moment. That seems to be the Evangelist's criteria for "the disciple whom Jesus loved."

The second criterion is *anonymity*. The Beloved Disciple appears as one anonymous. He is introduced in that role, even though the Johannine Christians knew his identity. The anonymous one is a universal symbol which includes all who never knew the earthly Jesus, and never saw the resurrected Jesus; but others can experience the One from above because of the witness of the Beloved Disciple, especially Thomas's experience, confession, and most of all Jesus' blessing on "those who have not seen and yet believe" (20:29). The drama ends with this blessing because of the dialogical relation between Thomas and Jesus. The drama of the GosJn moves at many levels; one is the gradual disclosure of the anonymous former follower of the Baptist as the supremely loyal, and fundamentally faithful witness. The drama is the gradual disclosure of the identity of the Beloved Disciple; in the final scene his mask is removed: he is Thomas.

The third criterion is *closeness or authority*. Thomas's significance in the GosJn becomes even more evident when one realizes that his name appears only once in Matthew, Mark, Luke, and Acts, but seven times in the GosJn (11:16, 14:5, 20:24, 20:26, 20:27, 20:28, and 21:2). Not only Thomas's significance, but also his closeness to Jesus is revealed in his questioning. He knows the most important question to ask Jesus: Where are you going and what is the way? (14:5). The entire drama in the GosJn is the way of Jesus from above, through the world below, until he ascends back to his Father. Jesus has come into the world to show the way to the Father and to reveal that he is the way (14:6). Thomas's closeness to Jesus is finally emphasized in that he is "in the bosom" of Jesus (13:23) as Jesus is "in the bosom" of the Father (1:18), and that he and Jesus alone share the closing climactic scene. Thus there is both an *inclusio* between the opening of the "Book of Signs" and the opening of the "Book of Glory," and an *inclusio* between the beginning and end of the GosJn, chapters 1 and 20.

The fourth criterion is *lateness*. Why is the clause "the disciple whom Jesus loved" mentioned for the first time in chapter 13? We have already seen that he is *present* in the narrative from the beginning. We have also perceived that he appears in the very first scene of the drama. He is the anonymous follower of John the Baptist who follows Jesus. Both the Beloved Disciple and Thomas are mentioned by name or epithet about the same time in the drama.

The clause "the disciple whom Jesus *loved*" apparently is used for the first time in chapter 13 for more than one reason. First, he—the Be*loved* Disciple—is introduced immediately after Jesus' somatic demonstration of what "*love*" entails, and just before Jesus' commandment based on his *loving* actions. Second, the Beloved Disciple is introduced as an intimate one in the scene which depicts Jesus' last meal with his disciples. Third, it is fitting and appropriate for the hero of the GosJn to appear with this epithet at the beginning of the "Book of Glory." The Beloved Disciple is first and foremost the one trustworthy witness to the glory which comes from above. The narrator chooses the Greek noun δόξα to explain the Gospel; he selects this noun and uses it more frequently than do the other Evangelists (7/3/13/*18*). The Beloved Disciple, present during the Last Supper and the speeches associated with it in the second edition, hears Jesus appeal to the Father to "glorify me ... with the glory which I had with you before the world was made" (17:5; cf. 17:22-24). Narrative art is thus well served by the place in the drama in which this epithet is introduced.

The fifth criterion is *cross*. The dramatic words of only one disciple named in the GosJn help us understand why only the Beloved Disciple is clearly with Jesus as he dies. Thomas entered the drama with the paraenesis to be with Jesus until the end; apparently that means to be willing to die with him. The harmony of the GosJn is clarified as we recognize that Thomas should be present at the cross, as the Beloved Disciple, anonymously representing all Christians.

The sixth criterion is *commendation*. Why does the author and editor of the GosJn feel compelled to commend the Beloved Disciple and to stress that his witness is true (19:35, 21:24; cf. 5:32)? Perhaps it is because of the disparaging ways Thomas has been portrayed, as well as the polemical ambience in which the GosJn took shape. This commendation has become even more important today, when we scan the disparaging comments about this hero that began to appear in and around Rome in the middle of the second century C.E. and are distressingly still present in many of the commentaries published in the last fifty years.

The seventh criterion is *fear and death*. The Johannine Community, if not necessarily the Johannine School, was shaken by the death of the Beloved Disciple. This requisite fits anyone mentioned by name in the GosJn; it admirably fits the witness of Thomas through whom Jesus blesses those who believe in him but will not have the benefit of experiences like his. The link with Jesus is through the truthful witness of the Beloved Disciple, who, in my opinion, is none other than Thomas, who grounds Jesus' blessing for those who believe because of Jesus' words to him (20:29). When the Greek was in uncials written *scripta continua* and without marks of punctuations, 20:29 could mean, "Jesus said to him [Thomas], 'Because you have seen me you have believed. Blessed are those who have not seen and [yet] believe.'" It may today have that meaning and could refer to Thomas's witness of Jesus' life from his time with John the Baptist to the revelation of Jesus' resurrected state. This meaning would link Thomas more clearly with the fear felt by those in the Johannine Community who believed because of his witness, and their anguish that perhaps Jesus had meant Thomas would remain until Jesus returned. Also, the blessing is not only on those who will not be able to "see" as had Thomas. Jesus' blessing is also on Thomas; moreover, the meaning of 20:29 seems to be the following: "Because you have seen me you have believed. Blessed are those who have not seen and (yet) believe (because of your trustworthiness and valid witness)."

The eighth criterion is *Peter*. Why is the Beloved Disciple almost always portrayed in a dramatic way as superior to Peter? The best answer is that Peter was supported as the head of the Twelve by the Roman church, which was on its ascendancy by the late first century. In contrast, Thomas, who was the beloved disciple of many eastern churches, needed to be portrayed as the one whom Jesus loved. He was superior to Peter, who is depicted in chapters 1 through 20 in such a pejorative way that a reinstatement was necessary and was achieved partially in the Appendix (chapter 21).

All of the eight criteria are impressively met by the recognition that Thomas is the Beloved Disciple. Obviously, no proof can ever be possible, because the Evangelist did not want to reveal in a pellucid manner who is the Beloved Disciple. But it has become clear that Thomas is a valid, perhaps the only trustworthy, candidate for the Beloved Disciple.[10] At least I have attempted to demonstrate how and in what ways I gradu-

---

[10] Although Peter Brown is referring to the Syrian church, his words also fit our exegesis of the GosJn in which we have seen that *mutatis mutandis* the Beloved Disciple performs some of the functions of the Paraclete. Here are Brown's words, "Thomas was the 'Twin' of Christ. He continued Christ's mission on earth" (*The Body and Society*, 97).

ally became convinced that Thomas is the Beloved Disciple. The criteria were developed at the outset and refined as the exegesis of the GosJn developed. They were then employed and finally double-checked. The answer is consistent with the method.

10.7 PARTIAL UNVEILING

Running throughout this monograph may well be a question that it is now time to confront: If the Evangelist sought to reveal who was the Beloved Disciple, he (or she) certainly did not do so without an accompanying and frustrating opaqueness. Why did the author not pellucidly disclose the identity of his leading character?

The question is an important one. Three answers seem most important.

First, the GosJn comes to us from something like a school. The purpose of the gospel was not so much to initiate believing (thus the avoidance of the noun "faith"); it was to deepen and stimulate the process of believing. Thus πιστεύ[σ]ητε in both 19:35 and 20:31 may well be originally a present subjunctive (πιστεύητε) or an aorist subjunctive (πιστεύσητε).[11] Hence, the verb either denotes durative action, "you may continue believing" (continuous present) or action qualitatively completed, "you may bring to perfection believing" (aorist perfective [punctiliar Aktionsart]).[12] Thus, the believer is taught about the deeper meaning of believing and living out the claim that Jesus is the One sent from above by the One who sends. The search for appropriate passages in the Hebrew Bible (and LXX) and the refinement of the interpretation of "scripture" (20:9)

---

[11] With ἵνα the Evangelist frequently uses not only the present subjunctive, but also the aorist subjunctive. This is true regardless of the fact that NT Greek prefers the aorist subjunctive over the present subjunctive 322 to 57. See N. Turner, *A Grammar of New Testament Greek*, 3:100–101.

[12] Metzger, on behalf of the UBS Committee, opined that the "aorist tense, strictly interpreted, suggests that the Fourth Gospel was addressed to non-Christians so that they might come to believe that Jesus is the Messiah" (*A Textual Commentary on the Greek New Testament*, 256). The argument that the aorist must be inceptive (or ingressive) is more an attempt to explain the origin of the variant. Some scribes may have changed the present to the aorist in order to imply that the GosJn was a missionary tract. The aorist, of course, may be perfective, denoting the completion of believing. It needs to be stressed that the aorist denotes a punctiliar action. One point is centralized, and it can be the beginning (inceptive aorist), the ending (perfective [or effective] aorist), or denoting that the action is represented as one focused point (constative aorist). I find a succinct description of these uses of the aorist with examples in J. H. Moulton's *A Grammar of New Testament Greek* (Edinburgh: T. & T. Clark, 1978 [3rd ed.]) 1:108–09.

was the task of scholars working together in a school. For the identity of the Beloved Disciple all of this means that the Evangelist did not want to proclaim the identity of the Beloved Disciple. He wanted to allow students to contemplate the name of the Beloved Disciple within the much more important tasks of studying God's word, following the way of the One from above, and worshipping the Creator.

Second, the Evangelist represents two levels of knowing. Those within the School know the truth and are free; those outside do not know the truth. D. M. Smith rightly points to the "insider-outsider language" of the GosJn: "As insiders to the distinctive message and language of the Gospel, they understand, while outsiders, however well-meaning, do not."[13] The end of the drama clarifies the presence of the Beloved Disciple within the Baptist's group; it also discloses the identity of the anonymous one, and Thomas's confession in 20:29 provides the basis for an exegesis of GosJn 1:1. Hence, Smith can claim that "what is said in 1:1 about the word is based on postresurrection knowledge and confession of Jesus."[14]

Misunderstanding functions not only narratively, but also to disclose that what the implied reader knows Nicodemus, the Samaritan woman, and οἱ Ἰουδαῖοι do not comprehend. Ironic intention in the narrative of the GosJn, as G. R. O'Day emphasizes, should be

> difficult to detect, because the essence of irony is to be indirect. A straightforward ironic statement would be a contradiction in terms. The ironist's challenge is to be clear without being evident, to say something without really saying it. The author must therefore provide the reader with signals to the irony without shattering the tension between the two levels of meaning.[15]

Thus the identity of the Beloved Disciple will always remain unknown and unperceived by those who do not indwell Johannine Christianity.

Third, there are three groups reflected in the GosJn. (1) The ones outside are those who are ignorant of the truth, and do not come to the truth. Some of them control the synagogue, and the author has Jesus separate himself from them with such words as 8:17, καὶ ἐν τῷ νόμῳ δὲ τῷ ὑμτέρῳ γέγραπται ... (8:17). They are not to know the identity of the trustworthy witness. (2) The ones in the Johannine Community who did not know Thomas personally are slowly shown how to recognize him in the accounts of the Beloved Disciple. (3) Those in the School who remem-

---

[13] Smith, *The Theology of the Gospel of John*, 114.

[14] Ibid., 115.

[15] O'Day, *Revelation in the Fourth Gospel* (Philadelphia: Fortress Press, 1986) 25.

ber him are joined with the Evangelist (19:35) and the redactor; they affirm that his witness as reported by the Evangelist is true: καὶ οἴδαμεν ὅτι ἀληθὴς αὐτοῦ ἡ μαρτυρία ἐστίν (20:24). This group does not need to be informed about the name of the Beloved Disciple. They remember him personally. And they—as all the Johannine sectarians who are consecutively reducing the circle of those who should be loved—do not want it clearly revealed.

Cumulatively, therefore, the identity of the Beloved Disciple must not be broadcast. Neither clear disclosure nor blind ignorance of the Beloved Disciple's name is appropriate for the narrator's art. It is in the story, which is a paradigm for believing, that the identity will be suggested. The Johannine drama is thus from voiceless anonymity with the Baptist to voiced personal confession and identity before "my Lord and my God."

10.8 RETROSPECTION

In retrospection we can report, moreover, that this search has helped clarify numerous issues. The Beloved Disciple cannot be a literary typos or fictional creation by the narrator because the Appendix reveals that the Johannine Community was devastated by the death of a real human being. Not only his credibility, but also the trustworthiness of Jesus' message was threatened until an unknown master teacher in the Johannine School, the editor who added chapter 21, explained the proper means of interpreting one of Jesus' logion. Jesus had not said openly that the Beloved Disciple would not die; he had said "if I will for him to reman"[16] until I come—that is, remain alive when Jesus returns in glory (cf. Mk 9:1 and 1Thess 4:17)—then what is that to you, Peter; "You come follow me!"

We learned that the author of chapters 1–20—the Evangelist who has given us both the first and second editions of the GosJn—is not to be confused with the trustworthy witness, the Beloved Disciple. The latter is the witness of the good news from the One above, and he caused the GosJn to be written (see chap. 1.4).

There is no consensus that the Beloved Disciple is John the son of Zebedee. In fact a study of gifted and independent New Testament scholars since the time of the Enlightenment, that is from about 1730 to the present, discloses that at least 22 hypotheses for the identity of the Beloved Disciple have been published. The research has exposed an unexamined presupposition which often appears in scholarly circles and publications. Many scholars have assumed that until Brown and Schnackenburg

---

[16] The importance of θέλειν and μένειν for Johannine theology does not need to be explained again; it is paramount and obvious in light of recent publications.

abandoned the hypothesis that John the son of Zebedee is the Beloved Disciple there was a consensus among experts that the Beloved Disciple was the apostle John. Such an assumption fails to represent the varied and creative reflections found in major works on the GosJn; it rather signifies a western, German and American-centered perspective.[17]

An exegesis of chapter 21 showed more than that the Beloved Disciple had died and was the witness—not the author—of the GosJn. It revealed an attempt to reinstate Peter as a leader of Jesus' group, but within the perspective that he is certainly not the Beloved Disciple.[18] For the Johannine School Peter was a confused person, according to chapters 1 through 20; he was "no Beloved Disciple." In an apparent attempt to heal differences between East and West, the School elevated Peter; but he was not accorded the stature of the Beloved Disciple. The Evangelist's endeavor to obtain peace and harmony among the churches was a hallmark of his age. About the same time, as Brown has demonstrated in *The Body and Society*, Ignatius of Antioch issued letters which "were magnificent statements of the ideal unity of each local Christian church: 'Give thought to unity, than which nothing is more sweet.'"[19]

10.9 A DRAMATIC PORTRAIT

An exegesis of chapters 1 through 20 exposed for us to see, metaphorically speaking, the Evangelist slowly developing the photograph, the portrait, of the Beloved Disciple. As an anonymous follower of John the Baptist, he appears in the first act of the great drama; he witnesses the Spirit descend and remain upon Jesus. He thence leaves John the Baptist and follows Jesus. He quietly listens; then he asks the incisive question, "What is the way?" The drama is thus set for Jesus to make a momentous proclamation, "I am the way ...." The anonymous disciple continues, now revealed to be "the disciple whom Jesus loved," at the place of honor and authority at the Last Supper. Peter turns to him for insight and access to

---

[17] It is surprising that many masterpieces in Dutch were ignored by German and English-speaking Johannine experts. This insight became apparent first in the search for one who claimed that Nathanael was the BD and surfaced again in a study of western and eastern Christianity before the establishment of Christianity in the fourth century.

[18] Another literary genius used the same narrative device for elevating the favored one. At the end of a poem which celebrates the beautiful women in his life Robert Burns concludes by putting all of them below one woman with the words, you were "no Mary Morrison." I am indebted to Hugh and Jean Anderson for delightful discussions of Burns' poetry. Hence the author of chapter 21 lauds Peter, but concludes that he was no Beloved Disciple.

[19] Ignatius, *Letter to Polycarp* 1.2; Brown, *The Body and Society*, 58.

Jesus. As Thomas, he leads the disciples through his paraenesis to follow Jesus fully and ultimately, even to his death. At the cross he alone of the male disciples is said to be present and thus he is the only male disciple to follow his own exhortation. The narrative shows him, and him alone, witnessing the death of his master. At the tomb, in contrast to Peter, he sees and believes. The implied reader, through the rhetoric of suspense, is enticed to wonder what he sees and what he believes. The only insight obvious is that he continues to believe that Jesus is the One from above. Thus he leaves Mary Magdalene weeping at the tomb and goes home. The reader knows that he must return again.

He does so in the final act. As Thomas, he is the only disciple said to be missing when Jesus first reveals himself to the disciples. Like the Beloved Disciple, Thomas alone among the disciples is not depicted as afraid and hiding. As the faithful paradigm for discipleship, he refuses to believe secondary reports. And as the Beloved Disciple, standing before the tomb with the burial clothes and face-cloth, continues faithfully, but will not jump to resurrection belief; so Thomas remains faithful to the crucified One, but will not base his resurrection belief on others' questionable claims. He demands to see the one distinguishing mark of Jesus' death, since only he, as the Beloved Disciple, has seen the thrust of the soldier's lance. Eight days after Jesus' appearance to some disciples he is confronted by the risen Jesus, who exhorts him to believe his co-disciples' report and experience for himself what they have claimed. He does and thus authenticates the experiences and belief of the first generation of believers, anchoring such belief in reality for subsequent Christians.

Thus the witness of the Beloved Disciple, Thomas, encompasses the good news from the very beginning, when Jesus leads a baptist movement, until the very end, when Jesus completes his final resurrection appearance. The Evangelist hails the Beloved Disciple, especially in 19:35 and 21:24, as the trustworthy witness. He is ὁ μαθητὴς ὁ μαρτυρῶν περὶ τούτων. The words "concerning these things" (περὶ τούτων), according to my interpretation of the GosJn, denote Jesus' entire ministry, from the very beginnings when he was baptized (3:26, 4:1) until he had ascended to his Father (20:17-31). The Beloved Disciple provides for the GosJn the valid witness to the ministry of the One from above. He witnessed the descent of the spirit upon Jesus and later the spirit's ascent from him. The Evangelist and editor can thus claim (using independent phrasing) that "his witness is true" (19:35, 21:24; cf. 5:32).

I have concluded, with some surprise and full conviction, that the best candidate for the identity of the Beloved Disciple is Thomas. His portrait reflects the ideal disciple. He watches, observes, and especially witnesses. He asks astute questions. He follows his bold paraenesis. He anchors Johannine belief in one incarnate life; he alone sees the death and confirms the physical resurrection of his master and grounds believing in the *continuity between the crucified one and the resurrected Lord*. Alone on center stage with Jesus, he is given the concluding testimony, "My Lord and my God." Thus, the Johannine Community can continue to affirm that they have been given the gift of life, and that their Community offers, through this One, not only life but eternal life.

Selected Bibliography

This bibliography focuses on publications devoted to the Beloved Disciple. Attention has been given especially to works that make a major contribution, and are from the time of the First World War to the present.

Agourides, S. "Peter and John in the Fourth Gospel." In *Studia Evangelica* 4, edited by F. L. Cross, 3–7. Texte und Untersuchungen 102. Berlin: Akademie-Verlag, 1968.

———. "The Purpose of John 21." In *Studies in the History and Text of the New Testament in Honor of Kenneth Willis Clark*, edited by B. L. Daniels and M. J. Suggs, 127–32. Studies and Documents 29. Salt Lake City: Univ. of Utah Press, 1967.

Armenillas, P. "El discipulo amado, modelo perfecto de discipulo de Jesus, segun el IV Evangelio." *Ciencia Tomista* 98 (1962): 3–68.

Ashton, J., ed. *The Interpretation of John*. Issues in Religion and Theology 10. London: SPCK; Philadelphia: Fortress, 1986.

Ashton, J. *Understanding the Fourth Gospel*. Oxford: Clarendon, 1991.

Bacon, B. W. "The Disciple Whom Jesus Loved." *The Expositor* 4 [Seventh Series] (1907): 324–39.

Bakker, J. T. "'De Moeder van Jezus was daar,': Ein reactie." *Homilectica en Biblica* 21 (1962): 51–54.

Barnhart, B. "Two Centers: Peter and the Beloved Disciple." *The Good Wine: Reading John from the Center*, 378–86. New York: Paulist Press, 1993.

Barrett, C. K. *The Gospel According to St. John*, 2nd ed. Philadelphia: Westminster, 1978. See esp. "The Origin and Authority of the Gospel," 100–34.

Bauer, W. *Das Johannes-Evangelium*. Handbuch zum Neuen Testament 6. Tübingen: J. C. B. Mohr, 1933. See esp. 173–75.

Baur, F. C. *Kritische Untersuchungen über die kanonischen Evangelien ihr Verhältnis und Ursprung.* Tübingen: Verlag und Druck von Ludw. Fr. Fues, 1847.

Becker, J. *Das Evangelium nach Johannes,* 2 vols. Ökumenischer Taschenbuchkommentar zum Neuen Testament 4/1 and 4/2, 2nd ed. Gerd Mohn: Gütersloher Verlagshaus, 1984, 1985. See esp. "Das Problem des Verfassers," 1:48–50 and "Exkurs 9: Die Gestalt des Lieblingsjüngers," 2:434–40.

Benoit, P. "Marie-Madeleine et les disciples au tombeau selon Joh 20:1-18." In *Judentum, Urchristentum, Kirche: Festschrift für Joachim Jeremias,* 141–52. Edited by W. Eltester. Beihefte zur Zeitschrift für die Neutestamentliche Wissenschaft 26. Berlin: Verlag Alfred Töpelmann, 1960.

Bernard, J. H. *Gospel According to St. John,* 2 vols. Edited by A. H. McNeile. Edinburgh: T.& T. Clark, 1928. See esp. "John the Apostle was the Beloved Disciple," 1:xxxiv–xxxvii.

Blank, J. "Der Lieblingsjünger (21,20-24): Die zweite Schlussbemerkung (21,25)." In *Das Evangelium nach Johannes,* pt. 3:208–15. Geistliche Schriftlesung 4/3. Düsseldorf: Patmos Verlag Düsseldorf, 1988 [2nd ed.].

Boismard, M.É. *Du Baptême à Cana (Jean 1.19-2.11).* Paris: Cerf, 1956. See esp. 72–73.

Bonsack, B. "Der Presbyteros des dritten Briefs und der geliebte Jünger des Evangeliums nach Johannes." *Zeitschrift für die neutestamentliche Wissenschaft* 79 (1988): 45–62.

Braun, J.-M. "Le disciple que Jésus aimait." In *Jean le théologien et son évangile dans l'église ancienne,* 301–30. Études bibliques. Paris: Gabalda, 1959.

———. "Saint Jean, la Sagesse et l'histoire." In *Neotestamentica et Patristica: Eine Freundesgabe Herrn Professor Dr. Oscar Cullmann zu Seinem 60. Geburtstag Überreicht,* 122–32. Supplements to Novum Testamentum 6. Leiden: Brill, 1962.

Bretschneider, K. G. *Probabilia de Evangelii et Epistolarum Joannis, Apostoli, Indole et Origine.* Leipzig: Sumtibus Jo. Ambros. Barthii, 1820.

Brodie, T. L. *The Gospel According to John: A Literary and Theological Commentary.* New York/Oxford: Oxford Univ. Press, 1993.

Brown, R. E. *The Churches the Apostles Left Behind.* New York: Paulist Press, 1984. See esp. "The Heritage of the Beloved Disciple in the Fourth Gospel: A Community of People Personally Attached to Jesus, 84–101; and "The Heritage of the Beloved Disciple and the

Epistles of John: A Community of Individuals Guided by the Paraclete-Spirit," 102–23.

———. *The Community of the Beloved Disciple*. New York: Paulist Press, 1979.

———. *The Gospel According to John*, 2 vols. Garden City, N.Y.: Doubleday, 1966; London: Chapman, 1971.

Brown, S. "The Beloved Disciple: A Jungian View." In *The Conversation Continues: Studies in Paul and John in Honor of J. Louis Martyn*, edited by R. T. Fortna and B. R. Gaventa, 366–77 (Nashville: Abingdon, 1990).

Brownlee, W. H. "Whence the Gospel According to John?" In *John and the Dead Sea Scrolls*, edited by J. H. Charlesworth, 166–94. Christian Origins Library. New York: Crossroad, 1990. See esp. "Who was the Beloved Disiple?" 191–94.

Bruce, F. F. *The Gospel of John*. Grand Rapids, Michigan: Eerdmans, 1983, 1992.

Bruns, J. E. "Ananda: The Fourth Evangelist's Model for 'the Disciple Whom Jesus Loved'?" *Studies in Religion/Sciences Religieuses* 3 (1973): 236–43.

Byrne, B. "The Beloved Disciple." *Anchor Bible Dictionary* (1992) 1.658–61.

———. "The Faith of the Beloved Disciple and the Community in John 20." *Journal for the Study of the New Testament* 23 (1985): 83–97.

Bultmann, R. *The Gospel of John*. Translated by G. R. Beasley-Murray. Oxford: Blackwell, 1971.

Carson, D. A. "The Authorship of the Fourth Gospel." In *The Gospel According to John*. Leicester, England: Inter-Varsity Press, 68–81. Grand Rapids, Michigan: Eerdmans, 1991.

Ceroke, C. P. "Mary's Maternal Role in John 19,25-27." *Marian Studies* 11 (1960): 123–51.

Chapman, J. "We Know That His Testimony is True." *Journal of Theological Studies* 31 (1930): 379–87.

Clergeon, C. H. "Le quatrième évangile indique-t-il le nom de son auteur?" *Biblica* 56 (1975): 32–36.

Collins, R. F. *John and His Witness*. Collegeville: Michael Glazier, 1991.

———. "John's Characters." In *These Things Have Been Written: Studies on the Fourth Gospel*, 1–45. Louvain: Peeters, 1990; Grand Rapids, Michigan: Eerdmans, 1991.

———. "The Representative Figures of the Fourth Gospel—I." *The Downside Review* 94 (1976): 26–46.

———. "The Representative Figures of the Fourth Gospel—II." *The Downside Review* 94 (1976): 118–32.

Colson, J. *L'énigme du Disciple, que Jésus aimait*. Paris: Beauchesne et ses fils, 1969.

Crossan, J. D. "The Race to the Empty Tomb." In *Jesus: A Revolutionary Biography*, 186–90. San Francisco: Harper, 1994.

Cullmann, O. "Εἶδεν καὶ ἐπίστευσεν." In *Aux sources de la tradition chrétienne: Mélanges offerts à M. Maurice Goguel à l'occasion de son soixante-dixième anniversaire*, 52–61. Bibliothèque Théologique. Paris: Delachaux & Niestlé, 1950.

―――. "Der Verfasser des Johannesevangeliums im Rahmen des johanneischen Kreises." In *Der johanneische Kreis*, 67–88. Tübingen: Mohr (Siebeck), 1975. [ET = *The Johannine Circle*, 63–85. Translated by J. Bowden. London: SCM, 1976.]

Culpepper, R. A. *Anatomy of the Fourth Gospel: A Study in Literary Design*. Philadelphia: Fortress, 1983.

―――. "Beloved Disciple: The Apostle in the Fourth Gospel." In *John, the Son of Zebedee: The Life of a Legend*, 56–88. Studies on Personalities of the New Testament. Columbia, S.C.: Univ. of South Carolina, 1994.

―――. *The Johannine School*. SBL Dissertation Series 26. Missoula, Montana: Scholars Press, 1975. See esp. "The Origin of the Johannine School," 264–70.

Dauer, A. "Die Mutter Jesu und 'der Jünger, den Jesus liebte' (19,26f.)." In *Die Passionsgeschichte im Johannesevangelium*, 318–33. Studien zum Alten und Neuen Testament 30. Munich: Kösel-Verlag, 1972.

―――. "Das Wort des Gekreuzigten an seine Mutter und den 'Jünger, den er liebte.'" *Biblische Zeitschrift* N.F. 11 (1967): 222–39.

―――. "Das Wort des Gekreuzigten an seine Mutter und den 'Jünger, den er liebte.'" *Biblische Zeitschrift* N.F. 12 (1968): 80–93.

de Jonge, M. "The Beloved Disciple and the Date of the Gospel of John." In *Text and Interpretation: Studies in the New Testament Presented to Matthew Black*, edited by E. Best and R. McL. Wilson, 99–114. Cambridge: Cambridge Univ. Press, 1979.

de la Potterie, I. "Genèse de la foi pascale d'après Jn. 20." *New Testament Studies* 30 (1984): 26–49.

―――. "La Parole de Jésus 'Voici ta Mère' et l'accueil du disciple (Jn 19,27b)." *Marianum* 36 (1974): 1–39.

―――. "Le témoin qui demeure: Le disciple que Jésus aimait." *Biblica* 67 (1986): 343–59.

de Solages, B. "Jean, fils de Zébédée et l'énigme du 'disciple que Jésus aimait'." *Bulletin de litterature ecclesiastique* 73 (1972): 41–50. [This fascicle is also the Elie Griffe Festschrift.]

Draper, H. M. "The Disciple Whom Jesus Loved." *The Expository Times* 32 (1920–1921): 428–29.

du Rand, J. A. *Johannine Perspectives*. [Johannesburg]: Orion, 1991. See esp. "Authorship," 75–91.

Eckhardt, K. A. "Wer war der Lieblingsjünger?" In *Der Tod des Johannes als Schlüssel zum Verständnis der Johanneischen Schriften*, 28–37. Berlin: Walter de Gruyter & Co., 1961. Also see "Was bedeutet 'Lieblingsjünger'?" 38–45.

Eckle, W. *Den der Herr liebhatte—Rätsel um den Evangelisten Johannes: Zum historischen Verständnis seiner autobiographischen Andeutungen*. Hamburg: Verlag Dr. Kovač, 1991; Grand Rapids, Michigan: Eerdmans, 1987. See esp. "Der Verfasser des Evangeliums," 10–26.

Eller, V. *The Beloved Disciple: His Name, His Story, His Thought*. Grand Rapids, Michigan: Eerdmans, 1987.

Erbes, C. "Der Apostel Johannes und der Jünger, welcher an der Brust des Herrn lag." *Zeitschrift für Kirchengeschichte* 33 (1912): 159–239.

———. "Der Jünger, welchen Jesus lieb hatte." *Zeitschrift für Kirchengeschichte* 36 (1916): 283–318.

Ernst, J. *Johannes: Ein theologisches Portrait*. Düsseldorf: Patmos Verlag, 1991. See esp. "Der Lieblingsjünger," 17–26.

Filson, F. V. "Author of the Fourth Gospel." In *A New Testament History*, 372–73. New Testament Libray. London: SCM Press, 1965.

———. "Beloved Disciple." *The Interpreter's Dictionary of the Bible* (1962) 1.378–79.

———. "Who Was the Beloved Disciple?" *Journal of Biblical Literature* 68 (1949): 83–88.

Fuller, R. C. "The Authorship of the Fourth Gospel." *Scripture* 5 (1952/1953): 8–11.

Garvie A. E. *The Beloved Disciple: Studies of the Fourth Gospel*. London: Hodder and Stoughton, [1922].

Godet, F. L. "The Discussions Relating to the Authenticity of the Fourth Gospel." In *Commentary on John's Gospel*, translated by T. Dwight, 8–28. Grand Rapids, Michigan: Kregel Publications, 1978, 1985 [reprint of 1886 edition].

Goettmann, J. "Jean, le disciple que Jésus aime, le témoin qui demeure." In *Saint Jean Évangile de la Nouvelle Genèse*, 284–91. Paris: Cerf-Pneumathèque, 1982.

Goguel, M. "Le témoignage de l'évangile sur son auteur le disciple bien-aimé." In *Introduction au Nouveau Testament: Tome II Le Quatrième Évangile*, 315–54. Paris: Éditions Ernest Leroux, 1924.

Goulder, M. "An Old Friend Incognito." *Scottish Journal of Theology* 45 (1992): 487–513.

Grayston, K. *The Gospel of John*. Philadelphia: Trinity Press International, 1990. See esp. "The Beloved Disciple," 110–11; and "The Beloved Disciple and the Editor," 176–77.

Griffith, B. G. "The Disciple Whom Jesus Loved." *Expository Times* 32 (1920–1921): 379–81.

Grassi, J. "The Role of Jesus' Mother in John's Gospel: A Reappraisal." *Catholic Biblical Quarterly* 48 (1986): 67–80.

———. *The Secret Identity of the Beloved Disciple*. New York: Paulist Press, 1992.

Gryglewicz, F. "'Niewiasta' i uczén, Horego milowal Jezus (La 'femme' et le 'disciple que Jésus aimait')." *Roczniki Teologiczno-Kanoniczne* 14 (1967): 39–48.

Gunther, J. J. "Early Identifications of Authorship of the Johannine Writings." *Journal of Ecclesiastical History* 31 (1980): 407–27.

———. "The Meaning and Origin of the Name 'Judas Thomas'." *Le Muséon* 93 (1980): 113–48.

———. "The Relation of the Beloved Disciple to the Twelve." *Theologische Zeitschrift* 37 (1981): 129–48.

Haenchen, E. *John 1*. Translated by R. W. Funk with U. Busse. Hermeneia. Philadelphia: Fortress, 1984.

———. *John 2*. Translated by R. W. Funk with U. Busse. Hermeneia. Philadelphia: Fortress, 1984.

Hawkin, D. J. "The Function of the Beloved Disciple Motif in the Johannine Redaction." *Laval Théologique et Philosophique* 33 (1977): 135–50.

Hengel, M. *Die johanneische Frage*. Wissenschaftliche Untersuchungen zum Neuen Testament 67. Tübingen: Mohr (Siebeck), 1993. See esp. "Petrus und der Lieblingsjünger," 210–19.

———. *The Johannine Question*. Translated by J. Bowden. London: SCM; Philadelphia: Trinity Press International, 1989. See esp. "Peter and the Beloved Disciple," 76–80; and "The Person and Development of the Head of the School and Its Relation to the 'Beloved Disciple,'" 124–35.

Herbert, M. and M. McNamara, "Texts Relating to the Beloved Disciple." In *Irish Biblical Apocrypha*, 89–98, 180–81. Edinburgh: T. & T. Clark, 1989.

Hudry-Clergeon, C. "Le quatrième évangile indique-t-il le nom de son auteur?" *Biblica* 56 (1975): 545–49.

Hügel, F. von. "John, Gospel of St." *The Encyclopaedia Britannica* (1911) 15.452–58.

Iafolla, P. "Giovanni figlio di Zebedeo e il IV Vangelo: II Partie La testimonianza dei sinottici." *Bibbia e Oriente* 149 (1986): 143–55.

———. "Giovanni, figlio di Zebedeo 'il discepolo che amava' e il IVº vangelo." *Bibbia e Oriente* 148 (1986): 95–110.

Johnson, L. "The Beloved Disciple—A Reply." *The Expository Times* 77 (1965–1966): 380.

———. "Who Was the Beloved Disciple?" *The Expository Times* 77 (1965–1966): 157–58.

Johnson, N. E. "The Beloved Disciple and the Fourth Gospel." *Church Quarterly Review* 167 (1966): 278–91.

Kaufman, P. S. *The Beloved Disciple: Witness Against Anti-Semitism.* Collegeville, Minnesota: The Liturgical Press, 1991.

Kilmartin, E. J. "'The Mother of Jesus Was There.' (The Significance of Mary in Jn 2,3-5 and Jn 19, 25-27)." *Sciences Ecclésiastiques* 15 (1963): 213–26.

Kickendraht, K. "Ist Lazarus der Lieblingsjünger im vierten Evangelium?" *Schweizerische Theologische Zeitschrift* 31 (1914): 49–54.

King, E. G. "The Disciple that Jesus Loved—A Suggestion." *The Interpreter* 5 (1909): 167–74.

Kragerud, A. *Der Lieblingsjünger im Johannesevangelium.* Oslo: Osloer Universitätsverlag; Hamburg: Grossohaus Wegner, 1959.

Kreyenbühl, J. "Der Verfasser des Evangeliums." In *Das Evangelium der Wahrheit: Neue Lösung der Johanneischen Frage*, 146–369. Berlin: C. A. Schwetschke und Sohn, 1900.

Kügler, J. *Der Jünger, den Jesus liebte: Literarische, theologische und historische Untersuchungen zu einer Schlüsselgestalt johanneischer Theologie und Geschichte.* Stuttgarter Biblische Beiträge 16. Stuttgart: Verlag Katholisches Bibelwerk, 1988.

Kurz, W. S. "The Beloved Disciple and Implied Readers." *Biblical Theology Bulletin* 19 (1989): 100–7.

Léonard, J.-M. "Notule sur l'Évangile de Jean: Le disciple que Jésus aimait et Marie." *Etudes Théologiques et Religieuses* 58 (1983): 355–57.

Lewis, F. W. "The Disciple Whom Jesus Loved." *The Expository Times* 33 (1921–1922): 42.

Lindars, B. *Gospel of John.* London: Marshall, Morgan & Scott; Grand Rapids, Michigan: Eerdmans, 1972, 1987.

———. *John.* New Testament Guides. Sheffield: JSOT Press, 1990.

Lofthouse, W. F. *The Disciple Whom Jesus Loved*. London: Epworth, 1936.

Loisy, A. *Le quatrième evangile*, 2nd ed. Paris: Nourry, 1921.

Lorensen, T. *Johannes 21: Eine traditionsgeschichtliche Analyse; zugleich ein Beitrag zur johanneischen Lieblingsjüngerfrage*. Doctoral Dissertation. Zürich, 1970.

———. *Der Lieblingsjünger im Johannesevangelium: Eine redaktionsgeschichtliche Studie*. Stuttgarter Bibelstudien 55. Stuttgart: Verlag Katholisches Bibelwerk, 1971.

Lützelberger, E. C. J. *Die kirchliche Tradition über den Apostel Johannes und seine Schriften in ihrer Grundlosigkeit*. Leipzig: F. A. Brockhaus, 1840.

Macgregor, G. H. C. *The Gospel of John*. Garden City, N.Y.: Doubleday, 1929. See esp. "The 'Beloved Disciple' and the Authorship of the Gospel," xliv–xlviii, continue to lxviii.

Mahoney, R. K. *Two Disciples at the Tomb*. Frankfurt: Lang, 1974.

Minear, S. "The Beloved Disciple in the Gospel of John: Some Clues and Conjectures." *Novum Testamentum* 19 (1977): 105–23.

———. "The Original Functions of John 21." *Journal of Biblical Literature* 102 (1983): 85–98.

More, T. *His Witness is True: John and His Interpreters*. American Univ. Studies 7. New York/Bern, Paris: Peter Lang, 1988.

Moreton, M. B. "The Beloved Disciple Again." In *Studia Biblica 1978*, edited by E. A. Livingstone, 215–18. JSNT Supplement Series 2. Sheffield: JSOT Press, 1980.

Morgen, M. "Devenir disciple selon Jean." *Cahier biblique* 26 (1987): 71–73.

Morris, L. "Authorship." In *Gospel According to John*, 8–30. Grand Rapids, Michigan: Eerdmans, 1971.

Muñoz León, D. "¿Es el apóstol Juan el discípulo amado?" *Estudios Biblicos* 45 (1987): 403–92.

———. "Juan el presbítero y el discípulo amado." *Estudios Bíblicos* 48 (1990): 543–63.

Neirynck, F. "The Anonymous Disciple in John 1." *Ephemerides Theologicae Lovanienses* 66 (1990): 5–37.

———. "ΕΙΣ ΤΑ ΙΔΙΑ Jn 19,27 (et 16,32)." *Ephemerides Theologicae Lovanienses* 55 (1979): 357–65.

———. "John 21." *New Testament Studies* 36 (1990): 321–36.

———. "Note sur Jn 20, 1-18." *Ephemerides Theologicae Lovanienses* 62 (1986): 404.

———. "The 'Other Disciple' in Jn 18, 15-16." *Ephemerides Theologicae Lovanienses* 51 (1975): 113–41.

Nepper-Christensen, P. "Hvem var den discipel, som Jesus elskede?" *Dansk Teologisk Tidsskrift* 53 (1990): 81–105.

Nunn, H. V. *The Son of Zebedee and the Fourth Gospel.* London: SPCK, 1927, 1932. See esp. 73–86.

O'Grady, J. F. "The Role of the Beloved Disciple." *Biblical Theology Bulletin* 9 (1979): 58–65.

Osborne, B. "A Folded Napkin in an Empty Tomb: John 11.44 and 20.7 Again." *Heythrop Journal* 14 (1973): 437–40.

Otto, H. P. *Funktion und Bedeutung des Leiblingsjüngers im Johannes-Evangelium.* Unpublished Dissertation, 1973.

Painter, J. *John: Witness and Theologian.* London: SPCK, 1975.

————. *The Quest for the Messiah: The History, Literature and Theology of the Johannine Community,* 2nd ed. Nashville: Abingdon, 1993.

Pamment, M. "The Fourth Gospel's Beloved Disciple." *The Expository Times* 94 (1983): 363–67.

Parker, P. "John and John Mark." *Journal of Biblical Literature* 79 (1960): 97–110.

————. "John the Son of Zebedee and the Fourth Gospel." *Journal of Biblical Literature* 81 (1962): 35–43.

Porsch, F. "Der Jünger, den Jesus liebte." In *Johannes-Evangelium,* 2nd ed., 145–47. Stuttgarter Kleiner Kommentar; Neues Testament 4. Stuttgart: Verlag Katholisches Bibelwerk, 1989.

Porter, J. R. "Who Was the Beloved Disciple?" *The Expository Times* 77 (1965–1966): 213–24.

Potter, R. "The Disciple Whom Jesus Loved." *Life of the Spirit* 16 (1962): 293–97.

Pétrement, S. "Apollos and the Fourth Gospel." In *A Separate God: The Christian Origins of Gnosticism,* 276–97. San Francisco: Harper, 1990 [French original is of 1984].

Quast, K. *Peter and the Beloved Disciple: Figures for a Community in Crisis.* Journal for the Study of the New Testament, Supplement Series 32. Sheffield: JSOT Press, 1989.

Rigg, H. "Was Lazarus 'The Beloved Disciple'?" *The Expository Times* 33 (1921–1922): 233–34.

Rogers, D. G. "Who Was the Beloved Disciple?" *The Expository Times* 77 (1965–1966): 214.

Roloff, J. "Der johanneische 'Lieblingsjünger' und der Lehrer der Gerechtigkeit." *New Testament Studies* 15 (1968–69): 129–51.

Ruckstuhl, E. "Der Jünger, den Jesus liebte." In Stuttgarter Biblische Aufsatzbände 3. *Jesus im Horizont der Evangelien,* 355–401. Stuttgart: Verlag Katholisches Bibelwerk, 1988 [1977].

Russell, R. "The Beloved Disciple and the Resurrection." *Scripture* 8 (1956): 57–62.

Salvoni, F. "The So-Called Jesus Resurrection Proof (John 20:7)." *Restoration Quarterly* 22 (1979): 72–76.

Sanders, J. N. "The Internal Evidence for the Authorship of the Fourth Gospel." In *A Commentary on the Gospel According to St. John*, edited by B. A. Mastin, 29–32. London: Adam & Charles Black, 1968.

———. " 'Those Whom Jesus Loved' (John XI.5)." *New Testament Studies* 1 (1954–55): 29–41.

———. "Who Was the Disciple Whom Jesus Loved?" In *Studies in the Fourth Gospel*, edited by F. L. Cross, 72–82. London: A. R. Mowbray, 1957.

Schenke, H.-M. "The Function and Background of the Beloved Disciple in the Gospel of John." In *Nag Hammadi, Gnosticism, and Early Christianity*, edited by C. W. Hedrick and R. Hodgson, Jr., 111–25. Peabody, Massachusetts: Hendrickson, 1986.

Schlatter, A. "Johannes Glaubte im leeren Grab Jesu." In *Kennen Wir Jesus?: Ein Gang Durch ein Jahr im Gespräch mit Ihm*, 4th ed., 418–20. Stuttgart: Calwer Verlag, 1980.

Schmithals, W. "Die Lieblingsjünger-Redaktion." In *Johannesevangelium und Johannesbriefe: Forschungsgeschichte und Analyse*, 220–59. Beihefte zur Zeitschrift für die neutestamentliche Wissenschaft 64. Berlin/New York: Walter de Gruyter, 1992.

Schnackenburg, R. "The Disciple Whom Jesus Loved." In *The Gospel According to John*, 3:375–87, 484–86. New York: Crossroad, 1987.

———. "Der Jünger, den Jesus liebte." In *Evangelisch-Katholischer Kommentar zum Neuen Testament*, Vorarbeiten, 2:97–117. Zürich-Neukirchen: Benziger Verlag Zürich, 1970.

Schneiders, S. M. "The Face Veil: A Johannine Sign (John 20:1-10)." *Biblical Theology Bulletin* 13 (1983): 94–97.

Segalla, G. " 'Il discepolo che Gesù amava,' e la tradizione giovannea." *Teologia: Rivista Della Facoltà Teologica dell' Italia Settentrionale* 14 (1989): 217–43.

Schillito, E. "The Beloved Disciple." *The Expository Times* 29 (1917–1918): 473–74.

Smalley, S. S. "Authorship." In *Thunder and Love: John's Revelation and John's Community*, 37–40. Milton Keynes, England: Word Publishing, 1994.

Smith, D. M. "Beloved Disciple." *The Interpreter's Dictionary of the Bible: Supplementary Volume* (1976) 95.

————. "The Beloved Disciple and the Attestation of the Gospel." In *The Composition and Order of the Fourth Gospel: Bultmann's Literary Theory*, 220–23. New Haven/London: Yale Univ. Press, 1965.

————. "Interpreting the Historical Origins of the Fourth Gospel." In *John*, 58–71. Proclamation Commentaries. Philadelphia: Fortress, 1976.

————. *The Theology of the Gospel of John*. New Testament Theology. Cambridge: Cambridge Univ. Press, 1995. See esp. 5, 47.

Spaeth, H. "Nathanael: Ein Beitrag zum Verständniss der Composition der Logos-Evangeliums." *Zeitschrift für wissenschaftliche Theologie* 11 (1868): 309–43.

Stibbe, W. G. "The Beloved Disciple." In *John*, 149–50. Sheffield: JSOT Press, 1993.

Strachan, R. H. "Authorship." In *The Fourth Gospel: Its Significance and Environment*. London: Student Christian Movement Press Ltd., 1941, 1946. See esp. 82–89.

————. "The Beloved Disciple." In *The Fourth Evangelist: Dramatist or Historian?* 45–59. London: Hodder and Stoughton, 1925.

Streeter, B. H. "The Fourth Gospel: The Problem of Authorship." *The Four Gospels: A Study of Origins*, 427–61. London: Macmillan and Co., Ltd., 1924, 1951 [seventh impression].

Sturch, R. L. "The Alleged Eyewitness Material in the Fourth Gospel." In *Studia Biblica 1978*, edited by E. A. Livingstone, 313–27. JSNT Supplement Series 2. Sheffield: JSOT Press, 1980.

Swete, H. B. "The Disciple Whom Jesus Loved." *Journal of Theological Studies* 17 (1916): 371–74.

Tasker, R. V. G. "The Apostolic 'Authorship' of the Gospel." In *The Gospel According to St. John*, 11–20. Leicester, England: Inter-Varsity Press; Grand Rapids, Michigan: Eerdmans, 1960 [reprinted 1994].

Thornecroft, J. K. "The Redactor and the 'Beloved' in John." *The Expository Times* 98 (1986–1987): 135–39.

Thyen, H. "Entwicklungen innerhalb der johanneischen Theologie und Kirche im Spiegel von Joh. 21 und den Lieblingsjüngertexte des Evangeliums." In *L'Évangile de Jean: Sources, rédactions, théologie*, edited by M. de Jonge, 259–99. Bibliotheca Ephemeridum Theologicarum Lovaniensium 44. Leuven: Leuven Univ. Press, 1977.

————. "Johannes 13 und die 'Kirchliche Redaktion' des vierten Evangeliums." In *Tradition und Glaube: Das frühe Christentum in seiner Umwelt; Festgäbe für Karl Georg Kuhn zum 65. Geburtstag*, edited by G. Jeremias, H.-W. Kuhn, and H. Stegemann, 343–56. Göttingen: Vandenhoeck & Ruprecht, 1971.

Titus, E. L. "The Identity of the Beloved Disciple." *Journal of Biblical Literature* 69 (1950): 323–28.

————. *The Message of the Fourth Gospel*. New York/Nashville: Abingdon, 1957. See esp. 215–21.

van Tilborg, S. *Imaginative Love in John*. Biblical Interpretation Series 2. Leiden: Brill, 1993. See esp. "The Relation Between Jesus and the Beloved Disciple," 77–110.

Tobler, J. T. "Ueber den Ursprung des vierten Evangeliums." *Zeitschrift für Wissenschaftliche Theologie* 3 (1860): 169–203.

Uechtritz, F. *Studien eines Laien über den Ursprung, die Beschaffenheit und Bedeutung des Evangeliums nach Johannes*. Gotha: F. Andreas Perthes, 1876. See esp. 49–57.

Völter, D. *Mater Dolorosa und der Lieblingsjünger des Johannesevangeliums mit einem Anhang über die Komposition dieses Evangeliums*. Strassburg: J. H. Ed. Heitz (Heitz & Mündel), 1907.

Voigt, G. "Der 'Lieblingsjünger.'" *Licht-Liebe-Leben: Das Evangelium nach Johannes*, 17–19. Biblisch-theologische Schwerpunkte 6. Göttingen: Vandenhoeck & Ruprecht, 1991.

Voigt, F. S. "O Discipulo Amado Recebe a Mae de Jesus 'eis ta idia': Velada Apologia de Joao em Jo 19, 27?" *Revista Eclesiástica Brasileira* 35 (1975): 771–82.

Volkmar, G. *Der Ursprung unserer Evangelien nach den Urkunden, laut den neuern Entdeckungen und Verhandlungen*. Zürich: Verlag von J. Herzog, 1866.

Watty, W. W. "The Significance of Anonymity in the Fourth Gospel." *Expository Times* 90 (1978–1979): 209–12.

Whitelaw, T. *Commentary on John*. Grand Rapids, Michigan: Kregel Publication, 1993 [but the work antedates 1917 when the author died]. See esp. "The Authorship of the Gospel," xxiv–xlviii.

Whiteley, D. E. H. "Was John Written by a Sadducee?" *Aufstieg und Niedergang der Römischen Welt* II.25.3. Berlin: Walter de Gruyter, 1985. Pp. 2481–2505; see esp. "The B.D. Died While Finishing John: He Was a Sadducee," 2492–2502.

Zelzer, K. "'*Oudepo gar edeisan*—den bisher hatten sie nicht verstanden': Zu Übersetzung und Kontextbezug von Joh 20,9." *Bibel und Liturgie* 53 (1980): 104–106.

Zumstein, J. "Le disciple bien-aimé." *Cahier biblique* 26 (1987): 47–58.

Index of Modern Authors

Subject Index

misunderstanding, 54, 175, 225, 269–
74, 277, 286, 433
paronomasia, 255, 301, 324, 347
repetition, 246, 275–76, 280
symbolism, 140, 179, 186, 189, 223,
247, 250–54, 260, 271–72, 286,
291–92, 332, 355
See also Anonymity; Rhetorical techniques
Luke (Evangelist), 193, 195

Malchus, 268, 350, 358
Mali, 380
Mandaeanism, 331, 365
Manichaean Psalmbook, 381
Manichaeism, 365–66, 373, 380
Marcion, 385, 397
Martha, xiv, 55, 92, 185, 187, 189, 191,
234, 270, 289–92
Martyrdom of Thomas, 361
Mary (mother of Jesus). *See* Mother of
Jesus
Mary, sister of Martha, xiv, xvii, 55,
188–89, 234, 289–92
Mary, wife of Clopas, 57–58, 227
Mary Magdalene, xiv, xvi, 6, 28, 57–62,
68–121, 123–24, 137, 227, 231–33,
242, 267–68, 278, 296–97, 304,
306–307, 317, 325, 335, 339, 419,
436
Masada, 56, 134
Matthew (apostle), 181, 239, 410
Matthias, 23, 27, 127–28, 154–56, 182,
189, 194, 223, 427
Mesopotamia, 179, 294, 367, 384
Minor Acts of Thomas, 361
Moses (Mosaic), 58, 76, 92, 134, 164–
66, 257, 266, 279, 355, 415
Mother of Jesus, xvii, 4, 6, 20, 31, 43,
55, 57–60, 62–63, 136–37, 140,
146, 155, 162, 164, 167, 170, 173,
186, 188–91, 194, 200, 206, 211,
214, 265, 273, 317, 378, 395, 400–
403, 423
Mount of Olives, 185, 187, 341, 402,
404, 411

Nadin, 264
Nag Hammadi Codices, 224, 362, 377,
386, 416–17, 419, 421
Nathanael, 35, 37, 39–40, 119, 128–29,

181–85, 189, 204, 223, 226, 231,
234, 243, 248, 250, 261, 295, 329,
427, 435
Nagarjuna, 134
Nazareth, 6, 39, 56–57, 232, 425
Nestorianism, 365
Nicodemus, xiv, 28, 58, 69, 91, 124,
140, 227, 234, 250, 259, 268, 270,
277, 317, 322, 340–42, 433
Nisibis, 364

Odes of Solomon, 38, 41, 380, 382–83,
416
Origen, 394–95, 406
Other disciple. *See* Anonymity, Anonymous disciple of John 1, Anonymous disciple of John 18

Palestine, 157, 179, 201–202, 208, 214,
232, 294, 361–64, 368, 387–88,
399, 404, 409, 413, 421
Palestinian Jesus Movement (PJM), 411–
12
Papias, 394, 398, 407, 421
Paraclete, 54
Parthia, 294, 367, 373, 384
Paul·(Pauline School), x, xx, 47, 58, 73,
80, 93–94, 142, 179, 190, 192–93,
195, 205, 315, 323, 384–86, 410,
415
As BD, 128–29, 138, 156, 159–64,
223, 427
Persia, 364
Peter (Simon Peter), xi–xii, xiv, xvi,
xviii, 5, 13, 19–20, 26, 31–32, 34–
45, 47, 49–50, 54, 58, 61, 68–123,
125–26, 135–36, 138–40, 142, 147,
149–53, 156, 162–63, 168, 172–73,
175–77, 179–81, 184, 189, 193,
195–96, 200, 202, 205–209, 214–
17, 228, 230, 234–41, 243, 245,
248, 251–53, 255, 259–61, 268–71,
278, 283, 285, 290, 296–97, 303,
309, 315–17, 320–21, 324–25, 329–
30, 332, 335–42, 344–58, 366, 375,
384, 387–88, 390–93, 402–403,
410–13, 415, 419, 425, 427–28,
431, 434–36
Petra, 130, 134, 364
Pharisees, xvii, 70, 154, 185, 286, 346,
348, 357

Index of Selected Greek Terms

Index of Scriptures and Other Ancient Writings